THE MISSION OF GOD

Dedicated in hope:
To my children, Naomi, Hannah and Isaac.

"For You are my hope, O Lord God;
You are my trust from my youth. By You
I have been upheld from birth;
You are He who took me out of my mother's
womb. My praise shall be continually of You"

(Ps 71: 5-6).

THE MISSION OF GOD

A Manifesto of Hope for Society

Joseph Boot

Wilberforce Publications
London

First published in Canada in 2014 by
Freedom International Press Inc.

Second edition published in Great Britain in 2016 by
Wilberforce Publications Limited
70 Wimpole Street, London W1G 8AX
in association with the
Ezra Institute for Contemporary Christianity, Canada

The author gratefully acknowledges the writers whose works are quoted in this book. The quotations have, where practicable, been referenced in the End Notes with details of the writer, the title of the book, the publisher and the date of publication. If any requirement for permission has been overlooked, the publishers would be glad to hear from the holders of the copyright.

ISBN 978 0 957572 56 0

Printed worldwide by CreateSpace
and in the UK by Imprint Digital, Exeter

Bold, provocative and illuminating *The Mission of God* is a potential game-changer for modern societies. It challenges the secular *modus vivendi* and summons the Christian church to applied biblical radicalism. By recognising the numerous normative connections between the complex wisdom of the Hebrew Bible and the ethical authority of Jesus' resurrection Boot successfully deconstructs Christian antinomianism and establishes the demands of Christian discipleship for a new generation. All who seek to benefit from past experience of biblical social transformation, in a world that is simultaneously secularising and desecularising, will be challenged and rewarded, even where they do not agree.

Jonathan Burnside,
Professor of Biblical Law at the University of Bristol
Author of *God, Justice and Society*

A hard-hitting *tour de force* which will no doubt inspire, encourage and provoke. We're spectacularly missing the point if we think we have to agree with every point of Joe's exposition. What we in the UK urgently need to take on board is his Puritan vision of Christ's comprehensive Lordship over all society together with Scripture's comprehensiveness to speak into every area, and where cultural mandate and great commission form one integrated mission manifesto. Recommended.

Dr Daniel Strange, Academic Vice-Principal and Tutor in Culture,
Religion and Public Theology, Oak Hill College, London.

A work of theology that can be exegetically profound, philosophically rigorous, historically aware, culturally illuminating, pastorally wise with a serious love for the church and the lost – and to be all of that at the same time is an extremely rare feat. It is not something that can be pulled off only by learning the mechanics of writing theology; it takes a certain kind of person to write a book like that, someone deeply integrated around Christ as King over their whole life to compose such a compelling and seamless vision of God's mission for His world. I know Dr. Joe Boot to be that kind of man and that robustly Theocentric vision is precisely what he has offered us in *The Mission of God* – a must read for anyone seeking a more comprehensive view of God's supremacy.

Dr. Thaddeus Williams (Ph.D)
Assistant Professor of Theology, Biola University
Assistant Professor of Jurisprudence, Trinity Law School, California

This volume is as comprehensive an overview of the church's mission in the 21st century as anything you will find presently available. Its vast vision includes a deep understanding of Church and Western philosophical history, a strong defense of the validity of God's law for righteous living, a passionate call for Christian education and the immense importance of the Christian family, a brilliant, well-worked out statement of the most effective apologetic for the postmodern world, an incisive description of the utopian Oneist character of the present Western culture, a moving exhortation to take up the task of evangelism, and a positive vision of the final outcome under the lordship of King Jesus. With such an enormous scope, readers will doubtless question certain "Puritan" emphases, though, at every point, will be intelligently challenged to engage in further God-honoring biblical and theological reflection. In a word, a great achievement!

Dr. Peter Jones (Ph.D)
Founder and Director, truthXchange
Scholar in residence, Westminster Theological Seminary, California

So many today attach the "missional" label to themselves, but do not actually do anything but blog or become celebrities at "missional conferences." In contrast, Joe Boot's life reflects the competence, credentials, and the character necessary for helping us understand and execute the actual mission of God. His international efforts in missiology, apologetics, and church planting uniquely inform his analysis—this is no dry as sawdust theoretical tome, though it is both scholarly and challenging. This work cherishes, but does not cling, to historically faithful expositions of God's mission, a mission that did not begin with Billy Graham, nor end with Thomas Aquinas. With incisive theological analysis, Boot unpacks exactly how the essence of the new covenant, the law written on our hearts, is central to graciously fulfilling God's mission responsibly, faithfully, and comprehensively during this time between the Cross and the Consummation. Though one may quibble with some of his formulations or conclusions, he cogently shows that the "stuff in the middle matters" to God and this work demonstrates the richness of God's provision for living faithfully, truly living missionally. Anyone interested in affecting his community for Jesus can't not be benefited by reading this important new work.

Dr. Jeffery J. Ventrella (J.D., Ph.D)
Senior Counsel, Senior Vice-President
Alliance Defending Freedom, Phoenix

Joe Boot is one of the finest apologists I know: a sharp mind coupled with a hearty passion to serve the cause of the Lord Jesus Christ. In this new work, something of a magnum opus, he turns his gifts and scholarship to analyzing the place of the law in the life of Christ's church and culture at large. Not all will agree with his convictions or be convinced by his reasoning, but this book's arguments cannot be lightly brushed aside. They demand a rigorous consideration of the ongoing significance of the Old Testament. And if by reading this book, some Evangelical preachers end their neo-Marcionite silence regarding large tracts of the Old Testament, much will have been gained.

Dr. Michael A.G. Haykin (Ph.D)
Professor of Church History & Biblical Spirituality
The Southern Baptist Theological Seminary, Louisville, Kentucky

You hold in your hands the most comprehensive and cogent argument for the perpetuity of God's moral law as it relates to civil legislation written in 40 years. This thesis, bold but thoughtfully nuanced, offers a breath of fresh air amid both the hermeneutical nihilism and pietistic retreatism that infests the modern church. Joe Boot is God's Reformer in Canada, and this book establishes him as an intellectual force to be reckoned with both by a rapacious secular culture and a timid church culture.

Dr. P. Andrew Sandlin (S.T.D)
President, Center for Cultural Leadership, California

We are facing the final demise of Christianity in Western society resulting from the failure of the modern Church to be God's mission to the world. What shall be the response of the Christian Church? Dr. Boot challenges us to look to the history of the Church and reconsider what has been lost in the eventual ejection of the Puritan paradigm. The answer, says Dr. Boot, can be found in the great Puritan hope of applying historic Reformational Covenant theology of the Holy Scripture into every area of life. Puritan thought sought to externalize its theology into a praxis that was life changing, in personal, family, and societal realms. This book is a must read for every Christian, whether laymen, scholar, or minister.

Dr. Kenneth Gary Talbot, (Ph.D)
President, Whitefield Theological Seminary, Florida

In an age in which liberal evangelicalism is the order of the day in many circles, Joe Boot's *The Mission of God* stands tall as a *tour de force* of historic Christian orthodoxy.... Boot makes his case with coherence, clarity and conviction as one thoroughly rooted in the authority of Holy Scripture.

Greg Downes,
Theologian and Missioner, St Michael le Belfrey, York

Dr. Joe Boot is one of the top Christian apologists writing and speaking today, as evidenced by both his published work and extensive debate experience. In *The Mission of God*, Joe demonstrates that he possesses more than mere rhetorical skill, for this book is an intellectual *tour de force*. Equally at home discussing the philosophical nuances of ancient Greek philosophy, the benefits of a Puritan view of God's law, and the intricacies of modern social problems, Joe is the best kind of guide through the serpentine maze of ideas that he tackles: simple without being simplistic, profoundly learned without being inaccessible, pastoral without being pedantic. Impressive in both breadth and scope, *The Mission of God* challenges Christians to apply God's law to all of life for the glory of God and the good of their neighbors.

Dr. Gabriel Fluhrer, Visiting Professor of Philosophy and Theology,
Reformed Theological Seminary Global Campus

'I could not put it down ... this book is destined to be a classic.'

Rev. Dr. Bishop Joshua HK Banda (Ph.D)
President, Southern Africa Region of the Pentecostal Assemblies of Africa

CONTENTS

I

ACKNOWLEDGMENTS

With a project of this size and scope, developed over a number of years, it is a difficult task to remember and give due credit and acknowledgement to all those who have had a hand in making this work possible. By the unmerited grace of God I have been given a wonderfully supportive wife and family who not only give me freedom to write, but have graciously enabled my labours in England, Canada, the USA and beyond, where much of the thought content of this book has been tried in the fires of educational, apologetic and pastoral ministry.

I owe special thanks to a number of individuals for enriching and challenging my thinking through hours of discussion and interaction, not to mention their keen interest in this project and the many articles they suggested for my reference – in particular my friends and colleagues Dr Scott Masson and Dr David Robinson have greatly enhanced the writing process and therefore the end product. All the staff of Westminster Chapel have been an enormous help to me and I owe them my sincere thanks. I am greatly indebted to my friend, colleague and editor, Ryan Eras, for his painstaking and steady work with me on the manuscript, sometimes on the sunny deck of my Toronto garden and sometimes on cold Canadian winter mornings – periodically arriving bearing gifts of hot chocolate and egg muffins! His contribution has been invaluable. I am also very grateful to my friend Dianne Foster-Kent for her careful proofreading and editorial suggestions. Nonetheless, for all errors and failures of the work, I bear full responsibility.

I also want to acknowledge and thank the Westminster Chapel board of elders and EICC trustees for their faithfulness and for allowing me room to think, write, and travel. Their friendship and gracious support has made the challenging years of church planting a joy and not a misery. In particular I want to thank my dear friend Randy Currie without whose labours the Ezra Institute would not have come into being or have been effectively founded. Not only has he worked tirelessly to see the Institute established, but has travelled many long hours with me to various destinations for conferences and debates, inspiring the work and strengthening my thinking at every turn. But more than all this, he

13

has sat in hospital waiting rooms with me in times of great distress and peril for my wife Jenny, and comforted me in my sorrow, for which I will always be grateful.

My thanks also to Brian and Colleen Semkiw and Giles and Ashleigh Sutherland for their enduring friendship, kindness and support in the context of church, Institute, and family life. Some of the most fertile passages of this book were written overlooking the lake during one of our many family retreats in their inviting home. Thanks are also due to the entire Westminster Chapel church family for allowing me to put the biblical content of this book into action in the life and ministry of the church. I am blessed and honoured to serve you all.

Finally my thanks are also due to Christian Concern, UK and *Wilberforce Publications*, my publisher, for believing in this project and capturing the vision for this book, promoting it throughout the United Kingdom and taking the 'risk' when other publishers ran for cover. The content is challenging and controversial in a biblically illiterate and politically correct time in our history and I thank you for having the courage and love of freedom enough to publish this work.

Soli Deo gloria

II

FOREWORD TO THE SECOND EDITION

The Mission of God is a Christian classic. As a Christian barrister and most latterly chief executive of Christian Concern and the Christian Legal Centre in the United Kingdom, I have been contending for truth in the public square since 1988. In that time we have seen laws pertaining to life, marriage, family and the uniqueness of Jesus Christ drastically eroded. We kill the unborn child when inconvenient but use fertility treatment to have a child when we want; two men can marry and have children by surrogacy; two women by donor insemination. We create embryos, experiment upon them and then destroy them, whilst we foster animal-human hybrids.

Our society is besieged by the opposing but cohabiting forces of secularism and Islam. Anything that is anti-Christ. It appears moreover that the Church is weak; in the desire to welcome we have become accommodating. Our frailty of conviction is matched only by our failure to speak, and so the gospel message is lost, taken from the people.

How did we get to this place? And what hope can we offer? *The Mission of God* gives us the answer.

*The Mission of Go*d showed me that Genesis 1–3 sets the stage for the gospel – the Cross is the centrepiece, the seed is sown in Genesis. Genesis 1–3 is the context for our message of reconciliation, the meaning for our meaninglessness and the hope for our redemption. It tells us how the cosmos got here, how it's structured, and what God intends for it. Genesis 3:15 – Revelation 22:21 tell us how God is working to restore — and expand — his plan that sin spoiled.

The Mission of God gives us the theological framework to understand our times; to show us what God intends and what he's doing in the world today. The book outlines the hope for our nation, our cultural mandate. The book gives us the theology to say that God didn't create the world simply to take people to heaven. He created the world to glorify himself, and we glorify God most when we act as God intended in every aspect of life: as an individual, in marriage, families, communities and nations.

This book is an intellectual masterpiece; it is first rate scholarship

– a theological and historical gem. But it is more than that. It is the theological apologetic to act out God's truth in every sphere of life in twenty-first century Britain and beyond. Thank you Joe. The book is changing lives.

Andrea Williams
CEO, Christian Concern and Christian Legal Centre, London UK

III

FOREWORD TO THE FIRST EDITION

You hold in your hands the most comprehensive and cogent argument for the perpetuity of God's moral law as it relates to civil legislation written in over 40 years. This thesis, bold but thoughtfully nuanced, offers a breath of fresh air amid both the hermeneutical nihilism and pietistic retreatism that infests the modern church. It is a trumpet call to the reinstallation of God's revelational standards in home, church and the wider society. But this far-ranging book is more. It is a veritable blueprint for a restoration of the Kingdom of God in a Western culture that at first drifted and is now rushing headlong into apostasy from the Triune God. Dr. Boot selects as the paradigm for his blueprint the grand Puritan vision, which bequeathed to the English-speaking world the benefits — spiritual, intellectual, educational, economic, vocational — that made it the envy of the world. Ironically, in jettisoning this cultural paradigm due to its (erroneously) alleged narrowness and dourness, our English-speaking world has severed our lifeline to the godly resources of cultural virility. Even more importantly, however, Dr. Boot argues that *this* paradigm is atop the most God-honoring of the available expressions of Christianity — the Puritan vision seeks to honor God in every area of life and thought. It was the original "if-Jesus-isn't-Lord-of-all-he's-not-Lord-at-all" Christianity. If you want to live a 24/7 life pleasing to God, you'll end up with a Faith that looks suspiciously like good, old-fashioned — and ever fresh and new — Puritanism.

This book is not for the timid or diffident souls who want, at best, a Sunday go-to-meetin' Christianity that makes no demands on their comfortable, self-centered life. But if you long to please God, and wish to see him pleased, not just in the church house, but also the school house, the state house, the courthouse, the movie house, and the art house, this book will show you the way. Dr. Joe Boot is God's Reformer in Canada, and this book establishes him as a spiritual and intellectual force to be reckoned with both by a rapacious secular culture and a timid church culture.

P. Andrew Sandlin, S. T. D.
President
Center for Cultural Leadership
California

THE MISSION OF GOD:

A MANIFESTO OF HOPE FOR SOCIETY

*He has shown his people the power of his works, in giving them
the inheritance of the nations.
The works of his hands are faithful and just;
all his precepts are trustworthy;
they are established forever and ever, to be performed with
faithfulness and uprightness.
He sent redemption to his people;
he has commanded his covenant forever.
Holy and awesome is his name!*
– Psalm 111:6–9

19

AUTHOR'S INTRODUCTION:
FRESH WATER, ANCIENT CISTERNS

0.1 Epochal Turning Points

What is the calling of God's covenant people in history? What is the kingdom of God and how does it manifest itself? What does the reign of God look like and how are we to discern God working? What is the relationship between faith and public morality and policy? What should be the relationship between church and state? Is religious pluralism a biblically compatible and workable theology of state? Does the church have a future in history? Are Christians called to transform cultures? In short, what is the *mission of God* and what part do we have to play? These questions have become increasingly pertinent for the church today, especially in the Western world, because it is widely recognized that Western civilization is facing an epochal turning point. The political philosopher and former president of the Italian senate, Marcello Pera has stated aptly, "The apostasy of Christianity is exposing the entire West to the risk of a grave cultural and political crisis, and perhaps even to a collapse of civilisation."[1] Those who profess to be Bible-believing Christians can no longer ignore a growing chorus of non-evangelical voices from theology, philosophy and politics, sounding the alarm concerning the growing threat to religious liberty, the rule of law, the freedom of the church, and survival of the family (and hence civilization as we have known it). This threat is engendered by a growing statist vision of society, increasingly committed to a neo-pagan ideology that is now permeating every aspect of the Western social order. Even certain European heads of state have started to appeal to Christianity as the only hope for Europe's recovery.[2] The Prime Minster of Hungary recently declared that European decline was a result of abandoning the Christian faith:

> The European crisis has not come by chance but by the carelessness and neglect of their responsibilities by leaders who have questioned precisely those Christian roots. That is the driving force that allowed European cohesion, family, work and credit. These values were the old continental economic power, thanks mainly to the development which in those days was done in accordance with [those] principles.[3]

This growing crisis has made the subject of missiology,[4] and its primary areas of concern, all the more important for our moment in history. The turning point our culture has reached demands an apologetic response from the church, one that articulates and defends a biblical perspective on our calling, equipping this generation of Christians to live faithfully and effectively, in word and deed. It is my hope that I may be able to play a small part in offering that apologetic response, by assisting in the equipping of Christ's church with a renewed vision of the gospel in our hour of danger, and yet, equally glorious moment of opportunity.

0.2   Autobiographical 'Apologia'

Working as an itinerant Christian apologist for a number of years, based in both Europe and North America, as well as serving as a churchman and pastor on both sides of the Atlantic, in urban London, England and downtown Toronto, Canada, has given me a keen interest in the critical missiological questions mentioned above. By the gracious work of the Spirit, it has also enabled me to see their urgency. I further believe that, by the same grace, these experiences, in conjunction with my reading, have given me an insight into the 'soft underbelly' of the Christian church in the West. There are critical areas, in both theology and practice, where we are weak, ineffective, exposed and as a result, in peril, haemorrhaging great numbers of congregants. This book is the result of my studies and scripture-centred reflection on my ministry labours over a number of years. It attempts to diagnose some of the reasons for the church's present weakness in the West, and offers some direction to the church for renewal, reformation, and ultimately revival. The work is far from any kind of final answer, nor do I presume to possess such an insight or ability. Furthermore, I claim no originality for this work, in the sense that I say nothing that has not been said in past generations by faithful Christians within the creedally orthodox, protestant evangelical tradition – that is to say, I draw on ancient cisterns for fresh water. So whilst not a new brook it may nonetheless provide a valuable synthesis of a variety of streams of thought from various disciplines, coming together into a fresh tributary to refresh the thirsty faithful in a parched generation. My greatest hope is that it might function as a constructive addition to missiological reflection on the *reign of God,* and so for some, be a potential starting point for provoking immediate and deeper consideration of the crisis facing the church in Canada (and the West generally) and the way out. I also hope it may be a means of introducing another generation of Christians to the foundational biblical truths that gave shape to our Christian heritage.

The primary purpose of the book then is not to simply add yet more academic speculation to the over-laden shelves of scholars – dense pages patiently awaiting critique and discussion – but rather to suggest, to every thinking Christian, that there is a prophetic urgency to the church's mandate in our time, applicable to us all, which we neglect at our peril. The Bible's anthropology makes abundantly clear that because we are a fallen, sinful and rebellious race, without a God-given vision, mission, or purpose directing our lives, anarchy and death ensue, "Where there is no prophetic vision, the people cast off restraint, but blessed is he who keeps the law" (Prov. 29:18). We desperately need to *recover* the prophetic vision of God's word for our lives and the blessedness of living in terms of it.

0.3 Back to the Future

It is interesting to note how both biblically and historically, prophetic ministry begins with a backward look. The Old Testament prophets called upon the covenant people to *remember* God's repeated acts of deliverance in their history, and to *remember* his Law, if they were to have a *future*. They also pointed back to faithful servants of God within that history – historical figures like Moses and the patriarchs – and used their lives and example as a means of challenging people to return to faithfulness to their God-given mission. Likewise, true reformation within the church begins with prophetic witness that looks back to the *word of God* and the example of the 'cloud of witnesses' in our history who have lived in terms of it, and asks where we have departed from fidelity to the truth. So, in order to be able to look *forward* with vision and hope for the future of God's church, we must first look *back* to learn from the past and be resourced by it, by our fathers, and recover what is of value. Only an impudent and blind conceit could lead us to the presumption that we do not need to learn from our forebears in the faith as we face the challenges and opportunities of today. It was once commonly accepted that modern Protestants, and especially reformed and evangelical Protestants, owed a great deal to the biblical vision of the gospel and God-centred social order bequeathed to them by the Puritans – one example of faithful witness in our history. The evangelical faith of these devoted men provided the sense of vision and mission that helped stimulate, not only international missions and evangelism for three centuries, but nation-building and the establishment of free institutions in both the British Commonwealth and the United States. In the early chapters of this book I will be defining the key distinctions of Puritan thought, but a simple summary offered by Charles Cohen is helpful by way of introduction:

> Puritanism has been defined variously in intellectual, political, or cultural terms...it is best understood as a religious sensibility centered around conversion – the Holy Spirit's regeneration of the soul – and the concomitant determination to restore the purity of the apostolic church and reform society according to God's laws. Theologically, Puritanism represents an emphasis within the Reformed Protestant (Calvinist) tradition...Puritan piety was characterized by a veneration of the Bible as the rule for living righteously and a pervasive sense that God providentially supervises all human affairs. Puritanism made a substantial impact on Anglo-America...Puritan moral values made New England a watchword for sobriety – it had a lower percentage of illegitimate births than other regions – and may have instilled habits of economic discipline that abetted commercial growth...from its doctrinal and experiential matrix issued not only New England Congregationalism, but also varieties of Presbyterian and Baptist practice. Updated by Jonathan Edwards in the mid-eighteenth century, Reformed Protestantism became America's leading theological tradition.[5]

Puritanism had a distinctly Bible-centred theology, anthropology and view of history that gave it a great missional vitality. The plain reality is that the biblical faith and sense of cultural mission that gave us so much in both the British Commonwealth and the United States, with the rule of law, a free market, representative government, freedom of conscience and religion, and the freedom and self-government of the Christian church and family, was given to us in large measure by the influence our Puritan forebears.[6] What is left of this heritage has been disappearing extremely rapidly in the past two generations, and as a result, our culture is slipping into a complete loss of restraint, gripped by ideologies with pagan roots that promote a way of physical, moral and social death. A new generation now drifts without purpose and vision, with little confidence that they have a future, leaving us vulnerable to a growing religious vision of state power and authority that sees its total regulation and control as the only solution to the collapsing social order.

It is in light of this reality confronting the church, and the challenge of presenting the gospel in such a context, that I have undertaken this study, in the hope of re-capturing the minds and hearts of another generation of Christians in Canada (and beyond) with a Puritan (Calvinist) theology of *the* mission – with its distinctive anthropology and philosophy of history – reminding them of the culture (indeed civilization) that this biblical vision produced. It is then my purpose to bring the Puritan hermeneutic of *submission* to God's word to bear on the major themes of contemporary missiology. For the sake of clarity, Johannes Verkuyl's definition of the academic study of inter-disciplinary missiology is comprehensive and helpful:

> Missiology is the study of the salvation activities of the Father, Son, and Holy Spirit throughout the world geared toward *bringing the kingdom of God into existence.* Seen in this perspective missiology is the study of the worldwide church's divine mandate to be ready to serve this God who is aiming his saving acts toward the world. In dependence on the Holy Spirit and by *word and deed* the church is to *communicate the total gospel and the total divine law to all mankind.* Missiology's task in every age is to investigate scientifically and critically the presuppositions, motives, structures, methods, patterns of cooperation, and leadership which the churches bring to their mandate. In addition missiology must examine *every other type of human activity*...to see if it fits the criteria and goals of God's kingdom which has both already come and is yet coming.[7]

In my view, since missiology is concerned with how God brings His kingdom into existence, most particularly by the communication and application of this *total gospel and the total divine law* through his people, authentic missiology is not just about constructing a theology *of* mission in the abstract, it is biblical theology and doxology *as* the mission. A biblical approach to mission is therefore *biblical theology externalized* and applied to every area of life. It views all theology as in some way expressive of God's mission to reveal himself and his purposes in history, call out a people for his own possession and establish his kingdom reign. The Bible is therefore the self-revelation of the missionary (sending) God; revealed through his missionaries by the inspiration of the Spirit; about the mission; for a missionary people!

It is obvious then that missiological reflection is not done in a theological vacuum but will be committed to certain presuppositions about the nature of God's word, how this word is inter-related in the covenants of Scripture, and how that same word is to be externalized in the world. As a Trinitarian and creedally orthodox believer, I look to the Calvinistic tradition as my primary guide to understanding Scripture and externalizing the faith, especially as expressed in the Puritan legacy. This is because I believe this framework represents both the most faithful reading of Scripture and the most influential tradition within evangelical Christianity, profoundly shaping culture and civilization in the West.

0.4 Puritans Old and New

Regrettably, the coherent and compelling contribution the Puritan direction of thought can make in diagnosing and addressing the critical issues facing the Western church and culture today, has been routinely ignored by contemporary evangelicals. Some of those claiming to be Reformed are overtly hostile to Puritan views on covenantal spheres of authority (what the later Dutch neo-Calvinists came to call 'sphere sovereignty'), community or national covenant, law, culture and by extension Christian civilization.[8] Yet even where the hostility isn't overt, there is a tacit suppression of the dominant Puritan view of biblical law and gospel as it related to culture, national covenant, church-state relationship, crime and punishment, and the eschatological kingdom of God. Certainly, there is renewed interest among evangelicals in Puritan piety, pastoral ministry, spirituality, church government and forms of worship; indeed, these things are often celebrated. But scant attention in the popular literature is paid to the nature and character of Puritan thought as it related to their primary concern – the kingdom and reign of God in the earth by his Spirit, through law and gospel. There appears to be either embarrassment or cowardly reluctance to raise the 'spectre' of the Puritan ideal of God's reign, given the pluralistic idealism of modern Western politics. Yet the sovereignty of God and his total lordship over all aspects of life was, in large degree, the centrepiece of the Puritan worldview, shaped in the rigor of social and civil conflict, and the challenges of nation building on both sides of the Atlantic. Indeed, in many respects, they added little by way of theoretical theological development to Calvin (though they extensively developed the theme of covenant). Rather, as the quintessence of practical Christianity, what they did was to rigorously *apply* reformed thought to each area of life (both private and public, personal and institutional) in terms of practical theology (which all theology should be) in a fashion even more comprehensive than Calvin managed in Geneva. There is no understanding Puritan thought without recognizing their view of Christ's reign and crown rights – rights that the church is called to assert and pursue in the earth till he comes. To study the Puritans, whilst ignoring their practical application of God's law to all life, or their view that God's kingdom and total sovereignty is to be realized in family, church, school and state, is to largely fail to understand them. Is it not disingenuous to claim an affinity for the Puritans, delighting in the vitality of their prayers and piety whilst ignoring its source – their vision of God's covenant and reign in history? There is no accurate understanding of John Knox, Samuel Rutherford, John Owen, John Elliot, John Cotton or Oliver Cromwell to be had, whilst ignoring their view of Christ's present reign at God's right hand as King of kings and Lord of lords, to whom all men are subject, under whose law all men are held to account (whether king or commoner), and by whose gospel alone men can find redemption and restoration.

It is then perhaps, in some measure, *because* of the contemporary evangelical indifference to these sixteenth- and seventeenth-century Puritan convictions, that their most consistent modern heirs in the twentieth and twenty first century – the theonomists – have so often been chastised and ostracized. Since the majority of those who style themselves Puritans today systematically ignore the full consequences of the present reign of God, describing those who do not as 'theonomists' is a tool for marginalizing them. It suggests the theonomists' emphasis is an obscure footnote in the present rather than a recovery of the keynote of the past. That is to say, they have been ignored or censured precisely because they have taken up and revived key elements in our Puritan heritage that the rest of the modern evangelical community has chosen to forget or ignore.[9] A small crop of theologians, churchmen and apologists within the Reformed, Puritan tradition, over the last fifty years or so, have sought to bring to the church's attention an area of Protestant theology and practice long neglected – a rigorous examination of the details of the law-word of God in both testaments, and their application to every area of life; both public and private, church and state, personal and familial, in terms of the absolute sovereignty of God. They have likewise sought to make Christians increasingly self-conscious of the antithesis that exists between a biblical way of *living* in and understanding the world, and a non-Christian approach. Christian thinkers, theologians and practitioners such as Cornelius Van Til, John Frame, Greg Bahnsen, Rousas John Rushdoony, Gary DeMar, Kenneth Talbot, P. Andrew Sandlin, Jeffery Ventrella, James Jordan, and many others, have sought to point in various ways, and with different emphases, to many of these critical Puritan themes, and their relevance for our cultural moment.

Despite harsh criticism, these broadly theonomic thinkers and practitioners have, in my opinion, been largely vindicated in their observations and critiques of contemporary culture and modern Western Christianity, since over the past fifty years, the rapid degeneration of our social order, and decline of the church, has proved their prophetic diagnosis remarkably accurate. It seems clear to me that, without being unduly anachronistic, the essentially 'Puritan' solutions they have suggested, which rest upon an essentially 'Puritan' diagnosis, warrant serious attention. This is because both the diagnosis and recommended cure are grounded upon the same theological and covenantal hermeneutic, making their biblical and cultural exegesis two branches from the same tree. If the diagnosis has proven correct, there is surely much to learn from the proposed solutions. In my judgement, the most important representative of the 'New Puritanism,' is the late R. J. Rushdoony. He stands out as pivotal in terms of re-laying these foundations and updating them for a new era, giving concrete shape to a revived vision of a Calvinistic social order, rigorously applying reformed theology to the cultural and missional challenge facing the church. Though most Christians have never heard of him, John Whitehead called Rushdoony, "the most influential theologian affecting the Christian Right today."[10]

Now as anyone familiar with modern political reality will know, since anybody that opposes abortion, euthanasia, gay marriage, big government and the coercive redistribution of wealth is almost immediately identified as part of the 'Christian Right,' this is quite a remarkable statement; although it is not a commendation that Rushdoony would have appreciated.[11] The historian Molly Worthen,[12] in her critical analysis of Rushdoony's work and influence[13] (an analysis that is less than sympathetic to the Reformed worldview), points out that little more than a superficial caricaturing of Rushdoony's important contribution has taken place within conservative Christian circles. In light of the 'illness' of the West, she rightly considers this a real mistake because, "When Rushdoony identified an intellectual crisis afoot in American Protestantism, he was right...; the crisis he perceived was real."[14] She also incisively perceives that he was seeking to "impose upon conservative Christianity an intellectual consistency that it lacked."[15] So, rather than being casually dismissive of a new Puritan patriarch, she identifies him as a "strange brand of theological genius whose ideas proved robust enough to sustain a movement."[16] Moreover, she correctly observes that Calvin, as the godfather of the Reformed tradition and mastermind of the Genevan theocratic experiment, was his spiritual and theological role model, whilst "The Puritans – Calvin's progeny on the British Isles – were the ancestors to whom Rushdoony...paid most frequent obeisance.... In his *Institutes*, Rushdoony aimed to resurrect the vision of Calvin and the Puritans."[17] There is no doubt that this is an accurate picture of his intentions. Whilst his synthetic mind and unusually wide reading gave him a brilliant depth of insight and compelling originality of expression, Worthen further points out that "none of [Rushdoony's] beliefs is unknown in the history of Protestant Christianity – nor are many of his inclinations wholly alien to British and American political conservatism – Rushdoony reformulated them in a creative critique of late-twentieth-century American society."[18] His accomplishment was that he successfully, "refashioned this web of reformed Christian and conservative libertarian principles into a massive cultural indictment of twentieth century America on biblical grounds."[19] As Worthen correctly points out, Rushdoony's essential thesis was that, "we moderns are guilty of the heresies condemned in the fifth century at Chalcedon: we blur human and divine and worship man and his creations."[20] This creative refashioning did offer the Christian community a more consistent, thoroughgoing and refined Calvinistic vision of God's reign than had been seen before in the Reformed tradition, and by applying it to the immediate challenges facing Christians in the culture, it came with fresh insight and contemporary relevance. In linking a robust reformed perspective to the immediate problems of modern life, there is some similarity in emphasis between Rushdoony and another of his role models, the Dutch theologian and statesman, Abraham Kuyper, "to whom he credited the modern Calvinist re-awakening."[21] The spiritual root of Rushdoony's (and the other theonomists') Puritan critique and manifesto is summarized well by Worthen, "Revelation, not tradition, is the source of legitimacy.... Rushdoony viewed his mission as an attempt to restore in humankind a personal loyalty to God."[22] In the Puritan thesis, obedience to the law of God and his covenant is the *essence* of loyalty to God and is thus the meaning of true Christian worship. Consequently, Rushdoony and the other theonomists called people back to faithful obedience to God's law, as both the expression of true sanctification in the Christian who has been regenerated by the Holy Spirit, and as the means of glorifying God and serving the reign of Christ. In this volume I am therefore urging, that instead of dismissing modern Puritanism, we must consider it carefully, taking what is of value for facing the difficult realities confronting the church today. Irresponsible and sensational journalism as well as superficial evangelical criticism has regarded Rushdoony, and the new Puritans generally, with suspicion, as though their focus on God's law represents some sort of threat to freedom and our political institutions. Worthen rightly debunks this myth:

> The real trouble with Rushdoony's influence today is not the spectre of Mosaic law...the tragedy, rather, is that too many Christians have picked up Rushdoony's language without reading his books or understanding his fundamental challenge: that evangelical Christians must find a way to reconcile the Bible with true pluralism.... Every religious tradition must broker a compromise with the society it inhabits. In America, that compromise has broken down. *If Christians reject Mosaic law, they still must seriously consider the relationship between the Bible and the pluralist public square* [emphasis added].[23]

0.5 The New Puritanism within the Context of Pluralism

This is the critical issue at the heart of the problem of contemporary missiology; one that occupies the minds of many of today's Western missiologists and theologians. How should Christians relate to an increasingly de-Christianized public square where people are becoming either ignorant of, or hostile toward, the worldview of the Bible? What are Christians to do when the institutional church is marginalized, the exclusive claims of the gospel are viewed as bigotry and the moral law in Scripture seen as repressive and intolerant? In a context where, increasingly, people of other religions, from secular humanists to Muslims, coalesce (not without growing tension) under one governmental structure, and we are informed that the new state doctrine is multi-culturalism, how are Christians to understand and relate the claims of Christ and God's law to public life – indeed should they seek to relate them at all? In addressing this renewed encounter between biblical faith and the humanistic, Islamic and pagan ideologies in our time, many Christians have decided to adopt overtly pluralistic or inclusivist perspectives on the gospel and mission (dealt with in chapter 15 of this book), essentially surrendering moral absolutes and the binding character of God's law altogether and re-interpreting the Christian gospel to be embracing of many social orders and many routes to God, without the need for a saving knowledge of Christ. Is this capitulation an adequate approach for Christians seeking to understand how the Bible relates with today's pluralism? Indeed can biblical faith be reconciled with the modern philosophy of religious pluralism at all? The Puritan perspective says no, and regards the acceptance of philosophically pluralist and inclusivist missiological solutions as idolatry. It must be stressed that what is *not* being said here is that Christians cannot live peaceably in a religiously pluralistic context – the early church did and Christians have done so all over the globe for centuries. The question is, *how* are we to live in that context, if biblical Christianity cannot be harmonized in a new synthesis with the religious pluralism of our day? So as Robert Bowman acknowledges in his essay on theonomy entitled, *The New Puritanism*, whether we like or agree with Rushdoony and the theonomists or not, they are, "certainly asking the right questions. What is the proper relationship between church and state? Is a Christian culture possible? If a culture were converted to faith in Christ, how would their institutions change? What would be the basis of such a culture's laws? Does the Bible have the answers to society's problems, and if so, what are those answers?"[24]

0.6   The Challenge of the 'Emergent Church'

One part of the modern church that has drunk deeply from the wells of contemporary missiology to frame and answer these questions is the emergent church movement; adopting an emphasis on pluralistic or inclusivist solutions to Christianity's encounter with religious pluralism.[25] Moreover, the emergent church, which differs little in doctrine from late nineteenth-century liberal Christianity (although it lacks the intellectual and academic rigor of its forerunner), is dominated by the radical egalitarian philosophy of social justice – co-opted from cultural Marxists and utopians, and baptized in the name of 'God's reign' or the 'kingdom of God.' The younger generation of evangelicals are often strongly drawn to this position, being concerned about justice and equity, without understanding the philosophical and theological assumptions that underlie such a perspective. Younger evangelicals are rightly distressed that there has been apparent lack in the fundamentalist and evangelical Christianity of the previous generation, in addressing how the Christian faith is to apply beyond the walls of the church and beyond an individual concern with personal salvation. They want to know what the implications of the faith are for the problems and difficulties we are surrounded by in our culture. What does Christianity have to say concerning poverty and social deprivation? What does it have to say about the environment and care for the creation? What does it have to say about politics and the major social issues of our time like gay marriage and so forth? The silence of much modern evangelicalism (including the reformed world) has been deafening on most of these issues. The reasons for this are varied. One reaction has been to dismiss these questions as socio-cultural matters of concern only to 'social gospel' peddlers aligned with liberal Christianity, so by definition, they cannot be relevant to evangelicals. Another has been a retrenchment in a kind of minimalist soteriology where evangelicals have simply said that our sole focus should be 'the gospel' (albeit a truncated definition concerned with little more than justification and personal salvation) and a collective reaffirmation of basic creedal statements, holding the line on the great evangelical confessions in the face of pluralism. Still others have developed theologically novel responses, holding that these wider socio-cultural challenges are all areas of 'common grace' endeavour that should be left to the state to handle – there are allegedly two kingdoms and the Christian's concern is only the reforming of the church institution, its confessions, liturgy and discipline, but not the shaping of a Christian approach to the pressing matters of our time and culture which would seek to transform it. With the large-scale abandonment of the Puritan legacy in the area of *applied* reformed thought to all of life, and the retreat of conservative evangelicals into various theological and cultural ghettoes where the doctrine of the *sufficiency* of scripture is cloistered, no longer applying to the world at large, younger evangelicals have been left floundering, looking for an authentically Christian response to the ideological changes in our culture and the urgent problems facing them in the social order. The only portion of the contemporary church, outside of broad liberal ecumenism, or the handful of new Puritan voices, that has been giving some kind of *concrete* response, has been the emergent church movement. They offer 'social justice,' in the name of the reign and mission of God – a new friendly Christianity that welcomes doctrinal change, embraces diversity and seeks to right the wrongs in the structures of society. This call to 'join the revolution' appeals to young minds and has been winning many converts. But can these young people be blamed for their interest in such appeals and subsequent defection to emergent groups that have abandoned confessional evangelical faith? Raised in a church that has offered them little by way of careful biblical exegesis regarding their relationship to culture, providing no tools from God's law for a right biblical understanding of justice and righteousness, they have been easy prey for the purveyors of the new liberalism. What I believe we need to offer them is the new Puritanism that provides robust biblical answers and a truly Christ-centred alternative to the hybridized offspring of the cultural Marxists masquerading as Christian conscience.[26] The new Puritanism's emphatic alternative is that biblical revelation is the only guiding presupposition that will yield true conclusions to these questions, and the law of biblical revelation the only legitimate framework for organizing a society in a manner that does not invoke the judgement of God.

0.7 Authentic Pluralism

This perspective is Puritan to the core because at the foundation of Puritan theology was the view that all factuality can only be properly understood in subordination to God. There can therefore be no indifference to good and evil. Thus, a pagan 'cosmopolitanism' that 'equalizes' all beliefs and faiths in a social melting pot was, in the Puritan view, little more than a Tower of Babel in pursuit of a dangerous and false unity.[27] This did not mean a rejection of religious toleration in terms of people's personal beliefs, or hostility to various people groups with other customs and ideas living in Christian lands. The Puritan thesis rejects a pluralism of *law structures*, or *moralities* as being humanistic, polytheistic, idolatrous and self-eviscerating. However, the same Puritanism promotes equality before *Christian law*, freedom of personal belief, and liberty of public worship of the God of Scripture (or freedom not to worship). The Puritan-inspired Toleration Act of 1650 in England repealed all acts requiring church attendance at church on Sundays (Catholic or Protestant). "The intention was to provide civil equality as well as religious liberty."[28] This meant complete liberty for the public worship of Christians in their various denominations – though it certainly did not mean that Muslims could build mosques or madrasas and start Sharia courts as a parallel social order replete with their own legal system as in modern Britain![29] The famous *Instrument of Government* reinforced a Christian law and order, and freedom and equality for Christian forms of worship, stating that, "the Christian religion, as it is contained in the scriptures, be held forth and recommended as the *public profession of these nations.*"[30] This further meant that, as long as people did not, 'cause civil injury or actual disturbances of others' they were free to publically practice Christianity as they chose – at this time in English history this did not extend to Roman Catholicism (for obvious geopolitical reasons) or to those who practiced licentiousness.[31] Notably however, not one person died for religion in Protectoral Britain. Under Cromwell the Jews were also readmitted to England and people's consciences were not tyrannized over.

"He proposed no legislation to prevent men and women from worshipping as they wished...a vast amount of theology he disapproved of was published uncensored; and he did not prosecute anyone for religious opinions they were reported to have shared with others behind closed doors and with like-minded folk."[32] Likewise, Rushdoony and the new Puritans see themselves as the *authentic pluralists* holding to the only kind of pluralism that is biblically viable, non-idolatrous and non-disintegrating – maximum liberty, plurality and freedom within the bounds of God's moral law. This in no way excludes realism in the face of current social reality in the West, nor ignores the challenge of functioning as God's missionaries in an idolatrous order. Observing that the modern humanistic state is seeking a radical enforcement of *uniformity* in terms of a neo-pagan faith through its public schools, that tolerates no dissent, Rushdoony writes:

A single culture is demanded, and the public school must create it.... [A] free pluralistic society requires the abolition of the public school and tax support of the school in favour of a pluralistic education. The competitive aspect will ensure the quality of education, and the cultural implications of various faiths, philosophies and opinions can be given freedom to develop and make their contribution.[33]

Here we see a missiological strategy. By pursuing educational freedom in a society now filled with competing philosophies and religious ideas, where Christianity has ceased to be the religious consensus within the establishment, Rushdoony believed that Christianity would inevitably win the cultural battle by virtue of the fact that *it is true*. The cultural implications of the faith would be proven so superior to all other competitors that the truth of the gospel, as it did in pagan antiquity, would again triumph in minds and hearts by the grace of God. This then is one way Christians can live peaceably under an alien law structure, and by it, steadily transform the culture and restore a Christian moral order that honours God. A Puritan missiology thus seeks to win and not whip people into the faith, pursuing true freedom under God. The new Puritanism (theonomy) as represented by Rushdoony and others envisions the progressive advancements of Christ's reign and the transformation of the social order by individual regeneration and self-government in line with God's word. Faithful and joyful obedience to God in the family, church, school and vocations then follows, and only then will we see the gradual and peaceful implementation of God's righteous law within all the various spheres of life. A Puritan missiological vision thus looks forward in hope. It is from firmly within this tradition that I explore the present challenge and opportunity facing the church in the West. I look to the Puritans, old and new, frequently drawing on the work and best insights of those called 'theonomists,' Rushdoony in particular, because I am convinced that this direction of thought exegetes both scripture and culture accurately, and puts us in the right path (faithfulness to God's total word) for finding answers to our present crisis. Whilst I differ with Rushdoony (and others amongst the new Puritans) in a number of areas and applications, and my extensive use of his work certainly does not commit me to all his distinctive views; nonetheless, overall, I am persuaded that the new Puritanism (in which I do not hesitate to say I include myself) has a prophetic role to play in the church today and holds an important key to the churches mission and the recovery of the gospel.

0.8 The *Missio Dei*

I am acutely aware that this perspective puts me in a real minority in the field of missiology to say the least. But in light of our cultural crisis and my study of God's word, I have come to believe that, for the most part, both contemporary missiology, and evangelical discourse generally, in its examination of the church's message and calling in light of God's kingdom mission, does not pay sufficient attention to the specifics of God's word. In particular, its neglect of *biblical law*, in its understanding of the gospel and the kingdom reign of God, results in its impoverishment. By *biblical law* I take Jonathan Burnside's definition to be normative: "Biblical law [is] an integration of different instructional genres of the Bible which together express a *vision of society ultimately answerable to God*."[34] This implies an acceptance of the material authority of the complete divine law and mankind's accountability in terms of it. Put simply, I believe that in general, missiologists and theologians guiding the church in dealing with critical aspects of the *missio Dei* and 'reign of God' in a pluralistic age, consistently look to secular social and political theories, drawn from non-Christian philosophical ideas, to help define and accomplish the work of the kingdom of God rather than resting in and building upon the clear instruction of God's word. In response to this deficit, I consider the material authority of God's complete word in the Bible to be the only standard for the defining of the 'Good News of the Kingdom,' the ordering of social relationships, the formation of culture and the shaping of socio-political theory – including concerns for our shared environment, economic relations, and the meaning of social or public justice. Rather than looking to theological liberalism, and political and social sciences, employing variations on the thought of Karl Marx, Jean Jacques Rousseau Herbert Marcuse, Antonio Gramsci, Georg Wilhelm Friedrich Hegel, John Stuart Mill, Michel Foucault, Faustus Socinus and many others, I would urge that *biblical law in all of Scripture* must be taken more seriously when considering the Great Commission, the Cultural Mandate and issues of justice, social order and the meaning and implications of Christ's atonement. So, the most important questions implicit in all the following studies are:

a) What is the relationship between biblical law and gospel, and a faithful Christian vision of the kingdom of God and the *missio Dei*?

b) What is the nature of our current crisis of civilization and what does Scripture have to say about religious pluralism?

c) How does the Biblical vision of the gospel of the Kingdom help us understand the causes of the present theological, cultural, and sociopolitical crisis?

d) In what ways does this vision of the kingdom of God point us out of the present morass and navigate us toward hope and a future?

e) What can we do as Christians in our present cultural moment to build for the future faithfully?

To avoid misunderstanding, it is necessary to briefly say something about the provenance of the term *missio Dei*, as its use in many circles has justifiably come under sustained attack for conflating God's mission with the historical process, thereby side-stepping the specific calling of the church and practically excluding evangelism. It seems this now controversial term was first used by the German missiologist Karl Hartenstein in summarizing the teaching of Karl Barth.[35] Barth's name alone immediately raises many concerns for the reformed and evangelical reader because of the questionable views of Barth on the authority of Scripture and Christian theology generally – but those issues cannot be discussed here as they lie outside the scope of this work. The perception of the term *missio Dei* is not helped either by its popularity within and association with, a broad ecumenism.[36] Nonetheless, despite its dubious parentage, the original intent of the term *missio Dei* was simply to communicate that the concept of mission must be rooted in the doctrine of the Trinity, because our mission flows from the inner dynamic movement of God himself in personal relationship.[37] Consequently, despite legitimate criticism of many missiologists use of the term, I can agree with Christopher Wright that, "the expression can be retained as expressing a major and vital biblical truth...the God revealed in the scriptures is personal, purposeful and goal oriented."[38] The *missio Dei* (mission of God) pertains then to the 'sending of God' (of His Son, the Holy Spirit and His church) and the universal 'reign of God' *(basileia tou Theou)* and is therefore not limited to earlier, somewhat truncated, soteriological, cultural or ecclesiastical definitions of 'mission.' The godfather of much contemporary missiological thought, David Bosch, with whom I differ profoundly in many areas, nonetheless affirms, in principle, a God-centred and not man-centred approach to mission and the kingdom; one that begins with the Triune God and recognizes that he is not limited to the institution of the church, whilst always utilizing His covenant people as privileged participants in his work. Bosch writes that the church has to be:

Service to the *missio Dei*, representing God in and over against the

37

world, pointing to God, holding up the God-child before the eyes of the world ... the church witnesses to the fullness of the promise of God's reign and participates in the ongoing struggle between that reign and the powers of darkness and evil.[39]

So, God's mission is not limited to the institutional church sphere, but it embraces the whole organic church – God's people wherever they are. This definition of the *missio Dei* as the universal implementation of the 'reign of God' will be considered normative for the purposes of this book.

However, it should be noted that the meaning and manifestation of 'God's reign' within the rubric of the *missio Dei* is also very much disputed by missiologists, with some scholars now viewing the very term *missio Dei* as a 'Trojan Horse' for various rival concepts of mission to be smuggled within the walls of an ecumenical theology of mission.[40] Hoedemaker thus notes that the term '*missio Dei*,' with its theologically broad definitions, can be used legitimately by people who subscribe to mutually exclusive theological positions.[41] It is into this ambiguity that covenantal hermeneutics and a Puritan approach to the 'reign of God' can speak with a fresh, albeit controversial clarity. I have then endeavoured in the following pages, to further biblical faith and life through what I hope is an engaging analysis of key themes in contemporary missiology through a reformed, Puritan lens. As an unexceptional cultural theologian, apologist and generalist, and given the scope of this work, I have no doubt that my commentary and analysis will be lacking in places and that much deeper work and reflection needs to be done in many areas. But I have, to the best of my ability, sought to engage the cultural challenges in a manner as faithful to Scripture as I can muster. This is done, not simply out of an academic interest in missiological concerns, but because I genuinely believe that the core elements of *Puritan* thought must be restated with relevance in our time, as central to both the recovery of the church, and the Western world itself from the brink of disaster – a cultural auto-homicide well underway. As already intimated, it is my sincere desire that this meager contribution to missological reflection will lead more people to take a fresh look at a reformed vision of the gospel *and* its corresponding social order. The primary obstacle to my modest hope in our time is due to what Marilynne Robinson called a, "collective eagerness to disparage without knowledge or information about the thing disparaged, when the reward is the pleasure of sharing an attitude one knows is socially approved."[42] She said this in reference to the attitude one encounters at the mention of 'the Puritans,' and their much derided evangelical form of civilization, since the very term is falsely associated with repressiveness and intolerance in popular consciousness. But to ignore and disparage evangelical law and social order, and the gospel of the kingdom which enlivened it is, "to make ourselves ignorant and contemptuous of the first two or three hundred years of one major strain of our own civilization."[43]

PART I

THE MISSION OF GOD:

STUDIES IN A BIBLICAL PERSPECTIVE

Chapter One

IN UNDERSTANDING BE MEN:
THE CRISIS OF OUR AGE AND
THE RECOVERY OF THE GOSPEL

The Puritans exemplified maturity; we don't. Spiritual warfare made the Puritans what they were. They accepted conflict as their calling, seeing themselves as their Lord's soldier-pilgrims…not expecting to be able to advance a single step without opposition of one sort or another…. Today, however, Christians in the West are found to be on the whole passionless, passive and one fears, prayerless. Cultivating an ethos that encloses personal piety in a pietistic cocoon, they leave public affairs to go their own way and neither expect nor, for the most part, seek influence beyond their own Christian circle…[but] the Puritans labored for a holy England and New England – sensing that where privilege is neglected and unfaithfulness reigns, national judgment threatens.

– J. I. Packer

1.1 The Lost Word

The great reformer Martin Luther once said, "No greater mischief can happen to a Christian people, than to have God's word taken away from them, or falsified, so that they no longer have it pure and clear. God grant that we and our descendants be not witnesses of such a calamity." There can be no doubt, however, that as Protestant descendants of Luther we are witness to this calamity in our time - in our families, our schools, our courts, in the corridors of power, and even in our churches. Any missiological analysis of the Western world that does not address this desperate reality is, to my mind, hopelessly compromised and essentially worthless. Tragically, much of the academic 'help' offered to the Western church to address our malady either does not see, or refuses to see, that Luther's calamity is indeed the worst kind to befall Christians and that it is very much upon us.

Commensurate with this, social and cultural decay has advanced to such a degree that we are now seeing early glimmers of a broader realization among cultural and political elites of the crisis facing the West due to its abandonment of biblical faith. In a fascinating article, the social and political commentator Dr. Samuel Gregg has noted that increasing numbers of secular commentators and leading politicians are slowly realizing the need for a decisive public return to the values and virtues of the Christian worldview if European and even North American cultural identity is to survive and social cohesion and civil order be maintained. One such politician recently making 'politically incorrect' remarks in Europe, he notes, is German Chancellor Angela Merkel. Gregg writes:

> Not only has Merkel upset the European political class (especially the Left and the Greens) by saying what everyone knows that – multiculturalism has "utterly failed" – but she also argued that the issue was not "too much Islam" but "too little Christianity." "We have too few discussions about the Christian view of mankind," Merkel claimed in a recent speech. She then stressed that Germany needs to reflect more upon "the values that guide us, about our Judeo-Christian tradition." It was one way, Merkel maintained, of bringing "about cohesion in our society." And as much as significant portions of European society would like to deny it, it's simply a historical fact that the idea of Europe and European values such as liberty, equality before the law, and solidarity did not suddenly appear ex nihilo in the late seventeenth-century with the various Enlightenments.... There is increasing recognition, for example, that the idea of human rights was first given concrete expression by medieval canon lawyers.

Having noted that much of the church has reduced its contribution to society to the vague humanitarian platitudes of NGOs, he points to a quite surprising and encouraging development:

> This makes it even more ironic that increasing numbers of secular European thinkers believe Europe can only reinvigorate its distinct identity and values through reengaging its Judeo-Christian heritage. This is certainly the conclusion of one of Germany's most prominent intellectuals, Jürgen Habermas. A self-described "methodological atheist," Habermas has been insisting for some time that Europe no longer has the luxury of wallowing in historical denial. As Habermas wrote in his 2006 book, *A Time of Transitions*: "Christianity, and nothing else [is] the ultimate foundation of liberty, conscience, human rights, and democracy, the benchmarks of western civilization. To this day we have no other options. We continue to nourish ourselves

from this source. Everything else is postmodern chatter."[1]

This is a telling statement from a leading secular intellectual, observing an historic and social reality that eludes many Christians in the West today. This includes many mainline and 'evangelical' missiologists, endlessly holding forth about the alleged sins of the West as they pontificate, 'post-Christendom' and 'post-colonial,' like feminist revisionists on the evils of all generations and classes save their own. This historical revisionism and pluralistic mushymindedness is utterly pervasive in the younger generation (my generation below age forty), and part of my motivation in writing this study is to help stimulate and encourage critical reflection on the biblical missiology that did so much to shape our liberties and free institutions that are eroding before our very eyes.[2] It would thus seem that even the secular world is slowly beginning to realize that the decline of Christianity in the West and the virtues of the law of God are leading us to an inevitable social collapse and cultural death. We are indisputably living through a time that Martin Luther prayed he would never see:

> Whoso has Christ has rightly fulfilled the law. But to take away the law altogether, which sticks in nature and is written in our hearts and born in us, is a thing impossible and against God. And whereas the law of nature is somewhat darker, and speaks only of works, therefore, Moses and the Holy Ghost more clearly declare and expound it, by naming those works which God would have us do and to leave undone. Hence Christ also says: 'I am not come to destroy the law.' Worldly people would willingly give him royal entertainment who could bring this to pass, and make out that Moses, through Christ, is quite taken away. O, then we should quickly see what a fine kind of life there would be in the world! But God forbid, and keep us from such errors, and suffer us not to live to see the same.[3]

Recognizing the sad reality that we have "lived to see the same," it must be said at the outset that the Christian faith is not simply a matter of social utility. Jesus Christ is Lord, King, and Savior who came to establish his kingdom. The Christian is to live for the glory of God and for the kingdom of Jesus Christ, even if it means suffering, persecution, or even death – not simply because it gives one a better life. Nonetheless, because of the resurrection power unleashed by Christ's conquest of sin and death by the omnipotent working of the Holy Spirit, the transformation of all life by the mighty dunamis (power) of God is an inescapable bi-product of the ministry of the gospel. The inherent power of almighty God residing in the believer by the person of the Holy Spirit means that the power of the new creation is already at work in the world. This redeeming life and power transforms and renews all life by regeneration, so that hope, forgiveness, joy, peace, righteousness, justice, restoration, healing, social well-being, and law-abiding faith characterize a Christian people. It therefore follows, as Luther makes clear above, that when men turn away from the gospel and God's kingdom law, social decay and every kind of evil proliferates. It is, therefore, not historical accident that modern Western history's worst tyrants have vilified the law of God and that many revolutionary intellectuals who have transformed the way we think about ourselves have openly despised God's law and sought to remove it from our consciousness, as Luther warned. This should not surprise us; in fact it is quite logical. Antinomianism is the spirit of lawlessness which is the very essence of the demonic. The Bible not only defines sin as lawlessness (1 John 3:4), which is the opposite of righteousness and sanctification (Rom 6:19), it also refers to Satan as the lawless one (2 Thess. 2:3,8). It is from this demonic power – the spirit of disobedience, and a life of lawlessness – that we have been redeemed according to St. Paul, who reminds us that Jesus Christ "gave himself for us to redeem us from all lawlessness and to purify for himself a people for his own possession who are zealous for good works" (Titus 2:14). The father of modern psychology, Sigmund Freud, is one example of this demonic urge in sinful man to abolish the law. He ended his days writing a book spitting out venom against the law of God, ejecting law and crime from the universe and reinventing Moses as a pagan Egyptian in Moses and Monotheism.[4] Likewise, national socialist Adolf Hitler, the twentieth century's most famous tyrant, who provoked the Second World War the same year Freud passed away, whilst claiming a belief in some kind of God declared:

> The day will come when I shall hold up against these commandments the tables of a new law. And history will recognize our movement as the great battle for humanity's liberation, a liberation from the curse of Mount Sinai, from the dark stammering of nomads who could no more trust their own sound instincts, who could understand the divine only in the form of a tyrant who orders one to do the very things one doesn't like. This is what we are fighting against: the masochistic spirit

of self-torment, the curse of so-called morals, idolized to protect the weak from the strong.... Against the so-called Ten Commandments, against them we are fighting."[5]

Hitler's god was not the God of Scripture; his god was a lawless principle of power and pleasure. Many people in our culture would not be particularly shocked by these words today because they agree with them (so long as Hitler's name was not attached to the reference). These words could have been spoken by many a theological or political liberal, because both theological and political liberalism (by political liberalism I mean the "progressivist," cultural Marxism of the Left) are viciously hostile to the law of God. Stalin's Soviet Union also sought the eradication of the law of God and tried to ban even the reading of the Bible. Our culture is swiftly manifesting a like vitriolic hatred for God's word, attempting to remove not only reference to the law and gospel of God in public discourse, but also public representations of it – a difficult proposition since many are attached to judicial and political buildings and monuments, including the Parliamentary buildings in Ottawa, Canada. All that said, since God's power is available to the believer by the Holy Spirit, Christians cannot merely blame the culture for the growing persecution of Christianity and lawlessness at work in our time. It has been rightly said, 'as goes the church, so goes the world,' and so our current cultural crisis can be traced to the compromises of the church, and the private and public loss of the law-word of God by the severing of the connection between theology (religion) and every area of life. This severance begins in the pulpit, radically affects the pew, and then spreads to the culture. The greatest and most celebrated British judge of the twentieth century, Lord Denning, in an important lecture on the influence of religion on law and the social order shows the character of the connection between religion and public morality:

> In primitive [meaning earlier] societies the influence of religion on law was obvious, but it is not so obvious in modern societies. In primitive communities, religion, morals and law were indistinguishably mixed together. In the Ten Commandments, for instance, you find the First Commandment, which is religious: "God spake these words and said, 'I am the Lord thy God: Thou shalt have none other Gods but me.'" You find the Fifth Commandment, which is a moral precept: "Honour thy father and thy mother, that thy days may be long in the land which

the Lord thy God giveth thee." You find the Eighth Commandment, which is a legal duty: "Thou shalt not steal." This intermingling is typical of all early communities. The severance of these ideas – of law from morality, and of religion from law – belongs very distinctly to the later stages of the evolution of modern thought. This severance has gone a great way. Many people now think that religion and law have nothing in common. The law they say, governs our dealings with our fellows, whereas religion concerns our dealings with God. Likewise they hold that law has nothing to do with morality... [but] without religion, there can be no morality, there can be no law.[6]

This statement makes clear the inextricable connection between religion and law, but also reveals that the present novelty is not with those seeking to uphold biblical faith and law in ecclesiastical, familial, social and cultural life, but with the 'later stages of the evolution of modern thought.' He goes on in this essay to show the biblical foundation of the principles of law in the Western tradition and the implicit influence of Christianity within it.

It seems inevitable then, that without a recovery of the gospel and God's total word, for church and society, without a return to the theological (religious) foundation of social order, our very freedoms and liberties, peace, justice, and truth will disappear until a faithful missionary endeavour can recover a degenerate Western culture.

1.2 A Puritan Response

With the above challenge in mind, in this volume, I am arguing for the necessity of a recovery of applied biblical faith to every area of life – a vision of human life and affairs that was, I am convinced, best exemplified so far in our history by the Puritans, prominent heirs of the Reformation. The Christian academic apologist, Cornelius Van Til, reflecting the Puritan tradition, once laid out the choice in life before all men and women as, 'autonomy or theonomy' – selflaw or God's law – and in past decades this antithesis has become increasingly evident in both ecclesiastical and civic spheres. At the root of all the struggles of our time is the one that Luther identified – the question of the place and authority of the Word of God – and it is here that the Puritan tradition has so much to teach us, proving its abiding relevance for the Christian church. For them, the Bible was a complete revelation from God which is final, authoritative, infallible, and to be applied to all of life. If they confronted situations that were not covered by the specifics of Scripture, they held that such matters could be clarified by reasonable deductions from the Bible. As Puritan scholar Allen Carden has written, "their absolute belief in the Bible and the God of the Bible was the fundamental motivating force behind their worldview and the establishment of New England.... Given the choice of the comforts of England where violations of God's law were rampant or the wilderness of America where God's Word would receive its rightful place, thousands chose the latter."[7] Thus the source of the Puritan worldview, the foundation stone of their conception of the Mission of God, was the Bible itself. As John Eliot declared, "the Law of God, written in the Scriptures of the Old and New Testament...[is] pure, holy, righteous, perfect, and good... the perfect System or Frame of Laws, to guide all the Moral actions of man."[8] Personal piety, whilst important, was not enough for the Puritan Christian. The Bible was a revelation that had been given to the world to teach the nations the gospel and law of God; it was central to all life and could not be imprisoned within the four walls of a place of worship or the private home. Thus, "biblical examples and teachings were constantly held up as the standard for a Christian society."[9] Whilst, in this sense, the Puritans were Biblicist in their orientation, they were anything but anti-intellectual. Founding both Harvard and Yale universities, their view of knowledge was holistic and non-compartmentalised – they didn't need to run courses on the integration of faith and learning because it flowed inevitably from their worldview. Consequently, the intellectual power and force of Puritanism has been recognised even by non-Christian scholars. As John Coffey points out, "secular scholars like Perry Miller rehabilitated the original Puritans as serious intellectuals, distancing them from ill-educated fundamentalists and holy-rollers."[10] One of the most famous intellectuals in the history of America was the Princeton theologian and philosopher, Jonathan Edwards, referred to by some as the 'last of the Puritans.' He has been widely regarded as one of the greatest minds America ever produced. At the same time, intellectual rigor and accomplishment was not sought by the Puritans for its own sake but rather as a means to glorify God by effectively understanding and applying God's word and will. They were not public intellectuals in the modern sense of that term – a group of self-styled elites who defend a status quo. On the contrary, John Owen, perhaps the greatest of the Puritan minds in Old England, reveals the foundational presupposition of

Puritan intellectual thought: "pin not your faith upon men's opinions, the Bible is the touchstone."[11] Carden sums up the Puritan mind effectively, that "in terms of an overall worldview that effectively integrated a knowledge of and response to God and biblical values into all areas of life, the Puritans...were not to be outdone."[12] This uncompromisingly Christ-centred view is, however, even less popular now than it was in the seventeenth century. The level of hostility manifest by some (even amongst 'Bible-believing' Christians) toward evangelicals affirming a robust 'Puritan' missiology remains considerable, and it is not just evangelicals who have high regard for the Puritans who are marginalized. The personal accounts related by the fair-minded Roman Catholic scholar John Morrill, whose ground-breaking and extensive scholarship in the Puritans, the English Revolution, and specifically Oliver Cromwell, are telling. His scholarly work has led not only to verbal insults and hate mail, but actual physical assault on his person whilst speaking at academic conferences![13] Certainly consistent Reformed theology applied to every sphere of life is not the darling perspective of our generation of Christians (as noted it is presently marginal at best), but therein lies a part of its striking relevance to our day. To avoid the characteristic blindness of our age, we need the clarity that the faith of the past builders of Christian civilization provides in shining a light into our dark places – this requires attention to the old faith and old books. The Puritans and early evangelicals surely had their blind spots, and we likewise have our own. Consequently, only what C.S. Lewis called the "clean sea breeze of the centuries blowing through our minds," can blow away the clouds obstructing our vision that we might see the cause of our current dereliction.[14]

1.3 Puritanism – Alive and Kicking?

I have, then, in the opening study of this book, already laid my cards on the table. As a cultural theologian, pastor, and Christian apologist, I self-consciously stand in the Augustinian, Calvinistic, and Puritan tradition. I do so because I am convinced that this is the most biblically faithful and consistent interpretation of the Christian faith. As such, this vision of the gospel is as relevant today as it has ever been. I grant of course that the very term 'Puritan' sounds dusty, prudish, irrelevant, and arcane to most modern ears, yet in a fascinating essay on the contemporary relevance of Puritanism, Pulitzer Prize-winning author, Marilynne

Robinson corrects this ignorant perception: Puritanism was a highly elaborate moral, religious, intellectual and political tradition which had its origins in the writing and social experimentation of John Calvin and those he influenced. Whilst it flourished on this continent – it appears to me to have died early in this century – it established great universities and cultural institutions and an enlightened political order.... Puritan civilization in North America quickly achieved unprecedented levels of literacy, longevity, and mass prosperity, or happiness, as it was called in those days.[15] Historical scholars actually can't agree about exactly when Puritanism allegedly 'died,' giving way to a less fervent English non-conformity and broader North American evangelicalism, but all agree that the impact of Puritanism has been so far-reaching it is difficult to fully describe and quantify. Although sixteenth and seventeenth-century Puritanism was first an ecclesiastical phenomenon concerned initially with reforming the Church of England,[16] as well as being a reaction against the values and ideals of the so-called Enlightenment, it came to shape the structure of our key institutions far more than the secular forces of humanism. From scientific enterprise, free-market economics, and companionate marriage, to representative political order (by consent of the people), equality before the law, moral and social reform, and the idea of a national mission, the culture of Puritanism gave shape to Western civilization. This profundity of influence in their nurture of freedom and prosperity is not exaggerated. In his discussion of Puritan political thought, George Sabine highlights that "The separation of church and state was...an essential element of Calvinism, but not in the modern sense that leaves the state a wholly secular institution.... In the sixteenth century the separation of church and state was regarded as a novelty fostered by Puritans and Jesuits." Moreover, because the 'Independent' Puritans believed that any body of Christians could form a true church and ordain its own clergy and establish its own forms of worship without civil or ecclesiastical authorization, "Church and state became quite definitely two societies, not only separate but in principle independent, with the power of coercion concentrated in the state but limited to purposes within the province of secular government." This meant first that there was "a general connection between the principle of free assent in religion and consent to government." At the same time, "they never meant to deny that government ought to repress idolatry." Sabine argues then that "Independency came to its greatest power in

Cromwell's New Model Army."[17] This meant ultimately a war on tyranny. Cromwell biographer Robert Paul agrees that in the Puritan quest for toleration and liberty of conscience, "the Independents were defending a principle of far more value than their individual safety."[18] And so for John Cooke, the English Puritan lawyer who brought King Charles I to trial and whose love of liberty helped him stay the course, "tyranny was a crime committed by absolute rulers who became tyrants not just by virtue of the servitude their position inculcated, but by their fixed intention to govern without Parliament or an independent judiciary or any other democratic check on their power."[19] Calvin's Genevan polity and view of commerce was thus essentially carried on and extended by his Puritan heirs. As David Hall notes, "The process of Genevan elections itself was a mirror of Calvin's view of human nature and the role of the state. In one of the earliest organized democratic traditions, Calvin's fellow citizens elected four new syndics (commissioners) from a slate of eight for an annual term." Hall goes on to note that "This Calvin shaped polity which appeared to be...daringly democratic for its day, provided checks and balances, separation of powers, election by residents, and other elements of the federal structure that would later be copied as one of Geneva's finest exports." Moreover, "where Calvinism spread, so did a love for free markets and capitalism." Calvin saw much of this social order as simply an outgrowth of the implications of Exodus 18.[20] It is exciting that the research in this area is not over. As John Coffey points out, "it would be a mistake for historians to stop asking big questions about the impact of Puritanism on the culture of Britain and America...and we should not overlook their most obvious legacy – ardent evangelical religion."[21] Although 'organized' Puritanism essentially collapsed after the restoration (when Charles II came to the throne) the impact of the Puritan commonwealth could not be swept away. Puritanism had laid the foundations for the first great political revolution of modern times, and it was to influence others to come. The comprehensively Christian social vision it gave to the settlers in the New World has never been equaled in America. As well as giving us the famous Westminster Confession and catechisms, which still today shape evangelicalism, the Puritan era gave the English-speaking world a group of uncompromisingly Christian political leaders such as Oliver Cromwell, John Winthrop and William Bradford, as have never been seen since. Given its undeniably formative influence in shaping the faith and culture of our civilization, surely the literary and historical legacy, and more importantly, the theological assumptions, and presuppositions of the Puritan mind, cannot and should not be despised. Despite its marginal character for over a century and a half, a quiet, but significant revival of Calvinistic Puritanism has been underway for some years in both England and North America and cannot be ignored any more by the church and seminary. Indeed, liberal Anglicans in England have themselves recycled the term 'Puritan' and used it as an insult against conservative evangelicals opposed to the ordination of gay clergy.[22] The 'funeral' of the Puritan legacy was premature, for it is alive and well within the rubric of Reformed evangelicalism today:

> Theorists of the Puritan legacy have tended to overlook the longevity and persistent popularity of the zealous evangelical religion that Puritans did so much to promote. They have been inclined to think of Puritan religion as a kind of booster rocket that propelled the spacecraft (of capitalism or democracy or American national identity) into orbit and then fell away once its job was done. Yet Puritan texts helped to feed revivals of hot Protestantism in the eighteenth century and beyond...precisely because Puritanism never really died out... much that counted as Puritanism was subsumed and perpetuated within the broader evangelical Protestant tradition.[23]

So, although Puritanism (consistent Reformed thought) with its biblical rigor may not be popular today for obvious cultural reasons in the context of an often compromised church, it remains alive and relevant, and I am convinced it is a large part of the answer to the decline of the church in the West. If this is the case, a good place to start would be to ask who these fervent, biblically faithful and passionate believers were and what their application of the faith looked like.

1.4 Who were the Puritans?

J. I. Packer, a specialist in the Puritans, asserted that "Puritanism was a world view, a total Christian philosophy, in intellectual terms a Protestantized and updated medievalism."[24] At the heart of this world view was a desire to make all of life 'holiness to the Lord.' Because of that applied vision, the term 'Puritan' was coined in the early 1560s as a form of insult to a growing movement, and became widely used as a slur against seventeenth-century evangelical Protestant reformers in

England by those who considered them anti-establishment perfectionists. These evangelical Englishmen, who considered the Church of England insufficiently reformed, heartily took up the term, regardless of the slander, and continued to flesh out the implications of the Reformation. The great Scottish Christian leader John Knox (who trained under Calvin at Geneva) is usually identified as the spiritual father of Puritanism – Knox himself saw Scotland adopt a Calvinist Parliament which sought to uphold the gospel and law of God. Oliver Cromwell is generally seen as the most important Puritan statesmen in European history. Their dream was that the church and state in England should be brought into conformity with the word of God and be a manifestation to the world of the character of Christ's righteous kingdom. Since God had dramatically delivered England from the Spanish Armada in 1588 and thus from the threat of being reduced to Papal obedience, the Puritans believed that England must honor God by being a model of godliness for the rest of the world. We may look on this from our vantage point as mere hubris, but it was not arrogant presumption. They genuinely believed in the providence of God over all history, and if God had delivered little England so remarkably, they reasoned it must have been for a purpose; they must have a calling and responsibility for which they were accountable. Queen Elizabeth was, for the most part, deaf to the pleas of the Puritans for reform. She died in 1603 and under the Stuarts, James I and Charles I (1603-1640), things went backward for the Puritans in terms of their hopes for reformation and a godly England. The kings appointed nominal formalists to positions of authority in the church who were not Calvinistic but Arminian men, largely unsympathetic to the theology of the Reformation. The years 1640-1660 have become known as the Puritan revolution; this 'revolution' was led by pastors, and was an era of unprecedented evangelism and Bible teaching across the country. Packer points out that Richard Baxter (a Puritan pastor) observed in his writings that godliness in England had increased during this period to such a degree that if their work in evangelism and teaching could have been carried on in like fashion for another twenty-five years, England was likely to have become a community of saints as the world had never seen; to put it another way, England had been in the grip of real revival. New liberties were being established; new colleges and universities for biblical education founded (Durham is one example); new charitable organizations to minister to the needs of the poor were flourishing; legal reforms toward a biblical justice were progressing, with the elimination of cruelty, barbarity, and torture. The sciences, industry, and international commerce were enjoying huge development and prosperity was increasing. Not only so, but England was emerging for the first time as a major European power and was respected throughout the world. But with the restoration of Charles II and the following persecution of non-conformists with around 20,000 Puritans spending time in prison over the next twenty-five years, the work faltered. By the time the toleration of non-conformity began again in 1689 the strength of the movement had been sapped. All this remarkable development of the social order is a far cry from the popular stereotype of the Puritans in black capes, pouring cold water over life, liberty, development, and pleasure. The lies and slurs leveled against Oliver Cromwell and Puritan England are manifold. Yet one of the most noted modern historians, Jacques Barzun, in his massive study *From Dawn to Decadence*, explodes a number of myths about them – including Cromwell. He writes that under the influence of the Puritans, "England and New England were not turned into places of systematic dullness and hypocrisy. Fifty years ago an English scholar delved into the records on both sides of the Atlantic and his findings explode the myth of the Puritan constipated in faith and thought."[25] Barzun reveals that the themes of sovereignty, the rule of law, obedience and revolt, truth and its attainment through revelation, reason, debate, science, nature and pleasure, and concern with the issues of justice and mercy are central in Puritan writings.[26] So, if the slurs were in fact religiously and politically-motivated lies, what were ordinary Puritans really like and what else did they believe? The first thing that must be said about them is that they were Bible-believing evangelicals who were concerned above all with godliness in each area of life (true piety) and were therefore also activists, because they believed that true Christians were the agents of Christ's renewing activity in the family, church, state, and all of life in this world. Whilst they saw themselves as pilgrims heading toward a new land, they focused their attention on the present world, knowing that they were called as God's servants to bring about the renewal of a fallen realm. Thus the Puritans had a warrior spirit – they were fighting Christians. Not in the sense of being naturally combative or antagonistic, but rather soldiers of truth committed to standing against what was wrong and seeking by faith and perseverance to put it right. The ideal Puritan

Christian was to honor God, give each person their due under God, and let God's word govern a life bathed in prayer. Christians must be the best husbands and wives, best children and parents, best employees and employers, best magistrates and citizens, best musicians and artists, best soldiers and servants – diligent, dutiful, respectful, honorable, in order to bring glory to God. The family was to be made into a church, where God was honored, God's word taught and God's glory sought above all else. Tenderheartedness and compassion were to mark the Puritan Christian and a spirit of generosity, mercy, and charity to overflow in a communitarian public spirit. Though life was warfare, the arms of that war were prayer and tears, because to the Puritan, the one who suffers conquers! This was the Puritan ideal and is found throughout their literature.[27] Consequently, to the Puritan mind, Christian piety was a priority. This implied that whatever else you did or were called to, personal godliness could not be sacrificed; it must come first. This meant not a monastic existence, but a deep commitment to biblical integrity in all of one's personal life. To deny the importance of this was to deny the rule and providence of God. You cannot glorify God by sinful living, no matter what you think you may be forfeiting by acting with integrity. Because personal responsibility before God was seen as so significant, the Puritans emphasized the importance of the individual moral agent and personal conversion. This did not make for individualism, but a community of individuals with mutual responsibilities – thus they were communitarian but not collectivist (communist). This sense of individuality within accountable community led to the biblical conviction that they were a community before God. Hence, society was a unit from which you could not opt out. You served God in the family, church and community, wherever God had placed you and to whatever state he had called you, for better or worse. As a community they believed that they were exhorted and instructed by God's covenant word and that therefore God viewed them and judged them as he did Israel. Family, church, and state were each seen as subject to blessings and curses in terms of God's word for obedience and disobedience, and since judgement in these contexts is corporate, what affects the community affects the individual – you stand with the community. So whether God is judging the community or nation or blessing it, the Christian must stand fast, be faithful to God, and intercede. There was no get-out clause.

They were motivated by goals that used to characterize most

evangelicals. First, they believed in the importance of justice, or *equity*. Justice meant receiving what one was due under God, not absolute *equality* where everyone gets the same as everyone else. People are all different, having different gifts, families, backgrounds and abilities, and most important, are morally differentiated. For the Puritans, justice was defined not by human imagination or social convention but by the law of God which covered all areas of life. As Puritan scholar Joel Beeke notes, "The law of God directly or indirectly addresses the world and the life of every individual."[28] The Puritan writer Richard Sibbes typified the Puritan mind on this, "There is not anything or any condition that befalls a Christian in this life but there is a general rule in the Scripture for it, and this rule is quickened by example, because it is practical knowledge."[29] Here, the right that we all have as human beings is the freedom to serve God and receive what we are due in terms of his law. There were many lawyers among the Puritans and they labored under English Common Law to free people to serve God and obey His law. The importance of obedience to God's law was a conviction they drew from the Reformation itself. The masterful Dutch Reformed theologian and contemporary of John Owen in England, Herman Witsius (1636-1708) expressed well the reformed and covenantal view of the law shared by the English Puritans:

> Seeing the Decalogue contains the sum of the law of nature, and, as to its substance, is one and the same therewith, so far it is of perpetual and universal obligation ... and who can doubt, that it is the duty of a rational creature, to acknowledge God as his supreme Lord and governor, to whose will, without any further examination, he ought to submit, saying, "Lord, what wouldst thou have me to do...." The people of Israel constituted the church at that time, and as Jesus Christ the Son of God, and king of the church, prescribed the Decalogue to them, it follows, that the same law retains its force in the church, till it be abrogated again by the king of the church. We are not to think, that the church of the Old Testament, which consisted of Israelites, and that of the New, though for the greatest part made up of Gentiles, were a quite different people. They ought to be looked upon as one Kingdom of Christ, who made both one (Eph. 2:14) and who grafted us, when wild olives, into that fat olive, (Rom. 11:17). And consequently, the laws which were once given to the church by Christ the king, are always binding on the whole church, unless Christ

shall declare, that he has abrogated them by some other institution. But it is absurd to imagine, that Christ abrogated the moral law, in so far, as he gave it by the mediation of Moses to the church of Israel, and directly confirmed the same law, of the same king, in one and the same kingdom, though that kingdom is now enriched with new accessions and new privileges; why should we suppose it abrogated and ratified again almost in the same breath?[30]

One of the most popular of the Puritan preachers and exegetes in London during the seventeenth century, Thomas Watson, is of the same mind when he writes in his *Body of Practical Divinity* from 1692:

The Scripture, as Chrysostom says, is a garden, and the moral law is the chief flower in it: it is a banquet, and the moral law is the chief dish in it. The moral law is perfect. 'The law of the Lord is perfect' (Ps. 19:7). It is an exact model and platform of religion; it is the standard of truth, the judge of controversies, the pole-star to direct us to heaven.... Though the moral law be not a Christ to justify us, it is a rule to instruct us. The moral law is unalterable; it remains still in force.[31]

Secondly, in terms of this law, they believed Christians were responsible to God for the care and compassion they showed to others. Neighbour love, or *philanthropy*, was a rudimentary requirement for believers. In the providence of God we are placed in a community (neighbourhood/church/family) to show compassion by taking responsibility for the needs around us. The Puritans did not contract this task out to the state and its welfare programs. Ryken explains that "The Puritans did not share the confidence of our century that social cohesion depends on governmental structures. Rather they understood the crucial role played by the spirit of community."[32] A public spirit was required of all believers, so a failure to care for social needs was believed to hold negative consequences by inviting the judgement of God. Help for those in need went well beyond giving alms to the poor. They funded students through university. They bought books and Bibles for those who could not afford them. They helped people find employment and start businesses. They cared for orphans, widows, and the destitute. At the same time they did not believe in 'indiscriminate charity,' which they considered a social menace, but rather responsible support for those in genuine need. Samuel Hartlib, for example, distinguished between the involuntary poor and unemployed, and the incorrigibly idle.[33] William Perkins in a fashion typical of Puritan thought said, "it is the good law of our land...agreeable to the law of God, that none should beg that are able to labor."[34] They regularly cited St. Paul: "if anyone is not willing to work let him not eat" (2 Thess. 3:10), as requiring discriminating common sense in the distribution of charitable aid. Thirdly, the Puritans believed in the earlier meaning of toleration – bearing with someone even if you believed their ideas wrong and disagreeable. They expressed this idea as liberty of conscience to interpret the Word of God – this meant that the idea of toleration was still tied to Scripture. This is over-against the medieval view that persisted in the church in Europe throughout most of the seventeenth century, that the church or church-state alliance must enforce a particular vision of orthodoxy, even to the point of death. The Puritan view did not encourage a disruption of community life by lawless heresy, but it meant permission for independence and liberty to exist where law and order were not threatened. Oliver Cromwell and John Owen were both great exponents of this ideal, stemming from their desire that England be governed by Biblical law.[35] Finally in 1689, the foundation the Old England Puritans had laid was formalized in the Act of Toleration. Modern political correctness has been reversing this Puritan legacy by seeking to impose and enforce a particular line of believing, speaking, and even thinking upon entire nations and punishing dissent through censure, fines, and human rights 'heresy courts' to prosecute offenders.

Fourthly, the Puritans were convinced that knowledge had to be universally spread by sound education, literacy, and Bible teaching. They preached expository sermons that were applied to life and could be remembered. They began schools and universities because they believed all truth was God's truth and could be properly understood only in the light of the teaching of Scripture. They valued all the major arts from poetry to physics, military discipline and strategy because they were practical people living in God's world as his servants, ready to do his will in every area. Education in all areas of life was necessary to be fully equipped to serve God and bring him glory.

The Rev. John Geree recorded a noteworthy summary of the character and goals of the Old English Puritan:

He accounted subjection to the higher powers to be part of pure religion, as well as to visit the fatherless and widows: yet did he distinguish between authority and lusts of magistrates, to that he submitted, but in these he durst not be a servant of men, being bought with a price. Just laws and commands he willingly obeyed not only for fear but for conscience also; but such as were unjust he refused to observe, choosing rather to obey God than man; yet his refusal was modest and with submission to penalties, unless he could procure indulgence from authority. He was careful in all relations to know, and to duty, and that with singleness of heart as unto Christ. He accounted religion an engagement to duty, that the best Christians should be best husbands, best wives, best parents, best children, best masters, best servants, best magistrates, best subjects, that the doctrine of God might be adorned, not blasphemed. His family he endeavors to make a church, both in regard of persons and exercises, admitting none into it but such as feared God; and laboring that those that were borne in it, might be born again unto God. He blessed his family morning and evening by the word and prayer and took care to perform those ordinances in the best season. He brought up his children in the nurture and admonition of the Lord and commanded his servants to keep the way of the Lord. He set up discipline in his family, as he desired it in the church, not only reproving but restraining vileness in his. He was conscientious of equity as well as piety knowing that unrighteousness is abomination as well as ungodliness. He was cautious in promising, but careful in performing, counting his word no less engagement than his bond. He was a man of tender heart, not only in regard of his own sin, but others' misery, not counting mercy arbitrary, but a necessary duty wherein as he prayed for wisdom to direct him, so he studied for cheerfulness and bounty to act. He was sober in the use of things of this life, rather beating down the body, than pampering it, yet he denied not himself the use of God's blessing, lest he should be unthankful, but avoid excess lest he should be forgetful of the Donor. In his habit he avoided costliness and vanity, neither exceeding his degree in civility, nor declining what suited with Christianity, desiring in all things to express gravity. His own life he accounted a warfare, wherein Christ was his captain, his arms, prayers, and tears. The Cross his banner, and his word, *Vincit qui patitur*. He was immovable in all times, so that they who in the midst of many opinions have lost the view of true religion, may return to him and find it.[36]

1.5   A Cromwellian Case in Point

We have seen then that the Puritans had a holistic, intellectually robust and yet heart-driven, passionate Christian faith. They delighted in God's word, relished all the arts and sciences, and though morally strict, upholding the standards of biblical law even in matters of crime and punishment, were equally concerned with liberty of conscience, personal freedoms, and charity. In short the Puritans were mature Christians who made a remarkable contribution to Christian civilization, who, if we are honest, make most Western believers today look like half-hearted dilettantes. As noted earlier, one of the greatest of all the Puritans, and as a consequence, both the most admired and hated among social historians, was Oliver Cromwell. He exemplified the Puritan spirit and sense of the mission of God. Some may be shocked by that statement because he has been popularly depicted as a cruel, self-serving, and vicious man. This image is a pure fabrication. Concerning Oliver Cromwell even Barzun acknowledges:

> The verdict on Cromwell himself is that he was not the cruel and tyrannical ruler nor the narrow-gauge Puritan of legend. His policies made England prosperous. By "navigation acts" he increased trade in English ships; he favored the colonies and furthered colonization; he may be called the founder of the British Empire...his successor Charles II had different concerns: staying in power, doing without Parliament by accepting periodic bribes from Louis XIV, and enjoying himself.... But within half a dozen years, according to Pepys, many people remembered "Oliver" with a sense of longing.[37]

From a French-born scholar and leading historian with no sympathy for evangelicalism, this is a significant admission. Cromwell's objectives were Puritan goals in action as revealed in his petition to Parliament on August 13, 1652, in which he and fellow officers asked for the adoption of reforms, including "spreading the gospel; reforming the law; adopting more stringent financial controls; ending begging and vagabondage; paying military arrears; making provision for widows and orphans; and setting in train the arrangements for a new Parliament."[38] In one of the most significant Cromwell biographies of modern times, J. C. Davis concludes that what distinguished Cromwell was a "reliance on Providence and his willingness to follow a living God, the God of Abraham."[39] This made him a "vigorous warrior in the cause of God and

His chosen people," and a man whose political instincts were "to seek moderate solutions to the civil problems of rule."[40] Out of the mess of the civil war and revolution where monarchy was being identified with Babylon in its degeneracy, "His greatness is that he did so much more than cling on to the debris."[41]

Cromwell had amongst his favourite co-laborers the Puritan giant John Owen – one of his chaplains and advisors at the height of his power. One of Owen's tasks was to reform the law, and Owen was, using the contemporary theological term, essentially theonomic in his outlook. Theonomy simply means God's law and implies the abiding validity of the moral law in every sphere of life, including the civil, so that the general equity of those laws with civil or judicial implications should be candidly applied in society.[42] This was a distinctly Calvinistic emphasis advanced by the Puritans. As Eidsmoe has pointed out:

> Calvin placed greater emphasis on the Old Testament than did Luther. He clearly believed in the Third Use of the Law (the didactic use by which the Law serves to instruct believers in sanctification), on which Luther was less clear, and he believed the Old Testament Law has a greater role not only in the life of the believer but also in the affairs of state.... Calvin argued that the moral principles of the Old Testament are of universal application, but methods of implementing those principles, such as the punishment imposed, may vary according to time and place.[43]

Cromwell's objective was thus the building of a God-fearing Christian nation (not a sectarian one with a denominational spirit), with liberty of conscience for all Christian subjects (with admittedly limited toleration for Catholicism at that time), freedom from tyranny with righteous biblical laws in a noninterfering, locally-governed social order. He wanted to see the glory of God through the life and witness of a godly nation; for him the best form of 'national security' was to be covenanted in faithfulness to God. Even those who criticized Cromwell during the period, like Richard Baxter, looked back on his great decade of influence as a golden season for Britain and were able, "with hindsight, to look back on the protectorate as, if not the Promised Land realized, a decent ante-chamber to it."[44] Dependence on God's sovereign providence and eschatological hope, combined with a passion for moral reform, liberty, justice, and hard work – these characterized the Cromwellian spirit.

This is not to say any movement or man is perfect – far from it. There is no perfection this side of the full inauguration of the kingdom of God, and many mistakes were made in religious, social, and political life by the Puritans. At their worst they could be too punctilious, partisan, moralistic, wordy, and insensitive to the feelings of others. But despite their faults the assumptions which governed their reformed vision gave them an indomitable spirit to which we owe the greatness of our Christian civilization.

What was the motivating source of this spirit? What lay at the root of this zeal for culture building, providing the social energy, vision, and patience for such an endeavour? Terrill Irwin Elniff offers this able definition of the Puritan motive force:

> Puritanism, whatever else it might have been or whatever other effects it may have had in the social and political life of the sixteenth and seventeenth centuries, was more a matter of theology than anything else. Puritanism was a theological interpretation of life: not only in religious creed, but a philosophy, a metaphysic, and re-organization of the whole of life – material, emotional, and intellectual – from the standpoint of the Scriptures. What brought the Puritans into clash with the civil and ecclesiastical settlement of England was its radical insistence on judging civil and ecclesiastical issues on the sole basis of the Bible, which they took to be the Word of God.[45]

In other words, the Puritan starting point in approaching every area of life and thought was theological and biblical not autonomous – be it pragmatic, rationalistic, existential or utilitarian. They may not have had their interpretations right every time, but their admirable goal was submission to God in the familial, social, economic, academic, political, legal, educational, ecclesiastical and every other sphere of life. Their principle of interpretation was the hermeneutic of surrender, not suspicion, and God's word was for them the final word in all things. I cannot think of a better definition of applied reformed thought than that – Scripture as the first and final word. That is surely the nature of a truly biblical faith.

1.6 Puritanism and the *Missio Dei*

Puritans then, in Old England as well as the colonies in America, advanced a missiological vision of God's reign with the covenant grace and law of God at its heart – for them, the gospel was a matter of covenant. Historian Mark Noll points out that New England ministers preached "a covenant of grace in regular sermons and a national covenant in occasional sermons."[46] For these men, it was because of this covenant that God required community faithfulness to his covenant-law, "God has provided...salvation by grace, from his mercy alone; saved sinners now have the right and privilege to serve God by following his law."[47] Christian philosopher, the late Greg Bahnsen, observed that the Puritans wanted a government that would take God's law seriously by applying God's covenant commandments and its sanctions, explaining that "the Puritans were foremost men of the word of God...they acknowledged the authority of scripture for all things, and this naturally led to their affirmation of the full validity of God's law ... to speak of the law's abrogation, said the Puritans, was to dishonour God himself."[48] They essentially carried on Calvin's emphasis on the normativity of the law for the believer as a rule of life which, "in turn promotes genuine liberty rather than antinomian licentiousness."[49] Because Jesus Christ is sovereign king and ruler over all things and since he calls all men and nations to covenant obedience (Matt. 28:18–20), the Puritans were concerned with the advance and spread of the gospel. The whole world was progressively coming under the dominion of Jesus Christ and so Puritan civilization served as a lamp on a hill for all to see and copy. Since Christianity as a whole and especially the post-millennial outlook (as common amongst the Puritans), is future-oriented and not past-bound (limited by what has already happened in history), God is always calling his people toward a progressive movement of covenant faithfulness in history. For the Puritan, the gospel commission was not simply an announcement of sins forgiven through the atonement (though it must begin there), but the teaching of all God's covenant requirements. This included the whole law of God if the mission of God was to be accomplished – this alone was true liberty. Samuel Rutherford noted for example, "after Christ has made agreement between us and the law, we delight to walk in it, for the love of Christ."[50] Another Puritan, Samuel

Crooke puts it another way, that "to the regenerate, the law becomes as it were gospel, even a law of liberty."[51] Because the Puritans were interested in life and liberty, they regarded the law of God as central to the *missio Dei*. To that end, Oliver Cromwell, the great champion of liberty in seventeenth-century England, in a speech to the British Parliament on January 23, 1656 -7, appealed to the House for a progressive faithfulness to the law of God:

> ...you have laws and statues and ordinances, which, though not so all of them conformable as were to be wished to the law of God, yet on all hands pretend not to be long rested-in, further than as they are conformable to the just and righteous laws of God. Therefore, I am persuaded, there is a heart and spirit in every good man to wish they did all of them answer the pattern. I cannot doubt but that which is in the heart will in due time break forth...and I am confident that among you will rest nothing, but a desire to promote every desire in others and every endeavour that hath tended or shall tend to the putting of these laws in execution. I do for this congratulate you. You have a gospel-ministry amongst you; that have you![52]

1.7 Puritans and the Present

We can see then that the Calvinistic and Puritan perspective has a long and influential history in North America, England, and Scotland. Those who, in the present time, argue for a return to these theological convictions amongst God's people are obviously far from 'novel.' It is not anachronistic to refer to this Puritan vision as not only covenantal and Calvinistic but as broadly theonomic. Reformed thinkers during the past fifty years or so who have been advocates of the Puritan theological and socio-cultural vision of God's reign have sometimes been dubbed 'theonomists' or 'reconstructionists' – terms now used largely pejoratively. John Frame explains its reformed genetics for the uninitiated:

> [T]heonomy is not absolutely different from other reformed positions, but only relatively so. Theonomy is a school of thought within reformed theology...the differences between theonomists and other reformed thinkers are not sharp but somewhat fuzzy. Theonomy... is an emphasis, a tendency.... Historically, Reformed thought has shown elements of both relatively theonomic and relatively non-

theonomic emphasis. I do not believe that either approach may claim unequivocally to be "the reformed position."[53]

There can be no question that the Puritans (in both England and New England) were reformed thinkers with a strong theonomic emphasis (that is, an emphasis on the authority and applicability of God's law in all Scripture, to all of life) and so, along with Calvin's Geneva and Knox's Scotland, their era of greatness serves as an excellent illustration of reformed thought applied to the covenantal concept of the kingdom reign of God. Even severe critics of a Puritan missiology readily grant that in the United States, The constitution arose from the Puritan idea of covenant. The first great document of the colonies had been the Mayflower Compact, and state after state adopted similar documents. It is interesting that the biblical book of Deuteronomy – the covenant book – was the most quoted source in political writings and speeches preceding the writing of the Constitution. There is ample reason to believe that the framers and ratifiers of the Constitution saw themselves as entering into a solemn covenant, an act of lasting and binding importance.[54]

This is the past however. How might the Puritan vision of the *missio Dei* for our present moment be summarized? What characterizes the theological and social contours of this vision of God's reign? There are several interrelated components that each rest upon a covenantal reading of God's word.[55] First, since God's saving activity is accomplished through sending his Son, his Spirit, and in turn, his called-out people, God's mission is not limited to any one institutional expression, including the institutional church. Notice that God's covenant is made with families (Acts 2:39), so the kingdom of God is not first institutional, but an individual and family movement that grows and develops through personal conversion and familial obedience to God. The starting point of our mission today as God's people is not with political or social reform, or even with the ecclesiastical structures of the church (important as all those are), but with the gospel, the renewed covenant in Christ, and its personal and familial application to life. The number one priority is consequently self-government (meaning a regenerated and thus free man's personal obedience) under Christ, and this can only be accomplished as Christians rid themselves of false humanistic assumptions about 'neutral' areas of life and thought and see all things in the light of the good news of Christ's salvation and Lordship.

It follows then, that like the Puritans, we must recognize that God's basic institution throughout Scripture, starting from the Garden of Eden, is the covenant family. From a biblical point of view, all modern forms of government are variations on monarchism, of rule from the top down, whereas in Scripture, the family is the central social government. It is a remarkable fact that until very recently most Western nations retained the death penalty for treason (including Canada until 1998); the ultimate offense being seen as treason against the state, because modern humanism sees the state as the most important and basic institution. In biblical law, on the social level, treason could only be against the family:

> The basic institution in scripture is neither church nor state but rather the family. Because the family is God's basic institution it is most protected by God's law. The offense of biblical law in the eyes of many is its strict legislation to protect the family, because treason in scripture, on the human scene, is to the family, not to the state.... The family is man's first basic government, church, school and vocation.[56]

We learn from the Puritans that the church and state are of equal importance to the family in their own sphere, but in the economy of life, the family is the most basic or foundational. This is not to say that the family is a 'superior' institution with a kind of ontological priority, nor is it to say that the family is eschatologically 'prior' to the church – after all, in heaven there will be no marriage. It is simply to say that in the economy of human life, the family lays the foundation for human society for the believer and non-believer alike and is the nursery of knowledge, worship, government, and all social order. Thus, when the family collapses, all society breaks down. Consequently, the institution of the family, which preceded the Fall of man and remained after the Fall, for the well-being of the human race, is the institution most protected by God's law and is the very pattern by which we understand both our relationship to God as Father, and the creational model by which the church is governed. We further see this centrality by the fact that in scripture, four of the Ten Commandments immediately concern the family (not the church or state) because the family controls welfare, property, education, inheritance, children, and cares for the aged. It is viewed as the basic government and consequently, when it is eroded or weakened, the social fabric of any society moves swiftly to decay regardless of what the state tries to do to replace it. The covenantal family is at the core of the Puritan vision for the reign of God, for without healthy and godly Christian families, all of society moves toward ruin; there is no social substitute for the family in either church or state, so the church today must labour to train, protect, and equip the family. The Puritans saw that the elder-governed church (as the visible expression of the gathered covenant people), was to minster the sacraments (covenant meal), provide for corporate worship, teach and apply God's covenant word to the people, and provide diaconal care, strengthening the families (including all non-married persons) of the family of God as they serve Christ and make known the gospel in every area of life. The qualifications for eldership are all familial (1 Tim. 3:1–7) and the church was therefore to model family (Eph. 3:15; 1 Cor. 4:15–17; 2 Cor. 6:16–18; 1 John 3:1). Thus the church must not and cannot limit the realm of God's Kingdom reign to ecclesiastical functions – this truncation of the Christian calling has led to much of the decline of our faith in the present generation. At the heart of God's reign is the godly family, living joyfully in covenant obedience to God. It is easy to miss the essence of this biblical missiology when it is not first seen as personal, familial, and covenantal. A serious error is made when people see the beginning point of the Puritan vision as social, political or ecclesiastical reform – these are all a consistent outgrowth and fruit of a reformed vision, not the root. Thus the Puritan, and to my mind biblical, vision for the development of God's mission in the world, begins with evangelism and an expectation of success for the gospel amongst individuals and families, not with nationwide coercive 'Christianization' as is often charged. Greg Bahnsen and Kenneth Gentry, two modern Puritans, make this point abundantly clear:

> How can Christianization occur without the priority of evangelism? According to the order in Matthew 28: 19–20, evangelism leading to baptism, comes first. Then follows teaching the converts all things Christ taught, with a full assurance of Christ's age-long presence with them to promote more evangelism and more teaching of all things He taught.... In the final analysis, "with God nothing shall be impossible" (Luke 1:37). All of this hope has but one foundation: the gospel of the resurrected Christ (Acts 4:12; 1 Cor 3:11)...[and] when the Lord returns, He will return to a wheat field with tares in it – not a tare field with wheat in it (Matt 13:24–30).[57]

This is the starting point – evangelism and familial discipleship. These things are primary in the mission of God as His covenant promise to

IN UNDERSTANDING BE MEN...

us and our children is made manifest by the ministry of the Holy Spirit (Acts 2:39). Moving beyond this, the Puritan mind today recognizes that the kingdom of God is not limited in jurisdiction to families and churches, rather, "it speaks to every form of authority as being at his command, whether in heaven or on earth. This is the authority of God almighty (Matt. 11:25; Amos 1:3-2:3; Oba. 1; Isa. 10:5-34).... He also has authority...in realms such as the societal, political, economical, and so forth."[58] Thus, the Puritan missiologist is keen to point out that if we limit the gospel to 'spiritual evangelism' and the forgiveness of our own sins, we have missed the richness of God's redemptive purpose. As noted missiologist Christopher Wright has rightly pointed out:

> Spiritual evangelism means that the gospel is presented only as a means of having your own sins forgiven and having assurance of a future with God in heaven – without either the moral challenge of walking with personal integrity in the world of social, economic and political society around us, or the missional challenge of being actively concerned for issues of justice and compassion for others. The result is a kind of privatized pietism, or one that is cosily shared with likeminded believers but has little cutting edge or prophetic relevance in relation to wider society.[59]

The biblical vision thus begins with evangelism and the milk of the word – a rudimentary understanding of repentance, forgiveness, and new life. But we are then called on in the mission to apply Christ's Lordship in every area because a whole gospel cannot be privatized! How are we to do this? The principles which govern how we engage these various spheres of life are given to us in God's lawword found in the totality of divine revelation. The Puritan spirit, both then and now, sees God's word as the kingdom charter or Christian manifesto. This charter is the law that is celebrated in Psalm 1 and 119, and expounded by our Lord in the Sermon on the Mount. This leads us to the expectation that God's purpose for his Kingdom to come on earth as it is in heaven (Matt 6:10), is best reflected in our lives and in society when the gospel is received, and God's law is obeyed. When the gospel of Christ and his law of liberty is truly seen in the glorious beauty of holiness (Ps 29:2), such a vision makes the heart glad and becomes our delight (Ps 119:14–16). John Frame recognizing this makes the striking remark that, when such a vision is grasped, "most of us would find attractive the prospect of living under something like the Mosaic civil law."[61] In sum, the motive force for the Puritans (both seventeenth-century and modern) is a grass roots reformation that begins with individuals, families, and churches. It begins theologically with all of life under the sovereignty and providence of God. It starts with gospel faithfulness, personal integrity and the joyous freedom of serving God. As the family, its individuals, and then the churches (gathered families) are faithful to God in all the areas God's word requires, living and proclaiming the gospel of the kingdom to those who do not know Christ, the reign of God will extend and his kingdom will become manifest in every sphere – including, progressively, the civil. Clarification of terms and purpose Although the rest of this work is not a study of seventeenth-century Puritanism but rather an examination of the mission of God, from a Calvinistic reading of Scripture, I use the term 'Puritan' from here on as representative of my perspective (one dominant aspect of the reformed tradition). I am fully cognizant that this self-identification is not exacting if we limit the definition of Puritanism to an historical movement – though I have tried to show that Puritanism did not die but survives in reformed evangelicalism. Theologically, this identification is complicated by the fact that not all Puritans believed exactly the same things; like all movements, there was diversity. Nonetheless it is, I think, a valid generalization to identify what informs my vision of the mission and reign of God as Puritanism. As we have seen, Puritanism is a theological interpretation of life based on Scripture as well as an historical movement, and it is this God-centred, Biblicist, theological interpretation of all life with which I strongly identify. Critical also to my purpose is to note that this Puritan vision might also be described as essentially theonomic. The challenge made to us by the Puritan hermeneutic has been well described by R. C. Sproul Jr:

> My theonomic friends are wont to drive us to one of two choices, "Autonomy or theonomy!" And of course they are precisely right. We will either have man's law, or God's law and only a fool would choose man over God. The question then rightly understood isn't whether we ought to have law as God would have us have it. The question instead is what law would God wish us to have...be careful not to heed those critics who have precious little understanding of theonomy.... Those on the left, both theologically and politically, delight to present these heirs of the Puritans as evangelical jihadists hell-bent on imposing a Calvinistic fascist regime on the rest of the world. Nothing could be

further from the truth. Theonomists, like the rest of us, long to see justice in the political realm. They long to see the nations discipled. They long to see the kingdom made manifest. They long to see every knee bow and every tongue confess that Jesus Christ is Lord. Who, within His kingdom, could ever argue with that?[61]

The Puritan divines penning the Westminster Confession argued that there is an abiding equity in the law of God, which, allowing for changes in practical, geographical and cultural circumstances, has a perpetual moral legitimacy and binding character upon men and nations.[62] More generally, as we have seen, the Puritan vision took up a holistic gospel and biblical law (theonomy) in terms of covenantal theology, combined with an optimistic eschatology, and applied it to family, church and the social order. As such, I believe the term Puritanism is the most fitting description for an authentically reformed approach to biblical missiology in general. In our pagan times, with hysterical criticism of evangelicals all around and theological spin doctors manipulating words for emotional effect, it is equally critical that we understand this theonomic vision either directly from the Puritans themselves or through its recent theologically sophisticated exponents, not from pop-bloggers and journalists crying out "dominionist" every time someone seeks to relate the Bible and some aspect of real life – especially the public sphere. Such people rarely have a real working knowledge of the reformed and Puritan system of thought, with its long and rich heritage in the life of the church, and usually no love for Christ.

1.8 The Cultural Mandate

Finally, as an incentive to persevere in exploring the Puritan vision in the chapters that follow, it should be remembered that we do not live in an era in which we can be complacent about the authority of God's word, the meaning of justice, the life and future of the family, the calling of the church, or the function of the state. We have just emerged from a century of fascist terror, Marxist murder and madness, totalitarian regimes, and slaughter on a scale that made all the previous centuries' conflicts look like *Lord of the Flies*! As we face, at the beginning of this century, a scientific manipulative state, a resurgent pagan occultism, vitriolic new atheism, a burgeoning and debt-ridden elitist bureaucracy, and the growing spectre of Islamization, all with their own visions of god, law, and culture, it is imperative that Christians understand and apply what the Word of God teaches if we would be faithful in a time of crisis and opportunity, preserving the freedom of God's church. The moment has come once again for the saints of God to believe, preach, and apply to our lives what the Scriptures tell us unambiguously concerning the identity of the Lord Jesus Christ, "the Alpha and the Omega, the beginning and the end ... who is and who was and who is to come, the Almighty." (Rev 1:8). The Almighty God, the Lord Jesus Christ, is "the faithful witness, the firstborn from the dead, and the ruler over the kings of the earth" (Rev 1:5). This is not future tense, but present tense and it is all in St. John's opening greeting to the churches in Asia. This king Jesus who is now ruler of all the earth has "made us kings and priests to his God and Father, to him be glory and dominion forever and ever" (Rev. 1:6). That is the power of the resurrection: the unstoppable regeneration and sanctification of Christ's chosen people who are sent out into the world for its renewal.

Biblical doctrine tells us that the kingly priesthood and dominion given to Adam in the Garden of Eden, lost by sin and rebellion against God, has now been re-established in and through Jesus Christ, the second Adam. Thus the apostle Peter tells us that "you are a chosen race, a royal priesthood, a holy nation" (1 Pt. 2:9). As a kingly priesthood, we are called to work and serve under the sceptre of our great high priest, the king of kings and Lord of Lords, applying the crown rights of the king in each area of life. This is not some vague theological idealism. Rather, in the Puritan vision, it is the concrete task of God's people applied in history – we are called to spiritual horticulture. We tend God's garden when we make known his gospel, uphold his law, serve his righteousness and bear his image, not just in evangelism and our personal lives, but in all socio-political and cultural engagement. For the Puritans, this spiritual service included nation building! Speaking of the American context in this regard, Jewish scholar David Klinghoffer notes that:

> John Calvin...took a much more Jewish view of the Hebrew Bible, granting high regard to the legal observance of the Old Testament precepts even apart from the Ten Commandments. It was Calvinist Protestants, the Puritans, who gave the initial religious inspiration to what became the founding of the United States, the most philo-Semitic country the world has ever known. This rapprochement of Judaism and Christianity found its most remarkable expression in American law, which from the seventeenth century on drew inspiration not only

from the Ten Commandments but from the entire Hebrew bible. The earliest legal codes of colonial Massachusetts and Connecticut were based explicitly on the Pentateuch's legislative system.... American law similarly assumes that right and wrong are a matter of objective reality, the Ten Commandments are at the foundation of our moral and legal culture. It's for this good reason that Moses carrying the two tablets of the Decalogue is carved on the wall of the U.S Supreme Court. The United States has long regarded itself as the continuation of the history of ancient Israel – an "extension of the Jewish church," as the Pilgrims put it in 1620.[63]

The theology which undergirds such social energy holds that God has created the world, not merely as the environment of his creatures, but also as a sanctuary, his resting place where he is enthroned (Ps. 132:13–14). We are to work and take care of all that God has made (Gen. 2:15; Num. 3:6–10), maintaining the sanctity of his sanctuary. The Mosaic tabernacle was a reflection of Eden and the original creation (as well as the cosmic Temple in heaven), where human beings ruled and served as kings and priests.[64] Now the mission of God remains the establishment of his kingdom rule. So the task laid upon God's new people, the redeemed priesthood in Jesus Christ, is to extend the Garden, to increase, fill, subdue and rule (Gen. 1:26–28), bearing and applying God's image in all things (Gen. 1:26–28; Eph. 4:21–24; 5:1). This is not simply a spiritual metaphor. The physical world in which we have been placed is important, not peripheral, in the calling of God's people (2 Chron. 7:14). We read in Scripture: "for the upright will inhabit the land and those with integrity will remain in it, but the wicked will be cut off from the land, and the treacherous will be rooted out of it (Prov. 2:21–22)." We see this principle at work throughout the Bible. The first land grant in Scripture, given by covenant love, was Eden, awarded to our first parents; for their disobedience, they were expelled from this land. The second covenantal land grant was Canaan, promised to the people of Israel, from which they were also exiled for disobedience. In the end, Jerusalem and the temple itself were razed to the ground in A.D. 70 and the people scattered. The third land grant, now given to Christ's chosen race, the new Israel of God, is the whole earth, which is made clear in Romans 4:13, Ephesians 6:3, Mark 10:29–30 and Matthew 5:5; 28:18– 20. Indeed, St. Paul writes to the church that "all things are yours: whether Paul or Apollos or Cephas, or the world or life or death, or things present or things to come – all are yours. And you are Christ's, and Christ is God's" (1 Cor. 3:21–23). This is the inheritance of the people of God in Jesus Christ now, and with this astonishing covenantal privilege comes great responsibility.

This is not to say that I believe the revolutionary founding Fathers of the USA during and after the war of independence in the late eighteenth century were actually all Christians. The extensive evidence from surviving letters and books by men like Thomas Paine, Thomas Jefferson, John Adams, Benjamin Franklin and George Washington reveals varying degrees of influence from Enlightenment rationalists and French sophists. Deism, unitarianism, masonic occultism, universalism and Jesuit Romanism are found amongst them. Many of these views were hidden during their lifetime but emerged in letters published after death, as in the case of Thomas Jefferson, who was supportive of the blood-letting of the French Revolution. That being said, these were not the views of the vast majority of Americans and so the Christian faith still dominated the social and political landscape due to the abiding influence of the pilgrim fathers, Puritan revivals, and Puritan institutions.

In this great task, God has promised his presence with us as we minister to the world and order all things in terms of his purposes. St. Paul considered his own evangelistic mission as his 'priestly duty,' regarding his life's work as bringing about "the obedience of faith among the nations" (Rom. 1:5; 16:26). The calling of the covenant people in all history has never been to simply keep the blessings for ourselves and get to heaven. Instead, as Christopher Wright observes:

> The purpose for which this covenant with Israel existed...was part of God's long-term mission to bring blessing to all nations and all creation... the covenant presence of God will be a return to the intimacy of Eden. Ultimately, God's presence among his people must point to the blessing of his presence in all the earth.... The presence of God in Israel's tabernacle and temple looked backward to his presence in Eden, and forward to his ultimate presence among all nations in a renewed creation.[65]

This describes well the trajectory of the triune God's covenant in history and indeed the grand narrative of all Scripture. The good news (the gospel) is that our covenant-keeping God has sent Jesus Christ, his only begotten Son, our prophet, priest and king and established him through his death and resurrection as both Lord and Christ (Acts 2:36). Now, the Lord of the covenant calls us to faithfulness and obedience to serve him as his bond-servants and ambassadors until, as God declares concerning his Son through the prophets, "I make your enemies your footstool" (Acts 2:35). This prophetic witness goes back to the very beginning of biblical revelation. In Genesis 49:10, the patriarch Jacob lay dying and prophesied concerning the coming Messiah that he would be King of the nations, the great lawgiver, and to him, 'Shiloh,' shall be the obedience of the people. Shiloh literally means, 'He whose right it is' to rule. This is a declaration of Christ's office, also set forth in Philippians 3:21, where our Lord and lawgiver is declared to be bringing all thing into subjection so that no area of life is outside his Lordship. Humanistic man declares war on Shiloh, asserting his own self-righteousness, Lordship and right to reign – a false Shiloh. But Christ our Shiloh is bringing all things into subjection to himself in terms of the promise of his covenant (Acts 2:39). It was this great vision of Christ's Lordship revealed in his covenant grace and law which actuated the sixteenth-century reformers and their Puritan descendants and which gives shape to a truly Reformed vision of the *missio Dei*. It is this same covenant grace and law which I believe must be recovered by God's people in our time, for the glory and praise of God and the extension of his dominion (Ps. 72:8), so that the earth may be full of the glory of the Lord as the waters cover the sea (Heb. 2:14). To reject this view is to embrace the alternative of dualism, by which we divide reality into two realms – in which Christ's lordship is radically limited. This is the subject to which we now turn.

Chapter Two

IN HIM ALL THINGS HOLD TOGETHER:
THE DANGERS OF DUALISM

A true believing Christian...lives in his vocation by his faith. Not only my spiritual life but even my civil life in this world, and all the life I live, is by the faith of the Son of God; He exempts no life from the agency of his faith.
— John Cotton

The Psalmist testifies that the Divine Law was his school-master and guide in leading a holy life. He thus by his own example, prescribes the same rule to us all; and it is highly necessary to observe this rule; for while each of us follows what seems good in his own estimation, we become entangled in inextricable and frightening mazes...the word of God is set in opposition to all human counsels. What the world judges right is often crooked and perverse in the judgement of God, who approves of no other manner of living, than that which is framed according to the rule of his law.
— John Calvin

2.1 Authority and Duality

Like most of the Reformers, including Calvin, the Puritans totally rejected the sacred-secular dichotomy.[1] This rejection of a division between holy or sacred aspects of reality and allegedly secular or profane areas of life and work has been common amongst many of the great names in the evangelical and reformed tradition. This is for the good reason that, "In his Word, God absolutely forbids every inclination and every effort to break up your life into two parts, one part for yourself, and the other part for him."[2] This conviction was also held by Abraham Kuyper, the noted Dutch Calvinist theologian, statesman, and former Prime Minister of the Netherlands, little more than a century ago. What did this mean in practice? Simply put, all of life is religious. There can be no duality, no artificial dichotomy between the spiritual and historical, private and public, faith and life, heaven and earth. All areas of life are created, sustained and governed by God; all things are through him and for him (Col. 1:16). Thus, as a Christian and statesman, Kuyper believed that:

77

Christians must serve God within the world, and not flee into seclusion, as monks and some Anabaptists have done. When Christians obtain positions of civil authority, they must operate in obedience to God, since the Lord has ordained their authority (Rom. 13:1-7). This, Kuyper argued, means that civil government must "restrain blasphemy, where it directly assumes the character of an affront to the Divine Majesty." The constitution of the state should acknowledge God as supreme ruler, and government should set aside its regular activities on a Sunday and protect it as a day of worship. Magistrates...should regard themselves as responsible to God in the discharge of their duties. They should punish public attacks upon God as crimes against civil law, which acknowledges God as the source of the state's authority.[3]

Such words and convictions would strike most Christians in the West today as alien and even ridiculous. Despite his historical proximity, Kuyper is unknown to most modern Christians, and worse, many would find it difficult to identify with the God of whom he speaks and the faith he describes; a faith integrated into every aspect of life and thought in God-ordained space-time history. Furthermore, an anti-dualistic view such as Kuyper's would be considered, by the great majority in our culture, woefully intolerant. Surely you cannot drag the God of the Bible into every area of life: the classroom, the courthouse, the ballot box, the office, the bedroom, the Houses of Parliament and the laboratory? Surely that would make us intolerant of a diversity of perspectives? Yet, as R. J. Rushdoony has aptly observed, intolerance is a fact of life:

Intolerance is inescapable. If we are Christians and abide by Scripture, we will be intolerant towards murder, theft, adultery, false witness, and other offenses against God's order. They will be to us a violation of our freedom and order under God, and an oppression of godly men. If on the other hand we are sinners and lawbreakers by nature, we will be intolerant of God and His people, intolerant of godly laws and restraints precisely because we tolerate and love sin. Our Lord stated the issues clearly: "no man can serve two masters: for either he will hate the one, and love the other"; or else he will hold to the one, and despise the other (Matt. 6:24).

It is necessary for us to love God and his Word, and, it is our nature to do so. This means that we therefore hate sin and regard it as an

offense against God and man, an intolerable violation of godly order...
similarly those who hate God want to eliminate Him, and us, and
everything which is an aspect of God's law and order and word from
their universe. They are savagely and bitterly intolerant. In other
words, what you tolerate says a great deal about you. It identifies
your loyalties and your love, and it classifies your nature clearly.[4]

What we tolerate then not only defines us and our nature, it also points
to our greatest love and identifies our source of authority (Matt. 6:24).
This authority will inescapably be located either in God and his word,
the autonomous self, or some other human source of lordship, power,
or expertise. We cannot ultimately be ruled or governed in our lives by
more than one source of power and authority; as Jesus declared, "no
man can serve two masters." All dualism in our lives inevitably leads to
the dominance of one influence or power over the other, one of which
will eventually be resented or despised.

2.2   The Consequences of Duality

Because we have increasingly done what Kuyper decries, and separated
life into two parts or storeys, the sacred and secular, personal and public,
spiritual and material, one part for ourselves and the other for God, the
'toleration' of sin in the 'lower storey' (an alleged sphere outside God's
direct moral authority for ourselves) has become a practical virtue. One
immediate result is relativism in the moral and social order. Such a view
is obviously a denial of Scripture. "There is an objective standard of right
and wrong established by God's Word, and I cannot be judge over it: it
judges me and all men. There is a hierarchy of values in God's universe:
I cannot place my interests, whether they are important to me or not,
above those things which God declares to be important. God by right of
creation legislates for all men (Isa 8:20)."[5] Clearly, this government of
God, in Jesus Christ is total, as Psalm 110:1–2, Psalm 2, and Ephesians
1:15–23 make abundantly clear. All things are under Christ's jurisdiction
and are relative only to God, not men.

Foreign as all this may sound to some Christians, it is, in fact, very
good news! Since God by his providence is interested in all aspects of
our existence, all of life and work is raised to a remarkable dignity as
truly ethical, spiritual, purposeful, and inescapably meaningful. All
life becomes thereby, a source of joy and fulfilment. The great Puritan

William Perkins wrote, "The action of a shepherd in keeping sheep...is as good a work before God as is the action of a judge in giving sentence, or a magistrate in ruling, or a minister in preaching."[6] Sadly, this recognition of the ethical, sacred, and spiritual character of all life has been eroded by the revival of dualism. The progressive re-Hellenization of the church since the Puritan era, by a severing of Hebrew (biblical) roots, is at the heart of our current disintegration of life.[7] This is seen not merely in terms of popular relativism invading the church; it is also manifest in an escapist mentality amongst Christians. Where these various dualisms have revived and gained prominence in the numerous denominations, confused believers often seek retreat and escape from the world (a supposed lower storey of existence), rather than the redemption of it. In his important study of the Jewish roots of Christian faith, Marvin R. Wilson points to the important fact that our time and life-abandoning tendency is the result of resurgent Greek philosophy and a loss of biblical memory. Consider, for example, that the first thing God sanctifies in Scripture is not a place or a thing, but time itself:

> "And God blessed the seventh day and made it holy" (Gen. 2:3)....
> Biblical history is not the story of celebrating space, but the revelation of how people learned to sanctify moments, events – time. Thus the essence of spirituality is for God's people to know the dynamic presence and quickening power of the heavenly Lord at work on earth in their daily lives and activities.[8]

God is in the details – not the devil! All time, all the earth, all of life is his (Ps.24:1ff) and is sustained by his ordination. The division of sacred and secular is an artificial and unbiblical distinction. We are accustomed to associating 'spirituality' with a heavenly mindedness; a modern pietism and quietism concerned with 'eternal' verities of the inner life and soul, the 'beatific vision,' not the practical realities of laundry, raising children, education, law, culture-making, and gardening! The very term 'spiritual retreat' (although we know what we mean by this) implicitly conveys a non-biblical orientation concerning the nature of the Christian life. But for Kuyper and the Puritans, true spirituality meant recognizing the sanctity of all time, and the government of God over all life in all creation. Though a fallen order, Christ is now reconciling all things to himself both in heaven and in earth, through his redemptive work and by his servant people, his new humanity – the kingdom of the redeemed. This was the faith of the biblical writers and of many of our evangelical forebears.

The obvious question then becomes, why, in the face of the aforementioned consequences, and the clear Scriptural opposition to this Greek philosophical duality, does the modern church seem so inclined to espouse it? For example, when we read St. Paul's words in Colossians chapters one and three, how is it possible to maintain these dualisms in our thinking and living?

> He [Christ] is the image of the invisible God, the firstborn of all creation. For by him all things were created, in heaven and on earth, visible and invisible, whether thrones or dominions or rulers or authorities – all things were created through him and for him. And he is before all things, and in him all things hold together. And he is the head of the body, the church. He is the beginning, the firstborn from the dead, that in everything he might be preeminent. For in him all the fullness of God was pleased to dwell, and through him to reconcile to himself all things, whether on earth or in heaven, making peace by the blood of his cross (Col. 1:15–20).

The scope of this statement is all-encompassing – everything in heaven and earth, all laws, entities, authorities, powers, the visible and the invisible; all things were created through him and notice, *for him*. All created reality consists by his word and power, and in everything, in every aspect of created reality, Christ is to be preeminent. St. Paul makes clear that by the cross and through his church (his body) of which he is head, Christ is reconciling all things to himself. There is no sacred-secular divide here, no philosophical dialectic, and no sign of any autonomous realms in creation. Then in Colossians 3:1–4 (often erroneously cited in support of dualistic thinking), Paul challenges believers to recognize their status and delegated authority as those raised with Christ, who now sits in the seat of all authority at the right hand of God. He tells Christians to set their minds on things above, not of earth. This is not the introduction of Greek dialectics. It is not a charge to be heavenly-minded and unconcerned with life on the earth. It is not a reference to 'creation' at all, but to the thinking and pattern of an earthly or worldly mentality, a carnal or lawless way of thinking, an unregenerate life that is not hid with Christ, 'in God.' That is, St. Paul reminds us of the high calling to live as those now 'in Christ.' The context of these verses makes this emphasis plain. The immediate challenge he offers is for Christians to demonstrate the reality of our being in Christ by our obedience to God's law in life:

> Put to death therefore what is earthly in you: sexual immorality, impurity, passion, evil desire, and covetousness, which is idolatry. On account of these the wrath of God is coming. In these you too once walked when you were living in them. (Col. 3:5–7)

St. Paul goes on to instruct the believer to put off all such thinking and behaviour and to put on the new self, which is being renewed in knowledge after the image of its creator (v. 8–10). Now clearly, if 'putting to death what is earthly in you,' meant the physical, material or created realm, the apostle would be advocating suicide! It is abundantly clear that to set our minds on things above is not a plea to be meditating on so-called spiritual reality or contemplating heavenly bliss as a superior and higher realm of life and existence, but rather it means our self-conscious renewal in knowledge through the regenerating and sanctifying work of Christ, by his Spirit; this conforms us to godly obedience to his law. The law reflects God's character, Christ fulfilled the law perfectly, and we are now being conformed to his image.[9]

Why then the dualistic emphasis in today's church? It seems that there are three interrelated reasons. First, a faulty eschatology; second a defective cultural memory; and third an artificial separation of the Old and New Testaments.

2.3 Faulty Eschatology: Old errors, New Outfit

Christian eschatology can become dualistic when it posits, in various ways, too great a discontinuity between human history, or the present age, and the age to come. Where discontinuity is overly stressed, heaven becomes increasingly unrelated to earth and the doctrine of the kingdom of God; the spiritual is largely disconnected from the material; the daily work of the present bears little relation to the future; and the kingship of Christ is shunted off from world history to eternity and from earth to heaven, where his reign is almost exclusively postponed till a future period. It is therefore worthy of note that there have been times in the life of the church where old dualistic heresies have re-emerged, gained popularity, and eventually posed as a new orthodoxy. In time, within the segment of the church in which an old heresy flourishes, the historic understanding of a doctrine is so eclipsed that old orthodoxy finds itself on the outside looking in – forgotten, rejected and cast out as dubious. For those unfamiliar with the history of Christian doctrine, the former orthodoxy is then viewed with suspicion, a foreigner and alien in its own land. One of the most conspicuous examples of this kind of a reversal of orthodoxy would be the massive resurgence of millenarianism of various stripes, or what was historically called chiliasm, during the past 150 years.

Whilst I respect and honour my brothers and sisters in Christ who hold to historic pre-millennialism (and/or dispensationalism), and am not trying to question their sincerity or integrity, the relevance of this eschatological vision to our present consideration of dualism cannot be overlooked without missing an important fact in tracing the retreat and decline of the Christian faith and social order in our time. It must be granted immediately that all discussions concerning the millennium as a concept are so fraught with complexity that saying anything about the history of this idea in the church runs the risk of dying the death of a thousand qualifications. However, what can be said with reasonable confidence is that the early church condemned the patristic form of this doctrine with strong censure (the idea of a literal reign of Christ from Jerusalem for a thousand years), and by the seventeenth century the three major branches of the Protestant church had condemned the eschatology that taught a politico-religious restoration of the Jewish establishment in a literal future thousand-year reign of Christ on earth from Jerusalem. The Lutheran Church's Augsburg Confession of 1530, the English Forty-Two Articles of Religion of 1552, and the Reformed Second Helvetic Confession of 1566 all unanimously rejected millenarianism.[10] In this they were following Augustine and the first generation of Protestant reformers.

For Augustine and the entire medieval period, the thousand-year reign of Revelation 20, like many uses of numbers in Revelation, was symbolic. This text, for them, was in fact dealing with the whole period between Christ's first and second advents at the end of history.[11] However, a belief in a 'golden age' for the gospel, still to be realized in the future of the church before the second advent of Christ, fitted neatly into the Augustinian perspective and was arguably held by John Calvin, as appears from his commentaries on Isaiah. Though elements of what we now call pre-millennialism[12] did appear in some of the seventeenth-century Puritan writings, the orthodox view (that the church age *is* the kingdom age) dominated the confessional landscape leading, with a sense of divine logic I think, to the Great Awakening and the eighteenth and nineteenth centuries' optimism concerning the future of missions.[13] This was expressed both in Edwardian post-millennialism that came to full flower in Charles Hodge and Benjamin B. Warfield at Princeton, as well as in the great missionary enterprises of William Carey and William Booth in Asia and England respectively – both of whom were post-millennial men. This optimism concerning the progress of the gospel in the church or kingdom age they had derived from their Puritan heritage. As Iain Murray writes:

> For the Puritans there was immense optimism in such doctrine. It was the same optimism which appeared in the prayers of Christian people in the age of decline between the Puritans and the eighteenth century revival, which came to renewed public expression in that great awakening and led on, as though irresistible, to the world-wide missionary enterprise of English speaking Protestantism.[14]

For the majority of the Puritans then, and most evangelicals (until the late nineteenth and early twentieth century), the term 'millennium' (where it referred to something more than simply a symbol of the church age), identified not a literal thousand-year period after Christ's return during a physical reign from Jerusalem, but to a coming period of time marked by a remarkable outpouring of God's Spirit – an era of unprecedented success for the gospel in history, for the church. This remarkable period of worldwide success for the gospel would be followed by Christ's return.[15] As seen in eighteenth and nineteenth-century missionary zeal, this did not diminish the passion for the age foretold by the prophets when the earth would be full of the knowledge of the Lord as the waters cover the sea (Is. 11:9). On the contrary, Christians saw themselves as privileged participants in the establishment of the kingdom of God in the earth. Carden notes that "many Puritans of New England, especially those of the founding generation, looked with keen anticipation for the millennium, the establishment of Christ's righteous kingdom on earth."[16] The difference between this 'millennialism' and the millennialism so popular today in North America was expressed well in the preaching of the Puritan John Cotton, who declared that "the millennium would be experienced not through Christ's bodily presence on earth but through faithful preaching, and revivals of unprecedented dimensions."[17] In other words, as the church faithfully preaches and lives the gospel, the Holy Spirit would be poured out upon the world and a time would come when the diffusion of the gospel would be so widespread in the earth that the words of Isaiah 11 would be made manifest. This was the conviction of the Puritans of the English revolution and New England, and consequently, of many of our evangelical forebears. However, significant changes were ahead amongst evangelicals, well-illustrated by debilitating events in Ontario, Canada. In mid-nineteenth century Protestant Ontario, millenarianism raised its head again in the form of the exported Irvingite movement (named after the English millennial preacher Edward Irving) and in the even more disruptive Millerites – followers of the converted American deist William Miller (by this point a Baptist), whose detailed calculations from biblical prophecy had him predicting the end of the world in the years 1843 or 1844, followed by a literal millennial (that is, thousand-year) reign. This eventually led to the founding of the Seventh Day Adventist church.[18] This was quickly followed in the 1860s by the dispensationalist millennial crusade of J. N. Darby and C. I. Schofield, a movement emerging from the Plymouth Brethren in England, teaching that the world would only progress in evil until a pre-tribulation rapture – a doctrine reputedly first announced by a twenty-year-old Scottish girl named Margaret MacDonald, whilst in a trance in the 1830s.[19] It gained popularity in the 1880s through 'prophetic conferences' mostly held in Canada near Niagara Falls, where it sought to gain a conservative theological respectability.[20] However, these were all part of a wider tide of pre-millennial fever exported from Europe that essentially presented a 'counter-perspective' to the dominant Christian view of history itself.

Historian William Westfall explains that "these groups were only the visible part of a general religious and cultural movement that included many other heretical movements with strong millennial associations. Hornerites, Campbellites, and perfectionists were active in the province, while groups like the Children of Peace tried to establish utopian communities."[21] Westfall is certainly correct in noting that the battle concerning eschatology was a battle "over the meaning of time itself... each side was expressing a different view of the relationship between how one acted in the world and the course God had set down for history to follow."[22] A characteristic millennial scepticism about history and God's plan for the world ran alongside a resignation to failure for the spread of the gospel and the disciple-making work of the Holy Spirit. This doctrine horrified the leading evangelicals and Protestant churches in Ontario. Christian missionaries, like the Presbyterian Rev. James S. Douglas, sought to combat this millennial threat, advancing the critical point that our view of the future impacts our activity in the present. For him, we must be, 'up and doing,' because Christ will only return when the gospel has been victorious and the nations discipled. To sit still, purporting to interpret prophecy and waiting for the second advent, was unacceptable to such men. Neither could they accept a view that foresaw Christ returning twice – first to a 'secret rapture' of the church, and then a second time to a satanically-ruined history for the slaughter of his enemies with supernatural military power, forcibly setting up a literal world-state from Jerusalem. Such a view seemed to undermine the very essence of the gospel and the power of God manifest at the cross and in the giving of the Holy Spirit to accomplish the task of teaching the nations. Douglas' view was summarised by the Protestant periodical, *Christian Guardian*: "We therefore conclude that the Kingdom of Christ is a spiritual kingdom on earth, which is to be carried on through the instrumentality of God's Holy Spirit.... This is the plan laid down by Christ, and to be duly attended to by His church to enlarge and spread our messiah's kingdom through the world."[23] As Westfall demonstrates, these pre-millennial and dispensational movements were roundly condemned as heretical sects by the evangelical Protestant community in Ontario in all five of the main denominations (Anglican, Presbyterian, Methodist, Baptist, Congregational), which he states all suffered under the millennial crusades. Because of this, Westfall notes that "their archives are filled with material on the outbreaks of what they regarded as a persistent and threatening heresy."[24] Of course the millennialists shared much in common with traditional Protestantism. Both believed in Christ's reign (at some point), both held to his second coming and judgement. But as a key doctrine of cultural analysis reveals, "heresy gains power and authority because it is so close to what it tries to oppose."[25]

Why was dispensationalism and pre-millennialism seen as so dangerous, even heretical? It was not simply that Protestant theologians did not find adequate ground for it when interpreting Scripture (which they claimed they could not); they were looking at the fruit of these doctrines in the lives of people, and were often horrified by what they saw. Until this point, for much of Canada, hopes of a great Christian dominion developing across the North through the spread of the gospel were nurtured, as revealed by the founding text of the Canadian Dominion (Psalm 72:8). On Parliament Hill in Ottawa, the Parliament buildings remain testament to this Christian vision, most notably, the Peace Tower and the Memorial Chamber, where Scripture is engraved everywhere, inside and out. But according to Westfall, the impact of these sects was very significant in undermining this vision. Indeed the Rev. John Caroll singled out Millerism as one of the most disruptive forces in the history of Methodism in Canada.[26] Of the broad effects of millennialism Westfall writes:

> Millennialism had a devastating effect on the institutional structure of the Protestant churches, which bore the brunt of the onslaught.... According to contemporary accounts the prospect of the end of the world caused many people to abandon the routines of their daily existence and adopt a watchful inactivity in secular and sacred affairs. The two problems were closely related – the millennial groups were able to disrupt religious institutions because they presented an interpretation of time that appealed to many people. By the same token the Protestant churches had to provide their own interpretation of time in order to stop the destruction caused by millennialism.[27]

The Protestant interpretation of time had already been well-laid at the founding of the dominion. In the opening chapter to his fascinating study, "The Dominion of the Lord: Protestant Ontario and the Study of Religion and Culture," Westfall highlights the vibrant theological vision that motivated and sustained the Fathers of the Canadian Confederation:

> The vision of a new dominion 'from sea to sea' captured the imagination of the Fathers of Confederation and sustained an ambitious program of nation building...the words of the seventy-second Psalm seem to capture the ethos and provide a fitting motto for the new dominion: *A mari usque ad mare*, a nation from sea to sea...in the biblical passage from which Tilley drew the phrase, the word "dominion" has a spiritual meaning. Here the geographical extent of the new land amplifies the social and moral qualities that will grace this future state. The Psalmist lifts up his voice in praise

of a time when the true justice of God's commandments will triumph over the selfishness and wickedness of men. It is the just King who 'shall have dominion also from sea to sea and from the river to the ends of the earth.' The Psalm is a commentary on power in society, but instead of dwelling on the means of gaining power, it describes the moral and social goals that power should pursue...the biblical passages foretell a new type of society on earth when the wilderness of sin and injustice will become the dominion of the Lord.[28]

This summarizes accurately the convictions of many Protestant evangelicals at this time in Canadian history, convictions we have seen they shared with the Puritans, and many earlier evangelicals. This Psalm summarises an eschatology of dominion for Christ through the power of the gospel and the work of the Holy Spirit. Instead of Christ leaving and returning to earth several times (three comings in all) in order to do the work of his Kingdom, Christ's cross was seen as sufficient to save sinners, and the Spirit regarded as having sufficient power to bring about the discipleship and discipline of the nations. As one Methodist writer at the time argued, millennialism was a denial of the very economy of grace.[29] But slowly, due to various economic and social pressures, theological dilution, two world wars and the resulting depression and despondency, chiliasm reasserted itself in various forms – the most popular of which is dispensationalism (historic pre-millennialism also remains strong). Thus today, for the largest portion of the Protestant Christian community in North America, pre-millenarianism in these two forms is popular 'orthodoxy' despite the fact that not a single world-class seminary in North America continues to teach classical dispensationalism, and the later progressive versions are yet to be systematically stated and defended.[30] This doctrinal shift is a stunning example of how an old orthodoxy can be left on the outside, looking in. Pre-millennial (and/or dispensational) Christians tend to react with shock, surprise, and at times horror that any other view of the eschatological question might be taken – millenarianism is now practically synonymous, for many, with evangelical or fundamentalist Christianity. To take a different view of history is sometimes even considered liberal or antiliteralist. Consequently, the historic post-millennial and a-millennial views of time and the future (the church age is the kingdom age), are jettisoned in favour of explicitly pessimistic views of history that have sadly produced, to a large degree, cultural retreat, social stagnation, and an escapist mentality amongst many believers. This modern chiliastic, historical phenomenon constitutes a kind of theological revolution in which a biblically-faithful and centuries-old doctrine of orthodox Christianity finds itself a poor persecuted cousin to a relatively new (dispensational), not to mention historically condemned (pre-millennial) perspective. Then in the midst of the revolution, some well-meaning revisionists get to work trying to remake the history of millennialism, allegedly exposing the old orthodox interpretation as a form of faithlessness, no matter how old or biblically faithful it is. I have experienced this in the context of pastoral ministry, where I have practically been accused of heresy for an optimistic view of the church's future. Why is all this important? How does it relate to the question of dualism? The answer is easy to see when formulated as a series of questions. To whom does human history belong? Is history truly of spiritual relevance or is real spirituality reserved for the *parousia* and heaven? Does history truly matter, or is this material world and its events inconsequential compared to heaven? Who will be victorious in history – God or Satan? Is God committed to the redemption of his creation, or the abandonment of it? The widespread teaching that the end of the world is imminent and that the kingdom of God refers almost exclusively to a future millennial order at the end of history centred in a reconstituted geo-political Israel after the return of Christ has without doubt contributed significantly to the dualistic view that Christ's reign is only 'spiritual' for church history, in the sense that his rule is presently restricted to the private 'heart' of the Christian. We can expect no transformation of society; no vast success for the gospel; no widespread turning to godly laws; no real Christianization of culture. Our only hope is in the second coming or the rapture and our escape from this world, which is often regarded as merely a sinking ship and a lesser form of existence. In this view, the kingdom of God will only be concretely manifest in the earth – that is in the 'material realm' – after the second advent and the alleged restoration of an ethnic Jewish nation-state with Jesus on the throne in Jerusalem.[31] It is easy to see how this idea can and has at times led to a retreat from the defence of the gospel (apologetics), Christian education, biblically-motivated social transformation, and culture and nation building.

2.4 Theological Amnesia: Recovering our Cultural Memory

A second major contributor to the resurgent dualism within the church is the fact that, for the most part, we have forgotten what our Christian forebears actually believed about the application of our faith to all of life. The historian Alexis de Tocqueville once said that "when the past no longer illuminates the future, the spirit walks in darkness." Increasingly, the deleterious effects of our biblical and historical amnesia regarding the meaning and implications of biblical faith are being keenly felt by non-evangelical and secular historians, as well as many social commentators. It is a sad and ominous day for the church when it falls to those outside of it to sound the alarm and point to the primary causes of our social decay and cultural disintegration. As a faithful, integrated (non-dualistic) biblical faith has waned in the Western churches, so a biblical morality, education, and thereby culture, have all but disappeared in Western society. What can be seen clearly in the midst of this process of decline is that when Christians retreat from or abandon the task of engaging culture by the application of Christ's lordship and word to all things, they have not thereby taken a neutral view of culture, but in fact have unwittingly subordinated the faith and word of God to the prevailing assumptions of the day. J. Gresham Machen warned against this response to cultural conflict early in the last century:

> Christianity may be subordinated to culture. That solution really, though to some extent unconsciously, is being favored by a very large and influential portion of the Church today.... Christianity [then] becomes a human product, a mere part of human culture. But as such it is something entirely different from the old Christianity that was based upon a direct revelation from God. Deprived thus of its note of authority, the gospel is no gospel any longer; it is a check for untold millions—but without the signature at the bottom. So in subordinating Christianity to culture we have really destroyed Christianity, and what continues to bear the old name is a counterfeit.[32]

Nowhere is this subordination of biblical faith to the spirit of the age more evidently manifest than in the area of law and the resulting social order that a law-order creates. In his massive history of law and revolution in the Western world, professor emeritus of law at Harvard, the late Harold J. Berman writes, "neither law nor history can be understood, and more than that, neither can be preserved, if the legal tradition of which they are both part is forgotten or rejected."[33] Berman contends that:

> In the early twenty-first century, the Western legal tradition is no longer alive and well...there is an element of prophecy in all historiography. It has been well said that a historian is a prophet in reverse...the decline of the Western legal tradition in our century illuminates the nature of that tradition in the centuries in which it flourished.[34]

Berman demonstrates in encyclopaedic fashion that not only was Western (European) law explicitly drawn from biblical law and elements of the Justinian code prior to the papal revolution of the twelfth century, but that the Protestant Reformation and its view of the validity of divine law decisively shaped all Western legal and social institutions:

> The Germanic codes contain strong exhortations in favour of more just and more humane legal values. The Laws of King Alfred, for example, start with the Ten Commandments and a restatement of the laws of Moses, a summary of the Acts of the Apostles and references to the monastic penitentials.... Christianity broke the fiction of the immutability of the folk-law. Gradually between the sixth and eleventh centuries, Germanic law, with its overwhelming biases of sex, class, race and age was affected by the fundamental Christian doctrine of the equality of persons before God: woman and man, slave and free, poor and rich, child and adult.[35]

In his second volume focused on the Protestant Reformation and the German and English revolution, Berman writes concerning the impact of the Puritans upon the cultural shape of the West and the central role that they saw for God's law:

> The English Puritans...shared the belief that human history is wholly within the providence of God, that it is primarily a spiritual story of the unfolding of God's own purposes.... They believed, further, that God willed and commanded what they called 'the reformation of the world,' and they emphasized the role of law as a means of such reformation. An additional element in the Puritan belief system that strongly affected the development of English political and legal institutions was its emphasis on the corporate character of Christian communities. Anglo-Calvinist Puritanism was essentially a communitarian religion. It emphasized the existence of a divine

covenant, under which the congregation of the faithful was to be 'a light to all the nations of the world,' 'a city on a hill.' This, in turn, led to an emphasis not only on the virtues of hard work, austerity, frugality, discipline, self-improvement, and other features of what has come to be called the Puritan work ethic, but also on the sanctity of human covenants of public responsibility, community service, corporate enterprise, mutual trust, and other qualities associated with the concept of public spirit.[36]

It is a very important fact, increasingly uncovered by legal historians in this long-overlooked area of study, that the Christian Bible, and in particular, the revealed law of God, was the essential foundation upon which the Western vision of life and law, justice and liberty, have been built. Natural law thinkers themselves drew from divine law, initially identifying them explicitly with each other. Indeed, Berman shows that:

> These fundamental characteristics of the Western legal tradition were founded on Christian belief, first in its Roman Catholic form, later in its Lutheran and Calvinistic forms. Deism, the religious faith of the so-called Enlightenment, substituted for the Christian belief in divine law a belief in God-given reason and the supremacy of public opinion. Nevertheless, in 1914 it continued to be widely believed in the West that the ultimate sources of authentic positive law are divine law, especially the Ten Commandments...[37]

This is a critical and relevant statement because first, in our time, inhabited as it is by a largely antinomian church, we are reminded that the fabric of our society was built on biblical law, especially through the Reformed tradition. And second, because we are told that the replacement of biblical law (and the positive law derived from the general principles of biblical law), with 'man's law,' was a product of Deism and the Enlightenment tradition, both of which were virulently hostile to Christianity, where the law of God was sacrificed on the altar of 'reason' and public opinion. Nonetheless, the Enlightenment vision only gained general ascendency after World War I, and arguably triumphed only after the second world conflagration.

Thus, the Western legal tradition and the overall fabric of our social order were explicitly built on a covenantal and Hebraic understanding of God, man, and our relationship to time and creation. This was a move away from Hellenistic thought. Wilson thus notes:

During the period of the Protestant Reformation...signs of the re-Judaization of the Christian faith began to surface, as certain Hebraic biblical categories were rediscovered. The Reformers put great stress on the principle of sola scriptura...the consequent de-emphasis on tradition brought with it a measure of return to biblical roots. Accordingly, during the two centuries following the Reformation, several groups recognized the importance of once again emphasizing the Hebraic heritage of the church. Among these people were the Puritans who founded Pilgrim America, and the leaders who pioneered American education.[38]

He goes on to show that the Puritans who left England for America considered themselves like the children of Israel fleeing Egypt for the promised land, with the Atlantic representing the Red Sea. They also considered themselves to be under the covenant of Abraham, and therefore governed by the covenant law. They were the leading Hebrew scholars of the day – founding Harvard University in 1636 after the Puritan minister, John Harvard – so much so that the early Congregationalists were better Hebraists than many Jews. [39]

With this historical context of Western culture in mind, it is evident that our forgetful and negligent society is in an advanced state of decay because the foundations of social order, the law and gospel of Christ, are crumbling around us. The prophetic words of G.K. Chesterton are proving all too accurate in our statist and bureaucratic age, that "If men will not be governed by the Ten Commandments, they shall be governed by ten thousand commandments." For many decades now, large quarters of the Protestant church have in impotence and silence surrendered to the spirit of the age and succumbed to all manner of 'new commandments:' the liberalizing agenda of the social planners; not surprisingly, church attendance figures have dramatically declined over the past sixty years. Still more troubling, many professing Christians are dismissive of, or openly hostile toward, their fellow believers who would uphold the standards of God's word today, seeking to recover our cultural memory in the hope of being part of seeing a reviving and transforming work of God. Berman's analysis clearly reveals that those hostile to God's law are in fact historically in continuity with the deists and Enlightenment philosophers who were self-conscious despisers of the gospel. If Berman is correct concerning the triumph of humanistic law since the early part of the twentieth century, it has taken less than one hundred years for the opponents of the gospel to extirpate from our culture the law of light and life.

Now the story of shifting attitudes toward millenarianism sketched earlier, is mirrored, I believe, in what has happened with the question of the place of the law of God (or the doctrine of the law) in the contemporary Christian worldview – the dominant historic perspective of Christendom has been forgotten and cast out as irrelevant or dubious. As one example, very few Christians in my experience, and sadly even many trained theologians, are not conversant with the Puritan perspective on the law and gospel, despite the fact that their vision shaped our legal, political, social and economic landscape decisively in Great Britain and North America. The liberties, freedoms and rule of law that remade much of Europe, England and Scotland – essentially inventing North America – cultivating Christendomic consciousness in the three centuries following the Reformation, are due to the direct application of Scripture to family, church and state, yet many of us remain blissfully ignorant of this fact.

This theological amnesia has opened up a gulf between old and new evangelicalism with respect to the relationship between law and gospel and as a consequence the relationship between the gospel and culture. In a typical statement of Puritan doctrine, in his exposition of the Shorter Catechism of the Westminster Assembly on the Ten Commandments (from *A Body of Practical Divinity*, 1692), Thomas Watson, a famed and popular Puritan preacher in London, wrote that "the moral law requires obedience but gives no strength; but the gospel gives strength; it bestows faith on the elect; it sweetens the law; it makes us serve God with delight."[40] Having discussed the senses in which the law cannot be seen or applied by the believer (that is, as a means of justification, or as an indictment of condemnation against us) he states:

> But though the moral law be thus far abolished, it remains a perpetual rule to believers. Though it be not their saviour, it is their guide. Though it be not foedus, a covenant of life; yet it is norma, a rule of life. Every Christian is bound to conform to it; and to write, as exactly as he can, after this copy. 'Do we then make void the law through faith? God forbid.' Rom III 31. Though a Christian is not under the condemning power of the law, yet he is under its commanding power...this I urge against the Antinomians, who say the moral law is abrogated to believers; which, as it contradicts Scripture, so it is a key to open the door to all licentiousness. They who will not have

the law to rule them, shall never have the gospel to save them.[41]

Because our forebears believed and practiced such an integration of law and gospel, they necessarily integrated faith and life, biblical truth and culture-making – it was both inevitable and natural to them. If Christ is our saviour and his law the rule of life, then law and gospel must be proclaimed to every creature and put into practice in all areas of life. Historian John Coffey writes of the Puritan mind:

> Like the reformed, they typically qualified Luther's antithesis between law and gospel, emphasizing the role of God's law within the Christian life and local community, and trying to recreate godly Genevas in England and America.[42]

Yet, even in the centuries prior to the Reformation, the centrality of the law of God to the church and to culture was unquestioned by believers. Consider Berman's analysis, which carries far-reaching missiological implications:

> The Church...would work for...the reformation of the world through law, in the direction of justice and peace.... Law came to be seen as the very essence of faith. "God is himself law, and therefore law is dear to him," wrote the author of the Sachsenspiegel, the first German law book, about 1220.... Law was seen as a way of fulfilling the mission of Western Christendom to begin to achieve the Kingdom of God on earth.[43]

Whilst I would not articulate the church's mission in quite the same vocabulary as these ancient scions of biblical faith, the point is well taken. Law, as an aspect of the church's teaching mandate, was seen as central to the building of the kingdom of God bringing justice, peace and blessing to the nations.

A major question to be considered then, if we are to see a recovery of the gospel in our time, is the place of the law of God in the mission of God, expressed in and through the Christian's work and witness to the gospel of the Kingdom of God? It is a sad fact that this question has been, in recent times, the source of much confusion and controversy. Many contemporary Christians are so accustomed to hearing and interpreting the term 'law' as a negative and repressive category (a completely modern phenomenon), that the notion that God's law might have a central role in the Christian life and the mission of God and his church appears bizarre and even alien. Yet for most of Western history, the law of God has occupied a critical and central place in the life of the family, church, and society. It has been recognized by many as God's charter for sanctification, justice, liberty and life, and it was the Puritans who stated and applied this most effectively amongst our evangelical forebears. It is time we remember their legacy and consider its relevance for us today.

2.5   Divorcing the Word: The Artificial Separation of Old and New Testaments

2.5.1   Christ and the Law

A third significant reason for the dualism which dominates the contemporary church landscape is a sharp and artificial separation of Old and New Testament, and consequently of law and gospel. In Matthew 5:17–19 our Lord declares the abiding validity of the law, asserting that he has come not to abolish, but to fulfil it. The term 'fulfil' (*pléroo* in Greek) has a number of implications. Much ink has been spilt by scholars arguing in technicalities about all the varied shades of possible meaning. I do not want to enter that debate here. But as the Greek lexicons show, fulfilment certainly denotes that Christ is the object (end) of the law and the prophets; he is also the perfect manifestation of its requirements, and as the Lord and giver of the law, he has also come to implement and put into force his law. All this is undoubtedly implied by 'fulfil.' The greatest mind of the Protestant Reformation, John Calvin agrees in his commentary on the Sermon on the Mount that "Christ intended to teach that in all the structure of the universe there is nothing so stable as the truth of the law, which stands firm, and that in every part."[44] Calvin also considered those who slackened the law unworthy of the church pulpit. The popular notion that Christ is correcting or altering the law in Matthew 5 was abhorrent to him:

> [It is] wrong to reckon this a revision of the law or that Christ was wishing to lift his disciples to a higher level of perfection than Moses could achieve…this has given rise to the idea that the beginning of righteousness was once handed down in the law, but its perfection was taught in the gospel. However, Christ in fact had not the least intent

of making any change or innovation in the precepts of the law. God there appointed once for all a rite of life which he will never repent of...so let us have no more of that error, that here a defect of the law is corrected by Christ; Christ is not to be made into a new law-giver, adding anything to the everlasting righteousness of his Father, but is to be given the attention of a faithful interpreter, teaching us the nature of the law, its object and its scope.[45]

It is certainly not unusual today to hear Western Christians complaining vigorously about the state of society, the dramatic moral decline since the 1960s, the rampant criminality and the dereliction of much modern youth culture. Yet should we be surprised at this? If the church is compromised or ambivalent with respect to the law of God, will not the culture follow suit? But try telling many Christians that the social problems begin with lawlessness in the church and they will immediately respond that we are, 'not under law but grace.' It is true that the expression, 'dead to the law,' is in Scripture (Gal. 2:9; Rom. 7:4), but here it has reference to the believer in relation to the atoning work of Christ as the believer's representative and substitute. A Christian is only dead to the law as a legal sentence of death against them, Christ having died for them; but they are made alive to the law as the righteousness of God. Since Jesus himself is the true mediator between God and man, he rejected the law as mediatorial, in order to re-establish the law in its God-appointed role as law – the path of holiness. Jesus fully recognized and obeyed the law. It was only the absurd interpretations of the law popularized by the Pharisees that he rejected. Jesus directly challenged the hypocritical teachers of the law, because as Stephen the martyr declared, the scribes and Pharisees were those "who received the law as delivered by angels and did not keep it" (Acts 7:53). Thus, as Ernest Reisinger notes, we are biblically obligated to recognize that "Christ, the Mediator of the new covenant, is not a new Lawgiver. It was His eternal law that was revealed to Moses in the first place. He need not improve upon it or replace it."[46] The great Puritan commentator, Matthew Henry, makes this abundantly clear in his comments on Matthew 5:17-20:

> The rule which Christ came to establish exactly agreed with the scriptures of the Old Testament, here called the law and the prophets. The prophets were commentators upon the law, and both together made up that rule of faith and practice which Christ found upon the

throne in the Jewish church, and here he keeps it on the throne. He protests against the thought of cancelling and weakening the Old Testament.... The Saviour of our souls is the destroyer of nothing but the works of the devil, of nothing that comes from God, much less of those excellent dictates which we have from Moses and the prophets. No, he came to fulfil them.... He asserts the perpetuity of it; that not only he designed not the abrogation of it, but that it never should be abrogated.... The Word of the Lord endures forever, both that of the law, and that of the gospel. Observe, the care of God concerning his law extends itself even to those things that seem to be of least account in it, the iotas and the tittles; for whatever belongs to God, and bears his stamp, be it ever so little, shall be preserved.... The Jews reckon the least of the commandments of the law to be that of the bird's nest (Deut. 22:6-7); yet even that had a significance and an intention very great and considerable. It is a dangerous thing, in doctrine or practice, to disannul the least of God's commands; to break them, that is, to go about either to contract the extent, or weaken the obligation of them; whoever does so, will find it is at his peril.[47]

Another and related artificial dualism, still prevalent today, sees the Old Testament as law and the New Testament as gospel. This is another fallacy that cannot in any degree be drawn from the teaching of Christ or the apostles: "It is not as though some books of Scripture are exclusively law and others are gospel, or that the Old Testament is law only and the New is gospel. The law and the gospel are declared in each of them."[48] The falsity of such an artificial division is clearly seen in the words of St. Paul to Titus:

For the grace of God has appeared, bringing salvation for all people, training us to renounce ungodliness and worldly passions, and to live self-controlled, upright, and godly lives in the present age, waiting for our blessed hope, the appearing of the glory of our great God and Saviour Jesus Christ, who gave himself for us to redeem us from all lawlessness and to purify for himself a people for his own possession who are zealous for good works. Declare these things; exhort and rebuke with all authority. Let no one disregard you (Titus 2:11–15).

Paul makes plain here the unity of Old and New Testaments, showing that the grace of God is manifest in Christ's work of redeeming us from 'lawlessness,' purifying us for his own possession. Such a redeemed people are zealous for the good works and the life of self-control prescribed in God's law. The origin of the false division of scripture into law (Old Testament) and gospel (New Testament) is found in the early church heretic Marcion. Marcion was a wealthy ship-owner from what is now Northern Turkey, who came to Rome around A.D. 138 and began to argue that the Older Testament was inferior to the gospels (though he rejected Matthew, Mark and John as hopelessly contaminated by Judaism) and some of Paul's letters recognized by the church, and so should not be regarded as authoritative revelation for the church. He was clearly influenced by Gnostic thought and its dualism. Borrowing from Platonists, he held with the Gnostics that the world was created by a demiurge – a cruel god of blood sacrifice and war, law and judgement. Such a god, which he held was revealed in the Hebrew Scriptures of the Old Testament, was not worthy of worship. Surely a world that contains evil cannot be created by a good God; therefore, he considered the Old Testament the work of a demiurge of lesser status. Consequently, "The Old was the great antithesis of the New and thus was demeaned as being imperfect, offensive and unedifying,"[49] whereas his suitably edited portions of the New Testament revealed the God of light and love coming from heaven.

In his effort to remove the Old Testament from its position of authority, Marcion sought to 'elevate' the writings of St. Paul (though he only accepted nine of his letters to the churches and Philemon, not the full collection), suggesting that Paul taught that Christians were 'free from the Law.' The gospel should not be seen alongside and in light of God's law but rather as its antithesis. He thus sought to rid the church of every trace of its Hebrew moorings. In A.D. 144 the Church in Rome finally excommunicated Marcion for heresy. One early church apologist, Justin Martyr, considered Marcionism the most dangerous error of his day. For the church today this same heresy is sometimes unconscious and at other times calculated and deliberate. Either way, the Bible of the early church (the Old Testament) is regularly ignored, minimized, slandered, mocked, and rejected by significant portions of the modern 'evangelical' movement. Many believers really only take seriously a quarter of the Bible – yet that quarter (the Newer Testament) cannot be comprehended without the Older Testament. As a result, by ignorance or deceit the mission of the church is greatly distorted. Wilson rightly identifies the great danger to the church where this attitude prevails, explaining that "this selectivity has had the effect of neglecting the totality of written revelation, severing the Hebrew roots of the Christian faith, and thus eroding the full authority of the Holy Scriptures."[50] Scripture everywhere affirms that there is one creator, one Lord, one law, one redeemer, one faith, one baptism, and one King. This God is the same from age to age and does not change (Mal. 3:6). Christ affirmed the Old Testament with the authority of God himself, because as God the Son, he was, with the Father and the Spirit, its author, and could no more repudiate the Old Testament than he could repudiate or revoke himself. Missiologist Christopher Wright sees this point clearly when he states:

> Jesus then, according to the consistent witness of many strands in the New Testament documents, shares the identity of YHWH, the Lord God of Israel, and performs functions that were uniquely and exclusively the prerogative of YHWH in the Old Testament. These include especially God's role as creator and owner of the universe, Ruler of history, judge of all nations and savior of all who turn to him. In all of these dimensions of God's identity and activity, New Testament believers saw the face of Jesus, spoke of him in exactly the same terms and worshiped him accordingly.[51]

2.5.2 Paul and the Law

A great deal has been written on the subject of St. Paul and his relationship to the law, but the evangelical and Reformed tradition has always recognized and highlighted the apostle's positive view of the law. Wilson offers this summary:

> Just as Jesus, 'born under law' (Gal. 4:4), recognized its authority throughout his life (cf. Rom. 15:8), so Paul upheld the validity of the Law. In his terms, 'Do we, then, nullify the law by this faith? Not at all! Rather, we uphold the law' (Rom. 3:31). Some eighty times Paul quotes from the Law to establish the authority of his arguments. He emphasizes that 'the law is holy, and the commandment is holy, righteous and good' (7:12). He also says 'I delight in God's law' (7:22). He recognizes the Law as 'good' (1 Tim. 1:8) and 'spiritual' (Rom. 7:14), and he builds his theology by drawing heavily on the Old Testament Decalogue (13:8–10).[52]

In writing to the Galatians, Paul makes it very plain that the law is of divine origin (Gal. 3:19), and that it is an evidence of God's grace

(v. 21). Paul's letter to the Galatians emphasizes the inadequacy of the law for bringing salvation, and his letter to the Romans emphasizes that despite the transgression of God's holy law, there is still salvation in Christ. Thus, in Paul's theology, law and grace serve to establish each other, not conflict with or abrogate one another. The law is the foundation, and grace and truth are the fulfilment or completion of the law. Together they form one glorious trinity where judgement, mercy and truth meet in perfect unity. As Reisinger puts it, "God's promises always accompany His precepts. His grace turns precepts into promises, and the spirit of grace turns precepts and promises into prayers. In this way, the law establishes grace and serves the gospel, rather than opposing it." [53] Indeed, if Paul had conceived of a fundamental opposition between the law and the Spirit, he could not have possibly described the law as holy, righteous, good and spiritual (Rom. 7:12). It is consequently impossible to maintain that Paul was antinomian in any sense. On the contrary, his first explicit exhortation in Galatians, to "love your neighbour as yourself," comes straight from Leviticus 19:18! The Reformed understanding that the Pauline critique of the law has reference only to its soteriological function is surely the correct one. The moral law and its various sanctions and applications (case law) are still operative, and ceremonial (or restorative) shadows are equally fully operative in Christ's redemptive fulfillment of them. Christians must then reject legalism (salvation by works) and antinomianism (rejection of the law) for an ethic of gratitude for our spiritual liberation (justification) secured at the cross. We now live a life of obedience to God's law, by the Spirit, in gratitude for God's measureless grace – for his perfect law has become our desire and delight. Indeed, St. John writes:

"For this is the love of God, that we keep His commandments. And His commandments are not burdensome" (1 John 5:2–3).

In the hall of faith heroes described in Hebrews chapter eleven, the faith of Moses gets seven verses (23–29). The great saints in this entire chapter are held up to us as examples of covenant faith. They obtained a good testimony through faith, although chronologically prior to the receiving of the promise (Christ), that they should not be made perfect apart from us (v. 40). Whether Hebrews is written by Paul or not, it is Pauline in theology. Christ is the fulcrum upon which new covenant life and faith hinged both before and after the incarnation, for Paul categorically declares that God by his word, "preached the gospel to Abraham" (Gal. 3:8). For Paul, we gentiles are grafted into this Abrahamic, covenant life of faith, noting, "therefore, know that only those who are of faith are sons of Abraham...so then those who are of faith are blessed with believing Abraham" (Gal. 3:7,9). Jesus himself said that "many will come from east and west and sit down with Abraham, Isaac and Jacob in the kingdom of heaven. But the sons of the kingdom will be cast out into outer darkness" (Matt. 8:11–12). Thus there is only one great covenant of law and grace for Jew and Gentile alike, announced to all the great saints of old. Christ renews this covenant at the Lord's Supper. There, by his blood, he establishes the true 'Israel of God' (Gal. 6:16). Reisinger sums up Pauline thought regarding the covenant law effectively:

> The law manifests the sin that is in man. Grace manifests the mercy that is in God. The law demands righteousness from man. Grace brings righteousness to man.... The law speaks of what man must do for God. Grace tells what God has done for man. The law brings knowledge of sin. Grace brings the remedy for sin. The law brings the will of God to man but gives no power to obey. Grace gives man a desire to do the will of God and gives him power to obey.[54]

2.6 The Augustinian and Calvinistic traditions

Despite the fact that the full authority of the Old Testament and centrality of the law are basic to church history, there are nonetheless many Christians, deeply influenced by dispensational hermeneutics and an antinomian posture, who will immediately reject the notion that God's law has any application today, however relevant it may have been in the past; this view is totally foreign to Reformed thought. My contention is that the church needs a robust return to a Reformed missiological vision that embraces the law of God as Christ and the apostles themselves embraced and applied it. We need to reunite law and gospel in the mission and vision of the church. For guidance we have plenty of historical precedent. The Reformers, for example, saw themselves as men simply seeking to restore the church to faithfulness to the word of God, to Pauline and Augustinian doctrine. In his classic writings against the Pelagians in the context of a discussion of God's law Augustine states:

> Surely no-one will doubt that God's law was necessary, not just for

the people of that time [the Old Testament], but is also necessary for us today, for the right ordering of our life. True enough, Christ took away from us that crushing yoke of many ceremonies, so that we are not circumcised according to the flesh, we do not sacrifice victims from the cattle, we do not rest even from necessary works on the Sabbath (although we keep the pattern of the seven day week), and other such things. We keep these laws in a spiritual sense; the shadowy symbols have been removed and we see them in the light of the realities they signified...[yet] who can say that Christians ought not to keep the commands which tell us to serve the one God with religious obedience, not to worship an idol, not to take the Lord's name in vain, to honour one's parents, not to commit adulteries, murders, thefts, false witness, not to covet another man's wife or anything at all that belongs to another? Who is so ungodly as to say that he does not keep those precepts of the law, because he is a Christian and stands not under the law, but under grace?[55]

Augustine goes on to state that Christ has not come to destroy the law but to fulfil it:

It is quite clear and the New Testament leaves no doubt on the matter, what are the law and the prophets that Christ came not to destroy, but to fulfil. It was the law given by Moses which, through Jesus Christ says, "He wrote of me" (John 5:46). For undoubtedly this is the law that was added that the sin might abound – words which you often ignorantly quote as reproach to the law. Read what is there said of the law: "The law is holy, and the commandment holy and just and good. Was then what is good made death to me? God forbid. But sin, that it might appear as sin, produced death in me by what is good" (Rom. 7:12-13)...the intent was that, being thus humbled, they might learn that only by grace through faith could they be set free from subjection to the law as transgressors, and be reconciled to the law as righteous people...so the righteousness of the same law is fulfilled by the grace of the Spirit in those who learn from Christ to be meek and lowly in heart; for Christ came not to destroy the law, but to fulfil it.[56]

Furthermore, it seems evident that for Augustine, the 'law' was not restricted to the two tables only (the Ten Commandments); these simply summarised the law. Rather, 'the law' encompassed all the law and the prophets in all Scripture - as indicated by Augustine's clear reference to *case law* in this same passage written against the Pelagians:

> But are we therefore to say, when the law commands that whoever finds another man's lost property of any kind should return it to him the owner, that this has no relevance to us? And the law has many other things like this, teaching people to live Godly and upright lives.[57]

Although this view of the matter was not fleshed out in systematic detail by Augustine (that had to wait until the Reformation), and he was certainly not entirely consistent in all his comments on the law, this essential orientation concerning the eternal law of God was basic to his thought. Moreover, God's law was a witness for God in the heart of every person, it was not restricted to Israel. "The Old Testament expressed that law negatively as the *lex talionis* and the New did so positively as the golden rule ... for love is the fullness of the law ... For by the law of Moses, God had placed in front of human beings what they should have been able to see through their conscience."[58] Thus, for Augustine, law and gospel were not to be seen as antagonistic to each other. Although under the law man finds himself incapable of obedience without divine aid, under grace, by the Holy Spirit, he is enabled to obey and do the good.[59] "Augustine was convinced that the law, whether the Mosaic law, or the life, teaching and example of Christ, avails nothing without the aid of the Spirit.... The Spirit, too, not only informs man of the good, but also moves his will to desire it, love it, and delight in it."[60] Thus, for Augustine, the law of God being written upon the hearts of God's elect by the Holy Spirit, had an eternal validity. Furthermore, it seems Augustine would not have regarded biblical penalties as severe, but rather as compassionate and humane, since in the ancient Roman world, barbaric torture was routine and even common thieves were punished with death, whereas biblical law forbids mutilation (maiming and torture) and requires only restitution from thieves. Moreover, Augustine considered sanctions against pagan idolatry in increasingly Christianized Rome as a fulfilment of biblical images and prophecy in Daniel 7.[61]

With this theological foundation having been laid by Augustine, in coming to the Reformation and the work of Calvin, Melanchthon, Bucer, Beza, Zwingli, Knox and others, we find a high regard for the law in God's purposes for the church and society. This could be illustrated to the point of exhaustion but it is important to document some salient facts to help set my whole missiological argument in its proper historical

ontext. Calvin's view of the Ten Commandments, likely influenced
by his friend and mentor, Martin Bucer, was that the revealed law of
God was necessary because, despite man being made in God's image,
general revelation, due to the fallen condition of people, was inadequate
for a moral compass and insufficient for the direction of magistrates.
Though he saw conscience as a valid monitor, human depravity had
touched every aspect of our being, leaving conscience seared and
unreliable.[62] Consequently, God did not leave man to himself in this
regard; thus the giving of the law was as *gracious* as it was *necessary*.
David Hall notes, "such a fundamentally positive view of God's law
would become a distinctive ethical contribution of Calvinism."[63] Even
though the natural man is not inclined toward obedience (Rom. 8:3–8),
the law, for Calvin, is the perfect rule of righteousness, "the Doctrine of
the Law remains therefore, through Christ, inviolable; which by tuition,
admonition, reproof, and correction, forms and prepares us for every
good work."[64] Of those who opposed the law Calvin said, "[sinners]
inveterately hate the law itself, and execrate God the lawgiver.[65] The
Calvinistic tradition then has usually seen a three-fold use for the law:
convincing like a mirror, restraining like a bridle for the lawless, and
arousing the godly to obedience.[66]

Calvin's extensive preaching in Geneva through the Pentateuch
is testament to his view of the law. His substantial exposition of
Deuteronomy 27 and 28 stands out as a clear example of his belief in
the abiding relevance of the law of God to all members of society.[67]
Calvin's exegetical comments on relevant New Testament passages are
no less clear. For example, his comments on Jesus' upholding of the
law in Matthew 5:17ff are particularly telling and worth quoting in full:

God had promised a new covenant at the coming of Christ, but had
shown at the same time that it would not be different from the first, but
rather this would be His object – the covenant that He had originally
struck with His people would be confirmed for perpetuity. "I shall
write", He says, "my Laws upon their hearts, and I shall forget their
sins" (Jer. 31:33): these words do not at all depart from the former
covenant, but rather declare that it will continue to be firm and
valid, when the new has come upon it. This is exactly the intention
of Christ's words, when He says that He has come to fulfil the Law.
Truly he fulfilled the deadness of the letter by reviving it with His
Spirit, and eventually displaying in actual fact, what had till then been

IN HIM ALL THINGS HOLD TOGETHER...

indicated figuratively. As for doctrine, we must not make out that there has been any abrogation of the Law in Christ's coming, for as the rule of holy and devout life is eternal, it must be unchangeable, and likewise God's justice is one and constant, as He composed it therein. As regards ceremonies, if we allow that they may be reckoned somewhat incidental, it is only their practice that was abrogated: their significance was actually given more confirmation. So Christ's coming did not take anything away, even from the ceremonies, but rather the truth behind the shadows was revealed, and served to strengthen them; seeing the concrete fact, we recognize that they were not vain or useless. So let us learn to preserve this connection of Law and Gospel inviolable – but many erroneously try to break it! It has no small effect on consolidating our faith in the Gospel, if we hear that it is no other than the complement of the Law, both in mutual agreement claiming God as their common author.[68]

This statement delineates both the structure of covenantal theology and what would become a Puritan view of the law. Calvin goes on to argue in this passage of commentary that "sooner will heaven crash, and all the fabric of the earth dissolve, than the fixity of the Law shall be shaken,"[69] and that those who refuse to teach God's people to obey God's law are "not worthy of holding position in the church, if they slacken the Law's authority in any part."[70] Calvin also equates Christ's establishment of the kingdom in the gospel with the teaching of the Law. Commenting on Matthew 5:19 he says that "the kingdom of heaven is taken as the restoration of the church...as even then was coming to be at the preaching of the Gospel.... Thus Christ says that teachers are not to be admitted to His Church, when it has been restored, unless they shall be faithful interpreters of the Law, and shall study to assert its entire teaching.[71] This conviction about the validity of the entire law led Calvin to conclude that:

As God gave rules for ceremonies on the basis that their outward use should last for a period, but their significance be everlasting, one does not do away with the ceremonies, when their reality is kept, and their shadow omitted. When Christ keeps out of His Kingdom such men as accustom others to condemn the law, then it is fantastic folly for them not to be ashamed of remitting, by blasphemous indulgence, the absolute demands of God...in order to do away with the justice of the Law.[72]

We can go further in noting Calvin's positive attitude toward the law. For example, concerning even judicial penalties (which we will discuss in a later chapter), Calvin's commentary on Deuteronomy reveals his practical support for them and his concern that pagan law was sometimes closer to God's law than certain Christian perspectives:

> Nay, by the universal law of the gentiles, the punishment of death is always awarded to adultery; wherefore it is all the baser and more shameful in Christians not to imitate at least the heathen. Adultery is punished no less severely by the Julian law than by that of God; whilst those who boast themselves of the Christian name are so tender and remiss, that they visit this execrable offence with a very light reproof.[73]

Because of Calvin's clear exegetical and practical stance, some have raised the somewhat anachronistic question of whether we can call Calvin a "Theonomist." Gary North and James Jordan, whilst recognizing the inherent complexity of such a question, conclude that the evidence reveals that Calvin should be considered a "theonomist" but not a "Theonomist" – the former being a practical and loose theonomic viewpoint rather than a theoretical and self-consistent one. Jordan's comments are very helpful here:

> An examination of Calvin's theoretical writings on the judicial aspects of the Mosaic law will reveal that he believed they were given to Israel in a rather unique fashion, and are not binding on modern civil governments. Yet an examination of Calvin's practical writings and sermons (such as the sermons on Deuteronomy) will reveal that he used the Mosaic law, including its judicial aspects, as the foundation for social, political and legal wisdom, and generally favoured imitating the Mosaic laws in the modern world. In viewing Calvin's thought in its own context, it would be better to view him in terms of the preceding thousand years of corpus Christianum...the primary concern in this model is with the godly ruler, rather than with the law of God in the abstract. The church labours to produce Godly sons, who will be Godly magistrates...who will make proper applications of the fundamental principles of the Bible to their societies. After all, in reforming the city of Geneva, Calvin did not deliver two hundred lectures on common grace or natural law, but preached two hundred sermons on the book of Deuteronomy. He made full and direct

applications from Deuteronomy into his modern situation, without apology. He viewed biblical law as foundational and as the starting point for legal and socio-political reflection.[74]

Calvin was by no means alone in his emphasis upon the abiding relevance of the law to church and society. Zwingli, for example, did not feel the need to separate law and gospel as antithetical. "Everything which God has revealed is either command, prohibition, or promise.[75] Zwingli wrote:

> I call everything 'gospel' which God opens to human beings and demands of them. For whenever God shows his will to people, it delights those who love God and thus it is to them certain good news. For this reason I call it 'gospel,' preferring that term to the term 'law'; for it is more fittingly named to suit the understanding of believers and not of unbelievers; and at the same time, we overcome the tension between law and gospel. Besides I know well that Christ is the sum and perfection; he is the certain manifestation of salvation, for he is salvation.[76]

We see then that from St. Paul, through Augustine and the Reformation, and on through the Puritan age, there was no artificial dichotomy or duality posited between law and gospel, Old and New Testament, the God of the Old Covenant and the God of the New. This holistic vision of the Christian life provided the integrated worldview and social vision necessary for the development of Christian civilization. There can be no doubt that the Reformers laid the foundation for the emergence of covenantal Puritanism as seen immediately in Calvin's disciple John Knox (the spiritual father of Puritanism), who was arguably more consistent in the application of God's law than Calvin himself.

A reformed missiology must therefore repudiate dualism in all its forms, bringing heaven and earth, past, present and future, world and church, under the authority of all of God's total word. Only in this way can we hope to see a recovery of gospel effectiveness and the extension of the kingdom of God in our justly judged generation.

Chapter Three

KNOWN UNTO THE LORD ARE ALL HIS WORKS: A CHRISTIAN VISION OF HISTORY AND THE WESTERN WORLD

History is the witness that testifies to the passing of time; it illumines reality, vitalizes memory, provides guidance in daily life, and brings us tidings of antiquity.

– Cicero

All nations of the world were created by YHWH, stand under his government in their historical affairs, are accountable to him morally and especially for the doing of justice. Like Israel, however, all nations have fallen short of the glory of God and stand in the same default position: under God's judgment. That judgment will come as surely on the nations as it fell on Israel. But beyond judgment there is hope, for there is always hope with the God of Israel.

– Christopher Wright

3.1 Books and Barbarians

Cicero once said, "Not to know what happened before you were born, is to remain forever a child." Such a life is not only sad, it can be dangerous. Juvenile thinking in action, especially *en masse*, can be a terrifying thing. After the London riots of 2011, which spread to several major cities throughout 'civilized' England, a number of commentators referred to the youth involved, several as young as ten years old, as barbarians. Some people were murdered, others maimed or beaten. Property was vandalised, and parts of the city burned to the ground in what was described as the worst unrest in decades. Children hid under beds in terror, tenants escaped from their apartments down drain pipes as smoke and flames forced them to abandon their homes, and others tried to barricade their shop-fronts from a hail of debris and make-shift fire bombs – London was burning.

The appellation 'barbarian' was remarkably appropriate for these youth because the original meaning of the term in Greek and Latin usage was essentially 'outlander' i.e. a foreign and *rootless person*.

To the Greeks and later the Romans, all those outside their culture or civilization were barbarians and to be thus rootless was to be considered barbarous.[1] The term was then later taken up by medieval Christendom to refer to the non-Christian. So an outlander or rootless person is one fundamentally disconnected from society, from its history or culture and so from civilization itself. As a result they have no real interest in the future because they are without the sense of particularity and direction that historial rootedness alone can provide. They have no sense of belonging and therefore no awareness of identity. Without consciousness of rootedness, a person is left with only the lonely existential moment which offers no guidance, just a demand to choose in terms of oneself. What was striking about these London hoodlums was their frightening ignorance and inability to articulate, even when asked, what they were doing and why. Most were unsure why they were involved in the wanton destruction except to say that it was "a laugh" and "great fun," and "because of the rich and the government." None that I heard interviewed actually knew the name of the Prime Minister and when asked why they were destroying their own historic community, the homes and shops of their own neighbours, they merely answered, "We're showing the police we can do what we want." Several historians and commentators pointed to the fact that many of the protagonists, although being British-born and bred, could hardly speak comprehensible English, despite their expensive state education. One thing was clear, the rioters (and their delinquent parents) displayed a startling lack of awareness – or a rejection – of traditional British values, and a rootless indifference to British culture and identity.

None of this should be surprising, however, because when a generation ceases to value and identify with the past (even if only to self-consciously reject its errors and so avoid past mistakes), there is no ability to navigate forward responsibly. As former U.S. president Woodrow Wilson once put it, "A nation which does not remember what it was yesterday, does not know what it is today, nor what it is trying to do." Those under the age of fifty in the West have been taught to devalue the past, to ridicule and scorn the tradition, virtues, and experience of previous generations, and to believe the fallacy that if something is recent or latest, it must be best. This is the myth of progress that can only be believed by those ignorant of history. In the current telling of this myth we have supposedly reached an age where rationality and value no longer have any connection – to be rational means only to be 'scientific' (empiricist), a position which offers no values. To affirm values may be done, but not on the basis of the real and rational. Consequently, we need not be informed by the past, we simply choose in the moment as those without history. God is dead for us, so any values that exist do so only by virtue of the fact that I subjectively choose them, will them, personally experience them, or find them useful.

One cannot help but think that Cicero was right; we must know something of what happened before we arrived in the world, or we will never truly grow up from the cradle. Adult-sized petulant children are a menace to society and indicative of its collapse. History should matter to us because history matures us. This is important because it reveals the perpetual, practical relevance of history for the future. Of course, history must be interpreted, and we can only root ourselves in it, learn its crucial lessons, and put them to use, if we approach and understand history correctly.

3.2 Historiography

The French-born historian and former history professor at Columbia University, Jacques Barzun, has written a sweeping survey of Western cultural life, *From Dawn to Decadence*. In this work his precise religious persuasions are unclear, and in many respects he takes a very traditional view of history, explaining he is seeking to get at the 'facts' by guarding against bias. However, his understanding of fact and historical eventuation reveals a common modern neglect of the doctrine of God in history. In his author's note we read:

> William James concluded after reflection that philosophers do not give us transcripts but visions of the world. Similarly, historians give visions of the past. The good ones are not merely plausible; they rest on a solid base of facts that nobody disputes. There is nothing personal about facts, but there is about choosing and grouping them. It is by the patterning and the meanings ascribed that the vision is conveyed. And this, if anything, is what each historian adds to the general understanding.[2]

He goes on to say that the more historians a person reads, the closer that person comes to understanding the full complexity of history, though for an absolute copy one would need access to "the mind of God."[3] It

THE MISSION OF GOD

is not clear whether this 'god' for him is a literary device, a limiting concept, or vague faith, but the point is that, for this essentially Western understanding of how we gain historical knowledge (critical realism), his statement about the nature of history, philosophically destroys it. In what sense is history destroyed on such a view? To an extent what he says is accurate concerning the 'choosing' and 'grouping' of facts – by such a process, pattern and meaning are conveyed and elucidated by the author, providing a vision of history. This is an essentially Christian view of history; that is, history can be understood and lessons learned from it by careful investigation because it does have an objective pattern and meaning. However, Barzun has said that "there is nothing personal about facts." From a Christian standpoint, this is a serious error which destroys Barzun's project. If the facts are impersonal – not created and governed by a personal God according to the counsel of his will – then there is no pre-established meaning in the facts to be discovered and no 'real' pattern to describe. Instead we are confronted with a shoreless, undifferentiated sea of data. Without a personal God whose providence governs history there can be no 'true' or 'objective' interpretation of history. The historian is then only the creator of fanciful illusions – his visions are delusions. Barzun, for all his great learning and erudition, seems oblivious to the reality that he cannot have the "solid base of facts that nobody disputes" in a universe of impersonal factuality where history is a subjective exercise in storytelling. That is to say, since facts, to be facts, are being interpreted in terms of a worldview, the historian would only have meaningless, unrelated raw data, if the facts are ultimately impersonal (uncreated and directed), thus making the work of the historian futile. In another interesting aside, Barzun relates concerning the process of writing his book that "Chance has also aided the enterprise: family, time and place of birth gave shape and direction to effort; insomnia and longevity – sheer accidents – helped to crystallize fleeting insights by obsessive recurrence."[4] Now we recognize that 'chance' is a word sometimes used just idiomatically, but here Barzun does seem to see family, place of birth, and so forth as all merely fortuitousness! This is obviously contrary to the biblical view that all things are governed by the sovereign decree of God and his providential appointment. If this were not so, there could be no history, only the meaningless juxtaposition of space-time accidents. Thus Barzun must borrow from the Christian worldview to be a historian, whether he is conscious of this or not.

This is perhaps inadvertently recognized when he refers to the Western approach to history in the modern Christian era saying, "Our distinctive attitude toward history, our habit of arguing from it, turns events into ideas charged with power. And this use of the past dates precisely from the years that usher in what is called modern times."[5]

Our historic use of history has been predicated upon Christian assumptions about God and the world. With the abandonment of God in contemporary thought comes, necessarily, the abandonment of true history, once the internal logic of atheistic assumptions is worked out. In contemporary thought, the work of earlier historians, not just the events he or she records and explores, becomes little more than the will to power, as the alleged power-motive is 'unmasked' to expose the creative illusions of the historian whose vision is being deconstructed. History then ceases to be a serious subject of study for its own sake. Instead it becomes a subset of the social sciences, where man's social sins are held up as the approved lens through which history is to be interpreted – and thereby become an ideological tool for control.

3.3   The Bible and History: The Christian Perspective

In contrast to acclaimed historical surveys like Barzun's, which will go through revisions and changes, and perhaps be ridiculed years from now in light of further research, Scripture is an infallible book of history because it is the Word of the absolute, all-conditioning God.[6] Consequently, Scripture must be foundational to the Christian's understanding of history.[7] Unlike all other religious worldviews, biblical faith rests upon an historical revelation of God into history through real persons and events. No other faith is like this. With respect to the claims of other religions and sacred texts, although the Bible has had later imitators like the Koran, it has no true rival. R.J. Rushdoony explains this well:

> Virtually all the religions of the world are non-theistic; that is, they do not believe in God, in one supreme, absolute, and perfect God. In fact, most religions are atheistic...they do not believe in God although they may recognise many gods, or, more accurately...various powerful spirits and forces. The Kamis of Japanese Shintoism are sometimes called gods by foreigners, but they are more correctly described as powers. The word Kami means superior, and the word was applied to any object, thing, person, or spirit believed to have superior

status or power. In Buddhism, Taoism, and Hinduism, not God but nothingness is ultimate. These are essentially atheistic religions and man's salvation is death and Nirvana. Animism believes in the power of spirits and holds that even inanimate objects have a personal life or soul. It does not believe in God, but rather in spirits. For in none of these religions is there the God in terms of whom man can say, "Thus saith the Lord." No religion has what claims to be the word of God except biblical faith. Nowhere in the ancient world was there any trace of such a faith or of such a book as the Bible.[8]

Other religious texts give us philosophical abstractions, arbitrary and creative ethical teaching and fanciful mythologies, but a concrete, predictive, historical word from God is unique to biblical faith.

The two most pivotal doctrines for a Christian understanding of history are creation and predestination. When we turn to the subject of history it is immediately apparent that there are only two alternatives when accounting for historical eventuation. We either live in a world of creation, governed by the providence and the predestination of God, or we occupy an impersonal world of chance or fate, 'directed' by the nothingness of the abyss which destroys both meaning and freedom. St. Augustine saw this antithesis when he wrote:

Those who believe in fate argue that actions, events and even our very wills themselves depend on the position of the stars (which they call "constellations") at the time when we are conceived or born. But the grace of God stands above not only all stars and all heavens, but all angels too. In a word, believers in fate ascribe people's good and evil deeds and their fortunes to fate. In reality, when people suffer bad fortune, God is following up their vices with due retribution, while he bestows good fortunes by undeserved grace with a merciful will. He does both the one and the other, not according to a conjunction of the stars in time, but according to the eternal and high purpose of His severity and goodness. We see then that neither belong to fate.[9]

Simply stated, for Augustine, God governs everything in his inscrutable providence. Sin has wrought misery in human experience since the Fall, and the canvas of human history therefore manifests both the judgement and mercy of God with respect to the manifestation of his justice in a rebellious world. Without creation and predestination all we have left is what Christian philosopher Cornelius Van Til called brute factuality, that is, the unrelated isolated data of experience. No two facts could have an identifiably meaningful relationship, because there is no order, no design plan; they are forever unrelated and meaningless products of chance. Thus we have only two alternatives: chance or predestination, God or fate?[10] The foundational question of origins or creation makes this an inescapable dichotomy. The only way to try and avoid this is to take the universe itself as a 'given' and refuse to ask the tough question of origins, that is, refuse to ask the question of the origin of the universe and take the universe itself as god (Mother Nature). But all this does is smuggle the biblical God back into the universe in the name of nature – a 'personification' of the physical world. Only by making the question of the origin of the universe and its order illegitimate can the sceptic seek to evade this dilemma. In fact, if we are to retain the very idea of a 'universe' as opposed to a 'multi-verse' (no source of unity to provide meaning), we are implicitly pushed back to the doctrine of God and his providence. God's predestining and electing purpose is, in Scripture, both general and personal (Rom. 8:28–39; Eph. 1:7–14; Acts 17:24–28). He governs what we typically call the 'laws of nature' (his ordinary way of working), but he also knows the hairs of our heads and not a sparrow falls to the ground without our Father (Matt. 6:25–34; 10:29–30). God's knowledge of us is deeply personal and individual, perceiving our thoughts from afar, being intimately acquainted with all our ways. He is the all-conditioning God as the Psalmist so beautifully points out (Ps. 139). Furthermore, Reformed thought maintains that Christ dies in history for his elect, 'for His sheep,' not simply for the world in general (John 17:6–21; John 10:1–11). If we deny this fore-ordaining power to God, set out clearly by St. Paul (Rom. 9), this prerogative is simply transferred elsewhere. The power to plan, ordain and predestine is then ascribed to the autonomous individual or to an elite group – to the political establishment or scientific planners to govern and control man, his environment, his life and his fate. Everyone believes in sovereignty or predestination, people just disagree about the source.

There is a further consequence of predestination. Grace, in history, is interwoven with predestination. Grace has to do with God's favour toward us in his electing love – not because of any merit in us. If God is not a predestining God then our salvation is the result in some measure of our own merits and not his grace. There is no doubt the Bible makes clear that whilst the proximate determination of a person's life is in their own hands, the ultimate determination is from the Lord. In the Westminster Confession of faith we read:

> God from all eternity did by the most wise and holy counsel of his own will, freely and unchangeably ordain whatsoever comes to pass; yet so as thereby neither is God the author of sin, nor is violence offered to the will of the creatures, nor is the liberty or contingency of second causes taken away, but rather established.

As creator, God's fore-ordination in history is not an act of violence to the creature, removing liberty from the creature, whose will is a second cause; rather God's providence is in perfect harmony with them. Foreknowledge is not equivalent to predestination, since if God only foreknows history, it is history itself which is ultimate and not God – an alien history would decree something of which God is simply an interested or influential onlooker. In such a view, man makes his actions ultimate and determinative, placing God as essentially a motivated spectator in history. Eternity is no longer ultimate, but process, time, and history itself take the place of God. Clearly there is mystery here with respect to a Christian view of history; we have to be ready to accept on the basis of God's self-revelation both his sovereignty and our moral accountability. If this doctrine offends us because it appears incomprehensible, Scripture warns us against seeking to peer too deeply into things to marvellous for us:

> Oh the depth of the riches both of the wisdom and knowledge of God! How unsearchable are His judgements and His ways past finding out! For who has known the mind of the Lord? Or who has become His counsellor? Or who has first given to Him and it shall be repaid to him? For of Him and through Him and to Him are all things, to whom be glory forever, Amen. (Rom. 11:33–36 NKJV).

In Romans 9:19-21, St. Paul deals with those who will question why God has made them the way he has, putting God into the dock. Paul asks, "who are you to reply against God? Will the thing formed say to him who formed it, 'Why have you made me like this?'?" The question then concerns the source of sovereignty in history; is it man's, or God's? If it is God's then man is accountable to God (he cannot be accountable to the impersonal determinism of chance). If fallen man is sovereign, he will call God into the dock to give account to him, which is the basic human urge since the Fall – to play God. An egocentric, man-centred universe, in which everything revolves around his own desires, is fallen man's dream. But God calls us to live in history as his people, seeking first his kingdom and righteousness (Matt. 6:33), doing all for the glory of God to accomplish his purpose, not complaining against him for his ways. Rushdoony writes:

> Our calling is not to ask idle questions attempting to reconcile His absolute sovereignty and predestination with our responsibility and accountability. He has declared that this is so, and it is our duty to believe it and act in terms of it.... Job was deeply troubled, in his misery, by many questions and even doubts, but, in the face of all this, the bedrock of his life was his faith. He could thus cry out, even as he argued with God, "though he slay me, yet will I trust Him (Job 13:15)."[11]

3.4 Competing Views of History

The humanistic poet Trumbull Stickney (1874–1904) anticipated an existentialist approach to history when he wrote, "Live blindly and upon the hour. The Lord, Who was the Future, died full long ago."[12] The place of God in any worldview (alive, dead or indifferent), determines that faith's philosophy of history. We know that purely metaphysical definitions of time and history are highly problematic because definitions involve limitations which often elude us. Such discussions are therefore interesting speculative reflections (Augustine's *Confessions* has a fascinating discussion about the mysteries of time), but is not of primary importance for living.

Practically, history is first and foremost a moral problem for human beings – how to live in it, how to learn from it, what to learn from it, and taking responsibility for our part in it. If we exclude God from history we discover we are unable to find meaning in it, and become incapable of affirming anything about history or time. Indeed the past and future both collapse. If no God and no purpose exist beyond history, there is no viable idea of the future (implying pattern, purpose) since there is no meaning and consequence in time to give us a concept of the 'future' (since the present is meaningless). The same holds true for the past. Rushdoony aptly comments:

> To surrender a concept of time which binds past, present and future in terms of a related meaning is to surrender "the reality principle"

for the "pleasure principle." The golden age of existentialism will thus be the end of progress and the eventual death of man.... By renouncing the past and the future for the existential moment modern man has demanded an apocalyptic moment, instant paradise without any history or future. Karl Marx never swerved from this hope.[13] For ancient Greek philosophy, history (time and change) was either static and therefore an illusion, as in the thought of Parmenides, or all history was immersed in perpetual, directionless, fortuitous flux, with no transcendent meaning beyond it to define it, as in Heraclitus. There was no supervening mind of an infinite personal and sovereign God. Over against these pagan ideas, as Christians we must redeem the time (Eph. 5:15–16) because progress in history, in terms of divine purpose, is mandated by God. The Kingdom of God is going to be established and evil defeated, for the Bible tells us that his purposes are advancing (Ps. 72:8; Hab. 2:14). "The kingdom of the world has become the kingdom of our Lord and of his Christ, and he shall reign forever and ever" (Rev. 11:15). But, wherever and whenever history (time itself), rather than God, is seen as ultimate, history collapses into self-negation and meaninglessness, which is the point at which modern philosophy has arrived. History is change, but change alone, without God-given direction and meaning, is simply terror and doubt for those who pass through it. If time, and not the triune God, is ultimate, all philosophies end in the negation of life itself with a final goal of escaping the 'illusion' of history, into the void, nirvana, or absorption into Brahma – the nothingness. Without transcendent purpose, man's only alternative to outright nihilism is to create a private meaning, and magically read this onto the irrational happenstances of time – this is the kind of superstition that has become so common amongst humanists. Both the ancient Greeks and moderns like Nietzsche and Freud were highly superstitious and fatalistic – Freud tried to predict his death several times with numerological superstition and failed.[14] The point is, without the God of Scripture, a new law of being and eternal decree must be projected by man onto reality to create 'history.' Many superstitions can be sophisticated, philosophical, and 'scientific;' they need not be primitive, but they boil down to a belief in magic where a human idea seeks to incarnate itself in time to realize man's sovereignty or determination and set aside the purposes of God. Since this is impossible – for God, not man's ideas, governs history – rebellion against God is always marked by hostility, futility, tragedy, and heartbreak. The famous existentialist Jean-Paul Sartre concluded, "Man is a useless passion." Only sorrow and despair can result from man's rebellion against God.

Today, the so-called postmodern thinker denies real history and creates another illusion by deconstructing the past in terms of a hermeneutic of suspicion in the name of 'justice' – a justice that goes undefined. According to this line of thinking there can be no objective, trans-cultural meaning of history, only 'histories' that uncover the will to power. This is simply an existentialist philosophy of history within a literary framework. In the Christian worldview, however, the Bible gives us an infallible history in terms of the justice of God, a direction and framework for the interpretation of all time from the creation of all things, to the judgement and reconciliation of all things. For the Christian, history has a definite *telos* and progress in terms of God's rule, whereby all things are being shaken, so that only those things which cannot be shaken will remain (Heb. 12:26–29). The glorious goal is the Kingdom of God and the new creation.

3.5 History and Politics

For the humanist ('Christian' or non-Christian) the perennial problem of definition remains. We have seen that without the transcendent, ontological Trinity and a personal creation in terms of which all things are known, planned and ordered by the providence of God, man has the impossible task of locating all definition and rationality in himself, imposing his abstract 'idea' of events upon reality, leaving himself confronted finally with the 'irrational moment.' If history itself does not begin with meaning, it has none at all. Thus agnostic and atheistic historiography begins with the assumption that the absolute, personal creator God of Scripture has nothing to do with history and as a result we are reduced to the position of wanderers in a mindless multi-verse. However, since humanity cannot abide such mindless chaos, or live in terms of it, the allegedly 'irrational' flow of time, which daily becomes 'history,' must be harnessed and controlled – but how? Control of reality is often thought to be best achieved by politics and technology (magical or scientific) and so an alliance between paganism and politics emerged readily in the ancient world. Quickly, political systems of 'salvation' (oblation, order, wholeness and healing) developed, as religion was seen as essentially a department of the priestly state. The chiefs, monarchs or elites functioned as priests or gods in the political theology of antiquity, either as incarnations of the gods themselves or as mediators of their power and authority.[15] Likewise, magicians, sorcerers, diviners – and later, scientific planners, in this paradigm – were quickly equated with divinity as controllers of ultimate reality. This belief was found not only in low civilization, but in the high civilizations of Egypt, Greece and Rome – their magical polytheisms all reflect this deification of political or priestly man. Rushdoony cites two further examples found in Scripture:

> Baal worship in the Middle East was the worship of lords, natural and political, who governed all reality. The political rulers readily adopted Baalism in order to command that total control offered by this politico-magical worldview. Moloch worship, with its demand for human sacrifice, was politico-magical, and Moloch literally meant King. The medicine men of American Indian tribes had little relationship to religion; their function was magical and medicine was one facet of their claimed control over reality.[16]

The medicine man or 'shaman' is also highly distinctive in antiquity and continues to the present in various cultures, most notably in North America amongst the First Nations. The social historian of medicine, Roy Porter, points out:

> Common in Native American culture as well as Asia, the shaman combined the roles of healer, sorcerer, seer, educator and priest, and was believed to possess god-given powers to heal the sick and to ensure fertility, a good harvest or successful hunt. His main healing techniques have been categorized as contagious magic, involving rituals to prevent disease, fetishes, amulets (to protect against black magic), and talismans (for good luck).[17]

The perversity of all this godless culture-building (ancient and modern, Western and Eastern) is located in the human effort to control reality (history) in contempt of God's covenant law and grace and his purposes for time. Rebellion against God's purpose always brings judgement in which civilizations crumble. History envisioned without God and his Word results in seeing all history as man's social experiment, where all the variables need to be controlled by magic, technology or the self-styled political elite. States are often then seen by intellectual elites as laboratories where a controlled environment must be created to bring about the desired outcomes, which, in turn, are defined by humanistic philosophy. This requires statism, mass regulation, and the loss of freedoms. Since man's magic and manipulation is a disintegrating and demonic power based upon satanic lies (Eph. 6:12), rebellious man is caught in endless frustration because God's word always comes to pass (Job 12:9–25); his purposes cannot be defeated, nor his law violated without leading to death (Prov. 8:35–36). If this is the result of rebellion against God's plan for history, what is the result of obedience to God and harmony with his purpose for time? What if Christians, through the power of the gospel, instead of being at war with God's purposes and incurring the judgement of degraded cultures, faithfully applied God's Word to God's world – would we then not expect God's will to be increasingly done and his kingdom (reign) to come in our lives and social orders, on earth as it is in heaven? Would we then not expect the principles of life, liberty and justice to be in evidence? If Christians applied their faith to all life, would we not expect to see civilizations unfold that reflected these principles of God's Word? Instead of the reign of paganism with its magic arts, 'scientific planning,' lawlessness, moral degradation and tyranny, would not more just, free, moral and prosperous cultures emerge and rise from the pages of history?

3.6 Western History and Culture

There can be little doubt that Western culture, or Christendom (imperfect as it has been) over the past 1500 years, characterized by the massive emergence of new freedoms, the rule of law, justice, prosperity, and social cohesion, is one of the greatest marvels in the history of world civilization. This is not said out of some misplaced sense of Anglo-Saxon or European supremacy, neither is it cultural imperialism or colonial arrogance – it is simply a fact of history. It is simply not possible to account for the liberty created by Western civilization without recognizing the specifically Christian and biblical faith that formed its actuating principle. As Vishal Mangalwadi has pointed out:

> The covenant of the Ten Commandments founded the modern principle of constitutionalism, or rule of law, by a perpetual written and binding law. Britain's submission to the rule of law was institutionalized with the Magna Carta (1215), founded on common law, tracing to the code of Alfred the Great. The Mosaic code was the foundation for such legal codes in the West. One-third of Alfred's

"Dooms" (AD 893) quoted biblical law while collating the laws of three Christian kingdoms. Ultimately the Word of God was the basis for law and government.... The regularization of England's judicial system began with the Magna Carta. Within three decades, one of England's most famous godly judges, Henry de Bracton, began to systematize English common law. By the mid-thirteenth century, he had explicitly derived from the Bible the principle of rule of justice rather than force. By 1258, England's House of Commons was formed. The "Model Parliament" of Edward I in 1295 consisted of bishops, abbots, peers, two knights from each shire, and two representatives from each town.[18]

The rule of law over-against the pagan concepts of the rule of might, or the rule of an intellectual elite, was not the only foundation stone of Western civilization laid by Christianity. Out of Scripture also emerged the idea of a division of powers and accountability of rulers to the people.

[The] biblical governmental principle of the rule of elders became foundational to modern constitutional republics as the rule by elected representatives and not by hereditary aristocrats as in Rome. The early church adopted the Old Testament approach to the leadership of elders. It was very different from the direct and vulnerable democracy in Greece.... Biblical history contributed another critical principle of just governance: the division of powers and checks and balances.[19]

Mangalwadi goes on to show how Israel appointed political authority independent of religious authority by regulations codified by Moses, whilst the prophets kept a check on any abuse of political power. Mangalwadi thus shows how, contrary to popular misunderstanding, our freedoms in the West emerged from the biblical concept of theocracy: "Does the American notion of 'one nation under God' or 'in God we trust' imply theocracy or democracy? The biblical tradition rediscovered during the Reformation viewed theocracy and democracy as necessary compliments: human rule flowed from God's rule.

The Bible depicts God as the ultimate ruler."[20] Many Western Christians then have made a great error, internalizing an artificially-imposed and masochistic guilt complex, cowering in ignorant embarrassment because of what cultural Marxists have told them about their civilization, the shame they should feel and the reparations they should make. Certainly an appropriately biblical sense of humility and perspective must be maintained, that since we are fallen beings, the sinful desires to domination and subjugation of others have been very present in the history of Christendom. This does not mean, however, that Christians' view of the past should be characterized by a false humility that scurrilously runs down all the hard-won cultural and missionary achievements of generations of Christians, in the interests of pleasing the purveyors of an anti-Christian ideology. The common historical, 'infallible criticism' (allegedly uncovering a cynical, raw will to power in Western history), and the accompanying masochistic demand to 'repent' of our history is pure pretence – a hypocritical mask used to hide an elitist hatred of biblical religion, which the statist engine of political correctness (cultural Marxism) has used to drive the Christian faith into hiding. In short, those hostile to biblical faith have developed an alternate theology of history. This vision offers us a new satanic empire: Western colonialism, and with it, a new plan of salvation. Its exponents' political theology suggests that the whole world is divided into two groups – the oppressors and the oppressed. All men and nations are not sinners and alike under God's judgement. Rather, sin is to be Western (especially white, male, and middle-class) and in possession of wealth, which is merely the product of oppression, not the rule of law and hard work. The oppressor nations are therefore Western European and North American nations – the colonials and their children, who allegedly stole the wealth of the rest of the world. These evildoers are now to be judged by a redistribution of that wealth through political coercion. Cultural destruction of the family, confiscatory progressive taxation, carbon taxes for the myth of Western, man-made global warming, and any and all means to asset-strip the productive are legitimate weapons. Freedom is irrelevant, property rights are irrelevant, rule of law is irrelevant; all must be equalized. Salvation for the world is justification by redistribution, with the primary sinner being the 'guilty' United States. Their place in the world (along with Britain, Australia and Canada) must be altered for salvation to be effected.

Interestingly, the major proponents of this mythic history and counterfeit salvation are Western political and media elites and liberal theologians. In reality, however, the essential cultural characteristics (coveted around the world) of what we used to call Christendom are simply unparalleled anywhere else in recorded world history outside of the nation of Israel. Clearly Christianity is not European in origin, nor were the apostles or most of the earliest missionaries. The faith penetrated deep into the Far East, even China, before Christendom existed. Furthermore, some of the most influential church fathers among those that framed the great ecumenical creeds were African. Yet, quickly spreading West, Christianity took root dominating and decisively shaping European history and culture.[21] As the centuries passed it eclipsed the church in North Africa and the Middle East, as much of it slipped into error or weakness, and was eventually pushed aside by a warmongering Islam when European tax payers no longer wished to foot the bill for Western military assistance against Islamic aggression. It is not sheer accident that this 1500-year period in our history is what has been called the Christian era and that we date our very calendar from the birth of Christ. Indeed for centuries, right up until the last few decades, Western European and North American nations observed a rigidly Christian calendar, including weekly recognition of the Sabbath. When God's Word has been applied by fallen people to life and culture (however fallibly), the result has still been the building of the most stable and just civilization known to man, and in recent centuries people have flocked to these nations from around the world for justice, liberty, prosperity and opportunity. It is not chance that made the West what it is. The myth of Christianity bringing about "Dark Ages" in Europe (the 600 years after the fall of Rome) propagated successfully by French philosophes has long since been debunked as spurious, the fifteenth edition of the *Encyclopaedia Britannica* in 1981 dismissing the label as completely unacceptable historically. In fact the early centuries of the Christian era in the West were, as Rodney Stark points out, "one of the great innovative eras of mankind, as technology was developed and put into use on a scale no civilization had previously known. In fact...it was during the "Dark Ages" that Europe began the great technological leap forward that put it far ahead of the rest of the world."[22] Indeed it was Christian theology and social order that provided the fertile soil for the development of scholarship, medicine, technology and science. As James Hannam has shown, "the most significant contribution of the natural philosophers of the Middle Ages was to make modern science even conceivable.... Their central belief that nature was created by God and so worthy of their attention was one that Galileo wholeheartedly endorsed. Without that awareness, modern science would simply not have happened."[23] Indeed the learning of the Middle Ages was the fruit of Christian labour and thought. As Stark has critically noted:

> "Muslim" or "Arab" medicine was in fact Nestorian Christian
> medicine; even the leading Muslim and Arab physicians were trained
> at the enormous Nestorian medical centre at Nisibus in Syria. Not
> only medicine but a full range of advanced education was offered at
> Nisibus and at the other institutions of learning established by the
> Nestorians.... Hence, the Nestorians "soon acquired a reputation with
> the Arabs for being excellent accountants, architects, astrologers,
> bankers, doctors, merchants, philosophers, scientists, scribes and
> teachers. In fact, prior to the ninth century, nearly all the learned
> scholars in the [Islamic area] were Nestorian Christians." [24] The
> Cambridge University-trained professional historian Philip Jenkins
> agrees with Stark regarding the importance of Christian Syriac
> scholarship. He writes:

> In 1026, Nisibus was the scene of a famous debate between the
> Nestorian bishop Elijah and a Muslim vizier. Arguing for the
> superiority of Syriac over Arabic, the bishop made the seemingly
> incontestable claim that Arabs had learned most of their science
> from Syriac sources, while the reverse had seldom occurred....
> For a thousand years, Syriac Christians produced scholars and
> thinkers who could be set beside the best of their Greek or Latin
> contemporaries, and who shaped the emerging world of Islamic
> science and philosophy. [25]

So then, over against the humanistic myths of a 'Dark Age' and
'Enlightenment,' or the contemporary myths of today's 'post-colonial
theology,' if history is governed by God, his covenant law and
providence, then social histories, our successes and failures in the varied
areas of culture building, will be a reflection, in large degree, of human
beings obedience and disobedience to God's purpose and word in any
given era. This view is the biblical vision of God's active work in history
to bless and curse in terms of his covenant (Prov. 14:34; Deut. 28). This
is a covenantal reading of history that characterised the Puritan mind. The
Puritans were themselves industrialists, scientists, inventors, educators
and pioneers who believed that God required them to turn creation into
the culture of Christ. These convictions therefore lie behind the successes
of Anglo-American culture. Obedience to God's law and gospel brought
blessing, disobedience brought curses. Consider, for example, the way

Oliver Cromwell spoke at the opening of the English Parliament on September 17, 1656:

> I did read a Psalm yesterday, which truly may not unbecome me both to tell you of, and you to observe. It is the eighty-fifth Psalm, that is very instructive and significant...it begins, "Lord, thou hast been favourable to thy land; thou hast brought back the captivity of Jacob. Thou hast forgiven the iniquity of thy people, though hast covered all their sins. Thou hast taken away all thy wrath, thou hast turned thyself from the fierceness of thine anger. Turn us, O God of our salvation, and cause thine anger towards us to cease. Wilt thou be angry with us forever? Wilt thou draw out thine anger to all generations? Wilt thou not revive us again that they people may rejoice in thee?" ...and then saith he, "Yea the Lord shall give that which is good and our land shall yield its increase. Righteousness shall go before him, and shall set us in the way of his steps." Truly I wish that this Psalm might be better written in our hearts, that we may say as David, "Thou hast done this," and "Thou hast done that," ...whither can we go to a better God, for he hath done it? It is to him any nation may come in their extremity for the taking away of his wrath. How did he do it? By pardoning their sins and taking away their iniquities. If we can but cry unto him, he will turn and take away our sins. Then let us listen to him, and then consult and meet in Parliament and ask him counsel, and hear what he saith, "for he will speak peace unto his people." If you be the people of God, and be for the people of God, he will speak peace, and we will not again return to folly...till God hath brought us to this spirit, he will not bear with us. "Aye, but he bears with them in France; they are so and so." Have they the gospel as we have? They have seen the sun but a little; we have great lights. If God give you the spirit of reformation, you will preserve this nation from turning again to these fooleries. And what will the end be? Comfort and blessing. Then "mercy and truth shall meet together." There is a great deal of truth among professors, but very little mercy. They are ready to cut the throats of one another. But when we are brought into the right way, we shall be merciful as well as orthodox.... I have done. All I have to say is, to pray God that he may bless you with his presence, that he who hath your hearts and mine would show his presence in the midst of us.[26]

It is abundantly clear here that the Puritans believed our personal, social and national good, our peace and prosperity in history, are directly tied to God and his word governing our personal and corporate lives, as opposed to fate, magic arts or man's ingenuity, ideas and planning. Furthermore, in the same way that God was faithful and true to his historic covenant with Israel, if we will obey and be faithful to God and call upon him, our nations will know his blessing and favour. For Cromwell, this conviction was not an abstract spirituality that had no real bearing on actual policy – a kind of 'Parliamentary devotional' before the real secular business of worldly affairs was done – on the contrary, he actively pursued biblical ends in Parliament:

> The authenticity of Cromwell's commitment to law reform is shown in the various ordinances that he personally issued in the months before the first Protectoral Parliament began sitting. Most notable were ordinances for probate of wills, for the relief of debtors and poor prisoners, for establishing a High Court of Justice.... Cromwell did not give up the struggle for juster laws. As Protector he reminded his second Parliament that, "there are wicked and abominable laws that will be in your power to alter. To hang a man for sixpence, thirteen pence, I know not what; to hang for a triffle and pardon a murder, is in the ministration of the law, through the ill framing of it. I have known in my experience abominable murderers quitted; and to come and see men lose their lives for petty matters! This is a thing that God will reckon for.[27]

There is no cold abstraction here. To the Puritan thinker, God will actively judge persons and nations on the basis of our actions in history, our faithfulness or unfaithfulness to his Word and his standards. Why? Because he governs history. Injustice must not be borne, for God, as Cromwell declared, will reckon for it. This then is a robustly biblical view of historical eventuation. God is not at a distance from history, uninvolved and on the periphery, an interested spectator or distant 'first cause;' rather he is governing all things by his providence and wisdom. As the Scriptures declare, "righteousness exalts a nation, but sin is a reproach to any people" (Prov. 14:34). As the Psalmist also tells us concerning the wicked, "truly you set them in slippery places; you make them fall to ruin. How they are destroyed in a moment, swept away utterly by terrors" (Ps. 73:18–19). No view of history is more obnoxious or offensive to the humanist than one which declares God's sovereignty over all things. To suggest that blessing and cursing follows obedience and disobedience to God is viewed as primitive and a kind of intellectual suicide.

Professor Philip Davies for example, who specializes in Biblical Studies, writing on the issue of the Bible and 'social justice' in history, considers biblical history and accounts of justice mythological and contradictory; he denies the original sin of man, and cannot disguise his abhorrence for the substitutionary atonement of Christ as an expression of 'justice.'[28] He considers historical divine judgement in the Bible as unpredictable and indiscriminate at best. He concludes, "Perhaps either the ways of God are incomprehensible, or that, there being no god, our own sense of justice is compromised and subject to variation, and that we simply project on to this supernatural 'supreme judge' the very confusion that we can see in ourselves."[29] Whilst orthodox biblical faith recognizes that God's judgements in history are beyond our comprehensive analysis and that God's judgement is always in light of eternity and his final judgement so that we do not always see justice done in every situation (far from it), it does declare that God is just, that history is not 'chance and accident,' and that faithfulness and disobedience do bring historical reward and punishment. Without this God, all we are left with is Davies' bewildered confusion. Now clearly we can observe important historical examples of the biblical attitude toward history in the nation-building of the West. It is often claimed by our American friends that the United States is the most Christian nation the world has known. The U.S. certainly had a wonderful beginning, with over 150 years of Puritan, evangelical life at its foundation, prior to the war of independence and the revolutionary constitutional period. That said, we might fairly dispute that post-constitutional America can claim to be the most 'Christian' nation in history, though it was without doubt (and remains to a certain degree), a great Christian land. In fact I would argue that historically, the case could be made that both Great Britain and Canada have been more explicitly and covenantally Christian as 'nations' than post-constitutional America.[30] Perhaps the best example of this covenantal attitude toward history is found in England's Solemn League and Covenant in 1643. Ian Gentles points out that from Cromwell's perspective, "all of English history had been merely a preparation for the events of 1640-53."[31] Following the example of some of Israel's godly kings in the Old Testament (i.e. Josiah's national covenant with God in 2 Kings 23:3), in 1643 the Parliament of England made a covenant with God, called the *Solemn League and Covenant*. Protestants of the period had no difficulty believing that nations could covenant with the Lord (in a similar way that we make a covenant of marriage before the Lord). The final paragraph of the Solemn League reads:

> And because these kingdoms are guilty of many sins and provocations against God, and his son Jesus Christ, as is too manifest by our present distresses and dangers, the fruits thereof; we profess and declare, before God and the world, our unfeigned desire to be humbled for our own sins, and for the sins of these kingdoms: especially, that we have not as we ought valued the inestimable benefit of the Gospel; that we have not laboured for the purity and power thereof; and that we have not endeavoured to receive Christ in our hearts, nor to walk worthy of him in our lives; which are the causes of other sins and transgression so much abounding amongst us: and our true and unfeigned purpose, desire, and endeavour for ourselves, and all others under our power and charge, both in public and private, in all duties we owe to God and man, to amend our lives, and each one to go before another in example of a real reformation; that the Lord may turn away his wrath and heavy indignation, and establish these churches and kingdoms in truth and peace. And this covenant we make in the presence of almighty God, the searcher of all hearts, with a true intention to perform the same, as we shall answer at that great day, when the secrets of all hearts shall be disclosed; most humbly beseeching the Lord to strengthen us by his Holy Spirit for this end, and to bless our desires and proceedings with such success, as may be deliverance and safety to his people, and encouragement to other Christian churches, groaning under, or in danger of, the yoke of antichristian tyranny, to join in the same or like association and covenant, to the glory of God, the enlargement of the kingdom of Jesus Christ and the peace and tranquillity of Christian kingdoms and commonwealths.[32]

There is no sense in which the Declaration of Independence or United States constitution can compare with this declaration of the English Parliament, in terms of fidelity to Scripture, gospel faithfulness, or explicit Christian faith and commitment. Indeed, the United States constitution does not mention Jesus Christ, which has proven to be a serious mistake.[33] As political scientist and commentator Michael Wagner points out, "This Solemn League and Covenant was a major document of seventeenth-century Britain."[34] It was taken by both the Lords and Commons, legally assembled in the mother of all Parliaments, and then by the general populace of England as a whole. It was even sworn by Charles II when he came to the throne, and was placed on the statute book, to remain a component of English law throughout all time. "That is to say, the legitimate governing authorities of England bound themselves and their nation to follow and obey the Lord God of the Bible."[35] Canada was likewise, in some sense, bound as a British colony to this covenant, and obviously the Canadian parliament is an offshoot of the British parliament. All these things simply reveal the historically intimate connection of the Christian church to national life, government, and the social order in our history. Throughout the seventeenth and eighteenth centuries, many evangelical believers remained convinced that Christian nations could and should covenant with God. For example, Archibald Mason, a Presbyterian minister in the late eighteenth century, wrote in manner characteristic of the convictions of many:

> When a nation is enlightened with the gospel, comes to receive the truths of Christ, makes a profession of his religion, and submits to his ordinances and laws, it is as much a theocracy, a people under the immediate and gracious government of God, and are as much bound, by covenanting nationally with him, to swear an oath of national allegiance unto the Lord, as ever the house of Israel and the house of Judah were to perform this service in the land of Canaan.[36]

It is simply a fact that in Canada, as much as England, our institutions, traditions, and principles rest upon the teaching and influence of the Christian faith and church. Our legal system inherited from England rests upon biblical principles of justice. Given this history, the historian Mark Noll likewise argues that "Canada has an even better objective argument for being considered a Christian nation than does the United States."[37] Practically, this meant that Canadian believers "mobilized to preach the gospel in new settlements spread over a vast frontier. Canadians also linked the progress of Christianity with the advance of civilization. And they succeeded in bequeathing a Christian tone to the institutions, habits and morals of public life."[38] Indeed, "Canadians transformed a wilderness into a significant Christian civilization."[39] Noll helpfully summarises the character of this Puritan approach to life and history that is embedded in our English and Canadian past:

> Puritans believed that God created society as a unified whole. Church and state, the individual and the public, are not unrelated spheres of life but are complementary, intimately connected by God's act of creation and his continuing providence... Puritans believed that God always works with people through covenants or solemn agreements. They believed that the Bible explains the terms and conditions of the covenants through which God approached the world...almost all varieties of Puritans also held that God enters into covenants with nations, especially those that are granted special insight into the truths of the Bible. Guidelines from the Bible indicate to nations what they must do to enjoy divine blessing, while scripture examples concerning ancient Israel provide harrowing warnings about what will happen to nations that violate their covenant with God.[40]

Should this be thought a quaint and long-dead Christian romanticism that had no meaningful impact on our present time, one further illustration is necessary. What we have been noting is that just as pagan views of life and history produced pagan political theology and social orders, so when a Christian view of life and history has been applied by believers, Christian social orders, with all their concomitant blessings, have emerged, and great transformation has taken place. If societal and national sin incurs God's judgement against that order in history as the Puritans believed, then righteousness and justice (as defined by God's law) must be pursued and injustice abolished as far as possible if we would see God's blessing upon our children and grandchildren. This view was shared by one of the most beloved and famous of all nineteenth-century evangelicals, William Wilberforce, the man pre-eminently responsible for, and synonymous with, the abolition of the slave trade in the British Empire. Many Christians love to cite Wilberforce's example with admiration. Yet it is remarkable how few people ask themselves what theological vision undergirded Wilberforce's moral crusade and tireless tenacity to seek justice. Thankfully he does not leave us in the dark; he possessed an archetypal Puritan mind. In *A Letter on the Abolition of the Slave Trade; Addressed to the Freeholders and other Inhabitants of Yorkshire*, published in 1807, Wilberforce wrote the following:

> Of all the motives by which I am prompted to address you, that
> which operates on me with the greatest force, is, the consideration
> of the present state and prospects of our country, and of the duty
> which at so critical a moment presses imperiously on every member
> of the community, to exert his utmost powers in the public cause.
> That the Almighty Creator of the Universe governs the world
> which he has made; that the sufferings of nations are to be regarded
> as the punishment of national crimes; and their decline and fall,
> as the execution of His sentence; are truths which I trust are still
> generally believed among us. Indeed to deny them, would be directly
> to contradict the express and repeated declarations of the Holy
> Scriptures. If these truths be admitted, and if it be also true, that
> fraud, oppression, and cruelty, are crimes of the blackest dye, and
> that guilt is aggravated in proportion as the criminal acts in defiance
> of the clearer light, and of stronger motives to virtue (and these are
> positions to which we cannot refuse our assent, without rejecting the
> authority not only of revealed, but even of natural religion); have we
> not abundant cause for serious apprehension? The course of public
> events has, for many years, been such as human wisdom and human
> force have in vain endeavoured to control or resist...though the storm
> has been raging for many years, yet, instead of having ceased, it
> appears to be now increasing in fury... if such be our condition; and
> if the slave trade be a national crime, declared by every wise and
> respectable man of all parties, without exception, to be a compound
> of the grossest wickedness and cruelty, a crime to which we cling
> in defiance of the clearest light...is not this then a time in which all
> who are not perfectly sure that the Providence of God is but a fable,
> should be strenuous in their endeavour to lighten the vessel of the
> state, of such a load of guilt and infamy?[41]

It is vital to notice that a large part of Wilberforce's motivation for
pursuing abolition was the alleviation of judgement and infamy from
Britain, by bringing to an end a crime revived by Enlightenment
humanists, which in Wilberforce's view, was incurring the righteous
wrath of God in the form of national judgement. One of his primary
motive forces in pursuit of abolition was therefore his great concern
for the prospects of his own nation. He believed wholeheartedly in

the active providence of God in history and that Britain was under corporate judgement during this era for sins committed against her better knowledge. Since man-theft and enslavement are condemned by God's law in both the Old and New Testaments (Ex. 21:16; 1 Tim. 1:10), he feared the decline and fall of England if she persisted in this gross sin against God. It is a great pity that the modern church does not take as seriously as it should the theological vision of history that lay at the foundation of Wilberforce's quest for the justice of God to be manifest in his culture.

3.7 Law, History and Political Life

In the biblical perspective, then, all men and women stand before God as either covenant keepers or covenant breakers; white or black, Western or Eastern, rich or poor. The prophet Isaiah speaking of God's judgement upon the whole earth (not simply Israel) in the time before the coming of the Christ declares, "The earth lies defiled under its inhabitants; for they have transgressed the laws, violated the statutes, broken the everlasting covenant. Therefore a curse devours the earth, and its inhabitants suffer for their guilt" (Is. 24:5–6). Clearly, God relates to the human race by covenant (2 Sam. 23:2–7; Ps. 25:10; Ps. 111:5; Jer. 31:33; 1 Cor. 11:25; Heb. 13:20–21) and is intent upon bringing about the justice of his kingdom in the world through covenant faithfulness. In the Christian worldview, since there are real consequences in time for obedience and disobedience to God, law and covenant play a critical role in all historical eventuation for men and nations. As God declared through King David, "The God of Israel has spoken; the rock of Israel has said to me: When one rules justly over men, ruling in the fear of God, he dawns on them like the morning light, like the sun shining forth on a cloudless morning, like rain that makes grass to sprout from the earth" (2 Sam. 23:3–4).

In every culture, law is religious in origin and so it must be recognized that in any social order the source of law is the god of that society and that to which the people have bound themselves. To change the law order is then an implicit or explicit change in religion – revealing a change of gods (allegiance) in that political realm. This further implies that no absolute disestablishment of religion is actually possible in any society. A culture can certainly disestablish one faith or church, but it merely replaces that faith with another one, be it Islamic, Buddhist or any other humanistic faith. This is clearly what has taken place in the modern West. We have traded the God of the Bible for the god of the state (man enlarged), where the 'will of the people,' personified by an elite bureaucracy, now redefines law in the name of the people, the new god. This has been in no small part due to a faulty theology amongst Christians and the consequent abdication of responsibility by the church in the socio-political sphere. Due to the philosophical dualism that has so greatly influenced the church (discussed in chapter two), modern Christians have tended to separate God's law and covenant from real history and implicitly assumed that the state is not actually accountable to God's standards. As Greg Bahnsen notes, "nominalism and dualism contributed to the separation of natural reason and scriptural revelation, which in turn assigned matters of politics to a realm independent of God's word and its norms."[42] This has meant that practically, "modern Christians have generally thought and acted in politics independently of their faith."[43] As such, during the nineteenth and early twentieth centuries, Christians started to adopt the myth of the neutrality of the state. This quite logically resulted in a disconnect between Scripture, law, and public policy: "Emancipated from its ministry of justice under God's rule, the modern state has turned away from Scripture's moral law as the standard of political and legal obligation within society."[44] This present situation is very different from what our Christian forebears believed and envisioned for history. For example, Martin Luther saw that the civil magistrate must be subject to the law of God in order for God's kingdom purposes to be fulfilled in history. Harold Berman writes:

> The fact that Luther and his colleagues consigned law to a secular realm under civil authority has misled many scholars to suppose that they had made law and religion mutually irrelevant.... From his theology Luther drew the implication that it is the duty of Christians to accept the Ten Commandments as divine law to be applied not only directly in their personal lives, but also indirectly, through laws of civil authorities derived from it, in their political lives. The civil ruler, Luther argued, holds his authority of God and serves as God's vice-regent in the earthly kingdom. His law should therefore respect and reflect God's law. The civil ruler is thus not free to rule arbitrarily. Luther found those principles of justice expressed most perfectly in the Ten Commandments, which he believed to be a summary of the natural law and thus accessible to pagans as well as to Christians.[45]

John Calvin went further in insisting upon the application of the law of God to the social order as required for the good of all society and the flourishing of true humanity in history:

> Civil government...prevents idolatry, sacrilege against God's name, blasphemies against his truth, and other public offenses against religion from arising and spreading among the people; it prevents the public peace from being disturbed; it provides that each man may keep his property safe and sound; that men may carry on blameless intercourse among themselves; that honesty and modesty may be preserved among men. In short, it provides that a public manifestation of religion may exist among Christians, and that humanity be maintained among men.... The law of God forbids killing; but, that murderers may not go unpunished, the Lawgiver himself puts into the hand of his ministers a sword to be drawn against all murderers.... Would that this were ever before our minds – that nothing is done here from men's rashness, but all things are done on the authority of God who commands it; and while his authority goes before us, we never wander from the straight path![46]

Calvin's religious conviction permeated much of the Protestant world[47] and led to great change in the law, with developments in liberty, freedom and justice by the application of biblical faith to political and social realities. As Berman points out, a society's view of history and the development of law are intimately related:

> At the heart of the transformation of English law in the seventeenth century was the Anglo-Calvinist belief that God had made a covenant with the English people, that England was an elect nation, chosen, as the children of Israel had once been chosen, to be 'a light to all the nations.' To this belief in a divine covenant was added the Calvinist doctrine that history is wholly within the providence of God, and that the history of the English people, including the history of their institutions, was the heritage on which their constitutional law was founded and which gave guidance for its future development. Calvinism in its English form also contributed to the revolt against royal absolutism and the establishment of the supremacy of a parliamentary aristocracy."[48]

Here Berman clearly shows that law was transformed because of a Calvinist belief in the covenant of God and his providence throughout time. That covenant meant responsibility to God with blessings and cursing as judgement in history. Because the Lord and sovereign was God himself, this also put the English people in possession of a principle of liberty against tyranny. It is important to remember here that England drew its idea of national mission and responsibility from the doctrine of the covenant and a Christian philosophy of history – God's providence – not a concept of national superiority.[49]

In the case of England, the gospel and rule of God's law was what they believed they were to share as a light to the nations. One concrete example of a change in the law that followed Calvinism and that brought about a more just society was seen in the development of jury trial. Berman writes, "perhaps the most dramatic change in the procedure of the English common law courts in the late seventeenth century was the transformation of jury trial through the introduction of witness proof at the trial stage."[50] This is quite obviously biblical, since the Mosaic Law has strict legislation requiring the presence and testimony of witnesses in order to verify accusations of felony, and regulations protecting against perjury (Deut. 19:15–21; 1 Tim. 5:19).

Another significant development was the covenantal and communitarian sense that it was a "community responsibility to apprehend and correct those who commit sins, and if their acts constitute crimes, to institute criminal prosecutions."[51] As a people accountable before God, crime was a community, not simply a 'police' problem. In the courts, the jury was seen as representative of the community at large, and thus, the jury executed the community's responsibility to correct and restrain sin. "By convicting the guilty, the jury fulfilled the community's responsibility to repress and correct sin. By acquitting, or by convicting of a lesser crime, it served to control that responsibility by its judgement as to the nature and circumstances of the alleged sin."[52] Another positive biblical development was the humaneness with which people were to be treated. It is hard for us to fully appreciate the arbitrary power and cruelty of monarchies which dominated prior to the Puritan revolution in the 1640s. For example, the Star Chamber – a secular court, made up of the King's Privy Council – regularly enacted and handed out arbitrary punishments which included the "loss of ears or nose or tongue."[53] This sort of cruelty is totally unbiblical in its replacement of restitution with mutilation. Steadily, as the law was reformed in a biblical direction, the number of crimes punishable by death decreased. Cromwell and many of the Puritans wanted the law of God to reform all law to that of Scripture, and during the period of the English Revolution the number of capital offences did drop to around thirty (still far more than the Bible allows). Within 150 years, however, that number had risen to over 200. We see in this period that the Puritan theological vision for history was the realization of justice and mercy, which encouraged the maximum severity of criminal sanctions as a matter of law, in the formal meaning of the word 'law,' that is, as a matter of stated legal rules, coupled, however, with a high degree of humaneness and conscientiousness in the application of those rules to concrete cases."[54]

The Christian vision for history and politics thus involves the manifestation of the kingdom of God by the implementation of God's law in the sociopolitical and cultural spheres. This is what our Protestant forebears believed, and we have lived off of the momentum of their hard-won victories for several centuries. God's Kingdom is manifest in history as his mercy, kindness and justice is made manifest, bringing freedom and liberty from tyranny and the arbitrary power of man – the rule of law and our equality under the law of God is one of the greatest privileges of Western history, and we surrender it at our peril. Our abandonment of the living God and his law for the god of pluralism, has given us a new law-order that is having revolutionary consequences today, seen in the increasing lawlessness, tyranny, and depravity of Western culture. As James Jordan has incisively noted, "the modern concept of pluralism' is to the political order what polytheism is to the religious order. Surely 'pluralism' is the devil's own lie, that society can be neutral, neither for nor against God. In reality, no zone of life is neutral, and 'pluralism' is heresy."[55] Do we want to be for or against God? Is British, Canadian and American history to record the complete abandonment of the God and Father of the Lord Jesus Christ for other gods, and our resulting covenantal judgement and disappearance as a Christian culture; or by faithfulness are we to turn around our precipitous fall from grace? We must return to God's law for our history if we want to see freedom, justice and mercy preserved and God's reign extended throughout our lands.

3.8 Conclusions: God's Victory in History

As we have seen, humanistic and pagan philosophies view history as meaningless frustration – if it cannot be manipulated and controlled, the only hope is death and escape. As the Calvinistic, Puritan vision of history and providence sketched in this chapter has faded, two corresponding emphases (control or escape) have emerged in the church. The more humanistic and antinomian that Christians become in their attitude toward time and history, the more frustrated and hopeless they will feel about life and its prospects. As a result some Christians have become captive to occultist, pseudo-Christian theologies that promise an ability to manipulate God and one's circumstances by the 'force of faith,' positive thinking or confession, visualization, and various actualizing techniques. Others have developed elaborate theologies of retreat and escape from the world, in which every newsworthy event is another omen of approaching apocalypse and our timely escape from history before it falls into ruin.

This frustration experienced outside of surrender to God and his covenant word is articulated well in the book of Ecclesiastes with regard to life "under the Sun," lived without submission to God. A life of meaningless or hopeless activity is the most destructive lie that can be sold to anyone. Such thinking must always result in either an attempt to force an illusory meaning and purpose onto history (human will) or despairing, suicidal inclinations. In keeping with this in Canada today, a staggering new phenomenon has emerged. Amongst young adults aged 15–24 and 25–34, suicide has become the leading cause of death outside of accidents.[56] An educational indoctrination in state schools positing life and history as meaningless, or for all intents and purposes godless, no doubt contributes significantly to this social disaster. The elite social planners of the modern state thus rush to come up with new techniques to fix a problem they don't even understand. If modern science is to be the instrument by which we force a man-made meaning on reality, social history becomes an experimental laboratory for 'making up' purpose, and consequently history becomes a 'social science' with anti-Christian foundations.

In biblical faith, however, history is the canvas of God's activity, purpose and plan (Acts 17:24–31). The centrepiece of that plan is Christ, supremely manifest by his incarnation (Heb. 1:1–3a). He is the centre of both Old and New Covenant revelation. Christ is the source and centre of redemption for the whole of the created order (Col. 1:15–20). We do not see, as the pagans do, endless recurring cycles, with gods and goddesses symbolising the processes of nature – natural necessity in an endless chain. Rather, man is God's creature and is revelatory of God's purpose and plan – we are therefore accountable to God. Consequently we do not seek a futile power over an irrational history and nature by scientific socialism, the engineering of the scientific and political elite; rather we must say, "If God be for us, who can be against us?" (Rom. 8:31). God gives meaning and unity to every event in history. Nothing is meaningless or without purpose. We are in a perpetual co-operation with God in history for the glorious purposes of his kingdom. Such Christians can sing with Martin Luther, "A mighty fortress is our God, a bulwark never failing.... And though this world with devils filled should threaten to undo us, we will not fear for God has willed, His truth to triumph through us." This confidence in God's victory was the basis of the faith of the apostles, Augustine, the Reformers, John Knox, and the Puritans – a confidence we need again for our time. It is tragic that much of the church today thinks in terms of defeat and surrender with a defeated God and a defeated Kingdom – insipid, weak, cowardly, and yet self-righteous. But in Scripture we do not see God or his church surrender history to the devil or to the world – rather history is God's handiwork in which Christ will have the supremacy in all things (Col. 1:18). Eastern perspectives reduce all things ultimately to one (monism) and see the particulars of history as 'Maya,' a veil of illusion. Dualistic religions posit two equal and opposing forces in an endless conflict with each other. Naturalistic perspectives collapse into atomism dominated by the meaningless swerve of atoms. And dialectics tries hopelessly to hold opposing views in tension without reconciling them. Only biblical faith gives us the one and the many in the triune God, where all historical eventuation finds meaning in his sovereign plan, eternal decree, and creative power – the particulars have meaning, as does the whole unity in God's being and purposes.

Ultimately the plan of the triune God assures us of victory, hope and meaning, even through suffering (Rom. 8:31–39). The source of our hope in history was the work of the atonement, a salvation accomplished through Christ's suffering: History without the atonement would be an endless tale of horror, a repetition of Towers of Babel, and a cycle of tyranny and slavery without end. There would then be no way of escape in and from history without death. Even now in many churches, because of faulty views of God's law and of the atonement, the only way of escape is by death or by a "rapture." There is no victory for them in history. It is God's law that declares man to be a sinner, and it is the atonement and

Christ's regenerating power that makes us a new creation in Him. A new power is unleashed in history because "the weakness of God is stronger than men." The atonement frees men from the burden of sin and death and guilt to make them more than conquerors in Christ (Rom. 8:37).

Without the centrality of the atonement, Christianity always recedes into impotence. Only God's way leads to victory.[57] Because of Christ, history is not unrestrained and unending evil, even though it is marred and fallen. God is interested in history and all the details of our lives. Christ's life, death and resurrection were not merely spiritual in their implications, but historical. His victory was eschatological and historical –it was not a rejection of the creation, but the source and promise of its total renewal. And, I believe that at the end of time Christ will have not a world in chaos, rebellion, and utter darkness, but an overwhelmingly redeemed world to present to his Father, where the gospel has filled the earth as the waters cover the sea, a sign and symbol of his pre-eminence in all things (Col. 1:18).[58] For Christ is now reigning, with all power and authority in his hands; as St. Paul writes, "But each in his own order: Christ the firstfruits, then at his coming those who belong to Christ. Then comes the end, when he delivers the kingdom to God the Father after destroying every rule and every authority and power. For he must reign until he has put all his enemies under his feet. The last enemy to be destroyed is death. For God has put all things in subjection under his feet" (1 Cor. 15:23–27, emphasis added). Christ's triumph pictured at the marriage supper of the lamb will forever celebrate the historical reality and victory of Jesus Christ the Lord. What is this victory that overcomes the world? "Even our faith!" (1 John 5:4).

Chapter Four

NO OTHER NAME UNDER HEAVEN:
THE RELIGION OF STATISM AND
THE SIGNIFICANCE OF CHALCEDON

Much popular Christianity is effectively Arian or Eutychian rather than Chalcedonian...that it is really God who is revealed and at work in Jesus is one fundamental of the Christian tradition which Chalcedon sought to preserve, and that Jesus was truly human and therefore able to relate to us and ultimately save us is the other fundamental at issue.
— Frances Young[1]

Puritan political philosophy and theology reflect a belief in an absolute standard, a fundamental law of right and wrong as spelled out in the Bible, a belief in the paramount importance of right conduct, and a high degree of awareness of the existence of evil and human failure. Because of these views, two things were unthinkable: toleration of heresy and absolute authority wielded by anyone less than God himself.
— Allen Carden[2]

4.1 The Significance of the Challenge

With the exception of the error of the anti-Greek and theologically aberrant Nestorians and Monophysite groups, which, as we have seen, persisted for a long time in parts of Syria, Egypt, and Asia, the Chalcedonian council effectively summarized Christian theology for both the Eastern and Western Churches (although controversy continued in the East). The Western church which remained consistently and faithfully Chalcedonian was not weakened by the rise of Islam; it was this expression of the church which built Christendom throughout the Western world, steadily giving rise to the basic principles of liberty we enjoy today. Indeed it has been argued that, "A. D. 451 is one of the most important dates of all history.... Chalcedon...established the Christian foundation of Western Culture and made possible the development of liberty. Chalcedon handed statism its major defeat in man's history."[3] The late church historian Roland Bainton concurs in seeing Chalcedon as critical to the building of Western civilization:

141

The creed of Chalcedon affirmed the full deity and the full humanity of Christ in two natures.... The Church, which in the East did so much to disintegrate the empire, in the West became the builder of Christendom, which however attenuated still survives as Western civilisation.[4]

Bainton points out that when the barbarians invaded the West and the Roman Empire's government collapsed, "the church stepped in to assume many of the functions of government. The great task was to convert the barbarians to orthodox Christianity...the process of their education and civilization also fell largely to the church."[5] Thus orthodox Christianity, recognizing Christ Jesus as God and king, both fully man and fully God, led to the flourishing of a free church that was able to assume godly responsibility in numerous areas of social and civil life. Simply put, Christianity won the argument with paganism in the ancient world, intellectually and socio-culturally.[6] So in what way did the verdict of the Council of Chalcedon help create this vision of freedom, and why is it significant for a biblical vision of God's reign? Firstly, pagan philosophy was essentially statist; substituting God, it saw the state as the incarnation or locus of the divine in history. This had been the view of all the great ancient realms, including the Egyptian, Babylonian, Persian, Greek, and Roman empires, where the rulers were viewed and worshipped as gods – as one example, the Pharaohs of Egypt were considered sons of the sun god. This was also a foundational assumption in all variations of Molech worship seen in the Old Testament where differences between gods and men were those of degree, not kind, and salvation was achieved by self-deification, not by grace.[7] In this view, with people graduating to the status of gods, it was inevitable for non-Christian philosophy to view the state (man enlarged) as the central institution and highest point of history, manifesting "the nascent or incarnate divinity of being either in the body politic, the rulers or in their offices."[8] Thus, in various guises, "this faith was the substructure of all pagan statism. Thus the issue for the church, very literally, was one between Christ and Caesar."[9] These facts came to vivid expression in the first century A. D. when the Roman emperor, Augustus Caesar, declared himself to be the saviour of the world, his government issuing the declaration that "salvation is to be found in none other save Augustus, and there is no other name given to men in which they can be saved."[10] It is noteworthy that Christianity's radical dissent from this was seen by the Roman state, not as a religious, but as a political offense.[11] St. Peter's rebuttal could not be more explicit: "And there is salvation in no one else, for there is no other name under heaven given among men by which we must be saved" (Acts 4:12). This was not only a declaration of Christ as saviour, but also resistance to a particular view of the state as ultimate lord and sovereign. This specific conflict which confronted the early church concerning the claims of the state and its limits is no less real in modern times. In an article reflecting on the alleged failures of the American government to prevent the terrorist attacks of September 11th 2001, Harvard professor and former leader of the Liberal Party in Canada, Michael Ignatieff, ominously articulates the modern concept of sovereignty: "A sovereign is a state with a monopoly on the means of force. It is the object of ultimate allegiance and the source of law." [12] There is no essential difference between this idea and that held by ancient pagan Rome. This is precisely the nature of the theological conflict causing the political persecution of the exploding 'unofficial' church in China today, a government which shares Ignatieff's view of the state. One BBC commentator has grasped the essence of the issue in China well:

> After the Communist victory in 1948...missionaries were expelled, but Christianity was permitted in state-sanctioned churches, so long as they gave their primary allegiance to the Communist Party. Mao, on the other hand, described religion as "poison," and the Cultural Revolution of the 1960s and '70s attempted to eradicate it. Driven underground, Christianity not only survived, but with its own Chinese martyrs, it grew in strength. Since the 1980s, when religious belief was again permitted, the official Churches have gradually created more space for themselves. They report to the State Administration for Religious Affairs. They are forbidden to take part in any religious activity outside their places of worship and sign up to the slogan, "Love the country – love your religion." In return the Party promotes atheism in schools but undertakes, "to protect and respect religion until such time as religion itself will disappear."... What the authorities consider non-negotiable is the house churches' refusal to acknowledge any official authority over their organisation.[13]

Despite this opposition, armed with a principle of freedom under God from the Scriptures, Chinese Christian communities continue to grow and worship Christ as the King of kings and Lord of lords. Christ, not the state, is seen as the ultimate source of allegiance and sovereign source of law. Today there are more Christians worshiping on Sunday mornings in China than all of Europe combined: over 60 million people. So the issue for the church in the first century, as now, was one of lordship and sovereignty. We must answer the same questions: Whose right is it to rule? Is Christ the object of primary allegiance, or is man enlarged (the state) to be assigned a role that supersedes that of God the Son?

4.2   Chalcedon and the Principle of Liberty

The Council of Chalcedon met in A.D 451 to deal with a critical point of Christology that, whilst theological and pastoral in character, would, in time, have a tremendous bearing on the future of the Western world.[14] First, they upheld the orthodox understanding of Christ's full humanity and full deity, but further clarified that this union of the two natures was without confusion, without change, without division, without separation.[15] This did not create two persons but preserved the unity of Christ's 'person' which brought together two natures in the incarnation. Whilst probably not the council's major concern at the time (nor did they likely appreciate the full significance of their work), the indirect result of their formulation was that true Christianity could never be melded with paganism or any form of anti-Christianity, because "the natural does not ascend to the divine or to the supernatural. The bridge is gulfed only by revelation and by the incarnation of Jesus Christ. Salvation therefore is not of man, nor by means of man's politics."[16]

This meant further that Chalcedon effectively barred "human institutions from professing to be incarnations of the deity and able to unite the two worlds in their existence."[17] If the state (or any other institution) could be conceived of as an immanent divine-human order, then there was no possible appeal above or beyond the state – it is the final order and man is simply a political and social animal, as many Greek philosophers held. But if we are defined by the body politic, what happens to liberty? On this view, "liberty was non-existent. Permission from the state to exercise certain areas of activities could exist, but not a liberty apart from and beyond the state grounded in man's creation by God."[18] Law and life would then be defined by government statute. The broad governance of society would thus be reduced to an aspect of state social policy. That is to say, with no God and no divine law, there is no appeal beyond the state – the state, not God, is now sovereign.[19]

For the Chalcedon Council, Jesus Christ was not a divinized man (that is, an ordinary man who is lent or ascends to divinity), nor are people and institutions divinized through Christ (that is, made gods or part of God). Rather, by revelation and incarnation, the man Jesus Christ is made our sanctification and redemption, and we participate in his perfect humanity – not in his divine essence – as the second Adam.[20] The state, as might be expected, resented the implications of Chalcedon and modified its divinity claims with a more 'Christian' terminology. But Chalcedonian theology was steadily closing the door, not only on the political 'salvation' of *pagan* statism which saw man as assuming divinity, but also, as Gerhart B. Ladner has argued, on the *iconoclasm* of the Eastern Empire, premised as it was on its claim to being the true incarnation of the divine and the visible Kingdom of God on earth.[21] Indeed, Chalcedon ultimately meant that God's reign is not mediated by people and their institutions, but by Jesus Christ alone, and all authority and power must serve him as his diaconate (Rom. 13:1ff), submitting to the law-word of God. Thus, the implications of Chalcedonian Christology militate against both ancient and modern statism, providing instead a principle of freedom. Jesus Christ declared that in him is true freedom: "if the Son sets you free, you will be free indeed" (John 8:36). We are no longer slaves to sin and the sinful structures that men use to dominate others – we can make our appeal directly to God, for only when individuals and communities recognize a transcendent authority beyond them is true freedom possible. In the modern era, the re-emergence of statism with the French Revolution (Rousseau's social contract) and the Hegelian politics of power, asserting that "the state is the Divine Idea as it exists on earth,"[22] is expressed in its efforts not merely to ignore, but progressively deny the right of the church to any independent existence.[23] As Hegel himself admits, the state "is that actuality in which the individual has and enjoys his freedom, *but only as knowing, believing, and willing the universal*."[24] The key problem that we face as Christians today with modern concepts of freedom is that they are political and not theological. However, when liberty is defined politically and not theologically, freedom is destroyed because non-Christian thought is dialectical – always trying to unite the opposing ideas of nature and freedom – and does not have the resources to keep a social order from collapsing into tyranny or anarchy.

Essentially the question for dialectical culture is how to have both unity and diversity without collapsing into either a tyrannical order in which the state regulates and controls an ever-increasing field of life (education, medicine, markets, property, etc.) or the unrelated particulars of an anarchistic social chaos. To avoid atomism (total anarchic individualism) in the natural order of things, the vision of the so-called 'Enlightenment' was to posit the state as a social contract between autonomous men.[25] At the same time, to avoid the collapse of the realm of values in the spiritual order, the mind was credited with an original creative power. Then, in order to prevent the breakdown of the social order under the pressure of autonomous thought and man's 'creativity,' the state was emphasized more and more in an effort to retain unity in a world where God and his law were vanishing into irrelevance. Thus, to understand what is logically entailed in the Chalcedon formula (whether or not the Chalcedonian Fathers self-consciously appreciated all its implications) is to understand the significance of an applied Chalcedonian missiology. The socio-political application of Chalcedon produces the mindset of a biblical libertarian, because we must see the reign of God, his sovereignty, salvation, and law as the source of human liberty; every other alternative is tyranny and slavery, since "instead of gaining utopia by abolishing God and his law, people gain instead a lawlessness in which they are victims."[26] The Christian's life and self-realization is not comprehended by the state, but by the triune God and him alone. Liberty can only re-emerge as the state's everexpanding claims are resisted by a Christian renaissance of biblical faithfulness, with the state progressively reduced to its scriptural role as a ministry of justice. Thus Rushdoony accurately saw history bore out that:

> On the foundation of Chalcedon, the formulation of biblical Christology, Western liberty has been built. Ignorance and neglect of Chalcedon has been basic to the decline of the church.... The alternative is Christ or Caesar, liberty or slavery, God or man. Is salvation man's upward reach or God's downward reach? Is it man's word or God's grace? Is God or the state man's savior? The answer of Chalcedon is emphatically for God and liberty. Western liberty began when the claim of the state to be man's savior was denied. The state then, according to scripture, was made the ministry of justice. But wherever Christ ceases to be man's savior, there liberty perishes as the state again asserts its messianic claims.[27]

There can be little doubt that we see this correlation in Western culture today, where more and more regulations, controls, agencies and laws seek to 'save man' by making him a slave, stripping the family, the church, and private organizations and enterprises of freedom and liberty. We see clearly in Rushdoony's penetrating analysis why the theological, social and political implications of Chalcedon are so central to a truly reformed missiological thought. William Edgar rightly noted that "central to just about every one of Rushdoony's writings is the notion that freedom must be preserved at the local level, so that God's law can be faithfully obeyed by all people, without interference from higher temporal powers."[28] If the church fails to keep this central in her thinking today, the heavy price will inevitably be a period of suffering under a viciously anti-Christian tyranny. If the 'reign of God' is the essence of a biblical missiology, then the kingdom of God (the blueprint of his reign) is the plan and goal for history. A king or sovereign has, by definition, a realm, a scepter and a law. In Christ, this is cosmic in scope. The establishment of that universal kingdom is the *missio Dei* and it can only be accomplished when "he has put all his enemies under his feet" (1 Cor. 15:25). The primary opposition and satanic strategy against God's reign is, and always has been, man's self-deification, reflected in the initial temptation of Satan in Genesis 3:5, "to be as God." This finds its most fertile expression when humanity puts forward a collective effort to establish a humanistic order in rebellion against God that seeks to join heaven and earth (by usurping the prerogatives of God) and re-create paradise in terms of man's word and social planning. This was the dream of Babel in Genesis 11 and has been repeated in history down to the present. Today, a global, elitist oligarchy, in league with the modern socialistic and interventionist state, is dreaming and planning further development of their world bank, world currency, tax structures and what modern politicians are calling 'a new world order.' Thus, any missiological vision which does not have in view the undermining of the pretensions of statism is deficient at best and working within a humanistic and statist paradigm at worst. Therefore to pursue God's kingdom and reign, the Lordship of Christ over all things must be asserted (Eph. 1:16–23). This centres upon the Chalcedonian affirmation that Christ alone is the God-man, representing God to man, and mediating salvation, as both God and man, in unconfused union – our prophet, priest and king. No other union of the human and divine is possible – no agency, institution or state can claim for itself the prerogatives of God. For the believer, no other ultimate sovereign is acceptable and no other law admissible to command our obedience. Where man's law commands what God forbids, civil disobedience becomes a Christian duty. Christ alone, in his word and by his Spirit, speaks the word of life and salvation, not the state.

4.3 Statism and Contemporary Missiology

In this calling to a persistent resistance to statism, the Puritan mind finds itself in intractable conflict with almost all mainstream missiology – a field which largely favours either a passive resignation to the powers of the state (whatever their morality) or the full use of the coercive state to enforce a particular vision of 'social justice.' In each case there is an implicit acquiescence to statism.[29] For example, Johannes Verkuyl suggests that "the church reflects her Lord more accurately when she is oppressed than when she dominates,"[30] which seems to mean when she avoids any hint of 'Christianization' of the social and political sphere. Although it is abundantly clear that Christ is the servant king who suffered at the cross at the hands of sinful men, we should also notice he is no longer on the cross according to Scripture, but is raised in glory far above all power and dominion in this age, with all authority in heaven and in earth in his hands (Heb. 1:1–13, Eph. 1:20–23; Matt. 28:17–20). Christians do and will suffer for his sake, but our sufferings, whilst meaningful and significant, are neither propitiatory, nor of themselves redemptive – they are a byproduct of being identified with Christ, sent out as sheep in the midst of wolves (Matt. 10:16). Suffering, persecution and marginalization are not things to be sought as intrinsically virtuous or vicarious. Rather, in the midst of persecution we are promised victory (1 John 5:4). This is because the cross of Christ meant not defeat, but victory, life, and liberty for all who surrender to Christ as Lord. Thus, for the Puritans, since Christ is both life and liberty we are to pursue a life of freedom under God. This life begins with self-discipline, not an anarchistic rejection of God's law, or an appeal to state coercion:

> [T]he beginning of liberty is the discipline of Christ. His Word, Scripture, is the means to freedom in every area of life, and that liberty is under law, and is not, as in the modern view, liberty from law. The freedom from law bestowed by Christ is not antinomian; it is freedom from damnation by the law into power to live by a new nature in the law as liberty. The Christian view requires discipline

and discipleship; the second requires freedom from discipline and restraints. The Puritans recognised that true discipline is self-discipline, and is therefore an inner rather than an outer compulsion. The outer compulsion should do no more than establish conditions for the development of inner compulsion.[31]

At the same time, although the Puritan mind prioritized liberty, freedom and self-discipline, being opposed to statism (the swallowing of all other institutions and spheres of life as aspects of central state government), because of the godless erosion of liberty it represented, they were not opposed to civil government or keen Christian engagement with politics. On the contrary, they regarded the government of men as one of the highest vocations.[32] However, what terrified the Puritans (as indeed it should terrify us) was the idea of consolidating all authority and power in the hands of any man or institution. Since man is a sinner and only Jesus Christ the true Lord and saviour of man, "the Puritans did not share the confidence of our century that social cohesion depends on governmental structures."[33] Rather than civil government interfering with, dominating and regulating every aspect of people's lives, as though subjects are slave-wards of state (today often called the nanny state), "magistrates, as well as ministers, were called to be servants of the people."[34] This did not diminish the important role of the civil government in God's economy, because church, family and state were seen as partners in creating a Christian commonwealth. Contrary to myth, the Puritans did not believe in an ecclesiocracy, with all aspects of civil society dominated by the church and clergy. Rather, church and state were to be distinct spheres under God, with the church enjoying freedom from state interference and *vice versa*.[35] Not only were church and state not to be antagonistic, they were to mutually support and reinforce each other. In New England in 1646, Puritan ministers summarised their view of an ideal relationship between the church and civil government: "the Churches desire, the Magistrate Commands; Churches act in way of liberty, the Magistrate in way of Authority. Moses and Aaron should go together, and kiss one another in the Mount of God."[36] There was to be a complementary and not a competitive relationship between the two, where the church ministers the Word and the civil authority bears the sword, both submitting themselves to the authority of God and his Word.

Thus, the state was to be God's servant and any political order that refused to be such was a tyranny that must be resisted wherever it contravened God's law. This Puritan view continued amongst *many* Christians well into the nineteenth century in the United States. The noted nineteenth-century minster and Professor of Theology in the Allegheny Seminary, James M. Willson, in his detailed exposition of Romans 13:1–7 entitled, "The Establishment and Limits of Civil Government," sets out this view of civil government:

> Paul here styles them the "ministers of God" – God's servants. The servant should know his master even among men. And still more he who professes to wield an authority derived from God, in administering an "ordinance of God," acknowledge, reverence and give due homage to his sovereign. This acknowledgement should be practical. It does not consist in a mere profession of belief in His being, or even in His providence. It implies the study of His will, and a constant aim and effort to please Him. The ruler, or the nation, that claims to be above all other authority, demanding an unquestioning obedience to mere human law – that denies the existence of a "higher law," is in rebellion against God – is not a "servant," in Paul's sense. And more than this, the acknowledgment must be direct, and in express terms – it must be an acknowledgement...of the supremacy of the Most High; of His laws, as the Scriptures teach them. Further still, this acknowledgment must be rendered, not to the God of the deist – but to the only true God – the Christian's God – to God in Christ. Does the refusal to acknowledge God invalidate the authority of a government as tyranny does? Why not? Surely, if God has ordained this institution for His glory – if He has put it under His law – if He has designed to exhibit in it something of His majesty, it is difficult to see how a government that denies their maker and Lord of all – or withholds from Him, from His law, and from His son, even an acknowledgment, can claim His sanction upon its acts?[37]

This powerful statement of biblical faith stands in stark contrast to the vague assertions and theological cowardice of much contemporary missiology and political theology. For example, in expounding the same passage of Romans 13 in relation to the role of the state, John Howard Yoder exemplifies the approach of passive acquiescence to church-state relations, arguing that "the whole point of the passage was to take out of their minds [Jewish Christians in Rome] any conception of rebellion against or even emotional rejection of this corrupt pagan government."[38] Indeed, he argues for a radical "subordination to whatever powers there be,"[39] whilst somewhat inconsistently agreeing that this must not constitute obedience to requirements of violence or killing. In rejecting the Calvinistic and Puritan view that Scripture sets out a godly social order for which we should strive and labour even in the face of opposition, Yoder argues that Scripture calls for a "non-resistant attitude toward tyrannical government."[40] So how does one determine what is due to the tyranny of Caesar? In rather abstract and vague language Yoder says this is judged by "whether what he claims is due to him is part of the obligation to love. Love in turn is defined by the fact that it does no harm."[41] Yoder's pseudo-utilitarianism is summed up with the incredible conclusion that Scripture instructs Christians to be "nonresistant in all their relationships, including the social."[42] In fact, according to Yoder, Scripture calls Christians to "be subject to the historical process in which the sword continues to be wielded and to bring about a kind of order under fire."[43] This romantic and pacifistic ideal that sees every state as a kind of permissive providence of God in a somewhat impersonal historical process, in which the state is not to be resisted even emotionally, whilst measuring good (loving) and evil (unloving) in terms of what 'does no harm,' should be viewed by every evangelical as pure humanism (with late Anabaptist roots). By contrast, in Scripture all of history, its empires, kings, governments and their fortunes, are the product of God's active justice to bless or curse, judge or elevate peoples and nations in terms of righteousness as defined by his law (Amos 1–2; Ps. 2, Isa. 26:1–9; Prov. 14:34; Rom. 1:18–32; Acts 17:26–31). God's law in Scripture is the very definition of what it is to be loving toward a neighbour, thus anything that militates against the law of God must be deontologically unloving and harmful and therefore opposed and resisted – for love is the fulfilment of the law – something Yoder should have known (Rom. 13:8–10; Matt. 22:39–40, 7:12). Logically, Yoder's position leaves the Christian without a principle of true liberty in history, without a temporal appeal above and beyond the state, or the clear mandate to resist tyranny and injustice by word and deed. Such a view is both unloving and essentially lawless.

At the other end of the spectrum, British missiologist Andrew Kirk does not settle for the historical process of Yoder to take its course through a delinquent state. Instead, for Kirk, the *missio Dei* demands that we make use of the godless and coercive state to redistribute wealth and enforce socialism. Kirk's neo-Marxist perspective is essentially communistic, requiring greatly expanded powers for the state in areas ranging from setting minimum and maximum salary levels, to coercive redistribution of people's holdings as well as steeply progressive taxation and other restraints on human liberty.[44] Never mind the eighth commandment (thou shalt not steal), Marxism (in fact communism) is apparently more compassionate than any other system of government Kirk can think of, and "contains a strong element of hope.... Marxism's crowning assertion is that communist society is the only place where man can find his own real humanity by discovering that of his neighbour."[45] This salvation by government coercion is basic to statism. Such statements lend a good deal of credence to Meic Pearse's critique of the popular assumption that the world's social and political problems are essentially economic conflicts in fancy dress, based on a model of economic determinism that stems from what he rightly calls "a discredited quasi Marxism to which our academic and chattering classes remain addicted more than a decade after the end of communism and fully fifty years after they should have learned to know better."[46] The Puritan missiologist, however, is neither a retreatist pacifist nor a neo-Marxist, but believes in the necessity of civil government, qualified by the biblical conviction that the state only has abiding legitimacy where it surrenders to its limited God-ordained role as minister (diaconate) of justice in terms of God's authority (Rom. 13:4):

> The office of priest was clearly separated from that of the monarch, and the prophet was the spokesman for God in applying the standard of God's law to a sinful social order.... In terms of Biblical law, the state is a very limited institution, hardly a state in the modern sense. Its taxing power is limited to a head or poll tax which is the same for all males 20 years of age and older. No other tax is legitimate. Basic to military defence is a citizen's army, with only a limited professional soldier possible in so limited a state. It is not surprising therefore that while in Byzantium the Greek tradition survived enough to create a strong state, in the West the state collapsed, not only militarily but also intellectually...in a very real sense, civil government and economics became household management. The re-growth of urban life was largely made possible by Jewish merchants applying biblical law to the management of trading centres, which developed into cities. Europe gave promise of developing the integrity and freedom of the various spheres.... Calvinism in particular began the development of

concepts which led to a stress on the freedom of each sphere under God. Church, state, schools, economics, the sciences, the family... each with an obligation to serve God, and each without authority to rule over the other spheres.[47]

As soon as the state steps outside this sphere it plays God and offers every form of counterfeiting of the Word of God. In such a case it will invariably persecute the family and church, destroying localism and people's freedom to obey God's law. Such a state will be judged by God and once a state commands what God forbids, if Christ is truly Lord, then the Christian has the religious *duty* to resist.[48] The necessity of localism is a theme strongly emphasized by the Puritans who sought to guard against overly centralized politics for the very purpose of preserving freedom.[49] Mark Noll observes one key reason for the decay of Puritanism in New England – an emerging vision of big government:

> Cracks began to appear in the Puritan Way during the early years of the eighteenth century not primarily because of flagging spirituality but because the outside world – in the shape of Indian wars, military taxes, and centralized political authority – finally disrupted the stability of local life.... New England Puritanism succeeded as a social system only so long as it preserved its localism.[50]

By moving outside its God-ordained sphere, the state thus progressively destroys localism and with it, liberty, as it asserts a messianic (saving) role for itself in the centralized politics of power that exists to serve itself. This is done by attaching to itself the prerogatives of God. It is fascinating to observe in this regard that the theological categories of God's word are inescapable to all people, and if denied to God are typically transferred to the individual (anarchism) or the state (totalitarianism). When examined through theological lenses, statism involves a pretending to deity by offering everything from usurped sovereignty and law (in terms of human autonomy and positivistic law-making), to providence (cradle-to-grave security through state welfarism), predestination (by social science and planning), incarnation (by the implementing of man's 'word' and idea), atonement (via political reparations, payments, and the politics of guilt), salvation (through a growing world order) and judgement (by threatened environmental and social catastrophe for disobedience) and thus a counterfeit kingdom – the dream of Babel.[51]

In sum, the choice before the early church is again the choice before the modern church: Christ or Caesar? And whilst the modern state has dropped most of its theological language concerning its role, its purported function, goals and purpose are no different from those of the Roman Imperial order. Thus, as early Christians discovered, in order for freedom to flourish and the kingdom of God to grow, the pretentions of statism must be resisted and eventually, the state must be reduced to biblical limits, not by political revolution, but by the power of the Holy Spirit manifest in the preaching of God's word, the new birth, faith, and repentance, leading to personal and familial obedience to God's revealed law in each area of life.[52] In God's order, social liberty and Christ's dominion are one and the same. Here we can agree with Verkuyl's assessment, "What is the ultimate goal of the *missio Dei*? The answer is easy to find; in both the Old Testament and the New, God by both his words and deeds claims that he is intent on bringing the kingdom of God to expression and restoring his liberating domain of authority."[53] Since the kingdom rule of God is being extended in history, and since the state, as James Willson showed us, is appointed as his minister of justice (Rom. 13:4) and is therefore a part of the expression of Christ's reign and government when submitted to Christ, we can be both more biblical and, consequently, far more optimistic about the future of Christianity in history than Yoder and the Anabaptist or non-reformed traditions. The state is not God, for Christ Jesus alone is Lord, linking the human and divine in himself as the source of all sovereignty, power and law. As Christians therefore, we must neither retreat from the task of bringing all things (including the state) into subjection to Christ by regeneration and discipleship, nor delude ourselves into thinking with the 'Christian' Marxists that the state can itself bring about or incarnate the kingdom and justice of God (however that is imagined). For all the real failures of the church in history, for all its errors and sins of both retreatism and the periodic impulse toward ecclesiocracy, where would history be without her? She is, after all, the covenant bride of Christ and the beloved apple of his eye, called out as salt and light in the world. Her task remains, as we emerge from all the lessons of twenty centuries, to apply Jesus' word to each area of life and assert the crown rights of Christ till the state itself is converted and submits faithfully to his Lordship.

It might well be asked, in this historic task, how much are we to expect in this medial time between Christ's first advent and his return? What hope do we have in history for this middle period? Peter J. Leithart's conclusion on this matter is telling:

> Yoder thinks...that the project of Christianizing the state is doomed. The time when that could happen has long ago passed away. If he is right, we are facing nothing short of apocalypse. I believe that here too Yoder is wrong, and that we can escape apocalypse. But this can only happen on certain conditions: only through re-evangelization, only through the revival of a purified Constantinianism, only by the formation of Christically centred politics, only through fresh public confession that Jesus' city is the model city, his blood the only expiating blood, his sacrifice the sacrifice that ends sacrifice. An apocalypse can be averted only if modern civilization, like Rome, humbles itself and is willing to come forward to be baptized.[54]

If we honour and serve Christ, if we cherish our freedom, if we love liberty now and for our children, then we must call all men and nations by the gospel, to humble themselves before the King of kings and Lord of lords. We must command them to repent and call them forward to the waters of baptism. In so doing we stand with the glorious promise of Scripture that assures us, "the kingdom of the world has become the kingdom of our Lord and of his Christ, and he shall reign forever and ever" (Rev. 11:15). In the mission of God we have a privileged part to play in Christ's victory over all satanic power and authority, because "the kingdom and the dominion and the greatness of the kingdoms under the whole heaven shall be given to the people of the saints of the Most High; their kingdom shall be an everlasting kingdom, and all dominions shall serve and obey them" (Dan. 7:27)

Chapter Five

I SAW SATAN FALL: UTOPIA,
THE COUNTERFEIT KINGDOM OF GOD

The Puritans did not share the confidence of our century that social cohesion depends on governmental structure.

– Leland Ryken

5.1 Kingdom and Utopia

There are few more odious men that emerge from the pages of European history than the first truly 'modern' intellectual, the professional hypocrite, Jean Jacques Rousseau, famed author of *The Social Contract*. David Hume, who knew him well, by bitter experience called him, "a monster who saw himself as the only important being in the universe." Voltaire thought him, "a monster of vanity and vileness." Diderot, after knowing him for many years described him as, "deceitful, vain as Satan, ungrateful, cruel, hypocritical, and full of malice." He is perhaps most tellingly summed up in the words of the woman who he claimed was his only love, Sophie d' Houdetot. In old age she said, "He was ugly enough to frighten me and love did not make him more attractive. But he was a pathetic figure and I treated him with gentleness and kindness. He was an interesting madman."[1] Following Plato, Rousseau was a utopian dreamer, yet without doubt was a debauched narcissist, who whilst presuming to lecture others on education, family and state, abandoned all five of his own children in infancy to a hospice where they almost certainly died. Yet in many ways, despite his infantile and vile character, his masochism and exhibitionism, his thought paved the way for the French Revolution and influenced the Russian revolution, as well as playing a real role in inspiring both communist and fascist regimes in the twentieth century. He was an intellectual forerunner of Karl Marx and saw in the state the key to Utopia. Paul Johnson has written:

> Rousseau's state is not merely authoritarian: it is also totalitarian, since it orders every aspect of human activity, thought included. Under the social contract, the individual was obliged to "alienate himself, with all his rights, to the whole community" (i.e. the state)… The function of the social contract, and the state it brought into being,

was to make man whole again: "Make man one, and you will make him as happy as he can be".... You must, therefore, treat citizens as children and control their upbringing and thoughts, planting, "the social law in the bottom of their hearts." They then become "social men by their natures and citizens by their inclinations; they will be one, they will be good, they will be happy, and their happiness will be that of the republic".... He did not use the word 'brainwash,' but he wrote: "Those who control a people's opinions control its actions." Such control is established by treating citizens, from infancy, as children of the state, trained to "consider themselves only in their relationship to the body of the state"...he moved the political process to the very centre of human existence, by making the legislator, who is also a pedagogue, into the new Messiah, capable of solving all human problems by creating New Men.[2]

When considering this, one immediately recognizes how 'modern' Rousseau is and how his utopian thought has so decisively shaped our political and social order. Today's cultural Marxists who are busy with their ideological subversion and demoralization of the West in the name of social justice, have Rousseau to thank for their core ideas. It is then of tremendous concern when anti-Christian utopianism is imported into mission theology in the name of the reign or kingdom of God – here a socio-political religion replaces Christianity. We have already seen in previous chapters that social justice is not biblical justice, nor can the utopian state acting as a new messiah substitute itself for the kingdom of God. When considering the *missio Dei* and reign of Christ, it is then imperative that Christians understand the difference between utopia and the kingdom of God, lest they be found advancing the cause of other gods and another faith.

5.2 The Utopian Imperative

The term *Utopia* originates with Thomas More's ideal society and it means "no place." More, a devout Catholic revered by churchmen and sainted in 1935, was far from biblical in his thinking. His famous treatise is a plea for the abolition of private property and the establishment of communism. More's work is anti-Christian and subversive to the church because 'nature' is the measure of reality and virtue, and ultimately demands control by the state, which becomes man's re-creator, provider and preserver. As for all utopians, unity was More's supreme virtue.

Peace comes through the state – the humanly-wrought oneness into which man is absorbed. More saw himself as an elite ruler in a new order in which men would be manipulated to remove all social divisions. It is not surprising that Lenin found inspiration in More's ideas.[3]

True Christian orthodoxy *cannot* produce such utopian illusions. The creator, redeemer God, in his complete word, has declared the future of his Kingdom and rule, established by his will and power. Since God governs history, the Christian, in faith, obedience and confidence moves toward God's predestined future (Eph. 1:3–14; Prov. 16:4). The triune, sovereign Lord, who by his providence and power sustains all things (Heb. 1:1–3), is the one in whom the Christian trusts. Bereft of such security, the non-believer must posit an entirely different worldview. Utopianism, which denies God's predestinating purpose, is more than a political idea; it is a philosophy of life, a religious theology. Man takes the place of the mythical, non-existent God of the Bible. Instead of seeing man's environment as a good (though fallen) creation under the providence of God, utopianism perceives man to be in a chaotic universe that perpetually threatens to crush him. The noted British utopian dreamer, Julian Huxley, encapsulates the modern humanistic temper:

> So far as we can see [the universe] rules itself...even if a god does exist behind or above the universe as we experience it, we can have no knowledge of such a power: the actual gods of historical religions are only the personifications of impersonal facts of nature and of facts of our inner mental life.[4]

In this view, 'nature' is as capricious as the pagan gods of Greco-Roman mythology or as man's own inner life of evil thoughts. As Thomas Molnar puts it, "our vision of the universe inevitably influences our vision of society and, hence, our organization of society. If the universe is hostile to us, we conceive of society, our little universe, as also hostile."[5] Having jettisoned the God of the Bible, utopians are confronted by a threatening world of flux. They see no God to give purpose, direction, or rationality to life. This world of chaos in which man's 'freedom' runs wild jeopardizes its own existence by its unpredictability. Man lives in terror, a victim of fate and full of self-pity. Man in a world without God has an insatiable desire for control, rooted in the hope that man can be liberated from unpredictability into the true freedom of necessity! As J. B. S. Haldane, a Marxist Utopian, put it, "There is no supernatural and

159

nothing metaphysical…freedom is the recognition of necessity. This is a paradox, but a truth."[6] But when man frees himself from the sovereignty of God, he discovers a serious problem: absolute autonomy (self-law) leads logically to total anarchy of thought and to social chaos. To avoid this disaster, the individual is inevitably plunged into a *collectivity* that will *assume the role* of God in creating, predestinating, saving, guiding and providing for the newly liberated man. The new man-god is the collective agency for organizing man's liberty and salvation. This collective divinity is a Nebuchadnezzar-sized idol that steadily *lays claim to all the attributes of the God it has replaced.* The utopian devotee may not seem religious, since he rarely mentions God, judgement, salvation, heaven or hell. But he constantly formulates new doctrine, ceremonies and sacrifices. Huxley, the key writer of UNESCO's founding framework document, is explicit:

> If we translate salvation into terms of this world, we find that it means achieving *harmony* between different parts of our nature, including its subconscious depths and its rarely touched heights, and also achieving some satisfactory relation of adjustment between ourselves and the outer world, including not only the world of nature, but the social world of man. I believe it to be possible to "achieve salvation" in this sense, and right to aim at doing so, just as I believe it possible and valuable to achieve a sense of union with something bigger than our ordinary selves, even if that something be not a god but an extension of our narrow core to include in a single grasp ranges of outer experience and inner nature on which we do not ordinarily draw.[7]

Huxley blends secular terminology with the language of pagan spirituality. The union with something bigger than the self is the whole, the one, the ideal of man divinized in and by his unification with himself (nature). Huxley goes on to argue that purpose lies in 'science,' namely the endless possibilities of the evolution of man by socialization, organization and technology, through which man gains *power over nature* (himself) to deliver and save him from suffering and pain, (intolerable to all utopians, including those found in Eastern and pagan spirituality). The possible implications of such a utopian vision were foreseen by George Orwell in his dystopian novel *1984*, where he envisages the problem confronting all Utopian dreams – fallen man's exercise of power is demonic – only power for the sake of power is expressed when man usurps the prerogatives of God. Orwell has O'Brien declare in a noted passage:

Power is in inflicting pain and humiliation. Power is in tearing human minds to pieces and putting them together again in new shapes of your own choosing. Do you begin to see, then, what Kind of world we are creating? It is the exact opposite of the stupid hedonistic Utopias that the old reformers imagined. A world of fear and treachery and torment, a world of trampling and being trampled upon, a world which will grow not less, but more merciless as it refines itself. Progress in our world will be progress toward more pain…already we are breaking down the habits of thought which have survived from before the revolution. We have cut the links between child and parent, and between man and man, and between man and woman. No one dares trust a wife or a child, or a friend any longer. But in the future there will be no wives and no friends. Children will be taken from their mothers at birth, as one takes eggs from a hen. The sex instinct will be eradicated. Procreation will be an annual formality like the renewal of a ration card…there will be no loyalty except loyalty toward the party. There will be no love except the love of Big Brother…there will be no art, no literature, no science. When we are omnipotent we shall have no more need of science. There will be no distinction between beauty and ugliness. There will be no curiosity, no employment of the process of life. All competing pleasures will be destroyed. But always – do not forget this Winston – always there will be the intoxication of power, constantly increasing and constantly growing subtler. Always at every moment, there will be the thrill of victory, the sensation of trampling on the enemy who is helpless. If you want a picture of the future, imagine a boot stamping on a human face – forever.[8]

Here we have a powerful image of man's sin coming to self-conscious realization where man, as the new divinity, gains the sensation of pseudo-omnipotence in the collectivist order. Playing at God, total terror and total destruction are the reality as the new man-god brings his perverse wrath to bear on the world. This is his route to godhood – the exercise of naked power. He starts with the rejection of God (anarchistic vision) and then proceeds to a re-making of man as nature (god) incarnate through the Parliament of man, the federation of the world, as Tennyson referred to it. The solution to man's disunity, his alienation from himself, is therefore seen in a collectivist order, and ultimately a world-state.

This concept reflects more than mere idealism or a sub-stratum of Western thought. It is a logical necessity born of a lasting, deep religious hunger in those who have rejected the God of Scripture. Man needs order, certainty and salvation, and where God's governance is denied, man will attempt to mimic it. Wherever man has sought an immanent (not transcendent) source of power, a *theology of state* has developed and a new doctrine of God has been fleshed out. Although explicitly theological language is often jettisoned, the new doctrine is expressed in the terminology of the social or scientific revolutionary or in that of the new occultist spirituality. All that impedes the revolution is the propaganda of priests, the family and the church. Consequently orthodox Christianity is seen as the ultimate enemy of utopia. As J. L. Talmon expressed it, "The messianic trends [of the nineteenth century] considered Christianity as arch enemy...their own message of salvation was utterly incompatible with the true Christian doctrine, that of original sin, with its vision of history as the story of the fall, and its denial of man's power to attain salvation by his own exertions."[9] So, man has replaced God and his word, and needs a new doctrine of God and a new word. In this re-imagining process, he transfers the key attributes of God to man and his agencies. Because man is a sinner, these utopian schemes must always be dystopian in their outcomes. Let us examine why.

5.3   A New Doctrine of God: The Unity of the Utopian Godhead

5.3.1   Justice

Utopian literature was one of the key markers of the beginning of the modern age, though Plato's *Republic* is basic to all such modern Utopias. From More to Bacon, Campanella and Harrington, man dreamt of restoring paradise to the earth. The essential ingredient in making this a reality is that the state (personified by elite philosopher-kings) must be allowed to 'organize' society through technology (power) and scientific socialism, in terms of man's new conception of *justice*, which now means liberation from God. Justice is no longer located in God and his law, but in radical egalitarian levelling as the route to reunification. Where differences exist to any degree, this unity cannot be achieved.

But why is inequality, moral differentiation, diversity and variety such a horror to man's utopian aspirations? First, we must notice that the doctrine of God is inescapable. If man pretends God is dead, his need for the doctrine of God does not disappear, it is transferred from the transcendent to the immanent realm. Now central to the doctrine of God is the *unity* of the godhead. God cannot be divided against himself! In the Christian faith we have one God in three persons in perfect relational unity, fully representative of each other, and equally ultimate. Satanically inspired thought always counterfeits these doctrines because they are inescapable categories. So both the doctrine of God and the kingdom of God are counterfeited in utopianism. Second, the idea of *alienation* is critical to the utopian worldview because it suggests man is alienated from his true being. This idea is not new. It is as old as ancient Greek philosophy. In Plato we are offered the form/matter scheme. Form or idea produces the copies in the tangible world which are increasingly imperfect in proportion to their distance from the original.

Man is therefore alienated from the *idea* of man and as such cannot find unity with or within himself. Hegel's philosophy is critically important here in understanding the development of this concept in the West: Hegel's system regards man as condemned to externalize himself, to cease being pure consciousness. Every interpersonal relationship, every relationship with the state, every economic relationship and every relationship with God and religion is reification (objectivization) of man's subjective essence.[10] Here, man is steadily alienated from his true godhood simply by consciousness of anything outside himself – the essence of self being pure spirit or pure consciousness. This same idea is central to Buddhism and Hinduism, in which the goal of existence is re-absorption in the *one*, Brahma or Nirvana. The goal of pantheistic meditation (i.e. yoga) is to recognize the ultimate oneness and unity of all things; that distinctions are mere illusions. In Buddhism, the ultimate goal is pure consciousness which is unconsciousness – the annihilation of the idea of self altogether. Thus in Hegel, West meets East intellectually, although the implications are developed in different ways. Hegel saw the differentiation manifest in history and the created order as scattered bits of 'god' (human consciousness, pure spirit) everywhere. Therefore, man can only realize himself (discover his godhood) by *reunification with the fragmented self.* The quintessential utopian, Karl Marx, claimed to have solved this problem of fragmentation within the communist society. Far from dead, the Marxism of the new left is manifest as ecological and spiritualized socialism that seeks an androgynous, classless, discrimination- and distinction-free world of 'social justice' – a world ruled by a scientific, socialist, pagan elite. The new Marxism uses the weapon of cultural Marxism (political correctness) to enforce its ideas. Marx held that man was alienated from nature (himself), but could become one with it through work, an action of *nature* manifesting itself through man. Nature is the object and man is the subject, so a history created and controlled by industry was thought to reconcile subject and object (oneness). Nature (god) recreates itself by man's work, which expresses his *one essence* with nature. Nature, realized in man, is really god, yet doesn't realize it because it has been alienated from itself by the Christian theistic doctrines of God, man and the world. Man must become self-conscious, aware of being his own creator through work – a consciousness created by the re-making of nature through scientific socialism. Today, the *sine qua non* of all victimhood is the planet or nature itself, standing proxy for all 'oppressed' groups everywhere. It is no longer the bourgeois oppressing the proletariat. Nature itself must be liberated in order for man to re-create himself. This liberation requires radical equalization that will stop the white, Christian, capitalist plunderers. The process involves the development of a panoply of human rights for groups that demand not just equal opportunity but equal outcomes for all. This schema alone will create social justice, and all who oppose this program are cast as the oppressors and the enemy of human liberation. In all forms of Marxist thought, human consciousness is the supreme divinity. The idea of God is retained only as the ideal of perfection, even though he has no concrete existence; god exists only potentially because it can concretize itself in socialist mankind. So, "we are confronted with this strange paradox: the Marxist utopian denies the existence of God, but he holds that man may become divine or may develop a combination of purity and power that will transcend any human form."[11] Essentially, Marxist man does believe in a kind of super-nature – collective man. This transcending of human form is achieved by scientific (organized) and technological work that accomplishes man's reconquest of his essential unity with nature. "When man conquers nature he acquires the decisive victory over himself; he possesses himself."[12] This new god, by industry, continues to create. By doing so he believes he defeats what to him is the problem of history, sin, suffering and laborious work. The dominant Utopian worldview then is evolutionary, pantheistic and materialistic. Spirit and matter are one or are in the inexorable process of becoming one. The individual is identified with everybody and everybody is then elevated to divinity. In order for the man-god to be reunited with itself, in order to achieve *the unity of the godhead*, socialization and *humanization* must take place. These *require the co-operation of all men* in all the common tasks laid down by 'science,' as well as the reduction of all things to the secular, to the human, defined by time and by this world alone, not in terms of God or eternity. By vague philosophic abstractionism, secular theologies (whether religious liberalism or secular) make the notion of God so incomprehensible as to become meaningless. Human qualities are then blown up to cosmic proportions, ultimately asserting a 'universal mind,' and the results are called divine. For Teilhard de Chardin, for example, this is the *Omega Point*. He looked forward to the geophysical Congress of 1955 at which scientists of all nations would convene and exchange ideas, to provide a model for his noosphere.[13] This is the occultic emergence of a united super mankind.

The confidence of many elites past and present has been in the unity of the new godhead – man. Born in 1872, Bertrand Russell was widely regarded as one of the twentieth century's most important British intellectuals. He was not only an atheist but an ardent utopian. He writes:

It is the conquest of nature which has made possible a more friendly and co-operative attitude between human beings, and if rational men co-operated and used their scientific knowledge to the full, then the world could now secure the economic welfare of all.... International government, business organization, and birth control should make the world comfortable for everybody.... With the problem of poverty and destitution eliminated, men could devote themselves to the constructive arts of civilization – to the progress of science, the diminution of disease, the postponement of death, and the liberation of the impulses that make for joy.... Take first, international government. The necessity for this is patent to every person capable of political thought...when all the armed forces of the world are controlled by one world-wide authority, we shall have reached the stage in the relation of states which was reached centuries ago in the relations of individuals. Nothing less than this will suffice. The road to Utopia is clear; it lies partly through politics and partly through changes in the individual. As for politics, far the most important thing is the establishment of an international government.[14]

Though he formally repudiated communism, Russell believed in a world superstate with total power and a form of collectivism that would involve severe restrictions on human liberty including that cloak for murder and eugenics – 'birth control.' For him it was essential that man, as the new god of nature, must unite 'by love' if the conquest of nature is to be complete and death itself postponed or even defeated.

5.3.2 Love

This points us to the other critical ingredient in realizing the unity of the godhead – love! Man must be made to 'love' all men and for the utopian ideology this love means social justice. This must not be equated with love and justice in the biblical sense which entails the love of God and neighbour as the fulfilment of God's law (Lev. 19:18; Matt. 22:38–39; Rom. 13:10). Rather, since love of the living God is rejected, man must love the new god, collectivist man, with absolute and unswerving devotion. The God of Scripture is thus abandoned in favour of 'divine' interpersonal relationships. For there to be unity in the new godhead there must be total equality and equal ultimacy among all people which means loving all things. This means that there can be no *discrimination* in regard to anything. To insist there is a *moral* difference between people and their actions in terms of right and wrong, truth and falsehood or good and evil, as an objective standard, constitutes *discrimination*. In this worldview to discriminate against anything (except Christianity) is a contradiction of the utopian's most basic premise – oneness or total unity. Indeed, how could anything be right or wrong, true or false in terms of truth status in an absolute sense, since for all evolutionary pantheism these terms indicating differentiation (right/wrong, good/evil, male/female, etc.) are simply labels for different items throughout the advance (process) of psychological, biological and social evolution? All absolute distinctions are either illusory, less than fully-real, or mere social conventions. Naturally then, all religions, cultures, sexual practices, gender expressions or lifestyle choices are equal. Without this equality, the utopian holds, there can be no unity. Given the idea that all people are 'fragments of god,' no fragment can be more ultimate than another; all things must be levelled, for there must be unity in the godhead. Moreover, since all values are really just social constructs (objectivization in Hegel's terminology) in a historical process where all things are becoming one (unity), all basic distinctions in created reality must necessarily be broken down. To bring this belief from the abstract and land it in the concrete realm of present social engineering and political utopianism in North America, we need only point to the 'queering' of all things as the new social reality. Today, all over the U.S. and Canada (and most of Western Europe) our politicians, having bought into international utopianism, are co-operating for the redefinition of marriage, sexuality, family and even gender. It is not only that the sexual, social, cultural, historical and innate norms of heterosexual masculinity and femininity are being condemned as heterosexism, transphobia and homophobia, it is that the very idea that there are two genders is being denied. The obvious biological and corresponding social realities entailed in the terms 'male' and 'female' are increasingly no longer being viewed as normative in education, law, politics or even medicine.[15]

Politically, this 'unification' in the name of 'love' and care, is extending right into the dressing room and washroom where your children prepare for sports. Increasingly, one can express whatever gender one feels, irrespective of biology, and these distortions are protected by force of law. We are told that there are now many gender identities and sexual orientations. There are the transgendered, the 'two-spirited' (a Native American pagan concept for having both genders inside you), cross-dressers, gender-queers, the gender non-conforming and the androgynous. These people in turn may be Asexual, Bisexual, Lesbian, Gay, Transsexual and queer – it is difficult to keep up with the litany of new gender-identities and sexual practices being promoted by the contemporary utopians. In Canada, a private member's bill, C-279, otherwise dubbed 'the bathroom bill,' was successfully passed through a third reading in the Houses of Parliament. It amends the Canadian Human Rights Act and the Criminal Code to offer special protection against 'discrimination' in regard to 'gender identity,' that is, to those who claim to be transgendered (gender-variant, transsexuals, cross-dressers or the androgynous).[16] If this bill passes through the Canadian Senate, it will become law. Aside from the massive philosophical, theological and cultural implications of such a law which would deny the very concept of stable, established, normative human nature – a reality that has always informed our civilization and all sane social orders – the immediate practical fall-out would mean, for example, that any biological male who self- identifies as possessing another 'gender identity,' must be allowed to use women's facilities, from washrooms to showers and changing rooms, without prohibition or discrimination. As Michael Brown summarizes it, "say goodbye to male and female, to masculinity and femininity, to 'biological sex' and say hello to genderqueer, gender non-conforming, transgender, and transsexual…if the categories of male and female are up for grabs in kindergarten, can you imagine what's coming next?" [17] To recognize, accept and celebrate these ideas as the highest social values is called 'love.' And to insist that all others recognize and celebrate them, and to require them as a matter of legislation and coercion, is 'justice.'

Therefore, by eliminating differences (discrimination) in economic prosperity, knowledge, health, gender, moral values and more, all mankind will be humanized and socialized, united as one universal mind and entity and the unity of the godhead will be achieved. At this dreamed-of historical moment, socialized humanity will finally be classless, stateless, family-less, gender-less, lawless, religion-less and an essentially structure-less collectivity of beings in harmony with themselves and the other (nature). Equality is here both ontological (in terms of our being) and political. This love and unity, the accomplishment of total social justice, is the one great imperative of the utopian. We see this particularly in the 'repressive tolerance' agenda of Herbert Marcuse that has become the new orthodoxy throughout much of Western higher education. Those who oppose this vision are to be condemned as heretics, disturbers of the peace and purveyors of the new atheism – belief in the God of the Bible. Such a view of reality based on a personal God who transcends time and his creation, who differentiates, judges, commands, and calls to repentance cannot be tolerated as it destroys the unity of the new godhead. The heretics must be sectioned, silenced or cast out. This absolute requirement for the unity (oneness) of humanity as the essence of justice or equity is the fundamental principle of the dystopian nightmare.

5.4 The Omnipotence of the Utopian Godhead

A second necessary aspect to any doctrine of God is *omnipotence*. Clearly, if God is not sovereign and all-powerful he cannot be God. Consequently, if sinful man's humanistic project is 'to be as God,' then as the new source of power, certainty and meaning, he must be omnipotent. What is then required is that man as the new god must ape and *acquire* the characteristics of the living God in order to realize his divinity. In order to be all-powerful, the new god, of necessity, must eliminate chance, impotence (powerlessness) and uncertainty from human affairs and this requires total control and omni-competence. We have already seen that utopians believe this will require a world-state with universal jurisdiction. It is only in terms of this theology of state that we can understand the aspirations of the United Nations with its goal of a one-world order, manifest in the proliferation of a litany of international bodies, treaties and institutions, from banks, to courts, to armies, lawmakers and cultural organizations for 'planning' humanity's 'free' future when we will all be one.

The irony of this *coercive* pursuit of freedom through unity should not go unnoticed. Utopian power and control require the political use of coercion with the state, functioning as 'man enlarged,' being the sole source of law and sovereign authority. It further requires the manipulation of nature in terms of organizational 'science' to eliminate uncertainty and demonstrate this omni-competence. Such a vision is obviously dystopian since it requires totalitarianism. This is not simply a technique for domination, it is a religious principle. Molnar observes: "It is a doctrinal necessity inscribed in Marxist theory. Totalitarianism prescribes total domination over man – over all his mental spiritual, creative and technical endeavors, and its organization of these activities is the *sine qua non* of restoring man to a direct relationship with nature." [18] Total power is then an essential requirement to bring about the new utopia which mankind is said to both need and be destined for. Even if most people don't understand this destiny, the new philosopher kings, the elite social planners believe they understand, and more importantly, know what is best for the rest of us.

To understand the reason for this we must note again an aspect of Marxist theory. In this worldview, the ideal world (from which man is alienated), is the *material* world (nature) reflected in the human mind and translated into thought forms. Human thought is then reduced, by radical reductionism, to rank materialism. As a consequence, true philosophy is not the love of wisdom, man reflecting carefully on human experience, both internal and external, it is rather 'work' or '*practice*' of the human sciences (total praxis). In other words, the concern of utopian thought is not with *describing* or explaining the inner and outer world, but with changing and *controlling* them. Since the human person is a part of the material of nature (all that is) and the progress of cosmic evolution, man is equally the legitimate object of scientific and social experiment. A totalitarian world of total control, of the science of organization and experimentation, thus replaces Christian theology and philosophy. Whether the utopian delusion is expressed as a form of Marxism, National Socialism (fascism) or some other political permutation, power is the central theme. Both Marxism and fascism are totalitarian ideologies; one centred in class warfare where people are divided up into oppressor and oppressed groups, the other in elitism in which the superior must crush the inferior and weak. One calls for the *dictatorship* of the proletariat or the common people, the other for the *dictatorship* of the supermen. Both are instruments of naked power for the creation of a utopian society where, one way or another, man is becoming a god. In the twentieth century, both resulted in the expression of naked power involving brutal and horrific slaughter on an unprecedented scale. Both engaged in repression, torture, mass murder and 'scientific' experimentation on human individuals, families, communities and whole nations. Whether through the SS and Gestapo, or by officials of 'the party,' both sought total control of all aspects of the social order to create their brave new worlds. In both contexts, dissent could not be tolerated. Likewise both regimes claimed to act on behalf of nature (materialistic evolution), advancing mankind toward its destiny in godhood.

The true and living God remains the main obstacle to man's lust for total power and the creation of his dystopian nightmare. Once the idea of the God of the Bible is eliminated the stage of freedom from God or the stage of 'necessity' has been reached. In this stage of necessity, *nature and history dictate all human decisions and actions* with a total authority surpassing that of God himself. These dictates of nature cannot be refused. Molnar explains why: "First, because these dictates are proclaimed in the name of nature; secondly, because man is himself part of nature and of history, nothing remains in reference to which he might say 'no.'" [19] If nature and impersonal processes of history dictate human actions, then there is no transcendent appeal possible for man, no higher authority to which he may appeal against tyranny and slavery. The new order of unity and salvation is then the scientific, socialist state. The 'One' (nature/ god) is totally immanent and so there is no escape from the incarnate truth. It becomes logical then that to resist this truth is evil. Man is thus absorbed into a *process* that is both necessary and irresistible. Accordingly, total predestinating power is demanded and sought by the state in the name of man's freedom – freedom to be part of nature and its determinative historical progress. In a profound irony, true freedom becomes the renunciation of freedom. The desire for individual freedom is seen as a kind of childhood of mankind, whereas collectivist freedom is to grow up into the maturity of mankind's freedom to fulfil his destiny. In such a view only the immanent god (nature manifest in statist man), not the transcendent God, can be allowed in human politics, since a God who is different from nature and claims power for himself, would always attract loyalty away from the one immanent god. With man as the only god, complete cohesion and unification is thought to be within reach.

5.5 Posthuman Omnipotence

So how might this vision of total power be realized in the real world? How might total control, total predestination – the necessary precursor to utopia – be achieved by man? One recent proposal pushes the belief in man's technology, scientific planning and providence to new heights. In the book, *The Last Prophet* by Haldane, communication by telepathy results in the emergence of a super-organism. The social consensus of humanity is conveyed by electronic waves automatically so that all community units (people) act in the common interest at all times. A similar idea is vividly expressed in the science fiction of *Star Trek*, especially in the feature film, *First Contact*, in which the Enterprise's heroic crew engages in a struggle for the survival of humanity against a collective consciousness called the *Borg*. The Borg's goal is perfection, by the assimilation of all peoples and worlds into the Borg 'collective.' The Borg, a race of part-organic, part-cybernetic automatons, are all interconnected by carrier waves so that there are effectively no individuals, or at least no individual wills, although there are millions of humanoid beings (drones). The Borg's claim in confronting races for assimilation is that their power is irresistible. All will be assimilated and 'resistance is futile.'

Granted, this is the realm of science fiction, yet such dreams of a new type of enhanced hybrid human actuate many scientists, technocrats and bureaucrats today – although the dream of man becoming a superman is nothing new, and goes all the way back to the ancient pagan world.

Surprising as it may sound, increasing numbers of ethicists, futurists and scientists hold that man can become a great deal more than he presently is by the use of emerging technologies that would include cognitive enhancement, behaviour modification, bionic implants and more. It is thought that these things may lead even to the defeat of death and mortality. Julian Huxley (1887-1975) first coined the term transhumanism in 1957. He claimed, "the human species can, if it wishes transcend itself – not just sporadically, an individual here in one way, an individual there in another way, but in its entirety, as humanity." [20] There are many current efforts underway to develop these ideas and move toward the reality of a 'transhuman' or posthuman world. James A. Herrick notes, "hundreds and perhaps thousands of university and corporate research facilities around the world are involved in developing artificial intelligence, regenerative medicine, life-extension strategies, and pharmaceutical enhancements of cognitive performance." [21] The goal is nothing short of self-salvation. As the Humanist Manifesto II makes clear, "no deity will save us; we must save ourselves." [22] Inspired in some measure by Nietzsche's 'Overman' (which glorified self-actualization), transhumanism (influenced by Gnosticism, rationalism, science fiction and developed in the thinking of British philosopher Max More) has become a global intellectual and cultural movement with a considerable following amongst the intelligentsia.

Built on the cultural myths of evolution, progress, the superman and the power of a collective intellect, the eugenic idea has returned emphatically in transhumanism, but with a difference. The eugenics movement of the twentieth century, exemplified by the Nazi utopians, held that progress in evolution cannot now be achieved accidentally, with natural selection left to take its course, but must be controlled by deliberate selection, since intelligent man has become the custodian of evolution. The posthuman believers agree with this thesis, but realize that the old eugenics breeding program was scientifically flawed; in terms of genetics we are not inevitably 'improving,' since genetic entropy (the progressive accumulation of harmful mutations) is working in the other direction. Accordingly, for the transhumanists, *enhancement evolution* is the clear next step. Evolution, it is held, has produced us, and through us it has produced technology so that we are at the point where we can transform our own species by technological manipulation. The essential hope is that it will soon be possible to so integrate human technology (nanotechnology, biotechnology, information technology, cognitive science) with our natural physical, biological systems, that an effectively new species of man will arise that blends the technological and synthetic with the organic; man and machine merge into the transhuman. It begins with mechanically augmenting the body, but they believe it will end in an ability to deposit essential human consciousness in mechanical devices. This gradual transformation would include the extensive use of pharmaceuticals to enhance or alter cognitive functions and would be combined with an emphasis on re-education of the population about human nature. As computer scientist Hugo de Garis has put it, "because of our intelligence that's evolved over billions of years, we are now on the point of making a major transition away from biology to a new step. You could argue that…maybe humanity is just a stepping stone."[23] What was previously considered magic and mysticism in ancient paganism will now be pursued by technological means. Today, genetic manipulation is very much a reality, nanotechnology is advancing and human DNA is being looked at as a possible information storage device whilst many techno-futurists genuinely believe that within a generation human beings may be able to interact directly with cyberspace by immediate access via the cerebral cortex. Furthermore, some computer engineers reckon that our rate of progress will result in an internet that is a trillion times faster than today's within forty years.[24] Not only is the emergence of the transhuman thought to be in the interests of enhancing human experience in progress toward something other, it is also reckoned to be humanity's only escape from extinction. Herrick writes:

> Professor Julian Savulescu is the head of the Uehiro Centre for Practical Ethics at Oxford University and a leading proponent of human enhancement, the school of thought that promotes the progressive use of biotechnologies to improve human intellect, moral reasoning, and other traits such as physical strength. Savulescu has argued that deep moral flaws and destructive behaviors point indisputably to the need to employ technology and education to change human nature; either we take this path or we face extinction as a species…according to Salvulescu, genetic science, improved pharmaceuticals, and moral education may hasten the emergence of a new and better human race.[25]

Such men genuinely believe that technology will conquer everything from outer space to death itself; human nature will thus be conquered, delivering humanity into the future as evolved demigods. Interestingly, in this process, the Internet is viewed as man's first great step toward a unified consciousness.[26] This vague idea of a unified consciousness is expressed in Teilhard de Chardin's "noosphere," in Kurzweil's "singularity," and in Bertrand Russell's, "world of shining beauty and transcendent glory" that will blanket the earth and pervade the universe.[27] This 'omega point' is a globally integrated, immortal race.

The pagan, religious nature of these ideas, though shrouded in the language of 'science,' is very clear. The ultimate goal is not simply the emergence of a bionic man with an interconnected consciousness through cyberspace. The basic belief is that evolution, or the universe itself (the process of nature) through its human and then posthuman offspring and their technological innovation, is moving toward complete omniscience and *omnipotence*. "Ambitious evolution is merely using us and our descendents as its cat's paw to snatch technological divinity from the cosmos's chaotic flames."[28] Ray Kurzweil has stated clearly, "the universe will wake up; it will become intelligent and that will multiply our intelligence trillions upon trillions...; it is called the Singularity. But regardless what you call it, it will be the universe waking up. Does God exist? I would say, "'not yet,'"[29] This faith is therefore a religious trust in the posthuman potential, a radical humanism that is fervently committed to the belief that man can transform his humanity to godhood, seizing the attributes of God and achieving immortality, universal knowledge, and unified globalconsciousness."[30] This faith is also an *organized* religion. As David Herbert has pointed out in his book-length study of Transhumanism, 'Singularity University (SU) was the brainchild of Peter Diamandis (b. 1961), physician and noted entrepreneur. The inspiration for this venture came about after reading *The Singularity is Near*. Soon after, Dr Diamandis successfully enlisted Ray Kurzweil, the author of the book, to join in him creating this unique educational institution." Their goal is disruptive thinking and creative solutions that solve the planet's most pressing challenges.[31] Kurzweil was made the university's first chancellor.

Now there is a necessary link between the goal of man transcending his humanity and the need for increased limitations on human freedoms – including freedom of speech and religion, the right of privacy and the erosion of free sovereign nations through the *seizure of power* by a global authority. In essence, to acquire power over nature (that is, himself), man will need total power over people. As Herrick explains, for Savulescu, "more is needed, including worldwide cooperation 'in a way that humans have never so far cooperated.'"[32] Once again global government and control is apparently necessary for man to reach his divine potential. According to some posthuman experts, "the near future will usher in a global culture enabled by a massively more powerful Internet...." Hugo de Garis takes as simple matters of fact that "technical progress will create within forty years...a global media, a global education system, a global language, and a globally homogenized culture," which will constitute the basis of 'a global democratic state."[33] This massive centralization of power for the common good will of course require us all to surrender our historic commitment to freedom. Savulescu writes:

> We could reduce our commitment to liberalism. We will, I believe, need to relax our commitment to maximum protection of privacy. We're already seeing an increase in the surveillance of individuals, and that surveillance will be necessary if we're to avert the threats that those with anti-social personality disorders, psychopathic personality disorders, or fanaticism represent through their access to radically enhanced technology.[34]

Total power means total surveillance and the elimination of privacy in order to neutralize the threat from those who have *anti-social personality disorders* or who are *fanatics*. Contemporary utopianism already identifies those who oppose the legalization and promotion of the queering of culture as 'mentally ill' individuals suffering from irrational phobias, and the fanatics are of course the traditional religionists, the Christians: "Traditional religion has been the *bête noir* of enhancement advocates, an anti-technological and anti-futurist force to be actively opposed."[35] Transhumanism is clearly a religious utopianism growing in strength and influence with a real faith in the singularity – the One. Here we meet not only the lust for total power, but once again the pursuit of unity in the godhead which requires the use of power to reach this end. The common creed, motivating a delusional craving for total predestinating power is that "ongoing evolution will 'eventually produce a unified cooperative organization of living processes that spans and manages the universe as a whole.'"[36] But since the leading transhumanists (aspiring bureaucrats for the universe), like everyone else, are being overtaken by death what can be done to save them for the singularity? Herbert tells us:

> Kurzweil has set in motion an alternate plan – cryonics. He has already made arrangements with the Alcor Life Extension Foundation to have his body cryopreserved.... Even though we do not presently have the means of reviving bodies cryonically preserved, technology, as always, will be the panacea to gain eternal life – and thus we "will be like God." [37]

If ever there were a working manifestation of the demonic urge 'to be as god,' this is certainly it – a cosmos-sized unified bureaucracy of 'living processes' inclusive of the technologically resurrected, managing the entire universe through the emergence of a cosmic mind, a counterfeit god.

It may seem far-fetched that men are seeking the *power* to alter the very essence of human nature into a grotesque hybrid of semi-cybernetic life, followed by assimilation into some form of universal collective, but this is the utopianism of humanism; it is in reality a dystopian aspiration. Decades before today's futurists, H. G. Wells, a utopian *par excellence*, spoke of the 'process of thought' of which all are a part, growing in range and power without limit! Wells believed man as a collective could be immortal.[38] In this quest, man's task is to subordinate himself to the 'immortal being of the race' – all are to give themselves to that which increases knowledge and power.[39] To the ensuring of this end there should be no delay. Wells writes, "My idea of politics is an open conspiracy to hurry these tiresome, wasteful, evil things – nationality and war – out of existence; to end this empire and that empire, and set up the one Empire of Man."[40] This will come about when man gives himself to the collective and to science. 'We can all be citizens of the free state of science.' The impediment to accomplishing this glorious 'state of science' as Wells saw it was people's feebleminded attachment to God. "[O]ur political, our economic, our social lives which have still to become illuminated and directed by the scientific spirit, are still sick and feeble with congenital traditionalism."[41] What is the solution? "A great release of human energy and a rapid dissolution of social classes, through the ever-increasing efficiency of economic organization and the utilization of mechanical power."[42] In other words, man's transcendental aspiration, to 'grow in range and power without limit,' require coercive political power to dissolve the classes and the use of technology, or scientific control. For the most part, contemporary Western intellectuals (especially the new left) believe power must be used to demolish the traditional family, the orthodox Christian faith and any hint of social classes – only then can the necessary economic transformation take place to advance the collectivist cause. The language of the sciences and social sciences are easily translated into the language of collectivism and totalitarian politics and such writers move seamlessly back and forth between them.

In the Nazi utopia, the vision of the superman (overman) was used to justify scientific 'experimentation,' and a variety of forms of eugenics, in the quest to improve the quality of 'the race' for a glorious future. Many of these ideas have been subtly re-introduced by the medicalization of society and politics. As far as the impact on human liberty is concerned, medical interventions and political interventions essentially amount to one and the same thing, from the advocacy of birth control, to abortion rights, infanticide, euthanasia, tax-funded sex change operations and state-mandated insurance coverage for birth control and abortion. Moreover, modern states are involved in a great variety of forms of genetic research, including recent efforts to mix male and female genetic material in a human embryo. This politicization of science and medicine in the name of equality, freedom and progress works toward the elimination of the normal sentiments of individual persons, to replace them with *enforced* 'public' sentiments of the whole.

The wielding of this total power to bring about a utopian order, with or without the dream of the posthuman cyborg, requires a vast nanny state bureaucracy by which the whole of life is scheduled. The transition to Utopia may be traumatic, we are told, but it is for the best. Gradually, various instruments of freedom and power are withdrawn from individuals and families so that power is concentrated in the source of divinity – the power state. Private property is one of the first such freedoms to be targeted. Progressive taxation of income, property and inheritance leads to open and brazen assaults on private property, including direct seizure of money from bank accounts and of land or goods.[43] Money, a form of private property whereby one form of property is converted into another, is therefore a means of power or dominion. Private property must be steadily abolished because it introduces a rival power or source of resistance to the power-state. Wealth and property must be equalized and become 'collective property,' owned by the state. All men then become children, dependent upon public assistance. The most powerful social entity then owns and completely controls the source of power. A moment's reflection reveals that today, the modern utopian is a good way toward realizing such goals:

> The fact is, that the concept of the state (or the community), completely dominating and regulating the lives of its citizens, has been, by and large, accepted in the second half of the twentieth century...the debate of the past several decades has been merely whether the state, the race, the ideological empire or World Government will stage-manage the last acts of the passage to a coalescing mankind.[44]

The utopian then sees the planet as a source of unlimited power. If that power can only be properly harnessed, all the potentiality of man and nature can be focused on the conquest of other planets, solar systems, death and God himself. The ultimate goal is therefore the acquisition of power over things and men; in essence, it is the will to be God.

The delusions of men in this regard are staggering. The scientific socialist future was the one that Orwell contemplated with horror. Science in this vision becomes only what serves man's purpose – which, as we have seen, is power and control as an end. Society itself becomes an experiment and an exercise in material manipulation. Human beings become little more than the guinea pigs of scientific planners. For any experiment to be valid, the basic requirement is total control of the environment – all the factors must be under controlled conditions. Therefore, in the utopian vision of society as social experiment, a totalitarian vision is a necessary starting point, without which the experiment will be neither valid nor scientific. This is what is said with regard to the failures of Marxism in its political regimes past and present – there was or is a failure to foresee or control certain factors. Having learnt from these mistakes, many in the intelligentsia believe the experiment can now function properly – unforeseen variables can be eliminated. No longer about understanding reality, science has become the task of controlling it. So rather than the Christian view of reality, which leaves predestination to God – thereby leaving man in a place of liberty by denying the right of total control to any human agency – the scientific society believes its desired social results can be obtained by means of controlled causation. This has led scientists, futurists and political utopians to discuss or pursue everything from cloning to the modification of human organs, the creation of a synthetic human being, control of the weather, elimination of crime, modification of food, colonization of the universe, development of an artificial sun, elimination of disease, creation of transhumans, forced sterilization, and postponement or deliverance from death.[45] This new tower of Babel seems terrifying and imposing, as intimidating as the great statue of Nebuchadnezzar doubtless appeared to Daniel and his friends, but the Christian must not, indeed cannot fear, nor can we yield because "The world of the future shall be God's world, and man in that world shall be only what the predestinating power and control of God intend him to be."[46]

5.6 The Wrath of Man

One further logical development of man's dystopian will to *power* is the arrogation to himself of the power to judge and pour out wrath as the new god; in a world rejecting the living God, the need for judgement has not vanished. If God's covenantal judgements in history are denied, man's word of blessing and cursing must replace them. If God's transcendent court and judgement are abolished in man's thinking, then man needs to create for himself a purely world-bound and temporal court for absolute judgement, and consign men to an immanent hell for disobedience. If history is all there is, judgement cannot be delayed. To delay judgement is to hinder progress toward Oneness and unity. As Albert Camus put it, "the judgement pronounced by history must be pronounced immediately, for culpability coincides with the check to progress and with punishment."[47] The Christian view of reality can give men maximum freedom under the law and need not insist on absolute and immediate judgement in history over all sin, because ultimate judgement and the judgement of men's hearts and motives belongs to God alone. Without the living God, however, the utopian state fills the vacuum in man's craving for judgement. The terror involved in such a view is that this de-facto god, the power state, has no transcendent critique since there is *no God in judgement over it.* The utopian naturally recognizes that not all the population will agree with his vision of a total order that doles out summary judgement against the structural oppressors[48] and resisters, so in political discourse the 'people' or the 'real' population (outside of a demonized 'religious right') are the abstract group upon which the new unanimity is established. This public is then indoctrinated and required to internalize the (politically) correct way of thinking and the non-conformers are then to be punished for their bigotry, intolerance, rejection of the democratic will, sexism, classism, nationalism, heterosexism and a variety of psychological phobias that multiply by the week. To the scientific planners the utopian worldview is allegedly so self-evident that only the perverted would resist it and must be put on trial, by media, politics or tribunal, for their violation of the new positive human rights – this is the presently tame expression of temporal judgement in the West. The brutal interference of the state in the Chinese 'commune' system is well-documented (including the regulation of the sex lives of married couples), and yet these horrors give Western intellectuals little pause. Molnar comes to the disturbing crux of the matter:

> All this is done in order to change the nature of man, extirpate his selfishness and instill collective conscience.... The Utopian leadership always claims that its function is merely to facilitate association among equal citizens, including among members of a family – or in the religious utopian language, communication between them and God. Under such a claim the citizen shows his virtuousness to the extent that he abandons the socially divisive attitude of looking out for his own and his family's interests, and with a complete loyal candor, trusts the leadership class to take care of his needs...conversely, doubt in, and resistance to, this ability (and love) show stupidity, obstinacy and viciousness: doubters and resisters must be punished...since they contradict the associative principle and break unanimity, doubters and resisters must first be excluded from the membership of utopia's citizenry, hence from membership in the human race. The utopian who has scorned and abolished the coercive power of the state, with its police, laws, courts and executioners, proceeds to restore them in the most matter of fact way...on the extermination of resisters to utopia all utopian writers are in agreement.[49]

So judgement, as an expression of total power, comes from the new god, personified in the scientific socialist state. Every worldview has its vision of judgement, heaven and hell. In much Eastern thought, hell is temporal existence and heaven is impersonal being or non-being. For the utopian, hell is the world of God's law and absolute values, and heaven is the coming collective consciousness where man transcends his humanity. The dystopian nature of this doctrine of judgement and its diabolic threat to freedom under God is made plain by Rushdoony:

> To transfer final judgement, heaven and hell from the eternal order to time is to absolutize history and to enthrone man as god. It means the destruction of liberty, because history ceases to be the realm of liberty and testing but becomes the place of final trial. Having made the final judgement temporal, the humanist cannot permit liberty, because liberty is hostile to finality; liberty presupposes both trial and error and the possibility of serious waywardness when and where man is sinful and imperfect. History cannot tolerate both trial and error and [also] insist on finality and the end of trial and error. The humanistic utopias are all prisons, because they insist on a finality which man does not possess. Accordingly, the socialist utopias demand the re-education of man in the post-revolutionary world, in the era beyond judgement. The "new era" is the new heaven on earth.... But history refuses to terminate on man's orders, because it runs on God's time, and not in terms of man's myths.[50]

Whenever man usurps the attributes of divinity and seeks omnipotence, he creates a hell on earth and those he claims to be liberating become victims of the vindictive wrath of a counterfeit god.

5.7 The Omniscience of the Godhead

The biblical doctrine of the holy Trinity includes the affirmation that the living God is all-knowing, and that this is basic to the being of God. A true God cannot be without total knowledge since this is logically required by creation, total government, predestination and total power. As Christians we believe that God knows us totally, from the hairs on our head to the content of our minds, and that he governs the life of man comprehensively in his providence. It is then immediately noteworthy that in the dystopian projects of the modern age, we have the man-god, the religious object of the utopian, through the organized apparatus of the state, pursuing a total knowledge of man by regulation and most importantly, *education*. This is because the new god must, like the living God he is seeking to usurp, be all-knowing. Omniscience must be co-opted into man's vision of himself if he would be as god. This god cannot settle for approximations, or tolerate provisional, uncertain conclusions about a nature whose re-creator and predestinator he believes himself to be. Within this claim to omniscience there is also the presumption of the right to gather information in minute detail on every citizen, manifested in the parallel proliferation of surveillance. Today, the United Kingdom is the surveillance state of Europe, with a vast network of cameras photographing the citizenry several times daily. Increasingly, by this control of an ever-shrinking sphere of privacy, various mental health programs and sensitivity training, as well as the now mainstream chemical 'treatment' of people's minds, the man-gods are seeking omniscience.

However, the most important strategy in the utopian plan for omniscience has been the unrelenting drive to control all the apparatus of education. Since the utopian does not believe in a permanent human nature but a socially constructed and evolving one in the hands of man's technology, the effort is continuously made to direct all education. The idea is not to civilize a person in terms of what it means to be a responsible human being, discerning right and wrong, truth and falsehood. The goal is again the development of a system that will *transform* both current and future generations of children into good, pliable participants in the utopian order. Historically, from ancient Sparta to the former Soviet Union, this has typically involved either the complete removal of children from the care of their parents, or the elimination of parental teaching and influence as far as possible, keeping the child in all-day 'education' from daycare to university, out of the reach of parental 'ignorance.' By breaking the Christian concept of the family and achieving its progressive disintegration, the re-integration of the new man can then begin. As such, utopian education is not preparation for life and freedom with the goal of enabling children to think critically, equipped with the tools necessary for a life of learning and inquiry. Instead, education is social activism, and the goal is a homogeneous, predictable product, less able, less critical, less inquisitive, more pliable, not nurtured in divisive Christian understandings of life but with feelings of equality, fraternity and dependency. Whilst formal, graduated education is on the surface still encouraged, its goal is no longer the achievement of excellence for the individual, but rather the fusing of the personality of the child with the common mass. Nothing should be allowed to undermine the achievement of a pale equilibrium. The objective then is a 'new creation,' a new human being, known totally by the man-gods who brought them to birth. Education is governed in the modern utopian age by the doctrines of *behaviourism*. The utopian believes in the perfectibility of humanity, born without a sinful nature or pre-established essence. As such, man is a neutral being and totally malleable. As a purely material creature, an aspect of the cosmos, a person is ruled by external impressions and environmental factors.

Accordingly, by applying scientific and social controls, the individual is made ready for use in the building of the city of man. History itself can be wiped out (as mere social construct and power relations in disguise) by the educational revolution, which leads to revolution in all spheres (political, legal, economic and scientific), creating a clean slate on which society can be re-created. As in Hegelian thought and Eastern pantheism, individual consciousness is the problem in the psychology of behaviourism, because it leads to alienation, fragmentation or disintegration. The fully empirical man (totally controllable and governed by conditions and environment) cannot have an independent, personal consciousness, which would lead him away from oneness (unity) and universal consciousness, as well as opening him to considering the existence of a personal soul and of a living God outside and beyond nature. Why is this radical rejection of true personal consciousness necessary? Because to admit the existence of personal consciousness and individual souls would deny the new man-god his *omniscience*, for who can control inner consciousness, the individual soul or the being of God? Individual, personal consciousness must be rejected. Behaviourism considers a human being only in evolutionary terms, and thus wholly animal. There is no qualitative, rational dividing line between a human being and a beast. This idea is promoted by leading ethical thinkers like Peter Singer, in the animal 'liberation' movements he helped spawn, and amongst pro-choice advocates.[51] Here man has no God-given soul and possesses no intrinsic superiority to or dominion over the animal world. All liberation movements are culturally Marxist, for the liberation they seek is *from God* into the world of the new man-gods and the freedom of necessity – the inexorable movement toward unity. These movements toward oneness, toward the breaking down of all differentiation, of all real distinctions, not only raise the ontological status of animals and vegetation, but level man and beast; human babies have no more right to life than do foxes, seals or pigs. Killing babies and aborting children is no different from drowning puppies. Furthermore, experiments and conclusions that seem valid in the animal sphere are treated as valid in the human, especially in the realm of psychology. Clearly then, there is no 'mind' basic to this view of man and education because there is no mind-body, soul-body, or subject-object relationship at the level of ultimate reality – matter and spirit collapse into one. Man is material and essentially passive, and the educator must go to work on him and make and condition him for the scientific socialist state. This materialism does not eliminate concepts of spirituality, which are a man-made means of accessing the god within and putting man in touch with the cosmos or nature, of which he himself is part. Materialistic or pagan concepts of nature and the cosmos nurture and produce such pantheistic and occult religious ideas.[52]

The chief aim is *omniscience* for the man-god. The outcome of omniscience is the ability to predict and control totally. A given stimulus will produce a given response. Since such control is difficult to establish in adults, the key is to re-make children by educational conditioning as early as possible. Utopians religiously believe that education will gradually change the universe to fit man's planned order. This progressivist freedom, in which children are raised and educated in a 'scientific' or experimental way to join the collective and help man reach total *unity* is the dominant view of state educators today. Rushdoony notes that two things become very apparent in utopian education: "1) When mind and body are made one, mind being resolved into body, thought and action are also made indistinguishable, and any priority of thought destroyed. 2) Man's only freedom is to be conditioned to act in conformity to 'group standards.'"[53] Once again we have divine attributes, which in Christianity are basic to the being of God and with some predicates to individuals made in the image of God (i.e. personhood, mind, planning), transferred to the new unified godhead. In the world of dystopian education, social engineering first reduces the human to the animal (material/nature) and then denies independent consciousness to the individual, whilst attributing thought, planning, power, predestination and omniscience to the collective – the immanent one. Mild language is insufficient to describe this vision; it is nothing other than a demonic beast, a monster bent on destroying man. For as Rushdoony notes every "attempt to create utopia has only brought man a step closer to the borderlands of a totalitarian hell."[54] Man is not omniscient, nor is he at the wheel of history, he is a creature and by his attempts to be other than he is by manipulation, experimentation, drugs and social engineering, he only reveals his enslavement to the machinations of dark spiritual powers likewise beyond his control.

5.8 Babel is Broken

Men's Utopias, the man-created and man-planned societies of the future, are always a dystopian nightmare because man is a fallen sinner in rebellion against God (Rom 5:10–21). Fallen man is in constant denial of this reality, and hates to accept that he is a creature, and a broken one at that. As such, he is dead in trespasses and sins and utterly incapable of saving himself, from himself (Eph. 2:1–3). His demonic urge and evil desire is transparently the one seen in Genesis 3:5, "to be as God" and his motive is to force the usurpation of the divine attributes, which, being falsified in the hands of sinful man, produces not a paradise, but a hell on earth. As Molnar expresses it, "utopianism has been shown to be not only wrong in the light of rational arguments and by the experience of life, but that it is also a demonstrably moral evil."[55] However, if man is *not* a sinner as utopian dreamers claim, he does not need a *savior* but an *expert*, a guru, or Lama – essentially an elite class to re-organize all things and plan man's liberation from what are in fact the results of his own sins. These elite believe that the new man-gods can move beyond good and evil (as defined by God) and, becoming their own maker, re-imagine and redefine all things from truth and justice, to human nature, family, gender and all things else. Human power, it is thought, through a central organization of society, can restore paradise and overcome the problem of sin (not moral evil, but man's disjoint from nature, his alienation) without the redemption of Jesus Christ. From Thomas More to Bacon's scientific elite who prepared the way for communist thinkers, to Karl Marx (with his many disciples and descendents), right through to today's cultural Marxists (the new left, international Marxists and religious environmentalists), man is driven by his lust for power and his hatred of God's order. The more deeply one is committed to the utopian illusion the less able one is to recognize one's own depravity and sin. In the final analysis, dystopia is produced because of man's prideful defiance of God and lawless desire to manipulate mankind's future by enlarging man to cosmic proportions. Molnar is to the point: "[The utopian's] real vice is, first, the desire to dismantle human individuality through the dissolution of individual conscience and consciousness, and then to replace these with the collectivity and coalesced consciousness."[56] His arrogance puts him on god's throne, possessing total power, knowledge and control, believing that only paradise is fit for the man-god.

As we thumb through the pages of utopian history, we walk into the abstract (no-place) world of human delusion. Utopias, when implemented in the social order, are as unworkable and destructive as they are cruel. Interestingly, the nineteenth-century utopians anticipated the nationalization of industries, the welfare state, socialized medicine, state pensions and more.[57] These seemed ludicrously radical then, but are now part of life for most Western people whose social order these utopian plans are steadily bankrupting and destroying throughout Europe and North America as I write.

5.9 A Religious Worldview

Utopianism is a religious worldview; it has religious views of God, nature, man and community. The universe is one substance, both self-creating and self-sufficient. This world substance is not yet fully divinized, but through the process of evolution and change the substance is being purified and made homogeneous until it becomes a spiritual whole – the omega point. For this point to be reached it is necessary that the imperfect be steadily changed or removed. As it stands, this final point is only a *potential* point in the future, so man, as part of history and world substance, must re-divinize himself by bringing about the reunification of man with nature. To this end, experimental knowledge is power, which was of course the temptation in the garden of God back in Genesis. In biblical terms, man now seeks vengeance against the God of the garden who drove him from paradise, by building his tower of Babel, and attempting to arrest history, as a monument to his own divinity – the city of man. In this sense, the utopian lie is the *original temptation* that can only produce dystopia. The gospel awakens men from their sinful dream and quickens them to recognize that they are not God; they can never be omnipotent, omniscient, transcendent or sovereign. Rather, men are made noble in the image of God, created as his vice-regents to serve, obey and glorify God, and in this to discover their true joy and original humanity, unity in diversity, both one and many. In Jesus Christ the fragmentation produced by sin is undone, and man is made a new creation, restoring his fellowship not with nature, but with the living God and his fellow men, illustrated for us in the communion feast and the life of the church. Then, as the new humanity in Jesus Christ, people are called once again to exercise, not domination, but dominion under God, making creation a culture, to turn the world back into God's garden by the ministry of the gospel and obedience to God's every word. God alone makes all things new by regeneration and sanctification and he alone brings history to a conclusion at his ordained time; only then will there be a new heaven and a new earth in which complete righteousness dwells. This alone is the answer to man's religious hunger – God's new humanity in Jesus Christ, in whom we are made one in the Lord. God is in total control. His purposes will prevail and our joy and peace, salvation and rest is in the worship of God and enjoyment of him, in fellowship with his people forever. Pagan man dreams of pure consciousness, which is in fact unconsciousness, but St. Paul summons all to awake from dreams that lead to death and declares, "Awake thou that sleepest, and arise from the dead, and Christ shall give thee light" (Eph. 5:14 KJV).

Chapter Six

YOU SHALL NOT PERVERT JUSTICE: RELATING EVANGELISM, JUSTICE AND THE KINGDOM

True morality, or the Christian ethics is the love of God and man, stirred up by the Spirit of Christ, through faith; and exercised in works of piety, justice, charity, and temperance.
                                                                – Richard Baxter

Puritan social action was based on a covenant theology that required people to pursue the common good of the community... one aspect of Puritan social action was a concern to help the needy in society.... Puritan social action was primarily voluntaristic and personal rather than governmental or institutional.
                                                                – Leland Ryken

6.1   Evangelism and the Kingdom of God

The etymology of the word 'evangelism' reveals that it centres upon the propagation of the evangel, the good news that was manifest in the person of Jesus Christ. The English word 'gospel' literally means 'good news.' Furthermore, the synoptic gospels add that this gospel is 'the gospel of the kingdom' (Matt. 4:23). This kingdom terminology is scattered liberally throughout the New Testament (Matt. 9:35; Mark 1:15; Luke 4:43; John 3:3). Clearly, the doctrine of the kingdom is central to a biblical understanding of evangelism.[1] Since a kingdom requires a king, Jesus' announcement that the kingdom is here, that it has come near and that it is now advancing in the world is also a declaration that the reign of God, our sovereign, has broken into the world visibly.

Jesus' earthly ministry further demonstrated that this good news was not merely a piece of abstract information to be communicated; it involved a concrete manifestation. The kingdom coming near meant forgiveness of sin, healing of the sick, freeing of the demon-possessed and care and concern for the materially and physically poor, the oppressed and the outcast. It even meant the breaking down of old social barriers between Jew and Gentile, signalling the end of alienation and division within the human family (John 4:7–27). Not only was the good news of the kingdom an announcement of the reign of a just and merciful God, it was also a declaration of victory over the world and all of its sin, evil and injustice. To all who feel worn down by sin or suffering, by trial or tribulation, Christ proclaims the victory of his kingdom as a source of new hope: "take courage; I have overcome the world" (John 16:33). The evangel declares and demonstrates that this eschatological hope is not just a future hope, but also a present reality. In noting the movement from the messianic ministry of Jesus to its eschatological fulfilment in the Christian community, Walter Klaiber points out how the church is to carry on this mission:

> It lives this mission in its service to the sick, the helpless, the captive and the needy.... Evangelism befitting the gospel is evangelism in service of the invitation. It relieves those of whom too much is demanded. It liberates the captive. It heals the sick and worn down and gives new courage to those who have failed. But it does that not on its own authority, but rather in the name of Jesus. "Naming the name" is the most important function of evangelism in the context of the integral mission of the church.[2]

This is the essence of evangelism – 'naming the name' by proclaiming Christ's Lordship, extending the gospel invitation, and continuing Jesus' ministry by bringing deliverance, hope and liberty to a world dominated by sin. Biblical categories can distinguish, but do not separate (dualism) the physical and the spiritual, the inner and outer life. Christ's rule extends over every aspect of life; the Christian faith is comprehensive. His kingdom rule cannot be confined to inner piety but embraces all existence and brings life in all its fullness as indicated by our Lord in John 10:10, "I came that they may have life and have it abundantly." This being the case, we should expect to see our evangelistic efforts affecting the social and moral character of individuals, families, and society, indicating the visible presence of the kingdom.

Evangelism, when conceived in terms of the kingdom, is thus intimately related to eschatology –the direction of God's activity in history – which will ultimately be the new heaven and new earth. This narrative of God's activity reveals Christ's mission as the inauguration of a kingdom now within the reach of all those who will repent and believe the gospel. The work of evangelism then, at the very least, is inviting people to respond to the announcement of the kingdom in the terms laid out by the king. Regarding this kingdom, William J. Abraham is helpful:

"If this vision is correct then there is good news for the world; there is indeed a gospel worth sharing. Moreover, evangelism is an activity of the followers of Jesus that should be rooted and grounded in this dynamic, mysterious, numinous reality of the rule of God in history."[3]

In reformed thought, evangelism is history- and world-affirming; the gospel declares Christ's universal providential government and cosmos-renewing intentions.[4] Thus, we must repudiate all notions of evangelism that are intent on purely inward, pietistic concerns, seeking to escape from this world into heaven rather than seeking his kingdom coming "on earth as it is in heaven" (Matt. 6:10). Evangelism is not only about saving souls, but about declaring Christ's redemptive activity for the whole person – what he has done, is doing and will do. This declaration mirrors the three interrelated aspects of the kingdom that has come, is come, and will come. The all-encompassing nature of the kingdom means that in our confession and proclamation of Christ's Lordship, nothing is left out. David J. Bosch rightly points out that for the early church, "the idea of 'religion as a private affair,' of divorcing the 'spiritual' from the 'physical,' was an unthinkable attitude in light of the all-embracing nature of God's reign ushered in by Jesus."[5] The modern evangelical tendency to reduce evangelism to a form of 'eternal fire insurance marketing' seriously impoverishes our ability to capture a vision of the Messianic kingdom that the evangel is meant to announce and embody. Johannes Verkuyl also correctly emphasizes this comprehensive nature of the kingdom:

> God's goal in his mission is his messianic kingdom. The kingdom does not only address the spiritual and moral needs of a person, but his material, physical, social, cultural and political needs as well. For this reason Jesus came not only as one who preached but also as one who served (*diakonos*). He made the signs of that kingdom appear: the blind saw, the crippled walked, lepers were healed, the hungry had food to eat, and the lonely discovered they were no longer alone.[6]

This kingdom power at work in the life of believers does not end with love for God alone but embraces love for neighbour also. The love of neighbours proves love for God genuine (Rom. 13:8–10).[7] Yet, it would be a serious mistake to jettison or in any way minimize the proclamation of Christ's atoning work and his unequivocal call to repentance and faith, and attempt to replace it with the alleviation of some temporal physical need. This approach falls short of heralding the reign of Christ. Biblically, evangelism has an inescapable verbal dimension centred upon the Christian's witness to the truth of the gospel events that includes an invitation to obey the gospel, aimed at evoking a personal response from those to whom we speak. Only when the salvation and Lordship of Christ is acknowledged and the fruit of repentance is visible is it true that the kingdom has come and "salvation has come to this house," as demonstrated by Zacchaeus in Luke 19:2–9. To reduce our evangelistic outreach to sociopolitical engagement to meet the temporal needs of the disadvantaged is, according to J. Andrew Kirk:

> [T]o miss the very centre of the Christian faith. Evangelism is a visible witness to society concerning the core of all its basic problems: "It is what comes out of a person that defiles. For it is from within, from the human heart, that evil intentions come…" (Mark 7:20–1) – and the fundamental solution is God's grace and forgiveness, reconciliation and a new beginning. Evangelism also points to the reality of a transforming power beyond daily political life.[8]

Having previously criticized Kirk for his efforts to baptize Marx, on this point, he is right. Thus, every stratum of society needs, first and foremost, reconciliation with God. As made clear by Paul in 2 Corinthians 4:16–5:4, eternity is not defined by temporal concerns, but rather, it defines and establishes the significance of time. Thus, there is a non-dualistic priority of the eschatological future over temporal concerns in a fallen world that is under the wrath of God. The world is destined for destruction as well as renewal. So evangelism, understood in the light of the kingdom, must hold the proclamation and demonstration of the good news in dynamic tension, with temporal priority given to the eternal dimension in the biblical paradigm. These are not two separate components of evangelism (making known good news) that have an autonomous life of their own, but inseparable and interwoven aspects of the church's task in the world. To strive for political justice, the rights of the unborn, the falsely accused, or to give physical aid to the needy are clearly distinguishable, in principle, from proclaiming the redemption of Christ in the cross, but they cannot and must not be artificially separated. In the same way that faith without works is dead, so words without deeds are empty and deeds without words are mute. This does not mean that deed and word must always come together mechanically to be authentic, but rather that the believer's deeds and witness are to be consistent in every aspect of life. The preaching of a gospel of righteousness cannot be divorced from the practice of justice and righteousness. So, the church is to continue in the footsteps of the Lord, who is the fulfilment of all the law and prophets, in heralding his comprehensive kingdom rule and enlisting others to join the community which will reign with him. Bosch states:

> Evangelism, then, means enlisting people for the reign of God, liberating them from themselves, their sins, and their entanglements, so that they will be free for God and neighbour. It calls individuals to a life of openness, vulnerability, wholeness and love. To win people to Jesus is to win their allegiance to God's priorities.[9]

Bosch here appears very biblical. However, the critical issues must be addressed. We cannot leave these things vague and undefined. If evangelism is enlisting people for the reign of God, what does the reign of God look like? If we are to win people's allegiance to Jesus, what are God's priorities, how do we identify them and where do we find them? How do we go about winning people over to Christ's reign? These are the questions to which we now turn.

6.2   Evangelism, the Church and the Pursuit of Justice

Given that evangelism heralds a concrete, not an abstract kingdom, the role of the kingdom people who do the work of evangelistic outreach must not be abstract either. The church remains central to the task of evangelism and the pursuit of justice. There tends to be an artificial division in much thinking about the church and evangelism. Some see the church as the goal of kingdom outreach; evangelism is simply incorporating people into the church, which is seen as basically synonymous with the kingdom. Others view the church as an agent of the kingdom, emphasizing Christ's future reign. This distinction appears artificial when one considers that Christ offers himself both as the way and the destination (agent and goal). Christ is both the road home and home itself.

Therefore, as the body of Christ, with Christ as the head (Eph. 1:23), the church, in some sense, is both agent and end in evangelism as well. That is, the church (as a called-out people of the king) is also both the path (agent) and the destination (goal) because Christ, the husband, is returning for his spotless bride. The marriage supper, at the consummation of the Kingdom of God, will unite Christ's church in perfect unity to Christ and each other forever. That said, as St. Augustine saw, the church should not make the mistake of directly identifying the visible ecclesiae exclusively with the kingdom of God – his kingdom is more than a visible institution. Although it is presently imperfect, the church is a sign, instrument and manifestation of the kingdom, because Christ is amongst us, as celebrated particularly at the Eucharistic feast. For, as noted earlier, the kingdom can only be said to have truly come when Christ's claims are accepted and people willingly participate in the covenant life of God. Evangelism thus makes known that there is no salvation outside of unity with Christ in his body, the just church of the redeemed.

A proper emphasis on the church is very important because it can be tempting to take unbiblical refuge in the equivocal idea of *missio Dei* as a means of escaping the apologetic complexities and apparent embarrassment engendered by the failings of the church, thereby neatly bypassing God's chosen instrument of creation transformation (Col. 1:15–20). The *missio Dei* can be interpreted in sufficiently vague a fashion so as to obfuscate the purpose of the church in the world. Andrew Kirk admits that some theologies of mission are trying to bypass the church altogether, seeing rather God's 'direct' activity aside from the church as the key to mission. The result is that, by denying the ultimate distinction between the two 'seeds' and two 'cities' found in redemptive history, these theologies collapse the world and the church into one. Ultimately, they supplant the church and establish the world as the place of salvation through a gradual process of humanization – the creation of social conditions for human beings to flourish.[10] The church becomes peripheral, and increasingly irrelevant.[11] But, this is clearly erroneous. Kirk is insightful on this point:

> In the Pauline captivity letters (Ephesians and Colossians), the church is placed at the very heart of God's purpose to "gather up all things in Christ" (Eph. 1:10). It is said not only to be an instrument of the gospel, but part of the Gospel (Eph. 3:6). The reason for this is clear, if often forgotten: God's reconciling activity in Jesus Christ (2 Cor. 5:19) has as its goal not only individuals (Rom. 5:10–11) and the cosmos (Col. 1:20), but human beings with one another.[12]

The church as the covenant people is a justified and righteous social order that is part of the gospel and is therefore part of the announcement and embodiment of God's kingdom (Matt. 16:18). God's goal in establishing his messianic kingdom of justice is unveiled to the world in Christ and his church; these two cannot be separated, they are as indissoluble as marriage. Therefore, the *missio Dei* is without content unless it is interpreted as the *missio Christi*, and the *missio Christi* is realized and manifest through Christ's body by the *missio Ecclesiae*. This means that the church is a sacrament (sign) of salvation for the world when it displays God's imminent reign where righteousness, peace, reconciliation and new life are manifest. Here and now, when men and women turn to Christ, when evil and injustice are overcome, the 'gospel of the kingdom' breaks in and this happens most visibly in and through God's church.[13] Thus, the *missio Christi*, manifest by the new humanity in Christ, must have a deep concern for public justice,[14] since Christ's rule will hold sway over all things: "For he must reign until he has put all his enemies under his feet" (1 Cor. 15:25). As John Stott notes, "the church is meant to be the kingdom community, a model of what the human community looks like when it comes under the rule of God, and a challenging alternative to secular society."[15] This vision of God's mission has historically been recognized by large segments of the evangelical confessional church. However, the effect of the rise of various strands of liberalism and millennialism began to undermine the essential unity of the task of proclaiming and embodying the gospel of the kingdom, justification and justice together. This process has been called "The Great Reversal" by historian Timothy L. Smith regarding the changing attitude and approach of evangelicals toward issues of justice and compassion.[16] Stott identifies several primary factors triggering the change.[17] First, the blossoming of theological liberalism in the early twentieth century, which denied many orthodox tenets of faith, was marked by its concern for 'social action' or 'social justice.' However, the underlying theo-drama of liberalism posited a direct identification of the kingdom of God with the 'humanization' of the world into a utopia here and now. This was understandably intolerable to evangelicals, who reacted by defending the 'fundamentals' of the faith, and radually deemphasizing social action, which in the eighteenth and nineteenth centuries, under the likes of the Clapham Sect in England, and Jonathan Edwards and Charles Finney in America, had been a high priority. The second point which Stott notes was the parallel development of what was called the social gospel. This view, interpreting salvation purely as the regeneration of human relationships, advocated a form of 'Christianized communism,' seeing the kingdom as synonymous with the humanization of society in terms of their social theory. But as Stott notes concerning the kingdom:

> Without a new birth it is impossible to see it, let alone enter it. Those who do receive it like a child, however, find themselves members of a new community of the Messiah, which is called to exhibit the ideals of his rule in the world and so to present the world with an alternative social reality. This social challenge of the gospel of the kingdom is quite different from the social gospel.[18]

In a further relevant observation, Stott notes the popular spread of dispensational and pre-millennial eschatological schemes (over against the historic Puritan post-millennial view), through J.N. Darby and the Scofield Bible, which presented this world as beyond redemption, sinking into darkness until the coming of Christ and his literal millennial reign on earth. This led in many cases to an evangelical withdrawal from social and cultural engagement.

In an effort to respond to this reversal, in July 1974, at Lausanne, Switzerland, the International Congress on World Evangelization was held. Recognizing the need to address the question of the relationship between evangelism and social engagement, representatives from 150 nations endorsed the Lausanne Covenant. Sections four and five of this document dealt with the nature of evangelism and Christian social responsibility, declaring that both evangelism and socio-political involvement are part of our Christian duty. But, as Stott notes, it makes no attempt to relate them.[19] Stott optimistically referred to the congress as, "the turning point for the worldwide evangelical constituency."[20] The effect of Lausanne was still being felt in November 1996, when the National Assembly of Evangelicals drafted the Bournemouth Declaration which included the following conclusion: ``We recognize that no area of life is outside God's sovereign rule. We take the incarnation and transforming work of Christ as our model for engagement. We affirm our commitment to releasing Christian people for involvement at all levels of society."[21] Although Bosch rightly sees a danger in leaving these elements 'unrelated,' as though each has a life of its own when viewed as 'components' of mission,[22] there is at least an effort at Lausanne to reinforce the importance of both manifestations of the kingdom. What is missing is the genius of the thought of the Puritans to effectively relate these elements together in a seamless garment, knitted with exclusively biblical presuppositions.[23] So, if evangelism can be defined as the proclamation and manifestation of the 'gospel of the kingdom' in word and deed, then these two fruits of the kingdom cannot be separated, nor one set over against the other. They are theologically distinguishable, but interrelated and interconnected like grapes from the same vine, because Christ's kingdom is a total, comprehensive reign. Therefore, when justice is understood in kingdom terms, the church's pursuit of justice among human beings (love and justice for neighbour), as well as justification with God (love and justice for, and from God) will not detract from one or the other, but rather complement and reinforce each other. Notably, the actual proclamation of the evangel is then an act of justice in itself. For what does the call to repentance and faith mean if not justice for God, where he is truly given what is his due – love and worship with heart, mind, soul and strength? Likewise, when God's people seek justice for others, they are imitating their creator in seeking the right order of love – loving their neighbour as much as they love themselves.

6.3 Defining Justice and the Social Theory of the Kingdom

It is striking that the definition of 'justice' is so rarely addressed by theologians in the field of missiology, especially given that it is such a frequently discussed theme of the discipline. Few subjects are more popular in contemporary theological literature, even in evangelical seminaries today, than the theme of 'social justice' and the need to 'do justice' and transform laws and social order so that what are called 'structures of injustice' are not allowed to persist. All such arguments presuppose a standard of justice; obviously justice must rest upon some criterion or another. Yet for many 'Christians' writing on the subject, as open antinomians, the Bible, "cannot tell us what justice is or how we can exercise it." [24] This necessarily means that something other than God's word defines justice for them. In biblical faith, however, law and justice are inseparable. In society, when law does not express justice, it no longer commands respect and obedience. Society left without justice becomes suicidal, as Proverbs 8:36 makes clear concerning the wisdom of God's law: "he who fails to find me injures himself; all who hate me love death."

For Scripture, then, justice is quite literally a matter of life and death for any society. The social disaster of our age is that civil governments have abandoned true justice and separated law from justice. In fact, the view of many jurists today, is that neither law nor justice have anything to do with morality, let alone religion. In this view, law – and thereby our approximation of justice – is simply what the state enacts. The modern state has conflated positivistic law and justice, rendering justice merely an aspect of the state. This contemporary humanistic view means that justice is no longer basic to law and society by virtue of being a part of the fundamental order of things created by the sovereign God. Instead, justice is at best a social policy and so justice is what the state does. This serious error makes it all the more important that when Christians speak about justice, they have some idea what the biblical view is, and some understanding of how humanism has departed from the Christian view of justice. Clearly the meaning of justice must either be grounded in God or human beings as our referent. From the Christian standpoint either the justice of God or human imagination about justice will govern our social relationships.

Consequently, attempts to define justice apart from God's law lead quickly to rationalistic moral theories and relativism – laws are then merely social beliefs that have triumphed and have no connection with true justice. For biblical faith, justice is something that is revealed by God that is intrinsic to his character and nature. This revelation is found in distorted form in the human conscience and human traditions (Rom. 1:32; 2:14–16), but with clarity in God's law-word, supremely in the person of Christ – the only perfectly just man to walk the earth. Indeed, Paul tells us that in the gospel, "God's righteousness (justice) is revealed" (Rom. 1:17). Consequently, our concerns for 'justice' must be pursued from a Christian standpoint; and only if this is biblically rooted is God's righteousness being truly revealed in our gospel. Inevitably, the pursuit of justice takes many forms, personal, familial and societal, inescapably involving engagement with the polis (city or state) to see unjust laws, statutes and judgements that oppress, abuse and propagate injustice revoked and replaced with righteous laws and judgement. It is therefore obvious that the church must define the source of law and justice so that we might be able to identify and oppose injustice. Reformed and Puritan thinker the late Greg Bahnsen shows that this challenge has been basic to the life of the church from the beginning:

> As the early church formulated its creeds it simultaneously reformulated civil law. Such a correlation was inevitable since, against the ancient pagan tradition that located the source of authority and morality in the polis, orthodox Christian creedalism asserted the sovereignty of the creator over history and the incursion of the Messianic God-man into history. Thus the early creeds were a declaration concerning, not only theology proper, but eschatology and ethics; the course of history and the source of ethical authority were both found in the...ontological Trinity.[25]

This is a pivotal observation. The early churches' vision of 'social' justice (or rather public justice) brought them into conflict with the statist establishment of their day, because they proclaimed the Lordship of the messianic king over all things (including the imperial authority) and therefore rested the notion of justice and law upon the Christian creed.

Another way of speaking about social or public justice is social order, and social order, of necessity, is based on a social theory. Every social theory, Christian or not, has a creedal basis; that is, it presupposes some form of ultimate concern, a religious perspective. Behind every religious perspective is a god, whether 'incarnated' by the state or in Christ the Lord. The, foundation of social order is sovereignty. Sovereignty can be either transcendental or immanent, resting either in God or being an attribute of man and his order. Basically, the two conflicting concepts are between God's sovereignty and the claimed sovereignty of the state.[26] This is important because the ground on which we stand for justice, the means by which we pursue justice, the motive behind why we strive for justice and the end toward which the struggle tends, will determine whether it is consistent with the gospel. It is in facing these questions that contemporary missiology, in my opinion, has been woefully lacking in self-criticism.

In the Bible, the original meaning of the word justice is coextensive with righteousness, so they are interchangeable or related themes that often come together in the same verse (Ps. 33:5; Job 37:23). They are related terms because justice is an aspect of God's righteous character, as are mercy and compassion.[27]

In the Old Testament a 'just' person is simply a righteous person who does what is right in accordance with God's revealed law (Ezek. 18:5-9). Likewise, in the New Testament, the Greek word *dikaiosyne*, can be legitimately translated as 'righteousness' or 'justice.' Thus one could adequately translate Matthew 5:6 as referring to the blessed ones who hunger and thirst after 'justice'. Equally, Matthew 6:33, using the same word, exhorts us to seek first the kingdom of God and his 'justice' or 'righteousness.' The word clearly has both a vertical (God-oriented) and horizontal (people-oriented) dimension because it is tied to God's law. The common Hebrew term for justice, *mishpat* is found more than 200 times in the Old Testament, and its central meaning is rule of law: "You shall have the same rule (*mishpat*) for the sojourner and for the native, for I am the Lord your God" (Lev. 24:22). Justice here requires impartiality and due restitution irrespective of race, social status or creed; justice is to give people their due, be that punishment, protection or care. Consequently, the religious meaning of the term is inescapable. Even the Latin word *justus* from which we derive our English term justice literally means 'upright.' In the ancient world, justice likewise implied giving a person his or her due; if they have not received it, an injustice has occurred. According to Aristotle, justice could be understood in general terms of universal justice, encompassing the ideas of virtue, charity and morality, and also in terms of particular justice.

This had three basic elements, which, for the sake of discussion, remains a useful categorization: commercial justice is concerned with fairness and honesty in economic exchange; remedial justice is concerned with criminal and civil law; and distributive justice is concerned with apportioning goods and burdens among human beings.[28] In the Bible, God's law alone defines justice, righteousness, mercy and love, and deals with all these questions of remedial justice as well as economic exchange, distribution and charity. All these areas of righteousness or justice are important in Scripture and clearly address such contemporary problems in the West as violence (including the pandemic of sexual violence in pornography); exploitation through kidnapping and enslavement; poverty; the collapse of criminal justice; fatherlessness and the destruction of the family (leaving 'welfare orphans' and widows); rampant moral degeneracy; murder of the unborn; the legalization and normalization of homoeroticism and prostitution; and physician-assisted suicide and euthanasia (amongst many other social ills). In spite of this, many missiologists, when referring to the 'struggle for justice' almost always have a narrow distributive justice in mind. This distributive justice is usually called 'social justice.' Ronald Nash notes, "social justice is viewed as that species of distributive justice concerned with the distribution of burdens and benefits within society as a whole, a distribution that is usually controlled by political authorities." [29]

As we will see, the concept of social justice in these terms has little relationship to biblical justice. Social justice claims to be essentially democracy – the people's voice as God's voice – and involves a victimization mentality – blaming a bad environment or certain groups or classes within society for systemic injustice and inequality because of unjust social and political structures that are perpetuated by the powerful and oppressive. Typically in this vision, everyone has the alleged inalienable right (as a matter of 'justice') to equal access to land, resources, education, opportunity for betterment, marriage, a good job, adequate income as well as various social services, and increasingly a right to positive outcomes in all these endeavours. This ever-expanding litany of demands does not define justice but merely presents a modern doctrine of entitlements. It must be asked, for example, whatever the merits of universal education or social services, what this has to do with being just and giving a person what they are morally due in terms of Scripture or the 'rule of law.' Social theory and the Bible's material authority are critical issues here because a significant number of Christian thinkers calling for 'social justice' seem to ignore semantics and context in seeking out biblical proof texts to support their social theory; often failing to distinguish the different types of 'justice' the Scriptures are referring to. As Nash observes concerning the typical misuse of the Bible:

> Some of these verses refer not to distributive justice but to remedial justice. This is clearly true in the case of Exodus 23:6 which warns against depriving the poor man of justice but makes it obvious that the justice in view is that found in a court of law. [30]

Deuteronomy 16:19–20 instructs us concerning the role of judges: You shall not pervert justice. You shall not show partiality, and you shall not accept a bribe, for a bribe blinds the eyes of the wise and subverts the cause of the righteous. Justice, and only justice, you shall follow, that you may live and inherit the land that the Lord your God is giving you. Clearly what God requires of us is a strict obedience to his standard of justice and his standard only. Showing partiality to the rich or poor and the acceptance of bribes are attempts to pervert justice and are therefore all unacceptable because God requires the rule of his law, not our emotions or personal preferences, to govern us.

6.4 Bosch and Brueggemann: Banishment of the Law

The deep cleavage between various forms of socio-political deliverance through 'social justice' and, by contrast, a theological solution to the social consequences of sin through biblical law and gospel is extremely important. Here again the reformed and Puritan mind comes into conflict with contemporary missiology, which is almost entirely disinterested in the details of biblical law for informing questions of justice. The Puritans recognized that the only way to have justice and righteousness was to have it on God's terms. Perhaps their greatest achievement was their communitarian social order that emphasized the common good through corporate responsibility in caring for the poor and needy. In this social order, charity, employment creation and training were achieved through a personal and voluntary obedience to God's law, not by coercive government and its agencies. This view grew out of their covenant theology that recognized the requirements of God's law.[31] By contrast, one searches in vain among leading contemporary missiologists for a serious treatment of the details of God's law as it relates to justice; on the contrary, it is common for the law to be essentially overlooked or dismissed. For example, David Bosch, in his more than 500-page *Summa Missiologica, Transforming Mission: Paradigm Shifts in Theology of Mission*, a revered work of contemporary missiology, spends less than two pages considering Jesus' relationship to the Torah and the law's abiding relevance to the reign of God. Instead, the law is quickly de-emphasized and pushed to the periphery, "what happens...is that the law is pushed back in relation to God's reign...in Jesus' ministry people matter more than rules and rituals."[32] At the very least, Bosch here implies that the Old Covenant law is relatively unconcerned with people. But is it not the same eternal Word who revealed these laws to Moses that is manifest in Jesus Christ, who again spoke to Moses and Elijah in a cloud upon the mountain (Mark 9:2–8)? For Bosch, Jesus simply takes it upon himself to "abrogate the law, or at least certain elements of it."[33] Yet in Matthew 5:17–20, Jesus declares he has not come to abolish the law but fulfil it (lit. 'put into force'), stating that this law cannot pass away so long as heaven and earth remain. Bosch does not agree. In a

YOU SHALL NOT PERVERT JUSTICE...

rather superficial consideration of Jesus' attitude to the Sabbath, whilst not wanting to sound completely antinomian,

Bosch's essential view is that Jesus merely disregards regulations (as opposed to properly interpreting them) when love for people required him to do so.[34] For Bosch, in 'pushing back' the place of the law, the ministry of Jesus really gives us a "new criteria for inter-human relations."[35] This is a monumental statement with massive theological and social implications, yet he does not show us what this 'new criteria' is. Remarkably, he provides no biblical defence of his position. He then spends the next thirty pages considering forgiveness and solidarity with the poor. But without God's law, how can we understand the meaning of forgiveness or our relationship to poverty?

In a similar fashion, theologian and missiologist Walter Brueggemann sidesteps biblical law, though in a more sophisticated manner, by reducing the law of God to the fallible interpretative struggles of Old Covenant 'Yahwism.[36] It is not clear whether Brueggemann actually considers the Exodus 'tale' historically factual since it comes to us through what he calls "a process of tradition-building and liturgic re-enactment."[37] Thus, Israel's (that is Moses') vision of justice, "emerge[s] in and from this narrative."[38] For Brueggemann, Moses (not God, apparently) is the person who has the difficult work of transforming "the narrative vision of the Exodus into a sustainable social practice."[39] The Ten Commandments and Case Laws, rather than being a direct revelation of the divine moral character by the finger of God, constitute "an attempt to lay down policy lines that will preclude barbarism and nihilism."[40] Consequently for Brueggemann, the Torah is merely the Mosaic community's practical extrapolations from the Commandments which make use of "non-Israelite materials."[41] He claims that in this interpretative activity, "Israel's social vision was significantly compromised and toned down, in order to accommodate what we might call, 'social realism.'"[42] Since the law as given in Exodus 20–23 does not meet all Brueggemann's ethical expectations, he considers some of its provisions callused, further claiming that its economic and social structures made, in places, the disadvantaged into commodities.[43] Because of the selfish vested interests that he believes have crept into Old Testament law[44] and corrupted the narrative vision of the Exodus, concerning Deuteronomy (the book quoted most by Jesus) he comments, "For all of its compromise, this tradition of interpretation of the commandments retains much of the clarity and radicality of the Exodus."[45] Quite how Brueggemann's 'pick and mix' approach to biblical revelation is able to determine the original meaning of the Exodus and its social vision is unclear. What is evident is that Brueggemann has a particular hermeneutical approach to the Old Testament that is foreign to Jesus and the Apostles, for, far from questioning Moses, our Lord declared in John 5:46–47 that "If you believed Moses, you would believe me; for he wrote of me. But if you do not believe his writings, how will you believe my words?" (See also Mark 7:6–13; Luke 20:37–40; John 7:19, 23; 1 Tim. 1:7–11; 2 Tim. 3:16–17).

Despite his evident desire to read a, "radical notion of distributive practice"[46] into the now lost (supposedly historically unrecoverable) but original hope and Passover vision of Israel, it appears Brueggemann's distaste for the details of the revealed law of God lies in its social and economic 'pragmatism.[47] Likewise, the book of Proverbs – which he rightly sees as a practical explanation and application of the law of God that has much to say about wealth and poverty – is intolerably 'self-congratulatory' to Brueggemann because certain passages attribute the cause of some poverty to idleness, wilful ignorance or disobedience (Prov. 10:4, 11:25, 13:8, 23:21).[48] He feels at liberty to 'critique' this ethic, seeing the book of Proverbs not as the Word of God, but as a selfish ethical interpretation rooted in, "social experience...thought by its adherents to be a legitimated form of Yahwism."[49]

6.5 Generous Justice?

It is disappointing to then turn to ostensibly conservative, reformed churchmen and find the understanding of justice amongst some of them not much better. Timothy Keller, for example, in his confused and confusing work, *Generous Justice* (the title alone being a contradiction of Deuteronomy 16:18–20) ties himself in knots trying to relate biblical justice to a vision of 'social justice' he somehow feels obligated to defend. As a capable evangelist and evangelical pastor, it is discouraging to think that Keller seems to have become overanxious to please the current culture and sound trendy.[50] His book is a good example of what happens when well-meaning evangelicals fail to clearly define justice and righteousness in terms of obedience to the law of God and instead import present cultural fads into their interpretative exercise: they end up with a hybrid abstraction that in the name of being biblical, reads humanistic views of justice onto Christianity.

Keller starts badly by using a contemporary story, not Scripture, to set up his discussion and define justice: "Although both Heather and Mark were living comfortable, safe lives, they became concerned about the most vulnerable, poor, and marginalized members of our society, and they made long-term personal sacrifices in order to serve their interests, needs and cause. That is, according to the Bible, what it means to 'do justice'."[51] Really? Do we have specific biblical testimony to support the idea that this is the meaning of justice? Again he writes:

> To do justice means to live in a way that generates a strong community where human beings can flourish. Specifically however, to "do justice" means to go to places where the fabric of shalom has broken down, where the weaker members of societies are falling through the fabric, and to repair it. This happens when we concentrate on and meet the needs of the poor.[52]

Certainly God's law, amongst many other important things, requires us to help the poor as an aspect of a righteous life, but how is Keller's definition of justice supported by *mishpat* – the rule of God's law? Is this really an adequate description of justice?

Keller makes several critical mistakes that need to be addressed in some detail, as they are now common errors in the Christian community. First, he does not explicitly make justice and righteousness virtues that are clearly defined by God's law, and consequently, 'doing justice' is not consistently viewed as being concerned with obedience to the law of God. Secondly, a failure to presuppose the validity of biblical truth and a misunderstanding of common grace leads him into concepts of shared ideals, learning experiences and cooperation with non-Christian visions of justice that are totally unbiblical. This leads to the dangerous result that the 'fruit' of the gospel is interpreted as congruent only with his particular vision of social justice, which inadvertently pushes the door ajar to a redefinition of the gospel. First then, although paying lip service to the law of God as having, "some abiding validity that believers must carefully seek to reflect in their own lives and practices,"[53] Keller does not appear to take the statement seriously enough to apply it, because he himself is not sure how or what to apply. According to Keller, Christians are no longer under God's theocratic rule and since the church is not the state (which, contrary to Keller, actually wasn't the case even in Israel), there is 'massive change' in the application of God's standards; although exactly what these massive changes are (beyond the obvious that we are not Israelites in the Promised Land) he doesn't tell us.[54] He adequately describes the fulfilment in Christ of ceremonial or restorative shadows in the law that pointed to the cross or our separation to holiness, but then with rather contorted logic he writes, "[D]o we still have reason to believe that the civil laws of Moses, though not binding, still have some abiding validity? Yes."[55] But this is confusing. If they are not binding (required), how can they have abiding validity? Isn't the law here reduced to useful advice or helpful pointers that have 'some' value? He admits that the law of God is grounded in God's moral character and so, "we should be wary of simply saying, 'these things don't apply anymore,[56] and we must find some way of expressing these ideas in our present practice. Yet at the same time, according to Keller, nations are no longer bound to the law of God and the worship of the God of Scripture.[57] After these muddled caveats he goes on to cite some useful illustrations of Biblical law involving care for the poor (short-term debt, laws of release, charity etc.) and rightly notes that Scripture reveals obedience to God's law would virtually eliminate a permanent underclass.[58]

However, the biggest weaknesses in this part of his argument include his total failure to deal with the details and significance of tithing in the law of God for social welfare; his denial that gleaning laws were a form of charity; and his serious misuse of the law of Jubilee as allegedly, "relativizing private property."[59] His neglect of a proper treatment of the tithe in particular is very surprising, because the tithe is required by God in his law (Num. 18:28; 2 Chr. 31: 5–6; Mal. 3:10). Furthermore, it is a matter of justice, because tithing is giving God his due. Not to tithe is explicitly described as theft from God and is thus a form of injustice (Mal. 3: 8–12; Mark 12:14–17; Matt. 23:23). By failing to give God his due, people are also robbed of blessing because the use of the tithe included education and meeting the needs of the poor (Deut. 14:28–29; 26:12; 33:8–10). As Ray R. Sutton has pointed out with respect to Keller's neglect of the law, "those who appear to be so much in favour of helping the poor abandon the most obvious Scriptural advice when they reject the application of the entire Bible."[60] The end result of Keller's pages on the law of God is decidedly odd to say the least. The flow of logic might be accurately summarised like this:

a) We are not under a theocracy, so biblical law doesn't bind us.
b) God's law reflects God's character, so it must have abiding validity [does bind us?].
c) Some of it is still valid somehow (no criteria offered).
d) When applied, God's law actually worked (in Israel).
e) However, we are not in covenant with God in our nations today, so we can't apply what worked for the nation of Israel.
f) All is not lost however. The goal of some biblical laws was to eliminate permanent, systemic poverty. Taking the ends but not the means of biblical law, we can still pursue that goal today.

What happens then is that the 'great care'[61] to apply God's law that has 'some abiding validity' becomes (perhaps inadvertently) an exercise in abstraction. Justice is abstracted from biblical law as though means and ends are not intimately related and appointed by God, and so abstracted ideas or principles can then be re-imagined and applied in place of biblical law. It is certainly true that detailed exegesis is needed in interpreting the law of God – there have been changes in administration since the Promised Land of the Israelites, but not changes in substance. To use biblical law as essentially a 'resource' for ideas that sound useable and pliable for a chosen end, rather than as the binding Word of God is simply unfaithfulness. Biblical law and justice are no more separable as means to the end, than the preaching of the gospel is separable as means from the end of the salvation of sinners. To bypass the details of gospel truth and proclamation (as some missiologists do today) by simply arguing that God's goal is the salvation of sinners so the principle of universalism is as good an idea as biblical exclusivism and far easier than preaching Christ in our pluralistic culture, (since it results in the same end) is likewise faithlessness that denies that God appoints means as well as ends.

   Keller's approach to the law is like the strategy of Formalist and Hypocrisy, two characters in Bunyan's *Pilgrim's Progress*, who attempt to take a shortcut and climb over the wall onto the path to Zion rather than going God's ordained way through the gate. When asked by Christian why they did not enter by the gate, they use human 'custom' or tradition as their excuse; yet the gate was God's only appointed means of entry to the blessings of Zion. Keller appears to be looking for a shortcut over the wall onto the path that leads to justice, a compromise with the world's customs or visions of justice in this regard, without the necessity of entering via the gate to justice in God's law. He wants the destination, but like many missiologists today, is not sure about the route. God's law lays out for us the way of love or charity (Rom. 13:10), the way of righteousness (Ps. 119), mercy and justice (Matt. 23:23). We must go to the whole of God's law in both testaments to understand all of these requirements. The righteous man or woman lives a life that is the opposite of lawlessness. He will obey the Ten Commandments, he will tithe (including the poor tithe), he will seek the welfare of the fatherless and widow, and pursue justice in the courts and much besides – this is what the righteous or just man or woman will do. But Keller, like most contemporary missiologists, because of a neglect of the whole law of God, tends to collapse all of these virtues into a sharp focus on the idea of a redistributive transfer of wealth and simply call it 'justice.'[62] He suggests that, "the Bible does not say precisely how that redistribution should be carried out"[63] (though he doesn't seem to doubt Scripture teaches it should be carried out) and he deliberately refuses to rule out the liberal policy of state-sanctioned coercion, suggesting one can find support for this in the Bible[64] – in fact he appears to support the idea.[65] Although he notes family breakdown in passing (identifying it as a 'conservative' argument regarding poverty) and some other social ills, he offers no serious treatment of many pressing issues of righteousness and justice today. He has space to speak of the civil rights movement and race relations as they relate to poverty,[66] but there is no discussion of abortion (a modern pogrom), or sexual slavery and pornography (except in passing as evidence of 'structures' of inequality), or crime and violence, or the prison system or capital punishment on their own terms. There is no treatment of the unjust political assault against the family or the high-handed imposition of homosexual indoctrination and other perversions on young children in schools. The sole factor is economic relations and poverty, which implies (whether he wants it to or not) that most social problems are essentially by-products of economic inequality. In one of his most strained statements, Keller even suggests that at the centre of the Mosaic legislation was the 'principle of equality.'[67] Considering this statement in the light of the biblical text, there can be no response but to state that this is sheer nonsense. At this point he seems quite intent on not upsetting his secular readers at all.

Thus, despite recognizing that true righteousness is broader than poverty relief, Keller nonetheless spends the bulk of his book discussing redistributive ideas of justice – redirecting resources from the haves, to the have-nots. Why? Because justice is, according to Keller, "one of the main things [God] does in the world. He identifies with the powerless, he takes up their cause." [68] But is that the meaning of God's justice, or in fact the borrowed language of cultural Marxism and liberation theology? In my view, this is not only an inaccurate definition of justice, it is a dangerous one. What specifically is the 'cause' of the nameless powerless or poor? And is the designation 'powerless' anything more than an abstraction used to promote class warfare? Keller doesn't really tell us – this is simply the nomenclature of leftist missiology.

Because poorer people are often without the social status or influence that money can offer, they can be more readily deprived of justice in the courts and political realm (for example they can't offer bribes or hire top lawyers) and so the Bible frequently refers to poorer people (not some abstract proletariat) as those at greatest risk of oppression, especially the orphan and widow, since their weakness (by virtue of being without a provider and protector in the figure of a father and husband) might be taken advantage of. Any injustice perpetrated against people because of their disadvantaged state is abhorrent to God; we are to give special attention to ensure the rule of law (*mishpat*) for all such vulnerable ones and oppose all injustice; we are to show mercy and compassion and open our hearts to them according to God's law. But this surely does not mean God takes up every 'cause' of marginalized (powerless) groups, or those on low incomes; surely powerlessness or poverty does not make a person's (or group of persons') cause just or righteous by definition? In Scripture, there is no inherent righteousness in poverty or powerlessness or the cause of those in such a condition. Keller is playing with fire with his definition of justice, because the cultural Marxism of our age says there is 'righteousness' inherent in the cause of the 'powerlessness' or poor that justifies revolutionary action. For them, justice is equalization, described as 'fairness.' Hence, the only qualification for special treatment in our society is proving that you are a part of a powerless victim group; women, the poor or low income earners, aboriginals, blacks, gays, transvestites, Muslims, atheists, prostitutes, members of former European colonies, and so on. Today, acquiring the status of a 'victim' can provide disproportionate influence and power as new 'histories of oppression' are told and retold. These alleged histories become ideas charged with power, being put to political use to create guilt. This creation of collective guilt laid upon 'society' makes the causes or objectives of all such groups (equality, wealth transfers, more Mosques, marriage licenses and adoption rights, brothels in homes etc.) a matter of 'justice' and 'liberation' and the price for society's absolution is reparations of some sort – be it affirmative action, payments, tax advantages or some other social privilege. The point being, is God's taking up a particular cause not qualified by the nature of the cause of the powerless or the poor? Which causes are legitimate and which are not? Keller simply fails to grapple with this seriously. For example, if I am a homosexual and part of a small, powerless and marginal group of activists seeking to redefine marriage and the social order, does God take up my cause as a matter of justice? According to emergent church author Peggy Campolo (wife of noted 'evangelical' Tony Campolo who glowingly endorses a recent emergent church offering, *The Justice Project*), God does indeed take up the cause of homosexuals as powerless victims of injustice. She cites the case of two homosexual men disallowed from adopting children in their U.S. state. She writes, "*justice* is denied this very special family because legally these two parents cannot be married to each other...justice requires that we find a way to respect and affirm the rights of...those families created by the marriages of God's GLBT children"[69] Leaving aside the shamelessly anti-biblical nature of her statement,[70] we should notice that she frames the matter as a justice issue because the same definition of justice is at work – identifying with the cause of the powerless.

As a relevant aside, it should be noted that there is nothing 'original' about Campolo's position on this, although many self-styled Christian intellectuals in her vein like to think they are ground-breaking thinkers. Back in the mid-eighteenth through early nineteenth century, the British deistic philosopher Jeremy Bentham was equally concerned to subject biblical law to critical evaluation based on his vision of reason and justice. In his work, *Not Paul But Jesus*, he argued that not everything in the Bible was the word of God, and tried to drive a wedge between the apostle and Christ.[71] Only the teaching of Jesus had to be taken seriously (an early 'red letter Christian'). He wrote a manuscript on the subject of homosexuality that wasn't published until 1978 because of the social unacceptability of homosexual behaviour until the late twentieth century. In his view it was unjust to censure homosexual acts because he didn't think it was any threat to society.[72] He even argued that the sin of Sodom was not homosexuality as such, but a lack of hospitality to strangers;[73] there is nothing new under the sun. Campolo's views, whether she realizes it or not, are just the recycled ideas of eighteenth-century deists attacking the authority of Scripture. The only difference being, they were too embarrassed to publish their views on homosexuality at the time.[74]

Taking another example, consider theft. If I am poor and plan to steal from those who have more than me, whether by burglary or the long arm of the state, will God take up my cause? Scripture teaches that God takes up the cause of the righteous, whether they are rich or poor, president or ploughman (Prov. 3:33; 10:24–25; 11:8; Ps. 9:7–8; 18:20; 34:15–16; 37:25–33, 37–40). He certainly pleads the cause of the poor when their poverty means they are deprived of their due (justice), but God does not plead a man's cause simply because he is without wealth or power. Such an idea is ridiculous because the poor are perfectly capable of oppressing the poor, "a poor man who oppresses the poor is a beating rain that leaves no food" (Prov. 28:3). If a poor man oppresses a poor man, whose side does God take? Is he left with an insoluble ethical dilemma because unjust structures led the poor to steal from the poor? Surely not; God takes up the cause of the righteous. If a poor man's lack of wealth deprives him of access to justice in his case, God takes up his cause according to the Bible. But the judge can show no partiality in hearing the case of the poor or powerless. The concern of God's word is with impartial justice and with righteousness. Nowhere does God permit partiality in men's dealings with men based on their economic status; such an attitude is a perversion of justice. This is precisely why Keller's anti-biblical vision of unconditional and coerced charity is mythological and dangerous. As Ray Sutton points out:

> If we support those who have become poor through their own immoral behaviour, then we are subsidizing evil. God does not call us to support evil. Satan does, however; such charity expands his kingdom at the expense of God's. We should resist his temptation. There can never be unconditional charity in a world of scarcity. To give charity to one person is to deny it to another. There can be no neutrality. The myth of neutrality undergirds the reality of the modern welfare state: compulsory wealth-redistribution.[75]

The second problem that emerges in *Generous Justice* is Keller's weak vision of Christian apologetics and the attendant misunderstanding of common grace that leads him to conclude non-Christians share much in common with believers in matters of justice, so that Christians can learn from non-believers regarding how to be just. He rightly recognizes that faith commitments and assumptions lie behind all visions of justice, but suggests, "...our ideas of justice are rooted in views of life that are non-provable faith assumptions."[76] This denial of an effective proof for Christianity implicitly weakens the Christians' confidence that they are in possession, by grace, of God's authoritative revelation with regard to the truth about justice. Rather than reducing Christianity to an appealing or most 'probable' choice amongst various views of life, the Christian claim must be that without the God of the Bible and his infallible word, there is no possibility of ever knowing what justice is for anyone. Indeed without this God, there is no proof of anything. Thus Christianity is established by the impossibility of the contrary – this is known as a transcendental argument.[77] If we are left wrestling with various concepts of justice without a clear proof for the validity of one or the other, then the best that Christians can hope for is a seat at the relativistic table of our culture, and hope that the biggest members sat around will not finally pull our seat from under us. The popular discursive language of having, 'a seat at the table,' sounds humble at first blush, but we must not forget that Christ doesn't ask for a seat at the table – he owns the table!

Without this conviction of Christ's absolute Lordship, compromise of God's word is cast as humility and a watered-down vision of justice becomes good enough. Keller writes, "Believers have many of the criteria for a righteous and just life laid out in the Bible. How easy it would be to disdain all non-Christian accounts of justice as being useless.... Christians' own theology should lead them to appreciate the competing views of justice...because they know from the Bible that they are all partly right."[78] Keller then outlines secular schools of thought that emphasize rights, virtue or the common good and says that according to the Bible all of these are crucial aspects of justice. But in all this Keller apparently does not grasp the significance of the problem of criterion. He says believers have many (but not all?) of the needed criteria for righteousness and justice in the Bible. In expressing it this way, he appears to be judging Scripture based on a wider, unnamed criterion, so that Scripture is contributing to a bigger picture of justice, rather than authoritatively prescribing a binding vision that cannot be enriched by other insights.

Furthermore, we are forced to ask, how is it possible for non-Christian accounts of justice (righteousness) to be 'partly right,' never mind partly right according to the Bible? It must be said that Keller is simply talking nonsense here. Moral principles and laws are either 'just' or 'unjust.' Moral actions are either 'righteous' or 'unrighteous,' they cannot be partly just or partly righteous. Just because utilitarians speak of the 'common good,' liberals of 'individual rights' and conservatives of 'virtue' – themes that are covered in Scripture, this in no way implies they are 'partly right.' One is only begging the question until we ask what constitutes or defines the common good, rights and virtue. The utilitarian's moral arithmetic is a far cry from the requirements of God's law; as are the panoply of human rights demanded by liberals in our day and the conservative humanist's vision of virtue. Keller should simply know better here. Scripture does not give us any ground to take social utility, man-made rights and humanistic visions of virtue as insightful and instructive lessons, or to inform the Biblical vision of justice and righteousness. Doubtless, Keller writes this way because he is anxious for Christians to make common cause with their fellow citizens who hold competing visions of justice; but he neglects to mention that these visions emerge from a fallen world, rebellious reasoning, and man's seared conscience. Far from suggesting sinful man is 'partly right' about righteousness and justice, God's word declares, "Those who forsake the law praise the wicked, but those who keep the law strive against them. Evil men do not understand justice, but those who seek the Lord understand it completely" (Prov. 28:4–5). A Christian in possession of God's word and the gift of the Holy Spirit can understand justice completely according to the Bible; they need no lessons from the wisdom of the world. But those who neglect and reject the law of God praise wickedness. This reality is taught throughout Scripture. As our culture has departed steadily from the law of God, our society increasingly praises evil and wickedness as God's word leads us to expect (Is. 5:20; Rom. 1:18–32). Keller's strategy to justify his position and avoid this problem is to appeal to 'the light of nature' or 'common grace' which he claims, "provides the basis for Christians to cooperate with, and learn from, non-Christians."[79] He quotes Ken Myers approvingly, saying that, "When Christians articulate cultural values, they should be values that non-Christians can embrace as well...because we have expressed values which are in fact common values." [80] This is a complete misunderstanding of the doctrine of common grace. First, there is no such thing as 'the light of nature.' Nature is a personification here – God alone is light and he makes aspects of his character and nature known by his creative and providential work (Ps. 36:9; Ps. 19). The common grace of God is also at work in the world in sending rain on the just and unjust, and making bountiful provision for human beings who do not deserve it (Matt. 5:45). All peoples can pursue arts and sciences, write plays, and compose beautiful music, because of common grace (they are God's creatures in God's world). Furthermore, despite our depravity and sin and although the thoughts and imaginations of our hearts are evil (Gen. 6:5; Ps. 53:2–3; Rom. 3:10), by the grace of God, we still know how to give good gifts to our children (Matt. 7:11). All men are not as evil as they could be because of the common grace of God at work in people's lives. By the grace of God, fallen man is not permitted to live in complete consistency with the principle of evil that is at work in his being because of sin. Critically, common grace also means we do know what is right (Rom. 1:19–20; 2:12–15). None of this is in dispute. But the whole biblical worldview makes clear that this revelation is enough only to leave humanity guilty and without excuse before God, but not sufficient to make us righteous (or just). It is not that man does not know what is righteous, he just doesn't practice it without the transforming power of the gospel (Rom. 7:18–24). In moral rebellion against the justice of God, we suppress the truth in unrighteousness (Rom. 1:18). Indeed, even when sinful man appears to do what is right by his actions, it is with the wrong motives, and not directed to love and glorify God, who is the foundation of all justice. Paul declares that it is simply impossible for unregenerate man to truly pursue righteousness and justice; indeed, none does what is good, not one (Rom. 3:10–12).

Keller has argued rightly that justice and righteousness are co-extensive (this is critical), yet now he wants to say that the unregenerate with their visions of justice can be 'partly righteous' or 'partly just.' This is in flagrant contradiction to the word of God, "For the mind that is set on the flesh is hostile to God, for it does not submit to God's law; indeed it cannot. Those who are in the flesh cannot please God" (Rom. 8:7–8). This is unambiguous and categorical. Sinful man cannot truly do justice (righteousness) because he cannot submit to God's law! This is the very foundation of the gospel. Only Christ can make us just in order that the, "righteousness requirement of the law might be fulfilled in us" (Rom. 8:4). None of this means that Christians and non-Christians cannot cooperate on social projects, or work to a common purpose to end prostitution in an area, or find housing for the homeless, or rescue girls sold into sexual slavery, or save the local parkland for children – we can and should do those very things. But not because we share 'values' that non-believers can embrace as well (for that is increasingly not the case as Christianity has faded); not because humanistic visions of justice are 'partly right' as far as they go; and not because we can learn more about what justice is from non-believers' competing visions of justice. We do it because God requires it; we do it to glorify him by letting our light shine before men; we do it because of the love of God and neighbour. Certainly we cannot restrict ourselves to articulating values that the non-believer can agree with because at bottom, there are no neutral values, we don't ultimately agree about anything, "for what partnership has righteousness with lawlessness? Or what fellowship has light with darkness" (2 Cor. 6:14). According to Paul in this text, true justice is doing what the law requires, but the unregenerate man in his heart, "does not submit to God's law" (Rom. 8:7). Scratch the surface of any social activist and you will soon discover, if they are not Christians, that the values which drive them are far from biblical. We don't need to share the same values or even goals to respectfully cooperate on many issues. In the Houses of Parliament or Congress parties can be completely at odds with each other's values but still have the House function properly and harmoniously. We need to rid ourselves of the notion that working with unbelievers requires or implies shared visions of righteousness. We are to be salt and light in the world (Matt. 5:13–16), and when a given social project or endeavour has an end congruent with God's word, using means that do not violate God's word, we can participate gladly. We are to work to conform all of life to the word of God and his law, so that increasingly, the laws and structures of our social order reflect the law of God, and the influence of the gospel changes our communities.

Keller's arguments, in the sincere desire to see Christians meaningfully and generously contribute to social well-being, are pragmatic and not theological, so what emerges is a knotted mess. He seems so concerned to appease non- Christian readers that biblical truth is compromised.[81] We see then that Keller's ill-conceived definitions of justice inadvertently lead to an implicit denial of the Bible and the gospel (an outcome he certainly does not want). In fact Keller's idea of 'generous justice' leads him to a redefinition of the very marks of a true believer, "A life poured out in doing justice for the poor is the inevitable sign of any real, true gospel faith."[82] Although helping the poor is certainly an important part of the Christian's calling, it is not 'the inevitable sign' according to Scripture. St. Paul states:

> Therefore, since we have been justified by faith we have peace with God through our Lord Jesus Christ. Through him we have also obtained access by faith into this grace in which we stand, and we rejoice in hope of the glory of God...because God's love has been poured into our hearts through the Holy Spirit who has been given to us (Rom. 5:1–5).

The first mark of true gospel faith is peace with God, hope and the gift of the Holy Spirit. The fruit of this inner working of love, hope and peace, is obedience. Thus, the apostle John says, "And by this we know that we have come to know him, if we keep his commandments. Whoever says, "I know him" but does not keep his commandments is a liar, and the truth is not in him, but whoever keeps his word, in him truly the love of God is perfected" (1 John 2:3-5). Peace with God and keeping his word are therefore the inevitable signs of a true believer. One aspect of keeping of God's commandments will be mercy, manifest in part by a concern and care for the poor.

In short, Keller overstates the soteriological centrality of identification with the poor or powerless and consequently comes dangerously close to liberation theology in his account of the true marks of faith. Commenting on the thought of liberation theologian Paul Knitter, Diane B. Obenchain writes:

> [R]eligion that does not seek to remove poverty and oppression "is not authentic religion." Like Hick, Knitter affirms that "from their ethical, soteriological fruits we shall know them." In other words, we can judge whether and to what degree a religion is salvific by the degree those of a religion actually work to remove social injustice. Knitter affirms further that recognizing liberation from social injustice as the center for the evaluation of religions is the first step toward dialogue among the religions. Moreover, that dialogue has a mission... the encounter of one religion with another is an opportunity for self-critique and correction, moving a religion in the direction of "the

mystery of Soteria" and thus the centrality of practice over doctrine.[83]

Whilst I do not think Keller's desire to help the poor or to learn from 'other visions of justice' is motivated by this kind of pluralism, he appears muddled and is creating confusion. The reason for this confusion is that, in wanting to make identification with the cause of the poor and powerless the essential fruit of being a Christian and the benchmark for doing justice, "all the various views of justice out there in our society" are then perceived as, "partly right,"[84] or simply, "incomplete,"[85] as opposed to being actually wrong or an expression of *injustice*. On Keller's definition of justice, this is logical; after all, lots of people are trying to help the poor by various means, or express solidarity with those deemed disenfranchised or powerless, and on Keller's reasoning must be practicing 'righteousness' or 'doing justice.' The same is true of pursuing 'human rights' or rallying around belief in the lowest common denominator principle of 'human dignity' – many people claim to believe in these things, yet in reality they are not even able to agree on what a human being is nor when life begins! Now, biblically, and contrary to Keller, justice and righteousness are what God's law declares them to be, and nothing else. Justice is inseparable from righteousness and law, and these are inseparable in the Christian worldview from the covenant. This is the point that Keller – and contemporary missiology for the most part – misses. In Scripture the covenant law represents the righteousness of God. Without this law there can be no mercy, because there would be no justice. Mercy to the sinner, the poor and oppressed, the downtrodden and destitute is not antinomian, it is an aspect of God's righteousness because it is central to his law, as Jesus makes clear (Matt. 23:23). It was an act of mercy that God gave his law to his people. For fallen people in a fallen world, to receive God's law is an act of mercy and redemption. Mercy is basic to the law because the essence of God's justice is restitution, the restoration of his order and purposes for creation. God's mission is to restore all things to their original beauty and goodness; since this is the goal of his justice, salvation, mercy, and compassion are a necessary part of it. If righteousness is to reign over the world, redemption and mercy are necessary. Thus the righteousness of God's law must reign in the Christian life (Isa. 1:17). Justice is part of God's covenant faithfulness, and salvation is his covenant act. In response to this mercy, we obey his covenant law and show mercy. We simply cannot separate justice or mercy from the word of God.

Thus, in the end, it is only regenerate men and women who truly know the meaning of justice, and are able to lead the way on the path of righteousness in our world. Justice is only done when God's law is obeyed because justice is the restoration of God's order and righteousness is obedience to his word. Thus for justice to be done in society requires the diffusing of the gospel and regenerate men and women engaged in every area of life and thought from biblical principles, for the glory of God. It requires whole communities and cultures to come under the hearing of the gospel and glad obedience to God's law, so that justice is made manifest. Some will clearly only obey God's law outwardly in such a society, and not as a matter of the heart (true righteousness); some are to be restrained from wickedness (crime) by the law of God against their will; some will rejoice in the law of the Lord, reviving the soul (Ps. 19:7).

But only when God's commandments are seen as the bulwark of justice and righteousness will justice be done for the poor or anyone else. When justice is truly concerned with God's righteous law in all Scripture, poverty is not the defining issue Keller makes it, neither is poverty seen as the worst thing to befall a person, "Better is a poor man who walks in his integrity than a rich man who is crooked in his ways" (Prov. 28:6). What matters most is integrity before God and a righteous life. On the other hand, if Keller's definition of justice is correct how can the poor themselves live righteously and 'do justice,' since they have no wealth to distribute? If justice is primarily about economic redistribution, how can the poor be just beyond political agitation for themselves? The Bible tells us it is by the gospel we are made rich in God, whatever our social or economic status (2 Cor. 8:9). In fact, the apostle Paul spoke of his own physical and economic poverty in the service of the gospel, as "making many rich," for though Christians face economic hardship, as having nothing, we yet possess everything (2 Cor. 6:10). For St. Paul covetousness is a snare (1 Tim. 6:9), but, "there is great gain in godliness with contentment, for we brought nothing into the world, and we cannot take anything out of the world" (1 Tim. 6:7). In addition, the biblical answer to man's powerlessness is not social liberation and transfers of wealth; a man may be wealthy and exceedingly influential, yet impotent in life (just look at our celebrity culture). The end result of all rebellion against God is frustration and powerlessness. There is only one true source of power, "you will receive power when the Holy

Spirit has come upon you" (Acts 1:8). Rich or poor we can be, "clothed with power from on high" (Luke 24:49), because, "God gave us a Spirit not of fear but of power and love and self-control" (2 Tim. 1:7). When Christians preach Christ as the deliverer and the Holy Spirit as our source of life and power, when we live these realities out in our lives, it will be clearly seen that, "the darkness is passing away and the true light is already shining" (1 John 2:8).

6.6 Charity, Justice and the State

With some warrant then, today's predominant missiological vision in the churches, could be perceived to be a project of the Christian Left, with its emphasis on a social theory and legislation that is deeply influenced by modernism, Marxist Liberation Theology and often indebted to the 'social gospel,' popular in the late nineteenth and early twentieth century. Of this movement, whilst noting the appropriate challenge the social gospel brought to pietists lacking genuine engagement with these issues, Verkuyl is rightly critical, "both in theology and in practice, the social gospel was far too optimistic. It paired the Kingdom of God with a belief in progress derived more from the enlightenment than from the gospel itself...the social Gospel disregarded the eschatological dimensions of the kingdom."[86] With this conclusion the Puritan mind would agree:

> Modernism's characteristic message is the social gospel and social action. Modernism is the statist theology of contemporary man. Its gospel...is that the state has an answer to all man's problems. Whether it be a burden of body or soul, poverty, cultural deprivation, mental health, disease, ignorance, family problems and all things else, the state has a program and a plan of salvation.[87]

Drinking deeply from contemporary missiological themes, some 'emergent church' writers put forward a very similar utopian vision.[88] Most missiologists see true social justice as requiring a coercive salvation through the powers of state to bring about the ideal order. For example, Dave Diewert, former professor at Regent College, in seeking biblical warrant for this kind of statism argues that a Deuteronomic vision of justice would require a mandatory redistribution. Indeed, he argues charity is a bi-product of injustice and should be effectively abolished by government action:

> Justice is not the same thing as charity. Charity can be practiced while

structures of inequality are maintained; in fact charity is dependent on such inequality for its very existence. Charity is a way to manage social problems without a necessary commitment or strategy to eradicate them...it does not address the social, political and economic structures of inequality and exclusion that...keep them in that state of deprivation. Justice is precisely about political and economic arrangements of power that ensure access to material and social resources for all members of the society...to live justly is to engage in the work necessary to establish and maintain just social, political and economic arrangements... political leaders and those with economic and social power must consider the lives of the needy...and it is the people who must press, provoke, challenge and impel them to ensure that this kind of justice is actualized.[89]

The velvet glove of Keller quite logically gives way here to Diewert's iron-fisted state coercion in redistribution, giving a messianic role to the state and totally distorting the biblical message. First, Diewert appears to set up a radical and unbiblical dichotomy between charity (or love) and doing justice, so that charity is not part of a righteous order and thus love, by implication, is not, 'the fulfilling of the law' (contradicting St. Paul in Romans 13:10), a law which included the requirement of generous charitable giving![90] Statists invariably dislike charity because it produces a form of rival government to the state. Second, almost every problem is seen as an aspect of the failure of public policy and therefore must have a statist solution – social problems can all be dealt with by the right political structures which the people must impel governments to enforce. Individual and familial sin, personal irresponsibility and the realities of a fallen world appear to play a minimal, if any, role in Diewert's utopian thinking. Instead all social problems are due to man's environment and his salvation will come when the state transforms the human environment by social planning and statute law. The logical implication of Diewert's view is that personal charity itself becomes a participant in sin because it supposedly manifests and reinforces inequalities in the society where it functions. The non-biblical idea of 'equalization' (removal of all inequalities) has become the normative principle; justice here means 'equality,' rather than the biblical concept of rendering all their due (rule of law) with kindness and charity as an equally important aspect of God's righteous law. Consequently, Diewert sees coercive redistribution as a manifestation, indeed a requirement, of the kingdom of God.[91] Such statements lend weight to Rushdoony's contention:

> The goal of politics today is messianic: its purpose is paradise regained, a perfect world order by means of law and technology. Man's problem is not seen as sin but as a backward environment... statist theology sees all problems answered by statist action; the goal of all men of good will must therefore be social legislation.[92]

No doubt many intellectuals like Diewert have good intentions and noble motives, and genuinely believe that the spirit of revolution through a 'benevolent' coercive order will bring about greater 'justice' in society. But this is the myth that all modern revolutionaries have believed, and what begins with noble intentions for 'liberation' (not liberty – an important distinction since this liberation involves state sanctioned robbery) finishes in a police state. For the Christian, the bottom line cannot be good intentions but must be the law of God. As David Chilton correctly observes, "If, in the name of 'love for the poor', I transgress God's law by supporting legal plunder of my rich neighbour to fund a poverty program, I am not really loving, regardless of my profession; for love is always concerned to fulfil the law of God."[93] Chilton's point here leads to an important question. By what moral principle do the state's welfare 'programs' take from one person and give to another? If it is claimed this is done on the basis of justice, then it is, by definition, immoral or sinful to have more than someone else. If this is a moral principle of justice, then what prevents any form of stealing from those who have more than I do from being ethically valid? At the very least, such a view leads to the necessary enforcement of these principles of 'justice' by the powers of state.

We see then that without obedience to God as the priority, man's good intentions result in the multiplication of coercive laws that rob people of their God-given liberties by a state in pursuit of ever increasing power. As one contemporary Puritan has put it:

> The number of laws given to us in the Torah is limited, 613 by rabbinic reckoning, fewer by Christian counts. Again, these laws are mainly enforceable by God, not by man. Those that can be enforced by man are, for the most part, placed in the hands of the family, the specifically religious agency, or the state. They do not empower any institution or agency to control man and life. The primary solution to problems is not by means of coercion, revolution, or punishment

but by means of regeneration. Force is not abolished, because it is needed in a fallen world, but it is limited. A culture that relies on force to maintain itself is already in a process of decay and dissolution. A civilization is constructed on the premises of a religious faith, and it wanes when the faith wanes.... When men play god, they are unable to regenerate any man. They cannot by their fiat will make of any man a new creation. They must rather rely on compulsion, from compulsory education to strict controls on every man. The state seeks to recreate man by means of coercion...George Orwell in the novel *Nineteen-Eighty Four* saw the end of the state's power as the naked exhibition of total power, a boot stamping on a human face forever.[94]

Thus, one cannot justify covetousness, theft and coercion in the name of relief of poverty; it is still tyranny, regardless of the language of 'social justice' used to dress it up. Having said that, the overwhelming concern for true justice in God's law, for the poor and oppressed, comes out emphatically in the contemporary Puritan work of R. J. Rushdoony, in particular in his *Institutes of Biblical Law*.[95] So does the biblical requirement of a minimal civil government and non-coercive charitable order (as a necessary part of God's law order) in which most of God's law is enforceable only by God himself and where tithes and offerings are given freely for the relief of the poor with the promise of God's blessing for such godly living and His curse upon the neglect of this responsibility.[96] Social financing must be provided – how it is to be provided is the critical issue. As we have seen, it should not be through state-sanctioned theft, however well intentioned (i.e. by progressive taxation, windfall taxes, inheritance taxes, and property taxes, where people's wealth is plundered for redistributive welfarism), which is the politics of covetousness, envy and civil war. We are commanded by Christ to give freely to the needy without display and without hypocrisy (Matt. 6:1–4). There is no indication in Scripture that such giving is participation in sinful political structures or that true 'justice' in society ever eliminates the need for various forms of charity; this is because equalization is not the goal of the kingdom of God. Only if 'justice' is falsely defined as total communism can justice conceptually (though not in reality) eliminate charity in a fallen world. In the days of the Soviet Union for example, captured as it was by Marxist-Leninism, charity was made illegal because it was considered revolutionary activity against the state and its social order. Biblically however, charity and true justice –

which is rooted in restitution not redistribution – are together manifest in the law. In the Decalogue, the prohibition against all forms of theft and covetousness (which clearly presuppose private property) is found along with the requirement of the tithe (three tithes in all – approximately fifteen to eighteen per cent of a person's annual income), of which only one tenth went to the priest for worship; the rest was for education and various forms of social provision provided through the Levites. Thus, for the Puritan Christian mind, to abandon God's law and means of provision for the needy – the tithe – and replace it with statist 'justice' and its provision through institutionalized robbery (state coercion) is profane and a double theft from God.[97] George Grant summarizes the issue well:

> The reason Scripture is so specific about the implementation of charity is precisely due to the unique interrelationship of law and love. Biblical love is not naive, guilt-provoked sentiment. Biblical love is not a feeling. Biblical love is the compulsion to do things God's way, living in obedience to His unchanging, unerring purposes.... Biblical law is the encoded mercy, grace, and peace of God. It is love's standard. Thus, biblical law does not lock us into heartless, soulless exercises in social control. Love and law are inseparable, working in tandem to the glory of Christ and His Kingdom. And when they are evidenced as such, the needs of the poor will be met by faithful adherents of authentic Christianity – in word and deed.[98]

6.7 Means and Motive in the Struggle for Justice

Because today the powers of distribution are largely in the hands of a centralized and increasingly totalizing state, the church has to navigate the difficult challenge of 'statecraft' as it struggles for righteousness in social relationships – each one receiving their due as a sign of the kingdom by obedience to the covenant law.

Because justice is a religious concept, when denuded of its biblical dress it inevitably becomes mythical, simply an expedient means of social control by fallen men and women. Rushdoony describes the problem well:

> If men of wealth control the state, the law becomes their tool to subjugate the poor and make them poorer. If poor men control the state, the law then is used to rob the rich and all hard-working men to

support those who want to live on the proceeds of robbery. In the one case it is called the maintenance of social order, and in the other it is called social justice and social welfare, but in both cases it is robbery. And today, because God's righteousness is despised, the nations of the world are becoming robber states and lands without justice.[99]

This is the challenge the church faces and has always faced in one form or another. As Augustine put it, "Justice being taken away, then, what are kingdoms but great robberies? For what are robberies themselves but little kingdoms?"[100] It is the religion of secular humanism, reinforced, endorsed and embodied by the modern kingdom-state that sees itself as the neutral arbiter in all religious matters, having divorced justice from the righteousness of God. Power and authority are now seen as located in the modern state, granted legitimacy by 'the people.' As Bahnsen notes, "no longer was government seen as resting upon the shoulders of the God-man, the Messianic Prince of Peace, but civil authority was taken to be the result of an ancestral or limiting-concept "social contract", thus centering in the sovereign consent of the governed."[101] The modern states' 'social contract' thinking has permeated a great deal of missiological thought, uncritically turning to statist means and humanistic social theory to try and bring about its desired ends. As we have seen, many Christian intellectuals have turned to various forms of Marxism, each claiming to have identified the 'real Marx' and proceeded to clothe him in Christian garb. Liberation theology, as we noted, continues in varying degrees, to be characterized by Marxist ideology,[102] though due to the notorious and murderous failure of socialism in the former Soviet Union and China, claims to offer 'better' interpretations of Marx (despite the growing revolution against Marxism in Eastern Europe).[103] Astonishingly, the patriarch of contemporary missiology, David Bosch, attempts to play down this fact speaking warmly of Marxist theory as a tool in social analysis of tremendous value. He believes that certain third world theologians have 'sound reasons' for subjecting traditional Christianity to a Marxist critique. He summarily dismissing the criticism of Liberation theology in parts of the Western church as, "understandable in the light of the bourgeois[104] nature of most Western churches and their complicity with colonialism and capitalism,"[105] as though both are unqualified evils, and as if only the middle class attend church in the West!

Noted British missiologist Andrew Kirk is similarly enamoured with

Marxism, "adaptations of Marxist thought have contributed both to new ways of understanding the message of Christ and to new ways of doing theology."[106] In reference to the apostle James admonition concerning the payment of wages in James 5:1–6, Kirk, in a classic example of 'reading in' humanist social theory, approvingly makes the incredible leap that "...James here is anticipating Marx discussion of surplus-value, the value added in the manufacturing process which is not returned to the worker but kept as profit, either to be reinvested into the business or paid to shareholders."[107] In actuality, James (a first century Jew) is making direct reference to the law of God in Leviticus 19:13 and Deuteronomy 24:15, where the employer is required to pay his hired servant the agreed wage on the day of his labour, and not hold it back till the next day or beyond because day-hired servants were invariably poor and depended on being paid on time (day of) to provide for themselves and their families.

Kirk's disdain for capitalism or the free market (regularly confuting free market economy with today's statist interventionism which creates monopolies), and his conviction that social justice can only be accomplished by a brand of state enforced socialism is outlined in his book, *The Good News of the Kingdom Coming*. It seems Kirk believes that the accumulation of wealth beyond pure necessities must be the result of violence, fraud, bribes or theft. All money earned above a maximum wage set by the state would be forcibly given to charity. This redistribution of peoples' holdings will be accomplished, by steeply progressive tax rates – confiscation. This government sanctioned theft is viewed as 'Christian' by Kirk, who regards Marxism as a strong defender of the dignity of human beings.[108] Here we see the results of embracing a social theory that has no direct foundation in the revealed law of God, that then, in pursuit of 'social justice' seeks to employ the powers of the coercive state to bring about signs of the 'kingdom' without covenant faith. This runs the risk of setting up a counterfeit soteriology to establish a 'just order.' Breese sounds a necessary note of caution regarding the pervasive influence of liberation theology, which has effectively become mainstream in evangelical circles in the name of social justice:

> What is liberation theology? It is the view that holds that Christ came into the world to be our economic liberator. It asserts that his first purpose was to free the poor and the oppressed from the shackles of economic constriction. In actuality, liberation theology redefines sin...sin is to possess wealth in the face of the worlds' poverty.

Righteousness is to redistribute that wealth, giving it to the poor. Evangelism is also redefined. It is seen as the announcement of the economic liberation of Christ and the invitation to the oppressed peoples of the world to join the revolution he ordains.[109]

This major infiltration of Marxism into Christian theology came to prominence in the 1970s in Latin America. One of the most influential figures was Gustavo Gutierrez and his work, *A Theology of Liberation.* In his theology, man fulfils himself by increased self-consciousness and transforming nature, realized through the building of a socialist society where life is thereby made more 'human' – this begins by recognizing the class struggle as a fact. The Kingdom of God is realized in a society of brotherhood and justice where all men enter into communion with God as the political is grafted into the eternal.[110] The secular idea of man's self-creation through labour meets Marx class struggle, becoming a social gospel of the kingdom of God by political revolution. Whilst the Bible does teach salvation is not simply for the soul and recognizes the effects of sin on social structures, liberation theology offers a civic gospel where the world is denuded of the sacred (secularized), man creates himself by a self-aware revolution, justice is man-centred and defined by man, salvation is mediated not by Christ but by an abstract economic group called the poor – the world and the church meld into one, and Karl Marx trumps the Bible. The tired and familiar anti-Christendom rhetoric of modern missiology is right out of Gutierrez who saw the previous eras in church history as characterized by the 'Christendom mentality,' which would be done away by 'liberation.' This is accomplished not by reviving biblical faith to transform life and the social order, but by moving away from it into total secularization. Man, as the new self-conscious agent and creative subject in history now determines his own destiny – this is seen as liberation. This new kind of Christian should want to celebrate faith in a non-religious world. The move here is away from Scripture and orthodox biblical faith to a totalizing subjectivism where human experience determines right and wrong, appropriate belief and opinion, and defines the human task. That is to say, 'revelation' is man's subjective experience, since he determines truth in a world that exists in its own right. Here we have echoes of Hegel and Marx – there is total independence from God where human reason is 'political reason', as man is emancipated in history by his own work. Therefore liberation theology (and its bastardized offspring, 'social justice') spells the end of Christianity. Salvation itself is nothing more than the building of the human community in terms of man's socialistic and equalitarian ideal. The kingdom of God is not where the gospel transforms and God's will is heard and obeyed, rather the kingdom is seen only as man struggles against alienation and exploitation and achieves 'social justice.' The death and resurrection of Christ steadily sink into irrelevance as the historical 'becoming' of mankind takes centre stage. The central moment of Israel's deliverance from Egypt in the Exodus which functions as a type of our salvation in Jesus Christ is manipulated to mean social praxis, desacralization and the extension of salvation by social transformation to all people. As a consequence, in the thought of Liberation thinkers (and the social justice movement) we meet God (whatever he is) in our encounter with the poor, not with Christ. Our salvation allegedly passes through the poor and oppressed, since they allegedly bear the meaning of history. In fact, in this theology, the oppressed will bring about liberation themselves, as God saves history by them. So to know God and reach God is to 'work for justice' and thus salvation is attained by works.

This attempt to meld secularism and Christianity, Christ and Marx, is doomed because it is impossible to join those things which stand antithetical to one another – Marxism and secularism are simply atheism using another vocabulary, practically if not always theoretically. Jean Paul Sartre believed that "Marxism, as the formal framework of all contemporary philosophical thought, cannot be superseded."[111] He expressed here the dominant faith of the Western academy today – the utopian dream of world socialism in a totally secularised social order. The church has been invaded by this vision of reality given by Marx and Hegel that looks back for inspiration to the French Revolution. In this humanistic myth, man's self-conscious development in history away from 'alienation' (from himself) is the process of liberation, where man transforms the world by taking the reins of his own destiny. Man predestines the future, not God. The dialectical method of trying to fuse Christ and Marx, two opposites into a new synthesis, to reach a higher stage of development is an Hegelian delusion, where finally to know God is just to know man and the church as the body of Christ and bearer of the covenant of grace disappears into irrelevance.

It is then difficult to see how David Bosch can write off all criticism of liberation theology from the 'Western church' as simply 'bourgeois,' unless defending the good news of Christ manifest by his substitutionary atonement has been redefined as a bourgeois act of repression. It is noteworthy that the numerical strength of 'Western'-inspired evangelicalism (historically critical of liberation theology) has shifted south and is increasingly found in Africa, Latin America, and Asia as well as in non-Anglophone churches in Western nations. In light of these things we are forced to ask whether these ideas are really motivated by a love for the poor or in fact a hatred for the rich, where the poor are merely useful tools to establish the dictatorship of the new ideologues. The preaching of this message is meant to stir the 'labourers' to hatred, violence and revolution to establish what the Marxist elite consider 'freedom' – their own rule. Thus the strong contemporary tendency that has found its way into evangelical missiology, to view institutionalized robbery in the form of state enforced socialism as synonymous with the pursuit of justice warrants critique.

There are some who say liberation theology is passé and a spent force. But this misses the fact that the reason we hear little of 'liberation theology' anymore is because it is no longer a new fringe movement; it has become mainstream and its foundational assumptions have become basic to contemporary missiology under the broad umbrella of social justice. Ronald Sider, for example, borrowing from Gutierrez, categorizes the Exodus of the Hebrews from Egypt as a 'liberation movement' to free the poor from oppression. By contrast, Scripture tells us it was the fulfilment of covenantal blessing upon God's people in terms of his prophetic promise to the Patriarchs, beginning with Abraham, as well as part of his sovereign purpose to bring judgement on the Canaanites (Gen 15:12-16). Thus manipulated, in Sider's thought, the concept of liberation functions as an umbrella abstraction under the rubric of which various forms of revolution and 'liberation' are justified.[112] Rather than seeing the Exodus as a covenantal event that demonstrated and depicts salvation from death, slavery and sin by the promise of God and the blood of the lamb, Sider views it as simply liberation from oppression. Given that only the people who placed the blood of the lamb on the doorposts escaped death (i.e. 'poor' Hebrew families that failed to do so would not be spared) and since many Egyptians (oppressors) left Egypt with the Hebrews (Ex 12:37-38) through believing God's word, Sider's interpretation strains all credibility. Yet this aberrant vision of the Exodus has led to the belief that a socialist revolution is a form of Biblically justified revolt. Ironically, this 'liberation' results in the destruction of liberty. As David Chilton powerfully points out:

> Sider's social reforms necessitate stern, coercive measures by an omnipotent state, controlling the lives of people at every level. Of course this is done in the name of liberating the poor from economic injustice. But what it really means is power. The intellectual who agitates for statist liberation always assumes that in the Workers' Paradise he will be at the top of the pyramid. Provided that he is the dictator – that his property will not be "liberated" when the revolution comes, and that his notions of justice will be enforced on the unjust rich – he has no reason to regard tyranny as anything but freedom... liberation will apply Sider's good intentions by force, at the point of a policeman's gun.... The Exodus provided the Israelites with both liberty and law. Sider's liberationist "exodus" is merely lawlessness, and leads back to slavery.[113]

In a similarly lawless cry for liberation, using a language that fuses the liberationist and environmentalist nomenclature, Brueggemann writes:

> Only a new and lively hope...can deliver mankind from the oblivion that is being courted by its unthinking pursuit of "progress"...the earth will not bear such plunder, nor will the poor of the earth for long submit to the redundancy to which the plundering few reduce them! Christian hope is hope "against" all the false hopes of those who do not reckon with the reality of a limited biosphere and a shared existence.[114]

Though Brueggemann may have many issues in view here, from modernity to unrestrained greed, we again can hear the clear echoes of Gutierrez fused with contemporary environmentalist philosophy. His statement represents a shift of the locus of hope from God in Christ reconciling a fallen world to himself in the gospel (2 Cor. 5:19) to a humanizing of the biosphere – a 'new' and lively hope that stops the plunderers of the planet and the poor. Whilst we dare not ignore the critical issue of poverty, we have been arguing that we must critique the means for accomplishing the desired end. Is our hope for the world and the kingdom of God found in Christ and the resulting love of neighbour, spilling out in voluntary generosity as a challenge to the world the means to alleviate poverty and bring social improvement to people's lives? Or is it revolutionary hope that requires coercive state intervention offering a gospel and apocalypse that is difficult to reconcile with Scripture?

When all is said and done it seems clear that the issue is not about a deep concern for the poor. If it were, clear Biblical answers would be practiced – it is in fact an ideological conflict that involves two plans of salvation and two different types of judgement.

The French writer and philosopher Pascal Bruckner sees this clearly and he shows the link between environmentalist and Marxist ideologies amongst secular intellectual elites in the West who prophesy our doom, offering salvation only in terms of their culture of death:

> Around the turn of the 21st century, a paradigm shift in our thinking took place: We decided that the era of revolutions was over and that the era of catastrophes had begun…. What replaced the world's human future was the future of the world as a material entity. The long list of emblematic victims – Jews, blacks, slaves, proletarians, colonized peoples – was likewise replaced, little by little, with the Planet, the new paragon of all misery…. Over the last half-century, leftist intellectuals have identified two great scapegoats for the world's woes. First, Marxism designated capitalism as responsible for human misery. Second, "Third World" ideology, disappointed by the bourgeois indulgences of the working class, targeted the West, supposedly the inventor of slavery, colonialism and imperialism. The guilty party that environmentalism now accuses – mankind itself, in its will to dominate the planet – is essentially a composite of the previous two, a capitalism invented by a West that oppresses peoples and destroys the Earth. Indeed, environmentalism sees itself as the fulfilment of all earlier critiques. "There are only two solutions," Bolivian president Evo Morales declared in 2009. "Either capitalism dies, or Mother Earth dies." So the planet has become the new proletariat that must be saved from exploitation – if necessary, by reducing the number of human beings, as oceanographer Jacques Cousteau said in 1991. The Voluntary Human Extinction Movement, a group of people who have decided not to reproduce, has announced: "Each time another one of us decides to not add another one of us to the burgeoning billions already squatting on this ravaged planet, another ray of hope shines through the gloom. When every human chooses to stop breeding, Earth's biosphere will be allowed to return to its former glory." The British environmentalist James Lovelock, a chemist by training, regards Earth as a living organism and human beings as an infection within it, proliferating at the expense of

the whole, which tries to reject and expel them. Journalist Alan Weisman's 2007 book *The World Without Us* envisions in detail a planet from which humanity has disappeared. In France, a Green politician, Yves Cochet, has proposed a "womb strike," which would be reinforced by penalties against couples who conceive a third child, since each child means, in terms of pollution, the equivalent of 620 round trips between Paris and New York. Environmentalism has become a global ideology that covers all of existence – not merely modes of production but ways of life as well. We rediscover in it the whole range of Marxist rhetoric, now applied to the environment.... They alone see clearly while others vegetate in the darkness..." [115]

This vile vision of the humanistic and leftist elite has infiltrated, to a considerable degree, contemporary missiological thought and passed itself off as a new orthodoxy, outside of which one incurs the ire and censure of many Christian academics and intellectuals. Increasingly, the godly, hard-working and productive, whether in terms of fertility or industry are the alleged enemies of social health and the life of the planet itself. The link between an eco-soteriology – where the planet needs to be 'liberated' from the scourge of mankind, and man must steadily pay the death penalty for his sin of befouling mother nature – and the traditional Marxist 'liberation theology' is abundantly clear and well documented:

> The poor and oppressed are hermeneutically privileged, and all social analysis must begin with their experience. This hermeneutical privilege holds true for environmental issues as well as for theology. Eduardo Bonnin writes that the option for the poor is the "hermeneutic key that helps us realise the importance of an authentic solution to the ecological problem for the construction of the kingdom of God in Latin America." Just as the poor of the land are central to theological discourse, they must also be central to ecological discourse...the reign of God occurs on earth as a process that makes historical, social, economic, and political progress central. [116]

It is important to notice here that social analysis does not begin with Scripture – God's plan for creation and its cultivation, the problem of sin, the revelation of the law and gospel, our need for regeneration by the Holy Spirit, or the renewal and restoration of all things in Christ. The kingdom of God is not being extended by preaching and living out the good news, instead it is by economic and political progress in terms of humanistic ideals. Structures of injustice, not rebellion against God, are then seen as the essential human problem, and man's salvation is therefore located in social ecology:

> Liberation theologians emphasize social sin and structural injustice over individual wrongdoing. They claim that environmental exploitation stems from structural injustices that affect both the poor and the nonhuman world; ecological problems cannot be resolved until structures of exploitation and domination are transformed. Leonardo Boff writes that "ecological injustice is transformed into social injustice by producing social oppression, exhaustion of resources, contamination of the atmosphere and the deteriorating quality of life."... The emphasis on structural injustice and economic, political and social institutions led liberation theologians to propose social ecology as the philosophical movement within environmentalism that best expressed the liberation perspective...both social ecologists and liberation theologians agree that no divide exists between social and environmental issues.[117]

To disagree with this vision is to be 'anti-ecological' and a participation in sin because sin is redefined in the ecology based cosmology. For Leonardo Boff, author of *Ecology and Liberation*, everything that co-exists, pre-exists, subsisting by means of an all-inclusive web of relations. All being constitutes a link in a vast cosmic chain coming from and returning to 'God.'[118] What we have here is simply a repackaged pagan pantheism positing an inter-connectedness of all things in an infinite evolutionary web, emanating from and returning to impersonal being. Boff thus re-defines sin as "breaking connectedness" not the violation of God's law.[119]

All this runs counter to the biblical view that human beings are given a stewardship and rule over the creation, to care, cultivate, develop and transform wilderness into gardens and raw materials into useful instruments of culture, commerce and civilization. Conservation and stewardship are a mandate in order that the creation is not plundered but cultivated and its resources developed and replenished for the blessing of mankind (Gen. 1:26-29; 4:18-22). Indeed, according to St. Paul, the created order groans for man to take his proper place as God's dominion people in Christ Jesus. The earth cries out for its cultivation in terms of the kingdom of God. Our freedom in Christ spells freedom for the creation which comes only in and through the children of God, as they live to the glory of God and the final hope of total freedom from corruption (Rom. 8:20–24)

However, if the gospel of the kingdom seeks to circumvent God's kingdom people and his law (a theological impossibility), and employs a hermeneutic of liberation and 'humanization', the strong tendency is to find the locus of salvation in the creation itself (socio-economic power) and hence in and through the powers of the state – whether it takes a Marxist/environmentalist or capitalist interventionist model. What emerges is a counterfeit soteriology which is not merely a distortion of the kingdom of God but a redefinition of it. The 'Fall' brought about the atomism and selfishness that dominates our fragmented society. The modern state, failing to recognize the problem of sin and consequent alienation from God and fellow human beings offers a pseudo-soteriology, trying to affect a peace by force, without the redemption offered by Christ. But only through the gospel and the church, where genuine friendship with God and neighbour are made possible within a community of love that obeys his commandments, God's love being shed abroad by the Holy Spirit, is true peace and justice made possible. Without this saving order, the new "love" must be coercive! Both church and modern state are aiming at brotherhood and community which can only be imagined in one of two ways. It is either enforced by requirement of state against peoples' will where a false semblance of brotherhood is obtained whilst liberty is lost; or community and brotherhood, by God's saving grace, are manifest in free associations and loving generosity in the family of God, with a state reduced to the biblical limits of restitutive justice. This model risks tension and division but offers true community, as well as personal and social freedom. If the means of justice is in terms of God's law and not humanistic social theories, and salvation is in Christ by incorporation in his new humanity, as opposed to humanization by the state, then our motive in the pursuit of justice must be the genuine unity brought about by atonement; Christ's saving order through the cross (John 17:21). The only alternative motive is masochism – self-atonement!

The theologies that de-emphasize the propitiation of Christ as the reality that overcomes the power and guilt of sin, seek to ostensibly 'transcend' the new kingdom community, the covenant people, by biosphere humanization. Yet they have not escaped the question of the guilt of all men and women. No amount of sentimental or revolutionary talk about the preferential option of God for the poor can bring salvation to the poor or the rich for that matter. Reading some contemporary western missiologists on 'social justice,' one is left with the distinct impression that there is a conscious or unconscious attempt to alleviate a sense of guilt for being the white, western, male, relatively wealthy progeny of colonialists and imperial powers, born in the lap of old Christendom. Perhaps by suicidal economic activity, state-sanctioned theft (redistribution) sentimentalism, self-punishment and various kinds of 'sacrificial' burden bearing, we can make up for past sins, real or imagined. This is a psychologically valid 'human attempt' to alleviate our pressing sense of guilt – the cornerstone of all neuroses – by our own power.

Liberationist and statist thought is, I believe, a telling illustration of attempted self-atonement that many Christians appear to have adopted from the world. Rushdoony's observation here is particularly penetrating:

> The reality of man apart from Christ is guilt and masochism.... [T]he politics of the anti-Christian will thus inescapably be the politics of guilt. In the politics of guilt man is perpetually drained in his social energy and cultural activity. He will progressively demand of the state a redemptive role. What he cannot do personally i.e. to save himself, he demands that the state do for him, so that the state as man enlarged, becomes the human savior of man. The politics of guilt, therefore, is not directed, as the Christian politics of liberty, to the creation of a godly justice and order, but to the creation of a redeeming order, a saving state. Guilt must be projected, therefore, on all those who oppose the new order and new age.[120]

Consequently, the vituperation targeted at the Western church in general, in much missiological thought, bears close scrutiny in light of this observation of guilt projection, masochism and the pseudo-soteriology of a redemptive state.[121] The dominant note of contemporary missiology in this regard then is Western guilt, the origin of which goes right back to Lenin and his 1916 propaganda tract, "Imperialism, the Highest Stage of Capitalism." Despite the fact that the evidence reveals the poorest and most backward nations and peoples are those who have had little or no contact with the West, whereas those that have, have made huge strides in material progress, the myth is propagated that Christendom is simply a story of systemic oppression and injustice.[122] Much of the church has bought into the myth and has acted accordingly, by buying into the secular gospel to deal with the guilt manufactured by their masochism. As Antonides has noted, "what are unbelievers going to do about the guilt which they nevertheless experience? Burnham believes that liberalism permits the translation of this guilt into principles that are egalitarian, anti-discriminatory, democratist, peace-seeking and liberal – that is, those principles generally compatible with socialism."[123] Confessing the alleged colonial sins of the West and prescribing a political route to absolution is a popular past time amongst cultural elites in and out of the church. Thus, what was the glory of the world is abandoned by the intellectual class in search of salvation in Cuba, China and Haiti and in comradeship with the world's dictators, butchers and totalitarian regimes.

6.8 Eucharistic Faith or Environmentalism

A Puritan missiology affirms that the only solution to the problem of injustice and lawlessness is the gospel of the kingdom, proclaimed and manifest by Christ's new humanity, the church. In any theory of social or public justice, sin and evil are the problem to be confronted. For political egalitarian humanism, evil is in the environment personified by the clergy, the family, the wealthy, the bourgeoisie, churches, Christian morality and private enterprise, property or organizations. The state's power to change this environment (whether socialist or interventionist) is a form of saving grace – the elimination of true Christianity thus becomes a political priority. The Christian faith faces the same problem of sin in two ways. First, human government as God's minister of justice (Rom. 13:4) is called upon to establish 'restitution' not coercive 'redistribution' as the basic premise of law and justice (Ex. 22:1-15). Second, the church ministers by word and deed the saving grace of Jesus Christ, bringing us into true communion with God and each other in a social order of true righteousness, manifest by obedience to His law. The Eucharist or communion feast which symbolizes the essence of the church's existence is thus a form of Christian libertarianism against the totalizing modern state with its counterfeit soteriology and false semblance of justice. The ineradicable desire for social reunification in the human race results from our loss of original unity in the garden of God with Adam as federal head, and our scattering in enmity against God and each other. This unity can only be restored, and our social fragmentation healed, by participation in the man of justice, the second Adam, Christ's body. Given that Christians are dual citizens, with ontological priority given to our heavenly citizenship, we do not seek escape from the struggle for justice in this world but declare the "radical interruption by the church of the false politics of the earthly city." [124] Because our worship is not purely inward but public, uniting, through Christ alone, heaven and earth (Matt. 6:10), and thus revealing that the earthly city lacks true justice because it fails to worship God and love one's neighbour, it interferes with statist social order. The announcement of the kingdom reign of God proclaims that Christ alone offers unity and real justice; this puts statist soteriology[125] in opposition to the Christian story. William Cavanaugh describes the satanic plot against the Lord and his anointed:

> The church, above all, must be defeated in order for salvation to take place...when Hobbes and Rousseau imagined the emergent state in the seventeenth and eighteenth centuries, they understood quite clearly the imperative to defeat the lesser associations within the state body in order to vanquish multiplicity...the intervention of the state in matters of kinship, property and inheritance; the conception of law as something 'made' or legislated by the state rather than 'disclosed' from its divine source...the abolition of ecclesial courts and the transfer of sole judicial proprietorship to the crown; the replacement of local duties and privileges by the rights of interchangeable individuals; the enclosure of common lands; the states securing of monopoly over legitimate violence.[126]

The modern state, 'swallowing' the church and other 'lesser' associations, thus seeks to enforce the unity of humankind by incorporation into a counterfeit communion; a copy of the real body of Christ where true justice is found and where unity in diversity, freedom and responsibility, love and justice may flourish amongst a free people. Until we recognize this, the struggle toward erroneous visions of justice in the social order that are proliferating in the churches will directly or indirectly oppose the churches evangelistic efforts.

Christians have largely accepted the integrating role of the state on the false premise that the 'secular' is a 'neutral apparatus' for resolving conflicts of interest. Recognizing the creedally false soteriology of the state reveals the inherent conflict between modern statism and the Eucharistic manifestation of Christ's Kingdom in his alternative society.[127] The just kingdom of Christ first manifest itself in the Hebrew nation and now is made known in and through his kingdom people in the world (Eph. 3:8-10). Augustine was correct in seeing history as a struggle between two societies, the City of God and the earthly city. All the kingdoms of this world with their pretensions to justice and virtue will pass away, only Christ's kingdom will stand. The living church (or covenant people of God) being the social union of true believers, is the primary instrument through which the grace of God can work in history.[128] Thus a true commonwealth, by definition, must be Christian. Commenting on Augustine's claim that no pagan establishment can realize true justice Sabine notes, 'It is a contradiction in terms to say that a state can render to everyone his own, so long as it's very constitution withholds from God the worship which is his due.'[129] An Augustinian conclusion logically follows:

> No state can be just, since the advent of Christianity, unless it is also Christian, and a government considered apart from its relation to the church would be devoid of justice. Thus the Christian character of the state was embedded in the universally admitted principle that its purpose is to realize justice and right.[130]

The Psalmist states it effectively, "Now therefore, O kings, show discernment; take warning O judges of the earth. Worship the Lord with reverence, and rejoice with trembling. Do homage to the Son, lest he become angry, and you perish in the way" (Psalm 2:10–12). If this Augustinian interpretation of the gospel of the kingdom and public justice is correct, where God's people are manifestation and model of true justice or righteousness, entered into through the gospel, then our role is twofold. First, "true justice for pilgrim members of the City of God consists in sharing with others the forgiveness of sins",[131] then living out that kingdom life as members of a trans-national, alternate society of justice, exemplified in reunification with God and others, symbolized by the Eucharist. Secondly, as salt and light, we will call upon, 'the authorities that exist' (Rom. 13:1) to conform governmental laws concerned with particular justice, to the law of God, 'disclosed' in God's total law (all Scripture), and so witness the seasoning impact of the gospel of the kingdom already at work in the *ecclesia* (called out people of the king), destroying injustice and steadily bringing liberty and freedom from tyranny and oppression to all.

This regeneration and transformation of the world is the glorious task of God's people, as all things are brought into subjection to him, "so that God may be all in all" (1 Cor. 15:28). By this opposition to counterfeit soteriology we see a perfect union of evangelistic outreach and the pursuit of justice. Justice or righteousness is something we are (justified) and live (righteousness) from the core of our being as we share and manifest the gospel. However, if statism combining with humanistic social theories are uncritically adopted by Christians in the mission of God, then not only are we distracting from the critical task of evangelism, we are unwitting partners in offering a counterfeit gospel that is no gospel.

Chapter Seven

STRANGE FIRE: UNDERSTANDING JUBILEE
AND ATONEMENT

Poverty also hath its temptations.... For even the poor may be undone
by the love of that wealth and plenty which they never get: and they may
perish for over-loving the world, that never yet prospered in the world.
– Richard Baxter

Socialism is a philosophy of failure, the creed of ignorance, and
the gospel of envy, its inherent virtue is the equal sharing of misery.
– Winston Churchill

7.1 Land, Liberty and Economics

We saw in the last study that much contemporary missiological thought
views the *mission of God*, the inevitable sign of true gospel faith, or
even the nature of salvation itself, as centred in identification with, and
liberation of, the poor or powerless by redistributing wealth; as one
emergent church writer has put it, "we live our identity as God's children
and the adventure of God's redemption as we engage God's mission of
distributive justice."[1] Although there were seventeenth-century Puritan
radicals and sectarians like the Antinomians, Diggers and Levellers, some
of whom advocated for the abolition of private property and a grand
levelling of all society,[2] the dominant view of the Puritans and reformed
tradition as a whole was that biblical faith and law must govern our
social philosophy, including economic philosophy and charity.[3] Social
justice is not a biblical concept but a humanistic doctrine that aims at
replacing Christianity with secularism, and the church with the state.
As Marcello Pera points out, "The church doesn't seem to realize that
much of this secularization is the result of the welfare state and of the
concept of social justice, to which its own social doctrine also appeals...
if the state gives you everything that your family, your parish, and your
community once gave you, why do you even need a church."[4] And yet
Christians ask why so many are disinterested in Christianity and don't
attend worship in the churches of Europe. God's word has much to say
about true justice and economic relations in light of the atonement and
it is to this issue we now turn.

One significant aspect of biblical law with respect to economics in Israel was the law of *Jubilee*. This particular law has been the subject of a great deal of discussion and reflection in theological circles and is popularly used today as a 'Christian' rallying cry for justice in the form of debt relief, redistribution of wealth or even the relativization of private property. Because of this special interest and the peculiar socio-political use to which this law has been put, as well as its very important relationship to the doctrine of atonement, it warrants more than a cursory examination.

As noted already, the sabbatical principle of Jubilee (the Sabbath of Sabbaths) is typically invoked by missiologists as an exemplary expression of a philosophy of radical emancipation – early egalitarian justice in the face of vested interest in property rights,[5] via debt cancellation and state-sanctioned redistribution. As one example among many, this motif comes through strongly in the work of Canadian academic theologian and cultural commentator, Brian Walsh. In a highly emotive lecture, Walsh sets out a statist, interventionist and socialist model of economics, which he claims is based in the "memory of Jubilee."[6] For Walsh, this model will restore economic justice to society. Those whose economic theory disagrees with his 'mixed economy' (state-controlled market) are, in Walsh's own words, on the side of those *raping* the world, and in fact, raping God himself. Since God is in covenant with humankind, according to Walsh, he finds himself wedded to an abusive partner; as a consequence God is portrayed as a cosmic victim. His suffering love took Jesus to the cross as our great example of non-retaliation, an act of solidarity with the oppressed. Thus, for Walsh, when this view of atonement is applied to economics, *Jubilee* or liberation must be declared.[7]

Walsh correctly links atonement and the laws of Jubilee, but what exactly is Jubilee? Walsh states, "[I]n the fiftieth year, Jubilee is proclaimed and all who have lost their lands or who have been sold into slavery are to receive their land back and to be set free from slavery."[8] It was Jesus, in the synagogue, who announced that the Jubilee of Isaiah 61 was being fulfilled today, in history (Luke 4:16-21). Walsh sees the following implications in Christ's messianic announcement:

> Today is the year of Jubilee. Today, in my presence and in my proclamation, is Jubilee. The poor hear good news, captives are set free from prisons, and the oppressed are set free. Today, the shocked

and awed people of South America hear good news. Today, the prisoners at Guantanamo Bay and Abu Ghraib are set free. Today, those who have been oppressed by IMF structural adjustment programs, trade liberalization, privatization and exclusion from economic life…today they go free.[9]

For Walsh, as for several other thinkers we have considered, humanity's central problem is the environment, the social and economic structures and the problem of privatization – bankers and employers raping the world. Jesus' announcement of his great Jubilee is then largely stripped of its supernatural connotations and reduced to a socialistic form of 'humanitarianism,' a word with which, like 'humanization' (meaning to make like that which is human or of mankind), modern missiology is enamoured. However, it should be noted the original meaning of the term 'humanitarian' is, "one who denies Christ's divinity and holds him to be a mere man."[10] Yet the word is now closely associated with the idea of love for humanity and benevolence. The implication being, those who deny Christ's divinity are the real lovers of humanity and true source of philanthropy or benevolence. The modern cynical manipulation of this word says a great deal about the philosophy of our age.

Despite such misunderstandings, it is nevertheless highly significant that Scripture links atonement and Jubilee. Their interpretation is certainly related. Rousas Rushdoony, one of the most noteworthy modern Puritans, deals extensively in his *Institutes of Biblical Law* and commentary on *Leviticus*, with the law of Jubilee and its critical relationship to the doctrine of atonement. Rushdoony's treatment of Jubilee is far more coherent than Walsh's and deals with its biblical meaning rather than artificially imposing the Marxist lens of liberation theology or employing the rhetoric of political leftism.[11] Instead, to the Puritan mind, the Jubilee is, "the supreme expression in the Mosaic legislation of the Sabbath principle, the Jubilee year, the Jubilee is begun by the sounding of the trumpet on the Day of Atonement."[12] As an expression of the Sabbath, its primary purpose was not humanitarian, since the poor could eat of the field in the Sabbath year and the law required gleaning rights for the poor in the field every year.[13] Rather, the Jubilee sets forth the "restoration and restitution of all things in Christ."[14] As an expression of full restitution and the redemption from slavery made by God's provision of atonement, seen in the Passover feast and escape from Egypt and later foreshadowed in the sacrificial system of the Temple, "Jubilee began on the evening of the Day of Atonement, it made clear the foundation of the new creation, atonement through the blood of the lamb of the Covenant." [15] Atonement therefore means that because God has forgiven our debts, through Christ, we are to forgive the debts of our brothers and sisters in the covenant. As we have seen, the basic premise of God's law is restitution. The God of Scripture exacts the death penalty for sin and without the shedding of blood there is no remission of sin (Heb. 9:22). This is why the blood of the Passover lamb was shed and why the sacrificial system pointed to Christ – the Lamb of God. The Day of Atonement brought all this to mind for the ancient Hebrews and the early Jewish church. Sin has created an insurmountable debt to God and Jubilee is about the cancellation of debt for the people of faith. Thus, at the Jubilee festival, in the Israelite economy, "rural land holdings reverted to their original owners; slaves were freed as on each sabbatical year." [16]

Considering the theology and history surrounding the law of Jubilee, it is important to notice that Walsh distorts the meaning of Jubilee in a number of ways. First, his primary application of its meaning is to economics and not to theology – that is, sin and redemption and debt cancellation by blood atonement, so that people can enter God's Sabbath rest. Secondly, in trying to shoe-horn statist politics into the meaning of the festival, he neglects to mention that biblical law puts the control of *property* and thereby the control of *production* in the hands of the private family and not the state. Jubilee applied to a Hebrew family's rural land holdings in the Promised Land (not properties in towns or cities, it should be noted) and, as Leviticus 25:13–17 makes clear, in buying and selling such holdings, people were 'trading' a maximum fifty-year leasehold and as such the value of rural holdings altered depending on the number of years till Jubilee – at which point the property returned to the family who owned the freehold, whether a bond-servant or wealthy businessman. [17] In Israel, the economic purpose of Jubilee was to stipulate that no *individual* had the right to endanger the future of their family or tribe by selling their private land (source of production) off permanently, turning their inheritance into a capital asset, and thereby disinheriting their children in the part of the Promised Land apportioned to them. As Paul Mills shows, the essential idea of the Jubilee was that "a family should not have been totally without means of independent support for more than a generation." [18] Jubilee land laws thus had *nothing* in common with later Greek notions of communism (i.e. Plato's Republic) and the forcible redistribution of people's holdings. Attempts to relate communistic or Marxist ideals to Jubilee are simply putting Scripture to an illegitimate use for the purpose of political activism; it is neither responsible exegesis nor sound biblical theology. In fact, by cruel irony, *disinheriting families* through 'inheritance taxes' is today one of the primary means by which socialistic states and big government bureaucracies (like the present-day United Kingdom) strip families of their assets for the purpose of 'redistribution,' in direct *contravention* of the law of Jubilee. The temporary Hebrew land model is closer to medieval feudalism than modern socialism and welfarism which Walsh is keen to defend. Assets were redistributed only in the sense that rural land was to be returned to the family that historically had the inheritance right to it, this was not utopian planning. As Jonathan Burnside notes, "there is absolutely no attempt to redistribute movable assets such as animals. If the law was idealistic, why not redistribute these as well?"[19] In biblical law, the family is God's basic and thus the most protected institution. Even princes and kings (the state) are judged for the theft of family land in Scripture (Ezek. 46:18). God severely judged King Ahab for the theft of Naboth's farmland.[20] All theft of private family property whether by fraud, criminal seizure, state policy or taxation remains a total violation of God's law. The particular system of land division in Israel amongst the twelve tribes however, is clearly no longer applicable because our nations are not divided up into tribal portions as the Promised Land was.[21] Gary North further explains our discontinuity with the specifics of the land law of Jubilee: "National Israel was disinherited in A.D. 70. The Kingdom of God was taken from national Israel and given to a new nation, the church (Matt. 21:43). The jubilee land laws (Lev. 25) have ended forever."[22] Thirdly, slaves (indentured workers) released every seventh year and at Jubilee restored to family lands, were Hebrews who had become bond-servants through debt or had voluntarily sold themselves as workers for provision and security. However, Jubilee did not apply to criminal workers making restitution or the unconverted foreigner amongst them who had not become a covenant member (Deut. 15:1–6); but they could convert and become eligible for release.[23] This fact pointed forward to the truth of the gospel because, "There was no cancellation of debt for the unbeliever...typifying thereby that only those who are in Christ...have satisfaction rendered for their debt."[24]

These factors make Walsh's and other like efforts to co-opt Jubilee for various humanistic political causes essentially erroneous. Walsh is in the modernist and Fabian socialist tradition with his economic and political agenda which he claims is based in a 'memory' of Jubilee; this memory is so faulty he appears to have theological dementia.

7.2 Debt, Atonement and Jubilee

The ongoing modernist addiction to various permutations of Marxism and institutionalized theft amongst Christian intellectuals is quite stunning given the utter failure and often cruel butchery of all such communist states in the twentieth century. Despite these historic disasters, as Western Europe has steadily adopted cultural Marxism and Fabian socialism, and embraced the new salvific panacea – environmentalism – they have developed debt-laden welfare economies, their economic life and survival going critical at the beginning of the twenty-first century and now hanging in the balance on life support.

Debt and larceny seem to be the primary motive forces animating what is left of the European economies. Yet from a Christian standpoint we are called to eliminate debt as far as is possible: "owe no man anything, except to *love* each other" (Rom. 13:8). This true love for mankind to which we are called means we obey God with respect to our neighbour: "the one who loves another has fulfilled the law" (Rom. 13:8). We cannot rob others either by long-term debt (coupled with inflation), mortgaging a people's national future, theft or redistributive taxation, in the name of 'love for the poor' because "love is the fulfilling of the law" (Rom. 13:10). All protestations to the contrary are a façade for another agenda since, as St. Paul declares, "though I bestow all my goods to feed the poor , and though I give my body to be burned, but have not love, it profits me nothing" (1 Cor. 13:3, NKJV). To be lawless is to be loveless.

Rushdoony remarks tellingly concerning modernism's loveless failure to deal with critical social problems, including poverty:

> Their solution to it has been statism, i.e., state charity or welfarism as the substitute for Christian action...both evangelicals and modernists contributed very substantially to the rise of the modern state. The evangelicals steadily retreated from Christian action in the areas of health, education and welfare, and the state moved in.[25]

Furthermore, he observes that historically, in lawless and criminal efforts to 'cancel debt,' social revolutions have taken place usually involving the killing of bankers, land-owners and the destruction of records. These are, in effect, efforts to *counterfeit* Jubilee:

> Men through their politics are trying to create a false Jubilee, a false atonement, a false cancelation of sins, but there is no Jubilee for the ungodly, because the debt cannot be repaid man's way, either by forgiveness which is no forgiveness, or by the destruction of the creditor and records we cannot have two plans of atonement.[26]

The relationship between Jubilee and atonement now becomes abundantly clear. Rushdoony argues that those like Walsh, who preach economic and political liberation as Jubilee and thereby a *civic gospel*, will inevitably offer a false model of the atonement and an alternate plan of salvation:

> The social gospel is really a civil gospel; it espouses salvation by the state and its laws, and its hope shifts from God to the state. This has a major impact on the doctrine of the atonement. In the 1930s a pastor who adopted the social gospel began to preach also against the orthodox doctrine of Christ's atonement; he ridiculed it…calling it "butcher shop theology".… *This juxtaposition of the social or statist gospel and the denunciation of the blood atonement doctrine was an essential and logical one.* If salvation is an act of state, the work of men who are essentially good and who unite to make a better world, to look for a change in men through Christ's atonement rather than through the civil gospel is not only false but misleading. As a result, whenever the civil revolution flourishes, Christianity is under attack.[27]

This hits the nail right on the head. If people are not rebels against God's law and under just sentence of death, in *debt to God* and in need of his *Jubilee* through Christ's *Day of Atonement*, then the cross ceases to be about the cancellation of the debt of sin and becomes a symbol of political solidarity, martyrdom and victimhood. The all-conquering Christ, the *Lion* and the *Lamb* of Revelation 5, the victor over sin, death and the devil, canceling debt and disarming rulers through the power of the cross (Col. 2:13–15; Rev. 5:9–14) becomes instead the powerless victim, showing solidarity with the so-called oppressed masses. Walsh quotes Andrew Lincoln with approval in this regard:

> The powers of evil are defeated not by some overwhelming display

of divine power, but by the weakness of Christ's death.... []he death of the victim, who has *absorbed the destructive forces of the powers,* becomes precisely the point at which their *domination* is decisively brought to an end. Their claims, their accusations, *their oppressive and divisive influence* have all been *subverted* by a very different power: the power of the *victim on the cross.*[28]

The carefully-chosen wording here is important; 'domination,' 'oppression,' 'victim' and 'subversion' – pseudo-political terms of cultural Marxism employed to describe what was going on at the cross. But Scripture states, "The Lion of the tribe of Judah, the Root of David, has conquered" (Rev. 5:5); this is a message of expiation and ransom by blood atonement (Rev. 5:9). Jesus is surely not a victim in the sense implied by Walsh. In the first edition of *Webster's Dictionary* from 1828, victim is defined as, "a living creature sacrificed to a deity or as a religious rite" (which cannot be properly applied to the atonement of Christ). But the second definition of a victim in *Webster's* gives us the common definition, "one who is injured or killed as by misfortune or calamity." In the same dictionary, to be victimized is to be, "a dupe, defrauded, swindled, or cheated." The Christ of Scripture was not a victim, nor victimized. He determined to go to Jerusalem to die (Luke 9:51; Matt. 16:21–28); he willingly offered himself for sin (Heb. 9:14–28), and laid down his life of his own accord, with power to take it up again (John 10:17–18), defeating the adversary, sin and death, by the foreordained will of the Father (John 10:18; Rev. 13:8; Heb. 4:3, 9:26; Rev. 6:15–17).

7.3 Strange Fire

Walsh's view of the atonement suggests the accuracy of Rushdoony's analysis – advocates of a *statist Jubilee* will logically de-emphasize or denounce vicarious, substitutionary blood atonement. Then, in the place of what God requires to be laid on the altar to satisfy his justice, man places his own offering of moral works, self-punishment and self-righteousness. This is the essence of moralism and Pharisaism; man's works of self-righteousness are employed as a substitute for God's justice and law becomes a means of making people good rather than regeneration. In Leviticus 10, two of the sons of Aaron, Nadab and Abihu, are slain by God because they offer 'strange fire' – that is unauthorized fire, to the Lord. They sought to approach God by means he had not commanded. It is possible they were using coals not from the altar, or had entered the Holy Place to serve at the altar of incense intoxicated (cf. Lev. 10:9). Whatever the precise nature of their infringement, it was presumptuous and a sacrilege before a holy and righteous God. Sacrilege is a *form of theft* directed at God where his sovereignty and authority are infringed as man seeks to *correct* or *improve* on God's word by his own arrogant presumption. The sons of Aaron offered 'strange fire,' presuming that they had a better means of approaching God than the offerings and oblations prescribed. Since Eden, men and women have often supposed themselves to be more holy or more righteous than God, and able to improve upon him and his word. This Pharisaic spirit is rife in today's church, where many theologians, churchmen and leaders see themselves as above the Word of God, superior in their sensibilities and more righteous in their judgements than God's law. Not only so, some consider that they have a better way of atonement, a superior way of salvation and a better incense to offer.

Today, even the evangelical church is full of strange fire. This is clearly evident in the popular 'emergent church' literature which expresses the same missiological themes articulated by Walsh. For example, the openly heretical Brian McLaren considers vicarious atonement, 'divine child abuse,' and replaces it with his 'powerful weakness' theory.[29] Steve Chalke, another purveyor of strange fire in the form of the civic gospel, quite logically given his assumptions, condemns the doctrine of original sin, literally mocks the Old Covenant Temple, and regards the vicarious blood atonement of Christ as a morally dubious and 'twisted version of events.' Chalke's cross is simply a 'moral example' and his gospel, 'social improvement' by means of copying that example.[30] There is nothing new here; such views were emphatically insisted on in the missiology of Unitarians in the nineteenth century.[31] Walsh's summary of the *meaning* of the atonement, in light of the Jubilee, is very revealing, having more in common with 'Liberty, Fraternity and Equality,' as defined by the French revolutionaries than the Mosaic Law and biblical system of atonement:

> Atonement is about setting things right; setting all things right. And when people are restored to community and when economic relations are set right again, then the master/slave distinction must collapse, the unjust division between rich and poor must be overthrown and the reality of some folks having possession of land and the resources for economic well-being while others are dispossessed and left destitute

must be rectified through a *radical economic redistribution*.[32]

This is not a gospel of restitution for sin by Christ's substitution, but *equalization* through political sadism – the process whereby guilty people lay the punishment for sin upon other guilty people. Rushdoony is astute enough to see that sin "is not a monopoly of the left or the right but common to all men."[33] He argues:

> The civic gospel...has not abandoned vicarious suffering and atonement by the innocent; it has merely transferred it from Christ to all men who must now suffer.... Humanistic atonement demands vicarious suffering and payments as well.... State imposed vicarious suffering has no regenerating power; instead it destroys those it punishes as well as those it seeks to help. Statist atonement is destructive, not regenerative, because the state is a false savior.[34]

Biblical law and gospel know nothing of equalization through coercive redistribution. They are concerned with restitution, which alone can 'set things right,' because it is the restoration of God's order, not humanity's counterfeit paradise. Critically then, denial of Christ's work of restitution, the vicarious, substitutionary atonement – the *Day of Atonement* to meet the debt of sin – is to deny of the *reality of the debt* and consequently it is a total denial of Jubilee. "For men who deny the realty of debt...there can be no Jubilee, because the meaning of Jubilee is the cancellation of debt."[35] In the process of invoking Jubilee, Walsh in fact denies it. Yet there is no other way for debt cancellation to be effected – no other fire is acceptable to God. There is no other hope of salvation. There is no other Jubilee than the propitiatory sacrifice of Christ for sin. All other offerings are strange fire and come under the righteous judgement of God. Our Lord himself prayed, "My Father, if it be possible, let this cup pass from me; nevertheless, not as I will, but as you will...if this cannot pass unless I drink it, your will be done" (Matt. 26:39, 42). No other way was possible, for there was no other way for us to be redeemed than by the shedding of the blood of the lamb of God for sin, that we might drink his cup of salvation (1 Pt. 1:18–19).

7.4 Service and Stewardship

This orthodox and Reformed view of the cross does not make the Puritan vision unconcerned about real oppression, poverty, or care for the creation. As John Frame points out, Leviticus 19 and 23 place a limitation on landowning harvesters for the sake of the poor – the edges of the fields were to be left for the poor to glean. This was hard work for the recipient of social assistance, but it was a real and respectful means of social provision, not a dehumanizing hand-out. In the sabbatical years the fields were to lie fallow, whatever grew in those fields was for the poor and what they didn't eat was for the animals (Ex. 23:11). Frame suggests that today this can be expressed by the giving of food to the poor by grocery stores and food banks. Rushdoony includes 'goodwill industries' in this, where the poor restore donated items for sale, which involves meaningful work on the part of those receiving help. These are contemporary equivalents to gleaning.[36] The Scriptures also urge on us a massive generosity and sharing, a joy in giving, and deep concern for our poor brother in need (Mark 12:42–44; 2 Cor. 9:7; 1 John 3:17).

At the same time, there are requirements in biblical law, including rest for the land, beast, and man, which constitute a binding obligation upon all people for the purpose of good stewardship of creation, life and blessing. There are laws governing how animals are treated, how land is to be used and rested, how even in war, wanton destruction of fruit trees is prohibited, and a great deal besides. Much is said today about nature or land and 'environmentalism,' and Christians (usually the younger evangelicals), often with good intentions, can get caught up in the 'save the planet' rhetoric and agenda. Those who do not, or who say nothing about care and stewardship of creation, are usually labeled exploitative anti-environmentalists. Both conclusions are wrong, and neither apathy nor idolatry are appropriate responses regarding our relationship to the natural world. We can neither endorse the religion of environmentalism which makes a god of the created order, nor can we accept a 'couldn't care less' attitude to God's property, which is given as a gift of stewardship to man. As an aspect of Jubilee the land was important. The restoration of land concerned the inheritance of the covenant people and their share in the Promised Land.

But the Promised Land itself was a conditional gift, and just as our relationship to God is fundamentally moral, so we see in the legal expression of the Jubilee land grant, that our relationship to the land and environment is ethical. In Leviticus 18:24–30, the land spews out a defiling people. God expels from the land lawless people, whether they be Israelites or Canaanites. God's standards – his law – apply to believers and unbelievers, foreigners or strangers (Lev. 18:26). If people become a poison to the land by their immorality, the land vomits them out. That is to say, the physical condition of our environment, the condition of our land and animal kingdom, our ecological cycles and weather patterns, are inescapably related to the moral conduct of man. When we disobey God's commands, the land is parched and is not fruitful (Deut. 11:17). A truly biblical picture of creation stewardship does not elevate nature to the status of God as the source and wellspring of life, nor does it give nature or land priority over man, but rather tells us that the land suffers because of man; and because God governs all things by his personal agency, the created order responds to our moral conduct. In Genesis 3:17 we are told that the land is cursed on account of man. It was sin in man that brought the effects of sin into the created order. The Fall resulted in the expulsion of our first parents from the Garden of Eden, as the land vomited them out. The Noachian flood was another comprehensive expulsion from the land because of man's sin and defilement of the earth. This radical judgement destroyed the whole antediluvian world, with its extended life-spans and productivity. The Canaanites were then expelled from the land, as were the Jews during the exile and the fall of Jerusalem; clearly Jesus in Matthew 24 is applying the judgement of Leviticus 18:24–30 to Judea.

History is full of such expulsions right down to the present, such as the displacement of the Christian church in North Africa and large swaths of the Middle East, and the decline and displacement of Christianity in Western Europe. Furthermore, in the biblical paradigm, just as the curse on man resulted in a bondage to corruption for the earth, our final redemption and adoption will mean freedom from corruption for the land (Rom. 8:20–23). But because most people today (even Christians) think in impersonal terms about the creation and the land and view ecological processes in purely naturalistic terms, they do not think about man's sin in relationship to the fruitfulness of farming, husbandry, forest health and animal populations. Nor do they take seriously the expulsion from Eden, the Flood, or the Fall of Jerusalem, because they are evolutionary in their thinking and deny the historical character of Adam and Eve, thereby denying the creation ever fell – rather 'nature' has always been red in tooth and claw. They reject the temporal judgement of the global flood as myth and deride the active providence of God in the rising and falling of nations. History and the land peoples inherit are seen as merely random and a product of human power relations, coercion and illegal seizure. Droughts, plagues, floods and the productivity of land are to such people purely random phenomena and are unrelated to the morality of a people.

Biblical creation care however, means obedience to God's law as it concerns God, man and the land. This means that the environmentalists of today, who claim to love *Mother Nature* and therefore want to save the planet whilst worshiping idols, advocating the killing of the unborn to reduce carbon footprints, pursue the theft and re-distribution of land and resources, seek a radical equalization of all things, viewing the wealthy, the church, the family and Christian marriage as the primary obstacle to planetary salvation, are in fact destroying the environment; the land, cursed on their account, will vomit them out. If we are concerned with responsible care for creation and want to see human flourishing in the land and blessing on our agriculture, cattle, wilderness and animal kingdoms, we must obey God's law. If we are parched in these areas, we need look no further than our sins. Obedience is green! Thus the Puritan mind actually takes the totality of the law seriously in these matters rather than arbitrarily picking bits from the Torah or prophets that might fit with a given ideology, then setting the rest aside as hopelessly outdated and inconvenient.[37]

The obvious contradiction in much contemporary missiology is in its repeated appeals to *Jubilee* and the words of the *prophets* about oppression, poverty and the like, whilst denying the abiding relevance and validity of God's law. Clearly the prophets were God's servants, sent to call God's people back to *obedience to God's law*. Their words are not abstract statements about economics that can be arrested from their context and given an alien meaning. They can only be understood in terms of the whole law of God in Scripture and only then do we understand God's solution for these problems. Puritan thought especially notes the intended *outcome* of obedience to God's laws for debt, charity and Sabbath rest; not an equalitarian order but, "a debt-free society which is also poverty free, and this is only possible in terms of God's law."[38] God's law of liberty (Jas. 1:25) is thus at the heart of a truly reformed vision for God's reign. This reign can only be realized through obedience to God's word and not humanistic ideals which rest on envy and covetousness. A debt-free and poverty-free community cannot be established by pursuit of an illusory equalized society that is charity-free through state action, but only by faithful obedience to the law and gospel. That gospel and law is one of restitution and free generosity motivated by love. Once again we see that the key is in obedience to the law of God, not the theories of men. Wealth and riches in themselves are not the enemy, but a blessing from God to be used, as God's property, for his purposes by faithful *stewards* of his trust. As the Psalmist makes clear, "Blessed is the man who fears the Lord, who greatly delights in his commandments! His offspring will be mighty in the land; the generation of the upright will be blessed. Wealth and riches are in his house, and his righteousness endures forever…it is well with the man who deals generously and lends; who conducts his affairs with justice" (Ps. 112:1–5).

Chapter Eight

SIT AT MY RIGHT HAND:
LAW, THEOCRACY AND CONTEMPORARY RELEVANCE

For the Word of the Lord is upright, and all his work is done in faithfulness. He loves righteousness and justice.... Blessed is the nation whose God is the Lord.

(Ps. 33:4–5,12)

To me it is a wonder that the Old and New Testament, which containeth an exact system and body of all morals...,should not be the only rule of all morals.

– Samuel Rutherford

8.1 History, Continuity and Relevance

In the ninth century A.D. King Alfred the Great inaugurated codified English law with the Ten Commandments. In A.D. 1540, King Henry VIII established seven cities of refuge based on the biblical model of Numbers 27:1-11. The Puritan settlers of New England self-consciously planned their commonwealth after the pattern of biblical law, as can be seen from the *Order of the General Court of Massachusetts* 1636 and the *General Lawes of Plymouth Colony* 1658.[1] English canon law was so substantially drawn from biblical law that, in regard to biblical regulations concerning inheritance and English inheritance law, the nineteenth century jurist Sir Frederick Pollock said of Numbers 27:1-11 that it was "the earliest recorded case which is still of authority."[2] When the civil government of Israel was established, God addressed the seventy elders of the people and poured out his Spirit upon them, meaning that the first 'Pentecost' was a civil affair, at the ordination of civil authorities (Num. 11:16-17).

A similar 'Pentecost' event later occurred at the anointing of Saul, which marked the beginning of a second form of civil government in Israel, a transition from a commonwealth to a monarchy (1 Sam. 10:1-7). The early church continued such rites of coronation or anointing. The form of the rite which highlights the role of God's law in our history remains with us. The Oath required of Queen Elizabeth II (the head of state of Great Britain and Canada) stated: "Will you to the utmost of your power maintain the Laws of God and the true profession of the Gospel? Will you to the utmost of your power maintain in the United Kingdom the Protestant Reformed Religion established by law..."[3]

After this Oath, the moderator of the General Assembly of the Church of Scotland brought to the queen the Bible, saying:

> Our gracious Queen: to keep your Majesty ever mindful of the Law and the Gospel of God as the Rule for the whole life and government of Christian Princes, we present you with this Book, the most valuable thing that this world affords. Here is wisdom; This is the royal Law; These are the lively Oracles of God.[4]

After the anointing, which cited the anointing of Solomon, the Archbishop of York presented the queen with the Sword of State during which she is charged to wield the sword of justice in God's authority by stopping the growth of iniquity, protecting the church, defending orphans and widows, restoring, punishing, and reforming where required, in service the Lord Jesus Christ. When the Orb with the Cross was then given to Queen Elizabeth the II, the archbishop declared: "Receive this Orb, set under the Cross, and remember that the whole world is subject to the Power and Empire of Christ our Redeemer."[5] Though the faith was perhaps absent, this whole service bore testament to the ancient coronation service in Israel, and to the abiding relevance and authority of biblical law to the socio-cultural and political spheres, clearly declaring that the civil order is directly under and accountable to God, being established by his decree as part of his kingdom reign. Formerly, when the incoming President of the United States took the oath of office it was done, not on a closed Bible, but on a Bible opened to Deuteronomy 28, invoking the blessings and cursing of the law for obedience or disobedience. These oaths were taken with great seriousness because God's law was seen as a serious matter. All this reveals the fact that biblical law has had a continuous history as an object of relevance and study that makes it unique amongst ancient legal systems, and gives it "a claim to historical influence unmatched by any other legal system of antiquity."[6] This history is traceable back more than two thousand years to the fall of the Temple in Jerusalem in the first century. It can be traced back another thousand years to the period of the kings of Israel, and indeed all the way to Moses in the late second millennium B.C.[7]

Yet its relevance is not limited to the study of the *history* of Israel and the West. Jonathan Burnside, professor at the School of Law, University of Bristol and reader in Biblical Law, has published a massive study showing not only how biblical law has shaped the Western world, but how it remains relevant to solving contemporary legal dilemmas, and based on its track record, "will continue to be a source of inspiration and debate when modern legal empires have long been forgotten."[8] He notes:

> Biblical law continues to exert a hold over popular culture at a basic level, including the structure of the working week and the idea of a day of rest, the constraints placed upon political authority, the use of everyday language (such as references to a "scapegoat"), the idea of mercy, employee rights, and the special significance historically attached to marriage and the monogamous family unit. The word covenant which is prominent in biblical law, used to be the standard word for a contract in English law and is still used in the law of property today....biblical law is also remarkable for its revolutionary breadth and depth of vision. It has the imaginative power to disturb the world....a great deal of modern law is an indirect engagement with biblical law (for example, the abolition of the English laws of blasphemy in 2008), but often it is so implicit that we are not aware of it. We have taken our understanding of biblical law for granted for so long that it has become unfamiliar. This is the immanence of biblical law: it is part of our culture – but it is alien....biblical law does not function in relation to English law or U.S. law as an external or parallel body of law (cf. Islamic religious law or sharia). This is because, unlike sharia law, biblical law is nascent in the history of English law and so continues to be an influence on many citizens. It is simply unrealistic to suggest that we live in a wholly secular legal system....nor have politicians been successful in finding a dominant alternative discourse to the ethical language of the Bible.[9]

The alien yet immanent character of biblical law is not just true for the political and legal spheres today; it is true in the churches, which are largely responsible for our cultural amnesia. In many of today's churches, the law of God has been pushed to the periphery. Most protestant liturgies formerly involved the weekly reciting of the law, and many churches displayed the Ten Commandments in a prominent position, keeping the relevance and validity of God's law at the forefront of people's minds and making for a God-fearing society. This is implicit in the idea of law because "law is a form of command whose validity is derived from social facts – chiefly, the fact of sovereign power and the fact of habitual obedience on the part of most of the citizens."[10] Law is thus a value-processing system that is bound up with the character and goals of a society. If the divine goals for the world remain those of the kingdom of God expounded in Scripture, then the Bible gives us God's value-processing system based on his sovereign authority, and for God's good pleasure as well as our own well-being, we are called to obedience to it. We find this requirement difficult in our day because we are obsessed with the absurd notion that what is new is to be valued more than what is old, as though laws were like cars – the latest models must be more sophisticated, more useful, and more appropriate for the time than the old. What may be true of motor cars (although classic car enthusiasts may take issue with that) is not necessarily true of law and morality. Antiquity is not a disqualification for the truth or relevance of moral precept and law. Just because something is, does not make it right, and just because we have been born in a century of legal revolution against the Bible does not mean that we have made 'progress.' Just because things are a certain way in society at present does not mean that they should be that way, or that they cannot be other than they are. Repealing laws against blasphemy, sodomy, abortion, types of divorce and the like, may be modern ideas and developments, but this neither makes them right, true, or beneficial to society. What is older in this regard may in fact be far superior, and in the case of biblical law, for the Christian it must be, since it is from God, who does not change. Indeed legal scholars have acknowledged:

> We find in biblical rules and judgements a level of insight that has rarely, if ever, been surpassed. Nor do we find any other legal system a more positive vision for humanity and the world than that found in the biblical legal collections....we should not assume that what is, is inevitable – especially when what is, is wrong. Biblical law reminds us that the world can be other than it is – and that the actual is merely the possible.[11]

This does not mean there can be no new applications of law to new situations. Law is not static in the sense of being wooden and unable to be appropriately applied to changing circumstances. As R. J. Rushdoony points out:

The law is given as principles (the Ten Commandments) and as cases (the detailed commandments), and its meaning is to be hammered out in experience and in trial. This does not mean that the law is a developing thing but that man's awareness of its implications develops as new situations bring fresh light on the possible applications of the law. The Psalmist in Psalm 119 clearly saw the law as a positive force in his growth and in his ability to stand up to the adversities of history.[12]

Biblical law then presents itself to us as a journey into wisdom, in which we are introduced to the essentials of justice and righteousness in a variety of literary forms. As we have already seen, the biblical view of law encompasses much more than the Ten Commandments. As Burnside rightly says, "Biblical law [is] an integration of different instructional genres of the Bible which together express a *vision of society ultimately answerable to God.*"[13] This is God's vision and the biblical vision of all the societies of men, that they are accountable to God and his law. St. Paul declares: "Now we know that whatever the law says it speaks to those who are under the law, so that *every mouth may be stopped, and the whole world may be held accountable to God.* For by the works of the law no human being will be justified in his sight, since through the law comes the knowledge of sin" (Rom. 3:19–20). Here the apostle cites the law as a collection of God's commandments and wisdom from all over the older Testament, since his quotations from the Scriptures are from Psalms, Ecclesiastes and Isaiah. He makes plain that knowledge of sin comes by the law and that the whole world stands accountable to God in terms of it. The salient question regarding the relevance of biblical law today is whether or not we still believe the societies of men in the earth remain accountable to God. The Christian must answer an emphatic Yes. All men are accountable to God, and for human society to flourish we must walk in the 'old paths' in the 'good way' if we would know life and rest (Jer. 6:16). The reason being, the Torah and wisdom about which St. Paul speaks are written into the structure of the physical universe and the reality of all that is (Ps. 19; Prov. 8:22ff).

Despite all this, for many Christians today, the law of God is either never consulted and thus not understood, dismissed as irrelevant for our time, or viewed as an embarrassment not to be discussed. To preach the law of God in much of the modern church is to expose yourself to ridicule and charges of Pharisaism, legalism, dominionism, and even heresy. This is rooted in the loss of the centrepiece of old evangelical theology, the relationship between law and gospel; rightly discerning this used to be regarded as the key to evangelical divinity. John Warwick Montgomery correctly identifies the problem:

> Confusion of law and gospel is possible in two directions. Law may be invested with the quality of gospel, thereby deceiving men into thinking that they can save themselves through personal or societal efforts. But gospel may also try to replace law, producing what Bonhoeffer has classically phrased "cheap grace." In the one case law swallows up gospel, and the result is legalism; in the other, gospel absorbs law, yielding antinomianism. The gravity of dispensing with law for any reason – even on alleged ground that grace renders it no longer necessary – is suggested by the New Testament use of the Greek word *anomos* ("lawless one") for the Antichrist. In contemporary theology the antinomian error is rife.[14]

This antinomian error has cost the church dearly in our day, as biblically illiterate and lawless Christians are left floundering without a guide or anchor in the relativistic and pluralistic confusion of contemporary Western culture. Without a concept of Christian law, and the clear teaching of God's law in the churches, young people find themselves adopting pagan and humanistic ethical theories and legal frameworks that are not only inferior to, but hostile toward biblical law. Moral progressivism in education leads many professing Christians to the conclusion that God needs to be updated, that what was morally true in the first, fifth or seventeenth centuries can't possibly be true today and that therefore God's word needs to be subject to radical revisionism or its authority essentially denied. In his important study, *The Mission of God*, Christopher Wright, drawing heavily on covenantal themes developed long before him in the Puritan tradition, makes some very important observations concerning the law of God and its timely relevance. Amongst the most significant is that the biblical claim for Israel's social uniqueness was made on a world-stage with many other claimants to admirable systems of law, including the famous law code of Hammurabi in the ancient near East.[15] Wright observes concerning Deuteronomy 4:5–9:

> Old Testament law explicitly invites, even welcomes, public inspection and comparison. But the expected result of such

comparison is that Israel's law will be found superior in wisdom and justice. This is a monumental claim. It grants to the nations and to the readers of this text, including ourselves, the liberty to analyse Old Testament law in comparison with other social systems, ancient and modern, and to evaluate its claim. And indeed, the humaneness and justice of Israel's overall social and legal system have been favourably commented on by many scholars who have done the most meticulous studies of comparative ancient law, and its social relevance can still be profitably mined today. From our missiological perspective, these verses articulate a motivation for obedience to the law that is easily overlooked but highly significant. The point is that if Israel would live as God intended, then the nations would notice... here we find that at least one aspect of that blessing of the nations would be by providing such a model of social justice that the nations would observe and ask questions.[16]

It is a great pity that Wright's flash of insight here is not more developed in his work, and its implications fleshed out in terms of the kingdom and reign of God in modern society. The church's broader failure to understand the relevance of this clear biblical vision to our present social crisis leaves many of us without critical tools for Kingdom work and service, and worse, leads to moral confusion and arbitrary moral judgements. The law is therefore relevant, for without it moral and ethical judgements, indeed justice and injustice, are impossible to define.

8.2 An Instituting Consideration of the Relevance of Law

The need of the hour, then, is for careful study of God's law in all Scripture and an exploration of its significance today.[17] One such meticulous study of biblical law with a detailed mining of its contemporary social relevance is the *magnum opus* of the noted modern Puritan, R. J. Rushdoony, *The Institutes of Biblical Law* (1973), a work four years in the making of over 800 pages. In his *Christianity Today* column of 1974, Harold O.J. Brown named it the most important book of 1973.[18] Throughout this chapter we will be returning to it as illustrative of the Puritan mind. Technically it is a work of Protestant casuistry – a discussion and application of biblical law to real-world situations.[19] William Edgar also acknowledged that this work showed Rushdoony "to be a man of extraordinary brilliance possessing an almost encyclopaedic knowledge of human affairs." [20] Little of real consequence had been published in the field since A.D. 1700, because Unitarian and Darwinian social philosophies gradually came to dominate the church's social philosophy. North summarizes the work and its significance:

> Rushdoony took the Ten Commandments as the ordering principle for the whole of Biblical law, Old Testament and New. He analyzed each of the case laws in terms of the Decalogue. He concluded that civil government must be shrunk drastically to meet Biblical standards, so that the free market and voluntary social action will flourish.... It represented a major transition in his writing career from detailed negative critical analysis to a detailed positive alternative...."you can't beat something with nothing." [21]

Like the Puritans, Rushdoony saw biblical law as not only the benchmark of personal sanctification and self-government, but regarded faith and law as God's revealed purpose for human society as accountable to God and therefore critical to the Christian's Kingdom calling in the world. We have seen that in the absence of biblical law, an alien vision of 'social justice' becomes the predominant standard of righteousness. Concerning this competing perspective, Rushdoony remarked, "Justice is not social: it is individual. The doctrine of social justice goes hand in hand with the doctrine of social guilt. Social justice is not only an attack on individual responsibility but also on the immunity of the innocent." [22] The central vision for law and goal of law in this competing legal paradigm is *equality*. This does not mean the equality the Bible speaks of and implies – equality in terms of the dignity of our creation as persons made in God's image and the derivative privilege of being equally under the rule of his law. Rushdoony articulates the notion of equality in social justice theory:

> Equality is a form of slavery, because it is an instrument whereby all institutions, families, and religious authorities are eroded and destroyed. The egalitarian state stresses destructive and erosive freedoms such as sexual license, abortion, homosexuality, euthanasia, drugs, and more, as a means of eroding the positive social forces such as family and church. Such a state presents itself as the champion of liberty because it enhances individual irresponsibility, whereas true freedom means responsibility and accountability...where radical

individual freedom triumphs irresponsibility reigns, and also the tyrant state. Tyrant states triumph in the name and under the banner of "Liberty, Fraternity, and Equality."[23]

We can conclude then that the kingdom of God is not manifest in the nations by man's lawless vision of social justice and equality, but only by the manifestation of the righteousness and justice of God found in all Scripture. This perspective on law was undergirded by Rushdoony's deep Calvinistic convictions. In light of the Great Commission (Mark 16:15), John Calvin wrote concerning the mission of God's people in his *Institutes*, "No fixed limits are given them, but the whole world is assigned, to be reduced under the obedience of Christ, that by spreading the gospel as widely as they could, they might everywhere erect his kingdom."[24] As historian Lucien Joseph Richard observed concerning Calvin's thought, "In a real sense, the Christian must become an agent of the restoration of order throughout the world."[25]

The order that we are called to restore by the gospel is God's law order as we serve the restitution of all things in Jesus Christ. In Rushdoony's *Institutes* (self-consciously named after Calvin's) it is clear that several such interrelated doctrinal convictions are at work resulting in this sweeping manifesto. They include the sovereignty of God, covenantal theology, Calvinistic soteriology, postmillennialism, biblical law as the foundation for ethics (exemplified in the Sermon on the Mount)[26] and a pre-suppositional method in apologetics.[27] These factors come together in the *Institutes* to form a consistent Puritan missiology, sketching the building blocks of a program for a Christian renaissance. The relevance of biblical law is seen in the kingdom charter it suggests for the Christian church.

8.3 The Source of Law: Nature or God

In our culture, the other vision of law that competes with the pragmatic positivist law of social justice theory is that of natural law, in a variety of forms. In his exegetical companion statement of kingdom ethics, a commentary on Deuteronomy, Rushdoony makes clear the choices before all people in their relationship to law and ethics. His analysis is worth quoting at length because it lays an important foundation for the rest of the discussion in this chapter:

In the main, three concepts of justice have governed men. First, for biblical faith, justice is God's nature and law. Justice is an expression of God's being and is therefore the inescapable standard over all things. God gives us His law as the rule to live by. Justice is thus in essence supernatural because a fallen, sinful world cannot be just.... Second, some see law and justice as the expression of Nature, and they speak of natural law. This view, even in its church-related formulations, has an inherent contradiction. How can a fallen world give us law? We can agree that there is a law over the universe, and that this law is operative within the universe, but it is God's law, not Nature's.... Natural law is usually invoked to evade God's law while having some transcendental reference. The specifics of natural law cannot be agreed upon. There is no given body of natural law. Third, law can be purely the expedient, temporal, and changing law of nations. It has no external validity and it is pragmatic in purpose. There is no absolute good nor evil, right nor wrong. If God's law is not the overruling government over all things, then some kind of super-state must provide it. As a result, a world of statist law-making bodies soon seeks to create a fiat world law, a world court, and a world state. If there be no God with a governing law over all things, then a man-made world order must replace Him. Thus the alternative to God and his law is inevitably a humanistic law and world order.[28]

This is an excellent summary of the basic character of conflicting opinions on the *source of law* and it sums up the aim of Puritan thought well – to drive the believer to the conclusion that the law of God has an essential and abiding relevance to every aspect of life in society and to the religious, social, economic and political crisis of every age. The choice is theonomy (God's law) or autonomy (man's self-law), and autonomy leads inexorably to either anarchy or totalitarianism.

The main rival to biblical law in Christian thought has been variations of natural law theory. Natural law theories are a speculative and complex combination of metaphysical and moral philosophy with a long history; notably articulated as far back as Aristotle, and then in some measure 'Christianized' by Thomas Aquinas, with some original insights and development. Thomistic scholar D. J. O' Connor explains, "the theory of natural law which is the basis of St. Thomas' ethics turns on the idea that human nature is constituted by a unique set of properties which can be understood and summed up in a definition."[29] The idea here is that things 'are what they are,' and so we must understand the 'essence' of things, including the human person, in order to develop or recognize rational moral action. The ideas of 'good' and 'being' are essentially equivalent terms because good is viewed as a property of all existing things. Evil is viewed as the absence of good in a manner analogous to darkness being the absence of light, or silence the absence of sound, or cold the absence of heat. In other words, "Evil is present in a thing to the extent that it lacks some degree of realization for which its nature fits it." [30] Thus by rational deliberation on the essence of things, one is meant to be able to come to understand right moral action. This moral action is not an identifiable body of laws but a highly controversial *abstraction*.

Considering the prevalence amongst many Christians of natural law theories, especially those involved in the study and practice of law, it is worthwhile expanding our brief discussion of natural law theories to demonstrate the clear problems associated with the concept. The notion of natural law put to use for political purposes was probably first developed by the Stoic philosophers of the late classical Greek period. After the death of Alexander the Great in 322 B.C. his empire fragmented into four realms and Greek culture became a state-worshiping culture. To maintain classical culture required a coherent and cohesive political order – the Stoics provided the glue, the doctrine of natural law:

> They argued that there is a universal law structure, and that all rational men can apprehend it. This universal law was said to be the basis of universal humanity, and therefore the basis of universal culture. The only trouble was (and is), they could provide no evidence that such a universal legal order exists, or that rational minds will universally agree about what this legal order is. In fact, self-proclaimed rational men have argued ever since about reason, "right" reason, and natural law "properly understood." Roman philosophers later adopted Stoic philosophy and used the idea of natural law to justify the Roman Empire. [31]

For the Stoic reason itself was *inherent* in the universe as an impersonal principle (god) and so the rational state became the locus of divinity. Epictetus, a student of Seneca, wrote: "When a man has learnt to understand the government of the universe and has realized that there is nothing so great or sovereign or *all-inclusive as this frame of things wherein man and God are united*...why should he not call himself a citizen of the universe and a son of God." [32] Here, we are again back to the illusory claim of autonomy and neutrality in knowledge (in this case especially moral and judicial neutrality), which lies at the root of paganism and the modern revival of monism. If creator and creature are not *absolutely distinct* in terms of the transcendent triune God of Scripture (a concept that did not exist in pagan thought), reality collapses into a *continuity* of 'being' – the essential 'sameness' of all things which is the essence of paganism. In such a universe human beings will deify creation, their reason, and themselves as an aspect of this self-generating, self-explanatory order and the human mind will furnish reality with truth and law and call it an expression of *nature*. This Stoic paganism which St. Paul confronted on Mars Hill in Acts 17 has experienced a huge revival in the twentieth century in the modified form of post-secularism, due to the impact of Romanticism and its 'nature worship.' The United Nations' dream of universal humanity, spirituality and culture under a one-world-order, and contemporary human rights theory based on the monistic obliteration of all distinctions (from creator/creation to gender and sexuality distinctions), are all based in a form of this doctrine and are thus an expression of resurgent paganism. The ideas of *international* law and the notion of *human rights* are thus contemporary expressions of stoicism and Romanticism. These laws and rights that express the oneness of all things (being) are allegedly inherent in nature or 'humanity,' and thus should be recognized by all nations as 'citizens of the universe' and 'sons of god' (gods). This 'vision' can only be understood and embraced when we transcend the distinctions of Christian theism (created and uncreated being; male and female, objective right and wrong, truth and falsehood, etc.) and realize the synthesis of religion and ethics in a new oneness. Various forms of pantheistic occultism then express the spirituality of the age and 'nature' gives us its law which unifies good and evil in a new and higher way.

In the ancient world, as classical religion and philosophy collapsed and the Roman Empire fell, the door was opened for a biblical and Hebraic understanding of the creator-creature distinction, revealed law and freedom from the tyranny of 'oneness' (which politically produces a totalitarian god-state) to take root, spreading freedom under God wherever it went. As a result, for Christians to try and save modern civilization by an appeal to natural law (disconnected from the God of Scripture and his revealed law), is to appeal to classical philosophy and constitutes a death wish. St. Paul certainly does teach that all human beings know the *work* of God's law even though they may not be consistently conscious of all its precepts – they recognize by created instinct the work of God's law on their hearts, their conscience bearing witness to this reality (Rom. 2:14–15). However, though people know the work of God's law, in rebellion they don't want to obey it. Just as they see God's attributes and power in creation but refuse to honour God and worship the creation instead, so they know God's requirement and sanctions in their conscience but rebel against it. As a consequence, God hands them over to a depraved mind (Rom. 1:24) and they then live in terms of that (Rom. 1:29–32). Thus the work of God's law known by common grace (not by natural law) serves only to condemn people in their sin and rebellion, and does not provide an *alternate* law structure to biblical law, since rightly understood (not perverted or suppressed), the law in man's being only confirms God's written law (Rom. 2).

As opposed to the doctrines of classical philosophy, Scripture teaches that the human problem is essentially ethical, not a lack of information, knowledge or enlightenment. Sinful humanity in the face of our better knowledge chooses evil – the fall radically affected human reasoning, not just a person's 'soul' and body. As such, *reason* with its self-generated moral and political order cannot save. Natural law has its appeal because it pretends to neutrality and so is perceived by many Christians as a 'non-religious' paradigm and therefore a useful tool for engagement with the 'secular' sphere. But the reality is, "Natural law theory serves temporarily as a believable political philosophy only when there is a common religious agreement beforehand. Shatter that religious agreement, and natural law theory becomes useless." [33] This is simply because as soon as the religious consensus is lost, people's vision of what 'natural law' is becomes totally disparate or is abandoned altogether. The emphatic shattering of the Christian consensus in the West came in the wake of Darwinism and naturalistic evolution – for how could an ethical 'oughtness' arise from a self-generating cosmic and biological 'is?' Consequently, Christians who refuse to accept biblical law invariably try to salvage moral transcendence from the Darwinian abyss by an unconvincing appeal to pagan natural law theory (usually in modified forms of Thomistic thought) as a basis for civil righteousness and social order. For without one transcendent law you are left with only the crumbs of judicial pluralism, always moving from one principle to another as expediency dictates. This is the relativism and lawless pluralism of our culture which in the final analysis amounts to polytheism. Sutton summarises well the desperate situation in the West today: "At present, civil government in the West wants liberty without the Gospel, morality without Christ, affluence without covenant. It is willing to do anything, including forfeiture of its own lands to Mohammedans, except submit its nation to Christ. Civil leadership is even willing to subsidize polytheism."[34] In his study of Puritan political theory, Richard Flinn discusses the important work of Samuel Rutherford and his classic work, *Lex Rex*. Rutherford was confronting in his time a similar question about the *source* of law. Some of the papists of his day had argued that the king *as a man* was subject to God, but in the practice of his *office as king*, he was not subject to God's law. Rutherford saw that this meant that the king was either above God, or co-equal with God, which are both "manifest blasphemies."[35] Flinn points out that at the heart of the Calvinist view of biblical political theory is that the civil government must be under God's law, or be blasphemous. Furthermore, "unless we are willing to grant this doctrine and build upon it, there can be no Christian politics; there can only be humanistic politics, which, when practiced by Christians, is idolatry."[36] The upshot then of natural law theories in whatever form it is presented is that authority is shifted from God to man, from revelation to nature and reason. Flinn sees the inevitable consequences:

> In summary, we find that natural law theorists argue that both the institution of civil government and its form or structure are grounded upon natural law and the exercise of human reason. The upshot is that civil government in both its form and ethical roots becomes arbitrary and autonomous. Eventually either tyranny or anarchy will result.[37]

Simply stated, how can anyone determine for himself or others a minimum content of natural law that binds all people and can therefore be coerced by legislation without being hopelessly arbitrary? O'Connor wrestles with the difficulty of providing precepts of social morality within natural law theories, showing that they can offer only a *description* of salient facts about the human species and typical human desires, followed by a recognition of the obvious that "it is necessary, if men are to live together at all, to have certain rules protecting their personal safety and property and ensuring that degree of mutual forbearance and respect that will make social living tolerable." Or, as he otherwise states it, "Do as you would be done by." [38] O'Connor thus sees the root of the natural law problem clearly, noting that such a view prescribes no unconditional moral imperatives. "We are given no reason why we ought to act in a particular way. And this fact emphasizes once again the difficulty facing any attempt to base *morality* on human nature." [39] The inescapable result of such thinking means, as Rushdoony has pointed out, that "lacking the transcendental standard which Scripture provides, other systems inevitably turn to an immanent one and absolutize the state, the individual, or some other aspect of life." [40] Absolutizing some aspect of the immanent realm then becomes the project of humanistic thought, including the possibility of absolutizing of the church amongst Christian thinkers:

> ...the institutional church, cannot be identified with the totality of the church or the kingdom of God and thereby make that order incarnated in history. Moreover, the authority of the church must be biblical, strictly ministerial and never legislative, in terms of the will and purposes of God as manifested in Scripture. The authority of the church is in the area of proclamation of the word of God, the administration of the sacraments, and the government of its own inner life as an institution. *Christianity destroys itself if it absolutizes an immanent authority.* [41]

The theonomic position recognizes that the *form* or expression of civil government does legitimately vary at different times, in the historical context of the people who are governed and in terms of the consent of that people i.e. kings, judges, parliaments, councils, senates, presidents etc. But the institution of civil government is not autonomous, nor under the church, but under God, and in exercising justice it must be governed by him and his word in the immediate sense, as representing and under his authority.

8.4 The New Puritan Perspective

The alternative to natural law theory and its quest for 'freedom' is obvious – God's revealed law and the freedom made available by the law of liberty (Jas. 2:12). Rushdoony's Puritan thesis in the *Institutes*, in light of these rival concepts of the provenance of law, is clear and constructive. Seeing the *root* of the human problem as sin and rebellion against God and his word (not people's environment, whether social or economic), with rebellion aimed at independence from God, Christ is revealed and Scripture given to redeem and govern the totality of a person's life. Obedience to God's word, by the regenerating work of the Spirit, leads to salvation by faith in Christ, blessing, life, hope, joy and *liberty*, for "man shall not live by bread alone but by every word that proceeds from the mouth of God" (Matt. 4:4). Disobedience leads to misery, tyranny, curses and death (cf. Deut. 28). What is true of obedience for the individual is true for the family, school, church, and nation. What may confound some critics is that this commitment to Scriptural standards in all God's law-word, made Rushdoony not a Pharisaic legalist (a heresy he repeatedly repudiated), but a tireless advocate of liberty in every sphere – political, ecclesiastical and religious. As a *Christian libertarian* in the Puritan tradition, he held that lasting personal, social and political liberty was not possible apart from orthodox Christianity and the upholding of God's law.[42] For God's law is the law of liberty, of freedom (Jas. 1:25).

Rushdoony's conviction that God is the source of sovereignty and his law must therefore be the standard for all time, which in turn demanded a limited state, an end to confiscatory taxation, and the flourishing and freedom of the private family, social and commercial spheres, did not make Rushdoony's research organization, *The Chalcedon Foundation*, uncritically supportive of the American Christian Right. Rushdoony did not even like the language of 'right' and 'left,' since it stemmed from the seating position of political figures in the halls of power during the French Revolution. Although the American tabloid *Newsweek* featured an article about the 'Religious Right' after the 1980 landslide win for the Republicans, and named Rushdoony's *Chalcedon* as the only 'think tank,'[43] Rushdoony was opposed to statism of every kind, conservative or liberal. Despite his staunch opposition to communism and socialism in all his works, he was *not* a pro-militarist conservative. For Rushdoony, politics of any stripe devoid of this critical foundation of biblical law and true Christian commitment, was just more statism writ small! This made him highly critical of the so-called 'Christian Right' at times.[44] In a passage chastizing partisan political conservatism he wrote, "The conservatives attempt to retain the political forms of the Christian West with no belief in biblical Christianity. Apart from vague affirmations of liberty, they cannot defend their position philosophically."[45] As a consequence, he felt they tended to merely fact-find amongst liberal humanists to document their corruption and abuse of office. If successful in this strategy, this leads the people only to "exchange one set of radical humanists for reforming radical humanists." [46] In either case what is on offer is political salvation. But in Rushdoony's Puritanism, man's social problems cannot be solved by humanistic concepts of *political progress* of the right or left but only theologically, by a return to Christ, biblical law, and creedal affirmations that shaped the pre-modern period in the Christian West. The contemporary relevance of biblical law then is seen from the fact that it is *God's law* and therefore freedom for man in the social and political spheres, without which politics becomes messianic and a tyranny to any people.

8.5 Theocracy and the Kingdom of God

A further aspect to the contemporary relevance of biblical law is the way in which it speaks to issues of civil government. With everything from anarchy to oligarchy, autocratic dictatorships, communism and democracy as competing ideologies in today's world, theocracy is becoming a question of renewed interest, featuring often in theological discussions about the Christian's relationship to culture and increasingly in political commentary – usually as a source of dread and potential oppression. Puritan missiology insists that, as the Psalms make clear, God reigns over all the nations, and is alone both King and Savior. The Psalms declare the biblical vision of God's rule. If this is so, however, if man's politics cannot save, then are we not faced with the great 'boogey man' of modern political pundits, this alleged specter of 'Theocracy?' If God's purpose is that his word, and not the autonomous deliberations of human reason, govern society; if Christ is indeed to be honored as the King of Kings, as we noted is made clear by the words of the Archbishop of Canterbury at the coronation of all English monarchs; then are we not advocating for a kind of Christian tyranny – a tyrannical theocracy? We must first ask what theocracy actually means:

> Few things are more commonly misunderstood than the nature and meaning of theocracy. It is commonly assumed to be a dictatorial rule by self-appointed men who claim to rule for God. In reality, theocracy in Biblical law is the closest thing to a radical libertarianism that can be had. In Biblical law, the only civil tax was the head or poll tax, the same for all males twenty years of age and older (Ex. 30:16). This tax provided atonement or covering for people, i.e., the

covering of civil protection by the state as a ministry of justice (Rom. 13:1-4). This very limited tax was continued by the Jews after the fall of Jerusalem, and, from 768-900 A.D., helped make the Jewish princedom of Narbonne (in France) and other areas a very important and powerful realm (in this regard see Arthur J. Zuckerman: *A Jewish Princedom in Feudal France 768-900*). This tax was limited to half a sheckel of silver per man. All other functions of government were financed by the tithe. Health, education, welfare, worship, etc., were all provided for by tithes and offerings. Of this tithe, one tenth (i.e., one percent of one's income) went to the priests, for worship. Perhaps an equal amount went for music, and for the care of the sanctuary. The tithe was God's tax, to provide for basic government in God's way. The second and the third tithes provided for welfare, and for the family's rest and rejoicing before the Lord (see E.A. Powell and R.J. Rushdoony: *Tithing and Dominion*). What we today fail to see, and must recapture, is the fact that the basic government is the self-government of covenant man; then the family is the central governing institution of Scripture. The school is a governmental agency, and so too is the church. Our vocation also governs us, and our society. Civil government must be one form of government among many, and a minor one. Paganism (and Baal worship in all its forms) made the state and its rulers into a god or gods walking on earth, and gave them total overrule in all spheres. The prophets denounced all such idolatry, and the apostles held, "We ought to obey God rather than men" (Acts 5:29). From the days of the Caesars to the heads of democratic states and Marxist empires, the ungodly have seen what Christians too often fail to see, namely, that biblical faith requires and creates a rival government to the humanistic state. Defective faith seeks to reduce Biblical faith to a man-centered minimum, salvation. Now salvation, our regeneration, is the absolutely essential starting point of the Christian life, but, if it is made the sum total thereof, it is in effect denied. Salvation is then made into a man-centered and egotistical thing, when it is in fact God-centered and requires the death, not the enthronement, of our sinful and self-centered ego. We are saved for God's purposes, saved to serve, not in time only, but eternally (Rev. 22:3). To be saved is to be members of a new creation and God's Kingdom, and to be working members of that realm. In a theocracy, therefore, God and His law rule. The state ceases to be the

SIT AT MY RIGHT HAND...

over-lord and ruler of man. God's tax, the tithe, is used by godly men to create schools, hospitals, welfare agencies, counsellors, and more. It provides, as it did in Scripture, for music and more. All the basic social financing, other than the head tax of Ex. 30:16, was provided for by tithes and offerings or gifts.[47]

How do we arrive at this meaning? In keeping with the Scripture, as we have seen thus far, a Puritan, theonomic missiology is fundamentally anti-statist because *that is the way the Bible* is.[48] Authority comes from God alone and not the state, as 'the people' enlarged:

> There are only two possible sources of civil power; power and authority comes either from God or the people. If the power comes from God, then God's law must prevail. If power comes from the people, then the people's will should prevail, and there is no law then higher than the will of the mob.... [I]f power comes from God, then God's law must govern in every sphere of life.[49]

This highlights the fact that *democracy* is only as good (or useful) as the people and their submission to God's covenant; it is not a good in itself as though participation of the people in government assures us of truth, righteousness and freedom prevailing. Democracy can function as the tyranny of the 51% if cut loose from truth and righteousness. Democratic institutions can slow down the advance of tyranny, but cannot prevent it. It is ironic in our time that the louder people shout about their freedom, the less free they have become. People can quickly *consent* to what is evil and a culture swiftly become corrupt even if 'democratic.' When the 'voice of the people' becomes established as the 'voice of God' (*vox populi vox dei*), democracy, when utilized merely as a secular ideology, becomes the tyranny of the mob and God's law is quickly turned on its head. In this form, a democratic vision cut loose from the God of Scripture degenerates from participation in consent to be governed, into idolatry that *replaces God with man* and is not freedom at all but self-imposed slavery.[50] As a result, the progressivism of the nineteenth century as represented by the likes of John Dewey consequently held that Christianity and the family were aristocratic and un-democratic.[51] Thus, whilst Rushdoony (and the Puritan movement in general) believed in the consent of the people to be governed (Cromwell's Puritan movement assuring us of parliamentary, representative government) and a familial form of *proportional representation*, he, like the Puritans before him, did not believe in the late-modern ideology of 'one person/ one vote.' Rather, only the responsible can take such a responsibility. For example, Rushdoony did not think criminals, or long-term welfare recipients should be allowed to vote.[52] Identifying the slow poisoning of society by man's 'democratic' lawmaking, he considered his *Institutes of Biblical Law* the humble beginnings of a biblical response for our time. Reflecting on American history and its decadent trajectory he noted that "Our country once was making tremendous strides toward a great and a glorious reign of God. This country was begun in terms of the law of God. Statute law was something that came in after 1860."[53] Thus democracy as an ideology of 'one person/one vote' does not equate directly with freedom. Rather, theocracy, the rule of God, within a range of possible forms of civil government, does produce true liberty and it is therefore no surprise that a theocratic vision of life lay at the foundation of arguably the most free nation the world has ever known, the 'land of the free,' the United States of America, birthed as it was from the Christian Commonwealth of England, the 'mother of the free.' It is a myth to think that most men and women have lived historically in freedom. For the most part, aside from Christianity, men and women have lived as slaves of state under the tyranny of humanistic rulers.

Although Rushdoony certainly saw early American Puritanism and its theocratic vision as a great start, he was not a primitivist seeking to recover a by-gone era; on the contrary he repudiated primitivism and was future-oriented, seeing a greater manifestation of the reign of God ahead (theological postmillennialism). It was this conviction that inspired him to write the *Institutes*, in which he comes to the source and heart of his *Puritan vision* for theocracy:

> It is a modern heresy that holds that the law of God has no meaning nor any binding force for man today. It is an aspect of the influence of humanistic and evolutionary thought on the church, and it posits an evolving and developing god.... This is not the God of scripture, whose grace and law remain the same in every age, because He, as the sovereign and absolute lord, changes not, nor does he need to change. The strength of man is the absoluteness of his God. To attempt to study Scripture without studying its law is to deny it. To attempt to understand Western civilization apart from the impact of biblical law within it and upon it is to seek a fictitious history.... The Institutes of biblical law has as its purpose a reversal of the present

trend.... It is intended as a beginning, as an instituting consideration of that law which must govern society, and which shall govern society under God.[54]

Here Rushdoony lays out the scope of his program for the *missio Dei* – the theocratic *reign of God*, brought about by his grace and law, manifest in the power and scope of the total gospel. Holding that regeneration by the Holy Spirit turns people's hearts toward obedience and love for God's righteousness, the law of the Spirit of life in Christ,[55] he held that "God's kingdom comes as His law is enforced. The law of God is the practical program for the...reign of God."[56] By 'enforced,' Rushdoony did not mean 'imposed' in a *top-down* ecclesiocracy.[57] Mark Rushdoony comments, "Theocracy is falsely assumed to be a take-over of government, imposing biblical law on an unwilling society. This presupposes statism which is the opposite of theocracy. Because modern people only understand power as government, they assume that's what we want."[58] In a telling interview in 1992 Rushdoony stated categorically, "I don't believe in compulsion in these areas. I believe that we must work to bring people into the faith, not whip them into it.... I am not trying to deprive anyone of their freedom."[59] This was not a pragmatic statement to disguise some Machiavellian agenda. He recognized that the Christian consensus had been lost in America and Europe and abhorred the idea of a *coercive* return to Christian faith and practice. His exposition of the book of Exodus deals repeatedly with the status of unbelievers under God's law, showing that in a Christian (covenantal) commonwealth the coercion of unbelievers was not acceptable. At the same time he pointed out that Scripture requires respect from the non-believer for the faith of the Christian land in which he dwells. In dealing with Exodus 12 he writes:

There is an aspect of Leviticus 17:11–15, which is common to much in the law, that must be considered here. It is clear that the law recognizes that not all people in the covenant land will be covenant believers. The persecution of unbelievers *for their unbelief* is nowhere permitted. However, disrespect by the unbelievers for the faith is not allowed. No penalty is set forth here, but the law requires respect for the faith of God's covenant people. Just as the godly have no right to abuse or penalize the unbeliever for his unbelief, so must the unbeliever observe a respectful attitude towards the faith and do nothing to show

273

contempt or disrespect for it.[60]

One law equally applied to both the believer and unbeliever without respect of persons and the non-believer was not obliged to take part in the rites and celebrations of the covenant people (such as the Passover).

8.6 Slander, Fallacy and False Charges

Nonetheless, despite these clear statements concerning the true nature of theocracy and how biblical law functions, the *Institutes* landed like something of a bombshell in the academic world and has since generated a great deal of hostility toward the term theocracy. Lazy and at times malevolent criticism of Rushdoony and other theonomists in general has been focused here, suggesting that a Puritan theocracy is about the coercive rule of men or the church in the name of God and therefore represents a terrifying fundamentalism threatening Western freedom like Islamic *Sharia* and violent radicalism.[61] Nothing could be further from the truth, and Karen Armstrong, a leftist thinker, participates in her critique in a longstanding collusion between Islamists and the left. As Andrew C. McCarthy, former federal prosecutor in the United States, and author on the subject of Islam and jihad has pointed out:

> Islamists and Leftists are frequent collaborators. Though their disagreements are several and not trivial (e.g., women's rights, gay rights, abortion), they are in harmony on basic, big-picture matters. Both ideologies are totalitarian in the sense of wanting centralized control of people's lives, down to the small details; both elevate the good of the collective (or the Ummah) over the individual; both are vigorously anti-capitalist (something most Americans still do not know about Islamist ideology); and neither can succeed in achieving its grand design without suppressing the liberties and self-determinism of the citizen.[62]

Setting aside the manifest ignorance (both historical and theological) of comparing the *Sharia* with biblical faith and law, such distortion raises the spectre of intellectual dishonesty in which Armstrong, a respected scholar, is clearly implicated. In a hysterical passage in her acclaimed volume, *The Battle for God*, she writes:

> Like Muslim fundamentalists, North and Rushdoony are principally

concerned about the sovereignty of God.... The key concept of Reconstructionism is Dominion. God gave Adam and later Noah the task of subduing the world. Christians have inherited this mandate and they have the responsibility of imposing Jesus' rule on earth before the second coming of Christ.... Their vision is a complete distortion of Christianity in its abandonment of the ethos of compassion. When the kingdom comes there will be no more separation of church and state.... The dominion envisaged by North and Rushdoony is *totalitarian*. There is no room for any other view or policy, no democratic tolerance for rival parties, no *individual freedom*.[63]

It is important to deal with this statement in some detail, because this irresponsible characterization has become the popular understanding of theonomy combined with postmillennialism, and constitutes a summary of some of the primary objections to the Puritan perspective. Indeed, Armstrong's accusations actually extend to the patently false charge that Rushdoony intended to bring back slavery – a mind-set and practice to which he was explicitly opposed.[64] In fact, beyond the assertion of the centrality of the sovereignty of God, every point addressed in the passage cited above is false and *emphatically condemned* by Rushdoony's own writings. These facts will be seen to be critical for understanding the true character and meaning of the reign of God and theocracy in Puritan thought and its relevance for today. First, dominion and theocracy are *not* about 'imposing the rule of Jesus.' As a liberal (not European liberalism/ conservatism) statist and product of the Enlightenment, it seems inconceivable to Armstrong that cultural and social transformation can happen in any other way than by means of the arm of civil government and its coercion. She thus imputes such a revolutionary motive to theonomists. Yet Rushdoony writes:

> The biblical faith is a vision and mandate of man as God's image bearer to exercise dominion over the earth (Genesis 1:26, 28). This requirement has been warped by fallen man into a mandate to exercise dominion over other men. In the realm of mankind, the mandate is very different: "Wherefore, putting away falsehoods, speak ye truth each one with his neighbour: for we are members of one another" (Eph. 4:25).[65]

Elsewhere he also notes that "dominion is an aspect of God's image in man.... Fallen man has substituted *domination* for dominion, and self-will for God's will."[66] Dominion does not mean domination, but responsible stewardship, under God.

In terms of the role of various institutions as agencies of the rule of God, Armstrong argues that Rushdoony's Puritan manifesto will abolish the distinction between church and state, with a group of clergy presumably running the new church-state alliance. This dubious conclusion overlooks that Rushdoony endorsed a form of Kuyperian *sphere sovereignty*, which held that each sphere, including, state, church, school, and family, is *under God* with different responsibilities and jurisdiction; in such a view, as we have already seen, the church authorities have no mandate to control the state:

> The church, in terms of scripture, has no jurisdiction and control over other institutions and *spheres of life* except a "spiritual" one, i.e. the proclamation and application of God's word and authority to every realm. To limit the church, however, emphatically cannot and does not mean the limitation of Christianity and the Triune God. Rather, the church must declare every sphere of life must be under the rule of God's word and under the authority of Christ the king.[67]

This again reflects the impact of the Puritans on Rushdoony's reformed thought. "The Puritans developed the concept of sphere law, each sphere of life being based on a particular covenant...each sphere of life was independent of the others in that one did not rule the other, but the spheres were also interdependent in that each was seen as only a single part of reality."[68] These various spheres are emphatically not to be power centres, but are all to be oriented toward Christ and submitted to him: "Dominion is not given to the state nor to the church but to man and to families.... It is a serious error to see theocracy, the rule of God, as a government over men by a group of men in the name of God. The biblical doctrine of theocracy means, the self-government of the Christian man."[69] The various spheres are thus 'sovereign' only in the sense that they are independent (though inter-related) areas under the supreme sovereignty of God alone and his word – this reality the church is called to declare prophetically. The Old Covenant law itself recognized the *separation of powers* of church and state, with the priestly and Levitical functions being purposefully separated from each other and later from the monarchy. Clearly, Rushdoony's own words deny the notion of the domination of human institutions in society, holding rather that *freedom* is predicated upon the *rule of God* and his word, not the institutions of human society that God intended to be servants and ministers, not centres of power and control. Armstrong further charges that Rushdoony's missiological manifesto abandons compassion, yet one of his most noteworthy contributions to the field of missiology has been an insistence upon the biblical requirement of compassionate charitable welfare for the poor as a top priority for the church through the administration of the tithe.[70] And not only so, but the explicit motivation for doing this is bound up with the theocratic reign of God and his salvation: "This salvation-victory we are to spread into every realm. Because the tithes are Levitical and not priestly, they must be used to fund kingdom activities in every sphere. Churches, schools on all levels, hospitals, welfare and more must be financed by Christ's people in the name of the Lord."[71] This emphasis has a long history and is typical of the understanding of the early church, the frontier age and medieval period, the Puritans and modern evangelical heritage of the eighteenth century,[72] as well as the Dutch Reformed tradition of Abraham Kuyper. Believing that Christian society should implement these biblical ordinances Kuyper wrote that "all state relief for the poor is a blot on the honour of your saviour."[73] Given what we have seen concerning Rushdoony's definition of *theocracy*, perhaps the most incomprehensible of Armstrong's charges is that his Puritan vision would lead to *totalitarianism* and the elimination of personal freedom. The 1997 edition of the Chambers Dictionary defines totalitarianism as "a system of government by a single party which allows no opposition and which demands complete obedience to the state." Totalitarianism means that one institution progressively *swallows* all others, making all 'lesser' institutions subject to its total censure, licensing, and control. In our time, that institution is the state. But as we have seen, the bulk of Rushdoony's scholarly work was directed specifically against the concentration of power in the state and an elite group of social planners. He devoted an entire volume, *The One and the Many: studies in the philosophy of order and ultimacy* (1978), to a study of the error and evils of totalitarianism and its opposite error, anarchy, which he argued were inevitably produced by systems of social order that denied the Trinity and therefore ended up affirming the ultimacy of the group (state) over the individual, or the individual interest over the group (anarchy); whereas the doctrine of the Trinity (unity in diversity) demands that both must be held in a biblical tension for a just society to flourish under God's law, the provisions of which alone maintain their equal value. This society could be realized only by a growing communion of saints in true covenantal commonwealth.[74]

Consequently, to claim that theocracy is totalitarian or that theonomists would support a totalitarian regime in which an unqualified obedience must be given to a coercive state proves either total ignorance of their work or deliberate deception. This may sound strong, but how is it possible for a serious scholar to make such misleading statements when the very bedrock of theonomic thought stands in diametric opposition to totalitarian ideas? For example, Rushdoony specifically addressed the issue when he wrote that "A Christian theology of the state must challenge the state's claims of sovereignty or Lordship. Only Jesus Christ is Lord or sovereign and the state makes a Molech of itself when it claims sovereignty (Lev. 20:1-5)."[75] In one striking analysis of the nature of freedom he declares:

> The word totalitarian is new, but the fact of totalitarianism is an old one. It was universal in pagan antiquity, and it is a central aspect of our reviving paganism. In the ancient state, there was no area of freedom, all kinds of activities were controlled by the state...there were no dissenters allowed from the policies of the state outside the narrow, ruling clique. The state was the ultimate order, man's only true society.[76]

In ancient Rome where just such an order existed, manifest in the cult of emperor worship, the claims of Christ asserted by the church, to being Lord and supreme potentate (Eph. 1:19–23; 1 Tim. 6:15; Col. 1:15–20) were seen as radical and revolutionary. Rushdoony notes the connotations:

> The implications of this were far reaching...this meant that the idea of a unitary state controlling all things, i.e. totalitarianism, was negated... by placing the triune God above all human powers, including the state, the Christian faith undermined the supreme authority of the state.... Christianity has given to men a concept of *truth and of freedom* which transcends this world. No human ruler nor court can define truth and freedom: God is not only the creator but also the definer.[77]

This transcendent appeal beyond the state which exists in no other system than the Judeo-Christian worldview (Islam is statist and totalitarian in political philosophy), is the basic premise of liberty and freedom from tyranny, *which is the meaning of theocracy*. These kinds of crystal-clear statements are all over Rushdoony's written corpus and not hard to find! Thus, in the face of a growing totalitarian mentality in our time, where governments seek to redefine life, the family, gender, sexuality, truth, and law – and over against the assertion of Armstrong that Rushdoony's manifesto means "an authoritarian state church could replace the liberal polity of the enlightenment," [78] – Rushdoony declares that God's total law-word, manifest fully in Christ, "provides men with a premise for resistance, and for the rebirth of faith and freedom." [79]

It is noteworthy that many liberals like Armstrong either cannot see or deliberately disguise the fact that it is *their position* which is totalitarian. Perhaps the best way to illustrate this is the shift from the idea of *religious liberty*, to *religious toleration* (a very different thing) that has taken place in our time. As we see in Canada today, in a society which endorses religious toleration, the state is paramount and in each sphere its power and reach is total; the state is the sovereign or Lord, the supreme religious entity or power. This means that the state decides and legislates what and who can exist (even in terms of life, gender, the family, the church), and the state establishes the terms of their existence. The state further reserves the power to license and tolerate one or more religions upon its own conditions, subject to state controls, regulation and supervision. It has been the Christian faith that has historically resisted the totalitarian impulse in terms of God and his law. This battle has gone on since the beginnings of the early church:

> The Roman Empire believed in religious toleration. It regarded religion as good for public morale and morals and it therefore had a system of licensure and regulation. New religions were ordered to appear before a magistrate, affirm the Lordship or sovereignty of Caesar, and walk away with a license to post in their meeting place. The early church refused licensure, because it meant the lordship of Caesar over Christ and His church. The early church refused toleration, because it denied the right of the state to say whether or not Christ's church could exist, or to set the conditions of its existence. The early church rejected religious toleration for religious liberty.[80]

Rushdoony recognized and criticized the church for its complicity at times in religious intolerance rather than supporting religious liberty, noting that state establishment and privilege for one church, a state subsidy, only made the church a wealthy slave or part of the bureaucracy. The *tolerated church* also became parasitic, depending on the state to collect tithes and dues – its existence then is not because of the faith of the people but because of state subsidy. Once bishops are appointed and controlled by the state, the freedom of the church is lost. Then the tolerated church becomes a *persecuting church*, tolerating no rivals, and hence the conflicts between Catholic and Protestants and our ugly record of intolerance.[81] The blindness of the Church of England in its persecution of the Puritans, for example, was astonishing. Then when the great champion of freedom, Oliver Cromwell, came to power, one of the biggest challenges with which he had to deal was the Presbyterians who became a one-issue party, wanting control of the Church of England – Cromwell opposed them fearing a reproduction of the same evils faced under Archbishop Laud. The Presbyterians later helped undermine the Commonwealth and restore the profligate Charles II, who promptly kicked them out of the Church of England anyway. In the American colonies of the era it was actually leading Baptists like Isaac Backus who helped maintain religious liberty. For him the defenders of establishment were 'Caesar's friend.' For Backus, "Religion (meaning biblical faith) was prior to all states and Kingdoms in the world and therefore could not in its nature be subject to human laws."[82]

Theonomist and student of the Puritans, Ray Sutton, has explored the implications of biblical faith for theocratic government in society and argues convincingly that freedom is indeed dependent on Christ's sovereignty: "Unless there is a Christocracy, society ends up in some kind of bondage."[83] He argues that the notion of *secularized* freedom, relatively recently foisted on the Western world, is a delusion for the very simple reason given in Scripture that "freedom apart from Christ is impossible."[84] To deny this and assert freedom apart from Christ is to divinize the state. Thus, "The Puritans believed that if transcendence is placed in the State, then this sphere becomes 'absolutized': the new 'priesthood.'"[85] What most modern Western people (including many Christians) are asking for in the name of 'freedom' is in fact a new slavery, when they attempt to secularize the public sphere and pursue freedom without the Lordship of Christ. To object to this by saying that non-believers are *not* accountable to God's covenant law (moral law) is finally to say that *we have no basis for presenting the gospel to the unbeliever*

– since Scripture defines sin as lawlessness and only lawbreakers need the gospel! It is noteworthy that it is not only evangelical commentators like Rushdoony and Sutton who have exposed the delusion of secularized freedom, a freedom conceived without the God of the Bible. European political philosopher Marcello Pera notes that liberal secularism has been transposed into a new absolutized religion that is as dangerous and insidious as anything seen in the fascist and communist terror of the twentieth century: "It does not wear the brutal face of violence, but the alluring smile of culture. With its words, liberal secularism preaches freedom, tolerance, and democracy, but with its deeds it attacks precisely that Christian religion which prevents freedom from deteriorating into license, tolerance into indifference, democracy into anarchy." [86] He goes on to explain that "individual freedom requires limits: a sense of sinfulness, of what is forbidden, unthinkable, non-negotiable. This limit cannot be established only by positive law, at whatever level, because a law could always be overridden. A moral, religious limit is needed... the Christian limit is not putting oneself in God's place..." [87] For this philosopher, without a Christian vision of God and the human person, political life is doomed to be a mere exercise of power, indifference, and selfishness. His conclusion is emphatic: "Paganism is not a source of democracy, despite what some European politicians may have said. Freedom cannot be nourished by agnosticism, atheism, secularism. If we desire peace, coexistence, and respect, we must believe in the values on which these depend." [88] If the rule of God means freedom, which I believe it does, then lastly, theocracy means the end of slavery of every kind. Returning to Armstrong's caricature of and charges against theonomists, we see the absurdity of accusing the Puritan vision (champions of liberty) of promoting slavery. Concerning kidnapping and slave-trading, far from promoting it, Rushdoony's *Institutes* reveal that both Old and New Testaments condemn it – God's law requiring the death penalty for man-stealing and enslavement (Ex. 21:16; Deut. 24:7). He draws careful and scholarly distinction between the ancient Israelite (as opposed to Roman) institutions of voluntary servitude, bond-service due to debts and war, and criminal restitution through bond-service, and the evil institution of man-theft and enslavement.[89] This careful treatment is incredibly important when analysing Scripture in our politically correct generation in which the popular claim is made that the Bible has endorsed what is in fact a pagan concept of slavery

that bore little resemblance to the bond-service found in ancient Israel. In his commentary on Leviticus, Rushdoony observes:

> Even if an Israelite chose to be a bondservant, he went free in the jubilee year: *freedom and responsibility were his inescapable duties...* the unbeliever could walk away if the conditions were unjust, or convert and become eligible for Sabbath year release. During the early medieval era, Jewish traders took in countless numbers of European slaves in trade for goods; these slaves usually adopted Judaism to gain their freedom and their descendants make up the major and overwhelming proportion of those who call themselves Jews. In the United States, in the early colonial era, blacks who converted thereby gained freedom. It became necessary to pass legislation *against the biblical law*, which was common law, to establish slavery in America.[90]

It is a very telling point that European and American law had to take steps *against biblical law* to establish kidnapping and slavery as institutions. Indeed, in another work, Rushdoony not only condemns the evil of slavery but implicates Enlightenment statism (which Armstrong defends), as its source and power centre, not Christianity:

> Because of this statism, many evils proliferated. Among them was slavery. Historians sometimes fail to note how various states subsidized slave ships. Only in 1698, for example, did Britain allow private slavers to operate, and then only on payment of a tax to the crown. Prior to that time it was a state monopoly.[91]

History shows that the institution of slavery declined during the height of Christian influence in the High Middle Ages, practically disappearing in Western and Central Europe by the end of the thirteenth century. It was rather enlightenment statism, militarism and expansionist ambitions that reignited the slave trade in Europe and North America. The story of the eighteenth and nineteenth centuries contains the church's protracted battle against the slave trade.[92] This battle was inescapable for the church because the whole history or trajectory of the covenant people is marked by freedom from slavery to sin, state and debt of every kind, beginning with the Exodus from Egypt and manifest in fullness at the Exodus Christ accomplished for his people at the cross (see: John 9:31; the Greek word here for 'departure' is *exodus*). Rushdoony points out that the whole meaning of the covenant was "freedom to do His will and to be his covenant dominion people."[93] He quotes the nineteenth-century commentator Joseph Parker approvingly in his analysis of God's covenant purpose:

> God will have no slavery of a social kind. He is against all bonds and restrictions that keep down the true aspirations of the human soul. God has always proceeded upon the principle of the enlargement and the inheritance of liberty.... God has no crouching slaves cringing around his altar and afraid to look up to the cross which has given them forgiveness...when all is right within us we run the way of God's commandments, we sing at our work, we turn the very statutes of God into songs in the house of our pilgrimage. What God has been doing for man in the first instance has been the breaking of yokes.[94]

Slavery therefore is something from which we are delivered and a Christian social order will work against all forms of slavery produced by sin and corruption. The relevance of God's law here again is that it is not the *source* of life, but the *condition* of life and freedom. Without it we are in bondage. Rushdoony sums the issue up in characteristically powerful terms:

> Apart from Christianity, we will have slavery. If men will not serve God, they will become the slaves of men. The Bible thus regards slavery as a deformation of man and of society, but also as an inescapable reality in a sinful world. The Mosaic law set forth the standard of liberty under God (Lev. 25:10) while regulating slavery as a social evil, seeking by law to limit it as far as possible...slavery has been extensively abolished as a private factor, but it exists today as a state monopoly, and slavery in this sense is more prevalent than ever before in history.[95]

The *Institutes*, by expounding God's law, thus asserts God's sovereignty over all things (Psalm 24:1ff) and since he created and owns all things, true *freedom* can only be under God and his law – freedom however, is not identical with *autonomy*, and here lies an important distinction. For the Puritan Christian, non-autonomy under the sovereignty of God is true freedom. Autonomy as 'independence' from God is an illusion. Terrill Irwin Elniff describes this belief as understood by the Puritans:

> The non-autonomy of man meant the absoluteness and sovereignty of God. It followed that there was not only to be no sovereign power

on earth, but that whatever power did exist should be so divided and diffused that no one man or group of men could gain or claim absolute or sovereign power. Sovereignty had been shunted off to heaven by Calvin...and therefore the foundation for individual liberty had been laid.[96]

Thus, for theonomists, in an important sense, we *already live*, whether we acknowledge it or not, under *theocracy*, for God's purpose and rule as the Sovereign God governs all. However, the Christian, by regeneration, is brought to increasing self-conscious recognition and application of this reality, now being a child of God. This, quite consistently, leads to a theocratic logic of freedom from tyranny. As R. C. Sproul notes concerning God's law as the ultimate standard, "We are not autonomous. That is, we may not live according to our own law. The moral condition of humankind is that of heteronomy: we live under the law of another. The specific form of heteronomy under which we live is *theonomy*, or the law of God."[97]

8.7 The Slow Development of Tyranny

If we will not have theocracy under Christ, (whether in the context of parliamentary democracy, congressional republic, monarchy or another form of government), we will have the erosion of freedom and the development of tyranny. This happened dramatically in the twentieth century when Germany and Italy, as well as the Soviet Union, turned overtly to paganism, and we have a growing tyranny in our own time in the West due to a pagan turn. Nazi Germany's development of the Gestapo is instructive for those who do not think such horrors can re-occur in our own day. Gestapo is an abbreviation for Secret State Police. Certainly some form of political policing has existed in free states in order to uncover conspiracy and protect the institution of the state from injury: in order to protect the free state from treasonous subversion and to guard the wellbeing of its citizens, some form of this is arguably necessary.

Today, agencies like the NSA, FBI, CIA, MI5 and MI6 have worked to uncover Islamic terrorist plots against Western states. The activities of these agencies are certainly not always justified nor always sanctioned by elected governments, and illegal infringements of civil liberties must be a serious concern to all citizens, but there is meant to be *accountability to the people being governed*. Even in Victorian England a force did exist to keep an eye on the activities of certain exiles and refugees from discontented lands. However, as Edward Crankshaw points out, historically, "The political police of Britain and America...exercise a purely defensive function, designed to uphold the *status quo* sanctioned by the people as a whole. The German Gestapo on the other hand, was an instrument not of defence but attack...throughout its career it was an instrument of aggression."[98] Once state agencies start to attack and coercively 're-program' law-abiding citizens by regulations, erosion of liberties, threats, human rights tribunals and other forms of coercion, it has become an agency of aggression. Hitler's Nazi regime started slowly and carefully with only one Nazi in the Cabinet. The establishment of totalitarian power was gradual but deliberate. The Gestapo's grip on power took a decisive leap forward when Hitler induced President Hindenburg to sign a decree tellingly called "The Protection of the People and the State." This 'protection' spelt the end of personal liberty that had been guaranteed by the Weimar Constitution. In the name of dealing 'with enemies of the state and the people,' the Gestapo now had a free hand; yet Hitler was still not dictator and the Nazis were only a minority party in a coalition government.[99] The revolution now started in earnest. The *Gleichschaltung* was the steady process of bringing all German society under Nazi control. This meant total state control of the schools, the eventual outlawing of home schooling (in 1938), restrictions imposed upon pastors and churches, and soon enough by 1933, "all parties were officially banned and the National Socialist German Workers Party was declared, 'the only political party in Germany.'"[100] Yet all this development was not a 'secret' operation. The Gestapo was not "a dark and sinister tyranny, compact and aloof, ruling first Germany, then most of Europe, alone...and unobserved."[101] On the contrary, once power had been achieved, the Gestapo "merged itself inextricably with the mood of Germany as a whole."[102] Crankshaw reveals that it was not possible to separate the cruelties of the Gestapo from the cruelties of the General S.S. and other major departments of state. They had successfully re-programmed a culture in terms of a new ideology.

It is complete ignorance and folly to think that people have grown to be beyond such wicked cruelty, or that we have learned the lessons of history regarding the danger of naked totalitarian power in the hands of the state. There are some who simply want power for its own sake, power that exists only to serve itself. Once we throw off Christianity, the rule of Christ and liberty predicated on God's sovereign power, though at times it may take decades for the implications to work themselves out in the social order, the exhibition of naked power in terms of man's lawlessness is just around the corner, and it can sweep up a nation in just a few years with very little opposition. The Nazi regime reveals this fact unequivocally. Man is a sinner and once he becomes an 'outlaw' (outside of God's law in his thinking and living) he is capable of anything. In Germany, for example, although the 'liquidation' of entire peoples was discussed or protested by a handful of officials, it was not the rightness or pragmatic necessity of liquidation that was in question, but the method; the wrong method might damage the German cause and reputation.[103] Because of the universality of sin such cruel potential is not characteristic of only one people but all mankind. Conquered peoples under the Nazi regime, such as the Ukrainians and Romanians, engaged in their own campaigns of massacre and mass murder with great zeal. According to Crankshaw, some native Ukrainians engaged in such a high-spirited slaughter of Jews that they became too much even for the Germans and had to be discouraged.[104] There is a beast of Belsen lurking in every people group, because man is a rebel against God, and a walking contradiction. Unregenerate man will not do for others as he would have them do for him, but in his lawlessness will inflict suffering, pain and cruelty upon others to achieve his desires. And we must not forget that many of these monsters, who were just the most notorious of the butchers at work during this period of history, would have appeared to be perfectly normal individuals. "Many of the characters in this narrative were good fathers of families, who bought sweets and Christmas-trees for their children, and then went out to do some more killing, killing of children and women and old people especially, because these could or would not work for Germany."[105] What was the basis of this heartless rejection of life? How did it come to this? The answer is that a new god, the state, had usurped the sovereignty of God, becoming the new source and definer and life and law – for Hitler opposition to the state meant death. If you would not work for the interests of the state you were dispensable.

What would lead a people to surrender their freedom under God for the brutal hand of a tyrannical dictator? I think Crankshaw intuitively finds a part of the answer, "a rejection of that reality which includes one's neighbours, and an attempt to substitute a *false abstraction*. It is idealism gone rotten."[106] That is to say, one's real living breathing neighbour is ignored in favour of a perverse utopian ideal, an abstract idea of man's creation. To lose sight of the sovereign law of the God of Scripture is to *reject reality as it is*, in this case, the reality of your neighbour whom the law commands you to love. In place of love to God and neighbour, which was Jesus Christ's own summary of the law, is placed an abstract ideal, a utopian order (counterfeit kingdom) ruled by man's 'enlightened' reason, realized in and by the totalitarian state as supreme lawgiver and judge. Once such an abstract (disconnected with reality as established by God), secularized and pagan religion is accepted and the new sovereign placed on the throne of men's minds and hearts, the new authority is obeyed without question, even when that authority endorses and commands what is evil. How did this process begin in Germany? Again Crankshaw is persuasive in suggesting there was a "fathomless German cynicism which *separated absolutely political action from private morals*."[107] This may have been the longstanding product of a misunderstanding of Luther on the relationship between God's moral law and the civil magistrate, or a product of continental pietism, but whatever the cause, the public and private, secular and sacred, law and morality, God and the state had been radically divorced. The separation was so terminal that they were blinded (with notable exceptions) as a broadly Christianized people, to what the new tyranny represented and German liberal Christianity, being without God's word, was utterly impotent in the face of the terror unleashed by the rise of lawlessness. At the very least the German people in general were lacking the moral courage to confront tyranny and criminality in the public sphere. In this respect they only did what most Christians in the West have done today, retreated from the world and its public affairs suggesting that God has nothing to say to politics, for religion is a 'private matter' of inner piety; that you can't legislate morality; that there are 'two kingdoms,' and that the world of special revelation in Scripture has no jurisdiction over the secular world! God has two laws, one for Christians and one for the world and we have no right to call men to obedience to it in public life. The state is the educator and lawgiver and the church just shares 'the gospel.' This typical dualism and pietism found in the modern church, even in the name of reformed theology, provides no basis for resistance to tyranny and naked power, and likewise, in the face of a growing new tyranny today, the very same weakness seen in the German people in the 1930s is manifest in the Western churches. We have separated political action from private morals which is indeed a 'fathomless cynicism.' History proves that what has happened before can happen again. Without God's law and gospel we will have the development of tyranny. Without Christocracy we are doomed to repeat history's mistakes.

8.8   Law, Sanctification and Theocracy

The Puritan mind thus holds that the *whole law*, codified in the Commandments given through Moses, exposited in the wisdom literature, and interpreted by Christ and the apostles, reflecting God's eternal unchanging nature, establishes the foundational principles for *a truly free society that is ultimately accountable to God*. This is theocracy and this alone is true freedom. It was this way of life that the prophets[108] continuously called Israel to return to in order to be a light to the gentiles (Deut. 4:5ff), a model for the pagan nations to follow.[109] As already noted, the 'law,' even in its narrow sense, is not limited to the Ten Commandments (Decalogue), but includes their applied meaning and relevance as set forth in case laws (illustrations of how the Ten Commandments were applied in the civil sphere in Israel). These various case laws are also clearly *moral laws*, because they reveal the meaning of the Ten Commandments, illustrating, for example, what dishonor of parents constitutes or what constitutes murder over against manslaughter, or criminal negligence. How would we understand the nature of theft or adultery without moral laws that illustrate as a minimal case what these *crimes* are? All laws are moral or procedural thereto, reflecting the moral will (or nature) of the lawgiver. Biblical case law is no different. These moral laws that have civil application (for some sins are crimes and others are not) constitute what is sometimes called by reformed scholars, the civil law, because they identify which sins are crimes which then come under the sanctions of the civil magistrate, providing for us the foundational principles and cases from and upon which a just law order can be built and extrapolated. We know these laws are moral in nature because all of God's law concerns holiness, righteousness and justice reflecting his moral nature. For example, homosexuality, incest and bestiality are not explicitly condemned in the Decalogue, but in case laws. In fact the *only* place bestiality is explicitly condemned in Scripture is in case law (Ex. 22:19; Lev. 18:23–30; Lev. 20:15–16; Deut. 27:21). Similarly the law against egregious cursing (malicious verbal assault, associated with rejection of parental authority or even violence) of parents which Jesus explicitly upholds in Mark 7:7–13 and Matt. 15:1–9 is *clearly moral* but not explicit in the Ten Commandments – it is implicit in the fifth Commandment. Thus the case law interprets and applies the moral implications of the Ten Commandments to concrete situations and these laws must be profitably mined to develop our understanding of how God's word applies to us.

True sanctification means that we as Christians place ourselves under God's law, under his theocracy, in joyful obedience. Our calling is obedience to God in our lives, but the implementation of public justice is not given to individuals, nor the church, but to the state. The state is accountable to God and will be judged accordingly. As a people we get the laws we ask for, and only when people turn again to God by willing obedience to the gospel and to his covenant law will people require their 'differentiated public' (the state) to also do justice in terms of God's word. The only laws that are ever enforced are those that people are already willingly enforcing in their own lives.

It might be asked, if the moral laws applied to the civil sphere are still relevant and applicable, what of laws that refer to separation, diet, and the priesthood? Critically, these restorative or ceremonial aspects of the law, though lapsed in the old forms, are not disappeared but *transposed* and put into force in the priestly function of Christ and his continuing intercession in heaven, and are also manifest in our separation as his people unto holiness. David Chilton has observed:

> It is most significant that when the Apostles speak of our freedom from certain Old Testament regulations, they cite only ceremonial laws – such as sacrifices, the priesthood, circumcision, feasts – which pictorially represented the work of Christ until he came. For example, no New Testament text condemns the practice of restitution (and in fact Jesus pronounced Zaccheus to be saved after he had demonstrated his willingness to obey this detail of the law).... Both Testaments distinguish between laws that were ceremonial (and thus merely temporary) and those which were moral. The moral law is the abiding definition of sin and righteousness (Rom. 3:20; 7:7; 1 John 3:4). The ceremonial regulations on the other hand, symbolically represented the means of restoration of God's favor through the mediator who was to come (Heb. 7:10). The moral law answers the question, "How should I live?"; the ceremonial law symbolically answers the question, "How can I be restored to God's favor after breaking His moral law?"

The distinction was also understood in the Old Testament (Isaiah 1:11–23; Hosea 6:6; Amos 5:21–26; Micah 6:6–8). The ceremonial law was never intended to be a permanent feature of the duty of believers. But the moral law has lasting validity.[110]

For the Puritan mind the holiness of the law is the righteousness of God we were created to reflect, thus Christ's coming and our purpose is in terms of the original creation mandate:

Christ as the new Adam (1 Cor. 15:45) kept the law perfectly. As the sin bearer of the elect, Christ died to make atonement for their sins, to restore them to their position of righteousness under God. The redeemed are recalled to the original purpose of man, to exercise dominion under God, to be covenant keepers, and to fulfil "the righteousness of the law" (Rom. 8:4). The law remains central to God's purpose. Man has been re-established into God's original purpose and calling. Man's justification is by the *grace* of God in Jesus Christ; man's sanctification is by means of the law of God.[111]

Rushdoony did not mean here that the *source* of our sanctification is obedience to the Commandments. The source is Jesus Christ by the Holy Spirit, "The Spirit gives us another mind, the mind of Christ."[112] Sanctification is both definitive and progressive, "our dedication to God is an accomplished fact by our union to Christ."[113] In this union, "there is growth in the principle of that new life. This is progressive sanctification."[114] He explains it this way: "The *agency* in progressive sanctification is the triune God, especially the Holy Spirit. The *means*, the way, and rule of sanctification is the law of God. The goal of sanctification is to bring all things under the authority of Jesus Christ, the King of creation."[115] In fact, the law, being written as *desire and delight* into the heart by the Holy Spirit, is the very nature of the new covenant promise in Jeremiah 31:31–34 and Hebrews 8:8–12. This is what it means to be truly human. As Rushdoony makes clear, "man is most truly himself, as God intended him to be, when he fulfils his vocation by living in the Spirit...our relationship to Him is closer and more thorough than with our husband, wife, children, parents or friends. Our relationship to the Holy Spirit, unlike any other we have is total."[116] We are being conformed to the image of God's Son, the man of righteousness and justice. Thus Rushdoony could also write:

Lawless Christianity is a contradiction in terms...the purpose of grace is not to set aside the law but to fulfil the law and enable man to keep the law. If the law was so serious in the sight of God that it would require the death of Jesus Christ, the only begotten Son of God, to make atonement for man's sin, it seems strange for God then to proceed to abandon the law![117]

Thus the Puritan manifesto of hope affirms the abiding relevance of God's law to contemporary society (not just for Israel or the Puritans), because as God recalls us to faithfulness to the creation mandate, to exercise dominion as his priesthood in terms of his law-word, the kingdom of God or the reign of God is established in and through his servant people – this is the meaning of *theocracy – the rule of God.* We will either live under God's order or that of an idol. *Theocracy* is thus an inescapable concept. Rushdoony summarises the subject most effectively:

That fact is that all law is "religious." All law is based on some ultimate standard of morality and ethics. Every system is founded on the ultimate value of that system, and that ultimate value is the god of that system. The source of law for society is the god of that society. This means that a theocracy is inescapable. *All societies are theocracies.* The difference is that a society that is not explicitly Christian is a theocracy of a false god.[118]

We will either work in terms of and toward a society of Satan (idolatry) or we will seek and pursue the kingdom of righteousness, the commonwealth of Christ.

Chapter Nine

GOD'S SERVANT FOR YOUR GOOD:
UNDERSTANDING CRIME AND PUNISHMENT

The law restrains malefactors and those who are not yet believers.
The Law is protection of the community from unjust man. The
second function of the Law is this: at least by fear of punishment to
restrain certain men who are untouched by any care for what is just
and right unless compelled by hearing the dire threats of the Law.

– John Calvin

But if you do wrong, be afraid, for he does not bear the sword
in vain. For he is the servant of God, an avenger who carries out
God's wrath on the wrongdoer.

– Romans 13:4

9.1 Whose Law and Dominion?

During a debate over the *Lord's Day* bill in the Canadian senate on
July 9th 1906, Liberal Senator, James McMullen of North Wellington,
Ontario declared:

> ...we must not forget that we claim to be a Christian nation, we are
> a Christian-professing nation at least, and as such we should respect
> the laws of God. We generally make our laws in accordance with the
> provisions of God's law. His law says, 'Thou shalt not kill,' and our
> law says that the man that sheds man's blood by man shall his blood
> be shed. God's law says "Thou shalt not bear false witness against
> thy neighbour,' and our law says that a man who is guilty of perjury
> is liable to be punished and imprisoned for a violation of the law....
> [W]e confirm all these commandments by legislation. Why do we
> not confirm that commandment which says, 'Remember the Sabbath
> day to keep it holy?'.... We are responsible to a higher authority. The
> responsibility is that we should recognise God's law that is established
> and published in His own word.[1]

It is significant that in this statement to the Senate, the then common
conviction was set out that, as a people, we are accountable to God
for adherence to both the *first* and *second* table of the law – that is,

for offenses *against God* as well as men. It was likewise believed that there would be real and serious national consequences for a failure to obey God's law in these regards. This was not a fringe opinion amongst Canadian political leaders. During the same series of debates on July 11th, Liberal Senator William Ross of Halifax stated, "Now the individual or the family, the community, province or the Dominion which observes the Sabbath day as it should be observed, is one that will prosper; and if we are to enter upon the down-grade by setting at defiance the fourth commandment, we will go down as a nation by doing so."[2] Summarizing the outcome of the debates over the *Lord's Day Act*, historian Paul Laverdure writes, "Sabbatarians implemented some of their theocratic vision of a righteous Canada, but religious fragmentation prevented them from winning a complete victory in the political arena."[3] It is telling that, as this historian notes, it was internal Christian divisions and fragmentation that prevented a more full and complete victory for the Christian theocratic vision in the late nineteenth and early twentieth centuries. Had Christians been more united in this objective, the Canadian story may have been different. Nonetheless what history clearly shows is that, "at least until a century ago it was confidently assumed by most Canadians that Canada was a Christian country, and that this was God's providential intention. Thus the Canadian churches viewed themselves as the conscience of the state – politicians were expected to judge all matters by Judeo-Christian values ..."[4] Since these values included, as we have seen, both tables of the law, criminal matters were to be equally assessed by reference to the law of God. This is readily acknowledged by the social critic, Tom Warner, who is not a Christian, but a veteran homosexual rights leader in Ontario:

> There was a time, not so long ago, when Judeo-Christian values were indisputably "Canadian values," when it was generally and willingly accepted that the role of the state was to promote and protect such values. This tendency was especially true in regard to the regulation of public morals. The state enacted and *enforced criminal and other laws* regarding contraception and abortion, sexual conduct, sexual expression, and family and spousal relationships. The public schools were mandated with indoctrinating children with Judeo-Christian moral values. The state's role was to nurture, strengthen, and resolutely protect marriage and family in accordance with Judeo-Christian beliefs and morality.[5]

Such a role for the state in preferring some values over others is, in any era, inescapable. Having set God's law aside, the state in Canada today nurtures, enforces, promotes and indoctrinates in secular humanistic religious values and because of the nature of the pagan state, regulation and control are extreme, drifting increasingly toward the totalitarian. No state can be impartial in these matters. A law order will inculcate values from some worldview, either with man and his agencies as sovereign, or functioning as responsible and accountable to God. Law professors Rex Ahdar and Ian Leigh in a 2004 article for the *McGill Law Journal* entitled, *"Is Establishment Consistent with Religious Freedom?"* made clear that every country has some form of established religion:

> For a modern state to remain entirely impartial is, we submit, an impossible feat. The idea of a purely neutral state in which there is no official endorsement of the true and good, of a political community that eschews the notion that it acts on the basis of substantive values, is a mirage...the established position will inevitably exclude the worldviews of some citizens."[6]

For Ahdar and Leigh the implications of this are obvious: "There is, we contend, always an established or state orthodoxy."[7] The subsequent striking down of the *Lord's Day Act* in 1985 by the Supreme Court of Canada and the advent of the Canadian charter in 1982 were key markers plotting the demise of the Christian law order and the establishment of the new humanistic state orthodoxy.[8] Similar revolutions against biblical law have taken place in the last seventy years throughout the Western world. How did Christendom move from the one state of affairs to the other? How did we go from punishing abortionists, rapists, perjurers and sodomites with criminal sanctions, and protecting the Lord's Day as liberty for people under God, to endorsing the killing of unborn children, removing legal protection for the family, trivializing perjury, re-defining marriage in favour of homo-eroticism, and declaring the Sabbath Day unconstitutional? There are of course long and involved political stories, court cases and proceedings which describe the *process* of this legal revolution, but the root cause of the change is not pragmatic, but theological. We cannot possibly understand the critical issue of crime and punishment and how it reflects the changing religion of our nation without identifying the theological collapse that preceded it.

9.2   Cheap Grace, Costly Law

In his classic work, *The Cost of Discipleship*, Dietrich Bonhoeffer exposes powerfully the fatal error prospering in the modern church: "Cheap grace is the deadly enemy of our church. We are fighting today for costly grace." What is cheap grace? "Cheap grace means the justification of sin without the justification of the sinner.[9] Moreover, "Cheap grace means grace as a doctrine, a principle, a system. It means forgiveness of sins proclaimed as a general truth, the love of God taught as the Christian "conception" of God. An intellectual assent to that idea is held to be of itself sufficient to secure remission of sins."[10] This leads to the reality that, "cheap grace.... amounts to a denial of the living Word of God, in fact, a denial of the incarnation of the Word of God."[11] Without the reality of man's lawlessness and sin being clearly set forth and God's judgement against sin being clearly made known, love and forgiveness are reduced to general abstract conceptions that have no real need of the historic incarnation and atoning death of the living Word, Jesus Christ. Cheap grace is in fact a denial of the gospel because it justifies man *in* his sinning, rather than justifying man *from* his sin, freeing him to be a man of righteousness in Jesus Christ. This grace is no grace at all. It is a grace that amounts to "the justification of sin without the justification of the repentant sinner who departs from sin and from whom sin departs... cheap grace is the preaching of forgiveness without requiring repentance, baptism without church discipline, communion without confession, absolution without personal confession."[12]

There was more that Bonhoeffer recognized in this regard. He also understood the relationship between the blight of cheap grace and lawlessness or antinomianism in the church. Identifying the Marcionism rampant in many modern churches he notes that Marcion had accused the Jews of tampering with Matthew 5:17–20 and so he had altered this text to read, "Think ye that I am come to fulfil the law and the prophets? I am not come to fulfil, but to destroy." Bonhoeffer suggests that much of the church has slipped into Marcion's error.[13] By contrast he declares the Christian is "bound to acknowledge the law" by virtue of the fact that Jesus validates its authority.[14] But which law? According to Bonheoffer:

The law Jesus refers to is the law of the old covenant, not a new law, but the same law which he quoted to the rich young man and the lawyer when they wanted to know the revealed will of God. It becomes a new law only because it is Christ who binds his followers to it...every letter of it, every jot and tittle, must remain in force and be observed until the end of the world.... Jesus manifests his perfect union with the will of God as revealed in the Old Testament law and prophets. He has in fact nothing to add to the commandments, except this, that he keeps them. He fulfils the law, and he tells us so himself, therefore it must be true.... If men cleave to him who fulfilled the law and follow him, they will find themselves both teaching and fulfilling the law. Only the doer of the law can remain in communion with Jesus.[15]

We have a church in the West today suffering from the scourge of cheap grace because the law of Christ (that is the law of God given by Moses) has been steadily abandoned and an abstract 'system' of love and grace has been put in its place – a love that is not love, since love is the fulfilment of the law (Rom. 13:10), and a grace that is not grace (Rom. 6:1–2). It is important to emphasize here what Bonheoffer points out, that the law of Christ is not a different law from the law of Moses. This fact St. Augustine made abundantly clear centuries before in direct contradiction to today's 'two kingdoms' theorists:

> But if loving one's neighbour fulfills the law and the love of one's neighbour is especially urged in the Old Testament also (in which, the same apostle says elsewhere, all the commandments of law are summed up), then it is clear *that the Scripture given to the earlier people is also the law of Christ*, which he came to fulfill by love when it was not being fulfilled by fear.[16]

What then does *cheap grace* and the *law of Christ* have to do with crime and punishment? In what way does this failure to rightly divide the word of truth in modern Christianity impact the social order? First, when cheap grace is the message of an antinomian church, and God's law is jettisoned in the thinking and lives of a people, they *logically* and steadily cease to believe in the need for real justification before a holy God, because without the law there is no true knowledge of sin (Rom. 3:20), and without an understanding of sin, our accountability (Rom. 3:19), and God's justice, there is no perceived need for Christ's work of *restitution* – his atoning death and justifying grace. Christ made restitution for lawbreakers at the cross by his death, in terms of the believer's relationship to God, and by this act for his people, we are justified. When we truly repent of sin and come to Christ by faith for justification by his covenant grace, from then on, we also seek as far as is possible, to make restitution to those against whom we have sinned (Luke 19:8–10; Matt. 5:23–25; 1 Cor. 11:27–31; Jas. 5:16). As we walk as believers in terms of the covenant in Jesus Christ we live lives of daily praise, confession, repentance *and restitution*, being restored thereby to intimate communion with Christ and with others. This is also the meaning of the communion feast, where we confess our sins, eating and drinking in a worthy manner by first dealing with our sins against others, being cleansed and renewed by the blood of the covenant. The apostle John reminds us:

> If we say we have fellowship with him while we walk in darkness, we lie and do not practice the truth. But if we walk in the light, as he is in the light, we have fellowship with one another, and the blood of Jesus his Son cleanses us from all sin. If we say we have no sin, we deceive ourselves and the truth is not in us. If we confess our sins, he is faithful and just to forgive us our sins and to cleanse us from all unrighteousness. If we say we have not sinned, we make him a liar, and his word is not in us. (1 John 1:6–10)

We see that at the root of the biblical truth of the gospel is a cosmic worldview relating law, justice, restitution and restoration, but when this view of reality falls out of society, restitution, justice and true judgement also begin to disappear from the social order. Where hell and judgement fall out of the church's theology, just punishment falls out of the justice system. Where the law of God diminishes and the meaning of the cross is undermined, restitution, retribution and restoration, as the basis for criminal justice, start to vanish. This is empirically observable in our society today. Since the church is salt and light in the world, where the church fails to uphold these truths of the gospel, society will inexorably tend to lawlessness. In such a context, sin and crime will steadily flourish with growing impunity and a professional criminal class will develop. *Cheap grace* then has the social consequence of producing *expensive law* – a costly proliferation of scientific planners, therapists, correctional systems, positivist laws and various techniques to try and justify and save man by another means; not because he is a sinner (lawbreaker) whose punishment must fit the crime, but because he is sick or maladjusted to his environment, fixable by manipulation, therapy and technique. The enforcement of law then becomes a massive *cost* because restitution and retribution are not delivered by the courts and system of justice. Instead, a pharisaic and legalistic scientific plan of justification is offered by man's ingenuity. Thus without the biblical gospel, people do not govern themselves in terms of God's law but become lawless. As society becomes lawless, the costs of keeping criminality at bay skyrocket and this is evidently what we are witnessing in our time.[17] Indeed, this is the inevitable outcome when cheap, counterfeit grace attempts to excuse sin, without justifying the sinner.

9.3 The Christian Mind

In our Western cities today we have become all too familiar with this growing criminality, lawlessness and social collapse. Just by talking to one's own grandparents and parents it is easy to discern that life has changed dramatically in regard to criminality in the last sixty years. As a result, many of our cities are increasingly dangerous places, with certain parts of major Western metropolises becoming no-go zones for police officers except in considerable numbers. The American city of Detroit, known as 'Motor City' was at the top of *Forbes'* list of the ten most dangerous cities around America in 2009. The magazine based its finding on violent crime statistics, which they obtained from the FBI's crime reports. There were a reported 1,220 violent crimes committed per 100,000 people in the city. As another example, New Orleans, the murder capital of the U.S., sees an average of ninety-five murders per 100,000 residents, which is incredibly high when you consider that there are only 300,000 residents in the city overall. This figure is even more disturbing when you bear in mind that *Time* magazine reported that Baghdad has a murder rate of forty-eight per 100,000 residents – almost half that of New Orleans.[18]

This is nothing new however. High taxation, state welfarism, political corruption, violent and sexually perverted entertainment, as well as widespread criminality (including the murder of their own leaders), were all part of the decline and fall of ancient Rome. Interestingly, after the collapse of the Roman Empire in the West, where at one point the population of Rome itself had dwindled to as little as 500 as its streets and markets were abandoned, the remaking of urban life was made possible, in part, by Jewish merchants applying *biblical law* to the running of trading centres that steadily developed into European cities.[19] In the biblical worldview, unlike that of the great pagan empires where the gods themselves were deified men, identified as hero-kings or lords of a given state, the priestly office is separate from that of the monarch and the prophet and Levite (or teachers) are to speak for God concerning the application of God's law to a sinful social order. Part of this biblical vision of godly social order is the application of God's justice in criminal matters. The early church continued in the Jewish vein, holding forth God's law prophetically as a testimony and example to men and nations. For example, Origen, the late second and third-century Christian apologist, in his *Contra Celsum*, responds to Celsus' critique of Christianity's relationship to Judaism:

> If anyone were to study carefully their [the Jews'] society in their early days when the law was given, he would find that they were men who manifested a shadow of the heavenly life upon earth (IV.31)....
> If anyone were to apply his mind to an examination of the lawgiver's intention and the society which he founded, and were to compare them with the present conduct of other nations, he would admire none more, since as far as it is humanly possible they removed everything not of advantage to mankind, and accepted only what is good (V.42).... Would that they [the Jews] had not sinned and broken the law...otherwise we might have an example of a heavenly city such as even Plato attempted to describe, although I doubt whether he was as successful as Moses and his successors when they trained an elect nation and a holy people, devoted to God, by means of doctrines which were free from superstition (V.43).[20]

As we have already seen in previous chapters, this mentality grew, the doctrine and place of the law was steadily worked out and continued to inform issues of criminal justice right through until the mid-twentieth century in the West. The widespread abandonment of God's word as having anything to say regarding crime and punishment is now openly on display in our courts. For example, on Wednesday September 5 2012, in the Canadian *National Post*, an article appeared concerning a man in the United States who had strangled his wife and as a result wound up in a federal prison. At the time of Kosilek's brutal crime in 1990 he wore a beard and had lived as a man. Shortly thereafter, he began to dress as a female and then demanded he be regarded as a woman called Michelle, in an all-male prison. He then proceeded to sue the Massachusetts Department of Correction in the year 2000 and then again in 2005 on the ground of discrimination, arguing that his demand for sex reassignment surgery, which had been rejected, was a medical necessity and basic right, as much as prisoners needing to be treated for heart disease. Speaking with the Associated Press, Kosilek said, "Everybody has the right to have their health care needs met, whether they are in prison or out on the streets." In a shocking decision, U.S. district judge, Mark Wolf, agreed. In a bizarre ruling, he became the first federal judge to order the prison officials to use tax-payers' funds to grant the man an expensive sex-change operation on the grounds of equality and justice. Some lawmakers have rightly asked on what conceivable grounds the taxpayer, in the middle of a national economic crisis, with millions of people out of work, should be forced to pay for convicted murderers to have what most medical insurance companies regard as elective surgery? [21]

Many such ludicrous accounts proliferate on a monthly basis in contemporary news. In September 2012 in the United Kingdom a British judge, Peter Bowers, caused outrage when in his sentencing he declared that a drug-addicted serial thief showed 'courage' in carrying out his acts of burglary and went on to spare him a jail sentence.[22] In another report the same month concerning a spate of shootings in East Toronto, Canada, in the summer of 2012, a series of murders were linked to a well-known city gang. They had so terrorized the community that the police were unable to find witnesses willing to testify against the criminals who, firing at each other in a garden party, had just shot and killed two innocent bystanders and wounded twenty-three others in full view of dozens of people. Yet the reason for the shootings was a gang leadership conflict produced as a direct result of the failure of the judiciary to punish previous offenders. As journalist Megan O'Toole commented, "The leadership battle comes as key members of the Galloway Boys emerge from jail after years in prison, sparking tensions between older gang leaders and the newer generation that stepped up to fill the vacuum."[23] Not only does this reveal the inadequacy of punishment for serious offenders, it reveals the failure of the prison system to correct and reform. With the setting aside of Christian law, today the judiciary is flooded with 'progessivist' judges, lawyers and attorneys who, indoctrinated with a false view of man as sick, but not a sinner, regard criminals as essentially victims of their environment and poor education. Worse, acts that were in living memory seen as *crimes* are now praised by lawmakers and magistrates as practical virtues or proud statements of freedom and liberty – hence the Western world's penchant for striking down laws against abortion, prostitution, pornography, sodomy, blasphemy and polygamy, not to mention turning a blind eye to infanticide, and protecting thugs, thieves and violent criminals against real consequences. Victims and their rights are heartlessly overlooked as in many cases activist judges pursue a political agenda in the alleged rehabilitation of criminals. Increasingly few people today expect justice from the courts, and the prison industry has become a multi-billion dollar business that profits from 'messianic' government programs offering to recreate criminal man by scientific technique.

By contrast to these pretensions, the Bible makes clear that God is faithful and just, and without injustice (2 Chr. 19:7; Rom. 9:14). Everything God says and does is just and true. God's justice does not correspond to the humanistic ideal of 'equality,' but concerns the restoration of God's order and purpose in all things. God thus defines justice for mankind in terms of his own being as the creator and sovereign lord over all things. God's law consequently functions for us as a *value processing system* designed to establish a vision of justice and society that reflects God's character. No godly person can celebrate injustice, and no person of real integrity could worship, serve and adore a supreme being who does not finally give justice as the moral judge of the universe. The justice, righteousness and blessing of all God's law and instruction is celebrated throughout the Bible, notably in Psalms 1, 19 and 119. It is exalted and applied perfectly in the life, teaching and ministry of Christ as illustrated in Matthew chapters 5–7, and it is defended and affirmed by St. Paul in Romans 7:7–14, being put to use against the lawless in 1 Timothy 1: 8–11, in accordance with *the gospel*. St. Paul writes:

Now we know that the law is good, if one uses it lawfully, understanding this, that the law is not laid down for the just but for the lawless and disobedient, for the ungodly and sinners, for the unholy and profane, for those who strike their fathers and mothers, for murderers, the sexually immoral, men who practice homosexuality, enslavers, liars, perjurers, and whatever else is contrary to sound doctrine, *in accordance with the gospel* of the glory of the blessed God with which I have been entrusted (1 Tim. 1: 8–11).

The student of biblical law will immediately notice in St. Paul's statement multiple references to the crimes dealt with in the Decalogue. Despite these biblical realities and their accordance with 'the gospel,' amongst many Christians today, the most common objection to the Puritan vision of the *reign of God*, is the alleged severity of God's law, especially in matters that God deems criminal. This 'severity' is seen by some to render theonomic missiology untenable and unrealistic.[24] For example, some Christian scholars considering the Puritan thesis come away with academic shock that anyone today could uphold the idea that the righteous sanctions of God's law against what God deems criminal should be upheld as just, in principle, by believers.[25] The first question which must therefore be asked is, why would God's law appear abhorrent to any Christian filled with God's Spirit, since the Holy Spirit is the author of the law? Can the Spirit of God be divided against himself? Why would any Christian believer find God's law repugnant? Certainly a Christian person may not understand all the law, may struggle to appreciate the significance of some of its provisions, may differ over details regarding the applications of case laws today, or be wrestling with questions about the place of the law in the redemptive work of God in history; but to mock, belittle, criticize or place one's own moral sensibilities above God's revealed law *cannot* be characteristic of the Christian mind. Indeed, "the law is holy, and the commandment is holy and righteous and good...for we know that the law is spiritual...for I delight in the law of God, in my inner being" (Rom. 7:12, 14, 22).

This inevitably leads to a rudimentary logical challenge. It must be the case either that God's moral requirements *and sanctions* given to his missionary people Israel, and confirmed to his church by our Lord (Matt. 5:17–20), are indeed good, righteous and holy, reflecting God's character, nature and goals for righteous human society, or that they are immoral (harsh, barbarous, culturally relative etc.), not reflecting the changeless character and revealed nature of God. Puritans original and modern have had the academic courage to be consistent with this affirmation of God's law, even in upholding the righteous character of the penal sanctions, despite knowing their unpopularity in our cultural moment; in this, the Puritan mind is clearly following Christ's own example with the Pharisees in Matthew 15:1–9; Mark 7:7–13.[26] In these texts it seems clear that Christ did not permit cultural sensibilities or human traditions to trump his law word and its sanctions.

9.4 Reformers, Puritans and Penology

As we look back over the history of evangelicalism we consistently find a high view of God's law and its application to the judicial or civil sphere. A good place to begin an analysis of Christian penology, then, is to consider how our Christian forebears have understood crime and punishment and its relation to God's law. It is important that we do not dismiss Christian social history on the grounds that this was all 'in the past,' as though moral laws and sanctions are merely relative to a historical moment. The passage of time does not make true moral principles false; the justice or injustice of a given penalty for crime is not arbitrary or merely socially conditioned. The Christian cannot be evolutionary or progressivist in their understanding of these issues, as though criminal justice were an ever-changing matter of social expediency based on broader political considerations, because God does not change and neither does his truth (Mal. 3:6). In the Christian worldview what is morally true and just today, is so tomorrow, whether politicians change their preferences or not. We may disagree with some of the reformers and Puritans on biblical grounds, but we cannot ignore or dismiss them simply on the basis that this was 'the past.'

During the Reformation we see the central role that God's law played in the Christian view of justice. Indeed for most of the reformers, and in fact for most of the Christianized world at the time, the validity of God's law for the civil sphere was simply unquestioned and presupposed. For example, the Reformer Peter Martyr Vermigli wrote:

> First, I said that the *magistrate* is the guardian of the divine law, which includes not only the second table, but the first also. Therefore he is the guardian of both the one and the other. I also mentioned the words of Augustine who said that both private men and kings should serve the Lord. It is written in the Psalms, When peoples gather together and kingdoms, to worship the Lord. In another place, Now therefore, O kings, be wise; be warned, O rulers of the earth. Serve the LORD with fear, with trembling. Augustine adds that a private man serves the Lord by confessing His name and living rightly. This, however, is not sufficient for a king or magistrate. He should serve the Lord with his authority and power by punishing those who oppose Him. Unless he does this, the magistrate appears to give his assent to blasphemy and heresy. When the king sees and suffers these men, he joins himself

to them and promotes their shameful acts. When Nebuchadnezzar first came to know God, he proposed a decree promising capital punishment for those who should blaspheme against the God of Daniel. Darius later made a similar decree. Our magistrate should stamp out all idolatry, blasphemy and superstition.... The law of God states that blasphemers should be put to death not by a private man or by priests, but by the magistrate (Leviticus 24:16).[27]

Although I don't agree with Vermigli's conclusions here without qualification (and this is not the place to discuss the nature and meaning of blasphemy), his clear statement should not shock or surprise us because it is typical of the Reformation age. Whilst we must recognize that the Reformation was a complex period and that there were diverse views on the exact nature of the relationship of Christians to the Mosaic penal sanctions, it can be safely stated that the law of God was highly esteemed and practically applied. Martin Bucer, the leading Reformer and mentor to John Calvin wrote, "But since no one can describe an approach more equitable and wholesome to the commonwealth than that which God describes in his law, it is certainly the duty of all kings and princes who recognize that God has put them over his people that they follow most studiously his own method of punishing evildoers."[28] Commenting on the justice of God's penal sanctions Bucer states, "May the Lord grant the shepherds of his people the gift of not wanting to seem wiser than God, or more clement and humane, so that they may at length see what a pleasing sacrifice it is to God and how necessary and how effective a remedy against the deadly diseases of mankind it is to impose just punishments on godless, criminal, and wicked men."[29]John Calvin's commentaries on the four last books of Moses reveal the same attitude to penology in the law. He writes in regard to heresy and blasphemy, "Whoever shall now contend that it is unjust to put heretics and blasphemers to death will knowingly and willingly incur their very guilt. This is not laid down in human authority; it is God who speaks and prescribes a *perpetual rule* for his church."[30] And again, with respect to adultery Calvin considered it a shame and disgrace if universal gentile law punished adultery with death, and Christians just overlooked it: "Adultery is punished no less severely by the Julian law than by that of God; whilst those who boast themselves of the Christian name are so tender and remiss, that they visit this execrable offence with a very light reproof."[31]

Many more examples could be offered here, but whatever we make of Calvin and the Reformers on this point, it should be noted that these perspectives were not seen as particularly controversial, because this was the judicial atmosphere of an increasingly Christianized and reforming age. Historian Harold Berman shows that many biblical laws regarding crime were embedded in Europe *before* the Reformation. It is noteworthy that biblical laws appear lenient by comparison to much medieval law. Typically crimes punishable by death in the Middle Ages included, "treason, homicide, rape, arson, robbery, riot, counterfeiting, forgery, blasphemy, and unnatural sexual behaviour." [32] Six of these crimes (unless they involved manslaughter) were *not* capital in the Biblical law. In the early sixteenth century, Johann Von Schwarzenberg, a man who has been called the greatest legislator of the Reformation era and one of the great legal thinkers in the history of Germany, became the principal author of the first modern criminal code. This document played a very significant role in the German revolution as the first systematic codification of criminal law, and was enacted ten years before Luther denounced the authority of the Roman Catholic priesthood, birthing the Reformation proper.[33]

In the historic *Bamberg Capital Court Statute* we find "the first systematic and comprehensive codification, in the full sense of that word, of a single branch of law, namely, the law of crimes punishable by death, twenty-six in all, ranging from blasphemy and perjury to robbery and murder." [34] Again, twenty-six exceeds those crimes considered capital in biblical law (eighteen – twenty-three, depending on how they are counted and without factoring in changes by the New Testament canon). Yet as Berman points out, "Schwarzenberg and his colleagues did not make up these crimes; most of them were offenses that had been identified, named, and punished – by death – under the customary law of the Germanic and other peoples of Europe as it had developed during previous centuries." At the same time, one of the most important changes that took place during the period was that, "High standards of proof were set." [35]

In the next century, the Puritans, continuing the Reformation emphasis, developed an understanding of law and justice, punishment *and* restoration that sought to conform itself closely with the mercy, compassion and justice of God's revealed law. Just as the Puritans sought to submit family, vocation and church, not to mention king and country, to God's word, so with respect to *penology*, the locus of authority had to be the Word of God, not some external standard. In this view, "Whatever the Bible said was absolutely true and not conditioned [relativized] by time and place, conditions or circumstances." [36] The historic *example* of the Puritans in this regard is noteworthy. For instance, *The Massachusetts Code of 1648* begins with this statement:

> So soon as God had set up political government among his people, Israel, he gave them a body of laws for judgement, both in civil and criminal causes. These were brief and fundamental principles, yet withal so full and comprehensive as out of them clear deductions were to be drawn to *all particular cases in future times*.[37]

This conviction was not simply an abstract ideal in Puritan thought and culture. They sought to follow biblical law faithfully, not simply endorse the dominant cultural perspective. Consequently, theft was to be punished by due restitution, *not death*, as had previously been common practice.[38] Yet where existing laws already conformed to biblical law, they supported them. For example, seventeenth-century Puritan, James Durham wrote concerning adultery in, *A Practical Exposition of the Ten Commandments*:

1. When both persons are married, as David and Bathsheba were, this is most abominable, and that which we call double adultery.

2. When the man is married and the woman solute or free.

3. When the woman is married, and the man free, these two last are both gross, yet the latter is accounted grosser, as having these aggravations, of disturbing the peace of our neighbour's family, the corrupting of his seed and offspring, and the alienating of his inheritance added unto it, therefore not only the first but even the third hath been ordinarily punished by death amongst men.[39]

Durham likewise wrote concerning adultery in his *Lectures on Job*, "It is a heinous crime worthy to be punished by the judge. The laws of man should take order with such a sin, and the moral law of God taught that such a sin deserved death (Deut. 22:22), not only in the woman, as some would have it only, but also in the man." [40]

Again, we may differ with some of the conclusions of the medieval,

Reformation and Puritan church in matters of interpretation or application, but the point here is to simply note their common assumptions and practice with regard to what the Bible deems criminal. For the Puritans, the truth and authority of Scripture is from a transcendent source and so cannot be relativized, despite it being revealed into history.[41] Thus they held that from the fundamental principles of God's law deductions can be made to all particular cases in future times – including criminal law. The vitality of all Puritan thought came from this non-autonomous submission to the total word of God in everything and it was this foundation of stable truth that provided the cultural energy for their nation-building. No nation can be built without law and the law proceeds from a source of authority – for the Christian, that authority is the sovereign God. The noted Puritan Thomas Hooker observed that those who reject God's authority in the matter of law make a futile attempt to, "Justle the law out of its place, and the Lord out of His glorious sovereignty, pluck the crown from His head, and the sceptre out of His hand."[42] As Beeke and Jones point out regarding the Puritans, "the judicial law became an appendix to the second table concerning civil government given to Israel to give a rule of public justice, to distinguish Israel from others, and to be a type of Christ's government. Insofar as the judicial law is of common and general equity, it remains in force."[43]

More recently, moving into the nineteenth century, the theonomic logic of an evangelical legend, the great Baptist preacher, Charles Haddon Spurgeon, is abundantly clear. This great Victorian churchman known to many historians as, 'the last of the Puritans' wrote a political manifesto that contemporary missiologists would do well to read. Spurgeon held that the civil sphere, like every other, was to be under the absolute sovereignty of God and his law:

> I long for the day when the precepts of the Christian religion shall be the rule among all classes of men and all transactions. I often hear it said, 'do not bring religion into politics.' This is precisely where it ought to be brought and set there in the face of all men as on a candlestick. I would have the cabinet and members of Parliament do the work of the nation as before the Lord....[44]

It was the precepts of the law of God that was Spurgeon's primary concern in this statement. This is evident in his published political philosophy for the Christian, (which was prompted by the *Education*

Bill of 1870 concerning the state takeover of education) which he framed in the form of a series of penetrating questions. In the first question he asks, "are not all mankind under law to God, and where and when did the king of all the earth announce that nations were to be free from His control, and free from all recognition of His existence and authority."[45] In his third question he asks regarding the nation state and private companies, "are not both government and the company still bound to the laws of God; as for instance, that which allots for one day in seven for rest...if it be true, that both are free from the allegiance to the law of God, where is this affirmed or implied in Scripture?"[46] In questions five and six he recognizes clearly that the rejection of Christian civil law is the *de facto* establishment of religious atheism that would inevitably persecute the Christian faith.[47] Thus in question eleven he asks, "is it not true that Parliaments, and kings and nations, may say, 'Let us break his bands asunder and cast his cords from us,' such language ill becomes Christian men."[48] Lewis Drummond correctly summarises the source of Spurgeon's convictions: "That philosophy grew out of his basic theology, namely, that God is sovereign over all of life, and that includes politics, business, the home and every other aspect of one's being."[49]

This same theonomic thinking was commonly found amongst evangelicals (like Jonathan Edwards) in the eighteenth century, on both sides of the Atlantic. The contemporary reaction to these great scions of biblical faith is very often incredulity or dismissal. Some ill-informed and ostensibly Christian social commentators point to false religions like Islam and make ignorant comparisons between biblical law and the laws of Islam (*Sharia*) as a means of dismissing biblical penology; it is commonly suggested a Christian law-order would be like the rule of the Taliban! The truth is that Christian and Islamic legal structures bear only a very superficial resemblance and essentially differ at almost every level. Most fundamentally, biblical law puts all people under the same law to God (Lev. 24:22; Num. 15:29) to ensure equity and justice and forbids all forms of oppression, religious, legal or otherwise (Ex. 22:21; 23:6-9) – which is how Western civilization developed the idea of the rule of law and freedom of conscience. *Sharia* recognizes no such equality. Non-Muslims do not enjoy the same rights as Muslims (See Qur'an: Sura: 9:5–14, 73; 61:11; 66:9; 34:33; 47:4), and the totalitarian objective of Islam is the total conquest and coercive imposition of *Sharia* on all *Kaafir* (unbelievers) through the process of *jihad*.[50] That said, any reference to Islamic or other legal systems to invalidate biblical law is a non sequitur. Regardless what penalties other civilizations have used (past and present) for various crimes, biblical law sustains its own internal logic of crime and punishment; as the great Puritan Samuel Rutherford noted back in the seventeenth century, "though heretics and Mohammad teach that heretics, as also they teach that manslayers, adulterers, paricides, should die the death, it followeth not that we are not to teach the same." [51] That is to say, the validity of biblical law is not undermined simply because a heathen, pagan or heretical law order happens to attach a similar penalty to a given crime. *Similarity in some respect does not make for similarity in all respects.* A school teacher who believes there is no God may still teach that there is a law of gravity; it does not follow that *because* a non-believer taught there is no God, we should not teach the law of gravity. In the same way, just because Islam teaches falsely about the Trinity and Christ's atoning death (amongst many other things), does not mean we should not teach that murderers of their fathers or mothers should be executed.

Moving to the twentieth century, Reformed theologian John Frame notes that theonomic thought past and present believes, "the civil penalties of the Mosaic Law were binding upon present day civil governments." [52] That is to say, the Puritan mind holds that all governments (past, present and future) are inescapably accountable to the standards of God's law in matters of crime and punishment (rightly interpreted), not their own, and will be judged by it. The law's binding validity, even in criminal matters, does not mean however, that it can be *imposed* upon an unwilling society. On the contrary, God's law can only be effectively applied when a godly people demand it in terms of oath and covenant, and this is how the Puritans viewed their society, as a missionary people in covenant with God. [53] As Rushdoony has critically pointed out concerning the death penalty, "the penalty applies to a covenant people directly." [54] Moreover Rushdoony writes, "In the long run, legal reform without religious reform is not a tenable hope. There must be religious reformation *before* there is judicial or civil reform, or the alternative is coercion. Coercion eventually produces greater evils." [55] Theonomists therefore are emphatically against coercion. Practically this means that our first task as Christians is evangelism and teaching all that God has commanded, whilst recognizing that the Old Testament laws continue in force unless rescinded or modified by further revelation, in light of Christ's eschatological mission as the fulfiller, interpreter and enforcer of God's law (Matt. 5:17–18; Acts 10:9–33). As Gustave Friedrich Oehler noted:

> As God's covenant with His people is eternal, so also are the covenant ordinances; they are, as the expression frequently runs, everlasting laws and statutes for Israel and the future generations (see Ex. 12:14,17; 27:21; 28:43, and many other passages). The Pentateuch knows nothing of a future change in the law, nor of an abrogation of it even in part; only the attitude of the people toward the law was to be different in the last times.[56]

Thus theonomic Puritanism is the belief that *all of Scripture in its totality is God's covenant law-word* and as such, properly interpreted, remains in force in every detail till heaven and earth pass away. As Vern Poythress notes, "At the heart of theonomy is the conviction that God's word is the only standard for evaluating all human action," whether in the social, personal or judicial sphere. Such a view, theonomists hold, deserves the support of all Christians.[57] In terms of the principles of the Reformation, these Puritan views on crime and punishment are at least logical. It could be argued for example, that theonomic missiology is simply the Reformed doctrine of the sufficiency of Scripture applied to the social and civil spheres. The doctrine of Sola Scriptura and its complete sufficiency is not merely an abstract or ecclesiastical doctrine – it is a total reality for life. Man cannot live by bread alone, but by every word that comes from the mouth of God (Matt. 4:4), and this word is sufficient for all the circumstances and institutions of life, from the family, to the church, and state.

It will not do, as some critics have urged,[58] to dismiss civil applications of the law on the ground that these historic movements, states and communities of the Reformation and Puritan era (or any other era), that have implemented God's law did not last very long or that they didn't 'work' sufficiently well in the past. We could say the same thing about marriages or families, the churches and the courts; there are countless examples of the fallible and broken character of all these institutions. On this logic we would never marry, have children, become a church member, or trust a magistrate; the result would be anarchy in society. The reality is, there are no perfect institutions, they are all fallible. Obedience is imperfect. But when a marriage fails, a church falls into heresy, or a magistrate is found to be corrupt, it is not because there is something wrong with God's institution of marriage, the church or the state. When a state or nation in the past that implemented God's law does not last a thousand years, or execute perfect justice, it does not indicate a failure in God's law, nor can we conclude that the law must fall into disuse.

We cannot then reduce the law to irrelevance because we judge it has not 'worked' sufficiently well in other times historically; this is a humanistic and pragmatic argument that has no basis in Scripture, in addition to being logically fallacious. Furthermore, it is simply not a judgement we are even able to make independently of God, for how can we assess what has 'worked' without a God-given criterion? To judge if something has worked requires knowledge of the end in view. Do we really want to place ourselves on the throne of the universe to judge whether God's law has 'worked' in any given period of history in terms of God's purposes? Furthermore, if the Kingdom and reign of God in terms of his righteousness is in fact the end toward which God is working in history, then how can we substitute God's law for man's laws of imagination? Clearly in 1 Timothy 1, St. Paul does not believe we can.

As important and interesting as the social history of Christian law is, God's law is not merely to occupy the interest of the antiquarian or historian of the Reformation and Puritan era. God's law can and does have a bearing on our understanding of justice and civil law today. Certainly the law (including the judicial explanations dealing with criminality) was given to an ancient people of a different culture living in an agrarian society, and it is true that we are not living in sixteenth-century Geneva nor seventeenth and eighteenth-century England or America now, but we cannot move logically from this fact to a cultural dismissal of the law. To such a dismissive attitude, Old Testament scholar Alec Motyer gives short shrift, "Certainly any simplistic or bland appeal to culture to sidestep or to eviscerate biblical law is out of the question." [59] That said however, just because many Christians in the past believed in the application of the penal sanctions of God's law in matters God deems criminal, does not, in itself, make it right, nor does their practice bind our interpretations. Historic precedents are relevant and important, but how are we to go about understanding this aspect of God's law today?

9.5   Foundations of Biblical Penology

The power of the sword, the legitimate legal power of a limited coercion to restrain evil, is given in Scripture to the lawful authority of the civil magistrate (Rom. 13:15) and as we have seen, the Puritans taught that the magistrate is to apply the standards and principles of God's law in the matter of crime and punishment. It is certainly the case that compared to twentieth and early twenty-first century penology in the West, biblical sanctions for sins deemed crimes appear harsh in a permissive age; though the charge that biblical penalties are severe, measured against historic European standards (which are more humane than the historic examples of the Eastern kingdoms) reveals biblical penology is compassionate and light.[60]

That said, there is a difference between penalties seeming comparatively harsh (to modern sensibilities) and being *unjust*. Here the question again comes back to the *source and definition* of law and justice – who defines these for man? In the cultural milieu of ethical and judicial confusion today, foundational questions must be asked afresh. What is the relation between crime and punishment? Which sins are crimes? How should various crimes be punished? Without the *specific* guidance of God's law we have no adequate answers to these foundational questions. The 'law of nations' often appealed to by Christians in previous centuries as an answer to such questions was actually broadly based on biblical laws from early European codes. But regardless of what it meant to some of our forebears, such an appeal has no force today because the consensus of Christendom has gone. Once unhooked from biblical law, man's legislation soon enshrines murder and perversity as legal rights (as witness abortion and sodomy). What must be clearly understood is that when changes are made to the *penalties* for crimes, we in fact witness a change in social *values*. Furthermore, foundational changes in the law order in terms of which acts are deemed criminal, indicate a change of 'gods,' and therefore a new source of sovereignty.

To grapple with biblical penology adequately, we must understand the basic presuppositions of biblical justice. At the foundation of biblical penology is the doctrine of restitution or just recompense; this is made plain by the *lex talionis* (law of retaliation, or like for like). Central to a biblical understanding of justice, crime and punishment, is the *lex talionis*, "an eye for an eye and a tooth for a tooth" principle of justice (Ex. 21:24). This was not a literal principle but an analogical one.[61] What this principle demands is not knocking out the tooth of someone who has knocked out the tooth of another, but *exact justice* and impartiality in human courts. The *lex talionis* could be therefore described as the *sine qua non* of biblical law and the essence of the meaning of restitution.

It is not surprising then that we find this principle under attack in antinomian responses to the law of God; yet Jesus Christ himself dealt clearly with this matter in what has come to be called *The Sermon on the Mount.* Some theologies today simply reject the *Sermon on the Mount* as irrelevant to the Christian age, positioning it in the Old Covenant era, and by so doing, presuming it is somehow rendered non-applicable to Christians today (classical dispensationalism). Others accept that this teaching is for Christians, but suggest that Jesus was giving a new law on the mount (the *law of Christ*) and was in some manner superseding or setting aside the details of the Mosaic moral law in the process (New Covenant Theology). In this theology, the law of Christ is characterized as different from God's law given to Moses in the Ten Commandments and case laws; although exactly how and in what way it is different is unclear to say the least and a matter of dispute amongst its exponents. It is clearly necessary that all Christians accept that Christ is the sovereign interpreter of his law (Matt. 5:21–26). Once we have accepted that his words *are relevant* for our own time and not relegated to the past only, we see that far from abrogating the law or introducing a new law, in the *Sermon on the Mount*, Christ corrects the misinterpretations of his contemporaries. Thomas Schreiner in his exegetical work gives numerous illustrations of how people have read Jesus *incorrectly* as somehow abolishing God's law when in fact he was upholding it and correcting misunderstandings and misinterpretations.[62]

For instance, the requirement to love one's enemies and neighbours is not something new introduced by our Lord as is often thought, rather he was confirming, not over-turning his law (see Lev. 19:17–18). Schreiner shows that discontinuity is apparent in the redemptive elements of Christ's fulfilment of types and shadows in the law (i.e. the sacrificial system), but continuity is apparent in his dealing with *civil matters.* Thus in discussing the commonly held view that the *lex talionis* (Ex. 21:22–27; Deut. 19:15–21) in Matthew 5:21ff was being abolished by Christ, Schreiner shows that Jesus was doing no such thing:

What Jesus spoke against here is the practice of applying the judicial principle that the punishment should fit the crime, to the *personal* sphere. Individually, disciples are to forgive and do good to those that oppress them. Disciples should not take upon themselves the task of righting the wrong of the world, as if they should personally dispense justice...governmental authorities, on the other hand, still assign penalties on the basis of just compensation. If the punishment is not proportional to the crime, then the basis for all justice is removed. Hence Jesus does not abolish the OT law but rather corrects a wrong interpretation.[63]

This principle of the *lex talionis* is central to a Puritan understanding of judicial justice and penology. It bears repeating however, that properly understood, as Jesus declares, it did not constitute an endorsement of revenge or retaliation in criminal matters in the personal sphere – quite the contrary. As Enoch Wines shows:

In our exposition of this law it is...important to observe that it did not authorise the retaliation of injuries by individuals and so make each man a judge and avenger in his own cause...in every instance of the application of the principle of the *lex talionis*, it was the duty of the legal tribunal to adjudge, and of the public executive power to inflict, the punishment.[64]

The law of retaliation then required exact justice in terms of restitution or recompense. Thieves were to restore what was illegally taken with damages on top (two-fold to five-fold) depending on the nature of the thing stolen.[65]

Financial restitution was to be made in a variety of cases of negligence, accident, or instances where the victim of serious crimes was willing to accept appropriate financial compensation as an alternative to insisting on the death penalty (excepting murder, Num. 35:31–32).[66] Corporal punishment was to be administered for certain criminal offences and capital offenders faced excommunication, exile or death.[67] In his work on the *Doctrine of the Christian Life*, John Frame lists all the capital offenses of the Old Testament, including murder, incest, bestiality, kidnapping, rape, witchcraft and sodomy etc., seeking to analyse how they might apply today. He opens the possibility that some of the capital penalties (i.e. witchcraft and blasphemy) were perhaps based on the special holiness of Israel living in the presence of God and so should not necessarily be enforced by present-day Christian governments.[68] He therefore writes, "It could be debated whether many of the capital penalties of the Pentateuch should be adopted in modern societies. Many of them seem to be given in view of the special holiness of Israel."[69] However he goes on to argue that capital punishment is in a certain sense a *creation ordinance* that has in no way been set aside. He also shows that the New Testament *does not* repeal the death penalty (Acts 25:11).[70] In fact, Frame clearly states that capital punishments should be used much more often in modern society, especially in cases of murder and incorrigible delinquency.[71]

Furthermore, Frame makes a number of important qualifying remarks that bear consideration. First, the law of God cannot be applied comprehensively in modern nations where there is no covenanting with God (clear profession of faith) amongst the people (as there *had been* with the Puritans) and no desire to obey God's standards.[72] We have already seen that modern Puritans equally hold that biblical law cannot be imposed upon an unwilling people, but only applied when a godly community or nation demand it. Second, Frame argues that for a variety of capital offenses people could ransom their lives from death by making restitution by *other means*. This he argues is clearly implied in Exodus 21:30 and Numbers 35:31–32, where financial restitution is set in all manner of cases, though the crime of murder was not eligible for possible alternative punishment.[73] The noted Hebrew scholar Robert Alter agrees:

> The preponderant view of Jewish commentators in Late Antiquity and the Middle Ages is that in each of the cases stipulated here [Exodus 21:23–24ff], the intention is for the liable party to pay monetary compensation for the loss incurred...monetary compensation for such losses was a wide-spread practice in ancient Near Eastern codes, and as some of the medieval commentators point out, it would have been unfeasible to implement the *lex talionis* literally with equity (e.g., how does one punish someone who has caused a man a partial loss of eyesight in one eye?).[74]

Not only so, but it seems to also be clear that the victims of crime had a say in how the offender was to be punished. The law of retaliation did not always obligate the victim to press for maximum charges or the ultimate penalty. Indeed, Wines argues concerning the rights of victims of crime:

The person receiving the injury retained always the natural right of remitting the punishment, if the other chose to compound the matter by apologies and pecuniary compensations. The law does not command an injured person to avail himself of the right of retaliation, without any alternative. It only fixes the punishment, to which the author of an injury must submit, if he cannot compound matters with the injured party. Such satisfactions were in fact so common, that Moses found it necessary to restrain the use of them in the case of deliberate murder.[75]

Interestingly, Proverbs, a practical application of the law, warns the would-be adulterer that an angry husband is unlikely to be in the mood to come to terms and accept financial compensation for this violation of his family's sanctity; he may well prosecute for the death penalty (Prov. 6:32–35). If he does so however, he cannot exempt his unfaithful wife from the punishment – both offenders would face the death penalty and this fact prevented malicious and criminal misuses of the law and the proliferation of false charges. It doubtless also led to a minimal use of the maximum penalty as a clement spouse would likely merely divorce the unfaithful partner. Rushdoony likewise agrees that the case law cannot be read in a wooden fashion in this regard. He cites Gordon Wenham approvingly in holding that whilst the law often cites the extreme penalty, it allowed for lesser ones depending on the case at hand.[76] John Frame is again helpful on this point and is worth citing at length:

The case laws are not intended to refer specifically to every situation that may arise. Rather, they address representative situations, guiding judges in assessing responsibility. The Decalogue leaves judges no discretion. They have no authority to make theft legal or to penalize people for worshiping the true God. But the case laws encourage judges to be flexible in considering how the principles of the Decalogue apply to each case. The judges may not contradict the case laws, any more than they may contradict the Decalogue. But since cases vary, God gives to judges discretion to relate the Decalogue to new cases in wise and creative ways. As in modern courts, the judges certainly had the power to determine mitigating and aggravating circumstances, to assess motives, and to determine probabilities in the evidence. The penalties attached to crimes in the case laws are also exemplary, not to be automatically applied. For example, it is evident that in many capital crimes there is provision to ransom the life of the criminal. Numbers 35:31 prohibits ransom for the life of a murderer. But that suggests that ransom was possible in other crimes for which the case laws specify the death penalty, even when the text does not specifically mention the possibility of ransom. Examples may be adultery, homosexuality and blasphemy. Exodus 21:30 specifically mentions the possibility of ransom in an otherwise capital case. It may well be that judges in Israel had considerable liberty to determine penalties for crimes, following general principles of law found throughout the Pentateuch.[77]

We might characterise Frame's view here of restitution and the *lex talionis* as 'soft theonomy.' It appears that this nuanced theonomic view is also held by the noted Old Testament scholar, Walter Kaiser. As Greg Bahnsen points out, "What Kaiser is arguing is *not that there has been a change in the penal sanctions from the Old to the New Testament*, but rather that even within the Old Testament itself the law of God did not necessarily absolutely require the death penalty for all the crimes where that penalty is mentioned."[78] Like Frame, Kaiser argues exegetically for this from Numbers 35:31–32 and Exodus 21:30. A similar view of judicial latitude in application of penalties is offered by Jewish scholar David Klinghoffer, arguing that the *biblical laws of evidence ensured latitude was necessary* and that a critical purpose of the sanctions was not simply punishment but also teaching:

> …written in the Torah's legal code we find a death penalty for egregious crimes, including some that we [modern secular people] wouldn't regard as criminal (like breaking the Sabbath or adultery to cite two sins prohibited by the Ten Commandments). But the rules of evidence and procedure were so strict that getting a conviction was practically impossible and so from the time the Jews entered Israel, capital punishment was carried out rarely…, so why make Sabbath breaking a capital crime, if it was only in theory? Because the Bible intended to create a teaching model, indicating the severity of the moral offense by attaching to it, as a matter of principle, if not practicality, the ultimate punishment.[79]

Whilst modern Puritans (theonomists) would not argue for a death penalty for Sabbath-breaking given the change in significance of the Sabbath in the New Testament, there appears to be a good deal of exegetical and historical substance behind these observations about the *lex talionis* that should be taken seriously in a theonomic missiological perspective. In short, just because a death penalty is mentioned in relation to certain crimes does not mean it is to be automatically or mechanically applied. The purpose of the *lex talionis*, of the principle of just restitution and recompense is, in the last analysis, God-centred rather than man-centred. Just punishments have as their ultimate goal God's kingdom purpose and the restoration of His order in the world. Consequently penology is essentially eschatological in character – it concerns God's purposes and the shape of his ordained future. God's law aims at making impossible the development of a professional criminal class and so has in view godly progress in the social order, or what we might call a post-millennial principle. Since the punishment of criminality indicates God's reign over all things, crime and punishment should be a critical issue for contemporary missiology to grapple with – though it is almost completely ignored, even by Reformed studies on the Puritans.

In sum, as part of the means to the *realization of God's reign*, God establishes his laws of justice that include punishment to restore his order in several ways. First, the offender is to receive a just penalty that corresponds to the criminal act. Second, punishment purges evil from amongst a people rather than having guilt rest upon a people for ignoring it. Third, punishment also functions as a deterrent to criminality with impunity (Deut. 19:16–21). Fourthly, punishment functions as a kind of civil atonement in that by effecting justice it helps reconcile the offender to society, resulting in God's healing for the social order. Fifth, punishment involves recompense or restitution to the offended (not fines to enrich the state), so that there is real justice for victims of crime.[80] Having then discussed the foundations of biblical penology in the *law of retaliation*, we can now move on to consider some specific questions of interpretation.

9.6 Guidelines for Interpreting Specifics in the Law
Principle and Practice

First, by way of review, in the Puritan, Reformed vision, if we are to rightly interpret the word of God with respect to penology, we must see *all* of Scripture as the imperishable Word of God, not to be taken lightly or toyed with – we must analyze it responsibly seeking to *submit* ourselves to what God is saying, however counter-cultural it may be.

Motyer reminds us:

> According to our Lord's teaching in Matthew 5:19, the commandments of his Bible are to be treated with the utmost seriousness: it is this that determines promotion and demotion in the kingdom...any sort of cavalier attitude to the writings which the Lord Jesus reverenced as his Bible and as the Word of God should be anathema to the Christian.[81]

Likewise New Testament scholar, Thomas R. Schreiner (who is not theonomic), in his study of Mathew's Gospel admits that, "Jesus emphasizes that he has come to fulfil rather than abolish the law, so that even the least of the commandments should not be relaxed but rather *enforced.*"[82] This does not mean however that there are no instances of discontinuity between the Old and the New Testaments. On the contrary, there are some very important changes. The new covenant fulfilment of the old covenant promises and types means that the new covenant surpasses the older covenant in power, finality and glory. With Christ as our great High Priest, and our paschal lamb, we no longer show ourselves to the priesthood of the Temple (which is gone) if we have been cleansed of a disease; we are no longer bound by the atonement laws (ordinances) in the system of animal sacrifices. The Temple is no longer present in its ancient form and the old priesthood has been abolished, having been replaced by Christ himself. In Christ we are now a kingdom of priests (Ex. 19:6; 1 Pt. 2:9) fulfilling, as God's church, what Israel as a nation had failed to be. Various laws that indicated Israel's distinction from the pagan nations around them, and their separation to a special calling have also been 'transposed' in their significance. That is, certain restrictions from the spheres of diet and customary social distinction from gentiles, primarily pointed forward to their greater fulfilment in the church's separation as God's people to life and holiness as priests unto God.

Circumcision as the mark of the covenant was also replaced by baptism, and we no longer celebrate the Passover in the old form since Christ our Passover lamb has been sacrificed for us (1 Cor. 5:7). In addition, the way a Jewish man trimmed his beard and cut his hair, for example, or did not enter a gentile's home to eat, are no longer binding moral requirements upon Christians, because they were given to teach and illustrate the covenant people's separation to God and to holiness. So the biblically imposed link between natural hair and beard growth and unnatural or marring styles, with holiness, related to the fact that pagans developed many customs of cutting, marring and decorating their hair and bodies that were religious in character (Jer. 9:26; 25:23; 49:32 refer to this typical Arabian practice). In such a context, God wanted a clear distinction to be seen with his people. The body was not to be marred nor unnatural styles cultivated (Lev. 19:26-28). That is not to say that many of these types of laws do not contain profound wisdom for life or wise guidance for health. Nothing God says is by mistake and where such practices as body cutting and marring again dominate and become religious in significance, these seemingly redundant laws would quickly take on new significance. Consider for example the huge popular resurgence in the practice of tattooing in the West which was considered a pagan marring of the body in the past. As we become more pagan the practice may again take on religious significance. And we should not forget the health risks associated with tattooing. Furthermore, various studies have demonstrated the value of biblical dietary laws[83] and the health value of circumcision is very well known, especially in the prevention of sexually transmitted disease. The Western world adopted biblical laws of animal slaughter very early (and continues to observe them for the most part) and if medieval Europe had observed many of the sanitation laws of Scripture, and the quarantine laws regarding infectious disease, many lives would have been saved. With modern medicine, biblical quarantine laws were revived. This is all to say that God's law is all relevant, because it is God-breathed, and useful for teaching and training in righteousness (2 Tim. 3:16f) but not all of its requirements are now morally binding for Christians. Thus the validation and enforcement of the covenant law in Christ is not wooden, but interpreted in terms of Christ as the eschatological fulfilment and confirmation of all its provisions. Christ is the Temple into which we are being built and he is our great High Priest who has offered himself as the atoning sacrifice once for all and intercedes for us now at the mercy seat in heaven.[84] However, recognising the importance of eschatology in interpreting the place of the law in the coming of Christ the king does not leave us in the bewildering world of typological obscurantism or academic elitism that leaves the layperson wondering which way up to read the Bible.

Meredith Kline for example, a very capable and influential Old Testament scholar, leaves one feeling that every Christian needs a Ph.D. in redemptive historical hermeneutics before they can grapple with God's law and ethics. His innovative and novel 'intrusion ethics' are, in this writer's view, both fanciful and excessively dependent upon endless typologies. For Kline, the eschatological kingdom 'intrudes' into history in the Old Testament law and theocracy. Somehow, the Old Testament theocracy, even though it was historically before the coming of the Messiah king, was in some senses closer to the eschatological kingdom of God than the church is under the New Covenant! This Old Testament theocratic kingdom simply 'intruded' into a common grace world – that is, it was the eschatological kingdom set forth in a typological manner. Kline's break with the traditionally reformed and Puritan understanding of the relationship of the covenants is, to my mind, highly problematic and is convincingly refuted by Greg Bahnsen.[85] Furthermore, whilst containing some valuable biblical insights, the implications of Kline's 'intrusion ethic' lead to unbiblical and untenable conclusions for the social order. For example, Kline's theory leads him to argue for a religiously 'neutral' state (a functional impossibility) based on less than adequate biblical premises, and rooted in too sharp a dichotomy between the Mosaic and the New Covenants.

Clearly then, sorting through the law and interpreting the Word of God correctly takes work, diligence and discipline, though that task is not restricted to an elite few. Reformed scholar Motyer is insightful in offering a helpful and simple principle of interpretation for dealing with some of the complexities of Old Covenant law which also gives us a valuable hermeneutical tool in our consideration of penology. How do we know which specific laws and sanctions carry over to the present, and which do not? The *principle involved* in the distinction between clean and unclean foods was the distinctiveness of the people of God, expressed by their distinct dietary habits. In this case, the practice belonged to one sphere (diet) and the principle it embodied belonged in another (spiritual status). The principle remains, the practice does not. But in the case, for example, of homosexual practice (Lev. 18), practice and principle coincide. There is no other way in which it could be said that the practice is now abrogated but the principle remains, or that the principle can be expressed along other lines. Where the practice and the principle have *only* an ancient cultural or biblically imposed link, the practice has lapsed but the principle it once expressed remains: where practice and principle are, in the nature of the case, inseparable, both remain.[86]

In other words, there is no way to argue that prohibitions against sodomy or adultery (as two examples in God's law from the sphere of sexual morality) embody or illustrate a broader spiritual principle belonging to another sphere, or something to be fulfilled for us in Christ – the principle and the practice coincide. How might one show from Scripture that the prohibitions (against sexual deviance) have been abrogated, but the principle behind the prohibitions remains? One would end up with the absurd idea that prohibitions against homosexuality or adultery are set aside but somehow illustrate our spiritual status in Christ, or point forward to the need for sexual purity – but obviously this law concerns sexual purity. It is clear from this hermeneutical principle that the Ten Commandments and the great majority of the case laws which illustrate and explain the meaning and application of those commandments remain binding. As a bare minimum then, where practice and principle are inseparable – which constitutes the bulk of the weighty matters of the law – both remain. Furthermore, where a particular illustrative practice has lapsed, the principle still remains. Related to this point then, is the general equity of the law remaining even when some of the examples of a *practice* are culturally obscure but illustrate an important abiding *principle*. For example, God's law required the fencing of roofs in Israel. This is because roofs were flat and people had social functions on the roof. There was therefore criminal negligence involved in having an unfenced roof if someone fell and was killed or injured. In our time, we don't usually gather on the roof of our residences and so don't fence them by law. But we are required to fence our swimming pools to avoid criminal prosecution if a child falls in and drowns. Thus, though the practice of fencing roofs in the West has ceased, the principle and equity of that law remains – in the same sphere – criminal negligence.

9.7 Law as a Value-processing System

A further key to understanding and interpreting biblical law is getting into the mind-set of the Bible, where penalties indicate and express specific values, many of which have been lost in our contemporary society. People often fail to understand biblical penalties because they do not share the value structure that the Bible aims at for the social order. Even many Christians tend to think that since Christ has died for sin, surely we should not punish the criminal in terms of biblical law, as though since Calvary, God no longer has a moral order he desires for the nations. But clearly religious forgiveness through the gospel and absolution in the church is not the same as judicial or civil pardon! Consider: a murderer can find salvation in Christ and still be justly executed for their crimes to restore God's order by restitution at the social level. The destructive implications of a murderer's crimes, both for the victim whose life has been unjustly taken, and the grieving family and friends left behind, as well as for the society of which they are all a part, are not addressed by a murderer's conversion to Christ. Furthermore, laws without penalties are not laws requiring justice, but simply advice. Whilst we can theoretically differentiate moral principle (precept) and sanction (penalty) we cannot artificially separate their intimate relationship which coincides in the term 'law.' This is because both conceptually and functionally the *value* (ethical and social weight) of a *precept* is comprehended by the *severity* of the *sanction* attached to it which consequently helps us to determine whether a piece of legislation is just or tyrannical. For example, if the penalty for jay-walking in a given society were death whilst the penalty for murder was a $50 fine, we would consider such a culture bereft of justice and incompetent to judge in moral questions. If the death sentence were required by a society for tax evasion whilst rape incurred $20 fines, we would again decry the injustice of that order, because whilst the *precepts* are morally just (legislation existing against murder, rape and tax evasion), the *penalties* are immoral (in light of the *lex talionis*) and therefore we would say the *law order itself* is unjust. Simply put, the punishment does not fit the crime. This clearly reveals that we cannot glibly dismiss biblical penalties, for they reveal to us the social and ethical value of God's precepts (the weightier and less weighty matters) and enable us to distinguish between crime and punishment; that is, there comes a point when punishments themselves, whether too lax or too harsh, become tyrannical or criminal in their perversion of justice. Thus, penalties essentially 'describe' the socio-ethical 'value' of the precept. Law is the legislation of moral statutes and precepts (or is procedural to such precepts) and constitutes, in practice, the union of precept and penalty, without which law would not be law, but advice. The relationship between them comes to the heart of the meaning of justice in relation to crime and punishment. If we find our way into the instructional genre of law in the Bible with diligence and respect, we soon discover that biblical law (precept and penalty) is utterly profound, providing a coherent, compassionate and hopeful vision of society under God.

9.8   Controversial Areas of Biblical Penology: Offenses against the Family

Perhaps the most misunderstood and offensive area of biblical law to modern sensibilities is the biblical legislation with respect to marriage and the family as it pertains to sexual conduct. Historically, gentile and Christian states have been inconsistent in applying the law in dealing with, for example, sexual crimes addressed by Scripture. The gentile nations have swung between severe cruelty such as mutilation, public torture and retaliation (all forbidden by God's law), and a nonchalant toleration in their approach to and punishment of adultery for example.[87] Scripture on the other hand steadfastly dignifies life, the family and sexuality as sacred, providing a positive understanding of well-ordered sexual relationships in the form of heterosexual marriage. This shapes our understanding of what constitutes a departure from God's norm. The Bible defines the good and from there flows the biblical view of human flourishing with regard to sexuality, protecting the good with serious legal threats for a violation of their sanctity. The Bible's criminal sanctions for sexual offenses then can only be understood in the context of a worldview that has stable marriage, family and community as the social priority.

Adultery is the archetypal sexual offense in Scripture because it is, "the paradigm case of sexual relations outside marriage. Likewise, other forms of sexual deviancy are characterized in biblical law, as *forms of adultery*."[88] Strictly speaking, adultery in the Bible is consensual intercourse between a married woman and a man who is not her husband – it is still adultery even if the man is unmarried. It is not adultery *proper* if a married man has intercourse with an unmarried (unbetrothed) woman because there is no husband (household head) whose marital and familial interests are being threatened.[89] Instead this is a form of fornication; a sub-type of adultery, which is illicit extra-marital sex contrary to God's norm, and is likewise viewed as both sinful and criminal – there is no double standard. However, there is no penalty in Scripture for the unmarried (unbetrothed) woman in such a case, whilst the man would have to marry her in the unlikely event the woman and her father demanded it. Likewise if the father didn't want to give her in marriage to the man, the offender would still have to pay the dowry, which is a heavy financial penalty.[90] The offended wife can also legitimately divorce her unfaithful spouse in such a case according to Scripture (Matt. 5:31–32;

19:9). The difference here is not regarding the criminal nature of the offense, rather the exemplary penalty is different because of the social consequences and impact upon the wider family and community. The emotional consideration of being betrayed by an unfaithful spouse, whilst important, is second to the familial and social impact.

The penalty of payment of a large dowry, or the requirement of marriage and the dowry were enforced forms of social welfare for the unbetrothed woman and her parents. The goal was to ensure the woman was not left destitute and un-provided for. An unmarried woman's marriage prospects (and therefore her chances of social wellbeing) would fall significantly in Old Testament culture once the community was aware of her fornication, therefore the man had to pay a dowry for her financial protection. The question of polygamy is raised here in so far as, in the Old Testament law, polygamy was at times tolerated as a means of social provision. However, Jesus makes clear this was a concession by Moses to deal with the social consequence of sin. However, it is not God's intention for marriage (Matt. 19:4–9; 5:31–32; Eph. 5:22–33; 1 Tim. 3:2–5) and so toleration of polygamy is ended in the New Testament era. We see at the outset then that God's law has much wider concerns than individual consent and personal gratification when it comes to legislation about sexual crimes.

Modern law has come to view *consent* as the sole issue of significance in determining legitimate sexual relationships, whereas biblical law seeks to direct sexual energy in a manner that creates *community* and mutual responsibility, not rugged individualism and irresponsibility. Our departure from the biblical view in the West means that the law and social order has few if any sanctions for punishing or discouraging the various forms of adultery; it is increasingly seen as a non-issue because concurrent with the trivialization of adultery has been the seizure of the family's powers by the state. Thus, as the family progressively declines, the state increasingly steps in to take on the responsibilities of the family in a futile effort to alleviate the massive social deficit familial erosion leaves behind. Consequently, in recent times:

> Because the state is steadily encroaching on the two basic social responsibilities of the family, the custody of property and of children, the state is relegating adultery to the realm of things peripheral and relatively unimportant. *Not until the authority of the family in this area is re-established will adultery again become a menace to society*

rather than a form of entertainment.... In all cultures where the families' authority over property and children has existed, or has been re-established, adultery inescapably becomes one of the most fearful crimes...the relationship is inescapable: where an offense is treason against society, there particularly severe penalties are imposed.[91]

In other words, the institution which is perceived to lie at the foundation of a healthy society (true community) will be protected by serious sanctions. Where the deleterious effects of the collapse of the family, its powers and responsibilities, are temporarily masked by the state's intervention, adultery can be viewed as merely a matter of consent and a form of entertainment because initially there seem to be few serious social consequences – the family has ceased to be the centre and foundation of community. But where a biblical view of the family, its responsibilities and freedoms is re-established, offenses against it are once again taken seriously. This helps us to understand why modern law has taken treason against the *state* so seriously – until the last few years most Western countries retained the death penalty for treason, because the state is viewed as the foundation, if not the 'god' of the social order. What is important to understand here is that *treason* has always been punished severely by nearly all political orders, even to this day. Where the family (not the state) is the basic foundation of community, being the source of welfare, property ownership and basic government in society (as prescribed in Scripture), treason will be seen primarily as a crime against the family, not the state:

> Biblical culture is family based; there are no laws of treason against the state, because treason is seen as action against the peace and unity of the family. As a result, there is a penalty of death for treason against the family, whereas in modern culture, treason is an offense against the state. Offenses against the family are seen as less and less important and, by many, are acts denied the status of an offense. For modern man, the Biblical law of treason is primitive and barbaric. From the perspective of Biblical law, to make treason an offense against the state is implicitly totalitarian and socially destructive. Sin in our era has been politicized. The law of treason is indicative of this: the family has been replaced by the state, and offenses against the family are being dropped by the law as a multitude of new sins against the state are invented almost daily. God has been replaced

by the state. According to 1 John 3:4, sin is transgression of the law of God, but sin is now seen as transgression of the law of the state. Politicizing sin tells us that the state is the new god whose laws must not be transgressed.[92]

But this counterfeit god, the state, cannot 'cover' for the collapse of the family for long. The welfare states of Europe are already falling into ruin because of their attempt to replace the functions of the family. As this collapse quickens the family will once again become much more socially significant. Setting sexual crime in the context of marriage and the family is important for another reason: the relationship between children and their parents. If God desires human flourishing in community by honouring the family, then sexual crimes are an attack upon the family and human well-being. In Leviticus 20:9–21, the underlying concern in regard to sexual offenses is the rebellious rejection of the authority of father and mother – the cursing of one's parents – which Jesus forthrightly addresses (Mark 7:8–13; Matt. 15:3–9).

This provides the logic for the list of sexual offenses that follow (Lev. 20:10–20), for the one who commits them holds cheap the honour of his or her parents, the people who brought them to life. If the modern reader wants to understand biblical law and penology, it is critical that this be understood. Burnside is very helpful on this point:

> This structural connection between cursing parents and sexual deviance seems unusual from a modern point of view. However, it is not surprising given what we know about the formation of Israelite marriage.... [W]e saw that one of the features of the normal sequence of marriage is obtaining the consent of the father of the bride. This shows respect for parents...biblical law views departures from this sequence as problematic. If respect for parents is part of the normal sequence of heterosexual marriage and if sexual deviancy is understood as a departure from what is normative, then it follows that the biblical characterization of adultery, and other sexual relationships opposed to marriage, will include the idea of disrespecting or cursing parents...the structural link may also reflect the reality that, in practical terms, parents are deeply affected by the sexual misbehaviour of their children (including adultery) because they are the ones who, in most cases, have to deal with the emotional, organizational, and possibly lineage implications. Adultery and sexual wrongdoing affects parents

because managing the fallout...makes demands on time and resources across a whole nexus of family relationships. If adultery takes place in a marriage, and this leads to a divorce, this will have knock-on effects on parents and siblings who may have the increased burden of looking after dependent family members.[93]

We see then that sexual deviancy from God's norm has massive negative implications for the *community*, and it is healthy and flourishing community at which God's law aims. Thus to understand biblical penology regarding sexuality we need to view seriously the legislation of Leviticus 20 which connects idolatry, the dishonouring of parents and adultery. First and foremost deviant sexual behaviour constitutes idolatry as it is a denial of the sovereignty and lordship of the God of Scripture and the authority of his law; it constitutes the worship of other gods (like Molech) manifest in conformity to other laws and customs. This naturally raises the question of the person's relationship to God. Second, sexual crimes involve the explicit dishonouring and despising of parents and their authority, holding cheap their role in bringing us into the world and nurturing us. This brings into question a person's relationship to their parents and siblings. Sexual deviance thus expresses spiritual and familial dysfunction that has shock waves which spread to impact the wider family, the nation and a people's relationship with God – all are interconnected. The Bible therefore places limits on sexual expression in order to honour God, honour the family, and bring about flourishing community.

Consent-based contemporary law by comparison is atomistic, individualistic, self-centred, selfish and destructive of community; our present social decline and the collapse of marriage are living proof of this. These factors begin to help us understand why the exemplary punishments attached to biblical laws regarding sexual conduct appear severe. Sexual deviancy constitutes idolatry, the cursing of parents, and *treason*. As such it undermines everything God's law aims at in the creation of a well-ordered, harmonious, prosperous, and safe community life.

As we have seen already, these laws did not mean that the death penalty for sexual deviancy was thrown around haphazardly. First, there was the requirement of two or more (lit. three) witnesses to corroborate any charge (Deut. 17:6), and given the essentially private character of sexual activity, this made convictions extremely difficult to procure.

Second, it is difficult in Hebrew to distinguish the mandatory "[he] *shall* die" and the permissive "[he] *may* die." So in Deuteronomy 22:22 we see that the husband had the choice whether he wished to prosecute the offenders or pursue the maximum penalty. Third, we have also seen already that the death penalty was not mandatory in all cases that were proven, since the death penalty could be commuted to monetary payment on certain conditions (i.e. Prov. 6:32–35) and other penalties may have included simply divorce (Jer. 3:8) or a shaming ritual depending on the details of the case (Ezek. 16:39). That said, the New Testament is no less clear on the capital character of such sexual offenses, but also seems to indicate judicial flexibility. For example, in *The Institutes of Biblical Law*, the contemporary Puritan Rushdoony uses a number of qualifying exegetical arguments when engaging the issue of penology and sexual offenses. For example, in discussing penology and divorce he writes:

> Jesus, by making the inclusive term *fornication* the valid grounds for divorce, thereby made adultery, incest, and other offenses that once led to divorce by death now grounds for divorce by bills of divorce. That this was recognized to be the case in the church appears in 1 Corinthians 5:1–5, where in the case of incest, the death penalty was mandatory (Lev. 20:11), but Paul instead required excommunication, a spiritual surrender to death and Satan. In 2 Corinthians 7:7–12, it seems that, on godly sorrow and with separation, re-admittance to the church followed. Had the death penalty still been *mandatory* Paul would have referred to it, but, while seeing the sin as a spiritual death, he does not see any legal ground for anything other than separation or excommunication.[94]

Here Rushdoony seems to allow for a large degree of judicial flexibility with respect to the penalties for adultery and incest (and possibly others), making clear that the death penalty for such offenses is *not always mandatory* in biblical law (scriptural evidence taken as a whole). He appears to argue that St. Paul allows for a modification or at least flexibility of civil penalty in this situation – though I think that this text is not the most convincing one he might have chosen for illustrating that.[95] It seems to me that Rushdoony is right in suggesting that *functionally* the death penalty is not mandatory for such offenses based on exegetical evidence. However, in this piece of exegesis he does appear to uncharacteristically muddle the jurisdictions of church and state. Other modern Puritans like Greg Bahnsen have argued that Paul is not dealing with the civil question (penalty) at all in this passage, suggesting that Paul's concern here is only the ecclesial matter of church discipline and the religious sanction of excommunication, since the church did not have the authority to execute anyone in Roman society and saw its role as different from that of the state. Elsewhere, Rushdoony himself recognizes this very important distinction. Again in the *Institutes*, referring to the same passage in 1 Corinthians 5, Rushdoony acknowledges that this critical text is, "a difficult one as to some details," and suggests that, "St. Paul does not deal with it legally as a case of incest," [96] but rather refers to the man more generally as a *fornicator*, which covers a variety of offenses; likely because the man in question was in an adulterous, not only an incestuous relationship, with his step-mother. Here Rushdoony interestingly interprets St. Paul's guidelines as "realistic legal aid for coping with the problem of capital offenses in a society which does not recognize them as such." [97] Furthermore, he suggests that, "a godly law-order will restore the death penalty, but the church must live realistically with its absence and protect itself." [98] In interpreting this Pauline 'legal aid' and wrestling with the distinction between the role of the church and of the state in such matters, he clearly separates the spheres and jurisdictions of each:

> St. Paul orders them "To deliver such a one unto Satan for the destruction of the flesh, that the spirit may be saved in the day of the Lord Jesus" (1 Cor. 5:5). Craig is correct in interpreting this as the death penalty. Thus, the death penalty is clearly God's law for incest and/or adultery. The church, however, cannot execute a man; the death penalty does not belong to the church. The church, however, must in effect pronounce the death penalty by delivering the man to Satan; i.e. the providential protection of God is withdrawn, so that the man might be *humbled and redeemed.* [99]

It is difficult to see how one might escape the fact that these verses are referring to a death penalty of sorts. St. Paul's direction to hand someone over to Satan for, "the destruction of the flesh" indicates recognition of the death sentence and that the churches were to take these sexual sins so seriously that they must behave *as though* a death sentence had been judicially pronounced even in the civil sphere. In this way the leaven is purged out of the church by not associating with *unrepentant* fornicators who have claimed to be Christian (1 Cor. 5:6–13). That being said, Rushdoony recognizes that on certain conditions such a one can be received back into the fellowship of the church. He also notes that St. Paul often speaks *ministerially*, not just *legislatively* in dealing with pastoral challenges in local churches.[100]

Despite the exegetical value of these qualifications which are clearly provisional, Burnside makes clear, "it remains the case that biblical law sees the death penalty as a potentially suitable response for some sexual relationships, at least in those cases where there was sufficient evidence and where the offended party wished to prosecute."[101] In Scripture, marriage is God's norm forming a family unit. It is a serious covenant (Hebrew *berit*) that impacts the whole community. So significant is this relationship that it is seen as the only lawful place for sexual activity – everything else is destructive deviancy. This bond of faithfulness and love is an expression of God's love for the covenant people (Hos. 1–3) and God's love for his new covenant people, the church, which is the bride of Christ (Eph. 5:22–33). So important is this to God that sexual immorality or deviance "must not even be named among you" (Eph. 5:3) Why? Because without repentance, "everyone who is sexually immoral or impure, or who is covetous (that is an idolater) has no inheritance in the kingdom of Christ and God" (Eph. 5:5). As the modern West has steadily abandoned Christianity as our public faith we have lost our ability to think and reason in these biblical categories, leaving us almost incapable of comprehending the relevance and power of biblical law. As Burnside notes:

> The fact that we do not regard these offenses as serious is probably because we do not see relationships as significant nor adultery as one of the worst breaches of trust and relational devotion. We are so committed to living in what Dale Kuehne calls the "iworld" of postmodern individualism that we are insensitive to the relational concerns of the "rworld," which is based on the belief that "humans are made for relationships and that we find our deepest fulfilment not when seeking self-fulfillment but when living and engaging in the full constellation of healthy human relationships."[102]

Because of this individualism where choice and consent reign as alone significant, modern law now treats the sexual crimes of the Bible as victimless crimes – harm is defined narrowly, constraining sexual choices only in cases of a lack of consent and abuse. The biblical view is far broader and communitarian – sexual crimes harm not only the offender and immediately offended but also the *mishpahah* (group of nuclear households).[103] Likewise, *consent* in biblical law has reference not merely to a sexual act not being forced, but involves the consent of certain family members. That is, the appropriateness of sexual conduct involves the interest of third parties being taken into account. It is a public sexual ethic oriented in terms of the interest of the community as a whole. "There is a choice to be made between two approaches. On the one hand there is 'covenant sex' which is characterized by commitment between the parties and the formal recognition that sexual relations have the power to make or break communities."[104] This involves channelling sexual desire in a manner that creates community. "On the other hand there is casual sex which is characterized by low levels of commitment and sexual relations with almost anyone you like, provided there is consent."[105] A social order built on the former requires hard work, commitment and community support. The latter is anarchistic, having a hugely destructive influence on all who have to live with the consequences. The former means relational order, the latter produces relational chaos that gives no thought to third parties. The value of biblical penology then clearly emerges: "it forces us to shift context and question the seeming normality of what appears to be the social consensus of late-modern liberal society."[106]

9.9 Homosexuality and the Family

Few subjects produce greater ire amongst Western cultural elites today than any criticism of the revived predilection for the social recognition, and indeed celebration, of what the Bible considers the *abuse of oneself with mankind* and an *abomination* (e.g. Lev. 18:22; 1 Cor. 6:19; 1 Tim. 1:10). These texts and many others deal with homosexual acts or behavior. The King James translation often uses the term sodomite to describe those practicing homosexuality (see: Deut. 23:17; 1 Kings 14:24; 15:12; 22:46; 2 Kings 23:7) because it is descriptive of the actual act and links it immediately with the crimes of Sodom in Genesis 18 and 19. However, to introduce the biblical texts that deal with homosexual practice, or to cite God's law with respect to them, is to bring down upon oneself a firestorm of abuse and vitriol. It is then relevant to note immediately that the very term 'homosexuality' was a word invented in the late nineteenth-century by a German psychologist, Karoly Maria

Benkert. The purpose of the use of this word (replacing in large measure the use of sodomy in both law and popular parlance) has been to identify and *normalize* the idea that some people have a homosexual (sameness) orientation, character and genetic reality that is fixed, so that moral action is not really a consideration in the practice – it is just a matter of 'nature.' The hatred of all criticism of this view is precisely because of the religious revolution against Christianity and biblical faith, and the revival of pagan worldviews in the form of evolutionism, pantheistic humanism, and Hindu and Buddhist philosophies that have come to increasingly dominate people's thinking in the West (whether they realize it or not). These worldviews all promote the idea of ultimate *sameness* or oneness underlying all reality – so 'sameness' eroticism is then seen as an expression of 'reality.' These religious perspectives deny there is a creator God distinct and transcendent over creation, who defines and differentiates (discriminates) between real objects, facts, events, persons, genders, and acts.

It is historically well-established that from their earliest mention in history, homosexual acts expressed, and were associated with, the worship of idols, religious orgies, and fertility rites, within a polytheistic or pantheistic worldview. The homosexuality found amongst the ancient empires and cults (Assyrians, Phoenicians, Babylonians, Greeks, Romans etc.) was largely associated with chaos cults, phallus worship, temple priests, and worship of the human body (i.e. Adonis). In other pagan cults, religious symbols associated with homosexuality included the maypole and totem pole. The act was therefore predominantly religious in its significance; this is clearly seen in the biblical material regarding Baal worship, which involved a phallic pole, and in Canaanite religion which featured Asherah poles. We see then throughout Scripture an unequivocal condemnation of *all* homosexual practice as an idolatrous abomination that is ruinous to the person who practices it, as well as socially detestable and destructive of the family since it is a complete overturning of God's norm for marriage and children (Gen. 19:5–7; Lev. 18:22; 20:13; Jdg. 19:22–23; Rom. 1:26-27, 32; 1 Cor. 6:9; 1 Tim. 1:10; Jude. v. 7). There is no ambiguity in Scripture on this matter and no amount of revisionist gymnastics can get around the biblical text or its historic interpretation in Jewish and Christian tradition. Hebrew scholar Robert Alter, in commenting on the significance of Leviticus 20:13 states, "this locution [a man who lies with a male as one lies with a woman]...leads the Talmud in Sanhedrin to characterize the act as "putting a brush into a tube" – that is, the particular homosexual act of anal penetration."[107] In other words, the Bible makes clear that the act of men sodomizing each other is in view, coming under legal censure, whatever the context, not simply because the act was often associated with a pagan rite. In Leviticus 18:22–23, both homosexuality and bestiality are condemned together because they deal with one subject – *abomination* (lit. filth or abhorrence) and *confusion* (lit. repulsive disturbance or audacious depravity violating the natural order). These terms are significant because biblically these acts are acts of chaos that flow out of a religious perspective that believes in primeval chaos, whereby social revitalization occurs when man returns to chaos by acts of chaos. They are chaotic because they confuse and mix that which God has deliberately and purposefully separated and differentiated for human flourishing, health, and the furtherance of life, not death. This is why the condemnation of homosexuality is alongside the condemnation of bestiality – both are 'confusion' that reduces man to the purely animal and the image of beasts, marring the image of God their maker. This also explains why sodomites are called 'dogs' in Deuteronomy 23:18 and Revelation 22:15, because the practice resembles canine behaviour, not the glory of God-ordained human sexuality. As a result, in the Bible, both bestiality and homosexuality were subject to a maximum sentence of death (Ex. 22:19; Lev. 20:13, 15–16; Rom. 1:32), because God's distinctions must be maintained for human society not to degenerate into a culture of death. The Bible warns of the consequences of a toleration or celebration of such practices; the defiling of persons, the defiling of the land itself, and the overthrow and spewing out of a people (Lev. 18:24–30). Alter translates Leviticus 18:22, 23, "And with a male you shall not lie as one lies with a woman. It is an abhorrence. And you shall not put your member into any beast to be defiled through it. And a woman shall not present herself to a beast to couple with it. It is a perversion."[108] His comments on this text are important:

> The explicitness of this law – the Hebrew for "as one lies" is the plural construct noun *mishkevei*, "bedding," used exclusively for sexual intercourse – suggests that it is a ban on anal intercourse and intercrural intercourse (the latter often practiced by the Greeks).... There is scant textual evidence to support the apologetic claim of some recent interpreters that the ban on homosexual congress is

limited to the preceding list of incestuous unions. One may apply here the proposal of Mary Douglas that this is a culture that likes to keep lines of categorical distinction clear: no human-beast couplings are allowed (in contrast to the imaginative freedom on this topic of Greek myth), and any simulation of procreative heterosexual intercourse by the insertion of the male member in an orifice or fleshly crevice of another male is abhorrent.[109]

By understanding the biblical distinctions of species, genders, and the priority of the family, we can begin to understand the penology associated with this particular form of deviance from God's norm. In fact, "Leviticus 20:3–6 emphasizes that applying the penalties for sexual offenses is essential to preserving the survival of the biblical family unit."[110] In July 2005, Canada became the fourth country in the world and first in the Americas to legalize same-sex 'marriage.' The state education system has been steadily remade in terms of a pantheistic, homo-erotic worldview to indoctrinate children from kindergarten up to accept not only the collapse of gender distinctions, but homosexual relationships as normative and equal in value to heterosexual marriage.[111] As a culture, we have become generally familiar with not only public parades celebrating sodomy and transvestite/ transsexual confusion, but television dramas that normalize homosexual activity and redefinitions of gender and family. It will likely then come as a surprise to many that such practices were condemned and punished by law for most of Western history since the sixth century AD in terms of biblical faith.

Homosexual acts are not singled out in Scripture for special treatment; rather, just as adultery is seen as destructive of God's norm for human flourishing, so sodomites and catamites are seen as those openly rebelling against God's order, and are therefore subject to criminal sanctions. In the Western world, for most of our history, punishment of open acts of sodomy included the possibility of the death penalty, including the centuries after the Reformation. At times, just as there were unbiblical acts of maiming or brutality against heretics and felons, so Europe periodically committed unbiblical and cruel punishment of homosexual acts, which in France included castration. This can be neither defended nor justified – maiming, torture and cruelty are utterly abhorrent to God and condemned in his word. However, Christian lands throughout Western history were clearly concerned for the protection of the family, and in line with Scripture, saw homosexual practices as acts of social anarchy and religious acts of chaos. Henry VIII therefore outlawed homosexuality in England in 1533 with the *Buggery Act*, with penalties including the loss of property or death by hanging. The police monitored brothels for male prostitutes, and those who indulged in such acts could be subject to the death penalty. This was a social reality that continued for centuries. The United States maintained the ultimate penalty of death for convicted sodomites until about 1779 when Thomas Jefferson proposed that Virginia drop the death penalty for the crime and replace it with castration, but England and Wales did not abolish the death penalty provision for acts of homosexuality until 1861. It was not until 1869 that the Dominion of Canada abolished the maximum sentence of death for sodomy. To put that into perspective, in England, Wales and Canada, right up until my great-grandparents were in mid-life, the law still threatened homosexual acts with being potentially subject to the death penalty. Again, to put that into historical perspective for Christians, whilst the great Baptist minister, Charles Spurgeon, was preaching in London, homosexual acts (open sodomy) were still threatened with the possibility of the death penalty.[112]

In the early years of Canadian life, offences such as treason against the state, certain types of theft, burglary, rape, pedophilia, homosexuality,[113] and unusual sexual practices like bestiality, were all considered punishable by death.[114] After Confederation however, a major revision of the statutes reduced the number of offences to only three general offences that were subject to a maximum sentence of death: murder (until 1976), rape (until 1954), and treason and mutiny (technically until 1998). Nonetheless, homosexual acts were still considered criminal offenses in Canada until 1968. The purpose of these laws against sodomy, as we have seen regarding adultery, was to teach and preserve Christian social values, not hunt people down for execution. Because of biblical laws of evidence requiring two or three witnesses, it can be seen right away that few homosexuals, if any, would ever be executed under such a law. So it is unsurprising to find that few homosexuals, if any, ever were executed in Canada (from what I can discover), because of the typically private character of the practice and the law's intention to *teach* morality. Instead, the real effect of such laws in the West has been to drive homosexuality far underground, subject to social censure, to prevent the decay of marriage, the family, and the social order. The only time such a law could result in the maximum penalty would be in the case of brazen open acts of sodomy either in terms of religious rite or as a public and deliberate act of social chaos. This brief survey of Western penology regarding homosexual acts is important in order to appreciate the biblical legal inheritance of Western civilization and culture, and to remind us that attitudes to such acts have been, until very recently, quite different to what they are presently.

None of these things mitigate the fact that the biblical view of homosexual acts as detestable and criminal will be viewed by many today as draconian, intolerant and unthinkable. Indeed, as Burnside points out regarding present sensibilities, the biblical references to sodomy, "will find themselves labeled as 'texts of terror,'"[115] and certainly in Canada, these parts of the Bible would be considered 'hate speech' by human rights commissions. This leads people to think that because the contemporary social context is in some ways hostile to biblical sexual ethic, biblical law must at best be irrelevant or, at worst, should be actively excluded from the debate. But this hasty conclusion is misguided in light of the present social crisis and current legal reforms. Burnside continues, "When we compare biblical law with recent sexual offenses reform...we will find that biblical law is not irrelevant. On the contrary, we will see that consent is not the only way of thinking about sexual offenses in modern society. Biblical law provides us with the idea of relational sexual order.[116]

But is Burnside right? Are penalties for sexual offenses necessary for preserving the survival of the biblical family unit? Is relational sexual order destroyed by the reduction of sexual offenses to a matter of individual consent? Social history, not just the biblical material, suggests he is right. Since the decriminalization of homosexuality in the West from the mid-twentieth century, and the more recent redefinitions of marriage in Europe and Canada, relational chaos has indeed ensued. After a decision of the European Court of Human Rights, it is now lawful for a father-in-law to marry his daughter-in-law and likewise for a son and his mother-in-law to wed. The result is 'scrambled parenthood,' which is a conflict of generationality where fathers and sons are sexually interchangeable.[117] Once marriage and family are redefined, the floodgates are opened to a bewildering world of confused, ruinous, relational chaos. It must also be said that this reality is not simply an unintended consequence of socially libertarian attitudes. Homosexual acts were decriminalized by political pressure in the West because a religious and ideological agenda underlies the thinking of many of the intellectuals and activists at the heart of the social revolution against the family. If there were any doubt that criminal sanctions are necessary for the survival of the biblical family unit (whether our culture wants it to survive is another question), the words of the noted American homosexual activist, Michael Swift should give food for thought. In the original editorial he described this piece as an eruption of rage, a mad dream of his desired America, where 'oppressed' homosexuals could eventually dominate the social order:

> We shall sodomize your sons, emblems of your feeble masculinity, of your shallow dreams and vulgar lies. We shall seduce them in your schools, in your dormitories, in your gymnasiums, in your locker rooms, in your sports arenas, in your seminaries, in your youth groups, in your movie theater bathrooms, in your army bunkhouses, in your truck stops, in your all-male clubs, in your houses of Congress, wherever men are with men together. Your sons shall become our minions and do our bidding. They will be recast in our image. They will come to crave and adore us. Women, you cry for freedom. You say you are no longer satisfied with men; they make you unhappy. We, connoisseurs of the masculine face, the masculine physique, shall take your men from you then.... Women, you say you wish to live with each other instead of with men. Then go and be with each other.... All laws banning homosexual activity will be revoked. Instead, legislation shall be passed which engenders love between men.... If you dare to cry faggot, fairy, queer, at us, we will stab you in your cowardly hearts and defile your dead, puny bodies. We shall write poems of the love between men; we shall stage plays in which man openly caresses man; we shall make films about the love between heroic men which will replace the cheap, superficial, sentimental, insipid, juvenile, heterosexual infatuations presently dominating your cinema screens.... Our writers and artists will make love between men fashionable and *de rigueur*, and we will succeed because we are adept at setting styles.... You will be shocked and frightened when you find that your presidents and their sons, your industrialists, your senators, your mayors, your generals, your athletes, your film stars, your television personalities, your civic leaders, your priests are not the safe, familiar, bourgeois, heterosexual figures you assumed them to be. We are everywhere; we have infiltrated your ranks.... There

will be no compromises. We are not middle-class weaklings. Highly intelligent, we are the natural aristocrats of the human race.... Those who oppose us will be exiled.... The family unit-spawning ground of lies, betrayals, mediocrity, hypocrisy and violence will be abolished. The family unit, which only dampens imagination and curbs free will, must be eliminated. Perfect boys will be conceived and grown in the genetic laboratory. They will be bonded together in communal setting, under the control and instruction of homosexual savants. All churches who condemn us will be closed. Our only gods are handsome young men.... The exquisite society to emerge will be governed by an elite comprised of gay poets. One of the major requirements for a position of power in the new society of homoeroticism will be indulgence in the Greek passion. Any man contaminated with heterosexual lust will be automatically barred from a position of influence. All males who insist on remaining stupidly heterosexual will be tried in homosexual courts of justice and will become invisible men. We shall rewrite history, history filled and debased with your heterosexual lies and distortions.... We shall be victorious because we are fueled with the ferocious bitterness of the oppressed.... We too are capable of firing guns and manning the barricades of the ultimate revolution. Tremble, hetero swine, when we appear before you without our masks.[118]

There is no mistaking the hatred, rage and perversion explicit in his neo-Leninist worldview, recast in terms of homoeroticism. Particularly noteworthy is the facet of misogyny in homosexualist thought, typically overlooked by feminists. There is an unconcealed hatred of women, as well as a desire to revive and normalize Greco-Roman pederasty (in schools and dormitories), and obviously the family must be utterly destroyed. Now obviously it is very important to be clear that not all those struggling with same-sex attraction or in homosexual lifestyles share Swift's sentiments – in fact many would outright reject them. But the intellectual stronghold and spirit behind the homoerotic worldview, one widely embraced by homosexual and queer activists and entrenched among much of the intellectual class, would endorse much in this 'manifesto.' A culture that decriminalizes homosexual practice is one on the brink of total revolution and cultural death. The sad reality is, reflecting on these words of Swift penned back in the 1987, a good deal of what he claims will be done, has already been done. From the overturning of laws against homosexual acts, to the criminalizing of speech against homosexuality (through the Human Rights Commission in Canada – hate crimes regulations) to the revolutionizing of gender and family identity, to the take-over of values in the entertainment industry, to the attempt to 'queer' children from kindergarten up, to re-writing history (gay history), transforming sex education and inserting "gay-straight" alliances into public schools in the guise of anti-bullying campaigns, many of these stated goals are already accomplished. Such a progressive sequence of perversion and evil is predicted in Leviticus 20:13–16. Moreover, as Burnside points out:

> The legislation of homosexual relations and the introduction of same-sex civil partnerships is seen, in some quarters, as paving the way for three-way civil partnerships and this, in turn, is said to create pressure for the legalization of bestiality. This mirrors the Levitical sequence of 20:13-16. Civil unions between three persons became legal in the Netherlands in 2005.… [T]here is no conceptual reason why the next three-way union could not be between two men and one woman, or even between three men – including a man, a father, and his son. In the United States, the case is being made by practitioners and academics for the legalization of bestiality. Singer argues…the pursuit of equality should allow sexual contact between humans and non-human species.[119]

It is in light of these present realities that Burnside sees biblical laws concerning sexual offenses as of "profound relevance."[120] Biblical penology points beyond anarchic consent to a positive vision for society founded in God's relational order. Our chaotic practices are indicative of our idolatry, the dishonouring of our parents and our adulterous ways – despising our children by treasonous attitudes to the family. Yet, there is always the possibility of change. As any people turns back toward the living God, the gospel of Jesus Christ and his inscripturated word, they will steadily return to God's law protecting the family and have regard for biblical sanctions against sexual crimes. One very good example of this today is Uganda, a formerly pagan country that over the last one hundred years has become increasingly Christian and biblical in social values. In 2009 their democratically-elected parliament tabled legislation for tougher sanctions against sodomy (already illegal), which would have included an exemplary sentence of death for the most serious violations of the new law (i.e. sodomizing a minor, or sodomy when infected with

HIV). This law was discussed in parliament because the Ugandan people were demanding it. Due to hypocritical Western financial pressures, interference and threats, Uganda backed off the death penalty provision, but as of this writing (by the end of 2012), legislation is planned to go into effect that will punish aggravated sodomy (on minors, whilst infected with HIV, or for serial offenders) with life imprisonment. Lesser acts of sodomy will be punished with prison terms. With some historical irony, Western state actors have threatened to cut aid to Uganda if 'gay rights' are not respected.[121] This same political class, fierce critics of Christendom, who allege a past of evil interference from the Christian West through colonial Christian missions in Africa, now patronise the African and Asian nations for not having laws like the modern Western liberal state and threaten them with various sanctions if they are found in non-compliance with our deviant vision of 'gay rights.' Clearly interference is not the real issue in Western history for these politicians and thinkers – it's the *type* of interference that they are concerned with.

We can see, then, that because our religious faith has been altered as a people in the West, our criminal laws regarding the family and sexuality have followed the new religion – an 'I' world of self-centred, self-gratification, a 'godhood' the individual delegates to the state, to enforce the new 'liberty.' But surely the Christian must agree, as Rushdoony points out, that the Puritan John Cotton was right: "The more any Law smells of man the more unprofitable." Humanistic law has led to social chaos and crisis. It is time to turn again with the Puritans to the words of Isaiah 33:22: "For the Lord is our judge, the Lord is our lawgiver, the Lord is our king; he will save us."[122]

9.10 Abandoning the Law: The Failure of Modern Penology

The magisterial Reformer Martin Luther points to the biblical use of the law in the civil and criminal sphere:

> God has ordained all temporal laws and statutes to prevent and hinder sin. But here someone may object: if the law hinders sin, then it also justifies. I answer: Oh! no, this does not follow; that I do not murder, commit adultery, steal etc., is not because I love virtue and righteousness, but because I fear the hangman, who threatens me with gallows, sword etc. It is the hangman that hinders me from sinning, as chains, ropes and strong bands hinder bears, lions, and other wild beasts from tearing and rending in pieces all that come in their way....

Therefore this is the first point concerning the law, that it must be used to deter the ungodly from their wicked and mischievous intentions. For the devil, who is an abbot and prince of this world, allures people to work all manner of sin and wickedness; wherefore God has ordained magistrates, elders, schoolmasters, laws and statutes, to the end, if they can do no more, that at least they may bind the claws of the devil, and hinder them from raging and swelling so powerfully in those who are his, according to his will and pleasure.[123]

What Luther affirms above is the explicit teaching of St. Paul on one of the legitimate uses of the law in 1 Timothy 1:8–11. Remember that St. Paul does not separate the message of the *gospel* from the *law of God* in this passage. He tells us that the law is 'sound doctrine' in 'accordance with the gospel.' Thus if we deny the law of God even in its civil application or explanation, we are denying a key to understanding the truth of the gospel – the righteousness, holiness and justice of God. St. Paul's particular concern here, in which he references a whole series of offenses against the law of God, is the law's role as a restraint against criminality. Without this restraint, any social order will run into decay and ruin with, as Luther points out, Satan being given free reign. Now we have already seen that there is no specifically judicial or civil law found in the Old Testament as a separate 'list' or 'table' of 'civil laws,' separated from the 'moral laws.' Rather, what we find in Scripture is the *basis* for a Christian legal system applicable to the civil sphere. The laws of the Bible, outside the Ten Commandments, are *case laws*, and I have been arguing that largely, the Reformed faith has viewed it as the duty of the Christian ruler to extend the *equity* of these cases to cover whatever details they find in their own society. This is significant, because it means it cannot be argued that what has at times been labelled 'the judicial law of Moses,' has been abolished in the New Testament era, because there is no such category in Scripture as 'the judicial law of Moses.' What we have instead of a systematized criminal legal code is a set of practical *explanations of moral law*. Therefore, what the opponents of the Puritan position on penology must argue is that the *judicial implications* of the *moral law* regarding crime and punishment have been abolished in the New Covenant period. Yet these judicial implications are precisely what St. Paul seems concerned to uphold in 1 Timothy 1:8–11. There is no evidence here, or anywhere else in the New Testament, that Jesus or the apostles intended to repudiate the explanations and implications of the moral law that applied to the civil sphere. As we have noted in a number of places, for most of our history in the West, whilst admittedly mixed up to a degree with elements of Roman law, biblical law has been regularly applied, perhaps most obviously in English Common Law and Colonial American law.[124] But our cultural move away from God's law in recent years has had significant repercussions for our society. The communal consequences of sacrilege (abandoning the law of God) in criminal matters are on terrifying display in modern Canada for example. We now live in a culture that refuses to execute murderers, sexual abusers, paedophiles, rapists and kidnappers, crimes that were emphatically dealt with as *capital* offenses just two or three generations ago. We coddle the criminal today and thereby show little care for the victim. At the same time we legally murder tens of thousands of unborn babies every year (right up to term in Canada as we are without any abortion law) and want to practice infanticide, euthanize the elderly and assist depressed people to commit suicide with a physician. Clearly then, the ending of life is not the real objection to capital punishment; we appear anxious to end innocent life in any number of ways – we just don't want to punish the guilty. Men always want to legalise and endorse sin when they move in terms of rebellion against God, so our current cultural situation should not shock us.

The biblical law regarding a stubborn and rebellious son (Deut. 21:18–21) has been routinely attacked by humanists (and some Christians) as an illustration of the supposed barbarity of biblical law because it is said to condone executing disobedient children. This is both ignorant and idle criticism. This law has in view the incorrigible juvenile delinquent who cannot be restrained from criminality by his parents – he is old enough to be a drunkard and therefore it is clearly not a reference to naughty children. Since the parents were required to testify against their incorrigibly delinquent youths before a legal tribunal, only the most exasperating cases would ever have been heard. This law therefore is not endorsing capital punishment for unruly adolescents. This law, which Jesus upholds in Matthew 15:3–6, deals with a drunken young man old enough to beat up his father (Ex. 21:15). Commentators ancient and modern agree that this law refers to an uncontrollable youth's intent on rebellion against authority, manifest by repeat offenses and parental assault. A form of this law remained on the statute books of many U.S. states for many years.

Despite Canadian pride in our peacefulness, according to UN international comparisons, Canada has a rate of police-reported criminal incidents among the highest in the world – almost double that of the United States.[125] Furthermore, our failure to punish incorrigible violent offenders and murderers with the biblically-required death penalty (Gen. 9:5–6; Num. 35:16; Deut. 21:18–21), in the name of 'rehabilitation' and an enlightened 'humaneness' has led to rampant evil. This form of judgement is precisely what the Scriptures lead us to expect if we fail to punish the guilty (Deut. 19:13; 1 Kings 2:9, 31–33). In the thirty-three year period from 1975 – 2008, some 508 serious violent offenders were released from Canadian prisons after social and psychological 'rehabilitation' and being deemed no longer a danger to society. After their release, these 508 convicted felons proceeded to murder 557 innocent Canadians.[126] Such rates of recidivism are admittedly startling. In the United States, 53% of arrested males and 39% of arrested females are re-incarcerated.[127] Canadian statistics are nearly as bad. There is a reconviction rate in the range of 41% to 44%, which clearly points to the complete failure of our ability to punish and reintegrate offenders into the community. England and Wales likewise have a reported 50% reconviction rate for adult male inmates and 45% for adult female inmates released from their prisons in 1995. In the 'Christian' United States, there are more people in prisons than any other country in the world; approximately 2,300,000 prisoners. To put this into perspective, it is more than China and Russia put together. This mind-boggling incarceration rate amounts to this: one out of every hundred American citizens is behind bars.[128]

These facts show that at the very least the correctional system is not working well.[129] This unbiblical approach to crime 'warehouses' criminals, giving them ample opportunity to conspire with others to commit further crimes upon their release. As a result we now have a growing professional criminal class motivated by money and the exercise of lawless power. In our system of failing justice they are without accountability to anyone or to any higher authority. They are largely without remorse, without forgiveness, and with little sense of justice, heaven and hell to impact their thinking. Without the preaching of the gospel of justice and restitution regarding the Savior that died for them, and by neglecting biblical law, we have created a class of people outside civilization. Clearly, repeat offenders have not been deterred by their incarceration (and therapies) from committing more crimes, and evidently most have lost their fear of going to jail. Having spoken to prisoners and family members of repeat offenders, some actually look forward to spending a periodic term in jail for the free shelter, free meals and social activities.

This approach to crime stems from the so-called 'Enlightenment' where new law codes and penal practices sprang up in Europe and North America based on secular conceptions of the human person that denied the reality of sin inherent in human nature.[130] The influence of Lockean thinking – which viewed the human mind as a blank slate that, having been written on by experience, habit, pleasure and pain, could be potentially wiped and reconditioned – lay behind the development of 'penitentiaries' and 'reforming' regimes designed to remake the delinquent individual. The monastic ideal of confinement and 'penitence' was given a humanistic expression. Legal historian David Garland writes:

> The model penitentiary regimes of the USA in the 1830s would begin by subjecting new prisoners to an extended period of silent, solitary confinement which amounted to a kind of prolonged sensory deprivation. But this treatment was originally designed not just to discipline individuals but literally to strip them of all the *evil impressions and bad associations which had brought them to crime, and thus recreate a kind of Lockian tabula rasa.* This *reconstituted* subject could then be exposed to a completely controlled environment in which only authorized and positive impressions...would be experienced.[131]

The basic idea here is environmentalism. People are seen as products solely of their environment which *conditioned them* for crime. This programming can be undone by a scientifically controlled environment to *remake* the individual. Thus, "modern penal policy endeavours to transform conduct by threats, penalties, behavioural training, psychological adjustment, and the manipulation of environment – it seeks to improve and correct by technical means."[132] This obviously denies the biblical worldview portraying man as a sinner and rebel against God, fully accountable for his actions. Furthermore, justice (the idea of God's order being maintained by punishment fitting the crime through restitution) disappears from view altogether. It is no longer *public* justice that matters but the scientific state's surreptitious reprogramming of its citizens for its own purposes. As Garland notes concerning these humanistic techniques, "these measures...are undertaken on the margins of society, out of sight of the public and without involving them in the operation."[133]

The Puritan mind, however, sees criminal justice and punishments as the public restoration of God's order, aimed wherever possible at the restoration of the individual to the community.[134] Garland thus points out that Puritan punishments "were conceived as an aspect of community life and which aimed for the moral reintegration of the offender; modern penality is seen as management of a problem, aimed at the containment of deviant groups."[135] Garland thus shows how the Puritans dealt with criminals according to Protestant theology, not secular humanistic principles, which, whilst recognizing the effects of people's environment upon them, *denied* that environment was the *primary factor* in producing criminality – neither could it be used in determining culpability or mitigating punishment:

> Such persons were understood as free moral agents, able to choose good and evil...within this understanding of the human subject, spiritual attitude was the primary determinant of conduct, while material circumstances were a minor and subordinate force. The criminal who had chosen to defy God and law was thus a sinner...and was punishable accordingly. However, even in the act of punishment, the offender's soul continued to be an object of concern and penal rituals were designed to encourage individual acts of atonement and redemption.... The penal authorities strove to produce a 'true sight of sin' on the part of the accused and the watching community, thereby revealing the truth of the human condition and the flawed nature of human subjectivity.[136]

The Puritan response to crime in terms of Scripture was thus not only true justice, but it was far more compassionate, concerned as it was with the *recovery* of individuals and their *reintegration* into the community (in noncapital cases). The Puritan social response to sin as crime, notes Garland, was, "at once punitive and redemptive: the offender had to be punished in the name of the Law and also for the salvation of his or her soul"[137] Punishment for the Puritans was thus not aimed at a vindictive, "vanquishing of the enemy, but instead at the re-inclusion of the atoned and repentant sinner."[138] In Puritan fashion Rushdoony writes:

Justice in the Bible means restitution to a very great degree. Restitution and restoration are the essence of justice. The prison system as an answer to the problem of crime is a modern and anti-biblical scheme: it does nothing to further either restitution or restoration and accomplishes little other than removing the criminal from society temporarily. It does not remedy crime nor does it remedy the criminal, as it purports to do.[139]

Just as biblical law is the foundation for a truly Christian response to the questions of poverty and oppression – over against the contemporary doctrine of social justice – so, in regard to crime and punishment, biblical law points us beyond man's humanistic manipulation of man, to the restorative justice of God and a positive vision of hope for true community. In sum, as Montgomery notes, in all these areas of life and social order, "the Christian will test all positive law by the pronouncements of Holy Scripture, endeavouring by every legitimate means at his disposal to bring man's temporal law into conformity with God's eternal law."[140]

9.11 Conclusions and Clarifications

9.11.1 Limits of Law

The bringing of man's temporal law into line with God's law does not mean, as some suppose, that Puritan Christianity requires governments to force people to be obedient to the gospel and the whole of God's law:

> Theonomic ethics does not call for every magistrate to institute the entirety of God's law. That would be a horrifying abuse of political authority, turning every sin (e.g. lust, laziness, discourtesy, coveting, backbiting, impatience) into *civil crimes*.... [T]heonomic ethics holds that civil magistrates may enforce only those provisions of God's law which authorize penal sanctions against *narrowly defined kinds of outward misbehaviour*. God's law sets an objective limit upon the magistrate beyond which he may not go, whereas other schools of thought have no way of arguing against the state growing into a "beast" that "lawlessly" claims every area of life as its jurisdiction (cf. 2 Thess. 2:3,7; Rev. 13:15–17).[141]

This perspective is in stark contrast to popular humanism and its view of the state's role, where human authority moves far beyond punishing narrowly defined areas of outward misbehaviour, to the point of supporting, funding and endorsing murder. Rushdoony insightfully observes why many who object to biblical law as harsh are thus in the grip of hypocrisy:

> [H]umanism is butchering millions of babies annually through abortion. This is murder. Not all the evils of heresy trials and the injustices of some witchcraft trials are equal to this, in their brutality and carnage. *It is arrogance of a fearful sort to believe that ours is an enlightened age, and earlier ones darker.*[142]

This fearful arrogance leading to a lack of a logical ending point to state authority is illustrated in a most pronounced way by the work of a popular hero of humanists amongst today's vocal anti-religious secularists. Sam Harris's book, *The End of Faith*, with all its adolescent shrillness, seriously considers religious education 'child abuse' and actually holds that some people (that is, certain 'religious people') should be *executed* on the basis of their *beliefs*; to be clear, not their *actions*, but their private beliefs: "The link between belief and behaviour raises the stakes considerably. Some propositions are so dangerous that it may be *ethical to kill people for believing them.* This may seem an extraordinary claim, but it merely enunciates an ordinary fact about the world in which we live."[143] This is what happens when we jettison God's law that limits the magistrate to a small jurisdiction in punishing evildoers on the authority of God's word, and allow humanistic reasoning to take its place. It is remarkable that such a man can sell thousands of hysterical popular books praising humanism and secularism which simultaneously promote the possible execution of people for *private beliefs* and yet the media and intellectual class are, for the most part, silent about it. But if a Christian in public life or a Christian commentator should suggest that our culture needs to recognize and restore its commitment to the standards of biblical law, the intellectual classes and media react with a vindictive witch hunt as though heaven itself were falling! The reason being, they essentially agree with Harris. One perceptive non-Christian social critic, the British doctor Theodore Dalrymple, has rightly noted, "For Harris, the most important question about genocide would seem to be: 'who is genociding whom?' To adapt Dostoevsky slightly, starting from universal reason I arrive at universal madness." [144] So much for a new and enlightened age. Harris has since objected that the context of this comment is the connection between ideas and actions and that there are some people who have dangerous beliefs who simply can't be reasoned out of them. Yet the point at issue, which remains, is the fact that someone would actually advocate killing others for what they *believe* on the basis of the possible or hypothetical future outcomes of their beliefs – not for what they have actually done. This is a reversal of biblical law and the Western legal tradition which does not punish thoughts and private beliefs. What Harris further misses is that he and those like him – not a transcendent authority – are made judge and jury over acceptable and unacceptable beliefs. His religious humanism is acceptable whilst other religious education is 'child abuse.' What if Christians can't be reasoned out of their religious education that humanists might deem dangerous – are they to be executed? Harris tries to backpedal using the most extreme illustrations he can like the 'thoughts' of Osama Bin Laden; but the cat is out of the bag and he does not retract the statement. Harris and others like him believe that if our humanistic culture finds some people's private beliefs sufficiently objectionable (martyrdom by terror today, perhaps belief in Christ as Lord tomorrow), they may be ethically executed. [145] Harris's words should not surprise us at all; on the contrary, they reflect precisely where humanistic thinking inevitably moves as it becomes more self-conscious in our time. Such people are anti-God's law because they are anti-Christ and hostile to his righteousness and redemption. Thus, "to deny covenant law is to deny that there is a covenant: it is to reject the salvation plan offered by God in Christ." [146]

The contemporary Puritan view, then, *does not* hold that the magistrate must execute apostates and heretics. It does not propose to eliminate political pluralism for a monolithic form of government; neither does it hold that democratic institutions and societies are contrary to biblical law. [147] In fact the Puritan spirit is seen in the English Puritans who were champions of freedom, a free parliament and a free people, with king and country subject to God's law; a free people electing their own representative government. Theonomists therefore champion democratic procedures for the state, including free elections, open debate, and competing parties. [148] The biblical law does not abolish pluralism, for the stranger and alien are protected in biblical law. Rather the theonomic state would redefine its present limits to be in line with biblical teaching

– every law order places some limit on the plurality of politically acceptable options (i.e. the Nazi party is illegal in Germany).

So then, we can broadly summarize what I am calling a theologically Puritan approach to biblical penology in the following way:

a) All human governments are ultimately held accountable to God, in terms of his law and standards, not their own arbitrary codes. However, biblical law cannot be imposed 'top down' by any authoritarian structure, but must be embraced by a society (the consent of the people) committed to Christ and his covenant law. Such a people will demand righteous biblical laws.

b) Taking into account all of Scripture, biblical law upholds the death penalty as exemplary. It is either mandatory (in cases of murder), recommended, or potentially appropriate for a number of serious criminal offenses against the sanctity of life, the family and marriage, as well as for flagrant and contemptuous assault on God and his social order by instigation and incitement to idolatry – constituting treason. All other offenses require monetary restitution, banishment or corporal punishment. Prison is not part of biblical law except for temporary custody whilst awaiting trial.

c) The death penalty is not mandatory in all capital cases, allowing for considerable judicial flexibility, taking into account the aggravated nature of the offense, particular circumstances and magisterial discretion. The death penalty can be commuted to various forms of restitution. It has also been modified by further revelation for certain offenses in the New Testament era (i.e. Sabbath violation)

d) The church does not bear the sword of the state, but must recognize (as St. Paul did) the validity of the death sentence and declare it spiritually by excommunicating unrepentant capital offenders from the life of the church. As modelled by the early church, in cultures which do not execute punishment against serious offenses against the law of God, repentant offenders can be restored to the fellowship of the body, but may be barred from communion for a significant period of time.

e) A Christian culture, similar to those seen in historical precedents like Calvin's Geneva, Zwingli's Zurich, Bucer's Strasburg, Reformed Scotland (John Knox), Puritan England (Oliver

Cromwell) and colonial America (John Cotton), would uphold the death penalty as exemplary (the example of maximum sentence for violation) in capital offenses; bearing in mind that monetary restitution, corporal punishment and exile are also available to judges and magistrates in cases excepting 'first degree' murder.

f) Because of biblical laws of evidence being purposefully rigid, securing convictions was, and would be, very challenging, and because of the serious character of penalties, judges and juries who had lingering doubts in a given case would commute the death sentence, as seen in Cromwell's England with regard to laws against adultery.

g) Capital crimes would be extremely rare in a Christian culture because the law acts as a restraint upon wickedness and because the gospel transforms lives. Where certain sexual practices God deems worthy of the death penalty were indulged, the social censure would be such that those practices would be driven underground and neither celebrated nor endorsed by society, thereby eliminating their public influence.

In concluding this survey of biblical penology in Christian thought and practice, it is critically important to make clear that contemporary representatives of the Puritan perspective *do not* advocate immediate judicial reform to introduce exemplary capital punishments into today's culture for witchcraft, idolatry, adultery and so forth. This is a completely baseless criticism that is made by detractors of a Reformed and theonomic missiology who have not read the arguments carefully. It is true that theonomists recognize the importance of facing squarely the challenge to biblical penology on the grounds of its alleged severity: "Either the whole of Scripture is defensible or it is not." But this task is not identical with defending the actions of the church in the past; "defending Scripture from false criticism is not to be confused with defending either the medieval church or the Reformation churches." [149] But in addressing the criticism that Reformed theonomic thought wants to start executing people wherever possible, Rushdoony, perhaps the most noted of the modern Puritan thinkers writes:

The death penalty in terms of God's law is in process of being dropped. It is gradually being replaced by a new doctrine of capital punishment: death for the murder of prison guards, policemen, presidents, and other public officials. In other words, life has meaning if it is state-life, and the capital offenses are against the state, not against God's law...treason becomes then a *refusal* to commit idolatry. Two systems of treason are thus in conflict, God's system and man's. We cannot avoid this conflict, nor can we avoid defining treason, either in terms of Scripture, or in terms of humanism. What then must Christians do? Some ask, *are we to work for the execution of all idolaters in our midst today? The question pre-supposes either stupidity, or malice, or both.* It is our duty to evangelize, to work for the conversion of men and nations to Christ as Lord and Savior. At the same time, as part of our evangelism, we witness to the meaning of covenant law, and, in our own personal dealings, we live by it: we practice the tithe, restitution, debt-free living, and much, much more. Only as God's law is made the practice of men can it become the practice of nations. *Only those laws are enforceable which virtually all men are already enforcing in their own lives, so that the state's law affects a minuscule minority.*[150]

Furthermore, this obviously means biblical penology could *not* govern society by imposition, but only when there is "common assent...you have to have the overwhelming majority of people believing that this is the way things should be"[151] before biblical laws and sanctions could again provide the basis of jurisprudence. These statements alone refute the vast majority of the simplistic and often ignorant criticism levelled against the theonomic and Puritan position. Consequently, the dishonest slur that theonomists are dangerous radicals wanting to execute people in terms of a tyrannical ecclesiocracy, like some Islamic Ayatollah, really needs to be treated with the disdain it deserves. The Christian and theonomic answer to the widespread destruction of society by fornication, adultery, the normalization of homosexuality and the consequent family breakdown, delinquency, criminality, and fatherlessness, which destroys the social fabric and bankrupts the economy, is not lobbying for severe penalties for adulterers. Rather, "the biblical answer...is to re-establish the family in its functions, protect its integrity, and then penalize offenders. In a healthy society, treason is a rare crime. In a truly biblical law-order, adultery will also be rare."[152] Note the order here. The process would likely take *generations of faithfulness*; first, re-establish the family's functions. Second, have the church protect its integrity (as seen in St. Paul's instructions discussed); only then could society move toward penalizing flagrant offenders in some way.

Certainly not all of the Puritans were agreed about all the details of how God's law was to be applied in their centuries. Likewise, modern Puritan thinkers are not all agreed on the precise details of how God's law could be creatively applied to our modern society – in part because we have moved so far from our historic faith, it is difficult to see into a future context of Christian revival. There are clearly some legitimate differences of interpretation amongst theonomic thinkers in details of application of the law, since the case laws do not constitute an *exhaustive catalogue of laws and penalties* for every situation. This necessarily requires positive legal development based on biblical principles and considerable scholarly work to grow in our understanding. This does not mean that theonomy dies the death of a thousand qualifications as some critics have urged. The direction of Puritan thought is clear on the binding standards of the law, and its abiding contemporary relevance when properly applied. The very term 'Reformed' represents a distinct approach to the law, and theonomy is an identifiable stream (and arguably the dominant stream) within this tradition. In my view, then, John Frame is correct in arguing that the degree of theonomic emphasis among historic Reformed thinkers is not determined by general theological principles, "but on the exegesis of specific passages."[153] Certainly there is no need for ungodly division or sharp polemics between Reformed Christians on this point but rather a humble submission to God's word and careful handling of the word of truth. Critically we must honour the word of God and never impugn God's law with the charge of injustice. To tamper with God's law is idolatry and treason to Christ, constituting an attack on God's kingdom.[154]

9.11.2 The End of Biblical Law

What then is the end in view for biblical penology? It is a vision of social peace, and hope for a godly culture that is surrendered to the righteousness and justice of a covenant-keeping God, whose great love is made manifest by the restitution effected by Christ's redemptive work, and his grace expressed socially in a system of restorative justice where human flourishing within self-giving community can take place. The Reformed missiologist thus envisages a future Christian culture where, like treason against the state today, open treason against God and the family would be extremely rare. This is neither utopian, nor wishful thinking. Man's utopian visions are godless counterfeit kingdoms created by revolution, where a humanistic elite rule in place of God in terms of man's ideas, where man's sin nature is denied, and where Christ's atonement for sin and the regenerating work of the Holy Spirit are seen as unnecessary. In this view, man, by his own power and will, recreates Eden. But the biblical vision for the reign and kingdom of God is Christ-centred, where, by the power of the gospel, and the regenerating, resurrection life of the Holy Spirit, God remakes man in the righteousness of Christ, puts in him a desire to love God's righteous law (Ps. 119), writes its precepts upon his heart (Jer. 31:31–34; Heb. 8:10–12) and grants him the power to obey and walk in all the covenant blessings of Deuteronomy 28. It is God-centred from first to last. When the whole gospel is freely propagated, the family and the church grow strong, and regenerate godly men and women are found in positions of influence, we have historical precedent for holding out such a hope of real reformation and increasing manifestation of the reign of God. As Ian Gentles, a historian specializing in Oliver Cromwell and the English revolutionary period, has pointed out:

> Demographers have determined that during the decade of the 1650s the rate of illegitimacy or bastardy sank to 0.5 per cent, the lowest in any decade during the nearly 500 years during which records have been kept. The historic rate, until the mid-twentieth century, usually hovered around 4 or 5 per cent. In the last half century the rate of births outside of marriage has exploded 30 or 40 percent in Britain, and even higher in the US. Less bastardy suggests less fornication, which in turn may suggest less drunkenness. The Cromwellian reformation of manners may have changed more lives than we once thought.[155]

Cromwell's understanding of godliness included, according to Gentles, "everything from social justice for the poor to the strict observance of the Mosaic law on sexual conduct."[156] In 1650 Cromwell's parliament made adultery punishable by a maximum sentence of death. Yet, at the same time, "prosecution rates for moral offences remained low.... The mute testimony of parish registers points to a definite change in human behaviour...perhaps Oliver knew what he was talking about."[157] Taken together, this means that in the 500 years since records began, England had never been so sexually moral and marriages so stable as during the Puritan decade of Cromwell's ascendancy, whilst at the same time prosecution for moral offenses was low. This can only be accounted for by the fact that Cromwell developed numerous commissions for the propagation of the gospel and lay lectureships throughout England and Wales – from the military to the peasantry, people were turning to Christ and increasingly wanted just laws.

Given the glorious kingdom-centred end in view in biblical penology – a gospel truly worth publishing – it is, in my view, somewhat tragic that the Puritan, theonomic perspective has been so commonly shunned, ignored or attacked by fellow Christians in recent years. This is perhaps most clearly seen in the thoughtless and at times shameful shunning by other academics of one of the more noted Puritan thinkers of the last century, Rousas John Rushdoony. Certainly there are things to disagree with and reject in parts of Rushdoony's social commentary and biblical exegesis, but there is also much to be learned. One of the most significant Reformed theologians of the past fifty years in the United States, John Frame, shares my sentiment. In the opening of his 1976 review of the *Institutes* he laments the academic ostracism inflicted on this notable thinker: "I have come to regard this, however, as a premature dismissal of an important Christian thinker...recent reading, particularly in *The Institutes of Biblical Law*, have convinced me that...Rushdoony is one of the most important Christian social critics alive today" [158] In my opinion, the premature dismissal of which Frame speaks is due in large measure to opponents' ignorance of Rushdoony's work and a distaste for Puritan views on the Mosaic penal sanctions under review in this chapter – views that we have seen were essentially shared by great Christian leaders of the past like Martin Bucer, Huldrych Zwingli,[159] John Knox and Oliver Cromwell,[160] as well as the majority of the framers of the Westminster Confession.[161] Indeed, among the great Reformers, Luther and Calvin, not just Bucer and Zwingli, reveal in varying degrees of consistency, an essential, theonomic logic.[162] Rushdoony's own "Christian Manifesto," laid out in ten biblical principles sets the context for Christian penology, and is worth citing in full:

1. Sovereignty is an attribute of God alone, not of man or the state. God alone is Lord or sovereign over all things; over state, school, family, vocations, society and all things else.
2. The Bible is given as the common law of men and nations and was for most of U.S. history the common law, as Justice Story has declared.

3. Salvation is not by politics, education, the church, or any agency or person other than Jesus Christ our Lord.
4. The myth of Machiavelli that, by state control at the top, bad men can make a good society is at the root of our cultural crisis and growing collapse. A good omelette cannot be made with bad eggs. Truly redeemed men are necessary for a good society.
5. Civil rulers who rule without the Lord and His law word are, as Augustine said, no different than a mafia, only more powerful.
6. The state is not the government, but one form of government among many, others being the self-government of the Christian man, the family, the school, the church, vocations and society. The state is civil government, a ministry of justice.
7. For the state to equate itself with government is tyranny and evil.
8. The Christian man is the only truly free man in all the world, and he is called to exercise dominion over all the earth.
9. Humanism is the way of death and is the essence of original sin, or man trying to be his own god.
10. All men, things, and institutions must serve God, or be judged by Him.[163]

It is an oddity that many Christians fail to take notice of what the holy God of Scripture required when he wrote with his own finger the constitution and law of his elect people, whose calling was a *missiological* one – as a people of the covenant they were to be a light to the Gentile world, so that the nations alienated from that covenant might be drawn into it, and come to *obey his law*:

> Keep them [God's laws] and do them, for that will be your wisdom and your understanding in the sight of the peoples, who, when they hear all these statutes, will say, 'Surely this great nation is a wise and understanding people.' For what great nation is there that has a god so near to it as the Lord our God is to us, whenever we call upon him? And what great nation is there, that has statutes and rules so righteous as all this law that I set before you today? (Deut. 4:6–8; see also Is. 42:6; Heb. 2:2; Amos 1–2).

This total law was explicitly given for the *blessing and health* of the nations; for without God and his law there is only misery and the way of death. Where God's law is abandoned sacrilege is involved; here blessing is forfeited and curses result.[164] For those who would doggedly deny the abiding validity of the law, we must consider such thinkers essentially part of the Marcionite legacy:

> Until the rise of the heretic Marcion, no distinction was made between Old and New Testaments: The Bible was seen as a unity, with one continuous revelation. Marcion saw the Old Testament as the revelation of a creator God who was unloving and whose word was wrath and law, whereas Jesus Christ was the revelation of a God of love. Much of the New Testament was also rejected by Marcion as Judaized. He was not only infected with Gnosticism, but was also the father of dispensationalism.[165]

Whilst we must take care to exhibit Christian charity toward those who hold to a dispensational reading of Scripture, there can be little doubt that the impact of a dispensational hermeneutic has wrought havoc on the average Christian's ability to effectively interpret Scripture for two or three generations, and thereby on the church's missiological outlook, leading in many cases to inertia and apocalyptic obsession rather than concern for rebuilding a godly generation.[166] In the face of growing social decline, eschatologies of defeat and retreat have proliferated, hand in hand with an antinomian attitude toward the law of God in church and state, with the *criminal* being the primary beneficiary of this lawless sentimentality.

Whilst I do not claim in this chapter that the Puritan perspective is the only one that can call itself Christian, I am convinced it is the best, most culturally pertinent and the most biblical expression amongst the Christian perspectives on law and penology. A theonomic missiology thus argues that the weakness and decline of the modern church and its relative ineffectiveness is directly related to its abandonment of the law. This in turn has undermined justice in the courts, contributing to the growing collapse of our society. All is not lost however. Christ is still on his throne and ruling at his Father's right hand. Faithfulness amongst God's people now can bring great change for the future if we will take responsibility and put our hands to the plough for the sake of future generations. As Ruth Mayers observed concerning the example set by the life of Oliver Cromwell:

> Much may be achieved by dedicated Christians dependent upon God, zealous for his glory and guided by his word. Godly rule may

be a thankless task, a constant uphill struggle, in which perfection is unattainable and temptations are multiplied. But earthly governments cannot be neutral in the conflict between sin and righteousness. Their policies will tend to serve either the one or the other.... The example of Oliver Cromwell shows that Christian withdrawal from politics on the ground that no good can be achieved is an abdication of God-given responsibility which ensures the short-term triumph of ungodliness.[167]

PART TWO

THE REIGN OF GOD

Chapter Ten

THE HIGHWAY TO ZION: CHRIST AND CULTURE

*How blessed is the man whose strength is in you, in whose heart
are the highways to Zion! Passing through the valley of Baca they
make it a spring.*

(Ps. 84:5–6)

"This is the victory that overcometh the world, even our faith...."

(1 John 5:4)

*It is not said that it will be victorious in a single fight, or a few, or
someone assault, but that it will be victorious over the whole world,
though it should be a thousand times assailed.*

– John Calvin

10.1 Christianity versus the Imperial Cult

In the second century A.D. Bishop Ignatius of Antioch in Syria was
hauled across Asia Minor and Thrace to be torn apart by beasts at Rome
for the entertainment of the mob. Polycarp, bishop of Smyrna and a
disciple of the apostle John, was arrested and burned to death about
A.D. 156. A relative of the magistrate who arrested him was a Christian
and had tried to persuade Polycarp to save himself by saying, "Caesar
is Lord;" he refused and perished in the flames. The question this raised
then, as it does now, is why should Christians make such a big issue of
so trivial-sounding a matter? Church historian Roland Bainton writes:

> The Christians added to the Jewish formulation, "Hear oh Israel, the
> Lord thy God is one Lord" the further confession, "Christ is Lord."
> Not only the God of heaven and earth but a malefactor crucified by
> the government of Rome was declared to have an authority exceeding
> that of the emperor of Rome. The cult of Christ and the cult of Caesar
> were incompatible.[1]

That statement needs to be reflected on and absorbed. To understand
the nature of the present cultural crisis in the West and the challenge it
represents to Christians, we must go back to antiquity and the religious

363

policy of Rome that led to the persecution of the church. The Roman emperor considered his military victories the victories of Roman gods over other gods. The clear implication of this was that, "The warfare of peoples was considered to be a warfare between their gods."[2] The '*cult*ure wars' here was indeed warfare between cults; someone's *god* would be victorious. This did not mean a lack of official 'toleration' for other religions (gods) because, "all religions were to be tolerated in the lands of their origin, provided their practices did not contravene the laws of Rome."[3] However, the law of Rome must reign supreme since the various cults of the period lacked the *universality* to act as the glue holding the empire together.

Thus, the central requirement of law in Rome, from which the pagan social order naturally followed (for religion and politics were no more separate then than they are today), was the recognition of the emperor as the ultimate object of worship and allegiance – the source of all sovereignty. Pliny, the proconsul in Bithynia, wrote a letter to the Emperor Trajan in the year A.D. 112 which makes clear that, "the sole offense for which the Christians were put to death was their refusal to worship the emperor...and the test is whether the accused refuses to curse Christ and worship the emperor."[4] State worship, personified in the emperor, was thus required of all Roman citizens and conquered peoples.

How does this historical reality help us understand our own cultural moment? It is certainly true that in Canada today (as well as most of Europe, and the United States) Christians are not being executed for their faith in the Lordship of Christ – though many people are in overtly communist and Islamic parts of the world. Nonetheless, whilst we are not being tossed to wild beasts, we are now largely under an official state doctrine of *tolerance* which, in the name of 'equality' and compassion, is determined to censor, in the public and increasingly the private sphere, the preaching of the gospel, the moral standards of Scripture, the prayers of citizens in the schools and corridors of power, as well as free speech that challenges in any way the pagan and secular ideology of our time. This cultural shift is due to a revived 'cult,' a form of humanism (paganism) expressing itself sociologically as cultural Marxism. In this worldview the Christian faith is portrayed as a regressive, patriarchal and draconian form of oppression which serves the self-interest of white, male, wealthy and middle-class misogynists using the private family and repressive Christian morality as a weapon for the promotion of capitalism and class domination. Consequently the war being waged against the Christian faith in the West is a culture war in the *realm of ideas* that is as real as the violent war waged against the early church.

There is nothing new about this current strategy. In A.D. 261 Gallienus issued the first *Edict of Toleration* in the Roman Empire, the purpose of which was not to favour Christianity but to oppose it with a strategy other than murder and violence – targeted strategic propaganda. As an emperor soaked in Hellenic culture, Gallienus preferred to contest Christianity in the field of ideas.[5] Today, the propaganda war against the faith is well-resourced and powerful. The ideas have infiltrated every public institution and many private ones as well. Sometimes the propaganda is framed in terms of the political ideals of multiculturalism that dominate our society; at other times it has centred on the official state policy of *political correctness* (or cultural Marxism) as it relates to restrictions on free speech and liberty. Interestingly, this strategy is steadily being exposed and periodically resisted.

For example, in March 2010 a debate in the Senate of the Canadian Parliament took place around a motion moved by Senator Doug Finley concerning the "Erosion of Freedom of Speech." Finley urged his fellow senators to recognize the extent to which the state-sanctioned doctrine of political correctness in Canada had placed free speech under siege through official censors in the Human Rights Commissions, media and universities – a direct violation of the tradition of free speech inherited from Great Britain and France. In recent years we have seen numerous examples of this censorship too plentiful to mention, from the cancelling of a speaking event for Anne Coulter at the University of Ottawa, to the banning of pro-life groups and debate on a number of university campuses, to fines, gag orders and sensitivity training requirements for clergy, Christian groups, or charities that dare speak against certain sexual practices or new state policy on 'marriage.' It is not surprising that these attacks come to focus almost exclusively on Christians and the occasional Jewish social conservative. It is once again the Judeo-Christian tradition that is under assault and in our time, this agenda is no longer hidden. Part of this 'freedom freeze' in Canada has happened gradually through the use of mechanisms like the Canadian Human Rights Act (section 13.1) which forbids any material or speech likely to cause offense to people on the ground of race, religion, gender or sexual orientation – here, proof of intent is not required and truth or reasonable belief in the truth is no defense.[6] It is obviously difficult to see how a Christian view of the family or even basic Christian evangelism could avoid falling foul of this religious policy of state, since the proclamation of the gospel requires the calling of all men and women who reject the salvation and lordship of Jesus Christ, to repentance, faith and a changed life that eschews anything the Bible considers sinful and idolatrous.

What then is the calling of Christians in the midst of this culture war being waged against us? Several things can be said by way of introduction. First, we cannot distance ourselves from culture, or hide from it. We must understand its meaning and learn to think in biblical categories about it. Christ is over and transcends culture as creator, redeemer and king. All things have been made subject to him and he remains the same yesterday, today and forever (Heb. 13:8); his truth, gospel and law are not culturally relative. The apostle Peter writes, "… the grass withers and the flowers fall, but the word of the Lord stands forever" (1 Pt. 1:24). Since Christ's purpose is the *reconciling* of *all things* to himself (Col. 1:20), the transformation of culture by faithfulness to the gospel and the total word of God applied to all of life is central to the Christian's calling. This calling is easily overlooked, even by faithful Christians. As Hegeman notes, "Christians, in their zeal to honor God for His abundant redemptive graces and to proclaim this salvation to the whole of creation, have all but lost a strong sense of man's original cultural calling. In far too many cases, a vision for man's vital role as cultural-maker is altogether absent from the believers' mind."[7] This doctrine was not lost on the Puritans, however, and remains basic to the Puritan mind when thinking about a Christian's relationship to culture. "The Puritans were committed to search the Scriptures, organize and analyze their findings, and then apply them to all areas of life. They had a confessional, theological, and Trinitarian approach that urged conversion and communion with God in personal, family, church and national life."[8] The whole orientation of the Puritan perspective was one that sought to "implement its vision of spiritual renewal, national and personal, in the church, the state, and the home; in education, evangelism and economics…"[9] All of life was to be brought under the rule of Jesus Christ, which meant all of culture was subject to his sway.

Secondly, we must be mindful that "the weapons of our warfare are not of the flesh but have divine power to destroy strongholds. We destroy arguments and every lofty opinion raised against the knowledge of God and take every thought captive to obey Christ" (2 Cor. 10:4–5). Our battle is spiritual and it is a struggle for the minds and hearts of people. In the conflict we must be cognizant of the presence and power of the Holy Spirit, who alone convinces the world of sin, righteousness and judgement, and not imagine that a Christian culture can develop through our ingenuity, creativity, or wisdom. Thirdly, to wage this spiritual war, we must be faithful in every area of life to apply God's word. Only in this way will we see the gospel transform us individually, our families, communities and therefore cultures. This means recognizing and living in terms of the relevance of God's word to every area of life. As legal scholar John Warwick Montgomery writes, "How tragic if we compartmentalize our lives, restricting biblical understanding to local church activities and personal relationships, never recognizing that every substantive aspect of our legal discipline can and should be seen in the light of Christ."[10] What is true for the legal discipline is true for every discipline and every part of life – we must see all of it in the light of Christ. Until we recover this understanding of the faith we will not be able to comprehend, never mind emulate, the martyrdom of the great Fathers of the church who could not treat as trivial the words, 'Caesar is Lord,' but instead died for the confession, 'Jesus Christ is Lord.' Indeed, without this comprehension we will remain irrelevant to the crisis of our age and the faith of our forebears will pass like wind in the prairies, driven by the propaganda of idolatry – the worship of man and state. David Klinghoffer asserts the result of what happens when a culture makes such a turn away from God and his law:

> …we have inevitably, by definition, turned toward idolatry. The Bible recognises only these two states of existence: You have either cast your lot with God or with the idols. The greatest codifier of biblical law, Maimonides, put the idea in stark terms: "All who affirm idolatry reject the whole of God's teaching, all the prophets, and that which was commanded to the prophets from Adam till the end of the world"… since both liberal religion and secularism deny traditional norms of behaviour as rooted in the Bible, both equally represent a turn toward paganism.[11]

The question of culture-making ultimately then, is a question of lordship – idolatry or true worship. Is Jesus Christ Lord, or some other god? The character and shape of our culture depends upon the answer.

10.2   What is Culture?

Herman Bavinck pointed out that "Genesis 1:26 teaches us that God had a purpose in creating man in His image: namely, that man should have dominion.... If now we comprehend the force of this subduing under the term culture, now generally used for it, we can say that *culture* in its broadest sense is the purpose for which God created man after His image."[12] So the first task is to ask, exactly what is this subduing? What is the meaning of the term culture? The historian Jacques Barzun was acutely aware of the difficulty with our contemporary use of the term *culture* when he wrote:

> Culture – what a word! Up to a few years ago it meant two or three related things easy to grasp and keep apart. Now it is a piece of all-purpose jargon that covers a hodge-podge of overlapping things.... How did...a simple metaphor from agri-culture, lose its authority and get burdened with meanings for which there were other good words?[13]

This bewildering array of applications leads to a good deal of confusion. In Christian social analysis, especially amongst those aping the liberal intelligentsia, the term 'culture' has been so overused and ambiguously applied that it has become a very slippery piece of lingo. We speak of urban culture, sub-culture, business culture, organizational culture, arts culture, gay culture, multi-culturalism and on and on, to the point that we are not sure what we mean and are therefore uncertain about how biblical faith relates to this 'catch all' concept.

The original and primary definitions of culture, a word derived from *cultivation*, have been almost forgotten. The Latin verb *colere*, from which we derive the term, refers to tilling the ground in order to grow things. Older dictionaries therefore render the noun *culture* as a "state of being cultivated" and "a type of civilization" respectively. Here, the state of being cultivated in individuals essentially forms or creates a *type of civilization* that grows as a result of this intellectual and moral tilling. Traditionally then, an educated, mature and civilized person was considered 'cultured,' cultivated in terms of a particular ideal. A person's ideal *state of being* is thus a profoundly religious question and we retain this basic association in our use of the related term *cult* to refer to a system of religious belief (*cultus*). *Cult*ure has consequently been accurately described as "religion externalized,"[14] or more simply, applied beliefs. If you visit Saudi Arabia you will experience Islamic culture, specifically manifest by its law and education. Go to certain parts of India and you will witness Hindu culture with its integral mythology and the resulting caste system. Come to the West and you now witness humanistic culture with strong remnants of Christianity in people's language, literature, beliefs and other cultural artefacts like architecture.

Civilizations (the communal development and application of beliefs/doctrines) or cultures rise and fall as beliefs take concrete shape in the laws, education, art, architecture, economics, literature and customs of a people, and then, under various stresses, collapse and fail. We have already observed throughout this book the widespread capture of the West by the humanistic *cult* of state-sponsored polytheism (philosophical pluralism) sociologically expressed as multiculturalism and cultural Marxism, concurrent with the evident encroachment of an opportunistic Islam, which together are steadily producing social decay and collapse from economic meltdown to family fragmentation, and the rioting and anarchy increasingly seen in our cities. It is in the midst of all this that Christians must ask how they are to relate the gospel of the kingdom to the decaying culture of our age.

10.3 Culture as 'prejudice'

We must begin by recognizing the fact that no culture can be *neutral*. It is impossible for any social order to be neutral – that is, neither one thing nor another. Every civilization is and will be inescapably committed, through the spheres and institutions of family, academy, law, art and government, to a religious or cultural consensus, be it humanistic, Islamic, Hindu, Christian or any other. The illusory idea of a neutral order or *prejudice-free* space for an equal toleration of all views (or gods) is a myth utilised only to facilitate the establishment of a new intolerance. The noted social critic Theodore Dalrymple has illustrated this well:

> To overturn a prejudice is not to destroy prejudice as such. It is rather to inculcate another prejudice.... When George Bernard Shaw characterised marriage as a legalised form of prostitution, he was not so much demanding justice and equality for women, as he was encouraging the dissolution even as an ideal, of permanent bonds between a man and a woman. Unfortunately, mass-bastardy is not liberating for women.[15]

The removal of one prejudice (the Christian concept of marriage for example) does not lead to a neutral approach to marriage, but rather a considered prejudice against the Christian conception of the family as the new cultural norm, a prejudice very evident in our time. Simply put, the idea that one can *cultivate* a prejudice-free civilization, one without real value commitments, is a dangerous lie that has been used by secular humanism as a precursor to the marginalization and persecution of Christianity. Political scientists and historians understand that dissent in any civilization can only be tolerated to a certain degree, beyond which that social order dooms itself – which is why treason has always been considered a serious crime and historically severely punished, even in the West. This is also why conversion to Christianity is illegal in many parts of India, is a crime in most Islamic states, and why a *free church* is illegal in communist countries – remaining under a cruel persecution in China and North Korea, amongst many others. These pagan governments logically fear (in terms of their cult) the cultural and social transformation that mass conversions would inevitably produce, and naturally resent the swift demise of their power in such a scenario. However, once cruelty and mass executions are resorted to, such suppression is almost certainly too late to salvage the pagan social order, whether 'democratic' or dictatorial, fascist or communist. We are gradually beginning to see in Asia, Africa and South America, Christian cultures emerge, despite the suppression and persecution of believers in many of these contexts.

10.4 Cult and Culture

As we have seen, the Roman imperial cult in the early centuries of the church saw the claims of Christians concerning the *Lordship* of Christ (i.e. Acts 4:12; Eph. 1:15–23; Col. 1:15–20) not simply as 'religious' in the modern sense, i.e. separated from the real *secular* world into a limited sacred realm, but as sociocultural and political in their scope. The Roman emperor and senate did not pretend (like many Christians today) that religion and politics were unrelated matters, but knew they were inextricably tied together. Caesar was 'Lord' and thus the 'saving' state had a priestly function as a god to the people. However, in Philippians 2:9–11, St. Paul challenges the priestly state when he declares the following:

> Therefore God has highly exalted him and bestowed on him the name that is above every name, so that at the name of Jesus every knee should bow, in heaven and on earth and under the earth, and

every tongue confess that Jesus Christ is Lord, to the glory of God the Father. The pagan world saw this apparently audacious claim and the church's related claim to a freedom and ambassadorial status in Christ (1 Pt. 2:16; 2 Cor. 5:17– 20; Eph. 6:20), as a threat to the survival of the pagan establishment – and they were right as history shows. Notice the passing remark (with astonishing implications) that St. Paul makes in his final greeting to the church at Philippi, a letter in which he has declared Christ's name (or authority) to be above every other name: "All the saints greet you, especially those of *Caesar's household*" (Phil. 4:22).

Already, at this early point in the life of the church, Caesar's own household had been invaded by a new Lord, a new priest and a new King. The Christ of Psalm 2 was already being made manifest, and pagan Rome's days were numbered. When Constantine came to power during the colossal emergence of the Christian faith throughout the empire, under the influence of that faith, he abolished the blood-letting of the Roman arena, reformed the law toward a more Christian perspective in a number of important ways, built churches and hospitals and funded poverty relief. Since "the arena was Rome," and basic to the pagan concept of sacrifice, that vital step in a Christian direction proved revolutionary.[16]

Applied biblical faith inescapably transforms those who embrace and are influenced by it, and this has far-reaching consequences for family, vocation, law, art, state and therefore, *culture*. Counter-revolutions away from Christianity have concomitants equally radical, and – since they are anti-Christ – invariably evil. Knowing the implications of the biblical claims concerning Jesus, Robespierre and his French revolutionaries could not tolerate a *free church* – murdering thousands in the name of a new religion based allegedly on 'reason' – nor could Hitler, Stalin or Mussolini, murdering their tens of millions in the name of their various *cults*. Of particular relevance today, in the same spirit, our Marxist thought police of the politically correct brigade, along with the new atheists, would love to silence all Christians. In many cases attempts have been made to 'legally' asset-strip believers in the name of human rights, remove them from academic positions or deny them tenure, arrest them for preaching openly, or even seek prison terms for the expression of biblical views.[17] This cultural shift in lands of formerly Christian consensus has not happened overnight. The utter contempt for the Christian faith established now for decades amongst the Western cultural elite is well-expressed by Bloomsbury novelist Virginia Woolf, in a 1928 letter to her sister penned at the news of T.S. Eliot's conversion to Christianity:

> I have had a most shameful and distressing interview with poor dear Tom Eliot, who may be called dead to us all from this day forward. He has become an Anglo-Catholic, believes in God and immortality, and goes to church. I was really shocked. A corpse would seem to me more credible than he is. I mean, there's something obscene in a living person sitting by the fire and believing in God.[18]

Ironically, what was 'obscene' to Virginia Woolf has been the undeniable source and principle of liberty in the West, a liberty that permitted her to express her revulsion and disbelief. Whilst we must readily grant historical exceptions to this generalization seen in times of political upheaval and church-state conflict – usually *over* the issue of religious freedom and freedom of conscience as in the English Revolution[19] – freedom of conscience and speech have *only* flourished in Christian-dominated societies. These cultures have granted the greatest degree of liberty to individuals within biblical bounds; people being free to believe a set of doctrines or values or *not* to believe them and express non-violent dissent, so long as the law is obeyed (since law and culture cannot be neutral). That freedom and equality under Christian law is disappearing fast[20] as the cultural elite reform law and seek to use the humanistic state's bureaucracy to increasingly control and regulate the thinking, speaking and practices of ordinary citizens in almost every area of life.[21]

The critical point here is to recognize that there are no *neutral cultures*. A society may be full of competing claims, but it is impossible for it to be neither one thing nor another. The culture shapers are tilling the minds of others with a specific worldview in mind. *Someone's* morality will be legislated, someone's philosophy taught in schools, someone's vision of beauty and reality idealised in art. As John Frame puts it, "People make things, because they already have a plan in view – a purpose, a goal, an ideal. The ideal comes first, then making things. First the norm, then the cultivation, the culture."[22]

Culture is therefore a question of religion, because we are talking about values and ideals. St. Augustine saw this readily when he identified only two seeds and kingdoms in history, the city of God and the city of man, true and false worship. Idolatry leads to a corrupt culture based on false worship. The worship of the living God in Jesus Christ will lead to a radically different (though imperfect) culture. Thus, the exercise of dominion (culture-making), which is essential to the nature of man, will either be done in terms of God's word of truth, or man's lie. This means there is a true law, true economics, true beauty, true justice, by which man is called to live and serve God. The alternative is lying laws, lying economics, ugliness and injustice.

10.5   Culture and the Fall

As well as recognizing the religious *source* of culture, we need to grasp a biblical *vision* of culture and its theological underpinnings. It is easy to get lost in the vast array of Christian cultural analysis available today, all pointing to a variety of 'turning points' in making their case against (or sometimes for) present-day culture. For some, the turning point is a given philosopher or modernism in general; for others, the counter-culture of the 1960s; for others the Industrial Revolution; and for still others the now somewhat passé post-modern criticism. There have also been influential utopian cultural dreamers and 'planners,' idealised by pagans and Christians alike who are looked to as pivotal, from Plato's communist order in the *Republic* to the revolutionary, Ernesto Guevara, concerning whom Dalrymple observes, "if it hadn't been for the photograph taken by the Cuban photographer Alberto Korda, Ernesto Guevara would have been recognized by now as the arrogant, adolescent, power-hungry egotist that he undoubtedly was."[23] In each case, a great deal of weight is placed upon a particular time, person or event as pivotal in bringing us to our cultural moment. Whilst these historical developments are very interesting subjects for analysis and important in a limited sense, they are not the starting point for examining the nature of the Christian's relationship to culture and our route out of the current crisis.

The primary turning point for us to understand is the fall of our first parents in the garden of God. All rebel cultures in history since that time have merely been a replay of that initial rebellion. The basic sin of humanity is the attempt to be one's own God, to assert one's autonomy and be the source of definition for truth and reality independent of God. By recognizing this, we will be less inclined to chronological snobbery, assuming that we live in the most unprecedented or 'pivotal age' in history, and less enamoured with passing fads and borrowed intellectual constructs that allegedly pave the way to the future via a new 'paradigm' or 'technique' for the church to follow in achieving 'cultural relevance' (whatever that means). We can blame the rationalists or irrationalists, the moderns or post-moderns, the industrialists or Marxists, anarchists or proletariat, but in the end, Adam and Eve were both rationalist and irrationalist, modern and postmodern in their response to temptation. Irrationalist in rejecting the authority of God's self-attesting word and attempting to reason in terms of a neutral, ungoverned reality; rationalist in thinking they could construct and define reality and truth for themselves by the reach of their own minds. Western history has not been a linear movement from the heights of Greek culture and its rationalism to the lows of modern existentialism, nihilism and anti-foundationalism (themes in fact present amongst Greek philosophers called Cynics). It has always been an interplay between these two ideas; both are an attempt to escape the claims of God. "So the problem is not history; the problem is sin. Culture is bad today, but Sodom and Gomorrah were probably not any better, nor were Tyre, Sidon, Nineveh, Babylon, Rome, Capernaum, Chorazin, or Bethsaida." [24] Thus we face fallen cultures (beliefs externalized and applied) in every age.

What are we to do in our own? We can begin by remembering that the cultural task was given by God and mandated for humanity in our dominion calling – theologians call this the cultural mandate (Gen. 1:28). The *filling of the earth* presupposes the family, the home and multiplication, and to *rule* means the development of the earth, to bring out its potential and turn the *creation into a culture*. We are not slaves in the earth of our environment or our DNA, neither are we victims of fate; rather we are given a regal role as God's vice-regents in the earth, spreading his glory throughout the world by fulfilling his purposes. Since culture is commanded by God it is always, in Scripture, tied to his commands, desires, and norms. As we go about our family life, vocational life, church life and every other aspect of life, we do so in terms of obedience to God, as St. Paul tells us, "whatever you do, in word or deed, do everything in the name of the Lord Jesus, giving thanks to God the Father through him" (Col. 3:17). The Puritans saw that our work in our vocations was a critical part of the cultural calling and our humanity as God's image bearers. William Perkins wrote that, "the main end of our lives...is to serve God in the serving of men in the works of our callings.... The true end of our lives is to do service to God in the serving of man."[25]

Nonetheless, since the Fall we see culture after culture that, instead of working and serving for the glory of God, acts and builds out of a hatred toward the living God. Indeed, St. Paul tells us this is inescapably true for unregenerate man (Rom. 8:5–8). This does not mean non-believers can do nothing good or useful in culture, in art and science and so forth; they can, but not in an ultimate sense (that is, directed toward God's glory). Furthermore, the limited (self-oriented) good they do is only possible by borrowing unacknowledged capital from God, by virtue of being creatures made in his image. However when a person is born anew into Christ, their whole life changes and is reoriented in thought, word and deed, so that whatever we do, it is to be done, with delight and excellence, for the glory of God and in terms of his kingdom purpose.

This must have, and does have, a dramatic impact upon culture, because *culture is what we make of God's creation* in terms of an ideal – cultivating in terms of an ultimate belief in his word of truth. Here, what the early church called the 'third race,' Christ's new society, family, nation or covenant community, declares and lives a new way of life, and consequently manifests a *new culture*; it cannot help but do so. This means that everything in our lives expresses the totality of the reign and purposes of God – every other worldview is equally all-encompassing. We must recognize, like the early church, that Jesus Christ is still *Lord* and so by the Holy Spirit, faithfulness to him in sharing the gospel and obeying his commands will make *new creations* out of people (2 Cor. 5:17), gathering a new race (1 Pt. 2:9-10) who build new cultures (1 Cor. 10:23–31; Is. 51:1–5; Ps. 2; Ps. 22:27–31; Prov. 29:1–18). This is not by revolution, but by regeneration, faithfulness and obedience. As Christ's new humanity, we are the first-fruits indicating the direction of all history. Rushdoony stated it well:

> For both Paul and James, Christians are the first-fruits whom all creation will follow (Rom. 8:18–23). God, who created all things, ordained that Christ and His people, the new humanity, should lead the way to the rebirth and renewal of all things. This is not a mystical vision of the future. It is God's work of renewing grace and our response of faithfulness to His every word that leads to this great cosmic renewal. When James 1:18 tells us that we are to be "the first-fruits of his creatures," the word creatures has reference to all of

God's created things apart from man. God's purpose is cosmic, not man-centred, but, created man in His image is the starting point in Christ of this new creation...in Christ we ourselves become the first-fruits, the required offering to the triune God...[making] it clear that our redemption is the beginning of the regeneration of all things.[26] So then, sin and the Fall did not remove the cultural mandate, in fact God repeated it to Noah in Genesis 9:1–7. Moreover, Jesus restates it for his church in the Great Commission (Matt. 28:19–20). This commission, like the cultural mandate, clearly calls for a new culture, "*All authority* in *heaven* and *earth* has been given to me. Go therefore and make disciples of all nations, baptizing them in the name of the Father and of the Son and of the Holy Spirit, teaching them to observe all that I have commanded you. And behold, I am with you always, to the end of the age."

We are told here to comprehensively teach the nations to obey everything that Christ has commanded, and the word *teach* in the Greek language (*mathatos*) means literally 'discipline.' As believers we are to discipline and organize nations into covenant-obeying peoples, baptised by Christ, just as Israel was baptised symbolically in the Jordan. This conviction, re-deployed during the Reformation and developed by the Puritans, has dominated historic reformed evangelicalism. For example, the great Princetonian evangelical Charles Hodge wrote emphatically:

It is our duty, as far as lies in our power, immediately to organize human society and all its institutions and organs upon a distinctively Christian basis. Indifference or impartiality here between the law of the kingdom and the law of the world, or of its prince, the devil, is utter treason to the King of Righteousness. The Bible, the great statute-book of the kingdom, explicitly lays down principles which, when candidly applied, will regulate the action of every human being in all relations. There can be no compromise. The King said, with regard to all descriptions of moral agents in all spheres of activity, "He that is not with me is against me." If the national life in general is organized upon non-Christian principles, the churches which are embraced within the universal assimilating power of that nation will not long be able to preserve their integrity.[27]

There are some who immediately consider Christians who take this view and read Scripture with a mind to faithfully applying it, who speak of this rule and dominion of Christ, as somehow power-hungry revolutionaries seeking to usurp authority and exert *domination* over others. This caricature is now a popular tool of propaganda in the media who have recently latched onto the term 'dominion' to excoriate various Christians involved in politics, public office or positions of influence. There is nothing new here – such a strategy was employed against the Puritans and is again being used as hostility to the faith grows. In fact as Puritan scholar Coffey notes, "with the rise of the American Religious Right, Puritan bashing once again became a popular sport. The reelection of George W. Bush in 2004 provoked fears that the Christian Right was out to 'repeal the enlightenment' and recreate a 'Puritan theocracy.'"[28] Thus, if a Christian holds to Scripture as their standard for all areas of life, they are identified by the secular cultural elite as bogeymen and labelled 'dominionists.'

Tragically some Christians have joined in this jeering and joined the ranks of those mocking the application of our faith to culture. One cultural critic, after showing that the cultural Marxists of the political left have overtly pursued illegitimate domination, writes:

The leftists sense – *rightly* – that true dominion theologians *don't* wish to rule the world like the leftists do, we want the reverse. We want greater freedom, decentralization, privatization, self-determination, local law and local law enforcement, less taxation; and an end to forced transfers of wealth, wage controls, debt-financed wars and welfare, and a billion other government strictures and regulations. We want freedom, free markets, and local government. And this is the greatest threat of all to these leftist dominionists. They fear most not merely the loss of political control, but a world in which such control *is no longer possible*. This is the biggest threat of all. For a mere temporary loss of control, a mere replacement of partisan leadership, means that the top-down seats of power are still there for the taking again at some point in the future. This leaves leftists the opportunity for control. But in a Christian...world, power is decentralized, and there would no longer be a *single central State agency* (or three) which leftists could grab in order to control everyone! And this is the ultimate nightmare scenario for leftists, who above all things covet power. For this reason, they must smear this thing called "dominion" in as far as it threatens their control of society.[29]

However convinced we are by the specifics of such reasoning, there is no denying we are indeed faced with a conflict between two visions of dominion, two visions of culture – the city of God and the city of man. Are the nations to be the *dominion* of Christ by his gospel as he commanded, under his justice, righteousness and truth, or is man, claiming the role and prerogatives of God, to exert his *domination* over the lives of other men and women? Is culture then to be redeemed or left to its own devices? As the gospel transforms lives are we to pursue a Christ-centred vision for arts, sciences, education, the university, law, economics, politics, business and so forth, or are all these activities neutral aspects of a 'secular realm?' The answer of the reformed faith is an emphatic *yes* – we must consecrate all aspects of life to God. As J. Gresham Machen put it almost a century ago:

Are then Christianity and culture in a conflict that is to be settled only by the destruction of one or the other of the contending forces? A third solution, fortunately, is possible – namely consecration. Instead of destroying the arts and sciences or being indifferent to them, let us cultivate them with all the enthusiasm of the veriest humanist, but at the same time consecrate them to the service of our God. Instead of stifling the pleasures afforded by the acquisition of knowledge or by the appreciation of what is beautiful, let us accept these pleasures as the gifts of a heavenly Father. Instead of obliterating the distinction between the Kingdom and the world, or on the other hand withdrawing from the world into a sort of modernized intellectual monasticism, let us go forth joyfully, enthusiastically to make the world subject to God.[30]

10.6 Cultural Cowardice

Alfred Edersheim, a leading historian of antiquity, has highlighted that few people today appreciate the influence of Christianity in the transformation of the cultural life and moral character of Europe in the early centuries of the Christian era, nor do they adequately recognize the role of the Bible in advancing high civilization. The Greco-Roman world, governed as it was in thought and practice by religious paganism, Stoic natural law theory and Greek metaphysics, when confronted by the biblical faith of the church, was swept aside with relative ease, in part because of the radical dualistic tensions in pagan thought which were productive of social and moral degeneracy. Edersheim writes:

If a faithful picture of society in ancient Greece or Rome were to be presented to view, it is not easy to believe that even they who now most oppose the Bible could wish their aims success. For this at any rate, may be asserted, without fear of gainsaying, that no other religion than that of the Bible has proved competent to control an advanced, or even an advancing, state of civilisation.... [I]n the case of heathenism every advance in civilisation has marked a progressive lowering of public morality.... [O]n the contrary the religion of the Bible (under the old as under the new dispensation) has increasingly raised, if not uniformly the public morals, yet always the tone and standard of public morality.... Few of those who have learned to admire classical antiquity has a full conception of any one phase in its social life – whether the position of woman, the relation of sexes, slavery, the education of children, their relation to their parents, or the state of public morality.... St. Paul's description of the ancient world in the first and second chapters of his Epistle to the Romans must have appeared to those who lived in the midst of it as Divine even in its tenderness, delicacy and charity.[31]

Despite these historical realities, it is nonetheless true that not all Christians share the view that believers should be concerned with the consecration of culture, its public justice and morality. Consequently it is important to understand theologically, the roots of impoverished evangelical approaches to the cultural mandate. Regrettably, Michael Horton, a faithful evangelical scholar, unveils one popular approach to culture in a recent article entitled, "Transforming Culture with a Messiah Complex,"[32] that manifests strong dualistic overtones which, I think, is a reworking of a moribund fundamentalism – a kind of neo-Reformed novelty attempting to sound historic.[33] The article offers a powerful illustration of a theological dualism indebted to Greek philosophy that characterizes many Christians' understanding of our relationship to creation and the meaning of the kingdom of God.

Horton clearly loves old evangelical soteriology and wants to preserve its faithful declaration, which is a necessary and noble task. Equally he does not want the church to lose its focus on heralding the good news of the grace of God manifest in Christ through vicarious atonement, and our redemption visibly represented by the sacraments of the church. With all this, I can heartily agree. I am also hopeful that the primary target of his criticisms in this article and other works are aberrant 'emergent' writers within the church, who, claiming to be 'missional' and concerned with 'social justice,' speak of the reign of God as a kind of human political movement of a Marxist character, whilst often denying the propitiatory sacrifice of the cross, the sufficiency and authority of Scripture and the exclusivity of the gospel. I can join him in his condemnation of such heretical ideas. But his concerns in this regard lead him, in my view, to a serious truncation of the gospel of the kingdom that warrants critique in the light of Scripture.

Horton's basic idea seems to be that of *double sovereignty* or *two kingdoms* (with similarities to the nature/grace dualism of scholastic philosophy). In the world, God's authority is seen through natural laws and common grace in the cultures, governments and laws of the nations – allegedly based on the covenant with Noah. This idea is seriously problematic because the covenant with Noah was a promise concerning the providential continuity of seasons and the regularity of creation, as well as an assurance that God would not flood the whole earth again. These promises have proven unshakable since the flood. But if this was supposed to be a promise guaranteeing shared ethical norms for regulating culture, that covenant is historically, demonstrably falsifiable. It is true that God instituted human government with Noah after the flood concerning, specifically citing the death penalty for murder, but this is a *prescriptive requirement* of God, *not descriptive* of all future cultures. The idea that cultural hegemony is a promise and by-product of this covenant with Noah appears totally fallacious. Regardless of this strange notion, the basic idea is that in the one kingdom of *the church*, God reigns through Christ, the Holy Spirit and the life of 'faith.' In the other kingdom (all other aspects of life), by creational ordinance and natural abilities we work, marry and raise families, do art, cook, establish government, and so on; but to find the higher purpose of the *future state*, we need to find God's saving grace, which the church ministers to people. The *neutral state* by natural laws and common grace takes care of the rest, from education, to arts, hospitals and science. These are not distinctly Christian and do not need to be since the average citizen next door supposedly shares our Christian values on the basis of natural law or common grace.

On this face of it, this idea has rhetorical plausibility, but on examination is exposed as sophistry. If it be said that the evidence for such a view is that most people in America, Canada or Britain do indeed share the values of honouring parents, the sanctity of life, honesty in business, or excellence in education (in other words cultural hegemony – an idea already palpably false with the loss of the Christian consensus in the West) without being distinctly Christian people, we only need ask, why do they share such values? Is this because of 'natural law' and the covenant with Noah (which appears to bear no relation to the question of whether Christians are to consecrate culture), or is it because of *the centuries of Christian teaching and preaching* that has changed and transformed the culture of our Western nations? Is there really a common cultural and ethical framework throughout the world, or is it the effectiveness of *Christian mission* that allows the 'two kingdoms' advocates to appeal to cultural hegemony in defence of not needing Christianity to transform culture? Two-kingdoms cultural retreatists prefer to appeal to 'neutral nature' to account for Western culture, after all, one does not need a distinctively Christian theology and method to prepare a stir-fry or teach children, according to Horton

I will allow a most unlikely individual to answer Horton's superficial view of culture with devastating clarity. On his world voyage on the H.M.S Beagle, Charles Darwin, despite his growing agnosticism and deistic religious confusion, found himself unable to overlook the profound impact of Christian missionaries in Tahiti and the Pacific islands. In the first work he ever wrote, before the implications of his theory gripped and ruled him, Darwin's Christianized background caused him to rain praise on the evangelical missionary – today's two kingdoms theorists would do well to take note:

> It appears to me that the morality and religion of the inhabitants are highly creditable. There are many who attack…both the missionaries, their system, and the effects produced by it. Such reasoners never compare the present state with that of the Island only twenty years ago, nor even with that of Europe at this day; but they compare it with the high standard of gospel perfection…. [T]hey forget, or will not remember, that human sacrifices, and the power of an idolatrous priesthood – a system of profligacy unparalleled in any other part of the world – infanticide, a consequence of that system – bloody wars, where the conquerors spared neither women nor children – that all these have been abolished, and that dishonesty, intemperance, and licentiousness have been greatly reduced, by the introduction of Christianity. In a voyager to forget these things is base ingratitude; for should he chance to be at the point of shipwreck on some unknown

coast, he will most devoutly pray that the lesson of the missionary may have extended thus far.... [T]hose who are most severe should consider how much of the morality of the women in Europe is owing to the system early impressed by mothers on their daughters, and how much in each individual case to the precepts of religion. But it is useless to argue against such reasoners; – I believe that, disappointed in not finding the field of licentiousness quite so open as formerly, they will not give credit to a morality which they do not wish to practice, or to a religion which they undervalue, if not despise.[34]

We see here with utmost clarity the fact that the cultural hegemony argument is completely untenable. Horton and company can only appeal to their culture because it has already been under the influence of the gospel, not because there is a vague 'natural law' or general grace which brings people to broadly agree on the nature of education, the family, sanctity of life and business ethics. Horton may like stir-fried chicken while some of the Pacific and Caribbean islanders had been very happy with stir-fried man-flesh. Perhaps there is a Christian way to prepare food after all! What agreement we have enjoyed in the West, is based on centuries of the success of a vision of cultural triumph for Christ and his gospel – for before the faith came to Britain, many Celts to the North, in a then pagan land, were drinking the blood of the dead. Darwin's keen observation in the nineteenth century, that in the event of shipwreck amongst the Pacific islands, pray to God that you land on one that has felt the impact of the gospel, applies fully to Horton and those who support his view. What is actually happening in two kingdoms thought is that the word of God is implicitly reduced to a helpful *supplement* for individuals living of necessity amidst the common order – the earthly kingdom. In this view Christ does not judge, convert, transform and redeem bankrupt cultures, he is a condiment to sweeten our journey through the veil of tears. Scripture however teaches us that 'nature' (Horton's common order) is hopelessly fallen, our minds corrupted and hearts deceitful – we need the special grace of God in *all things* to function as God intends (Rom. 8:5–8; Eph. 2:1–3). Thus to realize marriage or parenthood, education or government as God wants, we need Christ; to realize our vocation as God intends we need to approach our calling with biblical lenses and seek God's glory in Christ. Likewise, to govern social orders with true justice, we need, not a warped and sinful vision of justice, but the corrective justice of Christ and his law (see Matt. 5:17–18). To deny this, it seems to me, fails to take the Fall and depravity of man as seriously as Scripture does. But for Horton, in all these spheres, from education to military service, Christ (or applied biblical faith) is simply not necessary to please God in these 'secular' arenas of life; man just does it all in terms of a vague conception of common grace. Yet Scripture contradicts this idea emphatically; faith is nowhere something reserved for 'church ministry,' but is central to all the work and exploits of the men and women of God throughout history (see Heb. 11:1–40). These heroes of biblical history did all this in faith toward God (from building the Ark to conquering kingdoms and shutting lions' mouths), knowing that by obedient faith, leaving their own selfish interests aside, God is building his *unshakeable kingdom* in history – ultimately by his son, Jesus Christ. But according to the two kingdoms theorists, we are *not* to labour to see the kingdom of God: "We hope and act in the present not in order to save the world or build the kingdom of God, but because 'we are receiving a kingdom that cannot be shaken.'"[35]

This, at first blush, sounds pious and heavenly-minded, but it is clearly unbiblical. It is obvious that *we* do not 'save the world;' this is a very poor straw man argument, for every Christian must acknowledge Christ is the only saviour, and master builder of the city of God. But, we are taught by the Lord himself to pray, in the present, "thy kingdom come, thy will be done, *on earth* as it is in heaven (Matt. 6:10)." Our Lord commands us, "seek first the kingdom of God and his righteousness (Matt. 6:33)." Christ is saviour and redeemer and is seated at the right hand of power establishing his kingdom, bringing all things into subjection (Heb. 2:5–8). St. Peter therefore writes that Christ has, "gone into heaven and is at the right hand of God, with angels, authorities and powers *having been* subjected to him" (1 Pt. 3:22). Note that the subjection is in the past tense. This victory is *now* being made manifest in history. Moreover, we are part of God's great work in history. St. Paul reminds us that God causes the growth, not man (1 Cor. 3:6) and no other foundation can be laid other than Christ and we build on that foundation (1 Cor. 3:10–11). We are therefore "God's fellow workers" (1 Cor. 3:9) as he brings all things into subjection, reconciling all things to himself:

> He has committed to us the word of reconciliation. Therefore, we are ambassadors for Christ, as though God were making an appeal through us; we beg you on behalf of Christ, be reconciled to God. He made Him who knew no sin to be sin on our behalf, so that we

might become the righteousness of God in Him. And *working together with Him*, we also urge you not to receive the grace of God in vain... for what partnership have righteousness and lawlessness, or what fellowship has light with darkness? Or what harmony has Christ with Belial, or what has a believer in common with an unbeliever, or what agreement has the temple of God with idols (2 Cor. 5:19–6:1,14–16. NASB)

Notice that the message of God's *reconciliation*, which is cosmic in scope (Col. 1:19-23), has been committed to us as ambassadors, *working together with God* to the end of the full consecration of all things to God – we do not sit by passively waiting for the kingdoms of the world to become the kingdoms of our Lord. St. Paul also makes it clear in the passage cited that there is no 'common order' in which believers and non-believers share the same assumptions, beliefs and ideals. There is no partnership between righteousness and lawlessness, light and darkness, idolatry and God's Kingdom, Christ and Satan. The two kingdoms advocates' effort to turn most of life outside the ministry of the sacraments and preaching into realms of common grace and order that don't need to be wholly devoted over to Christ is treason to the king of righteousness, and is a doomed attempt to wed idolatry with true worship, righteousness with lawlessness. Education, law, politics, economics, even diet, are not neutral areas for man's autonomous desires to have free reign, they are either devoted and consecrated over to God or they are not; they are then working and moving either in terms Satan's kingdom or Christ's – they can't be both.

Scripture declares that everything is already subject to Christ's authority and is in process of being brought outwardly and visibly into subjection, "for he must reign until he has put all his enemies under his feet" (1 Cor. 15:25); the last enemy to be defeated will be death. But for Horton, the kingdom is almost entirely in the future (after the return of Christ), and Christ's present kingdom reign is *specifically limited* to the ministry of the sacraments in the church and, he tells us, has nothing to do with building hospitals, defending the fatherless and widow, or holding public office. Rather, "proclaiming the word, administering baptism and the Supper, caring for the spiritual and physical well-being of the saints, and bringing in the lost *are* kingdom work."[36] This truncation of the gospel and retreatism or absconding from the world has a name – pietism. On this view, aside from some personal evangelism and a little diaconal care for church folk, only the professional clergy actually do any kingdom work! Remarkably those who disagree with Horton's analysis are dismissed as apparently suffering from an 'over-realized' amillennialism or post-millennialism. This is stated off-hand as though the optimistic eschatology (postmillennialism) of Reformed giants like Charles Hodge, B.B Warfield, Jonathan Edwards, William Carey, and a large number of our evangelical forebears is dead, without any scriptural demonstration of the alleged funeral. Instead it is implied that these eschatological perspectives are trying to, 'save the world' by their own strength, like proverbial Constantinian bogeymen.

This is hardly an accurate picture of the Puritan mind he is attacking. As Beeke and Jones point out, "The Puritans believed reformation was an ecclesiastical matter that also had far-reaching implications for the *civil realm*."[37] Packer has stated that, "Their [Puritan] vision of reality was not fragmented; they did not need to argue the point that Christian concern may not be limited to church order or to the welfare of individuals, but must embrace both together, along with the politics, economics, *and culture of nations*."[38] In reality, it is not the Puritan mind that is suffering from an over-realized eschatology, it is surely the two kingdoms theorists who suffer from an under-realized soteriology! Salvation is limited to personal salvation and does not have the kingdom of God in view for history. But for the Puritans their unwavering hope was that New England could become, "a place to cultivate a uniquely Christian society, which they called 'a city upon a hill.'"[39] These convictions were born out of their Augustinian eschatology seen in his massive work, *The City of God*, which maintained that the millennial reign of Christ was inaugurated at Christ's resurrection and extended to the end of the world (Rev. 20). Luther and the Reformed tradition followed Augustine in modified form (historicist hermeneutic) filled with an eschatological optimism, holding that a future day of glory was ahead in which the gospel would triumph – on this the Puritans were likewise agreed.[40] It is therefore difficult to see how such a dismissive attitude to a culture-transforming gospel can be taken seriously from the historical perspective.

Horton tries to justify his dualism (two kingdoms) by claiming that, "the New Testament does not offer a single exhortation to Christianize politics, the arts and sciences, education, or any other common grace field of endeavour."[41] This rather disturbing and dangerous statement, to which every tyrant in history would be delighted to say 'amen,' reveals a number of serious errors. First, it seems a latent *Marcionism* is present in Horton's careful qualification that the *New Testament* allegedly offers no mandate to build Christian culture. Even if that were true, at what point did the evangelical faith restrict itself to New Testament scriptures as alone relevant to the present world? The Older Testament was the Bible of our Lord and the New Testament church and is filled with prophecy concerning Christ's messianic authority and his kingdom breaking into history and shattering paganism (Gen. 49:8–10; Daniel; Ps. 2; Ps. 28; Ps 72; Isa. 58; Ezek. 21:25–27; Num. 24:17–19). It is also filled with God's law requiring public justice for all and compassion and charity for the poor, including the care of orphans and widows, the stranger, sojourner and oppressed. This law, Jesus declared, has an abiding legitimacy till heaven and earth pass – until then it must be put into force (Matt. 5:17–20). Horton realizes that the Older Testament is filled with requirements for the social and therefore *cultural order*, and so implicitly gives a greater authority to the New Testament, which is a form of Marcionism, condemned by the early church.

Furthermore, arguing that the New Testament has no explicit exhortation to Christianize education, arts, politics, etc., and so we shouldn't do it, is as absurd as saying the New Testament offers no explicit command to build church buildings, care for the creation and practice animal husbandry, therefore we shouldn't do it. Or, since the New Testament doesn't offer explicit condemnation of bestiality, has no prescriptive commandment to marry and have families (except in the case of uncontrollable desires: 1 Cor. 7:9), nor any explicit statement of the doctrine of the Trinity, therefore we shouldn't apply these teachings. In the first instance, the case laws of Moses give us a condemnation of bestiality and that is sufficient for a Christian – it needs no restatement in the New Testament. In the second case, by definition, the New Testament's teaching on divorce, family relations and discipline *presupposes* the abiding validity of the mandate to multiply, rule and subdue, as indeed it presupposes the validity of all the Old Testament. In the third case, the doctrine of the Trinity is the church's historic, unerring and inescapable *inference* from the relevant biblical passages from the Old and New Testaments. The idea that, even if there were no explicit text requiring us to Christianize culture in the New Testament, that we then lack such a mandate, is simply preposterous.

The expected transformation and consecration of culture by the gospel and law of God is plainly stated a multitude of times in the Old Testament. For example, concerning the incarnation and ministry of Christ and its cultural results, the prophet Isaiah is clear in chapters nine (quoted in part in Matt. 4:13–16) and eleven, "for of the increase of his government and of peace there will be no end...the zeal of the lord of hosts will accomplish this."[42] Isaiah 65 develops the cultural results of the triumph of the gospel. I would also argue that there are several very clear New Testament passages which are explicit calls to transform the culture. In 2 Corinthians 10:3–6, St. Paul tells us that our Christian lives are a spiritual conflict in which we seek to destroy every stronghold of argument, and false knowledge or 'lofty opinion' raised against the knowledge of God, and to take every thought captive to obey Christ. How can such a call be restricted to the church and its sacramental activities? The Psalmist reminds us in Psalm 24 that the earth and everything in it belongs to God – nothing is beyond the dominion of Christ, so wherever there is false knowledge in all creation, we are to pull it down and lead all thought in obedience to Christ. What else can this be but making culture the culture of Christ? St. Paul tells us that this creation, being wholly God's, is being brought into subjection so it is simply not possible to read Ephesians 1 and Colossians 1 and reflect on Christ as creator and head over all things being given to the church, and rationally conclude that Christ's intention is not the transformation of all things through his people. This is why Paul stood on Mars Hill in Acts 17 at the Athenian court with confidence. A number of members of that ruling council were converted (Acts 17:34). Does Horton really think that their abandonment of false philosophy and idolatry would not have a direct impact upon the culture, since culture is best understood as religion externalized?

Matthew 16:18–19 must also be grappled with. Clearly here, the church of God is given an authority on earth of great significance that cannot be brushed aside as simply a 'Roman Catholic doctrine.' An authority is given to God's people, in Christ, that is backed by heaven. The powers of hell unleashed in the earth cannot prevail against Christ building his church. Since the church militant (that is, active and advancing in the world) is being built by Christ now *in history*, when through prayer, prophetic witness and obedience, we wage our spiritual war, the demonic Spirit at work in the children of disobedience is defeated and Satan's *culture of death* destroyed. When by prayer, faith and obedience a Christian people rescues the fatherless, or sees abortion ended, or man-theft and slavery abolished, or prostitution and the exploitation of women criminalized, or murderers executed, has not Christ's culture of life broken in? The prophetic and priestly role of the church is by definition a culture-transforming commission – for we are a *royal priesthood* ministering a message of reconciliation to the world.

The early church truly believed they had a God-given authority that clearly impacted kings and thereby cultures. In the fifth century, Bishop Gelasius I (d. November 21, 496), who was the third and last bishop of Rome of African origin whose bishopric was characterized by his call for faithful orthodoxy said, "There are two powers by which chiefly the world is ruled. The authority of the priesthood and the authority of kings. And of these the authority of the priests is so much weightier as they must render before the tribunal of God an account for the kings of men." [43] Kings were seen as both accountable to God and in need of the care and instruction of priests as they carried out their task in the world. This audacious claim to authority and freedom or independence under God led the church to recognize an accountability for the condition of our nations since, as intercessors for kings and governments, we are to remind them of their accountability to the King of kings by the standards of God's word. Psalm 2 requires the rulers of the earth to do homage to the Son, and the church is to call nations to this obedience.

Related to this mandate is *The Great Commission*, another explicit New Testament commission to build Christian cultures (remembering our definition of culture). John Frame sees in the gospel Commission a clear mandate for believers:

> The Gospel creates new people, who are committed to Christ in every area of their lives. People like these will change the world. They will fill and rule the earth for the glory of Jesus. They will plant churches and establish godly families, and they will also establish hospitals, schools, arts, and sciences. That is what has happened, by God's grace. And that is what will continue to happen until Jesus comes. [44]

Now we should also note that Horton claims that there is no New Testament commission for specifically Christian education, and further suggests that we *either* discipline the church *or* the culture: "What if, instead of trying to discipline a pagan culture, we restored the evangelical practice of church discipline in our own churches." [45] We certainly need and must restore godly church discipline, for judgement begins at the house of God, but why is Christian education and discipline (both explicit in the Great Commission, Matt. 28:16–20) to be restricted to the church when Christ sends us to the nations to do it? This command is based on Christ's supreme authority over all things, given to him by the Father. To make disciples and discipline nations to obey all that Christ has commanded in his total-word is surely an *educational mandate* that inescapably transforms culture, including the nature of education. A more appropriate question would be to ask where Horton finds biblical warrant for sending Christian children to be educated by pagans in humanistic idolatry, an inescapable inference from his claim that there is no cultural mandate to develop Christian schools since these are an arena of common grace!

The neo-Marcionite tendencies in Horton's view lead also to an antinomian tone in his writing. He states, "the law can guide us in godly living, but it can never – even after we're justified – give us any life. "'Deeds not Creeds,'" means 'Law not Gospel'...just as we cannot derive any life from the law, we cannot derive any confidence in our cultural triumphs in so many fields." [46] How does one get from noting that the law is not the 'source' of life, to the conclusion that this implies we can expect no cultural triumphs in the areas the law covers? This is very contorted reasoning indeed. I agree with Horton that 'deeds not creeds' is an absurd statement from a biblical perspective, but again we have a straw man here, as though those calling for us to recognize the intended cultural impact of the faith in everyday life emphasize *doing* over against *right belief*. Biblically, you cannot have one without the other. Right practice should follow right belief. Horton also posits a sharp distinction between law and gospel (again not a Reformed perspective) as though those concerned to see righteousness in our culture are legalists seeking cultural triumph rather than gospel life.

It is certainly true that the law cannot *give* life; it is not the *source* of life, but it is portrayed in Scripture as the *way of life*, and this Horton completely fails to see (see Ps. 1:19; 119; Matt. 5:17–20; Luke 10:28), leading him to a defective view of the cultural task. Because the law has so much to say about human relations and the application of the faith to concrete issues of living, Horton has to jettison the law with the customary 'law, not gospel' mantra, to avoid its culture-making implications. Yet Jesus was the living Torah and taught the way of life in his exposition of the law in the *Sermon on the Mount*. It is most interesting to note that when Jesus is asked about how to inherit eternal life in the account of the rich young ruler he responds, "if you would *enter life*, keep the commandments" (Matt. 19:17). Since as fallen, rebellious people, we could *not* obey the commandments from a true heart without the redemption of Christ and the regenerating work of the Spirit, the law became death to us, but as St. Paul teaches, not because of any fault in the law: "so the law is holy, and the commandment is holy and righteous and good" (Rom. 7:7–14). In fact the mark of a true believer is not only right belief, but as Christ declares in Matthew 25:34-46, right action, which our Lord's brother James affirms as obedience to the law of liberty (James 1:22–27). We cannot be justified by the law, but once regenerate, what was once a bill of indictment against us, becomes our joy, delight and way of life – in this sense the law does give life, because disobedience to it is death and obedience brings life and blessing (Deut. 27,28; Rom. 6:23). The covenant law is now a gift of grace in and through Christ, obedience to which brings greatness in the kingdom of God (Matt. 5:19).

Indeed, this is the new covenant, that the law is now written onto our hearts and is now, not the *source* of life, but the *way* of life to us by the power of the Holy Spirit (Jer. 31:31–34; Heb. 8:8–12). St. Paul makes this application of the law abundantly clear when he cites the fifth commandment, "Children, obey your parents in the Lord, for this is right. Honor your father and mother (this is the first commandment with a promise), that it may go well with you and that you may *live long* in the earth" (Eph. 6:1–3). Here there is the *promise of life* and blessing in the earth, in *family culture*, for obedience to the commandments, which the Holy Spirit equips us to obey. This means of course that a culture which is conforming itself to the law of God, because of fidelity to the Christian faith, is going to be a culture which promotes and protects life, and a culture that hates the commands of God will promote death. No social commentary is needed to see the value of this point in our Western context given our dramatic lunge toward death over the last sixty years as we have abandoned God's law.

10.7   An Absent Christ – An Abandoned Culture

So what is the primary source of Horton's misunderstanding? This seems to be rooted in a most strange interpretation of the ascension of Christ, which, for Horton, justifies a philosophically naive neutralism and dualism (two kingdoms and sovereignties). It leaves space for his 'secular callings' (religiously neutral spheres) and 'common grace' (or natural theology/law) as areas where a specifically biblical and Christian approach to life is completely unnecessary, from education, to arts, politics and science. We have already dealt with the myth of neutrality, but what of this strange dualism? Horton somehow sees the primary hope of the church as located in Christ's alleged *absence* from the earth, because it focuses the church on crying out, "Even so, Lord Jesus, come quickly." Horton writes:

> The resurrection and ascension of Jesus generate a remarkable paradox. Right at the place where the suffering servant has been exalted as conquering Lord, the first fruit of a new creation, and the head of a body, *he disappears*. Then, precisely in that place that is *vacated* by the one who has ascended, a church emerges.[47]

Then speaking of the *church* and its failure to recognize this paradox adequately, he states:

> It is this recurring temptation to look away from Christ's absence – toward a false presence, often substituting itself [Church] as an extension of Christ's incarnation and reconciling work, that distracts it from directing the world's attention to Christ's *parousia in the future*. Yet a church that does not acknowledge Christ's absence is no longer focused on Christ....[48]

Whilst we can agree that there are sad examples in history of the church usurping a messianic role for itself, illegitimately claiming a kind of derivative divinity incarnate in its institutions, with a damaging conflation of church and state jurisdiction in the process, I find Horton's statements here simply staggering for an otherwise redoubtable reformed theologian. The main reason being, he makes the doctrine of the Trinity, to all intents and purposes, *invisible*. We can begin by asking how our Lord himself characterises the purpose of his ascension and departure.

Is Christ truly *absent* from his people? Is the church's hope really found in the notion that Christ is absent and we are simply to await his return and point the world to the fact he is returning? For me this is the most seriously defective part of Horton's reasoning. Horton appears to have neglected the third member of the godhead – God the Holy Spirit – altogether. In orthodox Christianity we recognize that each member of the godhead is fully representative of the others. The Son is exhaustively representative of the Father and the Spirit, and *vice versa*, one God, three persons, equally ultimate and each fully God (Col. 1:15–20; Heb. 1:1–3; John 14:7–11). One of the most incredible portions in all the gospels is Jesus' discussion of the promise of the Spirit:

> If you love me you will keep my commandments. And I will ask the Father and he will give you another Helper, to be with you forever, even the Spirit of truth, whom the world cannot receive, because it neither sees him nor knows him. You know him, for he dwells with you and will be in you. I will not leave you as orphans; *I will come to you*. Yet a little while and the world will see me no more, but you will see me. Because I live, you also will live. In that day you will know that I am in my Father, and you in me and I in you.... The helper, the Holy Spirit whom the Father will send in my name, he will teach you all things and bring to your remembrance all that I have said to you. (John 14:15–20, 26)

It is interesting that here again Jesus ties being in fellowship with him to keeping the commandments – and this is all gospel! Our Lord's promise here is that even though in the flesh he will not be seen, we will not be left as orphans, but he will come to us in the person on the Holy Spirit and be with us forever. Jesus Christ never represented his ascension as a negative absence, but as a benefit for the church and the world: "You heard me say to you, 'I am going away, and I will come to you.' If you loved me *you would have rejoiced*, because I am going to the Father, for the Father is greater than I" (John 14:28); "Behold I am sending the promise of my Father upon you. But stay in the city until you are clothed with power from on high." (Luke 24:49); "But when the Helper comes, whom I will send to you from the Father, the Spirit of truth, who proceeds from the Father, he will bear witness about me. And you also will bear witness because you have been with me from the beginning (John 15:26)."

Christ's ascension to the right hand of the Father and sitting down in the place of authority meant the universal ministry of the Holy Spirit in and through his people and in regenerating power throughout all creation. In sitting down in the place of authority, his enemies become his footstool. And all this is for the blessing of God's people and the world. The apostles were told by the Lord *not* to be taken up with the times and seasons of *parousia*, but focused them on the task (Acts 1:6–7), "but you will receive power when the Holy Spirit comes upon you, and you will be my witnesses in Jerusalem, and in all Judea and Samaria, and to the ends of the earth" (Acts 1:8). Moreover, our Lord not only did not see his physical absence as negative for the church, he saw it as *essential and positive* in his redemptive purposes. Sorrow had filled the disciples' hearts when he explained his leaving, but he comforts them saying, "I tell you the truth: it is *to your advantage that I go away*, for if I do not go away, the helper will not come to you. But if I go I will send him to you. And when he comes, he will convict the world concerning sin and righteousness and judgement...when the Spirit of truth comes, he will guide you into all truth, for he will not speak on his own authority, but whatever he hears he will speak...all that the Father has is mine; therefore I said that he will take what is mine and declare it to you" (John 16:7ff).

These incredible words could be expounded at great length but the point is clear. Christ is *not* absent. He is very present by his Spirit, and this is to our benefit. We are nowhere told to focus on the physical absence of Christ, we focus rather on his *abiding presence* with us by the Holy Spirit and the glorious task he has called us to – seeking the kingdom and bringing the rule of God to every area of our lives and to every nation, by obedience to the gospel and law of God. In his final commission, Christ tells us of his abiding presence, not absence, "behold, *I am with you always*, to the end of the age" (Matt. 28:20). In Horton's *culture of paradox*, the Holy Spirit is practically invisible and thus the glorious ascension of our Lord is transformed from the regal sitting of Christ at his Father's right hand and the *glorious procession of the Spirit upon the church*, into a tragic absence – and therefore a means of sanctifying inactivity and compromise by restricting the kingdom of God to saving souls from an alien world which God does not govern totally and consistently through His Christ. Instead God has one rule for his church and another for the world of common grace, or natural law. What is that world? Do sinners share our moral framework? No, they suppress the truth in unrighteousness (Rom. 1:18–32).

Does the realm of nature lead men to develop education and ethics, politics and science in a manner that all Christians can approve and participate in, leaving no need for Christian schools, Christian approaches to science, biblical justice and so forth? That is easily answered. Recently a humanist Bible was published called, *The Good Book* and aping the various divisions of Scripture, has a section called, "The Lawgiver," offering humanist wisdom on the source of truth and law:

> For the human mind is a kingdom in itself, and wise rulers know where the borders of their own kingdoms lie...to seek to prescribe what must be accepted as true, or rejected as false, or what opinions should actuate men is wrong. All these questions fall within a person's natural right, which he cannot abdicate even with consent... judgement can be biased in many ways, sometimes to a great degree, so that while exempt from direct external control, it may also be so dependent on another person's words, that it can be said to be ruled by him; that is the way of proselytizers, demagogues and teachers of the young and credulous, Who use their authority to fill others with beliefs and ideas of their own choosing; But although this influence carries far, it has never gone so far as to invalidate this truth: that every person's understanding is his or her own, and that minds are as diverse as palates.[49]

This is what the godless do with their moral reasoning and judgement – they assert their own autonomy, their own law, and regard their own minds as their own kingdom in replaying the fall of our first parents. In so doing they create cultures hostile to Christ; education that insists on autonomy from God in every field; law that calls good evil and evil good; and wisdom that is darkness for light (Is. 5:20). This is why the prophet Amos wrote against the lawlessness of the pagan gentile nations; it is why Jonah was sent to preach in Nineveh; it is why Christ came to establish his kingdom and the "coastlands wait for his law" (Is. 51:4–5); it is why he commissioned his church to teach the nations, in his authority, all he has commanded. Horton's two kingdoms vision is not the one seen in Scripture where the sovereign Lord, uniting all things in Christ, in heaven and earth, works all things according to the counsel of his will (Eph. 1:9–12). Christ has not, 'vacated' the world, he fills it by his Spirit. In him we live and move and exist (Acts 17:28). He fills all things in every way (Eph. 4:10).

In Horton's dismal worldview, "the church is lodged in that precarious place of ambiguity and tension between these two ages [our age and the future kingdom] until Jesus returns, relying *only* on the word and Spirit."[50] The terminology here is telling; *only* the word and *Spirit?* What kind of Trinitarianism is this? Is Christ not the eternal *Word*, the *living Word* revealed in infallible Scripture, and the *Holy Spirit* not the third person of the Godhead (fully representative of God) who is bringing the whole world into conviction of sin, righteousness and judgement (John 16:8-11)? It is *precisely because* Christ is no longer seen in the flesh that the Holy Spirit performs the work of bringing this conviction to the nations. In his sincere effort to enthrone Christ and look forward to his return, Horton gives us a low doctrine of the Spirit and emerges barely Trinitarian. For St. Paul, the ascension of Christ does not lead to academic ambiguity and tension with a limp-wristed whimper about an absent Christ, rather, *hope is ours* because the Holy Spirit has been given to us (Rom. 5:5). Moreover, "if the Spirit of him who raised Jesus from the dead dwells in you, he who raised Jesus from the dead will also give life to your mortal bodies through his Spirit who dwells in you" (Rom. 8:11). Christ dwells in us, the very hope of glory (Col. 1:27). St. Paul sums it up when he says:

> No, in all these things we are more than conquerors through him who loved us. For I am sure that neither death nor life, nor angels nor rulers, nor things present, nor things to come, nor powers, nor height nor depth, nor anything else in all creation, will be able to separate us from the love of God in Christ Jesus our Lord (Rom 8:37-39).

There is no power in heaven or earth that can absent us from Christ, nor thwart our calling and victory in him. Such a people do long for his *physical* appearing, not to remove the ambiguity of an alleged academic paradox, but to finally see our Lord face to face, to know as we are known, to hear his "well done" faithful servant, and to see the Lord Jesus deliver the kingdom to God the Father, "after destroying every rule and every authority and power" (1 Cor. 15:24). Certainly our life and mission is fraught with challenges, trials and tribulations but our Lord assures us, "take heart; I *have overcome* the world" (John 16:33).

I am certain that it is in no small part due to this faulty and widespread dual kingdom outlook that the churches in the West are often empty, in particular, of godly men (whose calling is dominion); and those who are present are often hopeless in their faith and derelict in their duty to fulfil the law-word of God in family and vocation. Instead of laying before men their calling in Christ to minister God's Kingdom life in every area, in their families and vocations, as priests unto God, they are told that their family, work, money, the education of their children and leadership in society and culture is merely a 'creation mandate' that is not related to our redemptive calling – it is 'law' not 'gospel.' Men are drilled instead to believe that the kingdom work is the work of churchmen in their institutions (the sacraments) and that their 'secular' role in life is to be kind and 'loving' at work, to be a sanctified husband and father in personal piety and then pray for the return of Christ, and if possible, on route, snatch a few brands from the burning. The Holy Spirit in this view does not fully represent the Godhead in the earth today and is unable to equip the church to fulfil Christ's final command to bear the message of salvation and the restitution of all things to the nations.

10.8 The Culture of Christ

Scripture makes abundantly clear that the Holy Spirit does fully represent the Godhead, does equip us for the task of discipling the nations and consecrating culture, and is given not just for ecclesiastical purposes but for our life in the world in every part. All our abilities are God-ordained and an aspect of our calling. God is more involved in our skills, according to his word, than we are. We cannot restrict the Spirit's gifts and callings to ecclesiastical functions and vocations. Such a view is totally unbiblical. For example, consider Exodus 31:1–11:

> The Lord said to Moses, "See, I have called by name Bezalel the son of Uri, son of Hur, of the tribe of Judah, and I have filled him with the Spirit of God, with ability and intelligence, with knowledge and all craftsmanship, to devise artistic designs, to work in gold, silver, and bronze, in cutting stones for setting, and in carving wood, to work in every craft. And behold, I have appointed with him Oholiab, the son of Ahisamach, of the tribe of Dan. And I have given to all able men ability, that they may make all that I have commanded you: the tent of meeting, and the ark of the testimony, and the mercy seat that is on it, and all the furnishings of the tent, the table and its utensils, and the pure lampstand with all its utensils, and the altar of incense, and the altar of burnt offering with all its utensils, and the basin and its

stand, and the finely worked garments, the holy garments for Aaron the priest and the garments of his sons, for their service as priests, and the anointing oil and the fragrant incense for the Holy Place. According to all that I have commanded you, they shall do.

When God calls people, he equips them with wisdom and *knowledge* for the everyday skilled tasks, and practical callings laid upon them. Also, we notice in Exodus that it is the *Spirit of God* that grants these gifts, including all manner of workmanship (v. 5). Wisdom is given in Exodus 31:6 so that the purposes of God may be accomplished right down to practical craftsmanship and manufacturing. Exodus 35:10, 25-26 also make clear that a large number of men and women were called to the work, and all their various skills are called '*wisdom.*' God is the source and author of all wisdom. Thus, all skills are a form of wisdom which come to full flower (finding meaning, value, purpose, intentionality) only in the service of God. In Philippians 1:9, Paul prays that the church will abound in wisdom and discernment to approve all that is excellent. As the giver of all wisdom, God builds everything, built beautifully. There is a universal meaning in what God builds. In the compositions of J.S. Bach there is structure, development, harmony, unity in diversity and thus universality. In a John Cage composition, there is cacophony with only limited, personal or eccentric significance. Must we not credit the Spirit of God with the gifts bestowed on a J.S Bach, and can we not see such a man anointed like a David for such a purpose in the shaping of culture for Christ?

Clearly, the Holy Spirit has not only been given to anoint church officers and give special supernatural gifts; he has also been given for a more general and specific purpose in our lives than is usually appreciated. The doctrine of calling and vocation is therefore a key aspect of the Holy Spirit's work and the reformed missiological outlook. Whatever our gifts and vocations, we are instruments of the Holy Spirit and thus partners in the work of his kingdom. The Holy Spirit is present in all our daily tasks. He is empowering us for a work, and it is he who causes us to differ (1 Cor. 4:7). The Holy Spirit is the giver of gifts which are not an end in themselves! There is a work to be done – the work of the kingdom, a partnership in the gospel, a cultural mandate to serve, work and rule. Whatever our gifts, from sculpture to banking, nursing and carpentry, all are in terms of His kingdom, "for beauty and for glory" (Ex. 28:2); and it is all to the "praise and glory of God" (Phil. 1:11).

God is building his cathedral through our partnership in the mission and he will, "bring it to completion at the day of Jesus Christ" (Phil. 1:6). Then, his new community will be perfect and complete. God began it, he will bring it to completion because it is God's work, not man's, and he will not forsake the work of his hands (Phil. 2:13). On that day, his cathedral will be finished and every artisan rewarded. Till then, our labour and partnership continues.

We are therefore called unequivocally to spread the culture of Christ to all creation. It is interesting that the Lord Jesus Christ likens himself to a farmer *planting and cultivating* his seed of the kingdom of God throughout the world (Matt. 13:1–30). He sends out his church as bearers of the imperishable *seed* of his word (1 Pt. 1:23) and he equates the results of our sowing faithfully to the reaping of a harvest (John 4:35–38), the transformation of people's lives, and finally of all creation (Col. 1:20; Rom. 8:19). The gospel of the kingdom, which we are commissioned to make known, clearly concerns our state of being.

We are either regenerate, redeemed people in Jesus Christ, or we are lost in the kingdom of darkness. The Christian state of being, like the mustard seed, grows and creates, as it has done wherever it has been in history, a type of civilization, which, seen first in the church, spreads to impact all those around it as leaven transforms the whole loaf. Wherever God is served, worshiped and glorified, there the kingdom of God is. Wherever God's children are faithful in preaching the gospel and pursue the cultural mandate, to apply God's truth to every area of life, civilizations and cultures are re-created because people's state of being is actually transformed by regeneration. We are God's new humanity in Jesus Christ and wherever God's people are, by the power and mighty working of his Spirit, the culture of Christ inescapably flourishes around them. It is this kind of faith that led the American Baptist preacher R.C. Campbell some seventy years ago to write concerning the *gospel*:

> It has made conquest of individuals, communities, nations, and continents, and leapt across oceans. It has aroused the complacent, indifferent and dying churches into virility. It has caused the breath of God to burn in souls and flame on lips. It has as its prime objective the salvation of the world. Think of the opportunity given by God to win the lost, convert sinners, reform communities, transform nations, revolutionize continents and completely evangelise the whole world! It proffers salvation, radiates sunshine, binds broken hearts, opens

prison doors, liberates captives, soothes sorrows, preaches the gospel to the poor, as it points to the lamb of God, which taketh away the sin of the world...what did Carey do for India: Start paganism on a fast retreat...The progress of Christianity can be traced by the sacrifices of those who have given themselves for its promotion.... The gospel is our supreme possession. Its power will destroy the babel towers of this world...it will send the fragments of pagan thrones and dictator crowns floating down the streams of decay...the world's security does not lie in great standing armies and navies, impregnable forts, fertile soil, gushing oil wells, bank vaults nor in vast undeveloped resources. Our security lies in the proclamation and acceptance of the gospel of Jesus Christ...just think of having by our side the one who stood upon the hill of time and saw the rise and fall of empires; rapid in their growth, colossal in their maturity, and grand in their decay...yes he who stood at the rise of a thousand governments, walks, talks and companions with and gives strength to his children as they serve him.[51]

This faith, courage and theological vision for human culture expresses well the Puritan mind that is steadily regaining strength again in evangelicalism on both sides of the Atlantic. Such a vision is inspiring because it is one of *hope* for the future – a hope that the Puritans exemplified and left for us as a rich legacy from which we can draw strength. One wonderful example is the great Puritan missionary John Eliot (1604–1690), who "strove to plant Christ's monarchy among his Christianized Indians as a model for God's rule among the nations."[52] Eliot's work, that saw thousands of conversions to Christ, establishing towns of "praying Indians" in the New World, was so influential on the Puritan mind of his day that it is said it encouraged Oliver Cromwell himself to promote the reign of Christ everywhere.[53] By 1674 he had established nineteen towns of Indian natives who had embraced the gospel and made a solemn covenant "to give themselves and their children to God to be his people as the basis of a new civil government." This government was based on biblical law in keeping with Moses and Jethro's rule by elders model in Exodus 18. These towns were completely self-governing in terms of the Christian faith.[54] His translation of the Bible into the Native American language, the *Algonquian Bible*, is considered one of his greatest achievements. English folly in King Philip's War of 1675 led to the wanton destruction of these tribes by neighbouring pagan tribes or angry colonists – John Eliot stood with them in the midst of the church is one of hope and courage, us that the life and ministry of the church is one of hope and courage, wherever it is found, transforming all around it, by the power of God. When John Eliot was one day accosted by a Native American sagamore with a knife, Eliot said,

> "I am about the work of the great God, and He is with me, so that I fear not all the sachems of the country. I'll go on, and do you touch me if you dare."[55]

The Puritans remind us that one of the great keystones of the Christian faith is hope; the Puritan mind is characterized by hope, that the work of the gospel is the highway to Zion. As Iain Murray has written, the Puritan mind: ...taught men to expect great outpourings of the Holy Spirit; it prepared the way to the new age of world-missions; and it contributed largely to that sense of destiny which came to characterize the English speaking Protestant nations. When nineteenth-century Christian leaders such as William Wilberforce viewed the world not so much as a wreck from which individual souls must escape, but rather as the property of Christ, to whose kingdom the earth and the fullness thereof must belong, their thinking bore the genuine hall-mark of the Puritan outlook[56] Perhaps nothing is in more need of recovery in our age than a gospel of hope for the future and the life-transforming power of the Holy Spirit for men, cultures and nations.

Chapter Eleven

FILL THE EARTH AND SUBDUE IT:
FAITH, FAMILY AND REVOLUTION

The family is the test of freedom; because the family is the only thing that the free man makes for himself and by himself.
— G. K. Chesterton

A household is as it were a little commonwealth, by the good government whereof God's glory may be advanced, the commonwealth which standeth of several families benefited, and all that live in that family may receive much comfort and commodity.
— Robert Cleaver

11.1 The Social Revolution

The noted Puritan Isaac Ambrose declared that a husband and wife had the privileged task of, "erecting and establishing Christ's glorious kingdom in their house."[1] Indeed, for the Puritan mind, the family was, "a school wherein the first principles and grounds of government and subjection are learned."[2] The health of the family in this regard was seen as absolutely critical not only for the church, but also for society in general because well-ordered families, "naturally produce good order in other societies. When families are under an ill discipline, all other societies [will be] ill disciplined."[3] Such a biblical vision was one that saw the family as a critical ground of life, peace, liberty, social order and human flourishing, without which civilization would collapse. This biblical heritage has been speedily jettisoned in recent decades. For over a century and a half, various forms of evolutionism have taught five generations of Westerners that the family is in fact just a primitive stage in the evolutionary process, something that needs to be *transcended* and then *abandoned* for other more enlightened and evolved forms of societal organization, making space for much greater sexual 'liberty.' In fact a few months after the death of Karl Marx, Engels wrote, "it is a peculiar fact, that with every great revolutionary movement, the question of 'free love' comes to the foreground."[4] Engels' work, *The Origin of the Family, Private Property and the State* (1884), which he claimed also represented Marx' views, involved offering an historical account of the family's origin from a primitive evolutionary past, mixed with economic forces. Marx had picked up his anti-family and communist ideas during a stay in Paris in the early 1840s where, among others, the famed socialist and utopian idealist, Charles Fourier, had been writing on the subject of the family. Historian Richard Weikart notes:

> Fourier advocated the replacement of monogamous marriage with a system allowing much greater latitude for sexual passions, since he believed that monogamy was an institution contrary to human nature and was thus an impediment to human happiness. He also proposed that children be raised communally, so society would be one, big, harmonious family...[5]

Thus the contemporary hostility to marriage and the family as regressive or repressive is nothing new and has been revived vigorously by today's cultural Marxists (the new left).

The evolutionary eugenics movement of the last century, led by some prominent feminists in North America, often advocated for the total abolition of the family.[6] The evolutionary line of thought has had various tributaries and has led us down a road toward self-destruction. The well-known reality of demographic decline in Western nations – spelling increasingly unavoidable economic decline – is just one illustration of the immediate crisis facing the West and it is a direct product of our secular hostility to God's basic institution.[7] The total fertility rate in Ontario, Canada reached its lowest level ever recorded in 2002, at 1.48 children per woman; the latest figures place it at around 1.56 (2009).[8]

In addition, the radical feminism that has informed so much of the shift in social attitude toward the family, considers the scriptural perspective a form of slavery – slavery for women. Their anti-biblical egalitarianism has feminized both church and society to such a degree[9] that many today view the Puritan (biblical) perspective on family as a draconian form of patriarchy. As a consequence, the idea that the family exists to glorify God, raise children and is in many respects to be like a church – a society of Christians governed by God's word, with Christ as head and the husband as the delegated leader of his home in loving service to God, wife and children – is anathema.[10]

Nonetheless, the historical reality is that the biblical family came onto the western scene as a *liberating force*. The pagan family was clan-based, and 'past-bound' in ancestor worship. In the ancestral clan religions of the Roman Empire a father had the power of life and death over the child and could disinherit his wife at will – misogyny and familial tyranny were the result. Ray Sutton points to the important difference between pagan and the biblical view of the family:

> The clans were the final authority about everything, even to the point of executing one of its own members should he be found guilty of some 'capital' or, or rather 'familial' offense. The church attacked this clan view...it taught that the family can only draw true life from the family of God. Build God's family, and God will save man's family...it is important however, that the biblical hierarchy of the family be theoretically and historically distinguished from the pagan patriarchal or clan family system...the clan family simply cannot compete with the biblical covenantal family. The biblical family order is supposed to replace clans and patriarchs. Abraham, Isaac and Jacob are frequently referred to as patriarchs. Biblical patriarchs yes; patriarchs of a clan system, no. When Abraham sent Ishmael away, he broke from Ishmael legally (disinherited). Ishmael no longer had to take orders from Abraham...the patriarchs in the bible were not patriarchs in the sense of men who ruled a single pyramid of families beneath them. The sons and daughters in law were not expected to live in their father's house or even nearby.[11]

Thus the Christian, biblical family, replaced the clan system. Many modern radical feminists still appeal to Marx, Engels and other nineteenth-century socialists in portraying the biblical family as a form of slavery – slavery for women. However, under biblical law, the wife was co-heir with the husband and could both inherit and rule the estate after his death; this is why in getting married in the Old Testament period a man would at the same time *legally adopt* his wife as his 'sister' and thus make her his co-heir of family inheritance.

We see this in Gen 24:1–67 and in the Song of Solomon; it also explains why Abraham told Abimelech, the King of Egypt, that Sarah (his wife) was his sister (Gen 20:1ff) – he wasn't lying, he had *legally adopted her*, but he didn't explain the whole truth of the matter. This is also the reason why today, the wife still (usually) takes the man's name – they are now as brother and sister and thus co-inheritors together.

Proverbs 31 further reveals the godly woman as a wife, mother, business woman, investor and manager. This was the common practice in the Puritan period. Christianity thus broke the arbitrary power of the father in the family and steadily conformed Western culture to biblical law. We easily forget in our time how deeply indebted we are in the West to Christianity and the biblical model of the family for our cultural stability, or legal protection of the private family and what is left of our social liberty. The rapid abandonment of God and biblical social values, accelerated by radical feminism, has sped up our social collapse and the erosion of the freedoms that rested upon them.

Now the question must be asked, if the family is undermined, and God is jettisoned, what will attempt to take their place? G.K Chesterton held that once you abandon *the* God, the greatest threat to freedom is that the *government* becomes the de-facto God. In his penetrating book, *Standing on Guard for Thee*, political scientist and social commentator Michael Wagner analyses in detail significant aspects of the history of the social revolution in Canada and its focused attack against the *family* – a revolution well underway, if not complete, in most Western countries. He notes that, "those who want the government to be the supreme power in society, unrivalled by other institutions, view the family as an obstacle to state power." [12] Leading Canadian social critic William Gairdner agrees, "[I]n our Western civilization there is an inherent and deadly conflict between *statism* and the whole idea of the *private family*." [13] In an insightful statement about the centrality of the family to every aspect of a free, healthy and viable social order Gairdner writes:

> [T]he family as an institution is at the heart of an entire social order. It is no exaggeration to say that the family is the creative engine of all the crucial values of a free and private society. So it follows that for any other social order to dominate – say, any collectivist social order – the family must first be broken down. That is why Canadians – for that matter, all those living under welfare regimes – must realise that if they have any desire to preserve the cherished life of a free society for their children and grandchildren, they first will have to recognise, then take up moral arms against, all those who wish to destroy the family. [14]

This statement is no hyperbolic exaggeration. There are powerful and organized forces at work, both natural and spiritual (if we are to take St. Paul seriously in Eph. 6:10–18), whose objective is the utter destruction of the biblical vision of the family. This in turn is the way to attack the church because, as the Puritans recognized, the church cannot substitute the family and the church's health depends in good measure upon what happens in the family. The attack on the family then, will necessarily involve first, a removal of protection for the family, its sanctity and authority. The evaporation of legal protection for the family is a relatively recent phenomenon and direct product of applied humanism and statism. All societies have and will protect their most basic and central institution with serious sanctions. As we saw in a previous chapter, in the late-modern Western world, the *state* is seen as the most central and basic institution for societal health. As a result, Canada retained the death penalty for a number of offenses against the state (such as murder of police officers and prison officials until 1976) including *treason and mutiny*, until legislation removed all reference to capital punishment on 10 December, 1998, in the wake of a growing internationalism, pursuing international law and government, courts and human rights that are even more hostile to the biblical vision of the family. The decline of legal protection for the family has thus been a steady one. In a noteworthy collapse of protection for women and the family, 1954 saw *rape* removed from the list of capital offenses; today you will almost certainly go to prison longer for seriously defrauding the CRA than for committing the heinous act of rape.

Likewise abortion was previously considered heinous. For much of the twentieth century, performing an abortion meant life imprisonment. Today, to simply pray or offer free literature highlighting alternatives to abortion to women outside abortion clinics, can lead to – and has – a prison sentence.[15] This is because the elite statist planners view children and fertility as a form of slavery for women. To endorse and give state support to the murder of the unborn attacks and breaks down the perceived rival institution to state power – the family. So-called reproductive rights are simply tyrannical laws enshrining the modern concept of sexual freedom and 'equality' for the purpose of the destruction of the biblical family. Changes to legislation in regard to both rape and abortion are manifestations then of the social revolution against the family. In another twentieth-century development, an attack upon the authority of the family was progressed by the removal of protection for the parents of incorrigible delinquents, not to mention society as a whole, when

1956 saw a parliamentary committee recommend exempting juvenile offenders from capital punishment. In 1976, Pierre Trudeau effectively achieved the complete abolition of capital punishment in the name of 'reason' and a supreme confidence in the goodness of mankind.[16] Today, the family – from taxation, to marriage and divorce law, to abortion, and to rape – has increasingly lost privilege and protection The groups seeking the abolition of the family and the growth of statism are both national and international in their reach and goals.

The essentially Marxist character of much of the modern agenda (as Gairdner earlier implied) is evident in turning the pages of Marx's *Manifesto* (the communist program had *ten new commandments*), in which, as Theodore Dalrymple shows, an open hostility to the family, and women in particular, is expressed:

> On what foundation is the present family, the bourgeois family, based? On capital, on private gain...but this state of things finds its complement in the practical absence of the family among the proletarians, and in public prostitution.... The bourgeois claptrap about the family and education, about the hallowed co-relation of parent and child, becomes all the more disgusting, the more, by the action of modern industry... the bourgeois sees in his wife a mere instrument of production.... Our bourgeois, not content with having the wives and daughters of their proletarians at their disposal, not to speak of common prostitutes, take the greatest pleasure in seducing each other's wives. Bourgeois marriage is in reality a system of wives in common and thus, at the most, what the communists might possibly be reproached with, is that they desire to introduce, in substitution for the hypocritically concealed, an openly legalized community of women.[17]

As Dalrymple notes concerning this deliberate and flagrant distortion of reality, "there is no mistaking the hatred and rage of these words."[18] Marx despised the family, and savagely caricatured it in order to destroy it. This synthetic rage in the guise of love for mankind was the real hypocrisy. A man who himself lived a 'bourgeois' existence, bohemian and 'flamboyantly squalid' had a vision for replacing the family unit that required the seizure and overthrow of its capital, property, private character and independence and a legalized community of women for sexual relations. Thus, Marx was a *parent* who, intellectually, sought the abolition of the family as a social fact. Tragically, two of his daughters, Laura and Eleanor committed suicide, in part due to his hypocritical, perpetual interference in their lives. Weikart shows that:

> Both Marx and Engels accepted...that a period of sexual promiscuity without families existed in the earliest period of human history... according to this view, in primitive society every man had sexual access to every woman and vice versa. There existed no sexual taboos or prohibitions of any kind and even incest was acceptable.... Engels once argued that this sexual community was a natural state inherited from the animal kingdom.... [W]ith naturalistic explanations such as these, Marx and Engels had shifted to a position in which, not the family, but the absence of the family, was the original and natural state of humanity.[19]

The family's development and subsequent role in history for them was only *malevolent*, "it was within the family that private property and the division of labor first developed...private property arose within the family, since women and children became slaves of men."[20] The familiar sound of feminist voices can thus be heard loud and clear here in the revolutionary clamour of mid nineteenth-century thought. For Marx and Engels as for many modern intellectuals, the monogamous family is just the most recent stage of biological and social evolution, which is in the process of being replaced with a more 'natural' and 'original' social organization (their concept of progress allegedly taking them back to nature. Unreality and death characterized Marx and every aspect of his thought since. In keeping with this, as far back as the late 1940s, international bodies such as UNESCO, in pursuit of international socialism, were promoting a rabidly anti-family agenda in the hope of breaking up first *the family* and then any sense of *national identity*, to facilitate a 'new world order' – a term many modern politicians are now using freely.[21] UNESCO stands for 'United Nations Educational Scientific and Cultural Organisation.' The framework policy for UNESCO was written by the British atheist and evolutionary eugenicist, Julian Huxley, around 1946. It was a restricted-access document for thirty years and was finally published by UNESCO in 1976 when the social planners felt the cultural waters had drifted sufficiently in their favour. In a revealing statement, having asserted the necessity of an evolutionary understanding of human nature and social order, Huxley wrote:

The unifying of traditions into a single common pool of experience, awareness and purpose is the necessary prerequisite for further major progress in human evolution. Accordingly, although *political unification in some sort of world government* will be required for the definitive attainment of this stage, unification in the *things of the mind* is not only necessary also, but it can pave the way for other types of unification.[22]

Despite the manifold failures and abuses of the UN and its various bodies, these overall objectives and plans remain unchanged. As Janet Mefferd has more than adequately shown:

The UN has been responsible for a number of horrific scandals, from the 1996 Oil for Food debacle to the peacekeeper sex-abuse scandals. It wastes millions of dollars while routinely denigrating the US and Israel. The UN upgraded the status of Palestine to that of a "non-member observer state" in the fall of 2012. This was just one of myriad examples of the UN emboldening human rights abusers. In fact, after drawing heavy criticism for putting tyrants and dictators on the former UN Commission on Human Rights, the UN created a new Human Rights Council in 2006. As of 2013 the following countries are serving on this committee, intended to protect human rights: Saudi Arabia, China, Cuba and Qatar.... Daniel Greenfield sums it up this way: "The United Nations has closed its eyes to invasions, tolerated genocide and accepted injustice. Where there is tyranny, it is timid, but where there is freedom, it is vicious...." In 1995, the *UN Commission on Global Governance* – endorsed by the UN Secretary-General and funded in part by the UN – issued a report called "Our Global Neighborhood." In it, the commission recommended "global governance" that would include the following: UN authority over the global commons; a standing UN army; a global court of criminal justice; an economic security council; and global taxation.... The UN has an ever widening global reach and presence, in both manpower and infrastructure. Its worldwide structural presence ranges from UNESCO to the World Health Organisation (WHO) to the World Bank (WB) to the International Monetary Fund (IMF).[23]

For Huxley and UNESCO the clear starting point for this utopian vision of 'world governance' is the transformation of the thinking of children in the nation's classrooms. Thus in a UNESCO paper entitled, *"In the classroom with children under thirteen years of age"* the scientific social planners write:

> As long as the child breathes the poisoned air of nationalism, education in world-mindedness can produce only rather precarious results. As we have pointed out, it is frequently the *family* which infects the child...the school should therefore use the means described earlier to combat *family attitudes.* (UNESCO 1949, 58)[24]

Such statements bear out G.K. Chesterton's chilling warning that "The government did not have such power over us when it could send men to the stake, as it does now when it can send them to the elementary school." The family, for many humanist elites, is a source of *infection* and must therefore be destroyed, for it stands in the way of total statism and its ultimate triumph in a new world order.

This agenda has been successfully propagated for decades throughout the West and we are now seeing the social consequences unfold tragically before us. First, as these UNESCO documents make clear, the goal is to eliminate the *Christian concept of the family* (as an independent sphere) and then the very idea of the nation, or *national sovereignty* – a vision aggressively pursued in the pan-European 'Union,' largely without the permission of the various national electorates. Essentially, localism of every kind must be destroyed. Such a vision can only be realized if children are taken from under the influence of their parents in the family and ideologically reprogrammed in state schools and by ideologues in the university. This vision of an equalitarian, unitary statist order of Marxist character in which the family eventually disappears is being effectively propagated in a university near you! While writing this chapter, I received the following letter from a student at York University in Toronto:

> The equity doctrine is what I've been heavily facing in my classes at York. A professor of mine last year told our class we were being judgemental imperialists because we thought that female-genital mutilation in the Democratic Republic of the Congo should be stopped. She questioned why we thought we could "impose our culture" on people in the DRC and brought up this whole idea that "No Culture is Wrong". Later, when I challenged some of the equity ideology which she was militantly imposing on us, I was marginalized as a "white-supremacist" and "perpetuator of colonial oppression." The scary part was, that, although I saw absurdity in her teaching, the

rest of my classmates had no framework from which to analyze what she taught and so they were just confused…and found her arguments to be rather impressive. *A lot of our professors see student's minds as blank slates to be written on or sponges ready to soak up whatever they give them, and they are doing their best to promote the Marxist-Leninist ideals of an egalitarian world-order. One of my TAs this year openly advocated to our class a society in which there is "no money and no families, but all are equal." And my peers are eating it up.*[25]

It is worth being reminded at this point that there is no contradiction between statism and relativism. The 'equality' of relativism is realized in and by the total state. No money and no families, where 'all are equal' is equality as defined by the state and in terms of a person's relation to the state. In the West, relativism has worked to destabilize the Christian consensus, making way for the new state orthodoxy. The state then declares the necessity for a 'referee' between competing religious and moral claims, and demands to be acknowledged as the final arbiter of pragmatic 'truth' if you want to be free to practice your private beliefs. The goal of the new Marxism is the establishment of a totalitarian world-socialism that finally leads to the disappearance of the state altogether as a utopian, equalitarian order is realized. And for Marx, this could be accomplished through the democratic process, as people vote for more and more state control.

11.2 The Sexual Revolution

Academic reprogramming in this delusional thinking is just the starting point for the scientific socialists. Huxley's 'things of the mind' must be applied and worked out in the concrete realm of the body politic, remaking all social relationships to bring about the revolution. Gairdner is right to the heart of the issue when he writes:

> [A]ll revolutionaries quickly see that to change the social order you first have to change the *sexual order*. The traditional family, after all, is a sexual, procreative entity that dictates much of our social reality (sexual roles, economic roles, socialization of gender, etc.) So by redefining the sexual nature of the family, we can redefine society itself. The long and the short of this strategy is that those who wish to engineer society in any direction must first break *all the traditional moral and religious sexual allegiances*. Sexuality must

be progressively divested of all its spiritual, procreative, and *family meanings*, divested even of its connections with romantic love...and in its place must be put an increasing emphasis on *raw sexuality* as a pure and joyous expression of the autonomous self.[26]

Thus the sexual revolution was first a cultural revolution that then became a legal revolution. As we have already seen, the first implication of the sexual revolution is that legal protection for the family is steadily removed and various offenses against it (including the sexual) go unpunished. Second, in exploiting the now-unprotected family in favour of raw sexuality, we find anarchic libertarians, Marxist educators, radical feminists, homosexual activists, pornographers, as well as the courts and statist social engineers, turning their collective guns against the family, usually in the name of rights and freedom. In 1999, the Ontario Court of Appeal outlawed the reciting of the Lord's Prayer at meetings of municipal governments in the province; the same court then declared Canada's historic and Christian definition of *marriage* 'unconstitutional.' In the name of the *Charter of Rights and Freedoms*, 2005 saw the federal government of Canada alter its historic Christian laws concerning the family and legalize same-sex marriages throughout the country. The conviction of the modern state expressed here through the judiciary is made plain by the court's ruling on the matter:

It is our view that the dignity of persons in same-sex relationships is violated by the exclusion of same-sex couples from the institution of marriage. Accordingly, we conclude that the common-law definition of marriage as "the voluntary union for life of one man and one woman to the exclusion of all others" violates s. 15(1) of the Charter. ([2003] 65 O.R. (3rd) 190).[27]

These Ontario Court of Appeal judges then took it upon themselves to *rewrite the definition of marriage* that would take effect immediately in Ontario. The magnitude of what must be grasped here is that the modern state courts, with judges trained in the humanism of the modern university, see marriage and family not as something inseparable from religion, defined by God, by revelation, and embedded in the historic practice of centuries of Western life in Christian lands, but as merely a *civil institution*, defined and governed by the authority of the state and its functionaries, as malleable and changeable as the social planners need it to be. Life is what the state declares it to be. Marriage and family are what the state declares them to be. Centuries of common-law (biblical law) practice and tradition are irrelevant to pluralists and relativists in pursuing their vision for a culture of raw sexuality. As for the preamble to the *Charter* and its mention of the 'supremacy of God,' the Supreme Court of Canada has made clear that, in our pluralistic and multicultural society, the reference to 'God' is evidently not a reference to an identifiably Christian conception of God.[28] In fact, a B.C. Court of Appeal judge called any legal argumentation attempting to revive the relevance of the Christian God to sexual ethics in Canadian life (in this case the protection of children from child pornography) via the charter, an appeal to a 'dead letter.'[29]

Emboldened by the Western courts' legal revolution, the brazen character of the assaults against the family in the cultural and social sphere of North America is at times staggering. For example, homosexual activist William Eskridge has stated that he hopes gay marriage "will dethrone the traditional family based on blood relationships in favour of families we choose."[30] Michelangelo Signorile has told activists, "fight for same sex marriage and its benefits, and then once granted, redefine the institution of marriage completely...the most subversive action lesbians and gay men can undertake...is to transform the notion of family entirely."[31] And as lesbian feminist Barbara Cox correctly noted concerning those who simply oppose their 'weddings,' "I believe they fail to look beyond the symbol and cannot see the radical claim we are making."[32] Unfortunately, Christians, including many church leaders, have been very slow to understand the radical character of what has happened in our society, and even when they do grasp it are often unwilling to say or do anything about it.

The purveyors and profiteers of raw sexuality, *the pornographers*, likewise make a similar claim about human nature and the social order. In all revolutionary sexual attitudes the goal is the overturning of the biblical concept of the family and the social order it creates, in order to replace it with anarchic raw sexuality as a 'free' act of the *autonomous individual* in rebellion against God. As R. J. Rushdoony has rightly noted concerning pornography:

> Pornography stimulates prostitution, because it requires the irresponsible use of a person in terms of the imagination. *Marital sex requires mutuality and is an aspect of a life of responsibility.* The pornographic mind finds itself progressively impotent in a responsible context and progressively potent only in an irresponsible and lawless

context, in the realm where the imagination defies the responsibilities that the external world and other people impose.[33]

The legalization and celebration of prostitution logically follow the permissive pornographic culture of our time, heralding a further assault against the family. If pornography and prostitution are considered the norm or even normative, and thus protected as 'human rights,' while the family is left exposed, one can see why modern justices and legislators are not shy about enacting their hostility toward the family. In September 2010, the *Ontario Superior Court of Justice* handed down a decision (following an earlier decision that sanctioned three-parent families), using the *Charter of Rights*, to declare that prostitution and its accompanying activities are a *legal right* protected by section 7 of the *Charter*. What was left of the law on prostitution (three provisions that criminalized some aspects of it) in Canada was intended to protect vulnerable women and their children (i.e. the family; someone's wife, daughter or child) not to mention a vestige of social decency. Now, in a time of human sex trafficking and sexual slavery in Canada, where vulnerable women are abused and exploited, pimps roam the cities, and children are exposed to neglect and abuse, 'enlightened' provincial justices consider that establishing and living off the proceeds of a brothel is a *legal right*, and sex-trade promoters celebrate their 'emancipation.'

The fleeing of mutuality, responsibility, and the familial ties of blood is also manifest, not just in pornography and prostitution, but in our culture of easy, no-fault *divorce*. Obviously the relaxing and demolition of divorce law was one of the earliest steps in our Western 'emancipation' from the family during the sexual revolution. The abandonment of legal protection for the family in our radical alteration of *divorce laws* was part of the wider transition in the law previously mentioned. In earlier Canadian life, divorce and marriage were considered matters of significant *public interest*. However, as part and parcel of the social revolution, divorce was reclassified as a purely *private matter*. Faithlessly, the church has mainly followed the lead of the culture and accepted the essential privatization of divorce as no big deal. Since Scripture is emphatic in condemning divorce (except on grounds of adultery and other serious covenant violations), one might expect to find evangelical Christians regarding divorce as a central social concern. Instead, to avoid the possible alienation of church members, it has been practically ignored. This is intimately related to the *collapse of church discipline* within Christian congregations which is, in turn, the result of culture triumphing over Scripture amongst church leaders and pastors. As a result, a privacy zone is simply assumed by most church adherents, and divorce is considered only a private matter.

A further aspect of the flight from familial responsibility is the murder of unborn children – a crime *promoted* by those who have a deep-seated hostility to the family. For the pro-choice activist, abortion sustains an alleged *right* to irresponsible sex and freedom from the responsibility of children, as well as an autonomous and unaccountable control of one's body, thereby reducing the unborn child to the status of personal *property to be disposed of at will* – a chilling reminder of the claim made by European and American slave traders about stolen Africans. For the feminist, abortion overturns the alleged 'patriarchy' that marriage and children is said to entail, (supposedly reducing the woman to a position of servitude) and frees her from male domination. For the religious environmentalist, abortion is also a means of reducing the world's 'surplus population,' regulating 'carbon emissions' and thereby 'saving' the planet; a more indifferent kind of cruelty and perverse self-righteousness is hard to imagine. For the humanistic and atheistic ideologue, abortion is a useful tool in the struggle for total statism and the abolition of the private family and property.

It is not 'chance' that both homosexuality and abortion were *decriminalized* at the *same time* in Canada, since both are tools in pursuing the abolition of the family and integral parts of the revolution against it. Henry Morgentaler, the Polish-born Canadian abortionist, having served jail-time for performing what were then *illegal abortions* (approximately 5,000 of them), recently received the *Order of Canada* (the highest civilian citation) for his alleged 'contribution' to Canada's freedoms. How? By effectively ensuring there would be no abortion law (babies can be legally aborted at full-term in our 'civilized' nation). Today, induced abortion is a common procedure experienced by nearly a third of all Canadian women during their reproductive years. However, consistently, half of all women accessing abortion are now in their twenties.[34] In the generations since the sexual revolution, abortions have clearly increased. In Ontario, York Region has an 80% abortion rate among teens aged 15-19 (2009), followed by Halton (77.9%), Peel (71.7%) and Toronto (71.7%). The Ontario average is 59.1%.[35] This is the fruit of Morgentaler's work, motivated as he was by strong atheistic and humanistic convictions in his love of death. He was founder and first president of the Humanist Association of Canada and was flagrantly hostile to the family both in his murder of the unborn and his self-confessed serial adultery.[36] Social commentator Carman Bradley writes in less than glowing terms about a truly evil man:

> Abortion on demand fits well the morality of his atheist and humanist belief system. He was not seen as a feminist but as a humanist; he loved many women and couldn't be monogamous...his first wife... refuses to speak about her former husband and has as little as possible to do with him. Just months before a tribute to Morgentaler his second wife bolted from Montreal to Chile, taking their son, Yann, with her. Yann has said this was what he himself wanted. Morgentaler's eldest child and only daughter, Goldie, cut off communications with him many years before. He is not a family man in any traditional sense of the term.[37]

These social and judicial illustrations are sufficient to demonstrate that the objective of many humanist elites in their revolutionary activism, social planning and statist politics, involves, as a necessary priority, the abolition of the private Christian family. This is a key and essential step on the road to the establishment of a radically anti-Christian social order of autonomous self-gratification, irresponsibility and hostility to life itself.

Since our time is hostile to life in its attitude toward the family it is evidently hostile to true health. We know that children do not fare well (by comparison) in single parent families. They are at much higher risk of poor physical and mental health, more likely to be abused and less likely to develop healthy adult relationships.[38] The general levels of stress, anxiety and mental health issues have massively increased in children and adults as familial structures have collapsed. The cost of trying to patch the situation in Canada is about $7 billion annually.[39] In the U.K, the costs are twice as much as alcohol abuse, smoking and obesity combined. In the United States, we now have a situation where 1 in 5 high school boys and 11% of all school children are receiving a 'medical' diagnosis of ADHD – a 41% rise in the past decade; some states in the U.S. found 23% of high school boys had ADHD diagnosis. Two thirds of these children are on stimulants like Ritalin and Adderall, in a significant number of cases leading to addiction, anxiety and even psychosis. These levels are set to increase further as the American Psychiatric Association plans to alter the fuzzy definition of ADHD (which has no definitive test) so that more people can be 'diagnosed' and 'treated.' Normal childhood behaviour is deemed pathological as struggling families seek quick remedies for moral problems.[40]

Emotional health is in steep decline as the Christian family has collapsed in Britain and North America. This is not surprising when we consider that the British Prime Minister David Cameron recently admitted that currently, at the age when British children are sitting their high school exams, they are statistically more likely to have a smartphone than a father living with them.[41] Suicide has now surpassed car crashes as the leading cause of death for Americans. More U.S. soldiers died last year by suicide than in combat. One third of America's employees suffer chronic and debilitating stress, which is increasingly thought to play a role in the progression of cancer. Eleven percent of all Americans aged twelve and older are currently taking SSRI antidepressants – mood altering psychiatric drugs with the FDA's suicidality warning label. One in four American women in their forties and fifties now take anti-depressants. One major European study concluded nearly forty per cent of Europeans are plagued with mental illness. Then there are tens of millions of users on different types of psychiatric drugs, the twenty-eight per cent of Americans with a drinking problem and twenty-two million on illegal drugs...a picture emerges of a nation of drug takers for the most part trying to cover the consequences of the moral collapse of Western culture manifest in their health.[42]

The reality is that the Christian worldview predicts such results in a culture turned toward sin and rebellion. Because God deals with all men and nations covenantally, we invoke blessing and cursing in our lives for obedience and disobedience to God. The physical order responds to moral order in terms of God's word. Creation itself was cursed due to man's sin producing thorns and thistles, and disease and death. The Canaanites are driven out of the land which 'vomits them out' for their abominations. The Hebrew's grow sick and die for their disobedience and go into exile so that the land can receive its Sabbath rest. Nebuchadnezzar loses his mind as a result of usurping the prerogatives of God. Israel's economy suffers and harvests are weak due to their failure to tithe (Malachi). Disease is the result of sexual promiscuity and perversion practiced by the pagans according to St. Paul in Romans 1. Christians get weak, some fall sick and die for coming to the Lord's table in an unworthy manner in Corinth (1 Cor. 11:30). We can no more escape God's moral order and its impact upon health in society than they could. If we would be a healthy nation, we must return to the Lord.

11.3   The Family and the Basic Powers in Society

What is the Christian called to in such a context? The Christian task is clear: we must diligently make known, by word and deed, both the mercy and justice of God in the gospel of Jesus Christ. This will mean that prophetically, in the totality of our lives, the righteousness of God is being manifest amongst believing communities. This will require that Christians have been profoundly transformed by a full-orbed, biblical gospel, so that Christian *families*, and by extension the churches, will be transformed and increasingly prepared to live faithfully to the Lord and engage contemporary culture at every level. Words, articles and speeches must be backed up by biblical faithfulness and godly work. Families and churches *recognizing* the primary issues of the social revolution is the first step, followed by faithful biblical teaching on the nature, character and centrality of marriage, children, and the responsibilities placed in the hands of the family. The transformation of culture, indeed the potential for the rebuilding of Christian civilization, that is possible through the re-establishment of the Christian family, is immeasurable. As the great Puritan, Richard Greenham wrote, "Surely if men were careful to reform themselves first, and then their own families, they should see God's manifold blessings in our land and upon church and commonwealth. For of particular persons come families; of families, towns; of towns, provinces; of provinces, whole realms." [43]

History backs up the Puritan claim for the power and centrality of the biblical family, under God, for the common good. Part of the story of how we came to the Christian revolution in the life of the family and the force of power it became for transforming the West, providing freedom and promoting prosperity, is a largely neglected one. Many have never heard the account of the *Empress Theodora*. Born in the early sixth century, her father was an animal trainer for the Roman arena. He died when his daughters were still very young, six, eight and ten respectively. Theodora was just eight years old. There was no provision made for the children and so after their father's death, they were sold, at this tender age, into prostitution; a cruel, ugly and bitter life. By her teens Theodora was a high-price prostitute and accompanied a businessman into North Africa on a business trip. He became angry with her and abandoned her, and as a result, she soon became seriously ill. A Christian presbyter and his family took her in, and took responsibility for her nursing care and they began to daily teach her the Scriptures. Although not converted straight away, within one year she was back in the capital of the empire and thinking seriously about the Christian faith. During that time she became acquainted with a young lawyer who was the nephew of a powerful general of the Roman armies. Subsequently, they fell in love and married. In a remarkable turn of events, the Roman emperor died childless. To prevent civil war over succession, before his death, he made the old warrior general, Justin, the emperor, and when shortly after, the old general Justin died, his nephew and heir, Justinian (the young lawyer married to Theodora), became emperor. Consequently, Theodora, the girl sold into sexual slavery at about eight years old became, in her twenties, the empress of the Roman Empire and a devout Christian.

When Justinian (another devout Christian) later called for the recodification of all Roman law, it is clear that Theodora's powerful public and behind-the-scenes influence upon her husband was significant in directing the lawyers to ensure that the legal reforms were generally in conformity to the Law of God. Concerning that influence, Theodora scholar, James Allan Evans, Professor Emeritus of Classics at the University of British Columbia, notes that "in the senate, Justinian and Theodora would argue questions from different viewpoints while the senators listened, but it was suspected that they agreed beforehand which of them would win the debate."[44] Theodora's social reforms for prostitutes and work with women is well documented, though her interests and impact was wide ranging. "Justinian acknowledged openly that he consulted his wife about a regulation that prohibited the purchase of public office.... But there is a group of laws issued by Justinian that deal with matters that must have been closer to Theodora's heart, and although Justinian does not make any specific indication that he consulted her, we can rest assured that if he took advice on secular simony he sought it as well on these."[45] These laws essentially had to do with the status of women and *family law*. She wanted to ensure that what the Bible had to say about the family be written into the law of the empire, which was a promiscuous culture, hostile to women, placing arbitrary power in the hands of husbands and fathers. Prior to Justinian's reforms the family had limited status in Roman law. If a man died, it was common for the family to be tossed out into the street the next day or for the widow to lose custody of her children. The husband might have made a contract with a friend or mistress (concubine) in which all his possessions were alienated and thereby left to them or illegitimate children. Theodora's influence can be clearly seen in a group of laws intended to improve women's legal rights; as Evans points out, "she must have inspired directly or indirectly the legislation that sought to erase barriers to marriage between unequals in rank... 'In service of God, there is no male nor female, nor freeman nor slave.' So wrote Justinian in a law dating to 535, and it was probably his respect for Theodora that led him to this view." [46] Roman law under the influence of Christianity had been slowly yet significantly changing prior to this time, but Justinian's reforms were a climactic culmination and conclusion to the social and legal impact of the growing faith. Theodora was no proto-feminist, but she was a woman clearly acting in the biblical tradition that taught compassion for the weak and helpless and which saw male and female as equal in the eyes of God. [47] Evans' conclusion is telling regarding this remarkable woman, whose rags-to-riches story saw a former prostitute attending imperial councils and debating questions with the emperor in the senate, leading to a life-long nuanced participation in the work of government:

> Justinian promulgated a number of measures to amend the double standard for men and women of the Roman legal system. A woman had had the right to conduct her own business without a male guardian since the reign of Constantine; with Justinian, the right was extended: a widow could now be the guardian of her own children. Women's property rights were recognized. The rules were made the same for dowries and antenuptial donations. There is a concern for public morality in Justinian's legislation on marriage and the family that probably owes something to Theodora. Divorce by mutual consent could no longer be tolerated; instead Justinian listed the legitimate grounds for separation of man and wife. A husband had the right to kill his wife's lover but only after he had sent him three written warnings, duly witnessed. Adultery remained a crime.... A wife caught in adultery might no longer be slain but would be shut up in a convent, and she could leave only if her husband pardoned her within two years. There is both a dislike of the death penalty and a

streak of puritanism in Justinian's family law. We cannot guess at the exact degree of Theodora's input, but we can be certain that as long as she was alive these laws were a product of her discussions and debates with her husband.[48]

All this reform was broadly in keeping with the law given to Moses and it produced one of the greatest legal revolutions in the history of the world. In light of this we can see that what is going on in Western society today through education, the courts and governmental social engineering is a revolutionary effort to undo what Justinian and Theodora, by their remarkable partnership, accomplished by the grace of God.[49]

When we analyse culture we see that there are *three* basic powers in any society. The humanistic revolution we have been analyzing aims at the seizure and use these basic powers, placing them in the hands of the state. The first is the *control of children*. This is absolutely critical because to influence, guide and mould children is to govern the course of the future. This is one of the key reasons why modern state educational strategies, oftentimes seek to alienate children from their parents, religiously, generationally, ethically and relationally. As just one practical example of this alienation of parent from child in Canada, a child as young as fourteen in public school may become pregnant and report it to a teacher. Legally, she can be counselled and sent to an abortion clinic without even consulting the parents, and without the parents ever knowing their daughter was pregnant.[50] Furthermore, Christians often fail to appreciate that humanistic sociologists and educators have *invented* the sociological concept of the 'teenager' (or adolescence), with inevitable expectations of rebellion and sexual experimentation in order to destabilize the family, alter the beliefs of the young and alienate them from the morality and thinking of their parents.[51] This alteration of the thinking of children leads to what we call today 'the generation gap,' and the rapid creation of 'cultural generations' every seven years or so, artificially accelerates this sense of alienation. The control of children then is one of the three greatest powers in any society because it shapes the course of the future. The question is simply whose vision of the future is to govern our children and families.

The second basic power in society is the *control of property*. In biblical law, and through the Empress Theodora in the Western legal tradition, the control of property is given to the family. The father could not dispossess the legitimate children or wife. The wife was given a

420

legal right to the family property in order to preserve and provide for the family. Socialistic legislators and planners have sought to alter these laws in the modern context in terms of taxation (property taxes, inheritance taxes etc.) but still in its basic form, property is tied to the family. Thus the control of wealth is, like the control of children, given by God to the family, enshrined in our law from the time of the Justinian code and on through the Western legal tradition, deeply influenced as it was by the Reformation.

The third great power in society is *inheritance*. Inheritance is also tied, in the Bible and the history of Christendom, to the family. Scripture gives us laws of inheritance (Deut. 21:17; 2 Kings 2:9). The eldest godly child is to receive a double portion of inheritance. In return is the expectation that they will take responsibility for the care of their parents (Matt. 15:5–6). God expects that parents will leave their children an inheritance as an aspect of a godly family life: "A good man leaves an inheritance to his children's children" (Prov. 13:22). Today, through taxation, the modern state is increasingly claiming inheritance, as the usurping 'firstborn.' In Britain for example (though not presently in Canada), through the most iniquitous of all taxes, after a pitifully low tax-free ceiling, the state demands forty per cent of the inheritance before the children receive anything. Most families have to sell their estates (large or small) just to pay the inheritance taxes. This is state-sanctioned theft on a grand scale, through a confiscatory and redistributive system designed to strip the family of property and power, enriching instead the bureaucracy of the modern state, the new provider of welfare and security. This is deliberately designed to usurp the status, significance and authority of the family. The state thus claims to be the new integrating concept, the new surrogate family, the source of provision and welfare.

Yet critically, the biblical family is history's most important welfare agency. Every family supports the children usually until through university, which is a form of welfare. All that a family does and provides for itself is a form of welfare. Remove the family and think of the costs to the state; the breakdown of the family has cost the modern welfare state untold billions. Biblically, the responsibility for the nurture of children, the care of the elderly, of relatives, of parents, given to the family, means that the family's influence and power is staggering. The family provides motivation, guidance, and instruction. It is the first school, government and vocation of every human being. Subsidies come to couples, when they get married, from the family to help them establish themselves with a growing degree of independence. For example, my parents-in-law helped my wife and I raise the significant deposit to buy our first home. Tithes and offerings and charity come from the family. Quite simply, the family has great power for good toward the well-being of society and it has power in the church and through the church. That is why to attack the family is the surest way to destroy Christianity in a culture or nation and it is why the family must be protected and fought for. For without the Christian family, the church is destroyed. The spiritual enemy of the faith knows this very well. It is Satan who inspires ideologies of hatred toward the family in order to destroy both it and the church, and thus degrade human society with a descent into sexual anarchy. Modern Canada is living proof that you progressively destroy society, if you undermine the Christian conception of family.

It has been shown over and over that the family is a vital and determining force in the lives of children. It is neither ethnicity, nor economic status which determines success, but the family. It has become a social crime to say so (politically incorrect) but study after study in Western countries has shown again and again that a stable family is the key to the well-being and success of children and students at every level and in every area. One study conducted in the U.K. published their findings in a report called "Breakdown Britain." This study like so many others (including the massive U.S. *Coleman Report* during the presidency of John F. Kennedy) found that the family was *determinative* for the success of children. The relatively recent U.K. report found that the common cause of academic failure, depression, drug use, violence, and criminality was *fatherlessness*.[52]

Modern humanistic man has abdicated his responsibility and calling with regard to the family, fled godly responsibility and thereby robbed himself of blessing. As a consequence we are producing a culture of vogue men who do not want to be responsible providers and leaders in the home, loving, training and teaching their children. The model 'man' of our time is the childish playboy who cannot grow out of puberty; unable to commit, selfish, irresponsible and derelict in duty. Hence we have more than fifty per cent (sometimes as high as seventy per cent in some parts of Western Europe) of children growing up in a home with only one parent. The Canadian press recently reported that the traditional family is now the minority type of family in Canada. Only thirty-nine per cent of families now have a married mother and father with children. This spells social disaster and chaos for the future unless the church rises up to its responsibilities.

With this decay of the family come the suicidal inclinations of our time. Ideas such as zero population growth, and fanatical religious environmentalism that sees human beings as a virus or pest destroying the biosphere with Mother Nature poised, getting ready to wipe out this infectious outbreak, are a mark of our madness. And tragically, as a result, our children in Canada are growing up in increasing despair, with suicide being the second leading cause of death among young people aged fifteen to twenty-four, and the leading cause of death for young men aged twenty-five to twenty-nine.

However, for biblically faithful Christians, there is a victory that overcomes the thinking and patterns of this world – our faith (1 John 5:4). Most of the church down through the centuries was converted out of all this mess and brought to a living hope in Jesus Christ. The grace of God redeems men and women from a destructive way of life that leads to death, forgives us for the sins and failures of the past, and empowers us for a life of conformity to the image of Christ – our consciences washed, sprinkled clean by his substitutionary death and resurrection life. This is the glory of the gospel for every believer. Today Christians may, like many Christians in centuries past, have failed God's calling in the family, in marriage, or as parents, and sinned against God in adultery, abortion or same-sex practices. Yet the God the Bible speaks of is a God of restoration, redemption and renewal, where genuine repentance and faith are active. It is certainly the case that all the consequences of sinful actions don't just magically disappear when a person is converted and places faith in Christ, but the believer is enabled to turn their backs upon sin and death, and by the Holy Spirit see all things be made new. As St. Paul put it so clearly:

> Or do you not know that the unrighteous will not inherit the kingdom of God? Do not be deceived: neither the sexually immoral, nor idolaters, nor adulterers, nor men who practice homosexuality, nor thieves, nor the greedy, nor drunkards, nor revilers, nor swindlers, will inherit the kingdom of God. *And such were some of you. But you were washed, you were sanctified, you were justified in the name of the Lord Jesus Christ and by the Spirit of our God.* (1 Cor. 6:9–11)

Our message as the church in a decadent age must be that Christ is the only source of justification and renewal. The church is a place where, 'such *were* some of us' yet we have been washed, set apart and made right with God. Whilst cultural challenges abound, God is also at work in remarkable ways. As believers return to God's Word, a quiet revival of family life can and is taking place as increasingly Christian people are realizing the necessity for taking responsibility for the family. Christian schools and home schools are springing up in reaction to the decaying state system. Parents are beginning to strengthen the ties of the Christian family in a multiplicity of ways.

One critical key to the future and godly responsibility, which the church must understand in our time, is the need to develop and empower the Christian family, to recover the welfare aspects of the ministry of the family; to establish Christian schools and agencies, private charities and organizations to bring all things into captivity to Christ. When the family is again basic to society under God's Word, where spouses are faithful to the marriage covenant, where children obey their parents in the Lord, and as they grow into adulthood, honour the family, we are promised by God himself, life and blessing as the pattern and character of the life of a people (Eph. 6:1–4). God promises us in this text that it "will be well with you" (or you shall be blessed and made strong), and that you may have long life. The evil tide described in this chapter that has broke upon our land can be turned back by simple faithfulness, courage and hope. The key to godly transformation, the key to the future, is in our homes, as individuals living in humble obedience to Christ and as families saying, "as for me and my house, we will serve the Lord" (Josh. 24:14–15). This is the key to the flourishing of the kingdom of God.

Chapter Twelve

LET MY CHILDREN GO:
THE CHRISTIAN MANDATE TO EDUCATE

The end then of learning is to repair the ruins of our first parents by regaining to know God aright, and out of that knowledge to love him, to imitate him, to be like him.

– John Milton

Above all, the foremost reading for everybody, both in the universities and in the schools, should be Holy Scripture.... I would advise no one to send his child where the Holy Scriptures are not supreme.

– Martin Luther

12.1 Education: A Christian Heritage and Calling

T. S. Eliot observed concerning education what upon reflection becomes plainly evident, that "we derive our theory of education from our philosophy of life. The problem turns out to be a religious problem."[1] It is therefore a most remarkable fact that leading authors within contemporary missiology have given scant attention to the critically important issues of a philosophy of education and education as mission. In their analysis of the *Missio Dei* and *reign of God*, missiologists considering the Western situation have largely ignored the decline of Christian education and the rise of a humanistic public education.[2] When one considers the role of schools in the history of Christianity generally, and in the West specifically, this is a serious oversight. It is also remarkable because it is a truism to say that those who govern the minds of the young, direct the course of the future of civilization. As such, few things can be ranked in importance alongside education as a top priority for Christian analysis and biblical application.

The Puritan Ebenezer Pemberton said that "when ignorance and barbarity invade a generation, their glory is laid in the dust."[3] Few level-headed historians would deny that the former glories of Christendom are lying in the dust today, and it is this author's contention that one of the critical reasons for the present decadence is the collapse of Christian

425

education in our culture. It only takes a generation or two of defective and anti-Christian education to create a culture of barbarians (rootless ones). Given this fact, throughout church history, until very recently, Christians had seen education as a primary avenue for applying the *reign of God*, and a key arena for the building of a Christian world and life view. We see from the Old Testament period that the *family* was the first educational institution amongst the Hebrews as Deut 6: 4-9 makes clear. Mother and father taught the children and the Mosaic law was memorized whilst the son was also apprenticed in his father's trade. The Levites functioned as teachers and educators training both the priests and the people in God's law. After the Hebrews settled in Canaan prophets began teaching the people as well. Reading and writing were obviously important so that the law of God could be understood and applied by all.

During and after the Babylonian exile, people being disjoint from the Temple, the synagogue arose, and they developed a system of schools, giving Judaism a strong organizational and institutional basis. The primary purpose of the synagogue was instruction and study. After instruction at home till the age of six, the children received teaching at the synagogue and attendance was made compulsory from A.D 64 by the order of the Jewish High Priest, in the final days of the Temple, Joshua ben Gamala. The education was free and universal making elementary education available to all regardless of economic ability. Even class sizes were regulated as the students learned writing and arithmetic and mastered parts of the Psalms, creation and the Levitical law – the book of Leviticus was actually the first subject learned. They also studied the Mishnah (oral law) and Talmud (Mishnah and Gemara – a commentary on the Mishnah). We see in the New Testament that these synagogues were fertile soil for apostolic preaching and teaching in the first century, as witness Acts 17:11.

With the diaspora amongst the Greeks, Hellenistic Jews also adapted Greek educational practices to fit their educational purposes. In the early church, the synagogue model of education was largely adopted by Christians. The church in Alexandria (a city founded on the Mediterranean cost of Egypt by Alexander the Great) developed a ministry of catechetical instruction from the beginning – the first mention of a Christian school there dates from the second century. In A.D. 179, Pantaenus, a converted stoic, developed a broad curriculum covering a wide array of subjects that proved critical in the historic development of

Christian education. Moreover, all ages and both sexes were educated. Historians Reed and Prevost note concerning this school:

> Students confronted Greco-Roman classics, philosophers and academic disciplines. They were equipped to converse with the most educated non-Christians. Such conversation was necessary to the propagation and preservation of the gospel. They were taught that there was nothing to fear from open and honest inquiry into all thought and that such inquiry could serve a missionary and apologetic purpose. Clement of Alexandria (ca. 150-215) succeeded Pantaenus as the head of the school between A.D 190-200.[4]

Clement added rhetoric to the curriculum and was likely paid from voluntary fees and gifts from patrons. With the eventual legalization of Christianity in the empire, there were many benefits for Christian education. The institutional church, education and government became more involved with each other as the early Middle Ages dawned. The early monasteries required careful learning to study scripture. The monks not only read, but copied manuscripts and calculated dates for festivals. In the *scriptorium* they made books and copied scripture – their work was sophisticated and highly specialized. The *library* was an *educational facility* in the monastery, some of which accumulated hundreds and even thousands of titles. Duplicates were collected and exchanged through the work of the scriptorium. It is indisputable to say that monasteries produced many of the finest scholars of the middle Ages. The leading thinkers of Western Europe largely receiving their education in monasteries for hundreds of years. Out of this was born not only the parish school but the Christian University, still a pillar of Western civilization and the highest achievement of medieval Europe. The origin of the university was essentially church schooling.

With biblical faith increasingly actuating people and because of the centrality of Scripture, reformed Christianity in particular led incontrovertibly to the great advancement of literacy, printing, and the founding of schools and universities throughout the Western world. As one example, 2011 marked the 500th anniversary of the life and ministry of the great reformer Pierre Viret, long-time friend and co-labourer with John Calvin. In Lausanne, Viret began the first Protestant and Reformed academy of the French-speaking world, in January 1537. This academy had great instructors from across Europe, with Theodore de Beze as the principal for nine years. Many great Christian leaders received their training there, including the authors of the Heidelberg Catechism of 1562 and the Belgic Confession of 1561. Calvin's own academy in Geneva likewise equipped Christians from all over Europe to take a faith committed to education everywhere, including the British Isles, through men like John Knox, the father of Puritanism, whose Calvinist parliament pioneered a nation-wide Christian education. Knox admonished the Great Council of Scotland that "your honours be most careful for the virtuous education and godly upbringing of the youth of this realm...for the advancement of Christ's glory."[5]

It was again the Puritans who in the commonwealth and colonies did so much to advance a vision for Christian education to advance the reign of God. As Ryken has noted, "Modern historians of education credit the Puritans with great educational accomplishments. One of them says that 'in several respects the Commonwealth was a period when university studies reached a peak.'"[6] Indeed the founding of schools and universities was one of the hallmarks of Puritanism; Harvard University in Boston, and Durham University, stand as testimony to the Puritan's educational legacy. Oliver Cromwell founded numerous elementary schools and sent commissioners throughout the country to research the educational needs. It is of interest that it was radical Protestants called 'sectaries' in England, and their counterparts known as 'antinomians'(anti-law) in the American colonies, who attacked the Puritan emphasis on a robust Christian education – they were anti-intellectual, seeing faith and reason, or faith and knowledge as antagonistic to each other. But the Puritan biblical faith could not divide God's creation and rule into two realms, that of faith and a so-called secular realm, with reason or common assumptions governing one and faith commitments governing the other. Rather they saw all knowledge as an integrated whole under God (revelation in creation and in Scripture) where everything was to be studied and understood in light of the foundation of God's word. There was no division between the spiritual and the natural. As one rule at the early Harvard College made plain:

> Let every student be plainly instructed and earnestly pressed to consider well the main end of his life and studies is to know God and Jesus Christ which is eternal life, John 17:3, and therefore to lay Christ in the bottom, as the only foundation of all sound knowledge and learning.[7]

One of the ways of defeating the work of Satan was, they believed, a Christ-centred education. This was ultimately the responsibility of parents; schools were to be an extension of (but not a substitute for) the teaching of the home in the word of God and Christian doctrine. The Bible was thus at the heart of the Puritan curriculum so that Scripture reading and biblical theology were seen as the integrating foundation of all thought. In fact, "the Puritan's aim in the classroom was to measure all human knowledge by the standard of biblical truth." [8] Ultimately, the goal of education was to make a person a whole and mature Christian, who, in the process of sanctification comes not only to share in the character of God ethically, but to share also his love of truth and beauty, thinking his thoughts after him. Influenced as they were by Luther and Calvin, the Puritans advocated what we call the liberal arts curriculum (a classical educational model). They advanced seven liberal arts that they characterized as a circle of seven sections with God as the centre. Certainly their model was not without fault and was at times insufficiently critical of classical thought and culture, with elements of scholasticism creeping in. Due to the influence of the Renaissance, men like Aristotle and other Greek thinkers were evidently accorded too significant a place. However, their basic orientation, goal and practice, was a self-conscious surrender to Scripture as authoritative over every area of thought, even if in places this desire was inadequately applied. Their passion for learning was largely driven by a dual awareness that first, all truth comes from God and so rightly apprehended must lead back to him, and second, that education is a fundamentally religious task and is the surest means to transform the values of a culture.

Whilst this reformed view of education might seem radical to many Christians today, it is only our loss of contact with our evangelical heritage and an uncritical adoption of progressivist, statist education that makes it seem alien. A full-orbed Christian education is the logical outworking of biblical faith in obedience to the command to raise our children in the fear and admonition of the Lord (Eph. 6:4). In the biblical worldview children belong to God and parents are stewards charged with their care (Ex. 13:2; 34:19; Ps. 24:1–2; Ps. 127:3). As Christian parents, privileged partakers in the covenant of grace, we have a double responsibility and obligation to ensure that our children are educated in a God-glorifying and Christ-centred manner (Deut. 4:9–10; 6:4–9; Matt. 18:6; Mark 9: 42).

12.2   Education: A Religious Function

Education is therefore an inescapably religious task because it grows out of our philosophy of life and as such is implicitly grounded in religious assumptions. It is either the ignorance of an untaught church, or simply faithlessness and disobedience to God's word on the part of many Christians in the West today when they refuse to acknowledge or recognize that the content of their child's education is plainly religious and that their young ones are either being instructed in the truth or indoctrinated with anti-biblical premises and faith. This religious character of education has been repeatedly pointed out by many non-evangelical thinkers and philosophers. Perhaps the most noted of all Canadian political philosophers, George Grant, highlighted the relationship between religion and education and noted that there is no escape from religious assumptions and indoctrination:

> The origin of the word [religion] is, of course, shrouded in uncertainty, but the most likely account is that it arises from the Latin "to bind together." It is in this sense that I intend to use it. That is, as that system of belief (whether true or false) which binds together the life of individuals and gives to those lives whatever consistency of purpose they may have. Such a use implies that I would describe liberal humanists or Marxists as religious people; indeed that I would say all persons (in so far as they are rational beings) are religious.... Indeed the present controversy is not concerned with whether religion should be taught in schools, but rather with what should be the content of the religion that is so taught. It is perfectly clear that in all North American state schools religion is already taught in the form of what may best be called "the religion of democracy." That the teaching about the virtues of democracy is religion and not political philosophy is clearly seen from the fact that the young people are expected to accept this on faith and cannot possibly at their age be able to prove the superiority of democracy to other forms of government (if indeed this can be done). The fact that those liberals who most object to any teaching about the deity are generally most insistent that the virtues of democracy be taught, should make us aware that what is at issue is not religion in general, but the content of the religion to be taught.[9]

Because Christians have largely accepted the status quo and watched, over the past decades, as the remnants of the Christian faith have been expunged from public education and replaced with a new religion, it is not easy for believers (perhaps especially pastors) to accept that the decline of the faith, the emptying of the church and its failing influence in culture has been inadvertently supported by Christians unwilling to speak to the issue of education or withdraw their children from public schools. Worse, some Christians when challenged on this point will often go on the defensive, loudly proclaiming the wonderful merits of 'free' public education, or will spiritualize their theological ignorance (or unfaithfulness) as a desire to be 'salt and light,' criticizing Christians who dare to question the state system or their personal educational decision. The reformed critic, Rushdoony, who was instrumental in the defence of Christian schools and home schools in the courts of the United States, and whose books on education helped launch the Christian school movement there, concurs with George Grant in his analysis of the relationship of religion to education:

> Education has always been a religious function of society and closely linked to its religion. When a state takes over the responsibilities for education from the church or from Christian parents, the state has not thereby disowned all religions but simply disestablished Christianity in favour of its own statist religion, usually a form of humanism.[10]

At the heart of the religious nature of education is the question of the nature of man. The doctrine of man is a faith postulate and it shapes the character of society and thereby education generally. We condition children in terms of a view of their nature and the role in life that idea of nature gives them. So the question is: what is their nature and what is the goal of their conditioning? Today, the state-sanctioned view in the public schools is that human beings are advanced animals, and along with pagans like Plato, affirms we are political animals. According to modern neo-pagan educational doctrine we have evolved by chance from the void and can ascertain no ultimate meaning or purpose beyond that which we can determine and decide for ourselves – meaning is ephemeral. This is essentially a return to an ancient pagan religious understanding of reality that seeks to disconnect knowledge from God:

> Greek thought regarded the universe, not with the principle of discontinuity held to by biblical thought, but in terms of continuity. There was no radical distinction between Creator and creature, God and man, but rather a scale of being, with differing degrees of

participation in being. Man's autonomous reason was capable both of understanding and participating in this scale of being. There was no conception of God as self-sufficient and absolutely independent, nor was there a true concept of creation; neither was it necessary to know God in order to interpret creation. The human mind, freely and independently, was regarded as capable of knowing reality and understanding all the facts without reference to God.... [B]ecause Greek thought had no conception of an independent and self-sufficient God who is the source of all true authority, it could not develop the authority of this God-related reason. For the Greeks, authority came from the Polis [city state], not from God.[11]

Education and the social order have today returned to this essential point. As a religious faith, it is held there is no triune and sovereign God over man (made in God's image) and no source of authority outside man's own mind; a mind which participates in the becoming of cosmic evolution (being in general). Since man does not need God to know the 'facts,' each man can independently interpret reality. But in such a contest of wits, no unity can be accomplished for the social order without a replacement source of authority – the state or polis. We thus return to the pagan Greek philosophers' vision. The state becomes the basic institution and the essential *educational* institution. Education is then the vehicle of state activism, by which the 'political animal' is moulded to adopt the state's religious vision of the future. This naturally leads to the notion that since the state is the locus of authority, guiding the process of 'becoming' in the child that is a product of nature, it must also be a salvific institution. In order to 'save' people from themselves and their ignorance, the state and its educational apparatus becomes the new redeeming order; the classroom is the new pulpit, the curriculum the new bible, and the state educators the new priesthood. State education becomes the new cure-all for sin, crime, emotional and mental health problems, social disintegration and economic disparity – in short the means of social salvation. Instead of God in Christ regenerating people, transforming them by the Spirit and the word, humanistic state education becomes the primary means of moral reformation, the development of virtue, and the diffusion of human knowledge, remaking the individual to become useful citizens of the polis. It is therefore no surprise to find that the Tenth Point of Karl Marx's *Communist Manifesto* was a demand for free, state schools. For all utopians this has been the only means whereby society could be controlled, allowing 'nature' to reach its goal. It is therefore noteworthy that the advent of state education in the United States was directly related to the *breakdown* of Puritanism. The schools steadily fell into the hands of anti-Puritan forces that saw in the public schools "a new religion and a new established church whereby the commonwealths could be regenerated and sanctified."[12]

Clearly then, education is a religious endeavour in which there is no neutral stance. In Western education today our concept of ourselves is decidedly man-centred rather than God-centred. Our allegiance having shifted from God to self, a tremendous and crushing burden is placed on each individual, to play God or *delegate ultimate decisions* about life and reality to others – the delegation to 'the other' in our time is without doubt to the state and its schools, the new umpire to bring about the acquiescence of the autonomous masses. The result of such relativism is a growing social confusion and chaos. Inevitably in response, a growing regulatory state is seen as necessary to enforce a humanistic religious consensus, a 'collective will' through the control of the educational establishment. Education has plunged downward into humanism in Canada (and the West) for decades since Egerton Ryerson, the chief superintendent of education for Ontario from 1844, described Christianity as the all-pervading principle of Canadian life. But even then, what passed for non-sectarian Protestant Christianity in the schools consisted, inconsistently from one school to the next, of Bible reading, prayer and the Ten Commandments, not a strong emphasis on biblical doctrine or a clear explanation and defence of the Christian worldview (as valuable as the other instruction was). Political scientist Michael Wagner has convincingly shown that the decisive influence of Christianity on public education had waned by the 1960s and 1970s, and was completely uprooted by the *Charter of Rights and Freedoms*, applied as it was to education in a series of subsequent court rulings.[13] Having begun firmly in Christian foundations – where teachers were expected until the late sixties (according to Ontario's Mackay Committee in 1969) to "bring home to pupils, as far as their capacity allows, the fundamental truths of Christianity and their bearing on human life and thought"[14] – by the 1980s the Canadian court's guns were turned on what was left of Bible reading and prayer in public schools. The Christian faith was now banished: "On December 6, 1990, the Ontario Ministry of Education issued a memorandum ordering all public schools to end any indoctrination in a religious faith. Regulations governing education were changed accordingly. The era of Christianity in Ontario's public schools was over."[15]

Of course, the meaning of the demand to end indoctrination in a religious faith was merely the repudiation of Christianity in favour of indoctrination in the religion of humanism and democracy. In light of this seismic change, the typical missiological strategy of simply trying to 'win elections' to bring 'top-down' change in education in such an apostate context is to shut the gate when the horse has bolted, is long out of sight and now many furlongs away. A social revolution has already taken place in North America and Western Europe, and therefore effective change for Christ's kingdom and reign will not come about simply by direct political action or an activism to get Christians onto school boards (as helpful as that can be in slowing decline). The notion that lasting change can take place top down, and not by regeneration and faithful Christian schooling at the grassroots, has proven mythical. To transform the course of the future, the minds of the young must be regained and captivated by Christ and his word at the local and private level, and this involves the necessary recovery of Christian schools and a distinctly Christian education.

12.3 The Myth of Neutrality: The Purpose of Education

The re-emergence and dominance of the pagan doctrine of man as a brute coming up from the void has so infiltrated education for decades that many Christians are unaware of the way they have been affected by this mythology, and are unconscious of its impact upon the theory of knowledge and its far-reaching implications for education. The infiltration of the church by Greek dualism, especially since the Enlightenment (discussed in chapter two), has also meant the severing of the connection between God (the alleged realm of faith and spirituality) and history or facts of experience (the realm of nature and matter), resulting in an implicit separation of true education from God and Scripture. The result has been the widespread idea among believers that education can be *neutral*. Consequently, a non-Christian education supposedly represents no threat to Christian truth and freedom, or the teaching of God's word – the alleged 'realms of faith.' Nor, it is thought, will a 'neutral' education damage God's little ones in the public schools.

Neutrality however is a *myth*, a by-product of humanistic and pagan thought, because humanistic thought pre-supposes a cosmos of autonomous, self-generated and therefore meaningless factuality, that is, meaningless 'bits of reality' coming up from the void. The facts are meaningless because, from atoms to antelopes there is no sovereign creator and predestinating God distinct from the universe, and therefore no overarching design-plan that precedes existence and history; there is no pre-established relationship between the properties of the universe. Reality is therefore impervious to interpretation, because what *is*, is not rationally related. With respect to humanity, the human person has no definitive essence that precedes experience in the world – there is no God-given definition of personhood. The 'facts' are therefore uncreated, undirected and thus ultimately unrelated to any other fact; all facts are consequently, for the humanistic, pagan mind, 'neutral.'

The term neutral comes from the Latin 'neuter,' meaning 'neither one nor the other.' A neutered man is called a eunuch because in the full sense of the term he is no longer fully male, yet not female. The term has since come to mean an unbiased position, or an unwillingness to take sides. Now it is quite clear from the very origin of the concept, that an allegedly 'neutral' position concerning education logically entails (whether appreciated or not) important *beliefs about reality* that are anything but religiously non-committed. For the Christian, reality cannot be 'neither one thing nor another,' if it is created and governed by God. Thus, an ostensibly 'neutral' or unbiased education is an illusion – albeit a useful one to the modern state. The reason that the modern state has insisted on the 'neutrality' of its education (and many Christians have believed this fictitious claim), is because to admit that education is not neutral would be to concede that all education is inescapably religious and that the government has violated the politically correct sacred cow of the separation of faith (religion) from public institutions – itself another impossible myth. We have already seen that at the heart of the question of educational philosophy is the *purpose* of education, and like the *content* of education, the purpose cannot be neutral. That is to say, since all education has a purpose in view, and purpose presupposes direction (teleology), it is again obvious that education, as a vision within society, cannot be to *no purpose* (neither one thing nor another). So, it will be helpful to explore further the religious purpose of education before examining its religious content.

The terms 'liberal' and 'liberty' are both derived from the Latin *liber* (free). From the Greco-Roman world to the modern West, a liberal arts education has ostensibly meant education for *freedom*. But what makes a person free and what is the ground of their freedom? Philosophical progressivism in education, with roots in figures like Horace Mann and John Dewey (which has shaped the whole course of public education in North America through much of the last century to the present), has held that true freedom is *liberation from the past*, from authority or revealed truth, and ultimately from God himself. Freedom in this view is not the result of salvation in Jesus Christ; freedom means instead liberation from previous constraints. To deny this approach to education has meant coming under censure as regressive and reactionary.[16] This utopian freedom, it has been held, will be realized by a universal system of state-sponsored schools, nurturing loyalty to the state and realizing 'free expression' for the individual, eventually ushering in a modern golden age. Here the locus of freedom is quite clearly the state, not God, in Jesus Christ. Thus, if statism is freedom, then modern public education is very 'liberal.' However, "if the superimposition of the state on every order of life and every sphere of human activity is by no means to be identified as liberty, then education today is definitely illiberal." [17]

Clearly then liberty is not self-explanatory. With the Christian consensus in the West presently lost, if the goal of education is liberty, then *liberty* must be defined. Is it freedom *under* God and his law, or freedom *from* God and his law? The dominant view today is the utopian statist's 'freedom of necessity,' where the state expresses the freedom of nature and remakes man in terms of nature's plan – a plan discerned by an elite bureaucracy. Clearly liberty cannot be identical with anarchy or *license*. If all people are free to do as they please, then no one is truly free, because freedom requires *law* by which our mutual freedoms are defined and circumscribed. For example, if I am free to steal, then other people are not free to possess their goods in peace or leave their property unattended at any time. However, it is clear that law cannot legitimately be identified, in an ultimate sense, with any *institution; rather*, law is a universal aspect of the human condition, of our existence in God's created order, of the revealed will of God. When a human institution seeks to reduce law to an aspect of itself as the source and ground of law, it steadily destroys true liberty – because liberty has been grounded historically in the West in an appeal to a higher authority than any human order. In fact, what any 'divinized' human institution must of necessity create is a new tyranny because it leaves no appeal beyond itself. Man-made laws then become the pragmatic instrument by which the bureaucracy enforces policy and protects *itself*, not the interests of justice and truth for all people. Thus, unless law, liberty and life have a transcendent source in the God of Scripture, human institutions will claim to incarnate these conditions of life within themselves, undermining freedom.[18] In these circumstances, education will cease to be the *art of freedom* in terms of God's purpose and law, instead being redefined by a divinized bureaucracy through its social planners as that which serves the collective will – true freedom thus becomes the necessity of nature expressed by the state. State control then means little more than people-control as the new purpose of education – i.e. freedom is what the state says it is:

> The state is the order of liberty, and the school is the means whereby citizens are prepared for the good life. The state has become the saving institution, and the function of the school has been to proclaim a new gospel of salvation. Education in this era is a messianic and utopian movement, a facet of the enlightenment hope of regenerating man in terms of the promise of science and that new social order to be achieved in the state.[19]

The massive emphasis on state education over the last century (despite declining standards and the growing illiteracy it has produced)[20] is an aspect of the belief that the human mind is a neutral consciousness or apparatus, a *clean slate* to be written on, rather than an aspect of a fallen creation in rebellion against God. The clean slate is an ideal; history can be wiped out and revolution can change everything.[21] The human person is thus malleable and transformable in terms of a controlling environment. That environment, the modern state insists, must be the state school that will facilitate the realization of a future manufactured in terms of humanistic man's self-ordained purpose – creating loyal subjects for the state and its vision of the great society. In Ontario, Canada for example, many state 'visionaries' saw the creation of compulsory state education not simply as a means of reducing vagrancy and crime, but as a means of transforming society as a whole. Archibald Macallum, an influential teacher in Ontario in the late nineteenth century, represents effectively the arguments used for the introduction of compulsory state education:

> Society has suffered so cruelly from ignorance, that its riddance is a matter of necessity, and by the universal diffusion of knowledge alone can ignorance and crime be banished from our midst; in no other way can the best interests of society be conserved and improved than by this one remedy – the compulsory enforcement of this great boon – the right of every Canadian child to receive that education that will make him a good, loyal subject, prepared to serve his country in the various social functions which he may be called on to fill during his life; and prepare him, through grace, for the life to come.[22]

Although grace for the 'afterlife' (not this life one might add) was at this time tagged on as an appendage to the goal of education, the clear emphasis here is the creation of a good and loyal subject for the state and its functions, which the child will, in time, be called upon to fulfil. God's purpose, his law and gospel are not primary matters of concern; and the faith is that the state's diffusion of knowledge will banish ignorance and crime once its education is enforced. Here the human problem is not sin and the remedy salvation in Christ, the problem is the environment and the remedy is state education. The current condition of our major cities and their public schools, despite over a century of statist pseudo-soteriological education, makes Macallum's grandiose claims for education, however well-intentioned, almost laughable. *It is therefore impossible to see the project of education and its apparatus as neutral.* All education is developed and carried out in terms of a purpose and a program for freedom. The question is, who defines freedom and what is the end in view? Educational programs will either be in terms of the purposes of God and his creative and redemptive work in creation, or they will be in terms of an alien religious purpose derived from the god of this world and his falsehoods.

12.4 The Battle for the Mind and the Future

Because education cannot be neutral, it is a field of conflict, a battle for the minds of the young and a dispute regarding the shape of the future; it is a conflagration in which there can be no neutrality. As Grant pointed out, "The constitutional state has an interest in limiting pluralism of belief.... [W]hen the state has become secularized, it will quickly free itself of its use of the church. The religion of humanity and progress will reign monolithically in the schools."[23] He prophetically added that, "assuming their religion to be self-evidently true to all men of good will, they are forceful in advocating that it should be the public religion." He called this religion the religion of progress, mastery and power.[24] Mastery and power require, of necessity, the enforcement of the new public religion and this requires the indoctrination of children into the new faith if the religion of progress is to define the future.

Though the non-biblical educational philosophies of history have been variations on the theme of autonomy and neutrality, differing significantly from ancient Greece to today's progressivism, the challenge facing the covenant people of God is the same in every age – faithfulness or surrender! Syncretism and compromise for God's people never work and can never last, though they promise much; as Tolkien so evocatively put it in the *Lord of the Rings, Sauron* does not share power. The god of this world is not interested in power-sharing with God and his people and there is no fellowship between darkness and light according to Scripture (2 Cor. 6:131–5).

The historical narrative of the Old Testament tells of a particular siege in the Northern kingdom of Israel, when Ben-hadad, the King of Syria, surrounded the capital Samaria. The then king of Israel, Ahab, was hemmed inside the walls of the city with just 7,000 fighting men. As was common in cases of overwhelming odds, Ben-hadad offered the besieged Ahab terms of surrender; they were not palatable. The king of Syria required that the gold, silver and the wives and children of Ahab be delivered to him. This was not a random request, but carried enormous significance. To surrender his wealth would leave the royal treasury empty and Israel asset-stripped, with no ability for future resistance. To surrender his wives to be raped and placed in Ben-hadad's harem would humiliate and shame Ahab and greatly undermine what was left of his power with the people. The biggest and most significant demand, however, was that his own children be handed over (again this was not uncommon in antiquity). His sons and daughters would be taken and re-educated in terms of an alien faith, religion, and morality. The plan would be that when they were returned to succeed to the throne of Israel, they would *recognize and serve* the foreign imperial power that had indoctrinated and raised them.

Today, not unlike pagan antiquity in many respects, the state increasingly lays siege first to our property (through property taxes, progressive taxation and inheritance taxes in many western countries), then our families, by forcefully pursuing the overthrow of the Christian view of sexuality, marriage and family, and then lays claim to our children. Compulsory state education and its humanistic curriculum (with increasing restrictions, controls, and monitoring of those who seek education in private schools and home schools), is a requirement that purposefully enables state indoctrination of our children in terms of a *foreign morality and faith*. Originally, education in Canada was in the hands of the family and the churches; the family was the primary educator. From the mid-seventeenth century numerous church institutions for education sprang up. For example, one Jesuit College in Quebec made available classical studies, grammar and theology as early as 1635. In the 1660s Bishop Laval founded the *Seminaire De Quebec* which eventually became *Université Laval*. Steadily however, with modernity and progressivism eroding the centrality of the family and the church's role in society, visions for state-controlled education developed. Well-meaning Christians like Egerton Ryerson in Ontario, with the noble intention of developing greater Christian character in the young, and broader Christian education free from Anglican church monopoly, began visiting various developed nations in the 1840s to explore educational models as he researched and planned his public education proposals. Though the picture is complex across the Canadian provinces (since education is under provincial not federal control), within a few years, the civil government was steadily taking over education – tax-funded and state-controlled. Ontario took the first step toward introducing compulsory school laws in 1871. Parents were then obliged by threat of fine to have children attend school – this required the use of state police to round up those in non-compliance even though many were apprenticed in their parent's trades. Legislation in 1891 raised the compulsory limits to eight through fourteen. The new law was more definite in stipulating penalties for parents.

Today, the compulsory age in Ontario is 6 through 18 years, which borders on the ridiculous, especially given the normal aspirations to pursue skilled labor careers among many young adults, and outstrips the U.K. which requires compulsory attendance until only 16 years of age. Other Canadian provinces in the late nineteenth and early twentieth century were more resistant, including the Maritimes and the mid-West; some politicians in Alberta for example, considered the compulsory proposals unconstitutional. One of the last areas of Western Europe to adopt a compulsory system was England and Wales, where the *Elementary Education Act of 1870* paved the way by establishing regional School Boards. Attendance was finally made compulsory from age 10 in 1880. Presently, in some Western nations – Germany for example – home education is illegal, a crime for which you may be fined or imprisoned and your children taken from you. In the U.K., the state now demands the right to privately interview (without their parents) home school children to determine the 'appropriateness' of their education. Furthermore, when returned to their families from their state education experience, many Christian parents are shocked to find that their child has been alienated from the family and the faith, taught a godless morality, and subsequently abandons the church. For example, in the United States, the most 'Christian' country in the West in terms of church attendance, LifeWay Research found that seven in ten Protestants ages eighteen to thirty who went to church regularly in high school stopped attending by the of age twenty-three. A full one-third of those had not yet returned to the church by the age of thirty. This means that about one-fourth of young Protestants have left the church in a generation. This finding is supported by the Barna Group which found six in ten young people will leave the church permanently or for an extended period starting at age fifteen. In keeping with this, the 2012 Millennial Values Survey, conducted jointly by the Public Religion Research Institute and Georgetown University's Berkley Center for Religion, Peace and World Affairs, found college-age millennials are thirty per cent more likely than the general population to be religiously unaffiliated. Millennials report lower levels of religious engagement across the board. In the U.S., just one in four says he or she attends religious services at least once a week, while forty-three per cent say they seldom or never attend.[25] As challenging as it may sound, and recognizing that many faithful Christian teachers have been called as missionaries into state schools, in a time like our own, dare we pretend to 'neutrality' and hand our children over to the Ben-hadad's of our age to be alienated from us and God's calling?

To some this may sound like melodramatic scaremongering, but it is in fact the sober truth. One need only track what is being forced even into the publically-funded Catholic school system in Canada today by various special interest groups crying 'discrimination,' to see a radical humanistic conquest of all Canadian public education. This landscape is a far cry from what the Methodist minister Egerton Ryerson had in mind when first proposing nondenominational Christian schools funded by the state for Protestants in Canada. There can be no doubt that a social revolution has been completed. All this is logical and to be expected when we recognize and accept that *neutrality is a myth* and that our public schools are religious institutions.

12.5 The Myth of Neutrality: The Content of Education

Christians believe that the uncreated being of God created the universe and all things in it, sustaining all things in terms of his law and purposes – we have an infinite God and a created, finite universe. Non-theists (pagans) believe the exact opposite. For them the universe has created God (or gods). They have either a finite god as an aspect of an infinite or self-generated universe, or no God, dismissed as a concept generated by the mind of man (where man is god). Non-Christian education is thus by definition, god-less education, whereas Christian education is God-centred education. Consequently, what is most central and important to the Christian is entirely left out by 'neutral' education. The immediate implications of this are unmistakable. Godless education denies that we are created in the image of God and are responsible to God, which entails the notion that human identity is a social construct and we *cannot* transgress God's law. If man cannot transgress then he is not a sinner and if he is not a sinner he does not need Christ or the gospel. A child educated in such a view soon realizes he does not need to live and think in terms of the triune God of Scripture, but can think and live autonomously and for himself.[26]

Now the implications of this are not limited to the ethical or the moral realm so that, as long as we morally instruct our children, a 'neutral' education in all other subject matter and informational content will be fine. It is not simply that true Christian education seeks to bring the child face to face with a righteous God, whilst the non-believer is just confronted with a relativized, amoral, justice-free universe. Rather, by definition, non-Christian education holds that the child is surrounded by an essentially mysterious and ultimately unknowable universe and can only grope in the darkness. By contrast, Christian education holds that in Jesus Christ, who is the revelation of God, and through his infallible word, man is restored, in principle, to the light of God, in whom all things consist and in whose light we see light. As Van Til has put it, "Non-Christians believe that insofar as man knows anything, he knows

442

apart from God.... Christians believe that everything is dark unless the current of God's revelation be turned on."[27] That is to say, all things are only seen as they truly are when they are understood in the light of God and his revelation. To deny this is to affirm that 'methodological naturalism' or 'practical atheism' (the utter denial of God's relevance to knowledge and understanding of the created order) is an acceptable path for the Christian who professes to believe that the triune God of Scripture created, sustains, and governs all things – whose being, will and law, through his immanent, providential care, upholds the very essence of all life and thought. It is also to implicitly teach that knowledge and ethics have no relationship, that one's moral character and lifestyle have no bearing on knowledge. But such a view is a complete denial of the biblical teaching that knowledge is ethical (see: John 7:15–17; John 8:31–32). Jesus' own learning and teaching in John 7:15 is clearly the result of his obedience to God.

Doing God's will and abiding in the word of God are in these passages declared by our Lord to be the prerequisite of true knowledge (in a self-consistent and full sense of that term), and right understanding is said to be the fruit of obedience. The *doctrine of God* (including the identity of the Son) which is under consideration in John 7, is thus foundational to all knowledge – for in the beginning was the Word (John 1:1). Every worldview, indeed every person has a doctrine of God (or god), that is, a God-concept, and so by definition have an orientation toward God and the divine that deeply impacts what they can rightly know and know rightly. Our god is that entity which we consider to have non-dependent status, that on which everything else depends. Werner Jaeger, commenting on Hesiod's poem 'Theogony' (the genesis of the gods) writes:

> If we compare this Greek hypostasis of the world-creative *Eros* with that of the *Logos* in the Hebrew account of creation, we may observe a deeply lying difference in the outlook of the two peoples. The Logos is a substantialization of an intellectual property or power of God the Creator, who is stationed *outside* the world and brings that world into existence by his own personal fiat. The Greek gods are stationed inside the world; they are descended from heaven and earth...they are generated by the mighty power of Eros who likewise belongs within the worlds as an all-engendering primitive force. Thus they are already subject to what we should call natural law.... When Hesiod's thought at last gives way to truly philosophical thinking, the divine is sought

443

inside the world – not outside it, as in the Jewish Christian theology that develops out of the book of Genesis.[28]

Roy Clouser's detailed analysis of this antithesis between the biblical view and all others across the religious spectrum has led him to note a very important fact, the relevance of the concept of a *divine per se*.[29] Whatever gods, goddesses, or lack thereof may be posited in any system of thought, the religious kernel of all thought systems is found in their concept of the *divine per se*. The *divine per se is* "whatever is unconditionally, non-dependently real."[30] With all the disagreements about the nature and character of the divine, all systems of thought, all worldviews, have in common the belief that the *divine per se* is that which is characterized by *non-dependence*. The status of the non-dependent entity varies (matter, energy, spirit, nature, gods etc.) but the commonality is found in the belief in an unconditioned reality – *a divine per se*, that takes the place of the God of Scripture as the religious foundation of all worldviews. This doctrine of God not only affects all other beliefs, and therefore all knowledge, but it shapes how we theorize and reason about the world. Thus, the great gulf in purpose, content and theory between a Christian and non-Christian education rests here in the doctrine of the uncreated, absolute, sovereign and personal God who has spoken, a God who speaks into every area of life.[31] In biblical faith, this doctrine lies at the foundation of all truth and thereby all Christian education. Yet many Christians are accustomed to think of Christian teaching as a condiment that can be added to *flavour* otherwise 'neutral' areas of life, like education. Add some Bible classes to an otherwise humanistic state curriculum; send the children to Sunday school; do some devotions at home with the kids (valuable as these are), and it is thought one or more of these programs is a sufficient strategy for, and understanding of, Christian education. But this is a hybrid worldview indebted to Greek philosophical dualism, not biblical faith. By way of illustration, I vividly recall, a few years ago, sitting down for lunch in a cafeteria with a prominent evangelical pastor when our conversation turned to children and education. As I began to express my convictions regarding an immediate need for the recovery of a distinctly Christian philosophy and form of education in Canada, I was surprised to encounter strong resistance. His evident emotional discomfort with my comments quickly turned to agitated pronouncements concerning the *neutrality* of the purpose of education generally, and the 'facts' specifically, stating that "facts are the same facts to everyone; a table is a table and cats are cats, both to the Christian and non-believer alike." On the face of it, this seems eminently reasonable, but it is, upon examination, exactly what Van Til called it many years ago, 'a satanic falsehood.' And it is a falsehood to which many have fallen prey in our time, victims of a thoughtless continuity with the status quo amongst many churchmen.

It is true of course that in a certain sense cats are cats to the believer and nonbeliever alike – we point to the same creature and call it a cat. But is this really agreement about the nature of cats in anything more than the most superficial sense? Let's take another example to make the point clear. In the field of mathematics, we may have 'formal' or conventional agreement with a nonbeliever that 2 X 2 = 4, but that is as far as the agreement goes, and even this superficial agreement turns out to be essentially pragmatic and not substantive. As soon as you ask the most basic questions about this idea, the 'agreement' vanishes. Van Til points out:

> When you think of two times two as four, you connect this fact with numerical law. And when you connect this fact with numerical law, you must connect numerical law with all law. The question you face, then, is whether law exists in its own right or is an expression of the will and nature of God. Thus the fact that two times two equal four enables you to implicate yourself more deeply into the nature and will of God.[32]

So in the biblical perspective, the consistency, lawfulness, intelligibility, coherence and dependability of the created order, even at the abstract level of mathematics with its incredible explanatory power for the concrete world, is guaranteed by the religious presupposition that God is the author of all law and that in understanding and exploring these mathematical relationships we grow in our understanding of the wisdom of God in creation and our dependence upon him. However, When an unbeliever says that two times two are four, he will also be led to connect this fact with the whole idea of law; but he will regard this law as *independent of God*. Thus the fact that two times two are four enables him, so he thinks, to get farther away from God. That fact will place the unbeliever before a whole sea of open possibilities in which he may seek to realise his life away from God.[33]

So we see that in the most elementary of ways, the doctrine of God will at the outset impact our view and use of mathematics; do mathematical relationships (laws) take us into the nature and purpose of God, or bring us before a sea of infinite possibility? Math is an important illustration because it is the hardest sphere (being the most 'certain' of sciences) in which to demonstrate the myth of neutrality. Yet, when we look at theories concerning mathematics it is interesting to note that there is not even a consensus around the basic sounding question of what numbers actually are! If numerical laws of math do not exist as abstract entities by the mind and will of God, then what are they? Roy Clouser has shown, for example, that solutions to this question have been diverse; from the *Number-World theory* of the ancient Greeks and some Enlightenment rationalists, which held to the idea that numbers are eternal entities existing in another dimension upon which the visible world depends (the Pythagoreans sang hymns to the number ten and worshiped numeric law as the *divine per se*); to the pragmatism of John Dewey which held that numbers are *cultural products* which stand for nothing. For Dewey they are simply tools that help us do certain jobs and so mathematical equations are neither true nor false. Other popular theories include John Stuart Mill's notion of numbers as *generalizations about sensory perceptions*, and Bertrand Russell's view that they are actually *logical classes* – a shortcut to doing logic.[34]

This is not merely of passing interest. Clouser shows that how we answer the question of the *nature* of numbers and mathematical law, something that turns out to be an inescapably religious exercise, has a major impact on the way theory-making takes place. The consequences of this are far-reaching. He tellingly cites Morris Kline from *Mathematics, The Loss of Certainty*:

> The current predicament of mathematics is that there is not one but many mathematics and that for numerous reasons each fails to satisfy the members of the opposing schools. It is now apparent that the concept of a universally accepted, infallible body of reasoning – the majestic mathematics of 1800 and the pride of man – is a grand illusion...the disagreements about the foundations of the "most certain" science are both surprising and, to put it mildly, disconcerting. The present state of mathematics is a mockery of the hitherto deep-rooted and widely reputed truth and logical perfection of mathematics.[35]

It is in fact impossible to conceive of *any* subject area in an educational curriculum that is free from religious assumptions that might convey a religiously 'neutral' worldview or information – fact and value are inextricably related.[36] Clouser is particularly helpful at this point as he goes even deeper into this question by showing that because we cannot conceive of any 'thing' or 'event' which does not exhibit properties and laws (such as fiduciary, ethical, justitial, mental, aesthetic, economic, social, linguistic, historical, logical, sensory, biotic, physical, kinetic, spatial, quantative and perhaps other like properties), and because those properties and laws must be all *related* somehow, to make that thing or event intelligible, the question of *how* these properties and laws are related will affect every aspect of knowledge.

This warrants further reflection because '*how*' they are related is a *religious* question that takes us back to the doctrine of God. Anti-biblical views of the divine (*divine per se*) lead to a radically monistic view of the relationship between laws and properties. That is to say, non-biblical education is reductionistic, and usually reduces all reality into *one* of the above properties which must finally *swallow* or *absorb* all the others – like the *physical* property for materialists, or the *mental* property for pantheists. For them, all the other laws and properties are merely illusory or transitory manifestations of the ultimately physical or non-physical character of all existence – their *divine per se – the god concept on which all else depends.* But for the Christian, all the laws and properties of our experience are real and relevant since they are *not* dependent on, nor are they reducible to, one created property (the essence of paganism). Rather, they depend wholly upon the uncreated God.[37]

Consider the implications of this fact for every area of education. The reductionism that shapes all areas of anti-biblical education today is antithetical to the Christian approach. The Christian does not (indeed cannot) reduce history and social order to economics like the Marxists, or meaning and morality to linguistics like the deconstructionists, or science to the sensory like the materialists. Since God is the creative source and designer of the relationship between all the laws and properties of experience, there is a distinctly Christian way to approach history, economics, epistemology, linguistics, science and every other subject. Unlike non-Christian education, we do not reduce any aspect of reality to one or more created properties, but understand all things in terms of the sovereign and triune God of Scripture who is both transcendent and immanent in relationship to creation, and whose word and law governs all things in terms of the counsel of his will (Eph. 1:11). Christian education is thus God-centred and Word-centred in that it relates all knowledge back to God and his word. All truth is indeed *relative*! It is either relative to man and his mind, which must reduce all things to one manageable property so that he can play God, or truth is relative (related back) to God. If truth and thereby education is *not* relative to God, it can only be relative to man as god which is humanism and paganism. So again we see the far-reaching implications of the doctrine of God for education.

Moving away from the highly abstract and philosophic to something more concrete, we might also briefly consider the arts and their religious character as it relates to the doctrine of God. There is a glaring world of difference, for example, between the fragmented, abstract forms of modern art and the vision of reality they convey, and that of the worldview communicated by the painters of the Dutch reformation, which conveyed the beauty, reality and wholesomeness of God's creation. Much abstract, modern art, is an attempt to overturn the real world of God's creation and its meaning, redefining reality in terms of private 'meanings' imposed by the mind of man, that rejects God's order. In other words, one view of art makes the world relative to God and his word and the other, with nature as divine, makes all things relative to the mind of man. A more subtle example which reveals the role of the doctrine of God in the arts is seen in the paintings, on the one hand of Rembrant, which depict an evangelical view of the world, and that of Michelangelo which mixes Greek philosophical and Christian categories. Likewise, the musical compositions of J.S. Bach convey the worldview of a reformed Christian, and are markedly distinct from both the compositions of the renaissance and the modern fragmented 'noise' of the so-called 'composer' John Cage. Bach's work was characterized by purpose and forward motion; it embodied the principle of linear time, of progress from a clear beginning to a fore-ordained end, mirroring the working and purposes of God.[38] Some Western musical theorists want to see an end of Bach's 'Protestant ethic' expressed in the development of polyphony, tonal harmony and the musical forms based on them.[39] For such artists Bach is 'cramped' by his Christian worldview, whereas Claude Debussy rejects the Christian sequential logic and biblical vision, opening us instead to the limitless time of myth.[40] Thus, the arts can no more be a value-neutral sphere than can history or math. All these fields of human endeavour are distinctly religious, and implicit within them is a doctrine of God, a *divine per se*. All the arts convey a worldview, be it music, painting, literature, sculpture, architecture or film, and depict for us a view of 'reality' and a vision of beauty or aesthetic 'truth.' There is thus no way to teach the arts with integrity in a neutral fashion. Education in the arts will be as religious as education in history. Given these facts, and having established the impossibility of neutrality in the content of education, it is unnecessary here to cover the various religious accounts of origins (evolutionary or biblical), or law and ethics (Christian or pagan and humanistic) as fields of study and education which are manifestly and inescapably religious in character. These foundational views on human origins and the source of law give birth to, and are all well expressed in *political philosophy* that is a field explicitly infused with religious assumptions. Many examples could be offered here but one in particular stands out in contrasting a Christian view of man and law with a humanistic one at a pivotal time in Western history. The bloodless revolution of 1688 in England expressed some of the key thought forms of the Reformation and the earlier Magna Carta – limiting the king and balancing powers within government, establishing the rule of law and the freedom of the church. Even the French radical voltaire, a man who utterly despised Christianity and the church,[41] was deeply impressed by this 'freedom without chaos,' across the English Channel. The French revolutionaries, however, went on to try and accomplish a similar end (freedom) but with a different faith and religious basis – atheism embodied in the goddess of reason, as the *divine per se* and the commensurate vision of man as the noble savage. This differing doctrine of God when consistently applied to the socio-political sphere resulted in a bloodbath and the 'reign of terror' in which at least 40,000 people were executed by their government and its agents as the atheistic radicals sought to enforce their vision of freedom which they called the 'general will.' The new revolutionaries made 1792 'year one' in their new calendar for history, seeking to eject Christ from it altogether. The goddess of reason was thus hubristically enthroned in Notre Dame and Paris.

Then, out of the social chaos, Napoleon emerged to govern as a warmongering, though brilliant, commander and dictator. The twentieth century gives us ample illustration of the same phenomenon; when 'nature' was made god with religious fervour in the political philosophies of both Marxism (dialectical materialism) and Nazism (evolution and the emergent superman), the tragic results were manifest in the wholesale slaughter of untold millions. Clearly, what we believe about God and man, origins and law, governs our political and social philosophy and will determine what we teach our children about social and political relationships. Are we to be governed by the Ten Commandments, or the ten thousand commandments of the state or mob? Clearly in Canada today with the God of Scripture banished from public education, a new concept of life, personhood, family, gender, sexuality and ethics has been established – a concept rooted in a form of religious paganism.

We can therefore clearly see, in summary, that neither the *structure within* which we educate, nor the *purpose for* which we educate, nor the *content by* which we educate, can be neutral. Either there is an absolute, personal God, who governs all things and surrounds us as our ultimate environment, or there is not. If our answer is the latter, all interpretation of life at every level is without reference to God and reduces to the arbitrary, subjective and finally to an irrational surd – we are derelicts on a shore-less sea of futility and all our hope is thereby of necessity in 'progressivism' and the idea that out of the human phenomenon the possibility of gaining some sort of power and control over a chaotic environment might be possible – man must be made a god. Thus, if education is preparation for a free life by *adjustment to the environment*, then this leaves all of us with a stark choice with respect to the *kind of environment* we want our children adjusted to! If God is real and Jesus Christ is the eternal word and exact representation of God's being, sustaining all things by his power (Heb. 1:3), if in him we live and move and exist (Acts 17:28), then there is nothing more important to know about the facts than their relationship to him. The child who is taught (implicitly or explicitly) that she evolved by chance, from the goo, through the zoo, to you, will later deny she sees law and design in nature. The boy who is instructed that all meta-narratives are merely subjective storytelling (discourse) masking power-relations, or that history is the meaningless juxtaposition of random events combined with impersonal sociological forces, will soon see no final purpose in life. The child who is led to believe that all history's moral codes, conflicts and law-orders are simply disguised economic relations – social constructs to impose the will of the powerful or ruling class – will not see himself as face to face with the moral demands of a righteous God, but as confronted by a raw will to power against which he must rage. The child that is indoctrinated with the idea that God and his law are irrelevant to education will soon see no need for the gospel, and no need for salvation, since God is not the child's environment nor are they accountable to him. He dwells in an impersonal world, with nothing but the void behind and before. In light of such views, all education is rendered empty. But for the believer, Christ is the "power of God and the wisdom of God" (1 Cor. 1:24) and in him are hid, "all the treasures of wisdom and knowledge" (Col. 2:3). As the ancient king wrote centuries ago for our instruction, "the fear of the Lord is the beginning of wisdom" (Prov. 1:7; 2:6, 10).

12.6 The Curriculum of Christ

Given the truism that ideas have inescapable consequences, J. Gresham Machen pointed powerfully not only to the history-changing power of education, but also to the priority and urgency of a thoroughgoing Christian approach. His call to "mould the thought of the world" for the sake of its future, and pertinent warning concerning a growing anti-Christianity in the Western academy, is far more relevant and urgent today than when he wrote these prophetic words one hundred years ago:

> What is today a matter of academic speculation begins tomorrow to move armies and pull down empires. In that second stage, it has gone too far to be combated; the time to stop it was when it was still a matter of impassionate debate. So as Christians we should try to mould the thought of the world.... The real difficulty amounts to this—that the thought of the day, as it makes itself most strongly felt in the universities, but from them spreads inevitably to the masses of the people, is profoundly opposed to Christianity, or at least—what is nearly as bad—it is out of all connection with Christianity.... Under such circumstances, what more pressing duty than for those who have received the mighty experience of regeneration, who, therefore, do not, like the world, neglect that whole series of vitally relevant facts which is embraced in Christian experience—what more pressing duty than for these men to make themselves masters of the thought of the world in order to make it an instrument of truth instead of error? The Church has no right to be so absorbed in helping the individual that she forgets the world.[42]

The calling to take God's word and make it known, making knowledge an instrument of truth, and educating the world in terms of the faith, is not limited to an eccentric reformed missiology as some might assume. In fact it is noteworthy that the final commission given by the Lord Jesus Christ to his disciples contained an *educational* mandate: "All authority in heaven and on earth has been given to me. Go therefore and make disciples of all nations, baptizing them in the name of the Father and of the Son and of the Holy Spirit, *teaching them to observe all that I have commanded you.* And behold I am with you always, to the end of the age" (Matt. 28:18–20). In this charge we see first the total authority of our Lord declared over heaven and earth. Nothing in the universe is left out or exempted from his regency. His authority extends over every sphere and every area of life in all creation – this inescapably includes the realm of education. Second, it is because of Christ's authority that we take up this task with immediacy, humility and confidence. The power and authority to teach does not belong to us individually, neither does it originate with us. It is not arrogant presumption on the part of Christians to *teach* all nations because the authority to instruct is grounded in the regency of Christ; we are his ministers serving as High Commissioners or ambassadors of the crown. Thirdly, Christian initiation for the nations means far more than baptism, but *teaching* all of Scripture and its relevance to all of life.

Since Christ is the fulfilment and interpreter of all the law and the prophets, since he is the living Torah, it is the totality of divine revelation that is the content of our educational task; the curriculum of Christ. Our Lord said, "Man shall not live by bread alone, but by every word which proceeds from the mouth of God" (Matt. 4:4). Eugene Peterson has pointed out concerning the fullness of the Christian witness in history, and its educational significance, that *Moses* was chosen as giver of the law, and *Elijah* as the exemplar of prophecy, both pointing to the Christ as the fulcrum of witness, one that must impact all of life:

> Between them these two [Moses and Elijah] direct the attention of all humanity to Christ as Lord and Savior – God in our history for our salvation. Law and prophecy are the content of all witness. Law (Moses) is the revelation of God's truth. God wills us to know what is real. There is intelligibility in creation, and God shows it to us: intelligibility in rocks and weather, in morality and thought, in prayer and worship. Nothing is arbitrary. Nothing is haphazard. We do not make up an explanation of reality as we go along; it is given to us by

God. That is the importance of the Mosaic law: God speaks to us in such a way that we comprehend the intelligible givenness of reality. The universe is not a whim. Things do not occur by a throw of the dice. There is a reason and order and sense. Our minds, of course, cannot take it all in, but whatever we can take in makes sense. The man who denies meaning in life writes out his denial in grammar that he is sure will make sense to those who read it. We cannot escape this vast sense of givenness in which everything fits. The work of witness attests to this. When we witness we do not unpack the contents of our own emotional suitcases for the titillation of voyeurs, we point to what God has revealed. Prophecy (Elijah) is the immediate application of God's truth in current and personal history. Truth is not only an objective reality "out there," it involves us in an act of participation "in here." Prophecy is a call to live the revealed truth, not merely acknowledge it, and to discover new ways to live it in every aspect of life – while brushing my teeth, dialling the telephone, pulling a lever in a voting booth, signing a check. It is a proclamation that God's truth, evident in the "things that are made" (Rom. 1:20) must be embraced as the truth of my life in details, not just in general.[43]

Life and truth are found in Christ and his total word, and since his word defines the meaning and purpose of all things, the principles of God's word must govern our approach to every sphere of life and thought educationally and practically, be it science, history, art, politics, economics, law, or any other field of knowledge and endeavour. If Christ and his revelation of law (meaning) and prophecy (application of truth and meaning) are irrelevant to these areas, then his authority does not extend over heaven and earth and Christ is made a liar.

Fourthly, we should be reminded that Christ assures us of his divine aid and empowering presence as we pursue with diligence the educational mandate as witness to the world. Of course the Christian faith is more than true propositions and their communication, it involves the supernatural, regenerating and sanctifying work of the Spirit of God; no form of education can accomplish what is the province of God alone, we can save no one by education. But clearly, the Great Commission demonstrates that the task of education is embedded in the very nature of our calling as witnesses. People cannot believe and apply what they have not heard. To this task we must be faithful.

This mandate begins with our own children as Christian parents. A serious warning comes to all false educators of children, and perhaps especially to us who are Christian parents, when Jesus, in speaking of entrance into the kingdom of heaven declared, "whoever causes one of these little ones who believe in me to sin, it would be better for him to have a great millstone fastened around his neck and to be drowned in the depth of the sea. Woe to the world for temptations to sin! For it is necessary that temptations come, but woe to the one by whom the temptation comes" (Matt. 18:6–7). Whilst we can see that Jesus is referring to all childlike believers in the Lord in this passage, it seems clear that he specifically has vulnerable children in mind when he brings a child into their midst. If we cause them to stumble, if we are the *occasion* of their sins because we have thrown temptation in their way, we are culpable and are guilty of sin against the Lord. Is it not the case that today's radically humanistic education of our children in the state system of the West, and its indoctrination of children into a neo-pagan faith, is laying a serious stumbling block in front of our children; has it not become the occasion of sin to many of our little ones and led them away from the faith? Even though we cannot give our children salvation in Christ (only the Holy Spirit can do this), we must never be guilty of provoking them to sin by laying temptation to wander from the faith in their path by the education we provide. We cannot give them the gift of regeneration, but we can give them a faithful, God-honouring Christian education that rejects the idolatry of modern state education. Let us not as parents and pastors be the occasion by which temptations come and by it bring ourselves under judgement. To be led into sin leads swiftly to our young ones becoming slaves of sin (John 8:34). Do we not hear the voice of God in our time calling out as he did through Moses to Pharaoh concerning His 'son' Israel enslaved in Egypt, *'let my children go!'* As Christians, our children are not our own, they belong to God, they are his from the womb, from the very foundation of the world, and we are given the gift of stewardship as parents (Ps. 139:13–16). It is time for a great exodus of Christians from an apostate state education under modern Pharaohs to a redeemed education under Christ, the greater Moses; from instruction in a temple of idols under Pharaoh's priests, to the teaching of God's Levites in the tabernacle of God.

For the same reason, we cannot be apathetic or self-centred in our attitude concerning the educational and social situation facing our children and grandchildren. It is all too easy for older Christians to sit back and admit things are looking bad for the future, make pessimistic and pious-sounding pronouncements about eschatology, and then console themselves that they were blessed, missed the worst of the social decline, and that the hammer is unlikely to finally fall while they are still alive. In 2 Kings 20 an otherwise faithful king, Hezekiah, who did much right in the eyes of the Lord, ends his days in a tragic episode of short-sightedness, pride and faithlessness. He is miraculously healed of an infected boil that was about to take him into the grave and is granted by God's grace an extra fifteen years of life. Ambassadors come from Babylon with letters and gifts on news of his recovery from sickness and Hezekiah takes the opportunity to show off to Babylon's envoys all the wealth of the kingdom and all that is in his storehouses. Isaiah then prophesies to Hezekiah that the days were coming when everything which he and his fathers had stored up in the treasuries would be carried off to Babylon. He further declares, "And some of your own sons, who shall be born to you, shall be taken away, and they shall be eunuchs in the palace of the king of Babylon" (2 Kings 20:18). Hezekiah then utters some of the most blind and faithless words in the Bible; "Then said Hezekiah to Isaiah, 'The word of the Lord that you have spoken is good.' For he thought, 'why not, if there will be peace and security in *my days* (2 Kings 20:19)?'" Hezekiah was, astonishingly, *pleased* with the prophecy of Isaiah for the simple reason that he wasn't going to be around to see this disaster. There had been a degree of peace and security for him, so never mind about the children and their children. It is hard to envision a more self-centred response to the word of God.

Now I want to suggest that this account reflects the attitude of many Christians today toward the education of their children and grandchildren and the decline of our culture. Many are apathetic and contented with the fact that they have enjoyed a measure of peace and security in Canadian life (or life in the U.K, or U.S.) and haven't had to face what our children are presently facing and won't live to see all the consequences of an apostate education and cultural decline. In other words we say, "humanistic state education, so what, we were alright, our generation survived, we can enjoy our life and the treasury and spend our money on vacations and toys, racking up debts, and we need not make the sacrifice for our children's future to educate them in the faith – we won't live to see the darkest days." Put in this light, the neglect of our children in regard to education is the height of faithlessness. What happened to

Hezekiah's offspring? They were made eunuchs for a foreign faith and power – that is, they were neutered and rendered 'neither one thing nor another.' They were made 'neutral' and as a result had no future with no progeny to go forward in faith and obedience to God, robbing God of his heritage. The treasury of Christendom that we boasted in and then neglected has already been carried off; the wealth of the church has been decimated by negligence, faithlessness, compromise and idolatry. Our children are being religiously neutered by the state's education system today and unless we wake up, repent, and concern ourselves, in faithfulness to God with their future, whatever the sacrifice, our children will have no future. Moreover the faith itself will be neutered in the next generation and it will be because of our complacency and selfishness.

Thus, our choice today in education, as in every other sphere, is between two claimants to the throne of godhood and universal government: the state which claims to be our shepherd, keeper, and savior, and the Holy Trinity, our only God and savior. Covenant faithfulness or disobedience remain the only choices. To choose the latter means the self-government (faithful obedience to the word of God) of Christian people under the lordship of Jesus Christ, beginning with the individual, the family and the school. A renaissance of biblical liberty over against the tyranny of humanism will not be accomplished quickly by a non-violent revolution, by violent protest, by the barrel of the gun, or by top-down statist measures. Rather it will come by the steady, long-term, grassroots growth of self-government in the individual, in the church and the Christian family under God and by an uncompromising faithfulness to all of Scripture in the Christian school. And against all appearance what gives hope to us is the guarantee of the victory of God's reign, no matter how long it takes; as the Lord's Prayer reminds us in this connection to pray, "thy kingdom come" (Matt. 6:10).

Chapter Thirteen

DEFENCE AND CONFIRMATION OF THE GOSPEL: THE REIGN OF GOD AND APOLOGETICS FOR THE TWENTY-FIRST CENTURY

I have undertaken to defend the most glorious city of God against those who prefer their own gods to the founder of that city. The King and founder of this city...has made clear the meaning of the divine law in the Scriptures of his people, in which it is said, "God resists the proud, but gives grace to the humble."

– St. Augustine

When man thinks in self-conscious submission to the voluntary revelation of the self-sufficient God, he has therewith the only possible ground of certainty for his knowledge.

– Cornelius Van Til

13.1   What is Apologetics?

The task of Christian apologetics as it confronts us in the modern world may seem remote to Puritan concerns, after all those historically labelled Puritans were dealing with a very different context in a century where few people thought it intellectually compelling or socially useful to be agnostic about the existence of God, question the validity of their faculties of mind, or challenge the idea of revealed moral absolutes. Consequently the Puritans did not, indeed could not, address themselves to the subsequent philosophical challenges of the post-Kantian world.[1] It would be the Dutch Reformed tradition of the nineteenth century that would begin to effectively mount a specifically Christian response to these philosophical developments. Nonetheless, the core of the Puritan mind bears great relevance to the apologetic mandate. Whilst the issues of contemporary epistemology were not relevant to their time, as Christians they well understood the indispensable foundation of the Lordship of Jesus Christ to all fields of human knowledge and action. Moreover they believed in the infallible truth of Scripture and they pre-supposed its full authority for each area of life. As a result, the plain faith and confidence of the Puritans in the total sufficiency of the word of God make them honorary forefathers of a truly biblical approach to apologetics. Indeed, without a Puritan mind-set resting in the Lordship of Christ and the authority and sufficiency of his infallible word, it is difficult to see how one could begin an effective defence of the faith.

Two basic mistakes are common when many Christians come to consider the issue of Christian apologetics. The first is to assume that, as a discipline, it is of concern only to a narrow group of Christian elite, practiced in the art of a kind of Christian intellectual ninjutsu whereby opponents with tough questions are overcome and defeated; that is to say, it is thought of as a kind of evangelism for experts in philosophy. In fact, as the apostle Peter tells us in 1 Peter 3:15, apologetics concerns *all* Christian people in our readiness to share and defend the hope of the gospel which begins, not with an elite education and preparation, but submission to the Lordship of Christ in the core of our being. Furthermore, setting out the reasons for our hope in God and his reign is to be done in gentleness, humility and respect, so that we might have a clear conscience in regard to those who slander the faith, being put to shame by not only our words, but our conduct.

The second common mistake is to think that apologetics is to be academically confined as a subset of church dogmatics and limited to answering a handful of somewhat abstract objections to Christian doctrines; the existence of God; the problem of evil in light of God's being and attributes; objective moral truth in a diverse world of moral codes; the exclusive claims of Christ in a pluralistic society. Here, it is often thought, ends the task and scope of Christian apologetics. However, I believe we miss the significance and perennial relevance of apologetics when it is disconnected from the comprehensive Lordship of Christ and the *reign of God*. Far from being limited to answering a few common objections to the faith, biblical apologetics seeks to defend the lordship of Christ and the *hope* of the gospel of the kingdom in every sphere and area of life. This means we are to offer not just answers to certain isolated objections to certain Christian propositions, but a holistic defence of the Christian view of law, philosophy, education, art, science, politics, music, economics and each area of human endeavour. By limiting apologetics to answering a handful of classic or common objections to Christianity, it is made to appear irrelevant to Christians who find that their particular friends are not asking such questions, and irrelevant for our contemporary culture if addressing issues that were of concern only to those generations deeply committed to the assumptions of modernity. Such people are still part of the mix in Western society, but they are now in a distinct minority.

A further consequence of this truncation of apologetics is that it unwittingly sponsors the dualism of much modern Christianity in its retreat from the task of asserting and defending Christ's lordship over every area of life and thought. That is, where defending 'the faith' is limited to defending a handful of Christian doctrines that concern our 'religious' claims about God and Christ, we have tacitly endorsed a humanistic division of the religious from the secular. So a Christian enthusiastic about defending the faith may expend great time and effort in learning all the Christian theodicies (responses to the problem of evil), but not think it important to be able to defend a Christian vision of education, law, family, or culture. In my view, good apologetics is just the defence of good biblical theology, the queen of the sciences, from which all other disciplines derive their meaning, significance and coherence. Without theology there is no unity in the diversity of studies, and therefore no true university. The unnecessary and unhelpfully sharp division of apologetics from biblical theology and the wider concerns of Christ's total Lordship, is illustrated well by common definitions of apologetics. Theologian Alister McGrath provides a typical example: "In its basic sense, it is an *apologia* for the Christian faith...apologetics aims to lend intellectual integrity and depth to evangelism...the chief goal of Christian apologetics is to create an intellectual and imaginative climate conducive to the birth and nurture of faith..."[2] We see here the idea that apologetics is a kind of handmaiden to a more intellectual or robust approach to evangelism – its goal being to answer objections to the faith supposedly making people more receptive (a conducive climate) to the message of salvation. Now it is certainly part of the task of apologetics to give weight and intellectual integrity to our efforts in evangelism, for when we proclaim the gospel, we defend it, but there is surely more to apologetics than this rather truncated remit. The 'hope that is in us' which St. Peter calls us to defend, is not restricted to the reality of God's existence, sins forgiven and individual salvation; our hope is in the Lordship of Christ and his *total reign*. It is this Christ we honour from the core of our being (1 Pt. 3:15). The primary goal of apologetics is not to create, by argument, a mental climate conducive to faith, for we are incapable of making any sinner favourable to the claims of Christ; the Holy Spirit alone is able to do this. Rather, our task first and foremost is to *glorify God* by faithfully declaring and defending the truth. Then, by the grace of God and the omnipotent working of the Holy Spirit, we serve God's purpose of bringing *all thought* into captivity to Christ, under his reign, making all men accountable before him, where every mouth is stopped (2 Cor. 10:46; Rom. 3:19).

A more comprehensive, yet concise definition of apologetics, is offered by Cornelius Van Til: "Apologetics is the vindication of the Christian philosophy of life against the various forms of the non-Christian philosophy of life."[3] We see here, by contrast, the comprehensive character and wide application of the apologetic mandate. The Christian philosophy of life is all-encompassing and we are to seek to bring glory to God by vindicating it. We are defending an entire philosophy of life and thought that centres in the triune God. J. Gresham Machen wrote:

> The Christian cannot be satisfied so long as any human activity is either opposed to Christianity or out of all connection with Christianity. Christianity must pervade not merely all nations, but also all of human thought. The Christian, therefore, cannot be indifferent to any branch of earnest human endeavor. *It must all be brought into some relation to the gospel.* It must be studied either in order to be demonstrated as false, or else in order to be made useful in *advancing the Kingdom of God.* The Kingdom must be advanced not merely extensively, but also intensively. The Church must seek to conquer not merely every man for Christ, but also the whole of man. We are accustomed to encourage ourselves in our discouragements by the thought of the time when every knee shall bow and every tongue confess that Jesus is Lord. No less inspiring is the other aspect of that same great consummation. That will also be a time when doubts have disappeared, when every contradiction has been removed, when all of science converges to one great conviction, when all of art is devoted to one great end, when all of human thinking is permeated by the refining, ennobling influence of Jesus, *when every thought has been brought into subjection to the obedience of Christ.*[4]

This is the great task of Christian apologetics as it is integrated into every aspect of human endeavour – our priestly service to God is the defence and confirmation of the good news that Jesus Christ is Lord and this Lordship is to pervade all human thought as each area is brought into relation to the gospel (Phil. 1:7). Having defined the nature and goal of apologetics, in the rest of this chapter I will analyse various approaches to Christian apologetics as they confront contemporary culture, and argue that Van Til's presuppositional method is more biblically faithful, more effective in confronting unbelief and a necessity for the development of a consistently reformed approach to the *Missio Dei* that addresses every sphere of life.

13.2 Van Til: The Thomas Aquinas of Protestantism

Cornelius Van Til was born on May 3, 1895, in Grootegast, Holland. He was the sixth son of a dairy farmer. When he was ten years old his family moved to Highland Indiana in the United States. As a graduate student of philosophy at Princeton he was awarded a doctorate in philosophy after the completion of his seminary work. In 1926 he married Rena Klooster, his childhood sweetheart, and in 1927 completed his Ph.D. At Calvin College he studied under professors like Louis Berkhof, giving him a great appreciation for the Dutch Reformed tradition. He was particularly influenced by the work of Abraham Kuyper, (1837-1920) whose accomplishments as a Christian leader and thinker were remarkable, including serving briefly as Prime Minister of the Netherlands. At the heart of Kuyper's thought was the lordship of Christ over every area of life and thought.

Van Til was strongly opposed to the reorganization of Princeton Seminary along increasingly modernistic grounds by the Presbyterian General Assembly. In response to this reorganization, J. Gresham Machen, a noted Princeton professor of New Testament, along with other faculty, decided to begin a new seminary independent of Assembly control. This school would be in the Reformed tradition of Benjamin. B. Warfield and Charles Hodge. Machen was very keen to secure Van Til as professor of apologetics.

Eventually Van Til accepted, and in 1929 Westminster Theological Seminary opened. Here Van Til remained until his retirement in 1972. Van Til's scholarly published works are voluminous. Some of his most important are in the field of apologetics including, *The Defense of the Faith* (1955), *A Christian Theory of Knowledge* (1969), *Christian Apologetics* (1975) *Christian Theistic Evidences* (1976), and *Christianity and Barthianism* (1962). Regarding Van Til's significance, John Frame, professor of Systematic Theology and Philosophy at Reformed Theological Seminary in Orlando stated:

> If Kant taught the world of secular unbelief the essentials of its own [until then subconscious] theory of knowledge, Van Til did the same for the Christian.... If Kant's achievement makes him the most important secular philosopher of modern times should we not say that Van Til's achievement the makes him the most important Christian thinker of modern time?[5]

Interestingly, what makes Van Til such an important thinker is very simple: his starting-point. For Van Til, the ultimate criterion for truth in every area is either the eternal self-contained God of Scripture (ontological trinity) and his eternal decree, or an ultimate impersonalism. Christian and non-Christian thought thus stand in an *antithetical relationship* to each other in every sphere. The non-Christian has only the Cartesian self and ego as their beginning and ending point, the Christian has the ontological trinity. The breadth of the apologetic task is therefore almost unlimited. The goal is to push this epistemological antithesis by extending the presuppositional,[6] internal critique of other world-views to economics, education, history, politics, law, art, psychology, science and every sphere, thereby revealing the bankruptcy of anti-Christianity in all its forms, which then points to Christ and the totality of the Scriptures as the only non-disintegrating source of life, hope, meaning, truth and social order. Andrew Sandlin has indentified five key areas of development in Calvinistic thought reached by a consistent use of a Van Tillian starting point:

> First, the repudiation of all forms of dualism; second, opposition to the eternalization of any dimension of the temporal; third, the solidification of the historic reformed view of the law; fourth, the inherent historical progressiveness of the success of the Christian faith; and fifth, the reordering of all areas of human endeavour in terms of the Christian Faith as revealed in the Bible.[7]

Applied to apologetics, this theological starting point forces us to the conclusion that although we share common ground with the non-believer as creatures made in God's image, there is no *neutral* ground; no neutral way of thinking.[8] We must either think as consistent Christians in a comprehensively and self-consistently biblical fashion or we import some form humanism into Christianity and deny the antithesis. This insight is critical to understanding a consistently reformed conception of the 'reign of God' since it follows from these convictions that our understanding of the nature and shape of that reign must be derived directly from Scripture and guided by Scripture, resting our criterion for implementation of the *mission Dei* on God's infallible word. This rules out scholastic, Enlightenment and rationalistic forms of Christian thinking that posit nature or natural law as a 'neutral' foundation for knowledge, ethics and social organization.

Crucially, in Van Til's thought, truth is unified in God and his exhaustive plan for history. History itself is under rational control and governance, where prophetic prediction can be made by God, because reality is not subject to the happenstance of chance. Thus, when people deny that reality already has a structure and meaning by virtue of God's creative act and plan, they essentially try to separate fact and meaning (the inseparable). As a result, the unbeliever is left with only meaningless rationalizations that are applied to a random world where the whole idea of a 'system' of thought is a hopeless ideal, not a reality. In such a world, humanistic humanity retreats into irrationalism, irresolution and lawlessness (from logic to grammar to ethics) eventually committing intellectual suicide because they will not be honest with themselves and acknowledge that they are creatures of God, as such they stubbornly refuse to repent. This accords well with the divine voice of wisdom in Proverbs 8:36 as descriptive of human life, philosophy, social sciences and culture-building without Christ, "But he who sins against me wrongs his own soul; all those who hate me love death."

13.3 Approaches to Apologetics

It is important to notice then that not all apologetic methodologies are created equal, they are not monolithic. There have been, throughout church history, different methods and schools of apologetics which have different approaches to key philosophical subjects, critically epistemology, and are therefore *affected differently* by the current postmodern (or ultra-modern) and existential climate. As a broad but valid generalization, four main streams of apologetic method can be identified, though there is invariably considerable overlap in the practice of these schools. The first is *classical apologetics* which has historically been concerned with offering proofs for the existence of God (theism) from the works of nature, or from philosophical concepts such as causality and necessary being (ontology). The classical method has also been concerned about resolving apparent metaphysical problems like evil and suffering coexisting with an omnipotent and omni-benevolent God. Noted champions of this method include Thomas Aquinas and Rene Descartes. Their modern exponents would include apologists like Norman Geisler and William Lane Craig. This model is characterized by a *classical foundationalist* epistemology with roots in Aristotelian thought, which holds that certain beliefs have a 'self-evident' validity bequeathed by nature and provide a sound basis for rationally demonstrating the existence of God by human reason. The God 'hypothesis' can thus be established by reason as the best 'explanation' for the world. Quite naturally approaches to moral reasoning and ethics grounded in the concept of 'natural law' are emphasized.

A second method has been called historical or *evidentialist apologetics*. This approach is primarily concerned with historical, scientific, archaeological, textual, miraculous and prophetic evidences for the Christian faith as well as the corroboration of religious experience. For example, great stress has been laid upon providing historical evidences for the resurrection of Christ, and subsequent circumstantial evidences like the religious transformation of the disciples to show that it is *beyond reasonable doubt*, in terms of the notion of historical probability, that Christ was raised from death. This model has a fairly recent history in that it arose in order to respond to the rationalistic challenges of modernity, German higher critical theory and the attendant theological liberalism, although certainly we have apologists from the patristic era onward appealing to biblical prophecy and the miraculous as an evidence for the truth of Christianity; Blaise Pascal being a prominent seventeenth-century example of the skilled use of prophecy in Christian persuasion. Modern exponents of this method include apologists like Josh McDowell and Gary Habermas. This method in its contemporary form also usually assumes a *classical foundationalist* epistemology, holding that human reason is essentially a neutral tool and that evidences can be weighed on unbiased scales, potentially leading to Christian commitment, by analysing the *bare facts* to see where they lead and thereby achieving a balance of probability for the truth of Christianity. Moral law is again usually derived from a natural law ethic arguing that the universality of some moral principles and laws (like C.S. Lewis's argument for the *Tao* in *The Abolition of Man*) reveals a law inherent in nature that is accessible by all men.

A third method might be characterised as *existential apologetics*. This is not Christian existentialism. Rather, this approach seeks to grapple with the 'manliness of man,' the existential longings and felt needs of people, and proceeds to argue that the Christian account of life is the best explanation of the human condition. The contradictions in our nature (Pascal's *Pensees*), our moral consciousness, the sense of guilt and alienation we carry, our hopes, loves, sense of beauty, our doubts and despairing are all explored as *signals of transcendence*. Exponents of this method include Blaise Pascal and in more modern times, Os Guiness, Ravi Zacharias and to an extent C.S. Lewis. The epistemological moorings of this method vary from exponent to exponent and are not always readily apparent. However, it is clearly not rationalistic in orientation or motivation. As a result, approaches to grounding law and ethics tend to be diverse.

The classical, evidential and existential approaches outlined above do overlap in the practice of apologetics and are rarely strictly isolated. Each has made an important contribution to Christian apologetics over the centuries and offer key insights for defending the faith. That being said, it must be asked, are these approaches to apologetics methodologically the most biblically faithful, theologically consistent and helpful models for defending the faith today? The Van Tillian answer is no. It is *not* that apologists using these models are faithless, or theodicies unimportant, or evidences useless, or the human condition not an important signal of transcendence. On the contrary, all these considerations are very important in defending the faith. The issue is ultimately over whether biblical, theological convictions are defining the starting point for the defence faith. This starting point in turn affects both the method of apologetic approach and the scope of the mandate.

The fourth school of thought then in apologetics has been called *presuppositional*. This method has its historical and theological roots in St. Augustine and later St. Anselm and is characterized by the maxims, 'faith seeking understanding' or 'I believe in order to understand.' The modern development of this method is found in the highly original work of Cornelius Van Til. This view, in contrast to the classical and evidentialist model proceeds as follows: "Instead of trying to *prove* the truth of Christianity to the unregenerate, it assumes its truth at the outset and then challenges the natural man by demonstrating that on his pre-suppositions nothing is true, nothing can be accounted for, and his own thinking is invalid."[9] Thus, Van Til's goal was to show that the Christian worldview is the *only* rational and objectively valid one, in an indirect way, by revealing the *impossibility of the contrary*. His objective was to develop a God-centred apologetics, without compromise or cutting off communication with the non- believer. The presuppositional model does not employ the Socratic defensive method using autonomous and foundationalist 'tests for truth' to demonstrate to the natural man the validity of Christian claims. It is rather self-consciously God-centred. It holds that the almighty and all-conditioning God is not subject to the subjective and self-sufficient court of human reasoning, but is the very foundation and *pre-condition* of the possibility of human reasoning. In the presuppositional theological outlook, the basic assumption is that for human beings, self-consciousness presupposes God-consciousness and therefore spending time trying to "prove" God's existence directly is redundant. Rather, beginning with the ontological trinity we seek to show that:

> We either begin with the self-contained God and his eternal decree as man's ultimate environment, as derived from scripture, or we assume that chance is ultimate, in which case man can know nothing unless he knows everything. And to know everything is especially an impossibility in an evolving universe in which potentiality and possibility are unlimited.[10]

For Van Til it was impossible for people to suspend judgement and reason from 'self-evident' arguments and 'brute facts,[11] because all people have pre-theoretical commitments; every idea and sense datum is inescapably interpreted in terms of an over-arching paradigm. In presuppositionalism then, the apologist is urged to recognize that all ideas and arguments are located within a synoptic view of reality within which they make sense, so that our starting point, method and conclusion are always involved in each other. Consequently, facts are what they are as part of the Christian system of truth – facts are what they are because God is what he is. This method then is not underpinned by an Enlightenment story of human rational autonomy and a self-explanatory nature, but a biblical one under the sovereign Trinity, who made, sustains and governs all things by his own authority. Here we have an epistemology that is neither foundationalist (modern), nor post-foundationalist (post-modern) but rather pre-foundationalist and biblical. A biblically-derived epistemology that pre-supposes the truth of all Scripture, holding that its revelation is indispensable to valid thinking, means that law and ethics must find their foundation here and here alone. Thus Van Til's method has a pre-modern origin within the Augustinian tradition. Hans Küng's reflection on the biblical harmony in St. Augustine's Christian philosophy is applicable to presuppositionalism:

> Such a "Christian philosophy" is therefore not grounded in thinking as such but is reflective self-interpretation of the Christian faith, especially in regard to God and the human soul. Consequently, submission to divine authority is prior to all searching and researching. It is understandable that in this view – as opposed to the Cartesian – the principle *credo, ut intelligam*, "I believe in order to understand," should be mainly stressed.[12]

With notable exceptions like Anselm, until the time of John Calvin, the Augustinian emphasis (granting that Augustine himself was not self-consistent on this point) was largely abandoned by early apologists in favour of a reconciliation of Greek Socratic, Platonic and Aristotelian thought with Christianity. Thus a kind of scholasticism indebted to Greek philosophy has been the majority report amongst Christian apologists for the greater part of Church history.

13.4 The Story of Postmodernity

For centuries western thought was dominated by the conviction that all that exists is subject to God's immanent, providential activity and depends on him for its existence, while God still remains utterly distinct and transcendent, as the creator, not dependent upon the creation. There is created being and uncreated being and one cannot speak about these types of being as though they are part of one larger whole (being). However, beginning in the medieval era, certain Christian thinkers began to postulate that everything that is exists in the same way and in the same sense:

> Creation "is" only insofar as it participates in – or is suspended from – the creator. In contrast, Scotus asserts that "to be" is predicated univocally; that is, both the creator and the creature exist in the same way or in the same sense...the result is that the vertical suspension of creation from the creator is unhooked, and because being is "flattened," the world is *freed to be an autonomous realm*.[13]

Here the creature is granted an independent status of being, and is no longer explicitly dependent upon God. The Christian idea of transcendence (distinction of God) is also implicitly negated. Autonomy (self-law and rule) over theonomy (God's law and rule) thus invades human thought. This tendency to deny or ignore the truly transcendent has continued in western philosophy even though it appears in different forms – indeed it is at the very heart of the claims of *modernity*. It is essential then to understand the essence of modernity in order to notice where there is continuity and where there is discontinuity with modernity in the *postmodern* mood of our time. Though the *seeds* of secular, autonomous reason were sown long before, it was the Catholic philosopher and mathematician, Rene Descartes [1596-1650] in the seventeenth century who most clearly divorced the creator from his creation and thereby *knowledge and law from revelation* and laid the foundations upon which many after him would build. According to Descartes, we begin the project of knowledge with the self and doubt and hope from there to move toward certainty. Küng writes:

> With Descartes, European consciousness in a critical development reached an epochal turning point. Basic certainty is no longer centred on God, but on man. In other words, the medieval way of reasoning from certainty of God to certainty of the self is replaced by the modern approach: from certainty of the self to certainty of God.[14]

Peter Kreeft thus rightly contrasts the apologetic projects of Descartes and that of the Augustinian apologist Blaise Pascal. He observes that Descartes sought rationalistic certainty, utility, and ease, while Pascal was content to set aside an autonomous certainty for the kind of knowledge and understanding that comes through faith in Jesus Christ:

> His [Descartes'] chief critique of the ancients was that they lacked certainty, or "a sufficient criterion." Certainty, in turn, was his means to the end of utility, or efficiency, or "the conquest of nature." This technological conquest, in turn, was a means to the "relief of man's estate," that is, ease, comfort, the abolition of suffering. Yet these are precisely the three things his philosophy, and the civilization that has been seduced by it, not only fails to deliver but destroys. Life has never been so full of confusion and uncertainty. The average person has never felt so weak and helpless; and all social indicators show we feel exactly the opposite of ease and comfort.... Pascal is a prophet. Descartes is a false prophet.[15]

468

Küng equally notes the essentially Christ-less nature of Descartes' epistemological project: "There is nothing specifically Christian about his philosophy: Jesus Christ does not appear to have played any part in it." [16] Consequently *modern* philosophy is often said to have begun with Descartes. This established a new precedent, echoing ancient Greek scepticism, setting aside the thought of the Christian era by asserting that *knowledge must be established on the basis of humans, not God and revelation.* Descartes' now famous dictum "I think therefore I am," entailed the notion that valid knowledge could be acquired through methodological doubt, by finally finding an autonomous, *indubitable starting point* – the self. And from there, one could proceed to build a valid knowledge structure from the clear and distinct ideas that follow. However, other rationalists like Descartes, who wholeheartedly agreed with his project and method, came to differing conclusions about which clear and distinct ideas are 'self-evident' and what conclusions should follow from this autonomous starting point. Descartes himself went on to build a comprehensive philosophy of mind-body dualism.

The next significant figure in the unfolding story was Bishop George Berkeley [1685-1753], one of a trio of British empiricists that included John Locke and David Hume. He thought that all we can be certain of from this Cartesian starting point from human autonomy is *mental events* and properties. He reasoned that, since in human experience, our 'knowledge' comes from sense impressions processed by the human mind, how can we really know that there is a mind and body duality, as Descartes thought? He suggested that perhaps sense impressions come directly from God with no material world mediating the impressions in between – only minds exist, matter does not! Ironically, he developed this line of thought in an attempt to refute materialistic atheism.

Thus it was only a small and obvious next step to the thought of Scottish philosopher David Hume [1711-1776] who held that on this basis we cannot possibly know that there really is a God 'out there' sending us these sense impressions, we only know that we exist, and we cannot even 'prove' that deductively. If we are then merely a bundle of sensations (Hume was sceptical about the very idea of a self), how can we know that we have any real knowledge at all? Hume showed that the basic assumptions of cause and effect relations and inductive reasoning from particulars to general conclusions, are not rationally justifiable in themselves (by reference to the human mind), but are in fact 'beliefs' formed through 'custom.' That is, they are not proved but are 'believed' in order to make our experience intelligible so that we can have knowledge. It comes as no surprise that a radical scepticism was the result. Critically then, within a climate of mounting doubt and in an attempt to rescue science and knowledge from the scepticism of Hume, the German philosopher Immanuel Kant [1724-1804] thought he might find a way out of this *inexorable* plunge into the void, by offering a new method; a synthesis of rationalism and empiricism. He conceded that we cannot know *things in themselves*, what he called the noumenal realm or reality of things as they actually are, because our minds (faculty of intuitive beliefs) actually impose the ideas of causality, extension, space, and so forth upon the world of our senses. However, what we can know is the world as it 'appears to us,' that is the phenomenal realm, as an aspect of our experience, and so perhaps rescue the project of science.[17] Kant's 'Copernican revolution' is highly significant for understanding postmodern thought. Thus far in philosophic inquiry, he says, we have sought to conform and shape our thinking to objects or reality *out there*. But if we have no intuitive conception (ideas) of these things prior to our experience of them, then we are stuck with Hume's scepticism; we are merely receiving a bombardment of unrelated sense impressions about which we cannot have any real knowledge, because sense impressions don't give us intuitions and general principles (metaphysics). So Kant seeks to turn the tables and suggests that objects of knowledge (reality) in fact conform to the intuitive structure of our minds (space, time, causality, substance). His illustration from astronomy is quite helpful. For if reality is in fact structured by our perception and conceptions then we can 'know things' about the phenomenal realm before experience (*a priori*). Consequently he appears, in principle, not to fall into the radical empiricist trap of being bombarded with raw data to which we must conform our thinking, leaving us, in fact, without knowledge or any justification for the 'customs' of thought about which Hume speaks. So Kant tries to bring together the insights of rationalism's 'innate ideas' with empirical experience in the 'phenomenal' world. On this view however, in a very important sense, the subject (the observer) and the object (the thing experienced) become one and the same. Kant's philosophy implicitly elevates human beings to the status of creators of heaven and earth because these realities are in fact structured by human intuitive thinking. In this sense, the world may be seen as but a construct of our individual imaginations.

This idea leads to the conclusion that the human mind brings or *gives* rationality and meaning to reality in an 'original' fashion. Because humanity, in Kant's view, can only truly know things about the *phenomenal world of their experience* as structured by their minds, people cannot know things as they really are *in themselves*. He assumes then that our thought structure does not give us access to reality *as it is in itself.* Again, because of the ultimacy of the human mind shaping reality, for Kant, any god there may be cannot be known and certainly cannot speak to human beings by revelation; since any such revelation would itself be structured by the human mind. However, because human reason is severely limited by Kant, one can leave room for faith. One could therefore argue that Kant unwittingly built the superstructure for a postmodern 'openness' to spirituality combined with deep scepticism toward meta-stories; where science is really only a form of psychology that describes the human mind (more than it can the real world), and faith is a form of blind irrationalism that involves a Kierkegaardian leap into the unknowable noumenal. It was left to Georg Wilhelm Friedrich Hegel [1770-1831], however, to truly develop the consequences of Kant's autonomous man. If Kant's epistemology was right, Hegel concluded, then 'the rational is the real.' From this starting point Hegel saw that Kant's 'things in themselves' were an unknowable affront to autonomous thought. If human beings and not God are to be ultimate, *humanity's decree* must replace the divine decree, thus 'things in themselves' must not be left floating, leaving room for a transcendent God. How could Hegel eliminate the *thing in itself?* He does it by positing that Mind or Spirit is the *only* reality.[18] He builds the philosophy of consciousness to its apogee. His contention is that since it is preposterous to say anything at all about an object that can have no relation to our consciousness (the noumenal realm), that is to speak of a reality apart from a subject, the mind (rational subjectivity) must itself be proclaimed the ultimate unconditioned reality, the only true and real being. Thus to overcome Kant's dualism, Hegel gives us an absolute self-consciousness of mind or spirit as the *only reality*, a god realizing itself through the historical process, an evolving mind. With God ejected from reality, humans (the new gods) were now free to impose their idea, word and law on the world. Rushdoony concludes, "Hegel's radicalism was developed by his heirs fragmentarily.... From Kierkegaard through Sartre, the existential facet was steadily developed and exploited.... Hegel's radical humanism made man ultimate and freed him from the past as well as from the beyond." [19]

With people thus 'liberated,' the next critical figure and true father of the postmodern mood was Friedrich Wilhelm Nietzsche [1844-1900]. Nietzsche, a proto-existentialist, could not endure the notion of not being God if there were such a being, so he held that there are no gods. The truth or falsehood of such a claim was not relevant. Why give credence to man-made plausibility structures, logic, meaning, truth or even grammar and so establish a new 'beyond' over man? For him, untruth was a condition of life, the lie is necessary to realize oneself as god. The God of revelation, of Christianity, was dead and only the superman was left in his place. Nietzsche had followed the Hegelians in abolishing truth and the beyond. He openly acknowledged his epistemological starting point:

> The Hypothesis that, at bottom, things proceed in such a moral fashion that human reason must be right, is a mere piece of good-natured and simple minded trustfulness, the result of the belief in Divine truthfulness - God regarded as the creator of all things – these concepts are our inheritance from a former existence in a Beyond.[20]

Nietzsche, now beyond good and evil, truth and falsehood, is without any criterion for judgement. Why should life be considered better than death when even Hegel's "conscious world" cannot be a starting point for valuation? He cannot do without a criterion but it cannot be God, individual consciousness or collective consciousness – there can be no God over man. No *true* nature of being could remain, all must be a cyclical *becoming*, an eternal recurrence. Critically in the genealogy of postmodernity, clearly linking Nietzsche to Foucault, Rushdoony observes:

> In the concluding words of *The Will to Power,* Nietzsche admitted his inability to find meaning: he could only describe. "This world, do you want a name for this world? A solution for all its riddles?... This world is the will to power – and nothing more. And you yourself are this will to power – and nothing more." [21]

This is simply nihilism. Whatever motif it adopts, human rational autonomy ends here in ruin, annihilation and meaninglessness. It is pure negation. Nietzsche's final conclusion is telling:

What I tried to do was to stand on my own shoulders, to super-impose nature upon nature, denying a creator God, insisting that the world lives on itself; feeds on its own excrement, as I say somewhere among my notes. Where did Titanism of defiance lead me? To the same pit as Schopenhauer's Titanism of denial – to moral and spiritual exhaustion, to the nothingness of the Abyss.[22]

Later, existentialists like Jean Paul Sartre continue this theme of descent into the abyss in works like '*Being and Nothingness.*' Indeed with the Abyss as both the ending and the starting point, 'man is a useless passion.[23] Sartre thus plainly asserts the negation of God and divinisation of humanity: "The best way to conceive of the fundamental project of human reality is to say that man is a being whose project is to be God... to be man means to reach toward being God. Or if you prefer, man fundamentally is the desire to be God."[24] Having seen Nietzsche wanting to rid the world of a universal grammar, a twentieth-century contemporary of Sartre, Ludwig Wittgenstein (1889-1951), began to undercut the possibility of transcendent meaning in language. He held that our use of language occurs within a self-contained system with its own rules. Thus use of language is like a game, requiring knowledge of the rules of the game and an appreciation for the significance of terms to use the language; the conclusion was that the various language *games* have little relationship to each other:

> Wittgenstein explicitly abandoned any concept of truth as correspondence with reality, and instead he characterised it as a function of language. This means that no statement or proposition can be limited to a single meaning – its meaning is completely dependent upon context. And so all attempts at discovering truth or meaning are trapped by the language game in which they appear.[25]

The logical progression from this kind of language theory was toward the postmodern notion that there is no universal framework of meaning to language. Jean-Francois Lyotard argued that postmodern thinking requires a "war on totality."[26] We cannot assign universal meaning to anything since there is no God and therefore no universal overarching truth or reality. Critical to this development is the French philosopher Michel Foucault (1926-1984), the most-cited thinker in the humanities today. Though many postmodern thinkers deny they are true nihilists, Foucault was a self-conscious follower and admirer of Nietzsche, and like Nietzsche, he was a sexual deviant – dying of AIDS as a result of homosexual behaviour. He adored Marx and Freud, but it was Nietzsche who was most influential on his thought and to whom he gives most credit. Indeed, even Nietzsche's insanity simply "opened up the possibility for thinking about the distinction between reason and unreason."[27] Concerning Nietzsche's insanity Foucault writes in *Madness and Civilisation*:

> Nietzsche's madness – that is the dissolution of his thought – is that by which his thought opens out onto the modern world. What made it impossible makes it immediate for us; what took it from Nietzsche offers it to us...where there is a work of art, there is no madness; and yet madness is contemporary with the work of art, since it inaugurates the time of its truth.[28]

For Foucault, Nietzsche, even in insanity, was an artist (creating himself) whose masterpiece inaugurates the very time in which his ideas (art) are to be seen as a new 'truth.' The radical humanistic relativity of such a view has characterized much of the postmodern mood. The intellectual heritage implicit in this deep connection between these two men helps us to understand the contours of the postmodern mind. For Foucault, to call the dissolution of Nietzsche's thought madness is to classify, order and cover up the experience – such orderings need to be resisted to make room for novelty. As the philosopher of power, Nietzsche is echoed in Foucault's identification of the pursuit of truth as "a will to knowledge"[29] which tends to arbitrarily establish its own truth to be imposed on others, putting power in the hands of the writer or speaker. Foucault writes, "...power produces knowledge...there is no power relation without the correlative constitution of a field of knowledge, nor any knowledge that does not presuppose and constitute at the same time power relations."[30]

Here knowledge and power are seen as two sides of the same coin. Yet, how Foucault is able to use *words* to *unmask* power relations without falling into his own trap, or avoid the consequence of his own 'will to knowledge,' is unclear. The postmodern thinker Jacques Derrida, again working from the *presumption of atheism* and the ultimacy of the abyss, denies that language has a fixed meaning connected to a fixed, purposeful reality; that is, he denies the transcendental signified. To assign definitive meaning to language is to posit a realm of an *ultimate word* or thought, a *logocentrism*. However, since God does not exist for Derrida, no such meaning can be assigned. In this conclusion, Derrida is surely right – if there is no God, there can be no ultimate meaning assigned to anything. It is therefore clear, though ironic, that although postmodern thought is the direct descendant of Descartes, Kant, Hegel, and Marx, it *rejects* their certainties, meta-stories and totalizing schemes. For example, Hegel's *historical* dialectic is rejected because in order for all people to be their own gods, there cannot be a *collective consciousness* dictating truth, since such 'truth' is manifest in an 'oppressive' *confession* or *institution*. Such oppression is the *will to power and knowledge*, inevitably characterized by violence.[31] Naturally, history itself then also falls victim to relativism, in the eviscerating hands of the deconstructionist:

> The postmodern historiographer Greg Dening argues that recorded history is no more than an illusion of the past and that in reality it is determined by the cultural context and personal preferences of the historian. He claims, "History is something we make rather than something we learn."[32]

Since power relations are allegedly at the root of all such 'histories,' relativism is seen as a moral imperative. By it the deconstructionist is seeking 'justice' for the oppressed. The question is, on what does the deconstructionist stand as he slashes away at history? If all things are relative to man (not God) and ultimately subjective, what happens to the idea of justice to which they appeal? Nietzsche is again the forerunner of the postmodern mind in going to the heart of the problem. If moral categories are also relative and subjective, then moral values are only an 'appearance.' This being the case, how can one person's 'appearance' (personal preference or view) be a basis for condemning another persons' 'appearance.' For example, in telling his readers that there are 'no things in themselves' (following Hegel) Nietzsche writes:

> It is of cardinal importance that the real world should be suppressed... war against war the hypotheses upon which a real world has been imagined. The notion that moral values are the highest values belongs to this hypothesis. The superiority of the moral valuation would be refuted, if it could be shown to be the result of an immoral valuation – a specific case of real immorality: it would thus reduce itself to an appearance, and as an appearance it would cease from having any right to condemn appearance.[33]

If moral codes of the Christian era are in fact just disguised power relations to oppress others, then they are an 'immoral valuation' and so a mere appearance. Postmodern thinker Richard Rorty thus says concerning truth and morality, "...we can keep the notion of 'morality' just insofar as we can cease to think of morality as the voice of the divine part of ourselves and instead think of it as the voice of ourselves as members of a community, speakers of a common language." [34] Here morality is no longer the voice of God in the soul, but of a community of individual speakers. This moral and epistemological relativism embraces an autonomous individualism and communitarian relativism. Here the 'community' can change truth, morality and therefore law, as the majority see fit. Fundamental to all these opinions and implications is a total denial of any *transcendent authority* that can ground truth, language, history or moral law apart from individual tastes and an ever-evolving community consensus. It has been thinkers like Van Til, R. J. Rushdoony, Greg Bahnsen and others amongst the new Puritans in the modern era, who have emphatically demonstrated that if Christians are to be epistemologically self-conscious and not get caught in the same trap as the postmodern humanists, swimming in moral relativity, we must root ourselves in the transcendent authority of biblical revelation and its law to ground all moral judgements.

Postmodernism thus conceives of all religion, truth and morality as ultimately relative only to man, depicts history as a Nietzschean record of the raw will to power and knowledge, and exercises a general hermeneutic of suspicion toward all grand narratives. As such, in the name of justice, it gives rise to virulently anti-Christian thought structures and to "histories that implicate Christianity in a wide range of the cultures ills, racial conflicts, the ecological crisis, battles over sexuality and gender." [35] And since many postmodernists are insufficiently epistemologically self-conscious (unaware of their starting point or unprepared to push their thinking to its inevitable end), many insist that they are *not* advancing just another meta-narrative (i.e. nihilism), but are rather revealing the absence of one:

> I regret that I have been misinterpreted in this way...I totally refuse the label nihilism which has been ascribed to me and my American colleagues. Deconstruction is not an enclosure in nothingness, but an openness toward the other. [36]

However, deconstruction is supposed to be engaged in a reading of a text that depends upon a *primary reading* of a text; that is, it is a double reading that is parasitic on a primary reading. It seeks to locate a point of *otherness* to destabilize a dominant reading and does so in the name of 'justice' – a justice that is always on the horizon but never achieved since a definite justice would be a contradiction for post-modern thought. An 'arrived-at' justice would itself need deconstructing. Clearly, however, you cannot deconstruct from nowhere, without presuppositions and pre-theoretical commitments. Justice is a moral valuation, so the question of criterion has not been escaped by the deconstructionist. An ethical authority is merely being smuggled in by the back door, since openness to the 'other' is itself an ethical commitment! So despite its proponents' protestations to the contrary, postmodern thinkers have their own meta-story that seeks to trump modernism ('unmasking' all epochal stories as the naked will to power and knowledge). Yet ironically, the essential implication of postmodern thought is that ultimately no story can legitimately 'evaluate' the truth of another, since grand-scale narratives (worldviews) are subjectively and culturally conditioned. Claims to overarching meaning of an absolute or objective character are said to simply hide the motives of violence, power and control. All such claims are thus to be viewed with suspicion and rejected. Instead an 'infinite openness' to the 'other' and resistance to assign a definitive meaning to language, literature or life, is the *only right way* to encounter and understand text or human experience. What then is this, but another totalizing scheme in the light of which all history and literature is to be understood? The ostensible revelation of the *absence* of a meta-narrative, is itself a narrative with absolute intent! It is very telling that we have now reached a very clear antithesis between biblical faith and autonomous human thought. In our day Western thought has come to the dead-end of *deconstructing* life, meaning, morality and history into the void, from a platform of illusions. By contrast Van Til's reformed thought was concerned with seeking to *reconstruct* life, meaning and morality in terms of the infallible foundation of the Word of God.

Given its denial of the transcendent, one of the points of tension within postmodernism now becomes obvious. The relativism of deconstructionism in its quest for 'justice,' and the presumption of the power motive as the primary motive force, either constitutes a true 'story of stories,' capturing and 'unmasking' all others, or it does not. If it is not the true story that unmasks the others, it is, on its own terms, useless and

THE MISSION OF GOD

can be ignored. Now as we have seen, by its own narrative structure, way of speaking, and bold claims, postmodern thought inevitably exposes itself, on its own criterion, as another 'power play' with 'absolute intent,' disguised as newly enlightened, pacifistic, rationality. But if this is so, on its own assessment of knowledge and power relations, it cannot be a story that really 'accounts for' and explains the stories of other interpretative communities as it claims to do – its deconstruction is in fact hopelessly prejudiced. If the postmodern hermeneutic is 'true' and not 'false' (i.e. that all meta-accounts of truth, history and reality are in fact masks for a will to knowledge as power), it is found to participate in the very injustice of which it accuses all its predecessors and competitors, rendering it incapable of authentic evaluation. In short, we need only deconstruct the deconstructionist to expose the point of tension. Given this thorny problem and the fact that the lineage of the postmodern mood is traceable to the assumptions of modernity, it becomes all the more ironic to note that for the postmodern thinker, the alleged point of *discontinuity* with modernity is the quest for absolute meaning and truth:

> What postmodernism rejects about modernity is its alliance with the quest for absolute clarity (meaning) and certainty (truth) that, since Plato, has often been seen at the very heart of philosophy itself; more specifically, it is the rejection of the two dominant modern strategies for achieving absolute knowledge, Cartesian immediacy and Hegelian totality.[37]

In its desire to not assign absolute meaning and truth, postmodern thought tacitly, perhaps unwittingly, establishes the infallibility of its own criticism as a new totalizing standard. Thus in the postmodern hermeneutic of suspicion as it relates to modernity, the student has returned to chastise his own teacher, the disciple to slap his master.

13.5 Theological and Philosophical Implications for Apologetics

In considering the implications of these ideas for Christian apologetics, one core task is to ask which elements, if any, of the postmodern critique, are consistent with biblical presuppositions and which are not. First, Christianity can clearly affirm a *hermeneutic of finitude* that critiques the arrogant Enlightenment notion of *pure objectivity* through autonomous rational reflection, as right on target. Finite human beings, based on autonomous reasoning, cannot set up the objective universals necessary to give an authoritative and binding account of reality that must control valid conclusions. Such a role is for God alone. Second, in light of the biblical doctrine of the Fall, Christians can also grant some merit to subjecting claims for truth and meaning (outside of the clear biblical witness) to the hermeneutic of suspicion, asking serious questions about power, control and selfish desires (sin) as motive forces masked as truth and right.

That said, Christian apologetics must equally recognize the *continuity* of the postmodern mood with the religious *confession* of modernity. This continuity is most clearly seen in the 'unmasking' of their arrogant forebears from *precisely the same epistemological platform from which those forebears worked* – being part of the same self-destructive philosophic bloodline. That is, within postmodern thought, reasoning, thinking, judging and deconstructing are carried out on the presumption of autonomy and independence from the divine (or transcendent), a foundation-less platform in the abyss. In other words, the anti-Christian assumption remains that postmodernists have an *intelligible set of concepts to work with without reference to God.* Their epistemological project is thus begun from precisely the same self-refuting starting point employed by their modern forebears; forebears they malign for their arrogant certitudes. As Don Carson observes:

> What is striking...is the simple fact that both moderns and postmoderns begin the epistemological quest with the finite "I", even though they come up with radically different structures of thought. In fact...it is this continuity of the focus on the finite self as the starting place in epistemology that constitutes the chief reason why some thinkers prefer to treat post-modernism as a form of late modernism or even of ultra-modernity.[38]

James K. Smith rightly suggests therefore that what is often called *postmodern* thinking is in essence *modern* thought in a new outfit with some new terminology, pushed to its logical conclusions.[39] At bottom, they both hold to the idea that what exists, God or finite persons or objects, can be described independently of the transcendent God and his self-revelation. The foundation of epistemology for both modernity and postmodernity is the finite 'I,' the subjective self – where knowledge begins with autonomous man, he can never transcend himself and his subjectivity.

Given the intellectual lineage of postmodernity, the Christian apologist must recognize that there is an inevitable logic to the postmodern mood and train of thought that is more consistent and honest than that of their modernist, rationalistic forebears. In the absence of direct access to an objective reality, subjectivity, for them, is the *necessary* and only path to salvaging relevance and meaning. The presuppositions with which they work must lead them here as Rushdoony shows us:

> In a lonely universe, with man as the sole thinker, man can become subjective, because he is the only intelligent point of reference. All else is at best a blind order...and he alone can tell that tale, understand the universal meaninglessness and the cosmic surd. Meaning then is obviously subjective. In such a world-view, meaning requires subjectivity, because meaning cannot exist elsewhere by definition. Relevance in every area of life means subjectivity. If as modern philosophy holds, the world is man's will and idea, then to abandon subjectivity is to abandon relevance, meaning and truth.[40]

This is a critical statement since it reveals that we cannot understand postmodernity as the rejection of *all* meaning and truth, but the abortive attempt to *salvage relevance, meaning and truth* in the face of the abyss, by clinging to subjectivity alone.

13.6 Responding to the 'post' of Modernity

How is the Christian concerned with apologetics to respond to these salient facts? There are three possibilities. *First*, an insistence on objective meaning and truth located in the absolute triune God, and an infallible, transcendent referent in the scriptures, can be *abandoned* for a subjective and relativistic view of Christianity. This is clearly expressed in evolutionary perspectives on the faith set forth by some contemporary emergent church writers seeking to be self-consciously postmodern in their 'Christian' response to the intellectual climate. Barry Taylor who quotes theological liberals like Karen Armstrong approvingly has put it forcefully, "Religion is always a *cultural production* and the role of socio-cultural issues cannot be discounted from the ways in which we envision and understand faith."[41] For Taylor, in light of postmodern developments, the evolution of Christianity into something 'other' is essential for its survival:

> Whether Christianity has any future at all as a vibrant expression

of faith in the man from Galilee is a matter of debate as far as I am concerned. Perhaps the times call for something else, something other, not merely the repackaging of the old metaphors (playing 'relevant' game), but a new incarnation of what it means to follow Jesus.[42]

By way of further explanation as to his meaning he writes:

> To "go with the flow" might seem a trite way of describing theological engagement, but a commitment to fluidity and a willingness to swim in the cultural waters rather than insisting on one's own paddling pool is a necessary perspective. All these thoughts can be summarized as a commitment to weakness rather than strength. "Muscular Christianity" and "robust faith" are views that worked well in modernity's concrete world, but the viability of Christianity is not guaranteed by claims to power and declarations of strength and doctrinal postures.[43]

The postmodern themes of weakness, powerlessness, openness to the other, and a relativistic fluidity, are recurring motifs in emergent church literature, guiding an engagement with the non-Christian that desires, above all, a syncretistic Jesus acceptable to the atheist, Buddhist, Jew, Muslim and Hindu alike. The difficulty here, for anyone concerned with being biblical, is that emergent thought is a complete *capitulation* to the presuppositions and assumptions of *ultra-modernity* previously analyzed. These assumptions are alien and hostile to the Christian faith; a faith embodied in the doctrines of creation, sovereignty, the Fall, atonement, redemption and judgement. That is, at the heart of the postmodern worldview is a universe in which God (if he exists) is not totally sovereign, where human beings, not God, must interpret history and make it conform to their idea. In this dualistic world of idea and matter that are alien to each other – since not created and totally predestined by a sovereign God – man must, in 'original' fashion, bring them into fruitful relationship to shape a past and actualize a future he envisions, rather than *discover* and embrace the reality God commands and predestines. The *idea* must be realized in and through people since human individuals and communities frame the idea, incarnate it and actualize it. Thus the Hegelian and existential roots to postmodern 'emergent' responses to the apologetic challenge of our time are very plain and were clearly articulated more than a century ago:

> The interior spirit of any age is the spirit of God; and no faith can be

living that has that spirit against it; no Church can be strong except in that alliance. The life of the time *appoints the creed of the time* and modifies the establishment of the time.[44]

Those words could just as easily have been penned by Barry Taylor. The spirit and judgement of any age is thus inspired and so, by definition, for that age infallible. This is why 'orthodoxy' for some emergent writers is an evolving concept, with an evolving God, both being defined by the spirit of the age. As emergent church guru Brian McLaren writes, "I have become convinced that a generous *orthodoxy* appropriate for our postmodern world will have to *grow out of the experience* of the post-Christian, post-secular people of the cities of the twenty-first century."[45] On this view, Christian faith is an adaptation, the product of idea and experience (praxiology) evolving from the minds and practices of city dwellers in the twenty-first century. Consequently, the task of apologetics in its confrontation with anti-Christianity is *abandoned* by the emergent church and exchanged for a spirit of accommodation and reinterpretation. This is because the 'idea' of the people will reshape the very essence of orthodoxy, leaving the Christian nothing unchanging to defend. Taylor summarizes this perspective tellingly: "Religions exist in certainty and sanctity; faith lives in inquiry and fluidity."[46] Here, sanctity (respect for the sacred and Christian holiness) and certainty (confidence in objective truth) are to be given up in favour of the fluidity of 'faith' – a mere euphemism for syncretism. As a result, apologetics is viewed as irrelevant by definition since the existentialist orientation of the emergent writers destroys the decisiveness of the past and sacred authority, especially that of religious institutions and orthodox confessions.

This so-called 'Christian' reaction to the postmodern mood and postmodern thought, that reduces the defence of the faith to complete irrelevance, must be rejected as fatally flawed since it is built, like postmodernity itself, on humanistic and Enlightenment assumptions and rationalisations. As a result, emergent church thinking, representing the new liberalism, or 'progressive' Christianity, has already signed its own death warrant. Furthermore, despite its superficial appearance of being cutting edge, emergent church doctrinal concerns are as old as late nineteenth-century Christian liberalism. It is also the case that their prodigious effort to leap on the passing postmodern intellectual bandwagon was in vain, since postmodern hermeneutics have already become passé in the world of academia. It is fascinating to note that western culture is already facing rapid disillusionment with postmodern nihilism, subjectivism and rootlessness. Don Carson notes that in the year 2000 a consultation amongst twenty of the world's 'leading intellectuals' was convened at the Sorbonne and tasked with analysis of the current cultural situation; not a single paper presented even used the term postmodern. Carson thus rightly points out concerning the flurry of populist emergent literature and its fascination with postmodernism:

> Once again a movement that was on the cusp of intellectual endeavour half a century ago and popular in Europe four decades ago, and made popular on university campuses here a quarter of a century ago, is now the darling of popular evangelical writers trying to sound prophetic.[47]

The somewhat elitist and narrow 'emergent conversation' that implies the postmodern Christian's 'generous orthodoxy' has captured all that was good in the centuries before, and by eliminating the thinking of all the defunct absolutists who insist on propositional truth, has brought us to the cusp of a new and great era where 'everything must change,' is a hollow and naïve mantra. Michael Horton shares this scepticism:

> The cheerleading for the idea that we have entered a radically new era, a utopia of unprecedented opportunity fails to move me...because I just don't believe this hype. I think that every period has its pluses and minuses and that typecasting periods leads to demonizing or equally impulsive lionizing.[48]

The *second* possible response in addressing the implications of the postmodern mood for apologetics is the *classical, foundationalist* reaction. This view, separating the realms of nature (natural law and general revelation) and grace (special revelation), has reacted to the postmodern mood by seeking retrenchment in Aristotelian, Thomistic and Cartesian assumptions, working to reaffirm the ability of unaided human reason to establish God as the most plausible hypothesis, or inference to the best explanation for reality – certainly at least as good as any other account. This classical response is based on various appeals to reason, logic, and 'tests for truth' by correspondence with reality, internal coherence and empirical adequacy. It has also tended to insist on the possibility of human objectivity in considering arguments for God, and has also seen objective, absolute truth as something not only discoverable by the unaided human mind, but also acceptable to sinful men, even when it concerns God, his work and being. This is because on the classical view the reason of man is normative and not sinful and corrupted.

Now as we have already seen, the unholy alliance of autonomous reasoning and Enlightenment foundationalism has within it the seeds of its own destruction since it cannot escape the finite self, when the finite 'I' is the starting point for knowledge. As Herbert Cushman notes concerning the ultimacy of man's mind in Cartesian thought, "For Descartes reality is within the Self; and the next question before him is how to get out of the Self."[49] As a result, "the existence of God is an implication of human consciousness."[50] If you begin with the self as the ultimate ground for truth and reality, you can only end with the self, with truth as an aspect of individual consciousness.

Another related problem with this Christian response to postmodernity is the relatively superfluous role to which *special revelation* is consigned, as it relates to the apologetic task in the contemporary context. The classical method, often justly criticized for its epistemology by those concerned with reaching people in our culture (people who are now largely working with existential and relativistic assumptions about knowledge), grants that essentially, fallen, sinful people are on the right track as far as they go in terms of a *neutral* and autonomous method of reasoning; all they need is additional information and argument to establish the truth of Christianity. The *classical method* is thus obligated (given its view of neutrality in reasoning) to prove a bare theism first and Christianity afterward. With reason, meaning and logic *taken for granted* (that is, functional and intelligible irrespective of the existence of the God of Scripture) and considered capable of interpreting 'facts' of 'nature' that, in principle, may or may not be created by God, the believer and non-believer are thus far seen as occupying the same epistemological ground – rationalizing the particulars of experience in an original fashion to see if they do or do not lead to the conclusion of God's existence. Consequently, the classical method does not start with the presupposition of the triune God of Scripture and bring to the table the *Christian theistic story* as a whole. Rather it begins with an attempt to prove from the 'bare facts' a deformed theism, which others also might be concerned to prove (i.e. deists, cults, Muslims), from which to launch the additional attempt to show that Christianity, amongst the other theistic faiths, is more probably true. Cornelius Van Til insightfully criticized the classical method at this very point, for its unbiblical attempt to defend the faith in a piecemeal fashion, granting only a mere 'probability' for the truth of Christianity, allowing, in principle, for the possibility of meaning and rationality to exist independent of God – the gap between high probability and certainty for the believer being filled by an irrationalistic appeal to 'faith,' mystery and the 'heart' respectively. Van Til writing with great insight states:

> A truly Protestant method of reasoning involves a stress upon the fact that the meaning of every aspect or part of Christian theism depends upon Christian theism as a unit.... No proposition about historical fact is presented for what it really is till it is presented as a part of the system of Christian theism that is contained in Scripture. To say this is involved in the consideration that all the facts of the created universe are what they are by virtue of the plan of God with respect to them. Any fact in any realm confronted by man is what it is as revelational through and through of the God and of the Christ of Christian theism. But if this is true – and it would seem to be of the very essence of the biblical point of view to say that it is true – then it follows that the whole claim of Christian theism is in question in any debate about any fact. Christian theism must be presented as that light in terms of which any proposition about any fact receives meaning."[51]

In other words, the classical defence against the postmodern mood assumes that there are a group of observational 'common facts' outside of any pre-theoretical commitments or interpretive theory by which hypotheses can be tested – it assumes *fact and meaning can be separated* in an abstract world. The classical approach thus assumes that the *postmodern unbeliever* has, in terms of his own nature and reasoning and irrespective of God's existence, access to a rational world, intelligible standards and concepts, and a moral sensibility by which he may judge, test, verify or deny biblical Christianity; but this is something explicitly denied by Scripture (Ps. 14:1; Eccl. 9:3; Rom. 1:20; Rom. 8:7; Rom. 9:20; 1 Cor. 1:20–25; Heb. 11:6). The classical model, by underestimating the noetic effects of sin, thus proposes a line of argument that is supposed to lead the non-believer, if he would just reason cogently, from his autonomous unbelief and fictitious world of bare facts (uncreated and directed), to embrace the *antithetical conclusions* of Christian theism! In the first place, this approach is less than authentically biblical and logically self-defeating since neutrality in reasoning is already a *de facto* denial of the God of Scripture. Furthermore, this line of argumentation seems totally unacceptable to the postmodern mind in light of the abject failure of an arrogant modernity brow-beating people with 'self-evident' truths and ideas that seemed self-evident only to some and not to others. It therefore seems clear that the postmodern suspicion of classical foundationalism has some warrant at this particular point and that consequently a serious rethinking of the theological and epistemological underpinnings of Thomistic and Cartesian rationalistic apologetics is warranted in our time. As Albert Wells has incisively remarked:

> Nothing could be clearer than that a better way needs to be found for understanding reality than that which the modern philosophical tradition has offered. Representatives of that tradition have persistently hesitated to attribute any philosophical importance to the biblical revelation. They have perpetuated the prevailing conception of philosophy as a rational discipline that cannot admit any other source of authentic knowledge than what can be immediately known by the autonomous mind.... The record is clear that the modern philosophical tradition has not been able to provide an intellectual approach to reality that is adequate to the vastness, the diversity, and the complexity of reality, to say nothing of the ultimate meaning. Nor does the current existentialist posture in itself offer a permanent solution.[52]

The *third* possible response in grappling with the implications of postmodernity for apologetics is a *presuppositional* one. Theologically, Van Til was keen to point out that there is a fundamental difference in epistemology and methodology between Paul and the Greek tradition (Plato or Aristotle), and it is with the assumptions of Platonic and Aristotelian thought that the postmodern mind claims it wishes to break. For the Greeks, man and his 'ideas' are the measure of all things and the final reference point for truth, the ultimate epistemological court of appeal. Logic or reason (ideas) and fact (external reality) are brought into fruitful relation by human reflection and authority alone. For St. Paul however, it was not human beings and their autonomous reason, but God and his revelation that constitutes the final referent and ultimate criterion for knowledge (Col. 1:15–17; Col. 2:2–3; 1 Cor. 1:18–25; Acts 17:25–28). Human depravity and wilful suppression of the truth meant for St. Paul that fallen man's speculative thinking is never a suitable pattern for a defence of the faith. Moreover, being both sinful and finite, human knowledge can never be comprehensive, objective or absolute. Such knowledge is only possessed by God as the creator and governor of all things, since there is no realm of 'possibility' above him, no unconscious recesses within him, and no mystery or occurrence beyond him that can undermine his exhaustively comprehensive and infallible knowledge. Greg Bahnsen points out:

> The temporal realm, with its created unity and diversity, finds its interpretative unity in the mind and decree of God. God's selfsufficient, absolutely rational, comprehensive and coherent plan for creation and historical eventuation provides the integrating category of interpretation for man's knowledge. God's creation of the world establishes the reality of the particulars and yet provides a genuine, pre-interpreted order to things.[53]

Thus St. Paul, and the entire New Testament, teach that we know whom we have believed (2 Tim. 1:12) and can be both persuaded and '*certain of what we hope for*' (Heb. 11:1–3). Only a Johannine and Pauline epistemology (John 1:1–5; Col. 1:15–17) is able to avoid the dead end of scepticism, nihilism and solipsism which characterise the implications of post or ultramodern thought. God's Word must therefore be declared to be the ultimate standard of truth; truth that cannot be judged by any higher or exterior standard or principle. For the presuppositional apologist, God's Word is more reliable than man's ideas or sensations, the collective consciousness or the Hegelian state. Christ's Word is that which brings all other words into judgement (John 5:22; Heb. 4:12; Acts 17:30–31), not vice versa. His Word is not one hypothesis among many, but carries a self-attesting authority (Ps. 119:89; Prov. 19:21; John 10:35; Is. 40:8; 1 Pt. 1:25). St. Paul knew that God's Word does not have to pass man's subjective and autonomous 'tests' before it can be taken seriously, but rather that all factuality, logic and reason would be meaningless without God as their *source* and foundation. Sinful man arrogantly demands to 'test' whether the 'God hypothesis' and 'revelation' is admissible on the basis of his autonomous principles of reason, logic and evidence, whilst all the while those very principles prove to be unintelligible without the God of Scripture. Thus we may rightly ask how one could proceed to verify the Word of the God of all knowledge? On what possible basis could the Word of the creator, sovereign and all-conditioning God be verified or denied – by what standard? God declares who he is in Scripture: "I Am that I Am," that is to say literally, "I Am He who is" (Ex. 3:14), beyond all man's limiting definitions, because God is the source of all definition. When Jesus was challenged concerning the basis of authority for his teaching and activity, he declared, "Before Abraham was, I Am" (John 8:58). If the Word was in the beginning, as the source and instrument of all creation, how does one 'explain' the beginning of all explanations? What criterion is there outside of God that could be invoked as an alternate starting point for knowledge? So it is clear that one must *begin with the God of truth in order to conclude with either God or truth.* St. Paul's method, unlike Plato's, begins with the presupposition of the authority of God and his Word, and from this platform of certitude, directly challenges the non-believer to make sense of life and thought without God, showing in the process that God has rendered foolish the wisdom of the world (1 Cor. 1:18–25). This biblical approach to the defence of the faith is critically important because unless the apologist stands on a specifically biblical epistemology – revelational presuppositionalism – that is neither classical foundationalist nor post-foundationalist in orientation, he is unwittingly building on the same false assumptions as the non-believer and thereby undermining himself and his witness.

13.7 Methodological Implications

There is no proposition without presupposition. We all bring a *schema* or *synoptic view* of reality to bear in assessing 'fact' and 'evidence.' Since this is the case, the Christian must begin the task of defending the faith having presupposed the truth and authority of biblical revelation as a whole; the postmodern individual comes to the 'facts' and 'evidence' with another pre-theoretical commitment. Interestingly, given the power and importance of 'story' in the postmodern paradigm, a relevant and appropriate apologetic in our time consists of a defence of the *biblical story or account of reality as a unit.* In other words, the apologist is called to defend, like Paul in Acts 17, *Christian theism* as revealed in Scripture, not theism in general.[54] In the presuppositional method, this also involves ensuring that fallen people do not get the impression that they can, on their anti-Christian principles, arrive at truth in any consistent, ultimate sense, in any field of human thought. Instead they must be shown that when they discover truth in the 'phenomenal' realm (true facts and

488

observations) be they moral or physical realities, they do so only on 'borrowed capital' from the Christian worldview, by virtue of the fact they are God's creatures living in God's world – that is, they do so by being inconsistent with what they profess to believe. This does not mean that non-believers cannot know true things about atoms and antelopes. It means that unless atoms and antelopes and are ultimately understood in their relation to God (created, designed, having a specific place in God's exhaustive plan for history) they are not properly understood at all. The truth that is known about them by the unbeliever is partial at best and then shown to be irrational and arbitrary if the non-believer were consistent with what he professes to believe about reality – that there is no God, no design plan, no objective, no absolute meaning, and no pre-established relationship between the facts of experience. In such a world, where man is prisoner to his own consciousness and subjectivity, nothing could be known, nothing is true, and no concrete definition of anything in the realm of experience is possible. We must therefore show the postmodern individual, that whether they realize it or not, to function rationally in this world (even in the deconstruction of a text), they must live as intellectual parasites on the Christian worldview. Rushdoony summarizes the appropriate objective of the presuppositional apologetic well:

> The Christian should begin his thinking consciously committed to reasoning systematically on the pre-supposition of the ontological trinity, the self-contained God whose infallibly inspired final revelation to man is Scripture. No piecemeal assumption of Christian theism is possible: the whole must be presupposed, and the whole must be shown to be the only pre-suppositions which makes for rationality and gives the possibility of consistent knowledge.[55]

Amidst the postmodern atmosphere of our time, in the apologetic task, we can agree with the non-believer that there is no *neutral area* of knowledge in our discussion that is unaffected by our faith-based governing presuppositions, or our community story. But unlike the postmodern approach to knowledge that ultimately reduces to the finite 'I,' the fact that there is no neutrality and no proposition without presupposition does not negate the possibility of critique of other 'stories' (worldviews) or the reduction of competing accounts of reality to the absurd. Van Til, who never formulated his apologetic arguments syllogistically, but preferred theological and doctrinal formulations, writes that "Christianity must claim that it alone is rational. It must not be satisfied to claim that God probably exists.... [T]he Christian is bound to believe and hold that his system of doctrine is certainly true and that other systems are certainly false."[56] Other systems are shown to be false by demonstrating that without the theological truths and presuppositions given to us in Scripture, life and thought are rendered unintelligible on their own terms, because of the patent contradictions involved in the denial of an all-conditioning God. Christianity is thus proven true by the impossibility of contrary accounts or stories of reality.

James Smith, using a narrative-based terminology, explains in a similar way, this two-fold approach, which he calls a 'new apologetic':

> Christianity offers a much better story. The mode of cultural engagement in the market place of ideas, then, is not syllogistic demonstration but narrative persuasion…this narrative persuasion as a "new apologetic", begins by pointing to the mythical status of competing ontologies and narratives and offers a counter-narrative from the Christian story that is embodied in practice…*this does not negate the possibility of critique*. The focus of critique is on demonstrating the internal antinomies of secular reason…an immanent critique. The point is that because secular accounts do not properly recognize the status of the world as creation, their framework is plagued with tensions and contradictions that can be demonstrated ad absurdum.[57]

In light of the failed rationalism and irrationalism of contemporary thought, so evident in the postmodern predicament of epistemological enclosure in the self, whilst insisting on an operative openness to the other, Christian philosopher Alvin Plantinga is helpful in urging that we must defend the faith from a distinctively *Christian platform* and starting point. If we do not, we will find ourselves using the same autonomous method that is wholly inadequate to arrive at the desired destination: God, truth, and meaning.[58]

In sum, the reality of the postmodern climate and the dead end reached by Western philosophy in language games, highlights the necessity, perhaps more than ever before in the history of Christendom, of utilizing and honing a distinctly biblical apologetic, and this means telling the best story and showing why the biblical account is the true story of stories.

As Curtis Chang aptly puts it, "Lose the Epic and you risk losing the Epoch."[59] If we want to win our generation, we must tell the great biblical epic and capture all other stories. In the Christian story, the Word, the *logos*, was made flesh and dwelt among us. Our story centres not on the self as ultimate, but with the *mystery* of Christ made manifest in the man Jesus Christ. This story is a sweeping and grand epic beginning with creation, moving into an historic battle between darkness and light, culminating in the appearance of truth incarnate and the triumph of the kingdom of God. It is a history of God's self-revelation, of a cosmic conflagration that must be told and retold for our time.

Everyone must choose between competing religious stories, since all human philosophy is inescapably confessional or religious. To help the inquirer and sceptic confront this, today's apologist must reach back over a millennium past Descartes and there locate our true evangelical and catholic heritage in the apostolic witness to Christ. Thus we need to reject the rationalistic and scholastic dualisms of idea and matter, nature and grace, reason and revelation, instead unifying the spheres of faith or revelation and reason, intertwining philosophy and theology so that when we are thinking we are believing, and when we are believing we are thinking. There are too many artificially constructed, absolute distinctions between what is believed and what is known. But God's truth in the world and his word, both in the created order and special revelation, are one. They are interrelated and connected and so cannot be known adequately or properly apart from one another. Scripture must therefore again take its rightful place in providing the theological framework, philosophical presuppositions and narrative structure for the defence of the faith. Unifying these spheres, Andrew Sandlin writes with insight for the apologist in the light of the hermeneutical challenge of postmodernity:

> The Scriptures come to us in human language, but this language was in fact created by God to suit his revelatory purposes. The scriptures come to us by means of the writing of mere humans, but the mere humans were created by God to serve as vehicles for His revelation. The scriptures are transmitted to us in human history, but God predestines this history [and mainly his church in history] as the matrix within which His Word is preserved. The Scriptures address all sorts of topics, heavenly, earthly, -historical, ethical, scientific, artistic, and on and on; and the God Who inspired the

Word shaped every single aspect of the universe of which his word speaks. Therefore, we can never speak of any aspect of the Word of God as though it were contingent on the world, any more than we can speak of any aspect of the universe as though it were anything other than contingent on God.[60]

Such biblical apologetics will, by definition, brings competing narratives (worldviews) into collision. In the postmodern context of our day, the biblical story can take into account the *narrative-borne nature* of meaning in general, being sensitive to it, but then critically engage, account for and *reinterpret* rival stories, bringing them to final resolution in the gospel. In this Augustinian and presuppositional model, the apologist retells the Christian account of reality in a fashion designed to 'take in' the reinterpreted non-Christian stories. This involves first showing the challenger that their non-Christian account of reality leads only into the abyss, and then inviting them to look at the biblical view of reality, and by the work of the Holy Spirit, captivate their hearts with an epic that soars into eternity. It then becomes clear that the challenger's account of reality was only a minor subplot, with incidental characters, in the script of God's great theatre that is human history. As Curtis Chang writes:

> Like sanded pegs falling into the holes of a massive woodwork, all the reworked aspects of the challenger's story – whether they are the desires of its characters, the flow of its plot or the direction of its dramatic action – now find their final and true place in the gospel.[61]

Establishing the biblical story's superior explanatory power is crucial to showing that it can capture all other challengers' stories, because a meta-narrative must not only explain external reality in a way that other stories cannot, it must also explain the other stories themselves. This is precisely what Scripture and the presuppositional method do – they not only reveal the folly and futility of non-Christian accounts, they explain the significance of those accounts in the wider context of God's exhaustive plan for history. Even man in his sin is revelational of God. Human rebellion and myth-making reveal man's fallenness, blindness and depravity, as well as his need for salvation and the righteousness of God in Jesus Christ.

It can thus be said with complete confidence that today's understandable attack, by a form of ultra-*modernity* (postmodernity) upon *old modernity* for its hermeneutical violence and power-grab, does not constitute a fatal blow to biblical Christianity nor does it 'expose' the biblical meta-narrative as a cynical quest for power and control. This is because first, as we have seen, true biblical faith is not allied to the arrogance, errors or assumptions of Enlightenment rationalism and second, because the biblical narrative transcends all eras, empires and schools of thought, accounting for and explaining them all – including the postmodern. Indeed a presuppositional defence of the faith unmasks the absolute intent within postmodernity, revealing that it can only understand its own failures by submitting to the biblical paradigm, which is not a message of violence to lord it over others, but the *gospel of peace* (Luke 2:13–14; Rom. 10:14–15; Eph. 2:17).

There is the world of difference between willing and grateful *surrender to Christ* and a self-centred act of 'knowledge-violence' for the sake of power; a chief concern of postmodern thought in regard to meta-narratives. Chang rightly points out that the gospel of Christ involves a very real and joyful human surrender that implies no violent coercion. Rather, the sinner's repentant and thankful submission to Christ in the gospel, exposes "postmodernism's tragic attachment to pride and self-sufficiency that insists all surrender is obliteration and coercion. There is a self-surrender that is love: the love of Christ that unites humanity to God."[62] This is the *gracious victory of God*, effected through Christ at the cross, to free man from slavery to the sinful autonomy of the finite 'I', the wretched, ego-centric self, and to bring people to their predestined wholeness by love. Until human beings acknowledge the triune God as the source of all legitimate power and meaning, law and morality, men live under the tyranny of sin, exerting over one another a fallen 'will to power,' oppressing others in the name of a new morality, enlightened rationality and human 'freedom.' The biblical narrative ends all such oppression as it crescendos in the final judgement at God's throne, where justice is not 'on the horizon' yet never achieved, but is fully realized in the divine verdict. There, all apparent ambiguities, power-plays, human conceits and vain imaginations, all sin and evil, finally come under the immediate searchlight of perfect justice and are brought to an end, concluding the biblical epic that thus resolves all other stories into the meaningful conclusion of the total reign of God. Presenting and defending this epic history and destiny is the Christian task in the postmodern world.

This powerful theological account of reality forms the foundation of our biblical vision for the *missio Dei*. The absolutely sovereign and triune Lord of time and eternity, in terms of his all-inclusive plan for history, provides fallen man, by grace, his law and gospel. By incarnation, atonement and resurrection power, Christ reclaims the totality of the creation as His, and exercising in himself the right of eminent domain, effectually calls out by His Holy Spirit, for himself, a new humanity, charged with exercising the dominion mandate, to take *every thought captive* and bring all things under the Lordship of Jesus Christ:

> All things have been created by the sovereign and triune God out of nothing, the total possibility, potentiality and actuality of all things is completely determined by the creator.... All things that have existed, do exist or shall exist, have no being nor any history and possibility apart from the sovereign creating power and act of God. Creation and history have no surprises for God: he made all things and all things move in terms of his decree from all eternity.[63]

Since God governs all things in his providence, there must be meaning, even when we cannot see it, in every event, and therefore inescapable hope for history. And since Christ has conquered sin, death, hell and Satan, victory for God's people is assured through the spread of the gospel as we faithfully proclaim and defend the faith in today's marketplace of ideas. Despite all opposition, by regeneration and obedience to the Great Commission in the omnipotent power of the Holy Spirit, the eschatological vision of the kingdom of God is to be progressively realized in and through God's people, here on earth, in every nation, culminating and reaching perfection in the new creation. In short, either all of life and thought is deconstructed into the void – which is the way of death – or it is reconstructed in terms of the kingdom of God, the way of life in the gospel and law of God. There is no doubting which epic shall win the epoch.

Chapter Fourteen

MEN OF ATHENS: EVANGELISM IN A PLURALISTIC AGE

Truth feareth nothing so much as concealment, and desireth nothing so much as clearly to be laid open to the view of all: when it is most naked, it is most lovely and powerful.

– Richard Sibbes

Preach Jesus Christ and let us do it more and more. By the roadside, in the little room, in the theatre, anywhere, everywhere let us preach Christ.... A Christless gospel is no gospel and a Christless discourse is the cause of merriment to devils.

– Charles Spurgeon

14.1 Should We Evangelize?

Evangelism, like apologetics, should be pursued as an expression and outgrowth of the lordship of Jesus Christ over all things, extending his reign through the witness of the Christian believer. Yet at the present time in the Western church, our theological decline and compromise has reached the point where the very idea of evangelism as a legitimate calling for Christians is under threat, because the *evangel* (good news) itself has been steadily abandoned or redefined. In a context where the non-believing person is no longer seen as in the grip of idolatry and unbelief, standing under just condemnation and in need of Christ's redemptive work (John 3:18–21), there is no good news left to publish to the world, or defend before the sceptic; apathy, disillusionment and decay then ensue for the church. In this chapter, I want to show that both the apostles Peter and Paul, though their approach to evangelism is different, *presuppose*, by their very act of witness, the completely lost condition of all those alienated from the covenant in Christ. In a time when a syncretistic 'dialogue' with non-Christian worldviews has become the aim of many people professing Christianity, it can nonetheless be shown that biblically, evangelism, apologetics and efforts at conversion *take for granted* the exclusive uniqueness of Christ and his salvific activity, with the consequent *necessity* for evangelism being laid

495

upon the faithful church. In the following pages I will therefore show that the Apostle Peter's evangelistic engagement in Acts 10 undermines the assumptions of inclusivism and that St. Paul's evangelistic efforts in Acts 17 undermine both those of inclusivism and pluralism. I will further stress that both Paul's and Peter's preparation by God for these encounters, as well as their specific message and method on these occasions, were appropriately fitted for the context in which they found themselves and that their example remains the abiding model for the contemporary church in the twenty-first century.

14.2 Interfaith Thinking

It is noteworthy that St. Peter, a man untrained in Greek philosophy, gives us the 'magna carta' of Christian apologetics in 1 Peter 3:15: "But sanctify Christ as Lord in your hearts, always being ready to make a defence to everyone who asks you to give an account for the hope that is in you, yet with gentleness and reverence." The Greek word for 'defence' that Peter uses in this passage is *apologia* from which we derive the term *apologetics*. The Greek word *logos* used for giving an 'account' or 'reason' is the word from which we derive our term *logic*. In his first epistle then, the persecuted church is commissioned to give a logical and rational defence of the gospel whenever called upon to do so. Equally important, St. Paul tells us that his entire ministry is defined by the "defence and confirmation of the gospel" (Phil. 1:7). It is immediately obvious then, that the task of sharing and justifying the Christian message over and against competing religious claims was a central concern to the apostles Peter and Paul and indeed, is evident in the whole biblical witness (cf. Jude 1:3). In reference to Peter's exhortation to give a defence of the faith, Canadian church historian Michael Haykin notes:

> The task of defending the Christian faith in the face of unbelief and the open rejection of biblical truth and the Christian worldview is a responsibility laid upon every generation of those who love the Lord Jesus Christ.[1]

In light of this once common assumption in the Western church, it is important to appreciate that increasing numbers of Christians across denominational lines no longer feel bound to such a view, but in the name of dialogue and interfaith ecumenism, believe there is a more enlightened approach to non-Christian religions and worldviews. For example, despite the *fact* of Paul's standing before the Areopagus and Peter before the household of Cornelius to proclaim Christ and defend the faith, Catholic theologian Hans Küng feels forced to ask:

> Is it permissible for us Westerners and Christians still to talk about God as if our understanding of him is the only one possible...? Is it not a sign of provincialism if we raise universal claims from a very particular viewpoint? Might it not be evidence of a higher universalism if we remained continually aware of our socio-cultural limitations and restrictions even in the field of religion...? In this way, mutual contempt might give way to mutual appreciation, disregard to understanding, attempts at conversion to study and dialog.[2]

Setting aside the fallacious reasoning involved in assuming that efforts at evangelism (conversion) inevitably involve mutual contempt, disregard and unwillingness to dialogue, as though sharing the Christian faith with a fellow human being in the terms set out by St. Peter were an act of hostility, not one of love to Christ and neighbour, we see here a subtle shift away from the biblical understanding of evangelism to a more inclusivist paradigm. Thus Küng asks regarding the encounter between Christianity and other views of 'God' in the world religions that are essentially impersonal (the absolute, being, nonbeing, nothing etc.), "might it not perhaps be far better to interpret God more as super-personal and consequently not to give him a name at all?"[3] How one then interprets 'God,' and one's experience of God for Küng, "is always a decision of faith."[4] In other words, is there a respectful way to bring together the best or 'true' insights of all the world faiths (upon a humanly constructed, autonomous criterion for what is best or true) concerning the divine, and at the very least be enriched by them, and then find a way of proclaiming this 'true' God for all men within the various religions?

These kinds of questions are being frequently asked today, especially amongst younger Christians, including those in emergent 'evangelical' circles and so it is extremely important to understand some of the key ideas that are at work behind these questions, and be able to evaluate them in terms of Scripture. In broad terms, the common demarcation of Christian approaches to the status of non-Christian faiths identifies three primary views: *pluralism, inclusivism and exclusivism.*

14.3 The Challenge of Pluralism

We are constantly reminded on all sides that we now live in a pluralistic context in the West and, as such, exclusivist claims about God and the way of salvation are out of place, unenlightened, hostile or even barbaric. Some humanistic 'Christian' scholars still wear the garb of a scriptural terminology but have evacuated the faith of its biblical meaning entirely. For them, all religious claims are reduced to mythology and psychology (easily done with most world religions that are in fact based on mythology and psychology) in order to escape history and abstract a *universal religion* that acknowledges a nameless and mysterious divinity, or ground of being. Karen Armstrong for example, tells us that the *mythos* (myths) of ancient societies provided a sense of meaning in life by directing attention to a 'universal;' this *mythos* was rooted in the unconscious mind of worshippers. "The various mythological stories, which were not intended to be taken literally, were an ancient form of psychology."[5] These strange stories were "bringing to light the obscure regions of the subconscious realm.... [B]ecause of the dearth of myth in our modern society we have had to evolve the science of psychoanalysis to help us deal with our inner world."[6] For Armstrong, such 'myths' as found in the Bible only take on a semblance of 'reality' through ritual enactment and mysticism that potentially lead to 'intuitive insights.' God is therefore removed from history and made a product of the subconscious mind – not unlike Küng's super-personal, nameless God.

This denial of the biblical plausibility structure[7] inevitably leads to radical relativism in interfaith understanding. With biblical claims relativized and God redefined psychologically, to focus on historical fact or objective truth in events or statements it to entirely miss the point. Thus to "ask whether the Exodus from Egypt took place exactly as recounted in the Bible or to demand historical and scientific evidence to prove that it is factually true is to mistake the nature and purpose of this story."[8] The true purpose is apparently to inspire the mystical ritual of Passover as a rite of passage (supposedly like similar pagan rites) into a new reality. For Armstrong and academics like her, such stories must be mythologized and 'liberated from the past.' This abstractionism paves the way for a *totalizing pluralism that refuses to tolerate exclusivism.* In ruling out the personal, triune God of scripture who makes himself known in history, we discover a fatal bias of pluralists against the Semitic traditions. Thus in the name of respect for 'diversity,' Vinoth Ramachandra comments on the intellectual arrogance of pluralists:

> … [It] savages pluralism (religious) in the name of defending it. What is put forward as a humble way of relating to the rich diversity of human religious traditions quickly turns into a reductionist onslaught on the factual affirmations of those traditions, with the Semitic traditions taking the brunt of the assault. What we are left with is a series of Procrustean beds on which a new elite of self-styled 'progressive' theologians dismember the religions of the world.[9]

It is therefore of singular importance to notice that Luke, the *careful historian* who authored the book of Acts, notes both Peter's and Paul's insistence on the historical details of God's activity in history – this faith they proclaimed was not viewed as a product of their subconscious, a *mythos* of imagination, but spatiotemporal historical reality to which they were witnesses (Acts 10:37-41; Acts 17:26, 31-32). Just as some of the pluralistic Athenians sneered at the claimed historical physical resurrection of Christ because of their materialism and philosophical dualism, so today the historical claims of the Christian faith militate against contemporary pluralism. As radical 'Christian' pluralist John Hick admits:

> There is a direct line of logical entailment from the premise that Jesus was God, in the sense that he was God the Son, the second person of the Divine Trinity, living in a human life, to the conclusion that Christianity, and Christianity alone, was founded by God in person; and from this to the further conclusion that God must want all his human children to be related to him through his religion which he has himself founded for us; and then to the final conclusion, "Outside Christianity, no salvation."[10]

The biblical view, being non-egalitarian, thus invokes the sneers and ire of today's pluralist. *Exclusivist* views are simply unpalatable to the contemporary mind, so it is not uncommon to hear pluralists speak with admiration of Gandhi's or the Dalai Lama's faith perspectives. Küng notes, "In one way or another, many Europeans and Americans would subscribe to Gandhi's words: 'I believe in the Bible as I believe in the Gita. I regard all the great faiths of the world as equally true with my own…' "[11] Thus, *pluralism* is essentially the view that no religion can make the claim to absolute uniqueness or authority. Not only is there access to 'salvation' in Jesus, Jesus is only one means of salvation among many – a path among many paths amidst the world's religions and spiritualities. As such, to share one's faith with the goal of bringing about conversion would be both irrational and immoral. The consequences of such a view for biblical evangelism are clear; Peter's address to Cornelius and Paul's apologetic to the Athenians were unethical forms of 'thought violence,' and the entire enterprise of Christian missions a kind of cultural genocide. As Ajith Fernando explains, "A direct result of such thinking is that apologetics – defending the truthfulness of one's beliefs against opposing views – is considered undesirable and in need of replacement by dialogue. But dialogue here has the aim of mutual enrichment, not conversion." [12]

But as we will see, neither Peter nor Paul were engaged in an ecumenical, interfaith dialogue seeking personal enrichment or new insights from alternative faiths and spiritualities; rather, both were proclaiming the gospel with the object of bringing their hearers to repentance and faith in Christ. Therefore, it is difficult to see how interfaith pluralism could be considered as Christian in origin at all, for as Ronald Nash notes, "When people adopt pluralism, they must abandon every core doctrine of the Christian faith… " [13] Therefore, the very fact that Peter and Paul were involved in evangelistic engagement and efforts at conversion with non-believers demonstrates that they were not operating on pluralistic assumptions.

14.4 The Challenge of Inclusivism

Inclusivism is a modified form of pluralism. Inclusivism seeks to retain the idea that salvation is available only through Christ, but widens the means by which it may be appropriated by the individual. For the inclusivist, nobody can be saved apart from Christ, regardless of the religion to which he or she may ascribe. However, given that multitudes of people have not and will not hear a direct proclamation of the gospel in their lifetime, and since many pursue the divine and good will to their fellow men, God is able to provide access to Christ's redemptive work through almost any sincere 'religious' practice and devotion. That is, for people pursuing a life of peace, reconciliation and justice (a particular understanding of good works), God's 'salvific' grace is *already* shown to be at work in their lives. [14] Thus, Christ's unique *identity* is not usually denied, but his saving *work* is defined differently. The actual reality of Christ's redemptive work is seen as a necessary *ground* for salvation, but *knowledge* of Christ or *belief* in Christ are not necessary for those of other faiths, spiritualities or worldviews to enjoy the benefits of his atonement. The force and appeal of the inclusivist position lies in the sense that it is surely *unfair* of God to require *conscious knowledge* of and faith in Christ and his redemptive work as a *precondition* of salvation since access to such knowledge is evidently not based on an egalitarian historiography. This was an argument urged by early pagan critics of the early church's theology like Porphyry (232–303) and Julian the Apostate (332–363).[15]

The apparent success of this argument in winning minds is very evident in evangelical and Catholic churches today. Inclusivism has become so pervasive in contemporary Christianity that it is often carried to the new extent that salvific grace embraces those, not just ignorant of Christ yet sincerely practicing their own religion, but actively hostile to Christ and opposed to his deity, redemption, and Lordship. Samir Selmanovic, a pastor and part of the coordinating group for the *Emergent Village*, writes of his non-Christian friend Mark in New York who stated that, "to become a part of Christianity would be a moral step backwards,"[16] but who senses transcendence to his existence and believes it to be a gift. By turning to this 'grace' in his inner life, he seeks to be a channel of good to others even though he rejects Christianity.[17] Now in response, the apostle Paul would doubtless say, "having overlooked times of ignorance, God is now declaring to men that *all everywhere* should repent ..." (Acts 17:30). However, Selmanovic considers that this unbeliever's arbitrary opinion "...embodies the doctrine of creation, sin, salvation, and new life. That's Christ, embedded in the life of Mark, present in substance rather than in name."[18] This is the meaning of inclusivism. We shall examine whether Peter or Paul's missional approach supports such a view, and so whether Scripture can be used to support such arguments.

14.5 The Response of exclusivism

Ronald Nash summarizes clearly the essentials of the exclusivist view as it relates to both to inclusivism and pluralism:

> Christian exclusivism can be defined as the belief that (1) Jesus Christ is the only saviour, and (2) explicit faith in Jesus Christ is necessary for salvation. The first claim denies that there are or can be other saviours, a fact that distinguishes it from pluralism. The second claim denies that people may be saved without conscious and explicit faith

in Jesus Christ, which sets it apart from inclusivism.[19]

Consequently, for the exclusivist, beliefs and faith commitments logically incompatible with revealed, biblical Christianity, are false and cannot be salvific (saving). God alone is the author of salvation, accomplished through the work of the Lord Jesus Christ and applied to the heart by the Holy Spirit. No form of human effort, goodwill or merit can place us in right standing with God without the redemptive work of Christ and explicit faith in him (Rom. 3:9–31). In regard to those people truly responding to the general revelation of God in creation and conscience, drawn by his grace, *God will send* further revelation, so that explicit faith in his name and work is made possible (Matt. 25:29). Infants who die without reaching an age of comprehension and those mentally handicapped whose judgement is impaired are left in the just and merciful hands of God. Since our knowledge is so profoundly limited and God alone knows the heart, we are to occupy ourselves with what *is* revealed (Deut. 29:29) and not make pronouncements on things about which the Scripture is silent. We shall examine whether or not the exclusivist view is implicit in the engagements of Paul and Peter.

14.6 The Missional Approaches of Peter and Paul:

14.6.1 The Audience

Whilst the message of both Paul and Peter remains consistent with the whole apostolic witness, the missional or evangelistic *approach* of both Paul and Peter is dramatically shaped by the people to whom their message is to be addressed; from this we have much to learn as we confront the opportunity of our time. First, in Acts 17:16–34, St. Paul is confronted by a profoundly challenging context: a city full of idols (v.16). He first speaks with Jews and god-fearing gentiles and then finds himself *conversing* with Epicurean and Stoic philosophers in the marketplace. His themes being Christ and the resurrection, his interlocutors and are not complimentary, referring to him as literally a "seed picker," a kind of pseudo-intellectual who had picked up odd ideas here and there but without coherence (v.18).

It is instructive to understand that Athens was the philosophical centre of the ancient world. As part of the Roman Empire, it was characterized by state-sponsored religious pluralism and therefore reminiscent of many modern Western states. It was home to four prestigious schools: the Academy of Plato, the Lyceum of Aristotle, the Garden of Epicurus and the Painted Porch of Zeno, all dating from around 300 B.C.[20] Paul found himself addressing the disciples of Epicurus and Zeno. The Epicureans were ancient naturalists (atomists) who held that a naturalistic explanation for all events must be given. For them, lasting pleasure was the goal of existence, and once dead, a person's atoms simply disperse into infinite space. Zeno, the founder of the Stoic school, agreed with the Epicureans in holding that the senses alone can provide knowledge, but he exalted reason as governing all matter. However, his cyclic view of history precluded personal immortality for the individual.[21] These ideas help account for the scepticism with which Paul's proclamation of the resurrection was received. Furthermore, these views were only a sample of the many prevailing philosophical trends in Athens at that time. The intellectual climate of the period was one of perpetual uncertainty and turmoil – scepticism was thus the order of the day. Greg Bahnsen points out:

> ... [O]ver four hundred years of philosophical dispute with its conflicts repetitions and inadequacies had left many Athenians bored and thirsty for novel schemes of thought. Thus one can understand Luke's accurate and insightful aside to the readers in Acts 17:21, "now all the Athenians and the strangers sojourning there spent time in nothing else, but either to tell or to hear some new thing." [22]

Paul was therefore confronted in Athens with intellectual arrogance, radical philosophical pluralism, and biblical illiteracy which more than rivalled our own current context.

By contrast, St. Peter's gentile audience in Acts 10 was distinct in many ways from St. Paul's in Acts 17. After his dramatic vision and preparation, Peter finds himself in the gentile city of Caesarea in the home of a Roman centurion. This military commander, Cornelius, was likewise prepared for his encounter with Peter by a visionary experience. Cornelius is important because, even though he is a gentile, he worshipped the God of Israel; he was a "god-fearer". F.F. Bruce remarks:

> Many gentiles of those days, while not prepared to become full converts to Judaism (the requirement of circumcision being a special stumbling block for men), were attracted by the simple monotheism of Jewish synagogue worship and by the ethical standards of a Jewish way of life. Some of them attended synagogue and became tolerably conversant with the prayers and scripture lessons...[23]

Luke tells us that Cornelius regularly prayed to Yahweh and did acts of mercy and charity for the people of Israel. This response to God had "ascended as a memorial into the presence of God" (Acts 10:4). Thus, Peter was addressing a man in a similar condition to some of those worshippers gathered on the day of Pentecost (Acts 2:9–12) or the Ethiopian eunuch reading the prophet Isaiah, led to faith in Christ by Phillip the evangelist (Acts 8:25–39). Cornelius was a man who acknowledged the God of Israel in prayer, knew something of the scriptures, and was concerned to show mercy. As Bruce rightly notes, "Never had a preacher of the gospel a more promising audience."[24] The contrast then between the house of Cornelius and the court of the Areopagus could not be greater.

14.6.2 The Messenger

The respective missional approaches of the apostles Paul and Peter were not only shaped by the audience, but were the product of their divine preparation by birth, experience, education and miraculous calling. Here we find both similarities and contrasts. Paul was a Jew, a Roman citizen (either purchased or won by his father) and a citizen of Tarsus, a highly significant ancient metropolis, making him a man of significant social standing. Famed as a city of great learning, it was noted for schools devoted to philosophy and rhetoric. The great Stoic leaders of Tarsus included Zeno, Antipater, Heraclides and Athenodoras the Stoic. It is likely that this city exercised considerable academic influence on the young Saul of Tarsus, by way of exposing him to the major streams of Greek thought.[25] Paul proved to be an exceptionally gifted student (Gal. 1:14) and later studied under Gamaliel (Acts 22:3) in Jerusalem, one of the greatest rabbis of the era. Paul thus became a Pharisee of great zeal and some prominence. Bahnsen notes the significance of all this for his encounter at the Areopagus:

> ... [I]t is manifest that Paul was neither naïve nor obscurantist when

it came to a knowledge of philosophy and Gentile thought. Given his background, training, and expertise in scriptural theology, Paul was the ideal representative for the classic confrontation of Jerusalem with Athens.[26]

Furthermore, though the encounter in Acts 17 is not immediately preceded by revelation through a vision (as is the case in Acts 10 when Peter is prepared to meet Cornelius), Paul *already knew* his calling to the Gentile world through a vision of his own. He knew that he had been sent to the nations by God and that the gospel promises were extended to the gentiles in Christ (Acts 13:46–49). The very conversion of St. Paul was a sovereign act of God, selecting him as his *chosen instrument* for preaching the gospel to the gentiles (Acts 9:15). When Paul stood before the Areopagus in Athens, he doubtless recalled to mind the words he had heard from heaven on the road to Damascus as Christ himself commissioned him to go to the gentiles and "open their eyes so that they may turn from darkness to light and from the dominion of Satan to God, in order that they may receive forgiveness of sins and an inheritance among those who have been sanctified by faith in me" (Acts 26:18). In light of such a clear statement from Christ himself concerning the status of the gentile nations with respect to their relationship with God, there can be no doubt that the assumptions of contemporary religious pluralism and inclusivism did not even enter Paul's mind as he addressed himself to the Athenian court.

The Apostle Peter's preparation was equally miraculous, though as a man he was very different from Paul. He was, like Paul, a first-century Jew, but he was not an intellectual or trained rabbi. By contrast he was a fisherman of the peasant class who, growing up, would not have received the same level of privileged education of which Paul was a recipient. He was however in a more remarkable school for three years – the school of Christ! Now despite being called by Jesus to become a 'fisher of men,' and walking with him for three years, hearing the Great Commission (Matt. 28:18–20), seeing God move powerfully amongst non-Jewish proselytes at Pentecost (Acts 2:1ff) and doubtless hearing of the Ethiopian eunuch's conversion (Acts 8:25ff), Peter was still wrestling with the question of the universality of the gospel. His preparation was privileged and extensive as a close disciple of the Lord, but as a Jew and therefore devout follower of the law, development in his understanding was necessary and now about to take place. This certainly indicates that

Christ had not taught his disciples to violate any portion of God's law, but only to interpret it correctly, for Peter did not feel at liberty to break even the dietary laws of scripture as this passage makes clear. Further revelation was therefore necessary to reveal the true purpose of a certain aspect of the law, which was now being altered in significance.

Up to this point, to enter a gentile's house and accept the hospitality of that house was to be rendered *ceremonially* unclean because of the pagan worship of the gentiles, their dietary habits, lack of health laws, and their unconverted status (Lev. 11–15). Thus, it was necessary for Peter to understand that the ceremonial (or restorative) aspects of the law that consisted of types and 'shadows,' illustrating and teaching the separation to holiness of God's covenant people, had now been transposed in their significance and internationalized through Christ. Now Christ was setting both Jew and Gentile apart as one body for his holy purpose and it is the practice of sin from which we are all to keep ourselves completely separate, and not yoke ourselves to evildoers to be drawn away to idolatry (Deut. 7:3–6; 2 Cor. 6:14–18; Jude 23). This truth was what the temporary 'shadow' in the law (physical or visible separation of Jew from Gentile) was actually teaching. The realization of a transposition in the law's significance appears to have come much more easily to St. Paul, who later had to reprimand Peter for his practical if not theological inconsistency in this matter at Antioch, when having at first eaten with them, he proceeded to separate himself from Gentile believers at a gathering of church leaders, for fear of those of the 'circumcision' party who were insisting that gentiles had to be circumcised to become full covenant members (Gal. 2:11–21). In Ephesians 2:13–16, Paul points to the breaking down in Christ, of the wall of partition between Jew and Gentile (a possible allusion to the wall in the Temple that separated the 'court of the gentiles,' who were proselytes to the faith, from the Jews by birth), and the abolition in his flesh of the enmity between the two contained in *ordinances* of separation. By doing so, he makes of the two one new man in Christ, both being reconciled to God in one body.

Clearly then, Peter had not fully appreciated the significance of Jonah's preaching in Assyria, but God was about to teach him a similar missional lesson. His vision of the sheet filled with quadrupeds, reptiles and birds (Lev. 11) together with the voice from heaven commanding him to "kill and eat" begins a remarkable shift in his thinking. His initial response to the vision and command, protesting that he had never touched unclean things (Acts 10:14), is met with the assurance that God has cleansed these things so that they should no longer be considered unholy (v.15). This happens three times and as he ponders the meaning of the vision, a messenger from Cornelius' house arrives. The significance of the vision soon becomes clear to him, "the divine cleansing of food in the vision is a *parable* of the divine cleansing of *human being*s in the incident to which the vision leads up."[27] God had taught him, not that shellfish and lizards should be included in his new diet, but to call no human being profane or unclean (Acts 10:28). This was monumental from a missiological perspective. As Ramachandra points out:

> Here we are introduced to a stupendous sight, unimaginable in the ancient world, of a Jewish peasant under the same roof as a Roman military officer.... Peter, witnessing the same Holy Spirit at work in the Gentile's life, comes to a recognition of his own cultural prejudice under the deepening impact of the gospel on his thinking. Cornelius has come to a saving knowledge of Christ Peter has come to a deeper discipleship...[28]

God's preparation of his messenger involved shaping Peter's missional approach 'as he went.' By contrast, Paul's vision and conversion experience, which included a commission to go to the gentiles, as well as early travels among pagans, had already developed his thinking regarding the international scope of the gospel before he reached Athens. But Peter, as he encountered Cornelius, was being broadened to recognize that the God of Israel was never a tribal God of only one nation, but the God of all peoples (Gen. 12:3; Ps. 33:8; 97:6). The God of Abraham promised that through his seed (Christ; see Gal. 3:16), all the nations of the world would be blessed (Gen. 22:18). Suddenly, at the house of Cornelius, as the Holy Spirit descends upon the gentiles, Peter is aware that God is no respecter of persons (Acts 10:34-35).[29] Peter could thus be said to have been *taught* a missional approach in this incident that was to shape and transform his thinking for the future. Rather than Peter having a careful strategy to reach Cornelius, God had a strategy to reach Peter in this encounter with Cornelius. "Hence, both Cornelius and Peter had important things to learn."[30]

We see then that both Paul and Peter as *messengers* were prepared for these encounters so that just as character and plot can never be separated, so missional *method* and *messenger* cannot be divorced. In a critical sense the messenger embodies and incarnates his method so that God uses our whole being, background, family, education, proclivities and personalities, as well as his miraculous interventions to mould our engagements with the non-believer. Furthermore, both of these respective engagements reveal there are times when our encounters with non-believers serve to help us better comprehend the fullness, power and glory of the gospel message and further disclose to us its distinctiveness.[31]

14.7 Message and Method: Paul in Athens

Having considered both the audience (context) and the personal preparation of the apostles as messengers for these notable encounters between Christianity and the non-Christian world, we are now in a position to return to a consideration of the status of non-Christian faiths in relationship to the gospel. Does pluralism, inclusivism or exclusivism characterise the apostolic approach? The Apostle Paul's whole posture in Athens would seem to decisively decimate the pluralist thesis. We read in Acts 17:16–34, a rational presentation and defence of the gospel, combined with a critique of the Epicurean and Stoic opponents' worldviews. Paul's approach is therefore characterized by what we would now call 'Christian apologetics.' We see immediately then that gospel proclamation and apologetics cannot be artificially divorced. Alister McGrath correctly notes, "the New Testament brings the two together in a creative and productive interplay: to proclaim the gospel is to defend the gospel, just as to defend the gospel is to proclaim the gospel."[32]

What prompted Paul's encounter is itself important in addressing the challenge of pluralism and inclusivism (Acts 17:16–17). Paul is waiting in Athens for his companions and he is far from being impressed by Athenian culture, aesthetics and religious insights. He is evidently not looking to be personally enriched in a 'learning experience' with paganism. Rather, his spirit is *provoked* within him. The Greek word used for provoked (v.16) is the same word used in the Greek Old Testament for God's anger at Israel's *idolatry*. D.A. Carson points out that "the New Testament writers did not readily distinguish the pluralism of the day from the idolatry of the day: the destruction of the one was the destruction of the other."[33] Deeply distressed by the many idols on display, Paul began by *discussing* and *reasoning* in the synagogue and then in the marketplace with whomever was present. Paul's method was therefore appropriate to the context. Greg Bahnsen states:

The Greek word for Paul's activity recalls the "dialogues" of Plato wherein Socrates discusses issues of philosophical importance. It is the same word used by Plutarch for the teaching methods of a peripatetic philosopher. Paul did not simply announce his viewpoint; he discussed it openly and gave it a reasonable defence. He aimed to educate his audience, not to make common religious cause with their sinful ignorance.[34]

Now as Paul shares the gospel of Christ utilizing a Socratic method, some of his philosophically sophisticated hearers mistakenly consider him to be proclaiming a strange new divine couple; 'Jesus' (a masculine form) and the 'resurrection' (a feminine form) personifying powers of healing and restoration. Perhaps because of, or at least in spite of this confusion, the apostolic *kerygma* is sufficient to have Paul hauled before the Areopagus council (v.19). This council played an important part in Athenian life. Cicero tells us that the Areopagus assembly governed Athenian affairs of State – their jurisdiction and responsibilities were both religious and civil.[35] So it seems Paul is being accused of teaching about 'strange deities' (v.18) or at least being examined to see if he should be granted a license to teach, in the same city in which Anaxagoras, Socrates and Protagoras were tried for introducing new deities.

At Mars Hill, the apostle is confronted with total paganism – people who have never read the Old Testament, know nothing of the messianic prophecies and are not proselytes to Judaism or god-fearers like Cornelius. Consequently, Paul's approach is going to be different from Peter's in Acts 10 and even his own method in places like Antioch (Acts 13:13ff). The Epicureans were essentially materialists and the Stoics pantheists. Their monistic philosophies, by definition, denied the personal God of Scripture who speaks and reveals himself in history. Their use of the term *God* was a limiting concept (a way of avoiding an infinite regression) and little more than the deification of human reason or natural forces. It is interesting to notice then, that Paul's approach does not begin with an attempted classical 'proof' of the existence of a theistic God, based on the 'bare facts of nature,' so common in post-Enlightenment Christian apologetics. To do so would be to suggest that God may or may not exist (i.e. creation does not already presuppose this God) and that without God's existence, men still have an intelligible set of concepts with which to understand and interpret the world. Paul recognizes that such proofs from nature are largely redundant because men and women *know* that they are creatures of the living God but suppress (hold down) this truth in unrighteousness (Rom. 1:18–20). For Paul, the reality and knowledge of God is so evident to them, that they are without '*apologia*' (defence) for their sinful rejection of him (Rom. 1:20). Paul is thus confident as he embarks on his defence that he can take this fact for granted:

> Paul does not prove that God exists and is actually known by men. But, like the whole of the Old and New Testaments and incidentally the whole catholic tradition and also (unlike Barth) the Reformers, he takes these things for granted.[36]

Though bold and confident, Paul is not arrogant in his approach. He begins with courtesy and respect, noting their religious or superstitious orientation, but with no indication of viewing their religion or philosophy as an alternative way of salvation (v.22).[37] On the contrary, his mission to the 'wisdom lovers' of Athens afforded him further confirmation that, "in the wisdom of God, the world did not know God through wisdom" (1 Cor. 1:21).[38]

Although the specific question the Athenians had asked concerned the resurrection, Paul begins his address by identifying the true and living God. Again, it is of interest to note that there is no suggestion that Paul rallies various evidential arguments to bolster the claim of the resurrection. Instead of starting with this isolated fact – which, lacking the context of a biblical worldview, would have been seen by the Greeks as a monstrous story about a resuscitated corpse and thereby a meaningless occurrence – he lays the presuppositional groundwork so that the resurrection can later be interpreted in its proper framework. Paul astutely observes that between him and his hearers lies a total conflict in systems of thought. This is of course, very different from Peter's situation in Acts 10 whilst addressing Cornelius. In that instance, the hearers share essentially the same theological assumptions about reality so only more revelation of the *same kind* is required. Here in Athens, a total intellectual and spiritual re-orientation is needed.

To overcome this, Paul's strategy is to first identify a point of contact by exposing the suppressed knowledge of the true and living God found in inscriptions on the altar(s) in the city 'To an Unknown God.' Paul reinforces their self-confessed religious ignorance represented in their practices, which he later underscores as idolatry. He is evidently not establishing a 'natural theology' to argue from 'first principles' like a pagan philosopher, but is seeking to confront them with their sinful pride. There is a striking similarity of theme here, though with a different tone, to his discussion in Romans 1-3. F. F. Bruce emphasizes that:

> The knowledge of God, according to Paul in Rom. 1:19–22, was accessible to all in his works of creation, *but the capacity or desire to acquire it had been impaired by idolatry*. If the author of Romans 1–3 had been invited to address an Athenian audience on the knowledge of God, it is difficult to see how the general purport of his words could have been much different from what Luke here reports Paul as saying. The tone of the Areopagitica is different from that of Romans 1–3, but Paul knew the wisdom of adapting his tone and general approach to the particular audience or readership being addressed at the time.[39]

These exegetical factors militate strongly against Alister McGrath's view:

> Paul is able to base himself upon acceptable Greek theistic assumptions, while at the same time going beyond them. Paul shows a clear appreciation of the apologetic potential of stoic philosophy, portraying the gospel as resonating with central stoic concerns, while extending the limits of what might be known.[40]

While the gospel clearly deals with many human concerns, McGrath's view appears mistaken for several reasons. First, Stoics were not *theists* in anything resembling a biblical sense, but pantheists. Secondly, Paul gives no indication in the text that their *assumptions* are *acceptable*, quite the contrary. So it is difficult to see how McGrath reaches this conclusion. The message of Romans 1 and Acts 17 does not reveal a basic compatibility of the biblical worldview with Greek philosophy, but establishes it as the very *antithesis* of paganism. Third, Paul is not merely trying to 'extend the limits' of pagan thought as though it is right as far as it goes and simply requires some additional information to be true and complete. Rather, he challenges its very *foundational assumptions* as a sinful distortion of truth. That is, they have mishandled God's general revelation and have become fools (cf. Rom. 1:21–22). McGrath, it seems, is trying to *read in* to the text a natural theology argument, to support the Thomistic 'nature-grace' separation of classical apologetics in order to salvage a point of contact between believer and non-believer. But a point of contact is not lost by rejecting McGrath's perspective. A point of contact is always present in the fact that, as creatures of God, who are conscious that we are creatures living in God's personal and moral world, men and women cannot escape the self-revelation of God, manifest both within and without. Even in their rebellious religions and philosophies that worship and serve the creature or mysterious forces, rather than the creator, their culpability is betrayed by their tacit acknowledgment of the truths they have suppressed. As Bahnsen incisively puts it, "Paul was noting the basic schizophrenia in unbelieving thought when he described in the Athenians both an awareness of God (v.22) and an ignorance of God (v.23).[41]

Next, in verses 24–25, Paul explains the biblical doctrine of God and of creation. He therefore educates his listeners with a biblical worldview. Although he is not directly quoting from the Old Testament, there is no mistaking its origin in Scripture: "His argument is firmly based on biblical revelation; it echoes throughout the thought, and at times the very language, of the Old Testament. Like the biblical revelation itself, his argument begins with God the creator of all and ends with God the judge of all."[42] Furthermore, verse 26 speaks of a God who is sovereign over all of history. Events within history are not random but are providentially ordered in such a way that people will seek after God (v.27). It is this goodness of God that should lead people to repentance (cf. Rom. 2:4). Again, in this declaration concerning the nature of God's work in history, rather than finding common ground to make common cause with unbelief, Paul's view strongly contradicted the Epicurean and Stoic view of the divine. For the materialist Epicureans, the gods were made of very fine atoms and so lived in tranquillity in the spaces between the worlds – they were not involved in the concrete facts of human affairs. Moreover, the god of the Stoics was an all-pervasive, impersonal principle of reason, not a personal God who, by his sovereign power, works out all things in terms of the counsel of his will (cf. Eph. 1:11). So over and against the pagan views, Paul presents the God of Scripture as a transcendent yet personal God, distinct from his creation, governing all things and bringing all into judgement. Thus, "Paul contrasts divine will and sovereignty with human dependence and need."[43] The pagan fatalistic view of a cyclic history (with endlessly repeating ages) is then firmly refuted in terms of the doctrines of creation, providence and final judgement (v.31).

Paul continues his *apologia* by then quoting some of their own pagan sources to further manifest their guilt. Despite God's inciting of people to seek him, due to sin, they grope about for him, even though he is not far from us (v.27). Paul reveals that, by virtue of being God's creatures, even pantheistic Stoics are aware of the nearness of the personal God of the Bible. He cites Epimenides the Cretan from a quatrain in an address to Zeus: "in him we live and move and exist," (v.28) which is reminiscent of Paul's statement in Colossians 1:15-17. Paul uses this poetic quotation to emphasize the *total dependence* of people upon God for their existence. The second statement he cites, "for we also are His offspring," is quoted from his fellow Cilician Aratus in a poem on "Natural Phenomena" (echoed also in Cleanthes' "Hymn to Zeus").[44] In light of the contemporary claims of pluralists and inclusivists, it is critical to note what Paul is and is not saying here in his use of pagan sources. Is he commending Stoic doctrine or reducing Christian theology to Greek philosophical categories? Is this an inclusivist 'preparation of grace' whereby the Athenians are already sincerely on their way to a true knowledge of God? F. F. Bruce thinks not:

> In both these poems Zeus is considered…as the supreme being of Greek and especially Stoic philosophy. But did Paul intend to identify the Zeus of Greek philosophy *simpliciter* with the God of biblical revelation, whom in his letters he repeatedly calls "the God and Father of our Lord Jesus Christ"? Quite certainly not.[45]

It is clear from the context that Bruce is right. Paul is challenging paganism and identifying their religious worldview as idolatry. Truly, we are 'God's offspring,' in the sense of being his creatures, but not in the pantheistic sense of Aratus. Then what is he trying to accomplish with these citations from the poets? Is Paul equivocating with pantheistic terms and completely arresting the quotes from context and applying a totally foreign, biblical theistic meaning? Such a view is not plausible because he has *already defined* the God of which he speaks – Paul is not disingenuous in his utilization of these writers. He is not then embracing core elements of pagan theology as though it speaks truly of the God of Scripture as far as it goes, rather he is using "pagan expressions to demonstrate that ungodly pagan thinkers have not eradicated all idea, albeit suppressed and distorted, of the living and true God."[46] Bruce agrees, noting that "The delicately suited allusions to Stoic and Epicurean tenets…have their place as points of contact with the audience, but they do not commit the speaker to acquiescence in the realm of ideas to which they originally belong." [47]

Finally, St. Paul's typically Jewish polemic culminates in a clear admonition and a call to repentance. Paul has argued that the living God cannot be represented by a graven image, the handiwork of craftsmen. Then a further disapprobation of idolatry (v. 29) is followed by recognition and proclamation of God's mercy in overlooking this wilful ignorance and calling *all everywhere* to repent (v.30). As Bruce makes plain, "If ignorance of the divine nature was culpable before, it is inexcusable now." [48] The universal nature of this call to 'all everywhere' to repent unequivocally *destroys the thesis of pluralism*. Clearly, if many religious paths lead to the same God as pluralists claim, then there is certainly no need for such rational, educated, morally sensitive and spiritually aware philosophers to turn to Christ in repentance and faith. For pluralist theologians, Mars Hill would seem to be a futile, counter-productive and morally dubious engagement with the non-Christian world.

Likewise, the inclusivist is not helped by Paul's exemplary encounter in Athens. Why would Paul have stressed repentance so much if these pagans were sincerely reaching for the living God through their own religious tradition? Surely the inclusivist is forced to acknowledge that on their own terms, given the ontological reality of Christ's atoning death and the 'sincerity' and 'moral life' of the Stoic, these philosophers were better off *before* Paul preached to them. Since, for the inclusivist, the redemptive work of Christ may be applied to all people sincerely seeking God within their own religious contexts without explicit knowledge of Christ or faith in his death and resurrection, why interfere with their beliefs, pressing for conversion? Exposing the Athenians to a gospel proclamation would have only served to *condemn* the majority that did not turn to Christ, since most inclusivists would hold that their status before God would have changed after hearing and rejecting the gospel. It seems that the inclusivist thesis forces one to conclude that Paul should have left off his discourse in verse 28, or better still, not addressed these well-meaning philosophers at all. Ironically, the preaching of the gospel for the inclusivist may actually serve to accomplish the exact opposite of their desired ends – condemnation rather than inclusion for the 'sincere' heathen.

In the final analysis, it is doubtful that the apostle Paul of Acts 17 who penned the epistle to the Romans recognized any such category as the 'sincere' pagan genuinely seeking the living God through his own superstition (cf. Rom. 1:28–32; 3:9–19; Acts 17:30). After all, he was not asking the Athenians to adjust or refine their thinking a little but called for a total and radical change. At the close of his argument, Paul introduces the 'Son of Man' eschatology of the gospels (v.31). God has given to a true man, Jesus Christ, authority to execute judgement over all men (cf. John 5:27). Here we see a direct correlation with Peter's message to Cornelius (Acts 10:42). Paul then, has not departed from the apostolic witness, as though he were concerned that the pagan philosophers would find a clear gospel proclamation lacking in intellectual credibility. In fact, the resurrection is cited as the event which establishes the claim of Christ's right to judge all men. The ridicule that follows this conclusion is rooted in man's spiritual blindness and sinful suppression of the truth, expressed here in the familiar facet of neo-Platonic dualism. The physical world being inferior or evil and the immaterial or spiritual world being superior and good, the body being like a temporal prison for the soul, why would a divine being (God) wish to raise a physical being to life? Yet despite sneering from some, others wanted to hear him again on the subject and still others 'joined him' and became believers. Given the context, the fact that some from the council became disciples is astonishing and is testament to the power of the Holy Spirit at work through God's people as they faithfully preach Christ. Moreover, as Bruce notes, the speech "admirably summarizes an introductory lesson in Christianity for cultured pagans.... [T]he essential content of the speech is biblical, but the presentation is Hellenistic.[49]

Paul's missional method is thus seen to be one of *apologetic confrontation* between Jerusalem and Athens; Hebraic in content but Hellenistic in presentation. He sets out the entire biblical worldview for the pagan mind, *educating* his audience in terms of this new framework of interpretation, before introducing them to the Son of Man, the resurrection and coming judgement. His method and message never assumed a 'neutral stance' with respect to religious worldviews but rather accentuated the antithesis between Christian and pagan claims about reality. Yet this fact did not eliminate the point of contact which is always found in people's *common creation in the image of God* and God's self-revelation in creation (ourselves and the outer world) and history. Thus Bahnsen concludes, "The Apostles' apologetical method for reasoning with educated unbelievers who did not acknowledge scriptural authority turns out to be a suitable pattern for our defending the faith today."[50]

14.8 Peter and Cornelius

There are important commonalities worth noting between Paul's and Peter's addresses, as well as several differences in approach. Peter's message and method in Acts 10 is a tried and tested one, a classic example of the apostolic witness that mirrors previous sermons to God-fearing gentiles in Acts 2, and Jews in Acts 4 and 5. Like Paul, Peter begins his message to the house of Cornelius (Acts 10) with a highly significant statement, "sweeping away the racial and religious prejudices of centuries."[51] For a Jew to say that God does not show partiality (v.34) and to universalize the message of covenant grace to every nation was no small matter and resonates with the same demolition of racial prejudice found in Paul's defence in Athens (Acts 17:26–29). Both men recognized that God's choice of Israel was an act of grace and that God's providential and sovereign ordering of history was so that people would seek him. Peter also begins his address with an emphasis on the Lordship of Christ (10:36). Again, this is similar to Paul's affirmation in Acts 17:25. In Acts 10:40, Peter's words also turn to the theme of Christ's resurrection and he applies this historical reality to God's appointment of Christ as the judge of the living and the dead (v.42). Therefore, in both addresses we have first an affirmation of the universality of God's call in the gospel. Second, we have the concept of Lordship attributed to the triune God. And third we have the proclamation of the resurrection as proof of a final judgement through Jesus Christ.

That being said, there are also important differences in content and method between the two addresses. The critical phrase is found in Peter's words in verse 37, "you yourselves know the thing which took place..." Clearly, Peter's entire address presupposes not only a prior acquaintance with the Hebrew Scriptures (v.43) but a specific knowledge of the immediate events in the life, ministry and death of Christ (v.37–39). His message is essentially a summary statement of typical apostolic preaching covering the events from John's baptism to the resurrection. Noting that the scope of the address mirrors that of Mark's gospel, Bruce writes, "C.H. Dodd is no doubt right in suggesting 'that the speech before Cornelius represents the form of *Kerygma* used by the primitive church in its earliest approaches to a wider preaching.'"[52] The total ignorance of the pagans in Acts 17 of both Scripture and the historical details of Jesus' life and ministry precluded the use of such an approach for Paul. The force and persuasive power of Peter's discourse lay in his ability to proclaim Christ as God's "anointed" (v.38), literally God's messiah, foretold by the prophets (v.43). As God-fearing adherents to Judaism, these terms would have been comprehensible and meaningful to the household of Cornelius.

One unexpected element in Peter's encounter should not be overlooked. The descent of the Holy Spirit in such a dramatic fashion was clearly not anticipated (v.44)! This aspect cannot then be seen as an intentional methodology, the fruit of Peter's foresight, since Peter did not lay hands upon them. The coming of the Spirit was the spontaneous act of God alone. Why did the Spirit not fall on the Areopagus in the same way some might ask? The only adequate answer is God's ways are not our ways (Is. 55:8), but we can speculate as to some possible reasons. First, it seems doubtful that the 'sneering' pagans, not knowing the scriptures, would have understood the significance of this phenomenon in any event (Joel 2:28–29) and would have therefore misinterpreted it, perhaps viewing it in occultic terms. Secondly, it seems clear from Acts 10 that the gift of tongues was as much a sign for Peter as it was a sign for Cornelius' household (11:17–18); Paul was not in need of such a confirmation of the universal scope of the covenant or non-discriminatory availability of the gift of the Spirit.

Now, in what ways does Peter's encounter with Cornelius in Acts 10 help us grapple with the challenge of inclusivism that we are considering? It is to my mind bizarre that this passage is favoured by many inclusivists who believe that in it they find support for their position, particularly verses 34–35. For example, J. Andrew Kirk writes, "Cornelius stands for all God-fearing people who, because they pray to God regularly and give generously to those in need, are accepted by him."[53] Now it is obvious from the text that Cornelius believed in Yahweh and was thus in a similar position spiritually to a believing Jew of the time. But how does this support the claims of inclusivism? Ronald Nash states:

> The entire story is supposed to support the inclusivist distinction between believers and Christians. According to John Saunders, "Cornelius was already a saved believer before Peter arrived but he was not a Christian believer."[54]

Is the isolated statement in verse 35 really sufficient to support the notion that those who believe in a supreme being and try to live a good life are acceptable to God? Can we approach the Father without the Son in light of biblical testimony (John 14:6; 1 John 2:23)? The Pelagian assumption that good works can make one acceptable to God seems equally erroneous in view of unambiguous biblical teaching (cf. Rom. 3:9–20). When examined closely, taking Cornelius as the model, the inclusivist criterion for salvation would actually mean all god-fearing Jews and gentiles who affirmed the existence of God and were 'good people,' are saved. Thus the inclusivist Clark Pinnock describes Cornelius as "the pagan saint par excellence of the New Testament,"[55] and in the same light erroneously sees Paul's address in Acts 17:28 as an approving nod to pagan thinking.[56] The question then becomes what is the point of the apostolic witness to pagans, and what is the purpose of taking the gospel to God-fearers who affirm his existence, offer prayers and do 'good works?' Scripture makes clear that only those who put faith in and *welcomed the promises*, joining faith in those promises to obedience were actually saved (cf. John 8:56; Heb. 11:13–16). Multitudes of 'believing' Jews perished in the desert and in Korah's rebellion (Jude 1:5–11). The *promises to be believed* and embraced by faith concerned Christ, and our Lord himself condemns *believing Jews* who do not believe *in him* as the fulfilment of those promises (cf. John 8:31–39). Nicodemus was clearly a God-fearing believer who even recognized the work of God in our Lord's teaching, and yet, Jesus told him he needed to be "born again," without which he could not see the kingdom of God (John 3:3).

The oddity of inclusivists' use of Acts 10 as their key proof text is highlighted by the fact that in several places the passage itself directly refutes the inclusivist view. For example, Peter reports Cornelius' own testimony, "Send to Joppa and have Simon who is also called Peter, brought here; and he shall speak words to you by which *you will be saved*, you and all your household" (Acts 11:13-14). This expression employs the same Greek word used for our salvation in Christ and our deliverance by God. Clearly, Cornelius believed the angelic messenger and recognized that, despite his belief in God, prayers and works of charity, he was not yet "saved." At the conclusion of Peter's report to the apostles and leaders in Jerusalem, they glorify God for the salvation of Cornelius' house saying, "Well then, God has granted to the gentiles also the repentance that leads to life" (Acts 11:18). This clearly implies that prior to this event Cornelius had not experienced the repentance that leads to life. As a result, far from supporting inclusivism, this account strongly undermines it. Inclusivism appears to be more of an excursion in wishful thinking than it does a biblical teaching; a flight of fancy based on out of context proof texts and speculations that are not authorized by Scripture (cf. Deut. 29:29). Just as Paul and Peter trusted God to be the judge of the unbeliever, so should we (cf. Gen. 18:25).

It is then evident from both these texts that the kind of teaching propounded by Pinnock and other inclusivists, arguing that atheists hostile to the gospel who nonetheless 'love' their neighbour have in fact responded positively to God, despite their protestations to the contrary, is an indulgence in wishful thinking.[57] Not only these two passages, but the entire book of Acts seems to witness emphatically against both pluralism and inclusivism. Only by abstracting the atonement and resurrection of Christ into historical, epistemological and practical irrelevance can the pluralist or inclusivist models stand. St. Paul himself certainly would have passed with flying colours any tests to qualify for inclusivist salvation before turning to Christ in repentance and faith. Yet clearly his zeal for the God of Israel was not enough since Christ Jesus found it necessary to confront him on the road to Damascus to turn him from darkness to light.

In sum, Peter's and Paul's evangelistic approaches were both eminently fitted to the occasion. They were faithful to the apostolic witness, Hebraic in content, with Paul adopting a Hellenistic method of dialogue in Athens. Both encounters seriously undermine the challenges of both pluralism and inclusivism. Aside from confirming biblical exclusivism, the key lesson for our time is that we should not forget, "the Christian movement was born into a world every bit as pluralistic in ideology and behaviour as our own."[58] And even more important, the Christian movement has the same God active through his people. In the face of ancient pluralism, the apostles did not shy away from faithfully declaring the gospel. God prepared them for where he would send them and granted them wisdom and power for each encounter. God will do no less for us in our age where we are faithful. Thus Acts must remain the Christian model for truly biblical approaches to interfaith engagement. As in every age, we must evangelize or fossilize!

Chapter Fifteen

I WILL BUILD MY CHURCH: THE *MISSIO ECCLESIAE*

The life of the puritan was in one sense a continuous act of worship, pursued under an unremitting and lively sense of God's providential purposes and constantly refreshed by religious activity, personal, domestic and public.

– Patrick Collinson

Unto us Christians no land is strange, no ground unholy; every coast is Jewry, every house is Sion; and every faithful company, yea, every faithful body a Temple to serve God in.

– George Gillespie

15.1 The Mission of the Church

In discussing the mission of the church it is important to first offer a definition of the church; something all too readily assumed as obvious. The word *ecclesiology* comes from the Greek *ekklesia*, simply meaning *assembly*. The term is a compound of the Greek preposition *ek* (out from) and the verb *kaleo* (to call). It is fascinating to note that the most generic definition given by *Thayer's Greek Lexicon* is, "a gathering of citizens *called out* from their homes into some public place." This indicates that the church is a new citizenry with a public, not merely private calling. In the writings of the apostle Paul the term usually has reference to a group of believers in a specific city. For example, Paul's letters are addressed to the church of God in Corinth (1 Cor. 1:2; 2 Cor. 1:1), the churches in Galatia (Gal. 1:2), the church of the Thessalonians (1 Thess. 1:1) and so on. Moreover the New Testament picture of the church is that of a universal body (Eph. 4:4) of believers with many members but one head, Jesus Christ. So the church is a universal and organic (living and growing) body of regenerate believers (a new humanity or citizenry) who have been reconciled to God through the death and resurrection of Christ, called out to serve their king, finding regional expression in local assemblies (or embassies) of God's kingdom people. The theo-drama of the emergence of this great army and its part in the *mission of God* is a glorious one.

As we have seen throughout this volume, the *mission of God* is first rooted in the character and nature of the triune God of Scripture. In terms of the council of his sovereign will, and for his own glorious purpose (Eph. 1:11–14), the Father sends his Son and the Father and the Son send the person of the Holy Spirit (John 14:26). This sending God calls out and sends his *royal priesthood* into the world (*missio ecclesiae*), anointed and ordained by his Spirit as priest-kings of the second king Adam, to participate in the reconciliation of all things to God through Christ, re-cultivating all creation into God's garden and dwelling place in terms of his Word (Gen. 1:26–28; 9:1; Matt. 28:18–20; John 20:21–23; 2 Cor. 5:18–19; Eph. 1:4–10; Col. 1:15–20; 1 Pt. 2:5; Rev. 1:6–9). Christ Jesus reigns over all, for having been raised from the dead, ascending to sit down at the right hand of majesty and power, all authority and judgement is in his hands, and his royal court is now in session (Eph. 1:20–23; Heb. 1:3–4; Matt. 28:18; Phil. 3:21). Those born again by the Spirit of God are now sons and joint heirs with Christ, and are appointed ambassadors of his cosmic dominion. As 'new creatures' through whom the power of the new creation is already at work, God's people are sent out into all the earth to *declare the good news of Christ's reign and salvation and assert his crown rights in every area of life and thought* (Ps. 2; 1 Cor. 8:5–6; 2 Cor. 5:17–21; Eph. 6:19–20; Acts 2:29–36; 4:7-12; Phil 2:9–11; Rev. 1:5). As preparation and promise, this cosmic mission began with the patriarchs from Abel onward (Heb. 11:4–40; Gal. 3:7–9), and was expanded in the work and calling of the Hebrew nation as witness and blessing to the nations (Gen. 12:1–3; Deut. 4:6–8). Now in fulfilment of that covenant promise, at the end of the ages (1 Cor. 10:11; Heb. 1:2) and in the fullness of time (Gal. 4:4–5), the 'enlarged' Israel (John 11:50–52; Eph. 2:11–22; Rom. 2:29; 1 Cor. 10:1–4; Gal. 6:15–16), the church of Jesus Christ, the household of God and people of the King, both Jew and Gentile, fulfil their glorious mandate in terms of the Great Commission (Matt. 28:18–20). Clearly then, the mission of the church extends well beyond the reform of its institutional liturgy!

This is a distinctly reformed and Puritan perspective, and a world-changing one. In it the church militant on earth is salt and light, pillar and support of the truth, and the very embassy of God manifesting the manifold wisdom of Christ to all power and authority (1 Tim. 3:15; Eph. 3:10). This vision of the church's mission in the Western European context took decisive shape during the Calvinistic movements of the

Second Reformation in Holland and the Puritan era in England, Scotland and the American colonies. Calvin was in many respects the theologian of the Holy Spirit, not just in terms of explaining the Spirit's work of personal regeneration, but "the Spirit's activity of renewing the 'face of the earth.'"[1] This emphasis distinguished Calvinistic reformed thought from Lutheranism in terms of the theology of mission. Richard Marius writes:

> Luther never tried to make much of the present world, and a worldly age cannot make much of him. The Calvinists expected the world to endure, and they believed themselves to be instruments of God to convert it.... Calvinism has implanted...a perpetual dissatisfaction with our successes and a restlessness with the way things are.[2]

This view grew inexorably out of an understanding of the *regnum Christi* (kingdom-reign of Christ), exalted to total pre-eminence and therefore active in the world by his Spirit and through his people. Reformed thought could not tolerate the notion that the Christian faith could be *limited* to a vertical relationship between a person and God by individual regeneration, especially when used as a way of escaping from the responsibility of applying God's word to all things in the common life of mankind; such a view was seen as a denial of the incarnation. In a truly Reformed theology of mission, the church as God's kingdom people must not only be concerned with personal salvation, or institutional church affairs, but with the reign of Christ over all things. The church represents the exalted Christ to the secular order. As Bosch observes, such a view "could not but give rise to the idea of *mission* as 'extending the reign of Christ.'"[3]

It is particularly noteworthy that this theological outlook led to the birth of Protestant missions. According to Bosch, the "undisputed Protestant missionary pioneer"[4] was the Puritan, John Eliot (1604-1690). He spent the vast majority of his life and ministry working among the Indians of Massachusetts. Actuated by a wider vision of the *corpus Christianum* (Christendom and hence Christian civilization), the first Protestant society devoted wholly to missionary purposes was a Puritan development. Founded in 1649 it was called the New England Company; its focus was the funding of missionary activity in the transatlantic colonies. In 'extending reign of Christ,' Calvinism had added another element to mission that was diligently applied in Puritan mission theology and practice. Bosch identifies it:

> In the case of Calvinism, another dimension was added, that of theocracy. Wherever Calvinist missions were launched, the purpose was to establish in the "wilderness" a socio-political system in which God himself would be the real ruler. The missionary efforts of John Eliot clearly give evidence of this motif, particularly his "Praying Towns," a total of fourteen settlements in Massachusetts in which Indian converts were gathered and where the entire life of the community was organized according to the guidelines of Exodus 18. In similar fashion the Puritan colonies in North America were to be a manifestation of the Kingdom of God on earth. Christ's rule was to be made visible in both society and church.[5]

This was likewise the goal in the mother country, where Cromwell and many other Puritans were working toward a nation under God's law and gospel in which there would be a harmony between church and state, both submitted in their spheres to God. The ultimate goal of Puritan mission was therefore theocentric and not anthropocentric – above all the aim was the glory of God. All other proximate goals, though important, were not to eclipse this objective. The electing grace of Christ called for activity to that end. The church was predestined for a purpose in history and God's people must be about their task with zeal and joy for the love of Christ constrained them – love both for the believer and unredeemed humanity.

Puritan missionary zeal was likewise undergirded by the connection between the church's mission and eschatology – an aspect of predestination in history. The theocratic ideal, almost universal amongst the Puritans, was enlivened by the conviction that, as Calvin had held, God's people can expect in the last great epoch of history a great expansion of the church. Because of the nature of their theology of mission (extending the reign of Christ), these evangelical Christians didn't argue about whether to apply the faith to society or whether one could have a Christian culture, "it was simply assumed that people would live a better life once God's rule was established over their respective societies."[6] As such Bosch concludes, "because of its theocratic features the Calvinist branch of the Reformation put a greater emphasis than Lutheranism on the rule of Christ in society at large; this distinction also manifested itself in Calvinist missionary practice."[7]

One might well ask today, what happened? Where did the vital vision of John Eliot, Richard Sibbes, Richard Baxter, John Owen, Cotton Mather, Jonathan Edwards and other Puritan theologians for the church's mission disappear to and why? Whilst there always survived pockets and elements of the Puritan theonomic and theocratic ideal for mission, and some aspects of it were quickened by the eighteenth-century Great Awakening, it was not to be seriously revived again, updated and refined with theological rigor, until the emergence of the new Puritanism – the theonomic theologians in the late twentieth century. It is then essential to notice before moving on, that what undermined this early (and arguably original) Protestant vision of the church's mission as the extension of Christ's theocratic reign by law and gospel, was not a rival evangelical theological paradigm for mission within the church purporting to be more biblical, but the appearance and rise of the anti-Christian Enlightenment and its subsequent impact upon the church. Bosch's answer is emphatic: "The Enlightenment would shatter the theocratic ideal. Religion would be banished to the private sphere, leaving the public sphere to reason."[8]

It follows then that some of those today who attack the Calvinistic and Puritan vision of the reign of Christ within Protestant Christianity, do so as intellectual heirs of the falsely labelled 'Enlightenment,' whose creed was faith in mankind – for them the public sphere is not subject to God's revelation, but to reason, or natural law.[9] This new 'faith' offered a new plausibility structure, which, whilst not denying religion a seat at the table in adjudicating and regulating human affairs, relativized the absolute and exclusive claims of Christianity, thereby steadily pushing it from the public to the private realm. Furthermore, in this rebirth of human autonomy the "self-sufficiency of the individual over social responsibilities was exalted to a sacred creed."[10] Man was allegedly grown up now and no longer needed God and his law-word. Western man could thus embrace and pursue the ideal of a pluralistic 'secular society' and at least act in the public sphere as if there were no true and living God who had revealed his will authoritatively in Scripture. Bosch is insightful and helpful on this point:

> The individual experienced himself or herself as liberated from the tutelage of God and church.... [A]ll were born equal and had equal rights. These were however, not derived from religion, but from "nature".... [P]rior to the Enlightenment life in all its stratifications and ramifications was pervaded with religion. Legislation, the social

order, private as well as public ethos, philosophical thinking, art – all these were, in one way or another, stamped religiously.[11]

In our present cultural moment, the Enlightenment, having run its course and exiled transcendence, has left us the meagre crumbs of relativism, subjectivism, political pluralism and a concomitant return to esoteric pagan spirituality that is successfully merging itself with humanistic 'science.' Our moral, social, economic and political decline, the further we have departed from the faith, is now undeniable. In this context, many Christians are left asking, "can God still be the God of providence and grace? Can he establish an institute – the church – which addresses the human world with divine authority...? The unshaken massive and collective certitude of the Middle Ages has indeed vanished entirely."[12]

How has this crisis affected the church's view of its mission? The main responses to the de-sacralized predicament in which the modern church finds itself – where it hasn't entirely capitulated to the spirit of the age, like the Enlightenment-rooted 'Christian' liberalism of the mainline churches or the 'progressive Christianity' of the new liberalism that goes with the flow of cultural Marxism – vary from a kind of retrenchment in a 'reason-based' Christianity, to religious privatization, and theological flight and retreat. The first common response, still current and appearing mostly amongst Catholics and evangelical rationalists, essentially adopts the Enlightenment paradigm, wedding the 'age of reason' to Christianity, claiming that theology is a kind of natural science, the science of God, and that reason, through identifying natural law, can restore man to a truly moral and rational idea of himself, the world and God.

A second reaction, to escape the alleged threat from 'reason' and 'science,' divorces faith and reason, seeking to locate the faith essentially in human feelings and experience alone – a fideism of private esoteric experience. This is the perspective of much pietism, deeply influential in evangelicalism that sees little value in defending the faith or preaching and asserting the reign of Christ in the world of public human affairs. The goal of the Christian life and faith then becomes simply advancing one's personal spiritual growth. This response is often tied to an eschatology of escape and flight from the world as the ultimate hope of the church.

A third and most popular response amongst Protestants has been the radical privatization of the faith. Here, evangelicals in particular, like to think they can carve out a small domain in public affairs, having a 'seat at the table,' whilst leaving the rest of life to be considered a purely personal and individual realm, and allowing most of the public square to go its own way. A more sophisticated variation on this response has been the development of a 'Christian' political pluralism, which essentially embraces the globalist multi-cultural project of the modern left, and baptizes it as the church's *mission* in serving the common good – this *presupposes* the privatization and relativization of biblical truth. On this view, the very idea that biblical faith creates Christian culture or civilization is denied, and the Reformed view of biblical revelation effecting legislation is rejected as totalitarian. Rather, the Christian church has a common *mission* with people of other faiths – apparently exemplified in 'Christian' President Barack Obama's Cairo speech on June 4, 2009, which denied there is any clash of civilizations between Islam and Christianity – to come together and end disease, hunger, rights violations, and the abuse of creation, together creating a climate where people's greatest pleasure is 'love.[13] Miroslav Volf exemplifies this abstract unreality:

> Christianity is not a 'culture' or 'civilization;' it is a way of living centred on Christ *in* many diverse cultures and civilizations ... any form of imposition of a social system or of legislation allegedly based on God's revelation must be rejected. To affirm freedom of religion is to reject any form of religious totalitarianism and to embrace pluralism as a political project.... [T]he faiths that affirm social pluralism...can create a climate in which a love of pleasure has been exposed as empty and in which a robust debate is carried on about the most important question of all: "what makes for a life worthy of being called good.[14]

This kind of theological and socio-political infantilism not only fails to observe the manifest failure of the multi-cultural project across Europe, and the internal fault-lines and chaos of the Islamic world (and the so-called Arab Spring), but further, utterly fails to grasp the essential foundations of social order. First, culture *is* the *public manifestation* of the religious faith commitment of a people (be it Islamic, Christian, humanistic etc....) so in fact there is no avoiding religious 'civilization' and 'culture' where any given worldview predominates. That is to say, there is no such thing as a neutral culture. 'Multiculturalism' is therefore just a contemporary term for polytheism (many gods). But no society can be governed by more than one ultimate source of authority without provoking civil conflict and social chaos. This is for the simple reason that Sharia law is *not equal* to English Common Law; nor is the Hindu caste system *equal* to the Western legal tradition of equality before the law. Each system has a different source of sovereignty and thereby a different God or 'god' behind them. A community cannot function, for example, when both English Common Law and Sharia are perceived and treated as equally ultimate – the result of such irrationality can only be social suicide and judicial chaos.

The Roman Empire sought to 'solve' the challenge of its international cultic pluralism by politically sponsoring it, just as Volf proposes Christians should do. But the Roman world retained a semblance of cohesion only by ensuring that *ultimate allegiance* was to the emperor (the state) above and beyond any other religious commitment – there was no absolute religious freedom. This was true of all the polytheistic empires; ultimate power and authority lay with the king, emperor or ruler, i.e. the state. This pagan idea is the actual hegemonic reality that exists today in the West. The religion of the public sphere is a humanistic and pagan statism to which all lesser religious associations must submit. The state has replaced the authority of God and his Word, redefining everything from life, sexuality, marriage and family, to education, justice and truth. Furthermore, the doctrine of political pluralism itself must be 'enforced,' and today this is increasingly happening with totalitarian reach, without the consent of the governed. Clearly someone's vision of law and justice is going to be legislated and someone's vision of 'love' endorsed by the state – an 'establishment orthodoxy' that opposes rival orders is inescapable:

> You cannot escape the fact that, when you enact a legal system, you have an establishment of religion. Every legal system in the world is an establishment of religion. It may be Christianity, or it may be Humanism or Buddhism or Islam or Shintoism, but every legal system represents a moral and a theological structure.... [W]hatever we do legislate represents a moral judgement, whether it be good or bad, Christian or non-Christian.... Rome recognized that Christianity had a different moral system. It had a different sovereign, Jesus Christ, not Caesar. Rome recognised that its law was premised, not on the word of Caesar or the Roman Senate, but on the word of God. Therefore the Empire felt it was urgently necessary to oppose Christianity.[15]

Volf's 'ethical' rejection of revelation-based social legislation as 'totalitarian' clearly doesn't apply to the legislative *imposition* of religious and judicial pluralism – that is, political pluralism and therefore the enforcement of the law of other gods. This illustrates that the political concept of an unqualified or absolute freedom of religion is internally incoherent and functionally impossible.

The result of this muddled thinking is that Volf naively believes the world's states and religions can all work together toward the 'pleasure of love' by rejecting the 'love of pleasure,[16] but how is this possible outside of regeneration in Jesus Christ? Theologically, Volf doesn't take the problem of sin nearly seriously enough. Neither does he seem to appreciate that for biblical Christianity, "love is the fulfilment of the law" (Rom. 13:10). In other words, we must ask who defines love and the common good, God or man? Volf asks the world religions to collaborate on the question, "what makes for a life worthy of being called good?"[17] Yet Scripture answers God alone is good, for unregenerate men are in the grip of sin, who, in and of themselves, do not build a life worthy of being called good (Matt. 19:17; Rom. 3:20; John 8:31). Only in Jesus Christ can we be redeemed from lawlessness and conformed to the righteousness of God's law from the core of our being, so that love to God and man becomes our desire and delight (Titus 2:14). At the same time, sinful man's urge to lawlessness must be reined in by right use of God's law in the civil sphere to restrain evil (1 Tim. 1:8–11). A people that respects the Lord Jesus Christ will gradually demand such laws. Volf doesn't want the God of Scripture and his unchanging law to govern men, but prefers that the gods of the world and the doctrines of demons (2 Cor. 4:4; 1 Tim. 4:1) cooperate in saving man from his social problems by the elastic panacea of a humanly-defined 'love.' This 'modified' privatization of biblical faith and truth, calling for active support and promotion of political pluralism (public idolatry) in the name of Christianity, is fast becoming the dominant 'evangelical' perspective. Its cousin is the right-leaning two-kingdoms theology of conservative evangelicalism that supports the privatization of the faith with the notion that the public or secular sphere outside the institutional church is a realm of 'common grace' where specifically Christian revelation is not necessary to define and shape the common good. Biblical revelation is only for the church and Christian. Without denying that elements of Lutheran and Anabaptist thinking on church and culture have influenced modern evangelicalism's views in mission theology, it seems that the modified or 'qualified' privatization of Christianity in both camps (left and right-leaning) is largely an attempt to both cope with the Enlightenment's shattering of the theocratic ideal in Protestant mission theology, and to broker a deal with the crocodile of statism in the hope of being eaten last!

Biblically and historically, it is clear that the answer to the undermining of the *regnum Christi* in the West is not to be found in negotiating some kind of insidious compromise with anti-Christianity – the apostolic and early church approved no such treaty with the Caesars or cults around them. If the mission of the church is the extension of the reign of Christ by his glorious gospel and the rule of his kingdom law as Scripture would seem to indicate (Ps. 2; Ps. 110; 1 Cor. 15:25; Matt. 5:17–19; Matt. 6:10, 33; Rev. 1:5), then our task is a gracious, determined and faithful witness to Christ as the King of kings and Lord of lords. By word and deed, and with gentleness and respect we pull down false knowledge that sets itself up against God, taking every thought captive to Christ (1 Pt. 3:15–17; 2 Cor. 10:4–5). This is not accomplished by revolution (Rom. 12:19,21), but by regeneration, and multi-generational faithfulness to preach, teach, serve and obey in terms of the whole council of God. Faithful Christians are called to live godly, peaceable, honourable lives, seeking to live at peace with all as far as it depends upon them (Heb. 12:14; Rom. 12:17–21), without compromising God's word whilst dwelling in non-Christian social orders – this is precisely what missionaries have always done around the world and what Christians are once again doing in Western nations. Believers can love their neighbour, and pursue the good of the city and nation without socially, legally or politically approving and endorsing idolatry and the sovereignty of other gods. The early church faithful were often martyred for the profession of Christ's lordship over all things, and for refusing to participate in Rome's state-sanctioned political pluralism by offering incense to Caesar and accepting state license (as such they were considered 'atheists').[18] If another route were acceptable, they would have modelled it for us. Throughout various parts of the world today, and during all Christian history, believers have been marginalized, persecuted, displaced and hated for the sake of Christ, as he promised we would be. This is part of the church's calling because we do not belong to the spirit of the world (Matt. 10:22–23; John 15:18–19). True love for the lost outside of Christ is not manifest by complicity in a lie or tacit acceptance of wrongdoing, but only in doing God's will and declaring God's truth (1 Cor. 13:6; 1 John 3:18). As the apostle John reminds us, "the world passeth away, and the lust thereof: but he that doeth the will of God abideth for ever" (1 John 2:17 KJV).

15.2   The New Puritanism and the Church

If the covenant people's mission is not accomplishing a negotiated peace with the world's idolatry and antinomianism, then the answer to the shattering of the Protestant theocratic ideal by the Enlightenment lies somewhere other than the popular responses highlighted previously. The answer is in fact a simple return to the whole council of God in Scripture and a revival of a Puritan theology of mission that I have been detailing throughout this book. At the heart of a Reformed view of mission is the *Kingdom reign* of Jesus Christ and its extension throughout all creation. A king has a dominion, sceptre of authority and sovereign law. The missiologist Johannes Verkuyl summarizes the *character of that kingdom in* a manner that reinforces the true scope of the church's calling:

> The Kingdom to which the bible testifies involves a proclamation and a realization of a total salvation, one which covers the whole range of human needs and destroys every pocket of evil and grief affecting mankind. Kingdom in the New Testament has a breadth and scope which is unsurpassed; it embraces heaven as well as earth, world history as well as the whole cosmos.[19]

In developing a theology of mission then, we must neither romanticize the past (as though we are to be limited by it), as though history were static, nor accept the status quo as normative. Rather, as Lesslie Newbigin rightly observed, "The Church must in every generation be ready to bring its tradition afresh under the light of the Word of God."[20] The new Puritanism is seeking to do just this in our generation, whilst drawing upon godly precedent for refocusing the church on the *regnum Christi* through his law and gospel.

One such pocket of theocratic Christianity that survived the Enlightenment, elements of it becoming influential in the nineteenth and early part of the twentieth century, was Dutch Calvinism. This movement greatly influenced the new Puritanism (the theonomists). The noted statesman and theologian Abraham Kuyper (1837-1920) who served for several years as Prime Minister in the Netherlands summarized his Reformed missiological thrust this way – notice the centrality of Scripture to his vision of human affairs:

> One desire has been the ruling passion of my life. One high motive has acted like a spur upon my mind and soul.... It is this: that in spite of all worldly opposition, God's holy ordinances shall be established again in the home, in the school and in the state for the good of the people; to carve as it were, into the conscience of the nation, the ordinances of the Lord, to which the Bible and creation bear witness, until the nation pays homage again to God.[21]

We see here then the centrality of the glory of God and the law of God to the Christian calling as participants in the *missio Dei*. The Puritan mind thus sees the church's calling as expressly kingdom-oriented and therefore has a broader understanding of the *missio ecclesiae* than minimal institutional functions: "[The] church is more than the local building and congregation. The term is closer in meaning to the kingdom of God. It has reference to the called-out people of God in all their work together for the Lord."[22] This means that the structures of the church institution are never to be a limiting factor in extending the reign of God and pursuing the work of the kingdom – the work of ordained clergy and elders in their institutional role, does not exhaust the calling of church, leaving the laity to merely 'secular' tasks. Neither is the church to become self-serving by becoming a wealth and power center for its own sake. The church is to be a servant institution that equips, empowers and sends out every Christian in terms of God's glorious kingdom purposes. Rushdoony writes:

> The life of the church is not to be directed to developing an institution but to establishing God's saving power in their lives and in the lives of others, and in bringing dominion into the lives of men and institutions. Church members are the people of God, and they must further God's reign and government.[23]

God's people, the household of faith, function as a kingly priesthood in the earth in terms of Christ's government, which means that the church – the *ecclesia* or 'called-out' congregation – are being prepared by pastors, teachers, elders and evangelists for servant government in life under God. This task is eschatological and basic to our calling. St. Paul writes:

> When one of you has a grievance against another, does he dare go
> to law before the unrighteous instead of the saints? Or do you not
> know that the saints will judge the world? And if the world is to be
> judged by you, are you incompetent to try trivial cases? Do you not
> know that we are to judge angels? *How much more then, matters*
> *pertaining to this life* (1 Cor. 6:1–3).

Paul shows here that poor eschatology (understanding God's culminating
purposes in history) leads to bad ecclesiology, and bad ecclesiology
leads to a deformed theology of mission. As we come to understand that
our destiny in Christ is to judge the world and even the angelic beings,
we come to better understand our calling to judge and rule in matters
pertaining to this life. Many believers agree that one day at the return of
Christ we will somehow be involved in applying God's governmental
authority over the world, but they ignore Paul's key point in the text
which is this: given that the saints will at God's appointed time judge
the world at the last, *how much more* should we prepare ourselves and
be ready to govern ourselves, our families, churches and communities
in terms of God's word and authority. Calvin's comments on this text
are relevant:

> For all power of judging has been handed over to the Son in such a
> way that he will associate His saints with Himself in this honor, as
> assessors.… [A]s often as the faithful meet together in the name of
> Christ there is already in their assembly a certain reflection of the
> future judgement, which will be brought completely to view on the
> last day. Therefore Paul says that the world is judged in the Church,
> where there is set up the judgement seat of Christ, from which he
> exercises His jurisdiction.… [I]f all whom God has enlightened by
> His Word are possessed of so much authority that, by means of that
> Word, they judge not only men but also angels, are they not all the
> more eligible to judge concerning trivial and paltry matters?[24]

This is not to suggest that the church dispenses with the need for
magistrates and lawyers – on the contrary, Christians whose destiny
is to judge the world by God's Word, should pursue such honorable
vocations. The point is that given the church's calling in history, and
Christ's jurisdiction being manifest by his people, how much more are
we to be those who apply the standards of God's word to all the 'matters
pertaining to this life;' from the family, to courts of arbitration, schools,

healthcare, law, social provision, economics and more. For the church to realize its mission in history it must first be governed by God's word or it cannot manifest Christ's jurisdiction to the world. Consider, "The word designated church, ecclesia or assembly, signifies government, government in terms of the whole word of God. To be a government under God, the church and its members must first of all be ruled by the governing law-word of God."[25] This implies that believers are often working with truncated and sectarian definitions of the church and its calling, rather than one oriented by the kingdom of God and Christ's government in and through his people. Rushdoony writes:

> Rome has stressed the catholicity of the meaning of the *church* but identified it too closely with the institution. The Baptists have recognized the local nature of the worshipping group and the primacy of faith. The Church of England has seen the relationship of the entire people and their institutions to the church of Scripture but has reduced the church to the nation. Finally, the Reformed Churches have recognized the centrality of the covenant, but they have reduced the covenant to the community of institutionalized worshippers.[26]

In each case there is a 'cultural' and unbiblical limiting of the work of God within the confines of an institutional structure as though the institution itself encapsulates the Kingdom of God. The new Puritan conception of the *mission ecclesia* militates against this, re-appraising the nature of the church in light of Scripture and transcending the artificial limits that have been placed upon the calling of the kingdom congregation – whilst not side-stepping the church institution's God-given role and mandate in preaching, administering the sacraments and exercising church discipline.

Simply stated, the Puritan doctrine of the church is an *ecclesiology of the Kingdom*. In this view, the mission and the people are indivisible from one another – the Christian embodies the mission wherever they are, thus the mission of the people of God is not reducible to one institution. This does not mean a naïve or dismissive approach to the critical institutional aspects of the church, but a reorienting of perspective, for "while the church may be a building and an institution, and both can be important and needed aspects of its life, it is primarily a power and a government at work in the world."[27] The church and its calling are not then downgraded in Puritanism, rather they are expanded to look beyond the confines of its structures to a glorious vision of the universal reign of God. Thus, "the work of the laity must be seen as a chaplaincy, a carrying of the life of the faith into every area of life and thought. The layman does not leave the church when he walks out of the building."[28] It is important to point out that this perspective is only reviving and highlighting a forgotten dimension in the modern church's understanding of its mission – the new Puritans would therefore claim no originality here. Indeed the early church saw its role in much the same way as the Levites in Israel saw their responsibilities. From the first centuries of the church movement in history, it saw its calling as Christ's chaplaincy in the world:

> Hermas wrote of the Christian duty to care for widows and orphans, to relieve distressed believers, to practice hospitality, to reverence the aged, to practice justice, and to preserve their brotherhood. All the early literature stressed such responsibilities. Prisoners seized by raiders were ransomed. The church like the Jewish synagogue acted as a trustee for widows and orphans, and Cyprian compared the clergy with the Levites of the Old Testament in their responsibilities. The sick and captives were to be visited...; church buildings included rooms for storage of provisions for the needy. Basil the Great used monks to staff schools and orphanages and hospitals.[29]

The medical historian Roy Porter likewise points out the scope of the governmental ministry of the early church in terms of health and social provision:

> Jewish traditions of help and hospitality were extended, and Christ's instruction to his disciples to care for the sick and needy assumed institutional form through the appointment of deacons charged with distributing alms. By A.D. 250 the church in Rome had developed elaborate charitable outreach, with wealthy converts providing food and shelter for the poor ... Leontius, Bishop of Antioch from A.D. 344-358 set up hostels in his see; around 360, Bishop Eustathius of Sebasteia built a poor house; and St. Basil erected outside the walls of Caesarea 'almost a new city' for the sick, poor and leprous.[30]

This overarching sense of the mission of the church, so obscured in our time, is not one that those of us who would identify as contemporary Puritans think can be recovered overnight. However, linking eschatology and ecclesiology, I believe that a recovery of a missional theology of hope, dominion and victory, centered upon the kingdom of God and our priestly service to the king, would lead to a progressive renewal of the church's mission. Rushdoony's comment helps round up this discussion of the nature of that mission and the opportunity the church today is presented with:

> It is hardly likely, that after centuries of erroneous usage, we can readily return to the biblical usage which saw local congregations as outposts of Christ's Kingdom, as the church or kingdom in Ephesus, and so on.... [But] today, as the world more openly embraces humanism, our religious institutions, schools, families, and callings must see themselves as outposts of Christ's Kingdom, local gatherings of the citizens of the new creation. In the building for worship, the true church in a local community gathers to hear the word of God, whereby they are to go forth and exercise dominion.[31]

15.3 No Compromise

Not all evangelicals have failed to recognize the progressive truncation of the church's mission that has left us largely privatized in the West today. The noted twentieth-century evangelical leader, Carl F. H. Henry observed, "whereas once the redemptive gospel was a world-changing message, now it was narrowed to a world-resisting message.... Fundamentalism in revolting against the Social Gospel seemed also to revolt against the Christian social imperative."[32] For Henry this imperative included not just charitable help for the poor, but challenging the evil in political systems, secular modern education, racial hatred, unjust employment relationships, and international relations.[33] The influential English evangelical Anglican leader, John Stott, steadily came to recognize that the Great Commission had been inadequately interpreted by most evangelicals in the twentieth century. He wrote, "I now see more clearly that not only the consequences of the commission but the actual commission itself must be understood to include social as well as evangelistic responsibility, unless we are to be guilty of distorting the words of Jesus."[34]

Given the historical precedent for a theology of mission characterized by 'extending the reign of Christ' in the patristic, Reformational, Puritan and early evangelical church movements, as well as the hope, joy and victory entailed in such a view of the *missio ecclesiae*, why does this kingdom manifesto appear to be revolutionary or even threatening to many in today's church? I have come to the conclusion that the main answer to that is much less complicated than many like to think. One obvious reason is that this biblical understanding of the church's calling rejects compromising the faith. In a day of theological compromise, the comprehensive reign of Christ requires that a person "be a Christian in church, home, school, state, vocation and all of life. In going from one sphere to another, a man does not move from the realm of Christ to that of Mammon, Baal, Molech or any other god."[35] This obviously means equally that neither the "school, state, nor any other order of life can exempt itself from the...universal sway of God's rule and law. It is a sin to steal, bear false witness, or have other gods wherever we are."[36] This sounds obvious and initially uncontroversial, but once these basic premises are accepted and the challenge offered to apply them, the implications of the Puritan thesis become clear – uncompromising biblical faithfulness to the Lord, whatever the cost.

Nevertheless, it must be granted that this is not the only reason that theocratic and theonomic mission theology has met with such resistance. As we noted earlier, "with the Enlightenment, the churches limited their sphere, and God's sphere, to the spiritual realm. Before long, God became the absentee landlord of the physical universe. Polytheism was born thus within the church."[37] In practical terms in the life of the church, this meant that "the work of Jesus Christ was progressively limited to soul-saving.... [T]he Bible was read, not as God's law-word, but as a devotional book for pietists. The state (and most of life) was thus freed from God to follow a humanistic course."[38] Consequently the revived Puritan vision of the *reign of God*, with the church called to *extend the reign of Christ*, represents a radical departure from the neo-platonic, privatized and pietistic outlook of much of modern evangelicalism. And yet there is nothing radical from a biblical perspective about theocratic, Puritan, missional theology. It plainly expresses the heart of the very thing the Christian is commanded by our Lord to pray for. In this the Puritan mind concurs with Verkuyl's view that "the first three petitions of the Lord's Prayer summarize so well the deepest and ultimate goal of mission: 'Hallowed be Thy name; Thy kingdom come; Thy will be done on earth as in heaven.'"[39]

Now whilst the new Puritanism has encountered much hostility from within Protestantism that has viewed it as 'triumphalistic,' threatening to the status quo, or too far out of alignment with current Western social and political sensibilities, it has nonetheless garnered much interest and found support for many of its major themes across denominational lines, impacting not only the reformed but also the charismatic and Pentecostal churches. For example, John Frame believes that the revived Puritan or theonomic perspective has helped stir a new spirit in the church generally that includes "a passion for learning God's word in detail and applying it seriously, without compromise, to the world in which we live."[40] Similarly, in *The New Dictionary of Christian Ethics and Pastoral Theology*, J. G. Child highlights the benefit accrued to the church through the theonomic perspective. He writes, "by forcing Christians to grapple with the Old Testament's contribution to Christian ethics and a just society, and by offering insightful biblical solutions to the problems of the modern world, the Reconstructionists have enriched the church."[41] This broad, largely quiet and at times surprising spread of Puritan themes is in some measure due to the non-denominational, biblically-oriented and informal character of Puritan missional practice. Some critics have falsely regarded this historic theonomic missiology as some sort of revolutionary movement seeking to seize state power and enforce a theocracy on an unwilling society, but Michael McVicar in his PhD thesis on the theonomic 'movement' is correct in observing that "the process of Christian reconstruction happens in homes, living rooms, schoolrooms, board meetings, and in church basements. It is a slow, multi-generational process that builds slowly as women and men work to build the kingdom of God."[42] This quiet and progressive influence of Puritan missiology is also no doubt due to the weakness and evident inadequacy of current Reformed and evangelical missiological thought. The influential defender of Christian freedoms and trainer of Christian lawyers and attorneys through the Blackstone Legal Academy, Jeffery Ventrella, has commented, "it is humbling to see just how impoverished reformed missiology – indeed, evangelical missiology – is today."[43] In response, he directs Christians' attention back toward a vision of extending the reign of Christ: Theonomic postmillennialism – rightly conceived and practiced – demands our, promoting gospel primacy; demonstrating evangelistic zeal; cultivating christendomic consciousness; practicing cultural engagement; and habituating Christian humility."[44]

Understanding God's eschatological purpose in history, where his kingdom rule grows like a mustard seed into the biggest plant in the garden, means that we must actively choose today what God has purposed for tomorrow – his manifest rule and reign over all things through Jesus Christ. For Ventrella, this choice is ethical, "we must choose ethically, and therefore, we must choose eschatologically. Any other result would be, in a word, antinomian."[45]

15.4 Idolatry – The Root of Resistance

How then can the impoverishment of evangelical missiology be specifically and immediately addressed? How can Christian people and church leaders be encouraged to 'choose eschatologically' and thus choose to delight in and apply God's law and gospel to all of life? What lies at the root of our blindness to, and resistance toward, the reign of Christ in the church and world in terms of God's complete word? Tackling this problem is a largely forgotten aspect of the work of Christian apologetics, operating in a 'prophetic' role to the church. In the early centuries of church history, one of the key functions of the apologist was not only to defend the faith from hostile attacks from *without* (as it is popularly understood), but to "contend earnestly for the faith once for all delivered to the saints" (Jude v. 3). Some of the greatest works of apologetics – written by pastors and theologians it should be noted – have been directed, not against scepticism, but against heresy and idolatry *within* the professing church. This is seen in some of the work of Justin Martyr, Irenaeus of Lyon, Tertullian and Augustine.

Ordinarily, when we ask ourselves what the idols are hindering the mission of the church today that the apologetic pulpit must address, it is easy for our minds to turn toward the overt and obvious idolatry of pagan, humanistic sex cults that dominate our age, the worship of saints and images, or the religious environmentalism, occultism and materialism of our time. These idols are relatively easy to spot. Yet, the biblical condemnation of idolatry in the prophets is focused most significantly upon those who claim to be the *covenant people*. In Scripture, within the pagan world, idolatry is an expected and indeed judicial blindness *given* to covenant-violating nations for their punishment, discipline and correction (Deut. 4:19; Is. 6:9–10). But for the prophets, where idolatry is most dangerous and most devastating is amongst God's chosen people (his kingdom of priests). Why is this so?

It is, I believe, a truism to say, as goes the church, so goes the world. If the church herself is found in idolatry what hope is there for the peoples and tribes outside of kingdom life? Since the church's mission is to be a blessing to the nations, salt and light to the world, pillar and support of the truth and the manifold wisdom of God set forth before the world, God's word focuses upon his exacting *jealousy* for his bride – that she might be what she is called to be for the salvation and healing of the nations. The modern church is tempted to blame the humanists, pagans and Muslims, Marxists or other groups for the state of our culture and its idolatrous turn, but God calls his people to first take a long hard look at themselves in accounting for the decline of our social order.

In the remarkable and hard-hitting passage of Jeremiah 3:1–23, the prophet points to the faithlessness, through idolatry, of Israel and Judah. God likens the idolatry of his covenant people to an adulterous wife who plays the whore – it is a graphic and shocking image. In the text we learn that God's people took their adulteries (idolatry) lightly and thereby polluted their land (v. 9). They believed the lie, that the living God is not a jealous God (Deut. 6:5) or a consuming fire (Heb. 12:29); they believed God could be *domesticated* and made amenable to their faithlessness. The inevitable effect of idolatry amongst God's people was the decay of their faith, social order and nation. This theological and covenantal reality, as we have seen throughout this book, is unchanged! Yet, as always with God, his faithfulness remains, even when we are faithless. In the midst of the people's rebellion, there is hope. This hope is found in the invitation to return to the Lord. God calls his people to repent and turn to him; by this recognition of their idolatry, they can still find mercy, grace and restoration (v. 12–14). The faithful God of Abraham, Isaac and Jacob, the God and father of our Lord Jesus Christ, will give such repentant people shepherds (pastors and teachers) after his own heart, who will feed and lead them not into idolatry, blasphemy and lawlessness, but knowledge, understanding and faithfulness. Then, the Lord's presence shall be manifest as the Word goes out and the nations shall be gathered to it – a beautiful heritage (v. 15–18). Thus, the Lord calls out to his faithless people who have perverted their way with idolatry and forgotten their God, "return oh faithless sons; I will heal your faithlessness" (v. 22). The scope of this promise is personal, national and global.

15.5 Divine Jealousy

It is then a remarkable fact that one of God's own names (self-descriptions) is *Jealous*. In Exodus 20:5, we read a prohibition against all idolatry and there one of God's names is revealed, "for I the Lord your God am a jealous God." It is even clearer in Exodus 34:14, "for you shall worship no other god, for the Lord whose name is jealous, is a jealous God." This is restated in Deuteronomy 4:24, "for the Lord your God is a consuming fire, a Jealous God." This passage is quoted by the writer of Hebrews in chapter 12:29. Typically, this is not one of the names of God that believers often consider, but it is critical to our understanding of biblical faith. The word *jealous* is related to *zealous* and denotes exclusivity – another word our age has distaste for! Christians cannot domesticate this divine name, turn it into a cold abstraction by depersonalising it, nor write it off as an aspect of *progressive revelation* to a people struggling with the meaning of Jehovah worship – a name now superseded by an elastic and content-less principle of love. Love and jealousy are inseparably related and they are intimately involved in one another in the unchanging character of God, "For I the Lord do not change" (Mal. 3:6). We read in Hebrews 13:8 that "Jesus Christ is the same yesterday, today and forever. Do not be led away by diverse and strange teachings."

Jealousy, like God, is personal (as is love). Electricity is not personal. The murderer and the saint alike will both get electric shocks if they touch an electric fence because *current* is impersonal or non-discriminating in action. Thus, when people fail to discriminate in life between good and evil character and actions, right and wrong, truth and falsehood, they are depersonalizing and dehumanizing persons and life itself. Jealousy is intensely personal and is an aspect of real love. To offer a very concrete illustration, if a married man came home from a night on the town at 7 AM and sat down for breakfast after blurting out to his wife his illicit adulteries during his absence, and she simply responds, "Oh well, never mind. Eat your breakfast before it gets cold," the only truly cold thing in that room is the marriage, because the exclusivity of a marriage of love is jealous – it must be by its very nature. Thus, the married couple are jealous for one another's affection. As a father, I am jealous for my children, for their good and wellbeing. As a leader, I am jealous for God's church and I trust for the glory of God. This means that jealousy can be virtue because it is intolerant of *unfaithfulness*; its opposite is a complacent, indifferent and careless satisfaction. God's love for us is a *gift love*, (for our good and blessing), not a *need* love because his triune being is somehow deficient and in need of human love. If God *is* love, as the Scriptures say (1 John 4:8), then God *cannot* be short of it – water cannot get wet and he who is love cannot require what he is. Now clearly a God of accommodation to idolatry is not the Lord whose name is jealous. But the living God, his love is like that of a husband for his beloved bride – a deep longing for their good, their beauty (character or perfection) and their blessing and a passion for their exclusive allegiance and faithfulness.

The New Testament repeatedly uses the same language. St. James writes:

> You adulterous people! Do you not know that friendship with the world is enmity with God? Therefore whoever wishes to be a friend of the world makes himself an enemy of God. Or do you suppose it is to no purpose that the Scripture says, "He yearns jealously over the spirit that he has made to dwell in us" (4:4–5).

James here is concerned with the world's lawless way of thinking and living, infiltrating the church. Here, jealousy is quite clearly a good thing. The same is true of St. Paul's jealousy for the church in 2 Corinthians 11:1–4:

> I wish you would bear with me in a little foolishness. Do bear with me! For I feel a divine jealousy for you, since I betrothed you to one husband, to present you as a pure virgin to Christ. But I am afraid that as the serpent deceived Eve by his cunning, your thoughts will be led astray from a sincere and pure devotion to Christ. For if someone comes and proclaims another Jesus than the one we proclaimed, or if you receive a different spirit from the one you received, or if you accept a different gospel from the one you accepted, you put up with it readily enough.

Paul describes his jealousy as a divine jealousy; so what is he jealous for? Using the same metaphor as Jeremiah, he is jealous for the exclusivity of the marriage between the covenant people and Christ. And like the prophetic message of Jeremiah, what threatens the church's faithful betrothal to Christ, is idolatry, that is, being led astray by false gods –

'another Jesus' a 'different Spirit' and a 'different gospel.' We also see the reaction of the church at Corinth to such idolatry in their midst; they had "put up with it readily enough" (v. 4).

We see then the clear link, in both Old and New Testaments, between idolatry and divine jealousy, the covenantal illustration of marriage or betrothal functioning in both cases as the clearest picture of the righteous nature of God's jealousy for his people and the integrity of his name, 'jealous.' The apostles and the prophets therefore make abundantly clear that idolatry in the church leads to *jealous wrath*, and significant consequences. This is an unshakable aspect of real, genuine love – they cannot be separated. If we want a God of love, then we have to deal with the living God. This means that our attempts to liberalize, civilize or domesticate the God of Scripture are nothing short of idolatry. C.S. Lewis, the great twentieth-century British apologist, points out that to deny jealousy and wrath to God is misleading and destructive: "All the liberalizing and civilizing analogies only lead us astray. Turn God's wrath into mere enlightened disapproval and you also turn his love into mere humanitarianism. The consuming fire and the perfect beauty both vanish."[46] God's love is exclusive which means his love for his covenant people demands the eschewing of all idolatry.

15.6   The nature of Idolatry

The essence of all sin is idolatry and it was so from the first. The plan of the tempter was that every person would be their own god, determining what constitutes good and evil for themselves. Since all knowledge is ethical (human thought is either in submission to God and his word or not), this temptation included the idea of an autonomous definition of truth – the essence of the existentialist character of our age. Idolatry has many facets, but its most central is the worship of self. Man's favourite idol is himself and his own will. The *moral* fruit of all idolatry is then sin, since its root is sinful. In all forms of idolatry people succumb explicitly or implicitly, deliberately or inadvertently, to the notion that reality is to some degree chaotic and that forces (spiritual or material) can be placated, manipulated or bribed to conform to my own will. Put another way, in all idolatry man views the world not as it is, by God's created word, but as he would like it to be. In biblical faith, the triune God is the absolute Lord and sovereign over all things, providentially governing all creation by his grace, goodness and law. It is because of this that the Christian has rest, the Sabbath rest of God, because our absolute confidence and trust is in our unchanging, eternally faithful God who has revealed himself, and redeemed us in Jesus Christ, and spoken to us with finality in his infallible word. Outside of this faith, man's restless hope is in a futile illusion of 'control' through his incantations, words, ideas, manipulation and offerings. Finally however in the worldviews of anti-Christianity, even the gods (be they trans-humans or pagan deities) are subject to a cruel and blind fate.

As we have seen in this volume, the peoples of Western societies have steadily denied the God of Scripture and has turned increasingly to humanism, overt paganism, Eastern mysticism, occultism and a plethora of alternative spiritualities and with them finds no true rest – for there is no unchanging, sovereign Lord in whose providence and salvation they can find repose. Their restlessness and confusion is part of God's judgement upon their idolatry. So when the covenant people begin to take on the idolatrous ideas and patterns of lawlessness, the church is progressively destroyed and society goes with it. This is precisely why God declares in Exodus 20, "you shall have no other gods before me." Neither then is the church at liberty to make covenants with false religions – there is no 'common word,' nor a 'common brotherhood' outside of Christ – there is only covenant faithfulness or idolatry. There is then no middle way. God has emphatically declared that in the age of the church (that is, the age of the Messiah) he will, "cut off the names of the idols out of the land" (Zech. 13:2). So, when the church aligns herself in any way with lawlessness and idolatry she brings herself under judgement.

The two key forms of idolatry found amongst God's people in the time of Jeremiah were (and remain in today's church) *syncretism* and *false prophecy* in the name of the God of Scripture – and they usually come together. This was the specific sin that Jeremiah highlights in Jeremiah 3; what he calls the spiritual "orgies on the mountains" (v. 23). This religious promiscuity amongst the people of Israel entailed the idea that covenants (agreements and compromises) could be made with false gods, and that the Lord God is not exclusive, but *inclusive* and *pluralistic*. In Scripture, this is a form of testing God and provoking him to wrath. God declares through Isaiah, "I am the Lord, that is my name: and my glory will I not give to another, neither my praise to graven images" (Is. 42:8). The covenant people were forbidden any form of syncretistic worship, covenants and marriages. This requirement for the church of

Jesus Christ, the enlarged Israel, is repeated by St. Paul in 2 Corinthians 6:14–18. And the Lord Jesus is no less exacting. We cannot serve two masters (Matt. 6:24), and those not for Christ are described as against him (Luke 11:23). Christ declared himself to be the only way to the Father (John 14:6), and true love for Christ is clearly predicated on obedience: "If you love me, you will keep my commandments" (John 14:15).

In the modern church, we have people and movements who *claim* to want and worship a God of love; not a God whose nature includes law, jealousy, exacting justice, judgement and wrath. This pretence has always been the cry of those who would liberalize, sanitize, and domesticate the divine. But the love of which they speak is an abstraction, and their god an idol; an idea; a universalistic, and promiscuous god; an antinomian image without law, and therefore without grace: without justice and therefore without mercy. This 'progressive' god is evolving and changing as the spirit of the age appoints the creed of time. This is a god of man's making whose being and ways must conform to the shifting sands of popular culture. This god speaks no infallible word, for that word is now spoken by man for the *moment*. This profane image is a useless idol. The actual god in this theosophy is man. However much cloaked in theological or missiological verbiage, this evolving god is not the God of Abraham, Isaac and Jacob, the God and father of the Lord Jesus Christ.

Through the denial of the second commandment, the rejection of the God whose name is jealous, great numbers, indeed entire denominations in the Western church, have created and worshipped a god of their rebellious imagination. In too many quarters (including parts of the evangelical church), the Christian church has hitched up its spiritual skirt to play the whore against God, and our decline, our numerous church closures, our ruin and decadence are testament to our adultery. Many have, as St. Paul declared to the Corinthians, proclaimed another Jesus, a different spirit, and another gospel. This new Jesus and 'gospel' takes various forms. For some he is the mere man who was neither born of the virgin nor raised to life. Their 'gospel' is humanization and anti-supernaturalism. For them there is no triune God, though they wear the labels and garb of the ministers of Christ. Their pulpits are profane and their churches, synagogues of Satan (Rev. 2:9; 3:9). For others 'God' is acknowledged only to service their needs and interests; a self-help god working to improve personal self-esteem, make rich and give us what we want; a god that can be bribed or manipulated by various 'spiritual' and mental techniques. This new god is not exacting, thunders no law, speaks no unchanging word and is inclusive of idolatry and sin. For still others, the new spirit offers a hippie Jesus; an ecowarrior and inclusivist, engaged in class warfare and saving the planet from the plundering rich. This Jesus is an anti-Western pacifist and Marxist, with a gospel of social justice, identifying with the oppressed masses in throwing off the bourgeois family. This god is invariably letting all men into the 'kingdom,' be they Buddhist, Hindu, atheist, Wiccan or Muslim, as long as they are sincere, since 'love wins.' But he is not the sinless Lamb of God bearing away the sin and guilt of the world and taking God's wrath upon himself for all men (Is. 53). These spirits, and others like them, are the spirits of the age, not the Holy Spirit who takes what is Christ's and makes it known to us, the Spirit of Truth, who leads us into all truth and writes God's law into our hearts. These gospels are thus no gospel.

In our present culture, about sixty per cent of Americans co-habit before marriage.[47] In a study, titled "The myth of long-term stable relationships outside of marriage" that was undertaken by the Marriage Foundation, it was found that forty-five per cent of British teenagers between the ages of thirteen to fifteen are not living with both parents, and that nine out of ten children born to unmarried, cohabiting partners will be living in single-parent households by their teens. These figures are catastrophic.[48] In our time, as Christians have often silently looked on, marriage has been redefined, new genders have been invented, male and female roles have been redefined, education has been redefined, law has been redefined, justice has been redefined and throughout this theological and social revolution, much of the church has been in an 'open relationship' with the world – co-habiting with other gods – syncretistic to the core and too often a great advocate for and preacher of idolatry. Scripture warns us, and the Western church is discovering, that God does not co-habit! He is not in an open relationship with his people and his covenant word, in both blessing and cursing, is binding. It is important to notice what St. Paul writes in Romans 11 for the church's admonition. In discussing God's judgement against national Israel for idolatry and the grafting in of the gentiles he says:

> Then you will say, branches were broken off so that I might be grafted in. That is true. They were broken off because of their unbelief, but you stand fast through faith. So do not become proud but fear. *For*

if God did not spare the natural branches, neither will he spare you. Note then the kindness and severity of God. Severity toward those who have fallen, but God's kindness to you, provided you continue in his kindness. *Otherwise you to will be cut off.* (Rom. 11:19–22)

God's faithfulness to his covenant word continues in both of kindness and severity for his church throughout the ages. The Scripture binds us still, and calls us as a faithful bride to true and pure devotion to Christ.

15.7 Going the Way of Balaam

Syncretistic forms of 'Christianity' are inescapably involved in another aspect of idolatry, namely, *false prophecy*. When we consider what it is that leads God's people into idolatry, according to Scripture we find that the main culprit is false preaching and teaching. This is plainly taught in 2 Peter 2 and 2 Corinthians 11:4, as well as Jeremiah chapter 3. God promises the Israelites in Jeremiah 3, that if his people will return to him he will give them "Shepherds after my own heart, who will feed you with knowledge and understanding" (v. 15). The negative implication here is that a rebellious people will be given false teachers who lead them astray.

False prophecy (preaching and teaching) is not always easy to spot because it can and does use the name of the Lord and pretends to the real thing, which is the essence of hypocrisy. This is what Jeroboam did. He made two bull-calves of gold, established a new sanctuary, and said to Israel, "Behold your gods, O Israel, which brought you up from the land of Egypt" (1 Kings 12:28). Though taken lightly by many would-be teachers in today's church, it is a fearful thing, to invoke the name of God and our Lord Jesus Christ in idolatrous preaching and worship. Usually in Scripture, the false prophet is not an open idolater or pagan, but a prophet that arises from amongst the covenant people. This is typically the way in the modern church as well. It is not usually the loud humanist and open spokesman for Baal (sexual perversion, homosexual marriage, abortion, abolition of the family, queer culture etc....) who is the greatest danger to the church, but the audacious churchmen, masking their idolatry as faithfulness. Often gifted, eloquent, full of plausible-sounding argument and popular appeal, with media reach and glossy books and even an ostensibly 'evangelical' pedigree, such people can spin a new faith with words from the old. They may be talking of mission, justice, the kingdom of God, the 'real' or 'lost' message of Jesus, social justice and much besides, but inwardly can be ravening wolves. The critical mark and test of idolatrous leaders biblically, is that they will introduce *innovation* into the covenant and create a *new religion* out of the existing one. The true call of such false prophets is to say to God's people, "let us go after other gods." The more idolatry there is in the church, the more strife, restlessness, pointless innovation, frustration and impotence will characterize God's people. Idolatry always takes the church into a restless, Sabbath-less, gospel-less world of unbelief. And a church in the grip of unbelief is like the idol she has made, useless and powerless (Ps. 115:3–8). Her bell-towers fall, her sanctuaries will lie in ruin and her false ministers shall fade away.

Thus to turn God's covenantal jealousy into myth, or to equate it with a bygone cultural perception beyond which the church has now evolved, or to limit it to a past dispensation, is not only to create a false God by falsifying Scripture, it is to destroy *the very attribute* that those who would domesticate God wish to cling to – the 'love' of God. It turns out that their very concept of love is not the love of God at all, but the projection of fallen man's self-will onto the being of God, which is idolatry. This denuded, permissive and disinterested god is both powerless and unaffected, and what a man worships, that he becomes. The triune God of Scripture is a faithful, exclusive, loving, inexorable and jealous husband, and it is these very qualities (in the language of his gracious accommodation to our understanding) that make him a God of real love. This is brilliantly set forth in one of C. S. Lewis's most beautiful and telling passages:

The analogy between God's love for man and a man's love for a woman...is freely used in scripture. Israel is a false wife, but her heavenly husband cannot forget the happier days; *"I remember thee, the kindness of thy youth, the love of thy espousals, when thou wentest after Me in the wilderness."* Israel is the pauper bride, the waif whom her lover found abandoned by the wayside, and clothed and adorned and made lovely and yet she betrayed him. Adulteresses St. James calls us, because we turn aside to the *"friendship of the world"*, while God *"jealously longs for the spirit He has implanted in us."* The church is the Lord's bride whom he so loves that in her no spot or wrinkle is endurable. For the truth which this analogy serves to emphasize is that love, in its own nature, demands the perfecting of the beloved; that the mere "kindness" which tolerates anything except suffering in its object is, in that respect, at the opposite pole from love. When we fall in love with a woman, do we cease to care whether she is clean or dirty, fair or foul? Do we not rather then first begin to care? Does any woman regard it as a sign of love in a man that he neither knows nor cares how she is looking? Love may, indeed, love the beloved when her beauty is lost: but not because it is lost. Love may forgive all infirmities and love still in spite of them: but love cannot cease to will their removal.... When Christianity says that God loves man, it means that God *LOVES* man: not that he has some disinterested, because really indifferent, concern for our welfare, but that, in awful and surprising truth, we are the objects of His love. You asked for a loving God: you have one. The great Spirit you so lightly invoked, the Lord of terrible aspect, is present: not a senile benevolence that drowsily wishes you to be happy in your own way, not the cold philanthropy of a conscientious magistrate, nor the care of a host who feels responsible for the comfort of his guests, but the consuming fire himself, the love that made the worlds, persistent as the artist's love for his work and despotic as a man's love for a dog, provident and venerable as a father's love for a child, jealous, inexorable, exacting as love between the sexes...it is certainly a burden of glory not only beyond our deserts but also, except in rare moments of grace, beyond our desiring.... The impassible speaks as if it suffered passion, and that which contains in itself the cause of its own and all other bliss talks as though it could be in want and yearning. "Is Ephraim my dear son? Is he a pleasant child? For since I spake against him I do earnestly remember him still: therefore my bowels are troubled for him." "How shall I give thee up, Ephraim? How shall I abandon thee, Israel? Mine heart is turned within me." "Oh Jerusalem, how often would I have gathered thy children together, even as a hen gathereth her chickens under her wings, and ye would not."[49]

This is the living God, the father of the Lord Jesus Christ – a God of real love and faithfulness. And he calls his people to faithfulness, that they might share his endless joy and be partakers of his holiness (Heb. 12:9–13). Such love of God must be declared again in the church and this requires true preaching and true shepherds. It is hard to declare faithfully things that can make one unpopular, but the church's mission entails a duty is to the *whole* counsel of God. It is a daunting responsibility because Christian preaching and teaching is compared in Scripture (amongst other things) to a watchdog (Is. 56:10). Watchdogs bark a warning, but false preaching is likened to a dumb dog that cannot bark, like a lap dog that is sleeping or lying down. This leaves the church vulnerable and weak. But confidence and hope is stirred in the church when shepherds embrace and teach the kingdom mission, take Christ at his Word, and apply it to every sphere (Matt. 5:17–19). In recent decades, confidence and hope have been gradually sapped in the western church by a general failure to faithfully preach and apply the *whole counsel of God* in our churches. But this can be turned around if pastors, teachers and elders do what God in fact requires; that we declare his law-word faithfully, simply and directly, not abstracting it and forming it in our own image. We then summon one another as brothers and sisters in Christ to hear and obey, listen and act, read and apply. It is only the unadulterated word that will commend itself to everyone's conscience and grant God's church life and a future (2 Cor.4:1–5).

15.8 The Hopeless World

St. Paul reminds the church in Ephesians 2:12–13 of the Christian's former condition, "remember you were at that time separated from Christ, alienated from the commonwealth of Israel and strangers to the covenants of promise, having no hope and without God *in the world*." It is important to consider these words carefully. Paul says that when the gentiles were outside the covenant there was "no hope...without God in the world." Notice that the text is not about heaven, which is just a part of our hope; the focus is the world. We are told that the *ungodly* are without hope *in the world*. This is logical. Proverbs 8:36 is plain concerning the ultimate outcome of a rejection of God's wisdom: "all who sin against me wrong their own souls, all those who hate me love death." Without the sovereign God in their world, and outside of the covenant, men desperately plan their utopias, dream of creating cybernetic life and downloading their consciousness into a machine to escape death, and wonder how man will avoid the consequences of the evil in his own heart. Our culture in its restlessness and hopelessness is developing a love affair with death, hence the current obsession with promoting population control, abortion, homosexuality, euthanasia and physician-assisted suicide. By contrast Paul gives us the Christian pattern of life in Romans 5:1–5: "We rejoice in hope of the glory of God." According to the apostle, even our suffering and afflictions are meaningful and purposeful to produce in us character and hope, a hope that does not disappoint or put to shame. This means that nothing can happen to the child of God that is not able to produce in us further hope in the midst of our calling.

Though the church is called to covenant life and salvation, and is commissioned to spread this salvation victory to all creation, in the context of trials and tribulations, and the discouragements of idolatry (syncretism and false prophecy), it is easy to become despondent. But in Romans 4:17–18, St. Paul points to the biblical pattern for the covenant people set forth in the life of a patriarch, a man *called out* by God on a mission, Abraham, whom he calls the father of us all. Remarkably, "In hope he believed *against hope*, that he should become the father of many nations." This was astonishing hope in history concerning the future and mission of the covenant people. Indeed this shows us that hope for history and in history is not an abandonment of the faith, it is the maturing of our faith – it is following our Father Abraham. Who did Abraham put his trust in? God and his promises, or what appeared to be the facts around him? Again Paul tells us in whom we hope – our faithful and sovereign, triune God. In 1 Timothy 6:15–16 he reminds us, "He who is the blessed and only sovereign, the King of kings and Lord of Lords, who alone has immortality and dwells is unapproachable light, whom no one has ever seen or can see. To him be honour and eternal dominion. Amen." Yet, it is harder to hope and believe that the mission God has given his church can be fulfilled. It is easier to dress up faithlessness as realism, disobedience as a higher spirituality, or to succumb to hopelessness.

15.9   The Covenant of Hope

Two remarkable covenantal statements are made in Scripture relating to idolatry and the future – statements that should give every Christian cause for hope. The first is Exodus 20:4–5 and tells us of the judgement and consequences of idolatry, and the impact of its effects for three or four generations. Believers know the reality of this. We see the fruit of broken marriages, criminality and social decay all around us:

> You shall not make for yourself a carved image...you shall not bow down to them or serve them, for I the Lord your God am a jealous God, visiting the iniquity of the fathers on the children to the third and fourth generation of those who hate me...

The second is Deuteronomy 7:9: "Know therefore that the Lord your God is God, the faithful God who keeps covenant and steadfast love with those who love him and keep his commandments, to a thousand generations."

Notice the contrast. The consequences of idolatry amongst a people are seen to the *third and fourth* generation where hatred of God is present. But the covenantal faithfulness of God is to a *thousand* generations of those who love and obey him, despite our failures and backslidings. Think of the application of this for wayward families and children, churches, seminaries and universities; consider the application of this promise for our grandchildren and great grandchildren as yet unborn. The real question then becomes, how dare we have *no* hope? If God will hear the prayers of an ungodly man like Ahab, how much more will he hear those who love and serve his mission in the earth? (1 Kings 21:27–29).

By the grace of God, the church constitutes the people of the Jubilee (Is. 61:1–4). This declaration of Jubilee – liberty, freedom, salvation, healing and kingdom rebuilding in the ruin of devastations in former generations – was read by our Lord in Luke 4:16–21 before a Jewish congregation at the commencement of his ministry: And he rolled up the scroll and gave it back to the attendant and sat down. And the eyes of all the synagogue were fixed on him. And he began to say to them, "Today, this Scripture has been fulfilled in your hearing."

Jesus declared the arrival of the Jubilee in himself, in history. The covenant people in Christ are now the people of the Jubilee, continuing his work as the children of the King. The apostle John tells us in 1 John 5:3–4 that the victory is ours in Christ as we walk by faith in obedience to him:

> For this is the love of God, that we keep his commandments. And his commandments are not burdensome. For everyone who has been *born of God* overcomes the world. And this is the victory that has overcome the world – our faith.

Through faith in Christ, this law and gospel is hope and victory for time and eternity. It is a covenant of hope that must be shared and declared, defended and lived. Christ promised that he would build his church, and hell itself would not prevail against it (Matt. 16:18). We must again in the Western world recover the vital mission of the church that sees its calling as applying the reign of Jesus Christ in all creation. We must revive the spirit and vision of salvation victory that characterized the apostle John and inspired the great hymn writer who penned those potent words, "All hail the power of Jesus name let angels prostrate fall, bring forth the royal diadem and crown him Lord of all.... Let every kindred, every tribe on this terrestrial ball, to him all majesty ascribe and crown him Lord of all." G. Campbell Morgan commenting on Acts 28:16–31, highlights the keynote of the church's mission in our era. He writes that those who profess to be God's people must stand for:

> ...the Kingdom of God, not the caprice of a king nor the decision of a parliament, not the will of the people, which may be as mistaken as the caprice of a king. We stand not for monarchy, or democracy; but for Theocracy, for the Kingdom of God for the government of God, for the fact that He is King of the kings, for the fact that His law must be the criteria by which all human laws are measured, for the fact that only as His will is done can the people enter into the heritage of their own life. The Kingdom of God was the deepest note of the witness of the one man in Rome; and must be the deepest note of the witness of the Church in every city.[50]

It will require courage, fortitude and unwavering biblical faithfulness to rouse the church again to her mission in a generation that has lost its way in idolatry, and where many a prophet and priest have said "peace peace, when there is no peace" (Jer. 6:14). Yet in spite of all opposition, wherever a faithful kingdom people are found; wherever the church of Jesus Christ gathers as his embassy to serve as his ambassadors; wherever a willing and humble church will hear and obey, the rule and kingdom of God is present. For his Word is unchained, and when it is obeyed and declared by his royal priesthood, it *cannot* return to him empty, but will most surely succeed in the thing for which God sent it (Is. 55:11):

> Where the Christian witness is true to this Kingdom and to this interpretation, the issue is that the witness is unhindered; in spite of emperors, enemies, prisons and chains, "the word of God is not bound," and whatever may be the massed forces against its testimony, it is they which must crumble and pass and perish, as did Rome and Nero and not this word of the testimony. May it be ours to be true to that testimony in life and speech, to the glory of His Name. In proportion as we are so, the one word forever describing the Church will be the word with which this book ends, unhindered![51]

Propagandique imperii Christi, amen!

Rushdoony, Racism and the Holocaust

The Internet is a mixed blessing; with the many excellent research opportunities it provides come all the attendant hazards of navigating through bogus articles, shoddy scholarship, slanderous blogs and pseudointellectual nonsense. Millions of blogs and articles are available through a simple Google search that pass through no peer review, no publisher's scrutiny, and under no editor's eye; they are often not published in hardcopy journals and so nobody has put hard-earned money into making them available. All this tends toward the danger of misinformation in the ether being established as truth, and once it is out there, it is very difficult to retrieve or to nullify the effect. This fact puts Christians who write blogs and articles for the Internet under a serious obligation to be as truthful and honest as possible when writing about others – their character, claims and teaching. After reading an initial draft of this book, some trusted scholars of my acquaintance encouraged me, in light of its content, to briefly address a well-circulated myth on the web that has been employed as a whipping boy to encourage a quick disregard for the new Puritan thesis without giving it a fair hearing. If one can discredit a leading exponent of a theological position by misrepresenting their teaching, focusing on a given fault, or pointing to a disappointing incident or event in their life (consider the slander past and present used against John Calvin) it becomes much easier to dismiss their writings without actually engaging them.

In recent years, I have been saddened and distressed by some very unfair and indeed slanderous remarks (usually in the blog world) that have been made against one of the leading new Puritan thinkers of the last century, Dr. Rousas John Rushdoony (1916-2001), whose scholarly work is in some evidence in this volume. To put it charitably, as a way of discrediting him as a reformed scholar and Christian teacher, some bloggers and commentators have tried to suggest he was an ignorant racist who denied the Nazi Holocaust. This kind of poorly researched and scurrilous attack we might expect from secular ideologues, the new atheists and pagans whose agenda is often to paint every Christian as a purveyor of hate for believing the Bible, but it is not something we want to find amongst Christian writers. It is naturally then very disturbing when Christians write in this manner against fellow believers in Christ. So to set the record straight, contrary to some irresponsible commentary from certain writers and scholars who should know better – perhaps most notably, Carl Trueman[1] – Rushdoony *did not* deny the Holocaust, neither was he a racist or anti-Semite.

First, some background to Rushdoony's life is relevant in debunking the notion that he was a person interested in obfuscating or minimizing evil and the suffering of others, let alone denying genocide. R. J. Rushdoony was born in New York City on April 25th 1916, the son of Armenian immigrants to the United States. He bridged two worlds in more ways than one. He was conceived during a troubled time in Armenia and was raised in the New World in a community filled with recent memories of the massacre and persecution of Christians by Islamic Turks. His family settled in California where his father became the founding pastor of the Armenian Martyrs' Presbyterian Church. It was a church community made up of recent immigrants, who, like his own family, had fled the genocide. At this stage, young Rousas' first language in home and church was Armenian.

The Armenians as a people had officially converted to Christianity early in the fourth century A.D., though the Rushdoony household was able to trace their ancestry as far back as 629 BC to several Urartan Kings.[2] The family name actually means 'the royal town belonging to Rusas.' When Islam began to spread throughout Asia Minor, Mesopotamia and Syria, the Armenians held fast to their Christian convictions and were largely hated as a result. The later persecutions and finally the genocide of the early twentieth century are well known. Despite this terrible history, mission and Christian calling seemed to run in the Rushdoony blood. Rushdoony's great-grandfather was a priest in the Armenian Orthodox Church and his grandfather was studying to follow in his footsteps when he was blinded by Turkish soldiers in an altercation.[3] Rousas' father, Yeghiazar Rushdoony, was an orphan by the age of eleven and went to live with a relative in the city of Van, when a number of massacres left him again homeless in 1896. However, an American missionary, Dr. George C. Reynolds, brought him to his orphanage which eventually not only drew him to the Protestant faith but also to a close association with American missionaries. This relationship eventually led to repeated assassination attempts on Yeghiazar's life and four arrests. He was later to be educated in Edinburgh for his Master's and seminary degrees, and then returned to Armenia, married Vartanoush (Rose) Gazarian, Rousas' mother.

World War I provided sufficient international disruption for the Turks to carry out mass deportations, forced marches, murder, rape against Armenians, as well as their sale into slavery. In the state of Van, systematic massacres took place in one village after another. Rushdoony's ancestral home was destroyed and his extended family eliminated. A few days before the end of the siege of the city of Van, his older brother, Rousas George, died at just eleven months of age. A Russian advance had forced the Turks back briefly, but their subsequent retreat left the Armenian survivors exposed with little time to escape death by heading for the Russian frontier. At this point Rousas John's mother Rose was pregnant with him, and they narrowly escaped another Turkish massacre of Armenians preparing to cross the river Bendimahu. With Rose's dowry money they managed to get passage on a Russian steamer from Archangel to New York, arriving in October 1915. Rousas was born the following April, alive only by the mercy of God. His son, Mark Rushdoony, writes:

> The beginnings of my father's world and life view took shape in that setting of extended family and friends who all shared a horrific past. My father was aware that these people, his people, had lost all because they were *Christians unwanted in a non-Christian culture....* Despite the tragic experiences of that generation, my father always remembered them as a happy group that loved to laugh and sing. My father could see their character, their strength and even their greatness as coming from their Christian faith.[4]

From a young age Rushdoony was a voracious reader who loved Armenian and American history in particular. He went to Kingsburg High School and later attended the University of California at Berkeley, where he finally made a full transition in thinking from Armenian to English and graduated with a B.A. (1938) and M.A. degree, with honours, in English Literature (1940). He continued religious study at the Pacific School of Religion at Berkeley, a theologically liberal institution.

Rushdoony graduated from the Pacific School in 1944 and was ordained as an evangelist by the San-Francisco Presbytery of the Presbyterian Church, USA, since, rather than taking a pastorate, he wanted to become a missionary amongst the Indians of north-eastern

Nevada. This made him the eighth generation of Rushdoony's in the ministry. He worked amongst the Paiute and Shoshone Indians on an isolated reservation in Nevada for almost nine years, one hundred miles from any other missionary. Rushdoony became a true practitioner and not an 'armchair missiologist.' His son cites two reasons for his father's decision to go; first, a compassion for a neglected and mistreated people and second, a deep desire to learn how to effectively communicate the Christian faith and make it meaningful to people of another culture unfamiliar with it.[5] Analyzing the motivations behind his father's missionary zeal Mark Rushdoony stated, "He wanted to see if he could communicate with unbelieving people as a missionary. To do this he had to understand them. Indians saw Christianity as the white-man's leftovers, something the white man no longer had use for, like junk land and handouts."[6] In Rushdoony's ordination sermon, Rev. George Huntston Williams noted the great Christian heritage of the Rushdoony family and saw it as fitting that he should now labour to evangelize another culture:

> It is thus a moving and very fitting gesture, that you of this congregation…should provide the setting and occasion for the ordination of this scion of an ancient Christian house as an Evangelist, to be sent forth to still another people, the Paiute and Shoshone Indians in the mountains of Nevada.[7]

So began the ministry of R. J. Rushdoony amongst another people group and culture, whom he regarded as mistreated, suffering and in great need of the gospel. This biographical insight is relevant to the question of his personal beliefs because it reveals, not a racist, heartless denier of the suffering and persecution of others, but a man who, by family experience, knew what victimization and persecution were all about, knew what it meant for a whole community to suffer racial and religious persecution, and knew what it meant to serve for years a hated people group in great isolation, without anyone noticing and witnessing his labors.

Many years later, in the maturity of his thought, his ground-breaking *Institutes of Biblical Law* was published, in which Rushdoony develops arguably the most significant and comprehensive analysis of the law of God for the Christian life in generations. There can be no doubt that his family background, and missionary experience amongst Native Americans helped develop his conviction for the need of a recovery of God's law for the social order. The *Institutes* demonstrates (along with many of his books) to any fair-minded and informed critic, that Rushdoony was astonishingly well-read in human affairs with a genius for integrating diverse fields of knowledge and then developing sophisticated hermeneutical tools for the application of biblical truth to everything from philosophy and anthropology to psychology and sociology. He has written numerous instructive and influential works, some of which have helped launch important Christian movements and organizations, including the Christian and home school movements in the United States which are inestimably indebted to his work, *The Messianic Character of American Education* (1963).

Given Rushdoony's background, life-long scholarship and sacrificial service to Christ till his death in February 2001, we should surely expect that Trueman's, and similar articles dismissing Rushdoony's entire contribution to Christian life and thought, must be grounded on substantiated charges of serious and credible concern. However, this is not what we find. Instead, sloppy scholarship, and misleading argumentation have often led to downright false allegations being made, the most notorious of which is that he denied the Holocaust – and who can recover from such a charge? So, where did the notion of Holocaust denial come from? The very short section of the *Institutes* (1973) that is invariably cited out of context by his detractors to support their charge, concerns the ninth commandment and the sin of bearing false witness. In section 10 (*Institutes*, pages 585–590), entitled "The Lying Tongue," Rushdoony briefly examines Proverbs 6:16–19 and God's hatred of lying. As one of several illustrations of succumbing to the temptation of false witness, Rushdoony takes – injudiciously and very unwisely on such a sensitive topic it must be readily said – what was then some recent Holocaust scholarship, as one of his examples. It is almost certain that at the time, Rushdoony gave some credence to the idea in one particular book that the number of people murdered in the Holocaust may have been inflated.[8] Uncritically, and relying on what are now known to be very inaccurate statistics provided by Vicomte Leon de Poncins (*Judaism and the Vatican*, 1967),[9] who, in turn, was relying on the work of Paul Rassinier,[10] a French socialist, history teacher, journalist and activist, Rushdoony draws his application. That is, based on de Poncins' citations, Rushdoony notes that to inflate the number of Jewish deaths during the Holocaust is still false witness, however noble the intention. In other words, lying to create a greater effect on people's feelings, even in a noble cause, is still false witness.

Without mitigating the imprudence of the illustration offered given his inadequate exposure to historical expertise in this area, it should be immediately noted that discussions amongst historical scholars about exactly how many millions of Jews died under Hitler's regime, in what context, and by what means, or similar questions regarding how many Russians died in Stalin's Soviet Union, has been openly discussed in decades past without the hysteria it is attended with today. New information was still coming to light many years after WWII regarding the extent of the butchery of the Nazi regime, and after a world war, assessing the magnitude of mass genocide based on eye witness testimony, allied and Nazi documentation and census information, is not an easy task for researchers.[11] But, irrespective of this, and most important here, is that Rushdoony was not concerned in this passage, as the context plainly shows, to enter a debate he was not qualified to enter, about the varying merits of research into the numbers of deaths. His sole point was to say that our society has become so desensitized to violence, brutality and cruelty that citing murders in small numbers doesn't have the same psychological impact upon people anymore. To really affect people's minds and hearts you need to be able to cite incredibly large numbers. His comment was thus directed against any society that is unaffected by or dulled to real evil to the point where murder of one or a few, or even hundreds of thousands, is counted a small thing. He writes in the passage under consideration:

> Life had become so cheap and meaningless to these heads of state and their camp followers that a murder or two meant nothing. Likewise, a generation schooled to violence in motion pictures, radio, literature, and press could not be expected to react to a murder or two. The result was a desperately twisted mentality which could only appreciate evil as evil on a massive scale.[12]

Thus Rushdoony's reasoning was as follows: no matter how noble your opposition to evil may be in exposing it, even if by an exaggeration of numbers to show the heinousness of genocide, to inflate the evil of others is still false witness, as psychologically understandable as it is. In other words he was arguing in part, from a very well-known evil event (the Holocaust), that we should not magnify the evils of others for effect even if our cause is righteous. It is evident from the context that this is the only point Rushdoony was trying to make, even if the somewhat sloppy and hasty way he did it left him open to misunderstanding and criticism.

If the honest reader takes the time to read on in this same section of the *Institutes* closely, Rushdoony rightly goes on to castigate de Poncins for being "bitterly anti-Jewish" and "not ready to be distressed that *any* were brutally murdered."[13] The prejudicial motives of de Poncins in his ill-fated endeavour to defend the Roman Catholic Church's delinquency during the Nazi tyranny, despite its knowledge of the evils of the Holocaust, are now very evident to historians. Critically, it should be noticed that Rushdoony himself argues that de Poncins distorts the truth in his effort to protect the Roman Church and, as a consequence, was violating the ninth commandment, even while he was accusing others of violating it in their assessment of the numbers killed during the brutal extermination of the Jews. So, however inadequately these points were made, and however open to misunderstanding to the casual reader, it is abundantly clear from the *Institutes* alone, that Rushdoony had no intention of denying the historical reality of the Holocaust – indeed his obvious desire in the text was to show that God abhors all false witness. That being the case, it is simply not credible to suggest that his deliberate intention was to himself bear false witness whilst in the process of condemning it.

Now, Carl Trueman, a capable and professional historian, claims that Rushdoony should have known better than to trust Vicomte Leon de Poncins' use of Paul Rassinier as a source. Perhaps this is so, but it is clearly an anachronistic charge. Rushdoony's *Institutes* was based on lecture notes he had made in the 1960s which were edited and later published in 1973. Yet Rassinier's work was not even available in English until 1977, which was the same year any formal or initial rebuttal of Rassinier's writings first appeared.[13] Rushdoony was doubtless aware that what he was reading were de Poncins' arguments for a *revision* of earlier estimates of Jewish deaths in the Holocaust and that they were therefore controversial. But they were not transparently inaccurate, since, not only were they yet to be subject to academic rebuttal, but the passage he cites on page 586 of the *Institutes* invokes the name of one of the greatest Holocaust historians, the Jewish scholar, Raul Hilberg. Are critics like Trueman then justified in expecting Rushdoony – a theologian, social critic and generalist (not a professional historian) –

who was limited to his 1960s sources in the pre-Internet age, to interpret his reading through the lens of a body of research accumulated over the last forty or more years by expert historians specializing in Holocaust studies, that only rose to major prominence in those intervening years?

Others have also suggested that Rushdoony's passing reference to historian David Irving in a footnote on page 587 of the *Institutes* supports the notion that Rushdoony denied the Holocaust. This is not credible for two reasons. First, Irving did not identify himself as a Holocaust denier until 1988 and had written several highly influential works of history in the decades previous.[15] Rushdoony's book was published, as we have noted in 1973, fifteen years earlier, long before the Irving Holocaust controversy broke and was big news. No writer can be held responsible for views that a scholar they cite may articulate at a future date. Secondly, the reference in the *Institutes* is to Irving's international bestseller from 1963, *The Destruction of Dresden*, which described the Allied Bombing of the German city in World War II. Rushdoony's point here was to point out that the Allies attacked by air a hospital city without good military reason, killing tens of thousands, and that this was unjustifiable murder, and part of a murderous atmosphere in the twentieth century – it had no reference to the Jews or the Holocaust.

The organization founded by Rushdoony, the *Chalcedon Foundation*, clearly became distressed by the dishonest quote-mining performed on the *Institutes* on this issue, which distorted and manipulated a tiny fragment of this otherwise helpful and useful work, to slanderous effect. Doubtless they had become aware of the widely-circulated charge of Holocaust denial that was spreading as swiftly as an urban legend via the Internet, which naturally would discourage people from reading the reformed missiological vision of Rushdoony. In response, The *Chalcedon Report* printed an issue in the millennium year dedicated to the theme of racism called, "The Racialist Heresy." In this edition they published an article by Rushdoony called "Exaggeration and Denial" where he seeks to explain, in context, what he wrote in his *Institutes*. He writes:

> It is difficult to imagine that anyone can deny the reality of the mass slaughter that characterized the twentieth century, whether it be the Armenian millions murdered by the Turks, the Jewish millions murdered by the Nazis, or the untold millions murdered by the communists in China, Russia, and Cambodia.... In my *Institutes of*

Biblical Law, I noted that the scope of such mass murder had so numbed the modern conscience that the murder of a 'mere' thousand, or ten thousand, no longer shocked, tempting some to inflate the scope of lesser atrocities, lest they not seem sufficiently horrific. It was not my purpose to enter a debate over numbers, whether millions were killed, or tens of millions, an area which must be left to others with expertise in such matters. My point then and now is that in all such matters what the Ninth Commandment requires is the truth, not exaggeration, irrespective of the cause one seeks to serve. It is as wrong to exaggerate in order to shock as it is now clear happened in early reports of Serbian 'genocide' as to deny the reality of what the Nazis did, and in the case of the Communists, what they are still doing.... Historical revisionism condemns the future to play by the dangerous rules of exaggeration and denial. As I noted then, this will inevitably lead to even greater horrors as the bar of the capacity to shock is continually raised. This is the true danger of the myth of neutrality, where God's law is viewed as merely 'one side of the debate.[16]

It would be difficult to be clearer than that. Surely this statement alone is sufficient to end, once for all, the damaging and irresponsible charge that Rushdoony was a Holocaust denier. As I have shown, the real man Rushdoony (not the bogey-man of Internet slander) worked as a missionary to a mistreated and abused people, the Native American Indians, a people he loved and served for close to a decade on the most remote reservation in Nevada, one hundred miles from a paved road. He himself was one of the surviving children of a family of Armenians who narrowly escaped the genocide of untold thousands by the Turks after the outbreak of the First World War. These experiences made him sensitive to the plight and suffering of others, including the Jews, whom his lectures and books reveal he deeply admired as a people and revered as the bearers of the Covenant law, and seed of the woman, the Messiah.

Academic pedants can pick away at isolated citations, a footnote, and out of context statements in trying to build a flimsy case against Rushdoony as an anti-Semite, but nothing can substitute for first-hand personal testimony and witness from those that knew him intimately – especially if they happen to be Jewish. Just such testimony is in fact available for the first time publicly in this article. In this author's personal correspondence on this question, the Messianic Jew, Rev. Steve Schlissel, who worked with Rushdoony for years and was a close personal friend, kindly permitted me to publish some of his thoughts on the matter for this essay. He wrote:

As a long time correspondent, friend and associate of Rushdoony, I think I can safely say I have a familiarity with his views which is not entirely dependent upon what he has written. It was my close bond with Rush that moved his family to have me conduct his funeral and memorial services. That he would be considered by anyone as a possibly virulent anti-Semite is Twilight Zone material. He was not an anti-Semite in any form.... [regarding] the holocaust revision itself, the substance of that incident was Rushdoony giving a downward revision of the number of Jews who may have been slaughtered. I think he said it may have been two million rather than six. One must begin an assessment of such a statement with an understanding that the man read *a book a day*, every day. His goal was breadth of knowledge, I'd say, rather than a focused depth in a specialty. Consequently, his writings contain numerous examples of his having (necessarily?) relied upon less than the best distillation of data on a given subject in order to support this or that proposition. The authority of his writings come not from these instances, of course, but from his starting points, his rigorous commitment to God's Word and almighty authority, and abundant employment of "good and necessary consequence." That is where an assessment of the revisionist episode must begin, but it may only be concluded when full weight is given to his explicit purpose in offering the lower number. I have this by personal knowledge. It was not a case of, "You see those whining Jews, complaining over the death of supposedly 6,000,000 of their kind? Well, it was a full two-thirds less than those cry-babies claim. So there!" No! It was specifically to protest that it need not be 6,000,000 to leave a fully functional human aghast. His *point* was, "Supposing it were but two million? Would you just go about your business as if that was just fine? ... the context was a concern over the increasing felt-need for hyperbole in order to induce an effect (in this case, horror) which *he believed* should have been expected from any human with functioning senses, and that without jacked-up numbers. What happened from that argument of his was, ironically, a reverse of the very error which he was in that instance condemning. Instead of requiring too much to be moved to indignation, his critics required too little. Some can't generate human feeling for others without cant and great hooey, while others can find cause for offense in arguments intended to kick our compassion-reflex into gear at a much lower mark on the misery index. I can guarantee Rushdoony would assert that I have captured the issue in the correct perspective...

In Rushdoony, I knew a man who lived out of a gestalt, a man wrapped up in a worldview, a fellow who viewed things—all things—through a filter which was so profoundly, extensively and meticulously informed by "Old Testament" Scripture, that I'm convinced he could never be altogether certain that he wasn't Jewish. Don't misunderstand, please. He never averred to me that he considered himself such. My point is that he never needed to. The worldview handed down to me by blood— running and shed—is one which knows when it is in the presence of another A440 pitchfork [tuning fork]. Rush was swollen with like-mindedness with and appreciation for the Jews that extended even to the self-criticism which has marked us since we penned our universally distributed self-indictment, which is known under the name, The Holy Bible. If Rush articulated any alleged summary criticisms of Jewish people, I can tell you as a matter fact that they were to be understood as Jews in a typical political alignment and activity, not as—*never as* – Jews qua Jews. An example in reverse would be Rush's sincere pleasure derived from, and his easy endorsements of, the messages of Rabbi Daniel Lapin (South African born but, during Rush's last years, ministering on America's West Coast).[17]

In light of the clear clarifying statement above from Rushdoony himself, and the transparent first-hand testimony offered by his close Jewish friend who officiated at his burial and memorial, it is surely fair to say that only those with an intractable hostility to Rushdoony and his views could go on and continue to maintain that Rushdoony was a Holocaust denier or anti-Semite. And his books alone, if read, prove beyond all doubt that he was anything but incompetent as a scholar and thinker.

It is certainly right to observe that he was unwise in the *Institutes* to hastily lend credence to statistics that actually served de Poncins' polemical motive. Clearly, in hindsight, it was a significant error of judgement. Was it likewise injudicious to use such sensitive subject matter in a passing reference without clear clarification and a thorough treatment of the Holocaust question, when the issue at hand, and the way it was treated, was so open to misunderstanding? Yes. Did he make a serious mistake in citing these numbers that experts in the area now know are far too low? There is no doubt. But does any of that make him a Holocaust denier? Clearly not! It makes him as fallible as the rest of us and one equally prone to significant errors of judgement. And perhaps more important, does this human mistake justify writing him off or dismissing his theological and biblical arguments regarding the reign of God and his law? Surely not. It is the case that in the large corpus of his lectures, both written and audio-recorded, he occasionally made incautious statements about anti- Christian Judaism on socio-political or religious grounds, but never on racial or ethnic grounds. At the same time he had many warm Jewish friends and even close colleagues associated with Chalcedon, including Steve Schlissel (cited above), a messianic Jew who wrote regularly for Chalcedon and an essay for a *festschrift* in honor of Rushdoony (*A Comprehensive Faith,* 1996).

The fair-minded reader can also clearly see from Rushdoony's statement above that he was not interested in trying to defend de Poncins' statistical assessment as a matter of principle or historical conviction. On the contrary, he clearly states he wanted to leave that question to the judgement of the experts in the area, which is a clear admission of his own limitations in this field and readiness to acknowledge and accept the findings of recent, informed Holocaust historians. Rather, as he makes abundantly clear, the sum of what he was trying to explain was that whatever issue persons may be discussing concerning the actions of others, the ninth commandment requires the truth – not lies or exaggeration to promote our cause. How ironic it is that those who have falsely accused a man (who died over a decade ago and can offer no defense of himself) for what amounted to an error of judgement in the use of one illustration in an eight-hundred page volume on biblical faith and law, whilst expounding the meaning of the ninth commandment, should themselves be openly violating the ninth commandment with apparent impunity, by bearing false witness. The deliberate slandering of brothers and sisters in Christ is not a practice that commends us to the world, or advances the reign of God. To such people evidently in need of reviewing the meaning and implications of the ninth commandment, I can't think of a better place to start than Rushdoony's *Institutes.*

APPENDIX 2

Billy Graham, Evangelism and the Evangelical Tradition:
A Reformed Analysis

In the early part of the twentieth-first century, as modern evangelicalism faces the religious and social crises engendered by the collapse of the Christian consensus amongst both the cultural elite and general populace in the Western world, a huge re-evaluation of evangelism and mission (missiology) has been taking place. The cultural hegemony of the political and intellectual class in the form of multiculturalism and cultural Marxism has made deep inroads into the churches to the point that many Christians not only now question various methods of evangelizing, but the very need for and morality of evangelism. Long gone are the days when a Christian evangelist could visit a Western city and fill a stadium with non-believers; yet the Dalai Lama can! Many Christians are then asking not simply *how* we are to evangelize (method), but *whether* we are to evangelize (theology) and teach biblical faith and morality in a multicultural context.

As we look back on the past century, in facing this new one, there is much to appreciate and much to learn, much to celebrate and a good deal to bewail since our current situation reveals the overall inadequacy of mid-to-late-twentieth century evangelical evangelism. Billy Graham was certainly one of the most prominent and significant evangelicals of the twentieth century. He was, without doubt, a gifted evangelist of Christian character and integrity, clearly used by God around the world. In my view, understanding Graham, his theological and historical lineage, context and methods is instructive for understanding some of evangelical evangelism's successes and failures, and helps point to correctives for our century.

Billy Graham obviously did not arrive on the Christian scene by immaculate conception, but is located within the modern evangelical tradition that is rooted in the evangelical awakenings of the eighteenth and nineteenth centuries in Britain and America. Furthermore, Graham as an evangelist represents fruit from *one branch* of the evangelical trunk that goes in two distinct directions in both theology and practice during the mid-nineteenth century. The reformed believer historically has been as committed (if not more so) to the task of evangelism and mission as the Arminian Christian. I am convinced it is essential that in our time, reformed missiological thought emphasize the evangelist and the work of biblical evangelism as a priority for the twenty-first century church.

What is an evangelist?

The 'office' of the evangelist is a very important one in Scripture. In Ephesians 4:11, the apostle Paul identifies five offices established in the church with the function of equipping the church for works of service and building up Christ's body. Included in this list is the *'euangelistes'* or the 'evangelist,' which literally means 'a messenger of good' and primarily denotes a 'preacher of the gospel.[1] The term is applied to particular individuals in the New Testament. Phillip the evangelist was one such individual with this designation (Acts 21:8) who was not an apostle, yet whose ministry was 'itinerant' for at least part of the time. Though many of the apostles were also evangelists, not all evangelists were apostles; consequently, there is no suggestion that the evangelistic office in the church ceased to exist with the close of the apostolic era. St. Paul also charges Timothy to 'do the work of an evangelist' (2 Tim. 4:5). Clearly then, the offices of 'pastor,' 'teacher' and 'evangelist' have not passed away with the death of the first apostles and New Testament prophets.[2]

Given that the evangelist is an individual who performs a specific function and holds an 'office' in the church, there is clearly a distinction between the task of mission – the general witness of believers to the *'evangel'* through word and deed – to which all Christians are called, and the work of evangelism exemplified in the gift of evangelism and the office of the evangelist. The 'evangelist' in this sense is one who spreads the good news by proclamation, sometimes travelling far from home to do so.[3] I have had the privilege to serve in this function for a significant part of my ministry over the past twenty years.

The evangelist, both in the New Testament and in the history of the church, is one called and gifted to proclaim the gospel and equip others to do the same. Because evangelism centres upon the declaration of the 'good news,' the evangelistic call obviously requires effective communication. The primary means of communicating the thought content of the gospel is verbal, as in preaching and teaching. In 1 Corinthians 1:17, Paul writes, "For Christ did not send me to baptize, but to *preach the gospel*, not in cleverness of speech, that the cross of Christ should not be made void." John Armstrong offers a helpful definition of evangelism as "communication of the good news of Jesus Christ to sinful human beings with the purpose of converting them through and by the power of the Holy Spirit."[4]

The evangelist is therefore one peculiarly called to the task of preaching the gospel to those who have either not yet heard or not embraced the Lordship of Jesus Christ (Rom. 10:14–15). All believers are called to bear witness to and defend the truth of the gospel when asked a reason for their hope (1 Pet. 3:15) and to identify themselves with Christ; yet relatively few (in terms of all those called to belong to Christ's church) are specifically called to actually preach the gospel (1 Cor. 12:29; 1 Tim. 2:7). Now Billy Graham, undoubtedly the best-known Western evangelist of the twentieth century, was such a man (amongst many other godly Christian preachers), whose life and ministry testify authentically to his calling as an evangelist.

Billy Graham: The man and his ministry

Whatever one makes of his theology, it must first be made clear that Billy Graham is a remarkable figure whose renown is well-deserved within the history of Christian evangelism in the last century. Born in Charlotte, North Carolina on November 7 1918, he grew up on a dairy farm in a Christian family, enjoying a relatively happy childhood. His parents were committed members of the Associate Reformed Presbyterian Church.

In 1934, itinerant fundamentalist evangelist Mordecai Ham was conducting a 'crusade' in Charlotte and Billy Graham, who was seventeen years of age and somewhat cynical about the life of faith at the time, went to hear him. Having already determined not to be a clergyman, Graham was not expecting God to shake him to the core of his being and call him to preach. But the soul-stirring preaching of the evangelist brought him under conviction of sin and toward the end of the crusade he committed his life to Christ.

Initially, Graham successfully sold toothbrushes as a salesman but he soon enrolled at Bob Jones' College where he was told he was a failure, with more failure ahead; he left after just one semester. He then transferred to the Florida Bible Institute where he spent three happy and productive years. In 1937, with the help of his tutor John Minder, he was given his first preaching engagements. It was March 1938, when taking a walk at a place called the *Eighteenth Green* near the Institute, that he committed himself to become 'an Ambassador for Jesus Christ.'[5]

In 1939, he was ordained as a Baptist minister and the following year he moved to Wheaton Illinois to study anthropology. It was here that he met his future wife Ruth Bell. In 1941; they were engaged, and married in August 1943, the year of his graduation. This was just as Graham's ministry was getting underway. An important breakthrough came for him on the radio program 'Songs in the Night,' during which he met the man to become a life-long friend and ministry partner, the gospel singer George Beverley Shea. He also spoke in Chicago at the invitation of Torrey Johnson during a successful *Youth for Christ* Rally, and in 1945 he became that organization's first full-time evangelist. It is clearly significant and formative in Graham's life that in 1948, he attended the World Council of Churches' Congress in Amsterdam which set him on a lifelong course of ecumenical evangelism that would later become a persistent source of criticism from other evangelicals.

Perhaps the most critical moment of preparation for wider ministry in Graham's life came during a time of personal crisis. The noted evangelical preacher Charles Templeton (who later completely abandoned the faith), a friend of Graham's from *Youth for Christ*, became deeply impacted by the theory of evolution and its alleged challenge to the book of Genesis. He then began to share his doubts about the authority of Scripture with Graham. Graham was unable to offer sound and intellectually cogent answers to Templeton, which is not to his credit and certainly reveals shortcomings in his preparation for evangelism. Nonetheless, one night while at a conference in California, he walked alone and lay the Bible down in front of him, acknowledging before God his inadequacy intellectually, but committing himself to the full authority of Scripture by faith. This was a critical juncture that marked the start of a rapid rise to international fame.

That same year, the now-famous Los Angeles crusade was held. Some 6,000 per night were then in attendance. *Time* and *Life* magazines, among others, ran stories on the young 'hot-gospel revivalist.' Subsequent gospel events in Boston revealed that this significant publicity had preceded him, and he spoke to more than 100,000 in two and a half weeks. Around that time, in South Carolina, he attracted his largest single crowd with 40,000 in attendance, at which point people began to liken him to the flamboyant American evangelist Billy Sunday. The *Christian Herald* noted concerning these crusades that "West, East and South America is responding en-masse to the old-time Gospel."[6]

The recent development of mass media at the time certainly played a huge role in launching Graham into a ministry of great reach and significance. November 5th 1950 saw the beginning of his message and ministry going national with a radio program called "Hour of Decision" – a title which, in many ways, defines the theological and missiological emphasis of his ministry. The ABC network took the broadcasts coast to coast to a potential audience of nine million. Eight hundred stations broadcast it. In five short weeks, it became the most successful religious program in history.[7] With this exposure and overnight popularity, he found it necessary to launch the *Billy Graham Evangelistic Association* (BGEA) which committed itself, in the context, to an unusually high standard of integrity in matters of finance, accountability, interpersonal relationships and public relations. This admirable commitment to integrity and accountability was to prove critical in establishing Billy Graham as, not just an evangelist, but a Christian statesman respected around the world.

The next major breakthrough for his ministry came with his 1954 visit to London, England for the Harringay Crusade. Despite the terrible weather and the typically negative British press, the coverage only worked in his favour; thousands flocked to the stadium night after night and crowds poured forward to make commitments to Christ. The greater London crusade lasted eighty-eight nights, setting attendance records of over two million with around 40,000 registering decisions for Christ.[8] The crusade had such a visible profile and impact, that Winston Churchill himself conceded to Graham's request for a brief audience. Their meeting illustrates another central aspect of Graham's ministry; from then on he engaged many world leaders through private audiences. This fascinating encounter is related in Billy Graham's autobiography, *Just as I Am.*[9]

From this remarkable period on, Graham's ministry became truly international and his prominence on the pages of twentieth-century evangelism history was assured. In the providence of God, several historical and sociological factors seem to have conspired to make this all possible. First, Graham's ministry sprang up during the post-World War II gloom that was enveloping Europe, and to a lesser extent the United States. The failures of the League of Nations after World War I were obvious and depressing, and the illusory hopes of humanistic betterment in an enlightened 'golden age' of science and reason had been utterly shattered by a second global conflict followed by the spectre of international Marxism (communism) growing and spreading from behind the Iron Curtain. This despair, gloom and doubt contributed in God's sovereignty to the hearing that Graham received, especially in Europe. Secondly, the development of mass media never before available to earlier evangelists in the western world – like Wesley and Whitefield – was available to Graham. The rapid growth of television in the fifties and sixties served to put Billy Graham into the front rooms of millions.[10] Thirdly, his rise to prominence through simple gospel preaching predominantly took place in the largely Christianized West, where, at least nominally, the Christian worldview was still clinging on as the majority view amongst ordinary people in the middle decades of the twentieth century. He could therefore still rely on the fact that when he used his famous phrase 'the Bible says,' such a statement would carry with it into people's minds a recognized, accepted weight and even authoritative content that is largely unknown to the children of the seventies onward. Indeed, of the average of four per cent that came forward to make 'commitments' to Christ during his crusades, around ninety per cent acknowledged significant contact with Christians and the Christian faith prior to their coming forward, eighty per cent being brought along by Christian friends.[11] This residue of the Christian worldview, now largely lost, enabled him to connect with a mass audience in a way now essentially impossible for evangelical preachers in Western Europe and North America.

After the huge success in London, Graham conducted the massive New York crusade in 1957, which broke attendance records. More than 100,000 came to hear him at Yankee Stadium, the largest crowd to gather to hear any preacher in the history of the United States. The ABC network broadcasted live from Madison Square Garden. These programs launched the BGEA television ministry, the first nationally broadcast religious programming in the United States. Some seven million watched the telecast on Saturday evening primetime.

However, one cannot do justice to a brief survey of Graham's ministry without noting that it was not just massive gospel crusades and contact with world leaders that distinguished him. There were two other factors. First, he enjoyed, what were to many Christians, controversial friendships with U.S. Presidents, making him repeatedly a kind of informal 'chaplain' to the White House. Secondly, he had considerable involvement in national and international issues of peace, justice,

Christian unity and world evangelization. Some of this interest began during the complex civil rights movement in the fifties and sixties – the precise interpretation of which remains controversial amongst reformed thinkers and historians. Graham rightly believed that there was no biblical basis for enforced 'racial' segregation, since there is only one human race in Adam and Noah, and not many 'races' as evolution teaches, and that any other view was hostile to the gospel. He developed what would be a controversial friendship with Martin Luther King and even had him pray publicly at one of his crusades, to the consternation of other Christian leaders given some of King's political views, sympathies and sexual promiscuity. To his credit, on more than one occasion when doing crusades in the south in Mississippi and Tennessee, Graham personally tore down ropes that had been erected to separate black and white seating areas, to the fury of some committee members. In 1957, Graham invited a young black minister from Cleveland named Howard Jones to join his staff as an associate evangelist. This act was a massive and controversial statement about the injustice of segregation which angered many, but he courageously stood firm. Before Dr. King was killed by the assassin's bullet, he said of Billy Graham: "Had it not been for the ministry of my good friend Dr. Billy Graham, my work in the civil rights movement would not have been as successful as it has been."[12]

These things furthered Graham's growing popularity among the black communities and led in 1960 to a tour of ten countries in Africa. He avoided South Africa as a silent protest against apartheid – though one must question the wisdom of politicizing the gospel by denying the preaching of Christ to people on the basis of sinful and unjust social policy existing in their country; after all, is that not what the gospel destroys by the power of the Holy Spirit? The Christian evangelist is not a pop star, Hollywood actor or sportsman, denying 'entertainment' to populations with whom we disagree socially or politically, just to make a statement. In 1973, the South African government agreed to his terms for an integrated conference at which he preached to the first multi-racial meeting in the country; it was also the first time a religious service had been broadcast on national radio. Here he unashamedly declared apartheid 'sin.' The international campaigns increased during this decade and he visited Japan, India, Singapore, Brazil and the Far East during the next few years.

Another incident in his career worthy of special note was that he had the remarkable experience of praying in the Lenin stadium in 1959 that God would open the doors for him to preach in Moscow. His prayers were answered in October 1992, where Moscow's Olympic Stadium became the site of the largest crusade ever held in a former communist country.[13] Subsequent campaigns took Graham to Korea, where in five days he preached the gospel to 3.2 million people, and also to Hong Kong where his crusade reached 500 million, beamed via satellite across Asia. In 1992 and 1994, he held meetings in the self-professed atheistic state of North Korea. In each context he was given the opportunity to meet some of the highest-placed leaders of those countries. In North Korea, he notably said to those greeting him on his arrival, "I did not come to North Korea as an emissary of my government or my nation, but as a citizen of the kingdom of God."[14]

All of this quite remarkable account of Graham's ministry is mentioned without discussing the influential and, at times, complex relationship he has had with all the U.S. presidents since the 1950s, including Nixon before and during the Watergate scandal. In 1983, President Reagan awarded Billy Graham the Presidential Medal of Freedom, the highest citation that a civilian can be given. At the award ceremony Reagan said, "His contribution to the well-being of mankind is literally immeasurable. The world is a better place because of Billy Graham."[15] Furthermore, in the course of his career, Graham encouraged and supported numerous other major Christian initiatives, conferences and training programs. Geoffrey Hanks writes:

> To further promote the cause of evangelism, he initiated the World Conference on Evangelism in Berlin (1966) and conceived the idea that led to the Lausanne Conference (1974) which drew together a large number of World Christian leaders to discuss the issues of evangelism and social concern. In addition, he convened the 1983 Amsterdam Conference for 4,000 itinerant evangelists, mostly from third world countries in order to encourage them.[16]

This led to another congress in Amsterdam in 1986 for around 10,000 itinerant evangelists from around the world. Thousands have attended seminars at his schools of evangelism. The Billy Graham Centre in Wheaton, Illinois and the Cove near Asheville, North Carolina have trained numerous others. The BGEA claims that since 1947, over 83 million have attended Graham's meetings with 3,219,676 decisions for

Christ. Yet, it is praiseworthy to notice Graham has consistently refused to take any personal credit: "I cannot take credit for what God has chosen to accomplish through us and our ministry – only God deserves the glory."[17] Graham has also stated, "My goal is to proclaim the gospel to as many people as possible and to build bridges of friendship and peace regardless of political or economic systems."[18] Though the latter sentiment is noble, his varied involvement in political matters at times revealed what would be considered a well-intentioned naivety.

It seems clear then that any fair-minded analysis of Graham's impact, significance and international reach, even whilst disagreeing with some of his theology, methodology or approach to 'results' in evangelism, must acknowledge that Billy Graham was an evangelist raised up and greatly used by God.

A missiological genealogy of Billy Graham

Theologically, Billy Graham belongs to a historical family of evangelical preachers from which we can directly trace his missiological lineage. To do this, we must begin with the evangelical awakening in Britain and the United States, in order to note the particular influence of John Wesley and George Whitefield in the rise of modern evangelicalism. Both of these eighteenth-century men were great evangelists, preaching in Britain and America to large crowds, commanding and imploring people to repent and come to Christ. Both attracted listeners *en masse*, sometimes numbering as many as twenty to thirty thousand people at a time in the open air, before microphones were invented. Whitefield and Wesley were also great Christian statesmen. Wesley, who founded Methodist Bible classes across Britain, established and funded orphanages (a work which Whitefield was also engaged in) and both worked for social change. Wesley, along with Whitefield and his brother Charles, began to preach about salvation by grace through faith in the manner of the reformers in a time of moral and spiritual decline where unbelief was fashionable and superficial moralism was rampant in Church of England pulpits. Their message was not welcomed by the established churches, so as pulpits closed to them, first Whitefield and then Wesley took to the open air. They began to preach wherever people would gather, from fields and barns to town squares. Wesley, an itinerant, travelled some five thousand miles per year on horseback! Despite persecutions, he continued preaching the evangelical gospel everywhere and was still preaching in the open air at eighty-seven years of age, shortly before his death. Wesley was also a gifted intellectual and theologian who had studied at Oxford and mastered many languages; he touched every strata of society, as did the hymns of his brother Charles.[19]

George Whitefield likewise stands out as one of the greatest evangelists of all time. Armstrong notes:

> Certainly no English-speaking evangelist has ever preached the gospel with more effect and determination than George Whitefield.... He moved the masses as no one before him and hardly anyone since.... In thirty-four years of public ministry it is believed that George Whitefield preached more than 18,000 formal sermons.[20]

Here was a true itinerant evangelist whose preaching stirred the masses and planted the seeds of a new kind of evangelistic concept; a form of parachurch evangelism that would come to characterize the later forebears of Billy Graham. Whitefield had no self-conscious intention of doing this, of course, but his work would become something of a model for others. Harry Stout critically observes:

> His revivals were not really a church, nor were they connected to local communities and congregations. The appearance of Whitefield's audiences as religious congregations defied the traditional sense of the term. The audience changes with every meeting, evidencing no permanent structure or leadership aside from Whitefield's own charismatic ministry.... Whitefield's audiences and loyal supporters represented powerful new "parachurches" – voluntary religious associations based on marketplace organization and destined to characterize pan-Protestant "evangelical" organizations in the nineteenth and twentieth centuries. In an ironic process that Whitefield could not have foreseen and may not have realized; his revivals had become, in effect, an institution.[21]

That statement is critical to understanding the later development of planned crusade evangelism. Whitefield himself described itinerant preachers as gospel meteors that shot across the sky, dazzling with light and then disappearing from sight. Though Whitefield did not leave behind the formal structures that Wesley did, others in the nineteenth century would capture the momentum let loose by Whitefield's innovations and they would take it in a new direction.[22]

There are some obvious and striking similarities between the ministry of Whitefield and Graham. For example, neither occupied a settled parish (or local congregation) for any length of time; both held 'parachurch' initiative gatherings; both were involved in plain gospel preaching to the masses (though Whitefield was much more doctrinal and theologically robust); both led a transcontinental itinerant life with ministry conducted outside of church pulpits; and both focused on the calling of people to repentance. Yet there are also striking dissimilarities. For example, as Armstrong observes regarding Whitefield, "He did not count his converts or boldly pronounce a number of new believers after he left an area. Public appeals or any pressure to register physical response to the evangelists' message were never used."[23] No formal advertising or mass media was employed, nor was music used to help create a conducive atmosphere for a gospel appeal. So while methods and result assessment were different, Whitefield's itinerant oratory planted the seeds of a new movement for the nineteenth century.

The next critical figure in Graham's missiological genealogy is Charles Grandison Finney. His methods not only invented modern revivalism, but they split the evangelical community in two directions. He began to conduct revival meetings in the eastern United States where his evangelistic innovations came to be called 'new measures.' These included planned 'protracted meetings,' the first 'altar calls,' an invitation for the penitent to take the 'anxious seat' at the front, inquiry meetings in the 'anxious room' for people seeking salvation, and the repeated call for immediate action of will manifest in repentance and restitution. With respect to calling people forward to make commitments, Finney writes in his memoirs:

> If men who were under conviction refused to come forward publicly and renounce their sins and give themselves to God, this fact disclosed to them more clearly the pride of their hearts.... [T]his was one of the means used by the Spirit of God to bring them to present submission to and acceptance of Christ. I have long been of the opinion that the principal reason why so few are converted while under the voice of the living preacher was that they were not brought to that point and instant submission demanded of them.[24]

Here we see a remarkably direct lineage to the ministry of Billy Graham. Though some different terminology is employed, this could be a description of Graham's own ministry perspective and practice.

Now Finney was not only controversial for his invention of 'new measures' but for his arguably Pelagian theology – a development in New Haven theology, sometimes called the new school Calvinism. Here, through the influence of Scottish common sense philosophy amongst many New England divines, old Calvinistic doctrines like total depravity had been retained in name, but redefined in terms of man's free moral volition. As one implication of this theology, and anticipating Graham, Finney argued that one could *promote* 'revivals' because God had given certain means to create given ends; just as seedtime brings harvest in the natural world, so also in spiritual life. Emphasis was taken off the sovereignty of God in revival and placed on human planning, responsibility and immediate acts of the will in sinners. Finney consistently stressed this freedom and power of the human will, and the unity of moral action (in any given moment), redefining original sin and salvation in essentially psychological categories, views which invariably informed his evangelistic practice. Lane is helpful in identifying one of Finney's critical theological errors and its effect on his practice of evangelism:

> Morality is seen as a series of independent moral decisions, not the cultivation of a moral character. Thus the evangelist's aim is to bring about an instantaneous decision of the will rather than a radical change of character which in one sense is a life-long process. Finney's theology encourages a concept of evangelism as producing isolated decisions rather than radical changes of heart.[25]

This very criticism is one that has been repeatedly directed toward Graham. One of his biographers thus notes that "Graham feels that his ministry centres in preaching the gospel while the process of bringing new Christians to maturity is the responsibility of the local church."[26] This is all well and good, for there is a measure of truth in it. The itinerant evangelist cannot be responsible for bringing new coverts to maturity in the course of one or more presentations of the gospel. But the gospel *content* Graham's biographer is referring to, that characterized Graham's preaching, turns out to be radically truncated and at best, a bare minimum of Christian instruction.

An important contemporary of Finney's, whose experience and relationship with him illustrates the ensuing divide over the nature of conversion and revival in American evangelism, is Asahel Nettleton, a man who developed into arguably the finest evangelist of the era. He used none of the novelties or 'new measures' associated with Finney. Rather, adopting a theology and methodology strongly reminiscent of Jonathan Edwards, with a fairly intellectual approach to preaching Christian doctrine, he saw remarkable success for the gospel throughout New England and New York. He was noted especially for his sensitivity to people and his determination to involve the local church pastor in every aspect of his work.[27]

Nettleton became concerned about the 'new measures' and their results, and personally appealed both to Finney and to his powerful friends in an effort to avert schism and destructive fallout for the churches – though it is very important to note that he did not deny there was clear evidence of God's grace at work through Finney's ministry.[28] But as the New Haven theology of Nathaniel Taylor and Finney became more influential, abandoning the Augustinian doctrine of man and other hallmarks of Edwardsian, Puritan theology, Nettleton's wider support waned. His break with Finney and others associated with him became a paradigmatic case, illustrating divergent views on evangelism that have divided evangelicals to the present. Indeed, Armstrong says of Nettleton that "The story of his life, in reality, is the account of the seismic shift of both evangelistic theology and methodology in America."[29] Hardman likewise notes, "Nettleton saw this as a great rent in the body ecclesiastic, and he termed it, very accurately, 'a civil war in Zion – a domestic broil in the household of faith.'"[30] There is no doubt that of the two men, it is Finney, not Nettleton, who bears significant similarity to Graham in theology and practice, indicating which branch of evangelicalism came to dominate evangelistic theology and practice in America. This radical missiological shift in the first half of the nineteenth century permanently altered American evangelism and blazed a trail for the next famous American evangelist to precede and inform the ministry of Billy Graham; none other than D. L. Moody.

Dwight Lyman Moody was born in 1837 and died in 1899 at the dawn of the twentieth century. In 1871, when the Chicago fire destroyed the independent church he had founded, Moody felt called to a wider evangelistic ministry. Praying that God would baptize him in the Spirit for the task, his prayer was answered one day as he walked down a street in New York. Not unlike both Edwards and Finney relate concerning their own experience, Moody felt overpowered by the Holy Spirit, and his life and ministry would never be the same. For example, in 1871 on a visit to London England, after a week of meetings, one church welcomed four hundred new converts into membership.[31] Moody had developed a friendship with a man named Ira Sankey, a gifted singer whom he had invited to join him at his Chicago church; he led the congregation in singing. Sankey became song leader at all Moody's evangelistic campaigns, playing the pump organ.

Moody's evangelistic methods included inviting those who wanted to come to Christ to get up and come down to the 'inquiry room' where a 'personal worker' would give further counselling. His fame spread to Scotland and Ireland where he conducted successful meetings, finishing with a big event in London, England. Many people from every strata of life were converted. Moody and Sankey conducted many evangelistic campaigns together between 1864 and 1881 in cities like New York, Boston and Philadelphia. He also founded the Moody Bible Institute in Chicago in 1886 and Moody Press in 1895.

In what ways did Moody act as a bridge between the ministries of Finney and Graham? Some have argued that Finney was not really a 'mass evangelist' that held planned crusades with ecumenical city-wide campaigns.[32] Whilst this is an important observation, in my judgement, it also seems clear that Finney's revival meetings at places like Rochester did have many of the hallmarks of contemporary mass evangelism. However, there are definitely a number of things introduced by Moody that mark further development from Finney toward the later model of Graham. Hanks writes concerning Moody:

> ....more than any other he can be said to be the founder of the modern mass evangelism movement. While Whitefield and Wesley before him had attracted large crowds, it was Moody who pioneered evangelistic campaigns with a planned itinerary and funding, had meetings booked at specific venues, arranged publicity, introduced the inquiry room and, with Sankey, broke new ground in the use of religious songs.[33]

With Moody, a new era of American, Arminian evangelism that built on and developed the methods of Finney had arrived. Most notably, Moody extensively used religious music; employed wide publicity with planned campaigns; used temporary structures built for revival meetings; and had a parachurch emphasis that avoided the strictures of the local church and clergy. As Hardman points out, "By skirting dependence on clergymen and their churches, and by renting or erecting his own much larger halls, D. L. Moody was able to avoid the problems that beset Charles Finney."[34] Thus, in methodology, Graham most closely mirrors Moody. However, three important differences between the context and practice of Moody over-against Graham should be noted beyond the obvious changes in worldview and culture (i.e. presence of diverse people groups and decline of Christianity) between late-nineteenth and mid-twentieth century America and Britain. First, Moody's access to mass media was obviously limited to printing presses, without the advantages of radio and television. Second, Moody, like Finney and Whitefield before him, never kept tallies of converts like the BGEA does, due to the uncertainty of knowing which professions of faith were genuine. Finally, unlike Graham, Moody did not seek the company of the powerful and famous and never functioned as chaplain or confessor to presidents. He was always most at home among common people.

There remains one other American evangelist who deserves brief mention, occupying a position of prominence between Moody and Graham in order to complete our missiological genealogy —the former Chicago White Stockings baseball star Billy Sunday. Early in Graham's ministry, he was likened to Billy Sunday in style and method. In fact, when Graham was a small child, his parents took him to hear the flamboyant evangelist; he sat spellbound by the drama and antics of a preacher who would sometimes run across the platform and slide on his stomach up to the pulpit like stealing a base, to the delight of the crowd. Like Moody and Graham after him, Sunday had a famous song leader, Homer Rodeheaver, who sang rousing songs before the invitation to come forward for salvation was given, and again, most of his meetings took place in temporary tabernacles erected for a bigger space for the duration of crusades. His delivery was theatrical to say the least. Up to 20,000 people at a time crammed into the meetings. During his forty-year career, he was heard by some 100 million Americans with around one million 'hitting the sawdust trail' – going forward to shake hands with the evangelist to indicate conversion to Christ.[35] This of course indicates that some sort of record was kept of professed conversions. Janet Lowe wrote that "Sunday was part of an American tradition of travelling religious orators, who with passion and idealism, influenced America since its earliest colonial days. It was a heritage that Billy Graham would become part of."[36]

Implications, lessons and conclusions

This brief analysis of Billy Graham's missiological lineage reveals that he does indeed stand in a time-honoured tradition of mass evangelists going right back to the eighteenth century. However, as we have seen in the various chapters of this book, for cultural, theological and philosophical reasons, in our increasingly humanistic and pagan generation, a more theologically robust, educational apologetics and church-based approach to evangelism appears necessary for the church today. The Christian worldview has been so eroded in the modern West, and the appeal of hearing the Christian orator *en masse* so dramatically reduced, that it is very difficult today to even conceive (short of a miraculous general awakening) of an event like the Harringay Crusade of 1954. The apostle Paul did not draw such a crowd in pagan Rome or Athens, and it can be argued that ancient Athens is much more akin to where we are with respect to worldviews in the West today than London, England, 1954.

As we have seen, Graham was noted most as an evangelist for his ability to draw very large crowds to public venues to hear the gospel, calling people forward to give their lives to Christ. It should be readily pointed out that there have been many more polished and spell-binding preachers than Billy Graham over the past seventy years in the life of church, including evangelists, so it was not Graham's oratory alone that drew people. Neither is his name associated with revival as such, in the manner that a Wesley, Whitefield, Finney or Edwards is; no specific revival or general awakening of the faith is directly associated with his name. It was the American religious culture at the time of his prominence, the BGEA's effective use of media, the ecumenical model employed, and the acceptable type of evangelist that Graham represented in his time, not to mention God's overarching sovereign appointment, that mark his prominence and significance. His personal integrity and faithfulness to preaching Christ, not just the results of his ministry, will preserve his place as a great evangelical. Thus, it may well be that Billy Graham is the last of a certain mould of evangelists, the last great Western mass evangelist of our era standing in the tradition of American Arminian evangelists, notably diverging from the reformed tradition in the time of Charles Finney.

We have seen that assessing the significance of Billy Graham will be influenced by theological and missiological commitments, not just pragmatic considerations related to his results. One relevant facet that emerges in tracing Graham's theological genealogy is the noticeable decline in theological ability over the centuries amongst mass evangelists. William Abraham notes that people like John Wesley and Jonathan Edwards were pastors and evangelists, but they were also theologians of significant rank who made lasting contributions to Christian thought; their approach to evangelism was doctrinally and theologically rooted, as was that of Nettleton and Whitefield. Even Charles Finney was no theological incompetent, but a very gifted thinker and powerful intellect who wrote a systematic theology and established a theological college. However, an unhealthy disrespect for the confessions and landmark works of Augustinian and Reformed Christian theology crept in with Finney that, by the time of his key successors, Moody and Sunday, had degenerated into full-blown pragmatism and theological ignorance.[37] Graham, whilst being a contributing figure to a certain brand of ecumenism and neo-evangelicalism, and though certainly not as unreflective as a Moody or Sunday, has made no meaningful contribution to the theology of evangelism nor published serious missiological reflections on the strengths and weaknesses of his work and methods. Graham would be the first to admit that he is no intellectual and in his encounters with challenging questions from Charles Templeton and later, neo-orthodox thinkers like Barth and Brunner, he was not able to really engage the debate. Graham was a gifted and popular evangelist, making no claims to being a theologian or Christian thinker, and so should not be unfairly judged for this limitation. That being said, all thoughtful Christians are capable of thorough biblical and theological reflection. A lack of doing so can lead to significant theological errors, questionable practices and the decline of effective engagement with the culture.

The consequences of Graham's limitations theologically came into focus in a number of key areas. First, an undiscriminating mentality or overly simplistic approach to doctrine led to some arguably very unwise decisions. For example, as far as Graham was concerned, most denominations believed basically the same thing. The divisions were only over minor differences, so he says, "I made up my mind to fellowship with all those who love Jesus Christ with all their heart, and are seeking to serve him."[38] This rather fuzzy, semi-doctrinal minimalism led not only to a very broad ecumenism that grieved many faithful evangelicals, but also to a platform for liberals. To illustrate, Catherwood points out:

Often, eminent clergy whose views are far from Evangelical

and whose gospel is very different from the one which Graham proclaims, find themselves as honoured guests on his platforms, to the consternation of many local Christians, who have frequently had a terrible time with these people. This problem has grown the more famous Graham has become...[39]

Including liberals in major events and meetings succeeded in generating a good deal of frustration and confusion for Bible-believing Christians and seekers alike, prompting some significant churches not to participate in Graham's campaigns. Such a lack of prudence on Graham's part calls into question the motive for the broad ecumenism; had numbers in attendance and maximum participation in the big event become more important than gospel fidelity to the BGEA?

This leads to another valid criticism of Graham: the error of seeing evangelism, not the truth of the gospel, as the locus of unity. To co-operate for 'evangelism' with someone who denies the gospel (were such an oxymoron even possible) obviously does not bring about real unity, just a false semblance of it, thereby promoting hypocrisy. Francis Schaeffer put it well:

> It is because we are committed to evangelism that we must speak in antithesis at times. If we do not make clear by word and practice our positions for truth and against false doctrine, we are building a wall between the next generation and the gospel. The unity of evangelicals should be on the basis of truth, not evangelism itself. If this is not so, 'success' in evangelism can result in weakening Christianity. Any consideration of methods is secondary to this central principle.[40]

When theology and doctrine are made secondary to 'co-operation in evangelism,' we may witness an increase in 'decisions' for Jesus, but not an increase in disciples of the *Lord Jesus Christ*. Any fair-minded analysis of Graham's methods reveals that his priority was never maintaining and defending gospel truth and Christian unity, with clear evangelical theology and biblical doctrine informing the process of planning and executing evangelistic outreach. This is unlike many of the great evangelists before him who would never have compromised with, let alone honoured, those that denied basic tenets of the evangelical faith.

This theological fuzziness is a point at which Graham was justly criticized. Behind the broad ecumenism was a minimalist and weak evangelical theology. Weak theology always leads to questionable practice which eventually will undermine evangelism in the church. For example, although Graham's biographer, Lewis Drummond, makes a valiant attempt in his book on Billy Graham to imply there was a robust doctrine of God's sovereignty informing Graham's thought and ministry, the attempt appears abortive and unfortunately his book makes little effort to offer any sort of realistic critique of Graham on any front. Instead he fills the volume with page after page of unremitting praise and overstatement in what is more like hagiography than balanced and reflective biography. In one example of inadequate analysis, having tried to stress to the reader that Graham has a high view of the sovereignty of God, he goes on to tell us that "Graham's belief in instantaneous conversion as opposed to the idea of planting a seed that will grow and develop gradually overtime, brings home the urgency of the moment and the need to make an immediate decision for Christ."[41] Drummond himself does not appear to grasp the fact that those who have a high view of God's sovereignty in salvation do not believe that sinful men in their unregenerate condition are able of their own volition to make 'an immediate decision for Christ,' just because pressed to do so. Only as the Holy Spirit regenerates a person is true conversion and a decision to follow Jesus possible, and that very act of faith is ultimately in the hands of the sovereign God (Eph. 2:8-9).

Graham's brand of 'decisionism' – the pressing of hearers for immediate volitional and physical response on the view that conversion must be 'instantaneous' on the basis a person's 'decision' – is very difficult to square with Jesus' teaching concerning the four types of ground into which the gospel seed is planted (Matt. 3:3–23) and how these different types of ground respond. Indeed, the notion that conversion and regeneration (and it is unclear whether Graham clearly distinguishes these doctrines in his theology and practice of evangelism) have a readily identifiable instant or moment at a 'point of decision,' carries Finney's semi-Pelagian theological assumption of conversion as a sudden moral change in the will that is under man's immediate power, rather than a radical spiritual rebirth and transformation that is both act and process and fundamentally mysterious, because a work of the Spirit (John 3:6–8). The language of sovereignty may have been used by Graham and his colleagues, but as evidenced by the focus on labouring for and counting decisions, this view of 'sovereignty' is severely deformed or at best theoretical and not practical. The initiative in conversion and regeneration in the BGEA view is with people, not with God. The mode of appeal is the same each time in Graham's preaching: "I'm going to ask you to get out of your seats...get up and come right now...you may be the only one in your area – but you come." After a pause of a few minutes he added, "You can bring a friend with you to Christ today." Then, after a while, he declared, "You haven't come yet, and God is speaking to you." [42]

The belief of many evangelicals is that these methods or measures that include choirs and music, especially for altar calls, applying by formulae pressure on the will, are unnecessary human measures that fail to rely on the power of the Holy Spirit – a reliance modelled by evangelists of generations past like George Whitefield during general awakening – rather, they have a tendency to manipulate. The questions that naturally arise at out this are ultimately to do with trust and reliance upon God and the power of his word and Spirit. Are evangelistic strategies like co-operation with liberals, the overt use of celebrities to lend 'credibility,' and the calling and recording of decisions through pressure on the human will really about the glory of God and trusting his power, or are there other purposes mixed in? Would the worldwide invitations come if multitudes of decisions were not recorded? If immediate appeal is not made, how does one quickly measure the success and greatness of the evangelist?

Then there is the issue of working with the local church. Much has been made of Graham's helpful working with local churches to avoid some of the problems associated with the ministry of other itinerants who practically denounced the local church. In a typical crusade, 500–1200 area churches from 70–90 different denominations and groups were in some way involved in the ministry of BGEA. These workers included volunteers, counsellors, choirs and ushers. [43] On account of this Drummond again makes a huge effort to put Graham in favour with past greats: "There is little doubt that Charles Spurgeon, the great pastor-evangelist, would smile on Billy Graham's approach to couching his evangelistic ministry in the setting of the local church." [44] But this anachronistic statement is very doubtful indeed. First, Spurgeon was a Calvinist and, while warm-hearted, would not have approved of Graham's methods. Second, does the BGEA really work with and honour the local church and its leadership? For one thing, and in fairness to Graham, with that many churches involved, it is doubtful that on this mass scale such a thing is really possible, at least not in any level of depth. Certainly churches (once the invitation is made by a committee) can 'opt in' to a BGEA crusade and offer volunteers, but it would be somewhat irresponsible to suggest that this is operating *through* the local church. Graham has little or nothing to say on ecclesiology or the Eucharist or numerous aspects of Christian discipleship in which the church is central – all implicit when one accepts Christ as Lord. But they did seek to have all decisions followed up by a local church.

In Graham's favour, he clearly tried to address himself to some of these issues. He sought to build collegial relationships with local pastors. He tried to run his parachurch organization in such a way as not to supplant or replace the local church. In Graham's view, mass evangelism had only become necessary because of the failure of the church in evangelism and once this was addressed, the need for parachurch organizations like his would cease to exist.[45] This is surely right and Graham must be commended for these efforts and his recognition of the centrality of the local church.

Finally, how are we to assess results and what conclusions may be reached? Detailed research has shown that the great nineteenth-century, reformed teaching-evangelist, Asahel Nettleton, saw around 30,000 people come to lasting faith in Christ during a period when the entire United States population was only about nine million (compared to over 300 million today). These numbers are *not* the result of decisions registered or hands counted but are drawn from convert's subsequent faithful participation in the life of the local church. The local pastors themselves recorded that 90% who came to faith through Nettleton's ministry were still faithful believers ten, twenty and thirty years later. This is without parallel in our own time.[46] On the other hand, Charles Finney, the noted progenitor of the new measures declared of the new converts from his recent revivals in a lecture published in the *New York Evangelist*, "the great body of them are a disgrace to religion. Of what use would it be to have a thousand members added to the church to be just such as are now in it."[47]

Turning now to Graham's ministry, on average, four per cent go forward to make a decision at his meetings; so in a crowd of 100,000, this is about 4,000. At one major event in Bristol, U.K, some careful research on results was meticulously conducted. At that event, 2,642 came forward. However, of those who came to the front, only fifty-five per cent were professing salvation. As for the other forty-five per cent, fifteen per cent were seeking assurance, seventeen per cent were rededicating their lives and thirteen per cent gave another reason for going forward. Some of the converts interviewed were very unsure about what they had done. Interestingly, the BGEA's own statistics show that it is enquirers brought along by Christians from local churches that show evidence of conversion, not all of whom come forward at the time but who are prayed for and nurtured later.[48] Research has also shown that seventy-one per cent of those brought and then drawn into nurture groups were still active in the Christian life one year later. Tellingly, however, of those who came forward and did not join a discipleship group with a church, eighty per cent had nothing to do with the local church a year after going forward at a crusade.[49] Taking this event as representative, we can see from these results that:

a) On average four per cent of a crowd at a Billy Graham crusade go forward to make a 'decision.'
b) Of those, around half are not committing their lives to faith in Christ for the first time.
c) Of those that go forward and do not then get connected to a church, eighty per cent have nothing to do with the church a year later.
d) Around seventy per cent of those who make commitments to Christ and then are drawn into the local discipleship are active in the Christian faith a year later.

We can immediately notice several things. The numbers that pour forward at these events, having been called forward to make a decision are *by no means* all coming to faith, showing evidence of regeneration and conversion. Those that are genuine have usually been brought by a believing friend who has been witnessing to them and praying for them. Those that stick are those who are integrated into the local church, and the vast majority of those that are not, have no lasting contact with the church. Many do not go forward at the event but come to faith later – a seed having been planted! We can observe then the critical importance of the local church, the misleading nature of counting immediate 'results,' and that the Holy Spirit works in his own way in people's lives, in his own time.

Drummond disappointingly concludes his biography of Graham in the manner of a devotee with rose-coloured glasses, rather than with a considered scholarly appraisal. Surely, using *every available means* to proclaim Christ is not always the *best means* to proclaim him:

> Billy Graham has changed the old order of things in terms of how evangelism is done in the beginning of the twenty first century. He has made sure every available means is used to proclaim Christ to the nations. His ministry lines up with historical, evangelical evangelism, and yet it embraces the future...[50]

Billy Graham was indeed a phenomenon and a hugely significant evangelist in our time. God raised him up and used him in powerful ways despite some unbiblical methods, theological compromise and certain instances of theological and political naivety. That said, apart from his timely and effective use of mass media, his vast international reach largely due to modern communications technology, and his broad ecumenical methodology, I do not think we can accurately describe him as unique or as an 'innovator,' transforming an old order in evangelism and pointing us to the right pattern for the future. Rather, he belongs very properly to a specific lineage of nineteenth and early twentieth-century Arminian American evangelists, committed to crusade or 'mass' evangelism and revivalism. He is perhaps more accurately identified as the last of a particular breed of internationally prominent mass evangelists, rather than a practitioner who predicted future changes and developments (cultural, philosophic or missiological), blazing a trail for the next generation to follow in the twenty first century. It is certainly not clear how Drummond thinks that Graham has changed the old order of things for the twenty-first century, given that mass evangelism of this crusade variety is currently one of the most culturally impossible, inappropriate and unfruitful methods of evangelism in the Western world at present.

Accounting for Graham's successes in leading people to Christ is not difficult for an evangelical. It was doubtless Billy Graham's relatively unswerving focus and commitment to preaching a plain gospel on the authority of the Bible that enabled God to use him in a unique and powerful way. Moreover, he has been a man of genuine humility and integrity who wanted to work with others and pass on the grace that God had given to him. Graham's ministry reminds us that God can raise up a farm boy at any time he chooses to take the gospel to presidents and kings. It reminds us of the power of the gospel and it reminds us of God's sovereignty and providential working. Graham's ministry reminds us that though he may be the last of a particular breed of significant evangelists, he cannot possibly be the last great evangelist. For God calls faithful servants in every age and in every land to proclaim the gospel. Such faithful evangelists are found all over the world though we may never know their names.

NOTES

INTRODUCTION

[1] Marcello Pera, *Why We Should Call Ourselves Christians: The Religious Roots of Free Societies*, trans. L. B. Lappin (New York: Encounter, 2011), 62.

[2] BUDAPEST, Nov. 20, 2012 (LifeSiteNews.com) - Europe must return to Christianity before economic regeneration is possible, PrimeMinister Viktor Orban of Hungary said at a conference last week. According to Orban, the growing economic crisis in Europe is one that originates in the spiritual, not the economic order. To solve this crisis, he proposed a renewal of culture and politics based on Christian values to save Europe from economic, moral and social collapse. "An economic improvement is only possible for Europe and Hungary if souls and hearts rise, too," Orban said at the XIV Congress of Catholics and Public Life on "Hope and the Christian response to the crisis." Behind every successful economy, Orban said, there is "some kind of spiritual driving force ... A Europe governed according to Christian values would regenerate." In a Christian Europe the excesses that have created the economic crisis would not have been possible, he said. "A Christian Europe would have noticed that every euro is worked for. A Christian Europe would not have allowed entire countries sink into slavery to credit." He cited the new Hungarian constitution as a way forward for all of Europe, saying it is based on dignity, freedom, family, nation, fidelity, and love, with the express obligation to help the poor ... Orban said that Europe that forgets its Christian roots is like a man who built his house on sand. Hungary and Orban's leadership continues to be a thorn in the side of the statist, liberal consensus at the European Union. The Hungarian constitution has been under attack since its passage in May 2011. It explicitly defends the rights of the unborn and the definition of marriage as being between one man and one woman, and asserts that Christianity is the basis of the Hungarian national identity.

[3] Hilary White, "Abandonment of Christian Principles led to Europe's Economic Crisis: Hungarian Prime Minister, *Lifesite News*, last modified November 20, 2012, http://www.lifesitenews.com/news/abandonment-of-christian-principles-led-to-europes-economic-crisishungaria.

[4] The study of the mission of the church/Christians in light of God's revealed Word, in the context of our culture and context.

[5] Paul S. Boyer (ed.), *The Oxford Companion to United States History* (New York: Oxford University Press, 2001), 638.

[6] A good starting point for understanding the Puritans and their contribution are the series of essays brought together in, John Coffey and Paul C. H. Lim (eds.), *The Cambridge Companion to Puritanism* (Cambridge: Cambridge University Press, 2008).

[7] Johannes Verkuyl, *Contemporary Missiology: An Introduction* (Grand Rapids: Eerdmans, 1978), 5. Emphasis added.

[8] One good example of this strange hostility would be the work that emanates from otherwise Reformed scholars associated with the 'Escondido theology,' also known as 'two kingdoms theology,' the heartland of which is now at Westminster Theological Seminary in Escondido, California.

[9] From a scholarly perspective, omitting a keynote clearly distorts our entire understanding of Puritanism, and leaves the field of discussion of what most motivated the Puritans, which is obvious to their detractors, to those who hate them the most. That is no way to bring about a revival of Puritanism.

[10] Molly Worthen, "The Chalcedon Problem: Rousas John Rushdoony and the Origins of Christian Reconstructionism," Church History 77:2 (2008), 399–437, 426.

[11] This is because Rushdoony never considered himself either a political figure or a political activist, being largely skeptical of present Christian attempts to harness government by political involvement. He did not think that the language of left and right was helpful either when seeking to help people understand how God's word applies to various aspects of life and culture in the public sphere. He also believed that the desire of some to take over in Washington had corrupted a grassroots conservative movement.

[12] Worthen earned her PhD from Yale University and as of this writing is a professor at the University of North Carolina.

[13] Very little substantive work has been done on the new Puritanism (theonomy) by informed critics, but Worthen's analysis is better than most and at least demonstrates a genuine acquaintance with Rushdoony's own writings. Whilst she is not sympathetic to Puritan solutions from the law of God to our cultural crisis, and is critical of reformed thought, she is fair-minded in many aspects of her assessment and honest about the remarkable significance of Rushdoony, despite his being a relatively unknown scholar. However, I do not agree with some critical aspects of her analysis and assessment and would not recommend the essay as a starting point for those seeking a basic, introductory understanding of theonomy.

[14] Molly Worthen, "The Chalcedon Problem," 435–436.

[15] Worthen, "The Chalcedon Problem," 435.

[16] Worthen, "The Chalcedon Problem," 400–401.

[17] Worthen, "The Chalcedon Problem,'"420.

[18] Worthen, "The Chalcedon Problem," 401.

[19] Worthen, "The Chalcedon Problem," 406

[20] Worthen, "The Chalcedon Problem," 437

[21] Worthen, "The Chalcedon Problem," 413.

[22] Worthen, "The Chalcedon Problem," 421, 423.

[23] Worthen, "The Chalcedon Problem," 436–437.

[24] Robert M. Bowman, "The New Puritanism: A Preliminary Assessment of Reconstructionism," Christian Research Journal 10:3 (1988).

[25] Some have suggested that the emergent church movement is no longer current and that such references are dated, but that is like saying Liberation Theology is no longer an issue or that the Hippy movement is a spent force. The reality is that Liberation Theology didn't disappear into oblivion – it went mainstream and morphed into the social justice or progressivist movements in the churches of the West that now call for the humanization of the biosphere, propagandize regarding the concept of catastrophic man-made climate change, and call for the reorientation of the 'gospel' to the sites of the marginalized – the current Pope Francis is a product of this thinking. The Hippies were basically cultural Marxists influenced by the Frankfurt school. They didn't disappear either but simply got their hair cut (in most cases!) took places of influence in the universities and governments of the West and shaped a new generation – their major concerns are now largely implemented in mainstream Western culture. In like manner the 'pick and mix,' relativist and inclusivist 'gospel' of the emergent church movement has gone mainstream in much evangelicalism. The term may no longer be in regular use but that is because it is no longer needed. When egalitarianism, inclusivism, the normalization of homosexuality and social justice teachings are mainstreaming within evangelicalism, its major vehicle has served its purpose. No one speaks of 'The New Age Movement' anymore because the reenchantment of the West in terms of pagan religions is ubiquitous. So much so that some sociologists are speaking of the Hinduization of the Western world. Occultism is now popular culture.

[26] Peter Baklinski, "'Social justice' apart from evangelization drives youth away from Christianity, says new study," *Lifesite News*, last modified July 5 2013, http://www. lifesitenews.com/news/social-justice-apart-from-evangelization-drives-youth-away-from-christianity.

[27] Rousas John Rushdoony, *Intellectual Schizophrenia: Culture, Crisis and Education* (Philadelphia: Presbyterian and Reformed, 1961), 2.

[28] John Morrill, "The Puritan Revolution," John Coffey and Paul C. H. Lim (eds.), *The Cambridge Companion to Puritanism*, (Cambridge: Cambridge University Press, 2008), 67–88, 80.

[29] Christian pluralism doesn't pretend to be as expansive as modern political pluralism which is proving as unworkable as it is fatal to a culture – Islamic terror is making that all too clear. For the Bible and the historic Anglosphere, religious liberty did not mean polytheism and the state sponsorship of idolatry. To pretend that all religions and beliefs are equal is an absurd and transparent lie. Moreover, such humanistic polytheism or relativism is itself a religious perspective that is intolerant of those worldviews which reject it. And so modern 'multi-cultural' political doctrine is self-evidently a ruse to introduce a new legalized intolerance. This is precisely what Christians are facing today as they are arrested for preaching on the street in England, or fired from their job for not complying with diversity policies in the USA, or heavily fined for violating someone's

alleged human rights by the Canadian Human Rights Commission.

[30] Morrill, "The Puritan Revolution," 80.

[31] Morrill, "The Puritan Revolution," 81.

[32] Morrill, "The Puritan Revolution," 83.

[33] Rushdoony, *Intellectual Schizophrenia*, 50.

[34] Jonathan Burnside, *God, Justice and Society,* (Oxford: Oxford University Press, 2010), xxxviii.

[35] My basis for asserting this is solely the research of the noted missiologist Christopher Wright in his work, *The Mission of God: Unlocking the Bible's Grand Narrative,* (Illinois: IVP, 2006), 62.

[36] Especially noted in the field of ecumenical missiology is the work of Georg Vicedom.

[37] Wright, *The Mission of God*, 63.

[38] Wright, *The Mission of God*, 63.

[39] David J. Bosch, *Transforming Mission: Paradigm Shifts in Theology of Mission* (New York: Orbis, 1998), 391.

[40] My work would certainly be seen by ecumenists as using the term 'missio Dei' to smuggle in a rival concept of mission. However, they can claim no ownership of the mission or the reign of God! Its use in the context of Reformed thought is completely legitimate for entering the debate.

[41] Bosch, *Transforming Mission*, 392.

[42] Marilynne Robinson, *The Death of Adam: Essays on Modern Thought* (New York: Picador, 2005), 153.

[43] Robinson, *The Death of Adam*, 152.

CHAPTER ONE

[1] Samuel Gregg, "Europe, Immigration, and Merkel's Christian Values," Acton Institute Power Blog, last modified November 24, 2010, http://blog.acton.org/archives/20178-europe-immigration-and-merkel%E2%80%99s-christian-values.html.

[2] See as a good example, an article of one Canadian journalist and public intellectual, George Jonas, commenting on the February 2012 decision of the Canadian Supreme Court that ruled against the authority of parents over the education of their children. Jonas delineates the frightening implications for religious freedom. George Jonas, "Supreme Court puts the Final Nail in the Coffin of Religious Freedom," National Post, last modified February 28, 2012, http://fullcomment.nationalpost.com/2012/02/28/george-jonas-supreme-court-puts-the-final-nail-in-the-coffin-of-religious-freedom/.

[3] Luther, Martin Luther's Table Talk, 225. Emphasis added.

[4] R.J. Rushdoony, Freud (Vallecito, CA: Ross House, 2006), 38–39.

[5] Herman Rauschning, preface to The *Ten Commandments: Ten Short Novels of Hitler's*

War Against the Moral Code, ed. Armin L. Robinson(New York: Simon and Schuster, 1943), xiii.

[6] Rt. Hon. Lord Denning, *The Influence of Religion on Law* (Edmonton: Canadian Institute for Law, Theology and Public Policy, 1997), 17–18.

[7] Allen Carden, *Puritan Christianity in America: Religion and Life in Seventeenth-Century Massachusetts* (Grand Rapids: Baker Book House, 1990), 33.

[8] Carden, *Puritan Christianity,* 37.

[9] Carden, *Puritan Christianity,* 42. Emphasis added.

[10] John Coffey, "Puritan Legacies," in *The Cambridge Companion to Puritanism,* eds. John Coffey and Paul C. H. Lim (Cambridge: Cambridge University Press, 2008), 338.

[11] John Owen, *The Works of John Owen,* 16 vols., ed. William H. Goold (London: Banner of Truth Trust, 1966) 13:40-41.

[12] Carden, *Puritan Christianity,* 212.

[13] See John Morrill, *Oliver Cromwell* (Oxford: Oxford University Press, 2007), ix-x.

[14] C.S. Lewis, *God in The Dock* (Grand Rapids: Eerdmans, 1970), 202.

[15] Robinson, The Death of Adam, 150–151.

[16] Their efforts to 'purify' the church earned them the name Puritans. They were concerned that the Reformation had not been completed in the English church and that the influence of Rome was still too strong. It was from John Knox that they derived their passion to reform the church and from William Tyndale that they derived their commitment to Scripture and a theology of the covenant as the primary tools of reformation. By the time of James I many Puritans felt the task of reforming the church of England was hopeless and so they became separatists - some becoming 'Pilgrim Fathers' who after some time in Holland, established in 1620 the Plymouth Colony in what is now southeastern Massachusetts.

[17] George H. Sabine, *A History of Political Theory* (Holt, Rinehart and Winston: New York, third edition, 1961), 444-447

[18] Robert S. Paul, The Lord Protector: Religion and Politics in the Life of Oliver Cromwell (Lutterworth Press: Plymouth, 1955), 156

[19] Geoffrey Robertson, *The Tyrannicide Brief: The Story of the Man Who Sent Charles I to the Scaffold* (Anchor Books: New York, 2007), 193

[20] David Hall, *The Legacy of John Calvin: His Influence on the Modern World* (P&R Publishing: Phillipsburg, 2008), 25-29

[21] Coffey, *Puritan Legacies,* 340.

[22] Coffey, *Puritan Legacies,* 339.

[23] Coffey, *Puritan Legacies,* 337.

[24] Ryken, *Worldly Saints,* xvi.

[25] Jacques Barzun, *From Dawn to Decadence: 1500 to the Present – 500 years of Western Cultural Life* (St Ives: HarperCollins, 2000), 262.

[26] Barzun, *From Dawn to Decadence*, 263.

[27] One wonderful example of this vision is William Gurnall, *The Christian in Complete Armour*, first published between 1662 and 1665. It was republished by The Banner of Truth Trust in 1964.

[28] Joel R. Beeke, *Puritan Reformed Spirituality* (Grand Rapids: Reformation Heritage, 2004), 101.

[29] Richard Sibbes, *Divine meditations and holy contemplations,* cited in U. Milo Kaufmann, *The pilgrim's progress and traditions in Puritan meditation* (New Haven: Yale University Press, 1966), 46.

[30] Herman Witsius, *The economy of the covenants between God and man: Comprehending a complete body of divinity* (London, 1822; Reprinted, Escondido, CA: The den Dulk Christian Foundation, 1990), 175-177.

[31] Thomas Watson, *The Ten Commandments* (East Peoria, IL: The Banner of Truth Trust, 2009), 12.

[32] Ryken, *Worldly Saints*, 175.

[33] Samuel Hartlib, *London's charity enlarged,* cited in W.K. Jordan, *The development of religious toleration in England* (Cambridge: Harvard University Press, 1932), 213.

[34] William Perkins, cited in Christopher Hill, *Puritanism and revolution: Studies in interpretation of the English Revolution of the seventeenth century* (London: Secker and Warburg, 1958), 231.

[35] See James B. Jordan, "Calvinism and the Judicial Law of Moses: An Historical Survey," The *Journal of Christian Reconstruction: 25th Anniversary*, ed. P. Andrew Sandlin (Vallecito, CA: Chalcedon Foundation, 2000), 74–75.

[36] Rev. John Geree, *The Character of an Old English Puritan or Non-Conformist* (London: Christopher Meredith, 1646), http://www.reformedreader.org/character_of_an_old_english_puri.htm.

[37] Barzun, *From Dawn to Decadence*, 276–277.

[38] J.C. Davis, *Oliver Cromwell* (London: Arnold, 2001), 34.

[39] Davis, *Oliver Cromwell*, 200.

[40] Davis, *Oliver Cromwell*, 201.

[41] Davis, *Oliver Cromwell*, 201.

[42] A more expansive definition of theonomy is that it is a reformed perspective in theology and Christian ethics which holds that the totality of the covenant law of God in both the Old and New Testaments, when properly interpreted, remains binding upon Christians and upon civil governments as the standard to which all are and will be held accountable by God.

[43] John Eidsmoe, *Historical and Theological Foundations of Law: Vol III Reformation and Colonial* (Powder Springs, Georgia: American Vision & Tolle Lege Press, 2012), 1040-1041.

[44] Davis, *Oliver Cromwell*, 137.

[45] Terrill Irwin Elniff, *The Guise of Every Graceless Heart: Human Autonomy in Puritan Thought and Experience* (Vallecito, CA: Ross House,1981), 33.

[46] Mark A. Noll: *A History of Christianity in the United States and Canada* (Grand Rapids: Eerdmans, 1992), 46.

[47] Noll: *A History of Christianity*, 46.

[48] Greg L. Bahnsen, *Theonomy in Christian Ethics* (Nacogdoches, TX: Covenant Media, 2002), 526.

[49] Beeke, *Puritan Spirituality*, 110.

[50] Samuel Rutherford, cited in Beeke, *Puritan Spirituality*, 110.

[51] Samuel Crooke, cited in Beeke, *Puritan Spirituality*, 110.

[52] Wilbur Cortez Abbott, *The Writings and Speeches of Oliver Cromwell: Volume IV, The Protectorate 1655–1658* (Oxford: Clarendon Press, 1947), 389.

[53] Frame, *The Doctrine of the Christian Life*, 218–220.

[54] Wayne House, introduction to *Restoring the Constitution: 1787-1987*, ed. Wayne House (Dallas, TX: Probe, 1987), 8.

[55] A covenant is a treaty or contract or legal relationship between two parties. In terms of his relationship to mankind, God relates to us in terms of covenant where the parties to the covenant are unequal; here the greater gives his law to the lesser and man comes under God's grace and protection. Thus God's covenant with man is simultaneously one of law and grace.

[56] R.J. Rushdoony, *In His Service: The Christian Calling to Charity* (Vallecito, CA: Ross House, 2009), 23.

[57] Greg L. Bahnsen & Kenneth L. Gentry, Jr, *House Divided: The Break-Up of Dispensational Theology* (Texas: Institute for Christian Economics, 1989), 194–196.

[58] Bahnsen and Gentry, *House Divided*, 197.

[59] Christopher J. H. Wright, *The Mission of God: Unlocking The Bible's Grand Narrative* (Downers Grove, IL: Intervarsity, 2006), 287.

[60] Frame, *The Doctrine*, 222.

[61] R. C. Sproul Jr. "What is Theonomy?," *Ligonier Ministries*, last modified May 12, 2010, http://www.ligonier.org/blog/whatreconstructionism-what-theonomy/.

[62] For what seems to be an irrefutable demonstration of this, see Martin A. Foulner, *Theonomy and the Westminster Confession* (Edinburgh: Marpet Press, 1997). This work is an anthology of quotations from the Puritan divines involved in the drafting of the Westminster Confession.

[63] David Klinghoffer, *Shattered Tablets: Why We Ignore The Ten Commandments At Our Peril* (New York: Doubleday, 2007), 13–15.

[64] Wright, *The Mission of God*, 334.

[65] Wright, *The Mission of God*, 334.

CHAPTER TWO

[1] Ryken, Worldly Saints, 24–25.

[2] James E. McGoldrick, Abraham Kuyper: God's Renaissance Man (Ebbw, Wales: Evangelical Press, 2000), 245.

[3] McGoldrick, Abraham Kuyper, 163.

[4] R.J. Rushdoony, *A Word in Season*, Vol. 1 (Vallecito, CA: Ross House, 2010), 33-34.

[5] Rushdoony, *A Word*, 35–36.

[6] William Perkins, cited in Horton Davies, *Worship and theology in England: From Cranmer to Hooker*, 1534-1603 (Princeton: Princeton University Press, 1975), 66.

[7] 'Grecianization' here simply means a return to ideas stemming from ancient Greek philosophical categories of thought that are characterized by various dualisms – form/ matter, spiritual/material, ideas/events.

[8] Marvin R. Wilson, Our Father Abraham: Jewish Roots of the Christian Faith (Grand Rapids: Eerdmans, 1989), 178.

[9] The word 'secular' from the Latin '*saeculum*' essentially means 'relating to this world,' i.e. meaning not religious, spiritual, nor defined by the eternal. Anything considered 'secular' therefore is thought of as not influenced, controlled or governed by spiritual reality, revelation or religious authority. Thus secularism, as popularly understood, is the view that society's values and standards should not be influenced or controlled by religion. The fundamental failure here is to see that secularism itself is a religious perspective, the religion of humanism, where the source of definition for reality, truth and morality is 'of this world,' in the form of human reasoning and experience. Biblical faith denies such an artificial distinction between the 'spiritual' and 'earthly' and claims instead that all of life and reality, in every part, is created and defined by God and His revelation. Consequently there is no area of life or thought that does not come under his authority and lordship.

[10] Jeffrey K. Jue, "Puritan Millenarianism in Old and New England," in John Coffey and Paul C. H. Lim (eds.) *The Cambridge Companion to Puritanism* (Cambridge: Cambridge University Press, 2008), 259.

[11] Jue, 'Puritan Millenarianism,' 261.

[12] Christ must come before the millennium. The coming of the kingdom of God is thus largely 'postponed' till a literal thousand year reign of Christ physically upon the earth is established by heavenly military power.

[13] For a comprehensive discussion of Puritan missiology and the post-millennial hope see, Iain Murray, *The Puritan Hope: Revival and the Interpretation of Prophecy* (Bucks, England: Banner of Truth Trust, 1991)

[14] Murray, *The Puritan Hope*, 223–224.

[15] Today Christian theology speaks of three dominant millennial views: pre-millennialism, a-millennialism and post-millennialism. Both a-millennialism (no millennium) and post-

millennialism (after millennium) hold with the Augustinian tradition that the age of the church is the age of the kingdom of God that will be fully inaugurated at the return of Christ. However, between the first and second advent of Christ, they differ on how much success will be seen for the gospel. Post-millennialism has therefore often been dubbed optimistic a-millennialism, since those holding to post-millennialism are more optimistic about the success of the gospel in the church age and because the millennial period itself is usually interpreted as an indefinite age or era rather than a literal thousand years.

[16] Carden, *Puritan Christianity*, 95.

[17] Carden, *Puritan Christianity*, 95.

[18] William Westfall, *Two Worlds: The Protestant Culture of Nineteenth Century Ontario* (Kingston: McGill-Queen's University Press, 1989), 167.

[19] Bahnsen & Gentry, *House Divided*, xxxiv-xxxv.

[20] Westfall, *Two Worlds*, 168.

[21] Westfall, *Two Worlds*, 168.

[22] Westfall, *Two Worlds*, 188.

[23] Westfall, *Two Worlds*, 183.

[24] Westfall, *Two Worlds*, 169.

[25] Westfall, Two Worlds, 170.

[26] Westfall, *Two Worlds*, 177.

[27] Westfall, *Two Worlds*, 177.

[28] Westfall, *Two Worlds*, 3-4.

[29] Westfall, *Two Worlds*, 182.

[30] For a detailed analysis of the decline and theological collapse of dispensational thought, see the devastating critique by Bahnsen and Gentry in *House Divided: The Breakup of Dispensational Theology* (1989).

[31] This theological question is a separate issue from the present political crisis in the Middle East and is not anti-Semitic (though some commentators would suggest otherwise). One can be politically supportive of modern Israel as a state actor in the region, and concerned for its protection against Islamic fascism and UN hypocrisy, and yet deny theologically an eschatological political kingdom for ethnic Israel and/ or the idea that God has two peoples, the church and Israel.

[32] J. Gresham Machen, "Christianity and Culture," *The Princeton Theological Review* 11 (1913), 3–4, last modified November 17, 2011, http://homepage.mac.com/shanerosenthal/reformationink/jgmculture.htm.

[33] Harold J. Berman, *Law and Revolution II: The Impact of the Protestant Reformations on the Western Legal Tradition* (Cambridge, MA: Harvard University Press, 2003), 382.

[34] Berman, *Law and Revolution II*, 382.

[35] Harold J. Berman, *Law and Revolution: The Formation of the Western Legal Tradition* (Cambridge, MA: Harvard University Press, 1983), 65.

[36] Berman, *Law and Revolution II*, 10.

[37] Berman, *Law and Revolution II*, 16–17.

[38] Wilson, *Our Father*, 127.

[39] Wilson, *Our Father*, 128–129.

[40] Thomas Watson, *The Ten Commandments* (East Peoria, IL: The Banner of Truth Trust, 2009), 44.

[41] Watson, *The Ten Commandments*, 44.

[42] Coffey and Lim, *Cambridge Companion to Puritanism*, 3.

[43] Berman, *Law and Revolution* (1983), 520–521.

[44] John Calvin, *Calvin's New Testament Commentaries: A Harmony of the Gospels, Matthew, Mark and Luke* (Grand Rapids: Eerdmans, 1994), 180.

[45] Calvin, *A Harmony of the Gospels, Matthew, Mark and Luke*, 183–184.

[46] Ernest Reisinger, *The Law and the Gospel* (Phillipsburg, NJ: Presbyterian & Reformed, 1997) 139.

[47] Matthew Henry, *Matthew Henry's Commentary On The Whole Bible In Six Volumes: Vol. 5 - Matthew To John* (New York: Fleming H. Revell Company, Circa 1935)

[48] Reisinger, *The Law and the Gospel*, 133.

[49] Wilson, *Our Father*, 109.

[50] Wilson, *Our Father*, 110.

[51] Wright, *The Mission of God*, 121–122.

[52] Wilson, *Our Father*, 28.

[53] Reisinger, *Law and Gospel*, 145.

[54] Reisinger, *The Law and the Gospel*, 143–144.

[55] St. Augustine, *The Triumph of Grace: Augustine's writings on salvation*, ed. N. R. Needham (Ebbw Vale, Wales: Grace Publications Trust, 2000), 106–107.

[56] Needham, *The Triumph of Grace*, 107–108.

[57] Needham, *The Triumph of Grace*, 106.

[58] Gerald W. Schlabach and Allan D. Fitzgerald, Allan D. Fitzgerald (ed.) *Augustine Through the Age: An Encyclopedia* (Eerdmans: Grand Rapids, 1999), 324

[59] Carol Harrison, *Augustine: Christian Truth And Fractured Humanity; Christian Theology In Context* (Padstow, Cornwall: Oxford University Press, 200), 86-87.

[60] Harrison, *Augustine*, 110

[61] St. Augustine, Letters: The Works of St. Augustine; A translation for the 21st Century, ed. John E. Roselle (New York: New City Press,2001), 382.

[62] David W. Hall, *The Legacy of John Calvin: His influence on the modern world* (Phillipsburg: Presbyterian & Reformed, 2008), 18.

[63] Hall, *The Legacy of John Calvin*, 18.

[64] Graham Miller, *Calvin's Wisdom: An Anthology Arranged Alphabetically* (Bath, Avon: Banner of Truth, 1992), 191.

[65] Miller, *Calvin's Wisdom*, 193.

[66] Hall, *The Legacy of John Calvin*, 19.

[67] See James B. Jordan, *The Covenant Enforced: Sermons on Deuteronomy 27 and 28* (Tyler, TX: Institute for Christian Economics, 1990), xxxiii.

[68] Calvin, *A Harmony of the Gospels, Matthew, Mark and Luke*, 180.

[69] Calvin, *A Harmony of the Gospels, Matthew, Mark and Luke*, 180–181.

[70] Calvin, *A Harmony of the Gospels, Matthew, Mark and Luke*, 181.

[71] Calvin, *A Harmony of the Gospels, Matthew, Mark and Luke*, 181.

[72] Calvin, *A Harmony of the Gospels, Matthew, Mark and Luke*, 181–182.

[73] John Calvin, cited in Martin A. Faulkner, *Theonomy and the Westminster Confession* (Edinburgh: Marpet Press, 1997), 51.

[74] Jordan, *The Covenant*, xxxii –xxxiii. For a full survey of Calvin's use of the law see, Jack W. Sawyer, Jr., "Moses and the Majestrate: Aspects of Calvin's Political Theory in Contemporary Focus" (Th.M. thesis: Westminster Theological Seminary, 1986).

[75] Timothy George, *The Theology of the Reformers* (Nashville: B&H, 1988), 133.

[76] George, *The Reformers*, 133.

CHAPTER THREE

[1] *The New International Webster's Comprehensive Dictionary of the English Language: Encyclopedic Edition* (Trident Press: Florida, 1996). Note: Some encyclopedias suggest that the etymology of barbarian represents the apparent uncouth babbling of foreign languages to the Greco-Roman ear. See: *Encyclopedia Britanica Vol 3* (William Benton: Chicago, 1968), 147

[2] Barzun, *From Dawn to Decadence*, x–xi

[3] Barzun, *From Dawn to Decadence*, xi.

[4] Barzun, *From Dawn to Decadence*, xii.

[5] Barzun, *From Dawn to Decadence*, xviii.

[6] 'All-conditioning' refers to the creative and predestining sovereignty of God governing the entirety of the conditions of human life. See Cornelius Van Til, *A Christian Theory of Knowledge* (Phillipsburg, NJ: Presbyterian & Reformed, 1969).

[7] I am indebted to the thoughtful analysis of R. J. Rushdoony in his book, *The Biblical Philosophy of History* (1969) for my interpretation of Christian historiography in this chapter.

[8] Rousas John Rushdoony, *A Christian Survey of World History* (Vallecito: Ross House, 1999), 1.

[9] St. Augustine, 'Against Two Letters of the Pelagians', 2:12, cited in N. R. Needham (ed.), *The Triumph of Grace: Augustine's writings on Salvation*, 212–213.

[10] Here the irony is that 'chance' is simply another byword for determinism. Chance

isn't a power, force, or energy. It isn't anything substantive at all. It is a word which identifies our limitation in understanding the factors of causation in a given event. In other words, chance is a term that describes our ignorance. To say that history is the product of chance is therefore to say nothing more than history is fate (determination by powers unknown).

[11] R.J. Rushdoony, *Systematic Theology* vol 1. (Vallecito: Ross House, 1994) 223.

[12] R.J. Rushdoony *Systematic Theology* vol 2, (Vallecito: Ross House, 1994), 1080.

[13] Rushdoony, *Systematic Theology*, vol. 2, 1081.

[14] Rushdoony, *Systematic Theology*, vol. 2, 1086–1087.

[15] For a fascinating discussion of this concept at work in ancient Rome, see Peter J. Leithart, *Defending Constantine: The Twilight of an Empire and the Dawn of Christendom* (Illinois: IVP Academic, 2010), 47–51.

[16] Leithart, *Defending Constantine*, 78–79.

[17] Roy Porter, *The Greatest Benefit to Mankind: A Medical History of Humanity* (New York: W.W. Norton, 1997), 32.

[18] Vishal Mangalwadi, *The Book That Made Your World: How The Bible Created The Soul of Western Civilization* (Nashville: Thomas Nelson, 2011) 339-344.

[19] Mangalwadi, *The Book*, 341.

[20] Mangalwadi, *The Book*, 339.

[21] See: Tom Holland, *The Forge of Christendom: The End of Days and the Epic Rise of the West* (New York: Doubleday, 2008) for a sweeping study of the rise of the West.

[22] Rodney Stark, *God's Battalions: The Case for the Crusades* (New York: HarperOne, 2009), 66.

[23] James Hannam, *The Genesis of Science: How the Christian Middle Ages Launched the Scientific Revolution* (Washington: Regnery Publishing, 2011) 342-343.

[24] Stark, God's Battalions, 60.

[25] Philip Jenkins, *The Lost History of Christianity: The Thousand-Year Golden Age of the Church in the Middle East, Africa and Asia – and how it died* (HarperOne: New York, 2008), 77-78

[26] Abbott, *The writings and speeches of Oliver Cromwell*, 277–279.

[27] Ian Gentles, *Oliver Cromwell: God's Warrior and the English Revolution* (New York: Palgrave MacMillan, 2011), 170–171.

[28] Philip Davies, "Rough Justice?" in Matthew J.M. Coomber ed. *Bible and Justice: Ancient Texts, Modern Challenges* (Milton Keynes, U.K: Equinox, 2011), 46–47.

[29] Davies, "Rough Justice?," 54.

[30] It must be noted however that simply pointing to the federal Constitution of the United States, which sounds quite secular and does not refer to the triune God of Scripture specifically, is not sufficient for understanding the relationship of Christianity to the state in the United States. At the federal level the concern was with preserving maximum

religious liberty for all Christian denominations without any establishment of one church. At the state level however, most states were explicitly Christian and some even had established state churches.

[31] Gentles, *Oliver Cromwell*, 93.

[32] Cited in Michael Wagner, *Christian Citizenship Guide: Christianity and Canadian Political Life* (Ottawa: ARPA Canada, 2011), 6–7.

[33] There is no doubt, however, that the United States today has a far greater influence of the Christian faith upon social and public life than Canada or Britain – nations that have been in open rebellion against the covenant they made, and are suffering the consequences. The United States is tragically following swiftly in their footsteps at the present time.

[34] Wagner, *Christian Citizenship Guide*, 7.

[35] Wagner, *Christian Citizenship Guide*, 7.

[36] Archibald Mason, cited in Michael Wagner, *The Anglosphere's Broken Covenant: Rediscovering the Validity and Importance of the Solemn League and Covenant* (Lewiston, ID: Gospel Covenant Publications, 2010), 18–19.

[37] Noll, *A History of Christianity in the United States and Canada* (Grand Rapids; Eerdmans, 1992), 546.

[38] Noll, *A History*, 246.

[39] Noll, *A History*, 284.

[40] Noll, *A History*, 33–34.

[41] William Wilberforce, A Letter on the Abolition of the Slave Trade: Addressed to the Freeholders and Other Inhabitants of Yorkshire`` (London: Luke Hansard & Sons, For T. Cadell and W. Davies, Strand; And, J. Hatchard, Piccadilly, 1807), 4–6.

[42] Bahnsen, *Theonomy*, 2.

[43] Bahnsen, *Theonomy*, 5.

[44] Bahnsen, *Theonomy*, 7.

[45] Harold J. Berman, *Law and Revolution: The Impact of Protestant Reforms on the Western Legal Tradition* (Cambridge, MA: Belknap Press, 2006).

[46] John Calvin, *Calvin: Institutes of the Christian religion*, in two volumes Edited by John T. McNeill and trans. Ford Lewis Battles (Philadelphia: The Westminster Press, 1960), 1488, 1497.

[47] It should be noted that elements of Biblical law were well-represented in European law prior to the Reformation, in the form of the Roman Catholic Church's canon law. Berman notes, "'Modern' English, German, French, Italian, Swedish, Dutch, Polish, and other national European legal systems were initially formed in the twelfth and thirteenth centuries under the influence, first, of the new canon law of the newly independent hierarchical Roman Catholic Church, which governed the wide variety of 'spiritual causes' in all the territories of Western Europe..." Berman, *Law and Revolution*, vol. 2, 377.

[48] Berman, *Law and Revolution*, vol. 2, 376. Emphasis added.

[49] A sense of national calling can certainly lead to a sense of patriotism (and can develop into an unhealthy nationalism in some individuals), in a similar vein that leads many Americans to speak of their heritage and American exceptionalism – the idea that America and its institutions have something of value to offer and spread to the rest of the world. But this in and of itself is not unbiblical.

[50] Berman, *Law and Revolution*, vol. 2, 376.

[51] Berman, *Law and Revolution*, vol. 2, 319.

[52] Berman, *Law and Revolution*, vol. 2, 323.

[53] Berman, *Law and Revolution*, vol. 2, 310.

[54] Berman, *Law and Revolution*, vol. 2, 319.

[55] James Jordan, "Calvinism and the Judicial laws of Moses: An Historical Survey", in *The Journal of Christian Reconstruction*, 25th Anniversary ed. P. Andrew Sandlin (Vallecito, CA: Chalcedon Foundation, 2000), 57.

[56] Statistics Canada, ``Leading Causes of Death, 200-2004, 84-215-XWE,`` 2008, http://www.statcan.gc.ca/daily-quotidien/081204/dq081204c-eng.htm.

[57] Rousas John Rushdoony, "The Centrality of the Atonement," *Faith For All of Life*, March/April 2012 (Vallecito, CA: Chalcedon Foundation, 2012), 3,18.

[58] See B. B. Warfield, "Jesus Christ the Propitiation for the Whole World," in Kenneth L. Gentry, Jr. ed. *Thine is the Kingdom: Studies in the Postmillennial Hope* (Vallecito CA: Chalcedon, 2003), 79–81.

CHAPTER FOUR

[1] Frances Young, *The Making of the Creeds* (London: SCM, 1991), 76,78.

[2] Allen Carden, *Puritan Christianity*, 160.

[3] R. J. Rushdoony, *The Foundations of Social Order: Studies in the Creeds and Councils of the Early Church*, 3rd ed. (Vallecito: Ross House, 1998), 53. Emphasis added.

[4] Roland H. Bainton, *Early Christianity* (New Jersey: D. Van Nostrand Company, 1960), 81,83.

[5] Bainton, *Early Christianity*, 82–83.

[6] For a detailed study of the triumph of Christianity over paganism that supports Rushdoony's thesis in the *Foundations of Social Order*, see Charles Norris Cochrane, *Christianity and Classical Culture: A Study of Thought and Action from Augustus to Augustine* (New York: Oxford University Press, 1957).

[7] R. J. Rushdoony, *The Institutes of Biblical Law* (Phillipsburg: Presbyterian and Reformed, 1973), 30–40.

[8] Rushdoony, *Foundations*, 54.

[9] Rushdoony, *Foundations*, 54.

[10] Rushdoony, *Foundations*, 54.

[11] Rushdoony, *Foundations*, 54.

[12] Michael Ignatieff, "9/11 and the age of sovereign failure," *The Globe and Mail*, last modified September 9, 2011, http://www.theglobeandmail.com/news/world/americas/september-11/michael-ignatieff-911-and-the-age-of-sovereign-failure/article2160153/.

[13] Tim Gardam, "Christians in China: Is the Country in Spiritual Crisis?" *BBC*, last modified September 11, 2011, http://www.bbc.co.uk/news/magazine-14838749.

[14] For a full discussion of the theological issue see: Jaroslav Pelikan, *The Christian Tradition: A History of the Development of Doctrine, Vol 1, The Emergence of the Catholic Tradition 100-600* (University of Chicago Press: Chicago, 1971), 263 ff.

[15] Bainton, *Early Christianity*, 167

[16] Rushdoony, *Foundations*, 56.

[17] Rushdoony, *Foundations*, 56

[18] Rushdoony, *Foundations*, 56

[19] This attitude dominates our Canadian society today. One of the most shocking examples of this totalitarian vision is the arbitrary power given to certain government agencies today like the Children's Aid Society, including right of access, right of seizure, right to interview children without their parents and many more. For a detailed and shocking analysis of this power wielded by government today see the documentary, 'Powerful as God: The Children's Aid Society' at http://blackout.ca.

[20] Being made in God's image does not make us participants in his essence – there is an absolute distinction between creator and creature. In the same way, 2 Peter 1:4 does not collapse this distinction to mean that Christians share God's essence (become part of God), rather Peter reveals we partake in God's moral character and likeness, by the power and working of the indwelling Holy Spirit. Though the Spirit lives in the believer, we do not become part of God the Holy Spirit. It would appear some of the church Fathers, influenced by Greek thought, erred on this point using a language of participation that suggested divinization.

[21] See, Rushdoony, *The Foundations of Social Order*, p. 57

[22] Rousas John Rushdoony, *The One and the Many: Studies in the Philosophy of Order and Ultimacy* (Fairfax: Thoburn Press, 1978), 312.

[23] For a survey of this threat in the present time see, Janet L. Folger, *The Criminalization of Christianity* (Oregon: Multnomah Publishers, 2005).

[24] G.W.F. Hegel, *Reason in history: A general introduction to the philosophy of history*, trans. Robert S. Hartman (Indianapolis: The Liberal Arts Press, 1953), 49002E

[25] Rushdoony, *The One and Many*, 26.

[26] Rushdoony, *Salvation and Godly Rule*, Vallecito, CA: Ross House, 1983406.

[27] Rushdoony, *Foundations*, 66–67.

[28] William Edgar, "The Passing of R. J. Rushdoony," *First Things* (August/September 2001), last modified 2013, www.puritanboard.com/f54/passing-r-j-rushdoony-35542.

[29] The various offspring and permutations of liberation theology would be the best example of statist thinking in modern missiology.

[30] Verkuyl, *Contemporary Missiology*, 194.

[31] Rousas John Rushdoony, *This Independent Republic: Studies in the Nature and Meaning of American History* (Nutley: The Craig Press, 1964), 100–101.

[32] Ryken, *Worldly Saints*, 174.

[33] Ryken, *Worldly Saints*, 175.

[34] Carden, *Puritan Christianity*, 162.

[35] Carden, *Puritan Christianity*, 164–167.

[36] Cited in Carden, *Puritan Christianity*, 166.

[37] James, M. Willson, *The Establishment and Limits of Civil Government: An Exposition of Romans 13: 1–7* (Powder Springs: American Vision Press, 2009), 66–67.

[38] John Howard Yoder, *The Politics of Jesus* (Grand Rapids: Eerdmans, 1972), 202.

[39] Yoder, *Politics*, 203.

[40] Yoder, *Politics*, 204.

[41] Yoder, *Politics*, 212. One might rightly ask what defines 'harm' – God's law, or man's feelings? Yoder's view shares much in common with utilitarian approaches to ethics.

[42] Yoder, *Politics*, 214.

[43] Yoder, *Politics*, 214.

[44] Ronald H. Nash, *Why the Left is Not Right: The Religious Left: who they are and what they believe* (Grand Rapids: Zondervan, 1996), 47–48.

[45] Andrew Kirk, *The Good News of the Kingdom Coming* (Downers Grove: IVP, 1985), 44–45.

[46] Meic Pearse, *Why The Rest Hates the West: Understanding the Roots of Global Rage*, (Downers Grove: IVP, 2004), 26.

[47] Rousas John Rushdoony, Larceny in the Heart: The Economics of Satan and the Inflationary State (Vallecito: Ross House, 2002), 100– 102.

[48] Some reformed thinkers have argued that through legitimate officers of the state this resistance may finally take the form of force as was seen in the thought of John Knox, Oliver Cromwell, and the colonists during the American Revolution.

[49] Carden, *Puritan Christianity*, 168–169.

[50] Noll, *A History of Christianity*, 52–53.

[51] Rushdoony published a detailed study of this phenomenon, *Christianity and the State* (Vallecito: Ross House, 1986).

[52] See Owen Fourie, "The State Reduced to its Biblical Limits," in Andrew Sandlin (ed), *A Comprehensive Faith: An International Festschrift For Rousas John Rushdoony* (San Jose: Friends of Chalcedon, 1996), 200.

[53] Verkuyl, *Contemporary Missiology*, 195.

[54] Peter J. Leithart, *Defending Constantine*, 342.

CHAPTER FIVE

[1] Cited in Paul Johnson, *Intellectuals: From Marx and Tolstoy to Sartre and Chomsky* (New York: Harper Perennial edition, 2007), 26–27.

[2] Johnson, *Intellectuals*, 25–26.

[3] R. J. Rushdoony, *The One and the Many*, 269–71.

[4] Julian Huxley, *I Believe: The personal philosophies of twenty-three eminent men and women of our time* (London: George Allen and Unwin, 1944 reprint), 133–134.

[5] Thomas Molnar, *Utopia: The perennial heresy* (New York: ISI, University Press of America, 1990), 240. I wish to acknowledge my great intellectual debt to, and extensive dependence upon, the incisive analysis of utopian thinking offered in Molnar's book.

[6] Huxley, *I believe*, 111–112.

[7] Huxley, *I believe*, 134.

[8] George Orwell, *1984* (New York: Signet 1950 [1949]), 195.

[9] J. L. Talmon, cited in Molnar, *Utopia*, 20.

[10] Molnar, *Utopia*, 34–35.

[11] Murphy, Edward J. "Conflicting Ultimates: Jurisprudence as Religious Controversy," *Am. J. Jurls.* 35 (1990):129.

[12] Molnar, *Utopia*, 41–42.

[13] Molnar, *Utopia*, 70.

[14] Bertrand Russell, *A Fresh Look at Empiricism: 1927–42* (Routledge: London, 1996), 16, cited in Huxley, *I Believe*, 269–271.

[15] For a meticulously researched study of these dramatic changes see, Michael L. Brown, *A Queer Thing Happened to America: And what a Long, Strange Trip it's Been* (Concord, North Carolina: Equal Time Books, 2011).

[16] See http://openparliament.ca/bills/41-1/C-279, accessed April 2013.

[17] Brown, *A Queer Thing*, 95.

[18] Molnar, *Utopia*, 99.

[19] Molnar, *Utopia*, 113. Note that in both Marxism and Hitler's National Socialism, the doctrine of evolution in nature played a key role. For Marx, Darwinism justified the class struggle and verified his materialism, for Hitler, evolution justified the elimination of the weak in the creation of the man-god.

[20] Julian Huxley, *New Bottles for New Wine* (London: Chatto & Windus, 1959, 1957), 17

[21] James A. Herrick, "C. S. Lewis and the Advent of the Posthuman," John G. West ed. *The Magician's Twin: C. S. Lewis on Science, Scientism, and Society* (Seattle: Discovery Institute Press, 2012), 258.

[22] Paul Kurtz, ed. *Humanist Manifestos I and II* (Buffalo: Prometheus, 1973), 16.

[23] Cited by Herrick, *C. S. Lewis*, 255.

[24] Herrick, *C. S. Lewis*, 253.

[25] Herrick, *C. S. Lewis*, 235.

[26] Herrick, *C. S. Lewis*, 251.

[27] Herrick, *C. S. Lewis*, 251.

[28] Herrick, *C. S. Lewis*, 252.

[29] *Transcendent Man: The Life and Ideas of Ray Kurzweil. Directed by Barry Ptolemy* (DVD, Ptolemic, 86 min, 2009).

[30] Herrick, *C. S. Lewis*, 252.

[31] David Herbert, *Becoming God: Transhumanism and the Quest for Cybernetic Immortality* (Joshua Press: Ontario, 2014), 93

[32] Herrick, *C. S. Lewis*, 236.

[33] Herrick, *C. S. Lewis*, 253.

[34] Cited in Herrick, *C. S. Lewis*, 237.

[35] Herrick, *C. S. Lewis*, 256.

[36] John Stewart, cited in Herrick, *C. S. Lewis*, 251.

[37] Herbert, *Becoming God*, 98

[38] H. G. Wells, *I Believe*, 361.

[39] Wells, in *I Believe*, 362.

[40] Wells, in *Points of View: A Series of Broadcast Addresses* (London: George Allen and Unwin, 1930), 68. Available online at http://dspace.gipe.ac.in/jspui/bitstream/1/6186/3/GIPE-062996.pdf, accessed June 18, 2013.

[41] Wells, in *I Believe*, 363.

[42] Wells, in *I Believe*, 365.

[43] This happened in early 2013 in Cyprus, when the state directly seized assets from citizen's and foreigner's bank accounts in order to help meet requirements for a banking bailout and preserve their participation in the European Union. See http://www.humanevents.com/2013/04/01/cyprus-meltdown-asset-seizures-to-hit-50-60-or-maybe-even-100-percent, accessed April 16th 2012.

[44] Molnar, *Utopia*, 146.

[45] R. J. Rushdoony, *The Mythology of Science*, 25–42.

[46] Rushdoony, *Mythology of Science*, 43.

[47] Albert Camus, *The Rebel: An Essay on Man in Revolt* (New York: Vintage Books, 1956), 241.

[48] For the highly influential Michel Foucault (perhaps the most cited scholar in the humanities today), the Christian past involves the unjust preservation of an arbitrary worldview that pretends to be true or foundational. In fact, Focault held, truth or reality is merely a social construct, and past constructs should not bind us in the present. Thus, social reality in our time entangles people in a 'web of oppression.' The oppressor class are the white, male, heterosexual, wealthy, English speaking, able bodied, Christians – outside this group all others are victims of structural oppression to varying degrees.

On this view, the personal conduct of an individual is irrelevant to their participation in injustice and oppression. If you share wholly or in part, by birth or by hard work, a good number of the characteristics listed above, you are inescapably a structural oppressor to be judged and cast down to bring about social justice.

[49] Molnar, *Utopia*, 201-202.

[50] R. J. Rushdoony, *Foundations of Social Order*, 176–177.

[51] See the book that inspired the worldwide animal liberation movement, Peter Singer, *Animal Liberation* (New York: New York Review [1975] 1990).

[52] Yoga, meditation and various other forms of Eastern spirituality have also been shown to have the effect of pacifying people, making them more suggestible, 'open,' liberal in their attitudes and more unconscious of themselves. See the recent study conducted by University of Toronto Researchers, "February 22nd 2013, Moments of spirituality can induce liberal attitudes, U of T researchers say." http://www.artsci.utoronto.ca/main/newsitems/spirituality-induce-liberal-attitudes?utm_so accessed April 2013.

[53] R. J. Rushdoony, *The Messianic Character of American Education* (Vallecito, CA: Ross House, reprint 1995), 168–169.

[54] Rushdoony, *Messianic Character*, 169.

[55] Molnar, *Utopia*, 226.

[56] Molnar, *Utopia*, 227.

[57] See Molnar, *Utopia*, 232.

CHAPTER SIX

[1] R. Bowen, *So I Send You: A Study Guide to Mission* (London: SPCK, 1996), 60–62.

[2] W. Klaiber, *Call and Response: Biblical Foundations of a Theology of Evangelism* (Nashville: Abingdon Press, 1997), 48.

[3] W.J. Abraham, *The Logic of Evangelism* (Grand Rapids: Eerdmans, 1989), 39.

[4] R. J. Rushdoony, *Leviticus: Commentaries on the Pentateuch* (Vallecito: Ross House, 2005), 1–2.

[5] D.J. Bosch, *Transforming Mission: Paradigm Shifts in Theology of Mission* (Maryknoll: Orbis Books, 1991), 48.

[6] Verkuyl, *Contemporary Missiology*, 211.

[7] Rushdoony, *Leviticus*, 224–225.

[8] J.A. Kirk, *What is Mission? Theological Explorations* (Minneapolis: Fortress Press, 2000), 217.

[9] Bosch, *Transforming Mission*, 418.

[10] Kirk, *What is Mission*, 33-34.

[11] This is one of the reasons why the so-called 'emergent church' is often hostile to the institution, structures and authority of the church and its history. Christianity (by which they mean the visible institution of the church) is 'religion' which they suggest 'Jesus' is

against. Some emergent church pastors and thinkers are so 'low-church,' their forms of worship and institutional structures so loose, they conform to know historical definition of the life of the church. This is typically done in the name of 'contextualization,' 'inculturation' or 'incarnation.'

[12] Kirk, *What is Mission*, 35 (emphasis added).

[13] Bosch, *Transforming Mission*, 377.

[14] Most missiologists use the term 'social justice' which does not have a Christian but a Marxist origin. I therefore use the term public justice to refer to the vision of justice conveyed in Scripture.

[15] J. Stott, *New Issues Facing Christians Today*, 3rd ed. (London: Marshall Pickering, 1999), 28.

[16] Stott, *New Issues*, 8

[17] Stott, *New Issues*, 8-11.

[18] Stott, *New Issues*, 9.

[19] Stott, *New Issues*, 12.

[20] Stott, *New Issues*, 12.

[21] Stott, *New Issues*, 13.

[22] Bosch, *Transforming Mission*, 412.

[23] See Ryken, *Worldly Saints*, 173–186.

[24] Davies, 'Rough Justice?', 54.

[25] Greg L. Bahnsen, *Theonomy in Christian Ethics*, 3rd ed. (Nacogdoches: Covenant Media Press, 2002),

[26] R.J. Rushdoony, *The Foundations of Social Order*, 182.

[27] Righteousness/Justice (*tsedeq*), rightness, righteousness what is right or just or normal, rightness, justness (of weights and measures) righteousness (in government) of judges, rulers, kings of law of Davidic king, Messiah of Jerusalem as seat of just government of God's attribute righteousness, justice (in case or cause) rightness (in speech) righteousness (as ethically right) righteousness (as vindicated), justification (in controversy), deliverance, victory, prosperity of God as covenant-keeping in redemption in name of Messianic king: Old Testament Hebrew Lexicon - King James Version.

[28] R.H. Nash, *Social Justice and the Christian Church* (Lima, OH: Academic Renewal Press, 2002), 30–31.

[29] Nash, *Social Justice*, 31.

[30] Nash, *Social Justice*, 70.

[31] Ryken, *Worldly Saints*, 185.

[32] Bosch, *Transforming Mission*, 35–36.

[33] Bosch, *Transforming Mission*, 35.

[34] Bosch, *Transforming Mission*, 36.

[35] Bosch, *Transforming Mission*, 36.

[36] Walter Brueggemann, *The Covenanted Self: Explorations in Law and Covenant* (Minneapolis: Fortress Press, 1999), 48-58.

[37] Brueggemann, *Covenanted Self*, 49.

[38] Brueggemann, *Covenanted Self*, 49.

[39] Brueggemann, *Covenanted Self*, 49.

[40] Brueggemann, *Covenanted Self*, 49.

[41] Brueggemann, *Covenanted Self*, 50.

[42] Brueggemann, *Covenanted Self*, 50.

[43] Brueggemann, *Covenanted Self*, 51.

[44] Brueggemann, *Covenanted Self*, 50–51.

[45] Brueggemann, *Covenanted Self*, 51 (emphasis added).

[46] Brueggemann, *Covenanted Self*, 49.

[47] Brueggemann, *Covenanted Self*, 57.

[48] Brueggemann, *Covenanted Self*, 57.

[49] Brueggemann, *Covenanted Self*, 57.

[50] Timothy Keller's statist orientation and big-government socialistic bent was revealed much earlier than Generous Justice, in an essay published in 1990, "Theonomy and the poor: Some reflections," in William S. Barker and W. Robert Godfrey (eds.) *Theonomy: A Reformed Critique* (Grand Rapids: Zondervan, 1990) Keller's essay contains a series of serious misrepresentations of the theonomic outlook. This essay was effectively critiqued by Ray Sutton in, "Whose Conditions for Charity," Gary North ed. *Theonomy: An Informed Response* (Tyler, TX: Institute for Christian Economics, 1991), 231–254.

[51] Timothy Keller, *Generous Justice: How God's Grace Makes Us Just* (New York: Dutton, 2010), 2.

[52] Keller, *Generous Justice*, 177.

[53] Keller, *Generous Justice*, 24.

[54] Keller, *Generous Justice*, 21–22.

[55] Keller, *Generous Justice*, 22.

[56] Keller, *Generous Justice*, 22.

[57] Keller, *Generous Justice*, 23.

[58] Keller, *Generous Justice*, 26–28.

[59] Keller, *Generous Justice*, 27–28. (I deal with the subject of jubilee in detail in chapter seven.)

[60] Sutton, "Whose Conditions for Charity?," 239.

[61] Keller, *Generous Justice*, 29.

[62] This implies that anyone who doesn't pursue a vision for wealth redistribution ('social justice') and sacrificial living by subsisting on minimum requirements in order to give more money to the poor is both unjust and uninterested in justice.

[63] Keller, *Generous Justice*, 32.

[64] Keller, *Generous Justice*, 32.

[65] Keller, *Generous Justice*, 29.

[66] Keller, *Generous Justice*, 85–88.

[67] Keller, *Generous Justice*, 57.

[68] Keller, Generous Justice, 6.

[69] Peggy Campolo, 'Just Family Values: How Can Christians Advocate Justice for Non-traditional Families,' *The Justice Project,* edited by Brian McLaren, Elisa Padilla, And Ashley Bunting Seeber (Grand Rapids: Baker Books, 2009), 133–134, emphasis added. [For the uninitiated, GLBT stands for Gay, Lesbian, Bisexual, Transgendered]

[70] Homosexuality (sodomy) and lesbianism is everywhere unequivocally condemned in Scripture: 1 Cor. 6:9; 1 Tim. 1:10; Rom 1: 26–27, 32; Jude v 7; Gen 19: 5–7; Lev 18: 22; 20:13; Judges 19: 22–23.

[71] John Sandys-Wunsch, "Human Rights either Biblical or Useful," in Matthew J. M. Coomber ed. *Bible and Justice: Ancient Texts, Modern Challenges* (Milton Keynes: Equinox, 2011), 66–67.

[72] Wunsch, "Human Rights," 63.

[73] Wunsch, "Human Rights," 68.

[74] Wunsch, "Human Rights," 67.

[75] Sutton, "Whose Conditions for Charity," 254.

[76] Keller, *Generous Justice*, 155.

[77] I discuss the issue of Christian apologetics in detail in chapter thirteen.

[78] Keller, *Generous Justice*, 158.

[79] Keller, *Generous Justice*, 160.

[80] Keller, *Generous Justice*, 160.

[81] It seems to me that the other possibility is that as a student during the sexual and social revolution, like many of the boomers in the emergent church movement, Keller himself has simply not self-consciously cut himself loose from some of the cultural baggage that he has acquired in liberal America.

[82] Keller, *Generous Justice*, 189.

[83] Diane B. Obenchain, 'The Study of Religion and the Coming Global Generation, in Max L. Stackhouse, Diane B. Obenchain (eds.) *God and Globalisation, vol. 3: Christ And The Dominions of Civilization* (Harrisburg: Trinity Press International, 2002), 94.

[84] Keller, *Generous Justice*, 163.

[85] Keller, *Generous Justice*, 164.

[86] Verkuyl, *Contemporary Missiology*, 195–196, emphasis added.

[87] Rushdoony, *Foundations*, 62.

[88] One good example would be Doug Paggit in, 'This Is Just the Beginning: Living Our Great-Grandchildren's History,' Doug Paggit and Tony Jones ed. An Emergent Manifesto of Hope (Grand Rapids: Baker Books, 2007), 304.

NOTES

[89] Dave Diewert, "Living Justly," *Mosaic* (Fall, 2009), 5–6, emphasis added.

[90] Rushdoony, *Institutes*, 456–457.

[91] Diewert, "Living Justly," 7.

[92] Rushdoony, *Foundations*, 62.

[93] David Chilton, *Productive Christians in An Age of Guilt Manipulators: A Biblical Response to Ronald Sider* (Tyler, Texas: Institute For Christian Economics, 1981) 29.

[94] Rushdoony, *Institutes*, 155.

[95] Rushdoony, *Institutes*, 55–58.

[96] Rushdoony, *Institutes*, 54.

[97] Rousas John Rushdoony, *The Institutes of Biblical Law Vol. 2: Law and Society* (Vallecito, CA: Ross House, 1982), pp. 272–273.

[98] George Grant, *Bringing in the Sheaves: Replacing Government Welfare with Biblical Charity* (Windsor, New York: The Reformer Library, 1995), 50

[99] R.J. Rushdoony, *Law and Liberty* (Vallecito, CA, Ross House, 1984), 91

[100] Saint Augustine, *The City of God*, translated by Marcus Dods (New York, The Modern Library, 1993), 112.

[101] Bahnsen, *Theonomy*, 7.

[102] Nash, *Social Justice*, 155.

[103] Many of these contemporary reinterpretations of Marx stem from the thought of Herbert Marcuse, an unsparing critic of industrialized countries, especially the United States.

[104] The Marxist term for the class of citizens between the gentry and the laborers, usually referred to as the 'middle class.'

[105] Bosch, *Transforming Mission*, 440.

[106] Kirk, *What is Mission?*, 15.

[107] Kirk, *What is Mission?*, 107.

[108] R.H. Nash, *Why the Left is not Right*, 47–48.

[109] D. Breese, *7 Men who Rule the World from the Grave* (Chicago: Moody Press, 1990), 85-86.

[110] Harry Antonides, *Stones For Bread: The Social Gospel and its Contemporary Legacy* (Ontario: Paideia Press, 1985), 161–187.

[111] Jean Paul Sartre, cited in Antonides, *Stones For Bread*, 173.

[112] Chilton, *Productive Christians in an Age of Guilt-Manipulators*, 69–70.

[113] Chilton, *Productive Christians*, 71–72, 76.

[114] W. Brueggemann, 'Hope from Old Sources for a New Century', in W. Brueggemann (ed), *Hope for the World: Mission in a Global Context* (Louisville: Westminster John Knox Press, 2001), 16.

[115] Pascal Bruckner, 'Dazed and Apocalyptic: Why today's secular elites are prophesying a doomsday without redemption' *National Post*, Tuesday May 22, 2012.

[116] Lois Ann Lorentzen & Salvador Leavitt – Alcantara, 'Religion and Environmental Struggles in Latin America,' , Roger S. Gottlieb ed. The *Oxford Handbook of Religion and Ecology* (New York: Oxford University Press, 2006), 517.

[117] Lorentzen & Leavitt-Alcantara, 'Religion and Environmental Struggles,' 518–519.

[118] Lorentzen & Leavitt-Alcantara, 'Religion and Environmental Struggles,' 519.

[119] Lorentzen & Leavitt-Alcantara, 'Religion and Environmental Struggles,' 519.

[120] R.J. Rushdoony, *Politics of Guilt and Pity*, (Vallecito, CA: Ross House, reprint, 1995), 9.

[121] Walter Brueggemann's *Hope for the World*, offers a significant window into this trend, with eight different contributors from the Campbell Seminar on global mission echoing much the same thought.

[122] For evidence of these facts see the works of former emeritus professor of economics at the London School of Economics, P. T. Bauer, including: *Equality, The Third World and Economic Delusion; Dissent on Development; Reality or Rhetoric; and Western Guilt.*

[123] Antonides, *Stones for Bread*, 185.

[124] W.T. Cavanaugh, "Beyond Secular Parodies" J. Milbank, C. Pickstock and G. Ward eds., *Radical Orthodoxy* (London and New York: Routledge, reprint, 2003), p. 185. [Whilst I do not share Cavanaugh's socialistic tendencies I think his analysis of Statism and the progressive marginalisation of the church and its role is extremely valuable.]

[125] Soteriology, from the Greek term for salvation, concerns doctrines of salvation.

[126] Cavanaugh, "Beyond Secular Parodies," 191–192.

[127] Cavanaugh, "Beyond Secular Parodies," 198.

[128] G.H. Sabine, *A History of Political Theory* (New York: Holt, Rinehart and Winston, third edition, 1961), 191.

[129] Sabine, *A History*, 192.

[130] Sabine, *A History*, 192.

[131] R. Dodaro, *Christ and the Just Society in the Thought of Augustine* (Cambridge: Cambridge University Press, 2004), 111.

CHAPTER SEVEN

[1] Sarah Dylan Breuer, "God's Justice: A Biblical View," in Brian McLaren, Elisa Padilla, Ashley Bunting Seeber, eds. *The Justice Project* (Grand Rapids: Baker Books, 2009), 36.

[2] David R. Como, "Radical Puritanism," in John Coffey and Paul C. H. Lim, eds. *Puritanism* (Cambridge: Cambridge University Press, 2008), 253–255.

[3] Ryken, *Worldly Saints*, 180–181.

[4] Marcello Pera, *Why We Should Call Ourselves Christians*, 69.

[5] See Walter Brueggemann, *The Covenanted Self*, 50–51.

[6] Brian J. Walsh, taken from transcript of "From Shock and Awe to Shock and Grace: A Response to Naomi Klein's 'The Shock Doctrine 1,'" Presentation for "Empire

Remixed," University of Toronto, 26 November 2007.

[7] Walsh, "Shock and Awe."

[8] Walsh, "Shock and Awe."

[9] Walsh, "Shock and Awe."

[10] A. M. Macdonald, ed. *Chambers' Twentieth Century Dictionary: New Edition* (Edinburgh: W & R Chambers, 1972), p. 635.

[11] For his most detailed discussion of Jubilee, see Rousas John Rushdoony, *Leviticus*, 347–394.

[12] Rushdoony, *Institutes*, 140.

[13] Rushdoony, *Institutes*, 140.

[14] Rushdoony, *Institutes*, 141.

[15] Rushdoony, *Institutes*, 141.

[16] Rushdoony, *Institutes*, 141.

[17] Rushdoony, *Institutes*, 140–141.

[18] Cited in Burnside, *God, Justice and Society*, 204.

[19] Burnside, *God, Justice and Society*, 205.

[20] R. J. Rushdoony, *Chariots of Prophetic Fire: Studies in Elijah and Elisha* (Vallecito: Ross House, 2003), 5455.

[21] The new covenant clearly alters the significance of Jubilee laws concerning inherited property that applied to Hebrew families in the Promised Land. Since the new Israel of God is the church throughout the world, our inheritance is the whole earth (lit. Cosmos, see Rom 4:13) not just one parcel of land in the Middle East. The meaning of Jubilee is thus transposed in its significance pointing to its fulfilment in the gospel of the Kingdom.

[22] Gary North, 'Hermeneutics and Leviticus 19:19 – Passing Dr. Poythress' Test,' in Gary North ed. *Theonomy: An Informed Response* (Tyler: Institute for Christian Economics, 1991), 290.

[23] Rushdoony, *Leviticus*, 366.

[24] R.J. Rushdoony, 'Bringing back the King,' *The Crown Rights of Christ the King: The Dominion Collection*, audio lecture 6 (Chalcedon Foundation, 2006).

[25] Rushdoony, *Leviticus*, 361.

[26] Rushdoony, "Bringing back the King."

[27] R.J. Rushdoony, *Sovereignty* (Vallecito: Ross House, 2007), 272. Emphasis added.

[28] Walsh, "Shock and Awe." Emphasis added.

[29] Cited in D.A. Carson, *Becoming Conversant with the Emerging Church: Understanding a Movement and its Implications* (Grand Rapids: Zondervan, 2005), 166.

[30] Cited in Carson, *Becoming Conversant*, 183–186.

[31] Rushdoony, *Sovereignty*, 273–274.

[32] Walsh, "Shock and Awe."

[33] Rushdoony, *Sovereignty*, 273.

[34] Rushdoony, *Sovereignty*, 274–275.

[35] Rushdoony, "Bringing back the King."

[36] Frame, *The Doctrine*, 818.

[37] Rushdoony, *Institutes*, 142–145.

[38] Rushdoony, *Institutes*, 145.

CHAPTER EIGHT

[1] See Burnside, *God, Justice and Society*, xxv-xxvi.

[2] Frederick Pollock, cited in Burnside, *God, Justice and Society*, xxvi.

[3] *The Music with the Form and Order of the Service to be Performed at the Coronation of Her Most Excellent Majesty Queen Elizabeth II in the Abbey Church of Westminster on Tuesday the 2nd Day of June, 1953* (London: Novello and Company, 1953) 14.

[4] *The Music*, 15.

[5] *The Music*, 67.

[6] Burnside, *God, Justice and Society*, xxv.

[7] Burnside, *God, Justice and Society*, xxv.

[8] Burnside, *God, Justice and Society*, xl.

[9] Burnside, *God, Justice and Society*, xxvi–xxix.

[10] Burnside, *God, Justice and Society*, xxxvi.

[11] Burnside, *God, Justice and Society*, xxxviii.

[12] Rushdoony, *Institutes* vol. 1, 242.

[13] Burnside, *God, Justice and Society*, xxxii.

[14] John Warwick Montgomery, *Law and Gospel: A Study Integrating Faith and Practice* (Edmonton: Christian Legal Fellowship, 1994), 9.

[15] Wright, *The Mission of God*, 379.

[16] Wright, *The Mission of God*, 380.

[17] Jonathan Burnside's study, God, Justice and Society: Aspects of Law and Legality in the Bible, is a brilliant excursus for lawyers and legal students seeking to mine the insights of biblical law to address and interact with contemporary legal issues, challenges and problems.

[18] Gary North, "R.J. Rushdoony: R.I.P.," in *Chalcedon Report: In Memoriam*, 429, April 2001, 20.

[19] For Rushdoony, the term 'law' is used in a number of different ways. First, it can refer to the whole of God's word. Second, it can refer to the Old Testament as a whole, since the prophets were calling the nations (i.e. the book of Amos) to obedience to God's law given to Moses, and the wisdom literature contains celebrations of the law (e.g. Ps: 1; Ps: 119) and practical applications of the law in the book of Proverbs. Third, it can refer to the Books of Moses (the Torah) in their totality. Fourth it can refer narrowly to the Decalogue and case law (illustrations

of how the Ten Commandments were applied). Rushdoony saw the law as a unity, and did not favour the somewhat artificial distinctions of moral, civil and ceremonial. Rather, the ceremonial (or restorative) aspects of law were transposed by the New Testament to the priestly intercession of Christ in heaven (the book of Hebrews makes this clear) and civil law is simply an aspect of moral law. For example, God's laws against homosexuality and bestiality are 'moral laws' even though they do not appear in the Ten Commandments. Furthermore, wherever the New Testament appears to speak in negative terms about the law, it does so only, 1) Concerning a wrong use of the law (i.e. an attempt to be justified by it). 2) In declaring our freedom from the curse of the law. 3) In revealing the glorious fullness of ceremonial types in the law that have been fulfilled in Christ.

[20] Edgar, "The Passing of R. J. Rushdoony."

[21] North, "R.J Rushdoony: R.I.P," 21.

[22] Rushdoony, *Institutes*, 271.

[23] Rushdoony, *Sovereignty*, 200.

[24] John Calvin, *Institutes of the Christian Religion*, Henry Beveridge, trans. (Grand Rapids: Eerdmans, 1989) Book IV, Chapter 3, 318.

[25] Lucien Joseph Richard, *The Spirituality of John Calvin* (Atlanta: GA, 1974), 177.

[26] See R. J. Rushdoony, *The Sermon on the Mount* (Vallecito, CA: Ross House, 2009).

[27] See chapter 13 on apologetics.

[28] Rousas John Rushdoony, *Deuteronomy: Commentaries on the Pentateuch* (Vallecito, C.A: Ross House, 2008), 403.

[29] D. J. O'Connor, *Aquinas and Natural Law: New Studies in Ethics* (Suffolk: Macmillan, 1967), 15.

[30] O'Connor, *Aquinas*, 20.

[31] Ray R. Sutton, *That You May Prosper* (Tyler, TX: Institute for Christian Economics, 1987), 182.

[32] Epictetus, *Discourses, I*, ix (trans. P.E. Matheson), cited in Sutton, *That You May Prosper*, 182.

[33] Sutton, *That You May Prosper*, 183.

[34] Sutton, *That You May Prosper*, 192.

[35] Richard Flinn, "Rutherford and Puritan Political Theory," in *The Journal of Christian Reconstruction: Symposium on Puritanism and Law 5*, no. 2 (1978), 55.

[36] Flinn, "Rutherford and Puritan Political Theory," 55.

[37] Flinn, "Rutherford and Puritan Political Theory," 58.

[38] O'Connor, *Aquinas*, 83

[39] O'Connor, *Aquinas*, 84

[40] Rushdoony, *Intellectual Schizophrenia*, 55.

[41] Rushdoony, *Intellectual Schizophrenia*, 56.

[42] P. Andrew Sandlin, "R.J. Rushdoony: Champion of Faith and Liberty," in *Chalcedon Report: In Memoriam*, 429 (April 2001), 11.

[43] Mark Rushdoony, "A biographical sketch of my father," in P. Andrew Sandlin, ed., *A comprehensive faith: An international festschrift for Rousas John Rushdoony* (San Jose: Friends of Chalcedon, 1996), 29.

[44] An interesting publication appeared in 1998 by the Chalcedon Foundation, highly critical of the conservative American Right, *The Future of the Conservative Movement: A Chalcedon Symposium*, P. Andrew Sandlin, ed. (Vallecito, CA: Chalcedon Foundation, 1998).

[45] Rushdoony, *Foundations*, 185.

[46] Rushdoony, *Foundations*, 186.

[47] R.J. Rushdoony, "The Meaning of Theocracy: Chalcedon Position paper No. 15," in *The Roots of Reconstruction* (Vallecito, CA: Ross House, 1991), 63.

[48] Rushdoony, *Institutes*, 504.

[49] R. J. Rushdoony, 'Death and Restitution' (Chalcedon MP3 Archives, RR10777), www.chalcedon.edu, accessed November 2009.

[50] Rushdoony, *Roots of Reconstruction*, 24–28.

[51] Rushdoony, *Roots of Reconstruction*, 28.

[52] Rushdoony, *Institutes*, 100.

[53] Rushdoony, "Death and Restitution."

[54] Rushdoony, *Institutes*, 2.

[55] Rushdoony, *Institutes*, 3.

[56] Rushdoony, "Death and Restitution."

[57] See Howard Phillips, 'The Renewal of Christendom is R.J. Rushdoony's legacy,' *Chalcedon Report: In Memoriam*, 429 (April 2001), 29.

[58] Mark Rushdoony, "Interview with Joe Boot." It is noteworthy that 'theocracy' is technically compatible with various forms of government (i.e. monarchy or democratic republic) so long as kings, councils and parliaments subordinate themselves to the Word of God. Calvin's Geneva, Bucer's Strasbourg, Zwingli's Zurich, Knox's Scotland, Cromwell's England and Puritan New England, are all notable examples of essentially theocratic rule.

[59] R. J. Rushdoony, "Interview with Bill Moyer," God and Politics: On earth as it is in heaven, (PBS documentary: produced by Bill Moyer, 1992).

[60] Rousas John Rushdoony, *Exodus: Commentary on the Pentateuch* (Vallecito, CA: Ross House, 2004), 140.

[61] One such panic-stricken volume is Michelle Goldberg's poorly researched and journalistic, *Kingdom Coming: The Rise of Christian Nationalism* (New York: W.W. Norton, 2006).

[62] Andrew C. McCarthy, "Islamophobic Hysteria Becomes Conventional Wisdom," *PJ*

Media, last modified August 23, 2012, http://pjmedia.com/andrewmccarthy/2012/08/23/islamophobic-hysteria-becomes-conventional-wisdom/.

[63] Karen Armstrong, *The battle for God: Fundamentalism in Judaism, Christianity and Islam* (St Ives: Harper Collins, 2000), 361. Emphasis added.

[64] Armstrong, *The battle for God*, 361.

[65] R.J. Rushdoony, *In his service: The Christian calling to charity* (Vallecito CA: Ross House, 2009), 100.

[66] R.J. Rushdoony, "Christian reconstruction as a movement," 19.

[67] Rushdoony, *Christianity and the state*, 2.

[68] Terrill Irwin Elniff, *The guise of every graceless heart: Human autonomy in Puritan thought and experience* (Vallecito, CA: Ross House, 1981), 45.

[69] Rushdoony, *Sovereignty*, 31.

[70] Rushdoony, *Institutes*, 54–58.

[71] Rushdoony, *Sovereignty*, 34.

[72] See Ernest Marshall Howse, *Saints in politics: The Clapham Sect and the growth of freedom* (Trowbridge: George Allen and Unwin, 1953).

[73] Cited in Vincent E. Bacote, *The Spirit in public theology: Appropriating the legacy of Abraham Kuyper* (Grand Rapids: Baker Academic, 2005), 74.

[74] For Rushdoony, the state's role is limited to the administration of justice – courts of law, policing and the military. A small bureaucracy for the collection and administration of the poll or head tax and emergency services at the local level would also be envisioned. Beyond this, for Rushdoony, all other areas would be free of state interference.

[75] Rousas John Rushdoony, *Christianity and the state*, 3.

[76] Rushdoony, "Christianity and freedom," in *The Journal of Christian Reconstruction: Symposium on the Decline and Fall of the West and the Return of Christendom*, 13 (1994), 75.

[77] Rushdoony, "Christianity and freedom"' 76, 78–79.

[78] Armstrong, *The battle for God*, 362.

[79] Rushdoony, "Christianity and freedom," 81.

[80] Rushdoony, *Roots of reconstruction*, 147.

[81] Rushdoony, *Roots of reconstruction*, 148.

[82] Isaac Backus, cited in Rushdoony, *Roots of Reconstruction*, 149.

[83] Ray R. Sutton, *That You May Prosper*, 177.

[84] Sutton, *That You May Prosper*, 177.

[85] Sutton, *That You May Prosper*, 178.

[86] Pera, *Why We Should Call Ourselves Christians*, 5.

[87] Pera, *Why We Should Call Ourselves Christians*, 48–49.

[88] Pera, *Why We Should Call Ourselves Christians*, 106.

[89] Rushdoony, *Institutes* vol 1, 484–486.

[90] Rushdoony, *Leviticus*, 366.

[91] Rushdoony, *Sovereignty*, 19.

[92] For a useful discussion of these historic developments see *Encyclopaedia Britannica* Vol. 20 (London: William Benton Publishers, 1968), 633–641.

[93] Rushdoony, *Leviticus*, 382.

[94] Joseph Parker, cited in Rushdoony, *Leviticus*, 382.

[95] Rushdoony, *Politics*, 360.

[96] Elniff, *The guise of every graceless heart*, 45

[97] R. C. Sproul, *Essential Truths of the Christian Faith* (Wheaton, IL: Tyndale House, 1992), 17.

[98] Edward Crankshaw: *Gestapo: Instrument of Tyranny* (Ebbw Vale, Wales: Wren's Park Publishing, 2002), 18.

[99] Crankshaw, *Gestapo*, 70–71.

[100] Crankshaw, *Gestapo*, 72.

[101] Crankshaw, *Gestapo*, 228.

[102] Crankshaw, *Gestapo*, 228.

[103] Crankshaw, *Gestapo*, 230–231.

[104] Crankshaw, *Gestapo*. 231.

[105] Crankshaw, *Gestapo*, 246.

[106] Crankshaw, *Gestapo*, 246–247.

[107] Crankshaw, *Gestapo*, 73.

[108] See Amos 1–6.

[109] Rushdoony, *Institutes* vol. 1, 3.

[110] David Chilton, *Productive Christians*, 30.

[111] Rushdoony, Institutes vol. 1, 3–4.

[112] Rushdoony, *Systematic theology* vol. 1, 360.

[113] Rushdoony, *Salvation and Godly rule*, 409.

[114] Rushdoony, *Salvation and Godly rule*, 410.

[115] Rushdoony, *Salvation and Godly rule*, 410.

[116] Rushdoony, *Systematic theology*, vol. 1, 307, 324.

[117] Rushdoony, *Institutes* vol. 1, 4.

[118] David Chilton, *Paradise Restored* (Ft Worth, TX: Dominion Press, 1985), 219.

CHAPTER NINE

[1] James McMullen, cited in Michael Wagner, *Leaving God behind: The Charter of Rights and Canada's official rejection of Christianity* (Russell, ON: Christian Governance, 2012), 25.

[2] William Ross, cited in Wagner, *Leaving God behind*, 26.

[3] Paul Laverdure, cited in Wagner, *Leaving God behind*, 27.

[4] John Moir, cited in Wagner, *Leaving God behind*, 5–6.

[5] Tom Warner, cited in Wagner, *Leaving God behind*, 7. Emphasis added.

[6] Rex Ahdar and Ian Leigh, cited in Wagner, *Leaving God behind*, 12.

[7] Ahdar and Leigh, cited in Wagner, *Leaving God behind*, 12.

[8] For a full and detailed analysis of Canada's steady abandonment of its Christian heritage and biblical law order see Michael Wagner's important study, *Leaving God behind* (2012).

[9] Dietrich Bonhoeffer, *The cost of discipleship* (New York: Touchstone Books, 1995), 43.

[10] Bonhoeffer, *The cost of discipleship*, 43.

[11] Bonhoeffer, *The cost of discipleship*, 43.

[12] Bonhoeffer, *The cost of discipleship*, 44–45.

[13] Bonoeffer, *The cost of discipleship*, 121.

[14] Bonhoeffer, *The cost of discipleship*, 121.

[15] Bonhoeffer, *The cost of discipleship*, 121–124.

[16] St. Augustine, *Augustine's Commentary on Galatians*, ed. and trans. Eric Plumer (Oxford: Oxford University Press, 2003), 227.

[17] Canadian Centre for Justice Statistics, Justice Data Factfinder 1996, Juristat 16 no. 9 (1996), https://www.ncjrs.gov/App/publications/Abstract.aspx?id=163072. The police report about 2.6 million criminal incidents annually and violent crime steadily increased between 1962 and 1992. Young people are most overrepresented in incidents involving property crimes. Although young people are less likely to be charged with violent crimes than property crimes, they are still overrepresented among persons charged with violent crimes. Data suggest that adults and young people appearing in court are convicted of Criminal Code and drug crimes in equal proportions. All components of Canada's correctional system have experienced caseload increases in recent years, with average daily inmate counts rising for both adult and young offenders. Costs of operating Canada's criminal justice system are estimated at $9.6 billion yearly, or $331 per capita. The largest share of the criminal justice dollar is spent on policing (60%), followed by adult correctional services (20%). Youth corrections cost $488 million yearly, or $17 per capita [note: in developed countries the cost of fighting crime has risen to an average of 5% of GDP].

[18] "The 10 most dangerous cities in the world," Urban Titan, last modified September 2012, http://urbantitan.com/10-most-dangerouscities-in-the-world-in-2010/.

[19] See Irving A. Agus, *Urban civilization in pre-Crusade Europe*, 2 vols. (New York, Yeshiva University Press, 1966).

[20] Cels. IV.31; *Origen: Contra Celsum*, trans. Henry Chadwick (Cambridge: Cambridge University Press, 1953), 207, 297-298.

[21] Denise Lavoie, "Freed from his body: U.S. judge orders prison officials to pay for inmate's sex change surgery," *National Post*, Wednesday, September 5, 2012.

[22] Cited in J. John, "A matter of justice," *Philo Trust*, September 12, 2012, http://www. philotrust.com/blog/2012/09/a-matter-of-justice#.
UiYaTD_hdbA.

[23] Megan O' Toole, "Police need witnesses to nab gang," *National Post*, Wednesday, September 12, 2012.

[24] For a variety of reactions and responses to the theonomic vision see Bahnsen, Kaiser, Moo, Strickland, VanGemeren, *Five views on law and gospel*, ed. Stanley N. Grundy (Grand Rapids: Zondervan, 1993).

[25] Armstrong, *The battle for God*, 361.

[26] In late seventeenth and early eighteenth-century England, after the death of Cromwell, who had sought to steadily reduce the amount of capital crimes to the biblical categories, there was a massive proliferation of capital offenses added to the statue books under and following Charles II (after the restoration), in which over 200 crimes soon carried the death penalty – mostly for offenses against property. Cromwell had appealed to biblical law to reform an unjust criminal code during his years as Lord Protector. Today in Canada there are no capital offenses! The last were abolished in 1998 when the death penalty was abolished for mutiny and treason. This has meant the abandonment of Canada's historic moorings in God's law. For example, forgotten by many today, until 1954, rape (a capital offense in the Bible) was still punishable by death in Canada.

[27] Peter Martyr Vermigli, "Of a magistrate, and the difference between civil and ecclesiastical power (1561)," in W. J. T. Kirby ed., *The Zürich connection and Tudor political theology* (Leiden and Boston, 2007), 116–17.

[28] Martin Bucer, cited in Foulner, *Theonomy and the Westminster Confession*, 49.

[29] Bucer, cited in Foulner, *Theonomy*, 50.

[30] John Calvin, cited in Foulner, *Theonomy*, 51. Emphasis added.

[31] Calvin, cited in Foulner, *Theonomy*, 51.

[32] Berman, *Law and revolution*, vol. II, 136.

[33] Berman, *Law and revolution*, vol. II, 137–138.

[34] Berman, *Law and revolution*, vol. II, 138.

[35] Berman, *Law and revolution*, vol. II, 140–141.

[36] Terrill Irwin Elniff, *The guise of every graceless heart: Human autonomy in Puritan thought and experience*, (Vallecito, CA: Ross House, 1981), 38–39.

[37] "The Book of the Laws and Liberties Concerning the Inhabitants of the Massachusetts," *The Puritan Tradition in America 1620–1730*, ed. Alden T. Vaughan (Columbia, S.C: University of South Carolina Press, 1972), 163.

[38] See, Foulner, *Theonomy*, 31–32.

[39] Foulner, *Theonomy*, 31.

[40] James Durham, cited in Foulner, *Theonomy*, 32.

[41] With regard to the notion that Jesus repealed the justice of the possibility of a death

penalty for adultery in John 8, I would refer readers to Greg Bahnsen's work, *Theonomy in Christian ethics* (Nacogdoches, TX: Covenant Media Press, 2002), especially pages 288–320.

[42] Thomas Hooker, cited in Elniff, *The Guise*, 42.

[43] Joel R. Beeke & Mark Jones, *A Puritan theology: Doctrine for life* (Grand Rapids: Reformation Heritage Books, 2012), 563.

[44] Charles Haddon Spurgeon, cited in Lewis Drummond, *Spurgeon: prince of preachers: A new look at the 19th century's greatest preacher* (Grand Rapids: Kregel, 1992), 517–518.

[45] Spurgeon, cited in Drummond, *Spurgeon*, 518.

[46] Spurgeon, cited in Drummond, *Spurgeon*, 518.

[47] Drummond, *Spurgeon*, 518–519.

[48] Spurgeon, cited in Drummond, *Spurgeon*, 519.

[49] Drummond, Spurgeon, 520. During the early part of Spurgeon's career in England the death penalty was still common. But after 1861 capital punishment was only retained for four crimes, murder, piracy, arson in the Royal Dockyards and high treason – notice three are offenses against the state and only one retained for offenses against persons. These changes mark the progressive shift from a familial culture to a statist one.

[50] For a detailed analysis of the present day jihad taking place in the West see: Sam Solomon and E Al Maqdisi, *Modern day Trojan horse: The Islamic doctrine of immigration, accepting freedom or imposing Islam* (Charlottesville, VA: ANM, 2009).

[51] Samuel Rutherford, cited in Foulner, *Theonomy*, 15.

[52] John Frame, *Cornelius Van Til: An analysis of his thought* (New Jersey: Presbyterian & Reformed Publishing, 1995), 392.

[53] See, Beeke & Jones, *Puritan theology*, 779-781.

[54] R. J. Rushdoony, *Leviticus*, 255.

[55] Rushdoony, *Deuteronomy: Commentaries on the Pentateuch*, 291.

[56] Gustave Friedrich Oehler, cited in Rushdoony, *Leviticus*, 280.

[57] V. S. Poythress, cited in Alec Motyer, *Roots: Let the Old Testament speak* (Glasgow: Christian Focus, 2009), 26.

[58] See, Norman L. Geisler, Christian Ethics: Contemporary Issues and Options (Grand Rapids: Baker Academic, 2010), 213–214. Geisler's critique at this point is quite simply astonishing for an ostensible evangelical. He rejects the Reformed Puritan thesis on the alleged ground that 1) It didn't work, in that he thinks it was tried and failed; 2) He thinks it is a violation of the First Amendment of the U.S. Constitution; and 3) Because such a view is bigotry and presumption since we live in a pluralistic world. In rejecting the Puritan claim for the sociopolitical authority of Christian revelation he writes, "Lest Christians be tempted to say 'a Christian revelation,' we need only be reminded that there is a Muslim revelation too. In a pluralistic world, no-one's religious revelation is

going to be accepted by all others as the basis for government. The Bible (plus other religious books) can certainly be informative yet not normative for government. It can be a source without being used as a divinely authoritative source." Here Geisler denies the absolute sovereignty of God and presumes that religious polytheism (philosophical pluralism) can provide a stable and normative basis for civil law and government; he contends that Islam offers a credible competing claim to revelation and asserts that neutral human reason, utilizing various religious books and resources in a humanistic secular structure, can provide better justice and government than using the Bible as the divinely authoritative source. Here, in Geisler's thinking, man's autonomous reasoning (his religious humanism) provides a substitute for God's law and government. Somehow this new law of man (from a variety of sources) is going to be apparently acceptable to all in a manner that God's law is not. Geisler is simply not self-conscious enough to see that modern secularism views man's mind and experience as 'normative' and superior to Christian revelation, and that such claims are religious by definition. For Geisler, man's law is more normative than God's.

[59] Motyer, *Roots*, 27.

[60] E. C. Wines, *Commentaries on the laws of the ancient Hebrews*, (Georgia: American Vision Press, 2009), 272.

[61] Rushdoony, *Deuteronomy*, 291.

[62] Schreiner, *New Testament theology: Magnifying God in Christ* (Grand Rapids: Baker Academic, 2008), 617–671.

[63] Schreiner, New Testament Theology, 630. [Note: Thomas Schreiner is not a theonomic thinker. It is quite remarkable to me, that having understood these critical exegetical realities in his comments on Matthew's gospel, theologically, Schreiner fails or refuses to recognize their theonomic implications in his writings].

[64] Wines, *Commentaries on the laws of the ancient Hebrews*, 272. Wines argues that the Mosaic penal code is one of the most ancient on record and is founded on divine government and accords with natural equity. He shows how the principle of lex talionis was practiced by ancient and highly civilized peoples including the Athenians and Roman's - the laws of twelve tables. He argues that the law of Moses is a declaration of the general principles essential for the safety and good order of any society and goes on to show that in a literal administration of the Mosaic law, more liberality and compassion is found than in the history of Britain and Europe, where in recent times men were executed for the value of a sheep, a guinea and even a twelve pence farthing. He also refutes the absurdity of pitting Moses and Christ against one another regarding the lex talionis, showing that Moses addressed the perpetrators due penalty and Jesus addressed the injured party in forbidding indulgence in private vengeance 270 – 284.

[65] Frame, *The doctrine*, 696.

[66] See Robert Alter, *The five books of Moses: A translation with commentary* (New York:

W. W. Norton & Company, 2004), 441 (note 30).

[67] Rushdoony, *Leviticus*, 276.

[68] Frame, *The doctrine*, 701.

[69] Frame, *The doctrine*, 702. I don't find Frame's argument particularly compelling here. Since all God's law was given by a holy God to a people living in his immediate presence, if this fact somehow means a different standard of penology for Israel than the other nations, why would some of the capital punishments remain binding outside ancient Israel? If the criterion of just punishment for crime rests on the proximity of the presence of God in the temple/tabernacle (rather than the *lex talionis*), then on what ground is murder still worthy of death but rape and bestiality are not? This argument also overlooks the missiological significance of Israel's calling as a light to the nations, in part being models of justice to be copied, and further overlooks that the Church today, as the new priesthood, fulfils a prophetic function in calling the nations to obedience to God's law due to his presence in the world by the Holy Spirit, a world being re-made into his temple. Surely therefore a Christian people would seek to apply God's law in view of his perfect justice and abiding presence? Frame seems to leave the question open ended and does not appear convinced on this point. In my judgement he would be better to stick with clear exegetical inferences that build in flexibility into the application of the law than search for a vague principle that might imply abolition.

[70] Frame, *The doctrine*, 701–702.

[71] Frame, *The doctrine*, 700.

[72] Frame, *The doctrine*, 699.

[73] Frame, *The doctrine*, 702.

[74] Robert Alter, *The five books of Moses*, 440.

[75] Wines, *Commentary on laws*, 272.

[76] Rushdoony, *Leviticus*, 276.

[77] Frame, *The doctrine*, 205–206.

[78] Greg L. Bahnsen, 'The Theonomic Reformed Approach to Law and Gospel,' in Stanley N. Gundry, ed. *Five views on law and gospel*, (Grand Rapids: Zondervan, 1996), 136.

[79] Klinghoffer, *Shattered tablets*, 35.

[80] See Rushdoony's discussion, *Leviticus*, 275–276.

[81] Motyer, *Roots*, 23–24.

[82] Thomas R. Schreiner, *New Testament theology*, 627. Emphasis added.

[83] See Don Colbert M.D. *What would Jesus eat: The ultimate program for eating well, feeling great and living longer* (Nashville: Thomas Nelson, 2002).

[84] The book of Hebrews is perhaps the most important New Testament letter for helping us understand the change in the priesthood and significance of the Temple in the New Covenant era.

[85] See Greg Bahnsen, *Theonomy in Christian ethics*.

[86] Motyer, Roots, 27. It is interesting to note here that Rushdoony did consider the dietary laws of the Old Testament as valid and useful; though it is not immediately clear whether he considered them 'moral laws.' However, the principle outlined by Motyer was clearly followed by Rushdoony in his exegesis of the law in many instances. For example, as is clear from the Institutes, he clearly applied this principle to the laws concerning the land of Canaan, the Jubilee, the sacrificial system, the laws of separation, and the Sabbath; it is particularly noteworthy that Rushdoony, unlike most of the Puritans, was not Sabbatarian in the traditional sense laid out in the Westminster Confession. In each of these cases, he saw that a specific practice (shadow that typified some aspect of redemption) had ceased with the death and resurrection of Christ, (who is Lord also of the Sabbath) but the principle remained. His reading of Scripture was not wooden. All of Scripture was the law-word of God and had to be understood in terms of the whole.

[87] Rushdoony, *Institutes*, 399–400.

[88] Burnside, *God, justice and society*, 347.

[89] See Burnside, *God, justice and society*, 367. Because, in the Bible, married men are seen as the protector and provider with a delegated responsibility and authority in the family, passing family property to legitimate heirs for the preservation of family and community required certain knowledge of the paternity of their offspring. If a wife is unfaithful the husband is therefore wronged by two parties and the legitimacy of offspring can be called into question. In the case of a married man consensually sleeping with an unmarried woman, the offense is against the woman's father and is therefore illicit, but not strictly adultery. The woman's father could demand he take her as a wife and/ or pay a dowry.

[90] Burnside, *God, justice and society*, 369.

[91] Rushdoony, *Institutes*, 400.

[92] Rushdoony, *Leviticus*, 267–268.

[93] Burnside, *God, justice and society*, 351.

[94] Rushdoony, *Institutes*, 410–411.

[95] In my view, regarding 1 Corinthians 5, Rushdoony makes an exegetical error in suggesting that Paul has the civil or judicial question in mind. It seems clear that Paul's concern in 1 Corinthians 5 is ecclesiastical only, and that he does not address the civil question directly (only indirectly by handing the person over to Satan for destruction of the flesh). I would therefore be inclined to say that Rushdoony's discussion on pages 398–401 of the *Institutes* is the clearer exposition of his viewpoint on the penology for sexual crimes.

[96] Rushdoony, *Institutes*, 399.

[97] Rushdoony, *Institutes*, 399.

[98] Rushdoony, *Institutes*, 399.

[99] Rushdoony, *Institutes*, 399.

[100] Rushdoony, *Institutes*, 412.

[101] Burnside, *God, justice and society*, 365.

[102] Burnside, *God, justice and society*, 365.

[103] See discussion in, Burnside, *God, justice and society*, 377.

[104] Burnside, *God, justice and society*, 382.

[105] Burnside, *God, justice and society*, 382.

[106] Burnside, *God, justice and society*, 385.

[107] Alter, *The five books of Moses*, 632.

[108] Alter, *The five books of Moses*, 623–624.

[109] Alter, *The five books of Moses*, 623–624.

[110] Burnside, *God, justice and society*, 379.

[111] An examination of the website of the Toronto District School Board alone is enough to demonstrate this. The following resources prove the radical goal in Ontario's education strategy: The Accepting Schools Act http://www.ontla.on.ca/web/bills/bills_detail. do?locale=en&BillID=2549

Ontario's Equity and Inclusive Education Strategy, 2009 http://cal2.edu.gov.on.ca/april2009/EquityEducationStrategy.pdf

Ontario's Equity and Inclusive Education Strategy Guidelines, 2009 http://www.edu. gov.on.ca/eng/policyfunding/inclusiveguide.pdf

OSSTF "Shout Out" http://www.osstf.on.ca/adx/aspx/adxGetMedia. aspx?DocID=0c42ad90-0d22-41f4-a6cedcba45381e61&

MediaID=8241f51d-df44-41ef-8e9a-559ffa3293ed&Filename=shout-out. pdf&l=English

Toronto District School Board Curriculum http://www.canadianvalues.ca/SCC/ TDSB_Equity%20_%20InclusiveCurriculum_Seepage%20 10%20_.pdf

Hamilton Wentworth Equity Policy http://www.peacehamilton.com/pdf/policy.pdf

TVDSB Diversity Resources http://www.tvdsb.ca/programs.cfm?subpage=188593

TVDSB Podcasts – "Homophobia is Gay" video http://www.tvdsb.ca/podcasts.cfm

Public Education Advocates for Christian Equity http://www.peacehamilton.com/index.php

[112] I am not aware of any sermon preached in which the evangelical Baptist, Charles Spurgeon, condemned as unbiblical the legal sanctions against homosexuality in England.

[113] Hamish Copley, "The End to the Death Penalty for Sodomy in Canada," *The Drummer's Revenge*, last modified September 9, 2007, http://thedrummersrevenge. wordpress.com/2007/09/09/the-end-to-the-death-penalty-for-sodomy-in-canada/.

[114] Studies show that a majority of Britons, Canadians and Americans still support the death penalty, at least in the case of murder. Reporting on the poll "Canadians Split on Pot, Death Penalty: Poll," March 18, 2010, CBC News said "Those who support the

reintroduction of capital punishment tend to be Conservative supporters (53 percent), residents of Alberta (48 percent), men (43 percent), seniors (45 percent), high school grads (48 percent), and college grads (46 percent). However, Angus Reid Public Opinion (January 25, 2010) finds "Most people in the United States, Britain, and Canada support relying on the death penalty for homicide convictions, according to a poll by Angus Reid Public Opinion. 84 percent of respondents in the U.S., 67 percent in Britain, and 62 percent in Canada share this view." See Rupert Taylor, "Will Canada Bring Back the Death Penalty?," *Suite 101*, last modified December 1, 2010, http://suite101.com/article/will-canada-bringback-the-death-penalty-a315608.

[115] Burnside, *God, justice and society*, 375.

[116] Burnside, *God, justice and society*, 375.

[117] See Burnside, *God, justice and society*, 378–379.

[118] Michael Swift, Homosexual Manifesto, first published as 'Gay Revolutionary' in 'The Gay Community News,' 1987. http://panindigan.tripod.com/homorev.html, accessed, November 2012. The article was found to be of serious concern in the United States and so was reprinted in full in the Congressional Record. Nervous of this exposure, the claim of some homosexualists that the piece was satire has proven completely hollow – the cultural changes effected by homosexual activism in the twenty-five years since its publication have proven otherwise.

[119] Burnside, *God, justice and society*, 384–385.

[120] Burnside, *God, justice and society*, 385.

[121] "Uganda to Pass Anti-Gay Law as 'Christmas Gift,'" *BBC*, last modified November 13, 2012, http://www.bbc.co.uk/news/worldafrica-20318436. The bill was strongly condemned last year by Western leaders, including U.S. President Barack Obama who described it as "odious."

[122] Rushdoony, *Institutes* vol. 1, 792.

[123] Luther, *Table Talk*, 218.

[124] See some useful illustrations of this in, Rushdoony, *Institutes* vol. I, 782–793.

[125] William D. Gairdner, *The trouble with Canada ... still* (Toronto: Key Porter, 2010), 330.

[126] Gairdner, *The trouble with Canada ... still*, 373.

[127] Christy A. Visher, "Transitions from Prison to Community: Understanding Individual Pathways." *The Urban Institute, Justice Policy Center*, District of Columbia Washington, 2003

[128] Taken from the television documentary "Billions Behind Bars: Inside America's Prison Industry," *MSNBC,* originally aired October 18, 2011.

[129] J. Bonta, T. Rugge & M. Dauvergne, *The reconviction rate of federal offenders*. (User Report 2003-02). Ottawa: Solicitor General Canada, 2003.

[130] David Garland, *Punishment and modern society: A study in social theory* (Chicago:

University of Chicago Press, 1990), 269.

[131] Garland, *Punishment*, 269.

[132] Garland, *Punishment*, 75.

[133] Garland, *Punishment*, 75.

[134] Rushdoony, *Institutes* vol. II, 32–35.

[135] Garland, *Punishment*, 76.

[136] Garland, *Punishment*, 269.

[137] Garland, *Punishment*, 207.

[138] Garland, *Punishment*, 207.

[139] Rushdoony, *Institutes* vol. II, 32.

[140] Montgomery, *Law and gospel*, 9.

[141] Bahnsen and Gentry, *House divided*, 77–78.

[142] Rushdoony, *Institutes* vol. II, 469.

[143] Sam Harris, *The end of faith: Religious terror and the future of reason* (New York: W. W. Norton, 2004), 52–53. Emphasis added.

[144] Theodore Dalrymple, *Not with a bang but a wimper: The politics and culture of decline* (Chicago: Ivon R. Dee, 2008), 88.

[145] Sam Harris, "Response to Controversy," *Sam Harris*, last modified April 7, 2013, http://www.samharris.org/site/full_text/response-tocontroversy2.

[146] Rushdoony, *Institutes* vol. II, 469.

[147] See, Bahnsen and Gentry, *House divided*, 78–79. The criticism of democracy found in contemporary theonomic writings is only in the stipulated sense of a philosophical view that sees the voice of the people as equivalent to the voice of God – the will of the mob then defines all standards and there is no authority above the whim of the 'people.'

[148] Bahnsen and Gentry, *House divided*, 79.

[149] Rushdoony, *Institutes* vol. II, 466.

[150] Rushdoony, *Institutes*, vol. II, 468, emphasis added.

[151] R.J. Rushdoony, interview by Bill Moyers, PBS Home Video: "God and Politics: On Earth as it is in Heaven," *PBS*, 1988.

[152] Rushdoony, *Institutes*, 400.

[153] Frame, *The doctrine*, 220.

[154] Rushdoony, *Institutes*, 38–39.

[155] Ian Gentles, *Oliver Cromwell: God's warrior and the English Revolution* (China: Palgrave Macmillan, 2011), 100.

[156] Gentles, *God's warrior*, 99.

[157] Gentles, *God's warrior*, 165.

[158] John M. Frame, *The doctrine*, 957.

[159] See Timothy George, *Theology of the Reformers* (Leicester, England: Apollos, 1998), 32–36.

[160] For a study of the views of Martin Bucer, John Knox, John Cotton and the Calvinistic tradition, see *The Journal of Christian Reconstruction: Symposium on Puritanism and Law* ed. Gary North, 5 (1978) and for examples of Cromwell's thought on law see John Morrill, *Oliver Cromwell* (Hampshire: Oxford University Press, 2007), 96–98.

[161] See Martin A. Foulner, *Theonomy and the Westminster Confession* (Edinburgh: Marpet Press, 1997).

[162] See Martin A. Foulner, *Theonomy*, 49-51; and John Calvin, *The Covenant Enforced: Sermons on Deuteronomy 27 and 28*, James B. Jordan (ed.) (Tyler, TX: Institute for Christian Economics, 1990).

[163] Rusdoony, *Roots of reconstruction*, 1114–1115.

[164] Rushdoony, *Institutes* vol. II, 32–35.

[165] Rushdoony, "Christian reconstruction as a movement," 30.

[166] See Timothy P. Weber, *On the road to Armageddon: How evangelicals became Israel's best friend* (Grand Rapids: Baker, 2004).

[167] Ruth Mayers, cited in Michael A. G. Haykin, *The Reformers and Puritans as spiritual mentors* (Joshua Press: Kitchener, ON, 2012), 123.

CHAPTER TEN

[1] Roland H. Bainton, *Early Christianity* (New Jersey: D. Van Nostrand Company, 1960), 23.

[2] Bainton, *Early Christianity*, 21.

[3] Bainton, *Early Christianity*, 21.

[4] Bainton, *Early Christianity*, 22.

[5] Bainton, *Early Christianity*, 27.

[6] "Canadian Human Rights Commission Free Speech Controversy," Wikipedia, last modified January 3, 2013. http://en.wikipedia.org/wiki/Canadian_Human_Rights_Commission_free_speech_controversy.

[7] David Bruce Hegeman, *Plowing in Hope: Toward a Biblical Theology of Culture* (Moscow, ID: Canon, 2007), 29.

[8] Beeke & Jones, *A Puritan Theology*, 5.

[9] Beeke & Jones, *A Puritan Theology*, 5.

[10] Montgomery, *Law and Gospel*, 1.

[11] Klinghoffer, *Shattered Tablets*, 39.

[12] Herman Bavinck, cited in Hegeman, *Plowing in Hope*, 31.

[13] Barzun, *From Dawn to Decadence*, xiv-xv.

[14] Henry R. Van Til, *The Calvinistic concept of culture* (Philadelphia: Presbyterian and Reformed, 1959), 200.

[15] Theodore Dalrymple, *In praise of prejudice: The necessity of preconceived ideas*

(New York: Encounter, 2007), 25.

[16] That is not to say Constantine was a consistent biblical Christian, but he was not the mythological bogeyman of contemporary missiology, nor was he simply bad news for the church with his part in the emergence of a Christian order. For an excellent study regarding the impact of Constantine on the demise of the pagan empire to the beginnings of Christendom see Peter J. Leithart, *Defending Constantine: The twilight of an empire and the dawn of Christendom* (Illinois: IVP, 2010)

[17] See Janet Folger, *The Criminalization of Christianity: Read this book before it becomes illegal!*, (Colorado Springs: Multnomah, 2005).

[18] Virginia Woolf, cited in Peter Hitchens, *The rage against God: How atheism led me to faith* (Grand Rapids: Zondervan, 2010), 24.

[19] See J. C. Davis, *Oliver Cromwell* (India: Arnold, 2001).

[20] See the Harvard scholar, Harold J. Berman's massive study *Law and Revolution*, in which he demonstrates the demise of the Western legal tradition.

[21] This phenomenon in Canada has been almost exhaustively documented in William D. Gairdner, *The trouble with Canada still: A citizen speaks out* (Toronto: Key Porter, 2010).

[22] Frame, *The Doctrine of the Christian Life*, 857.

[23] Dalrymple, *In Praise*, 8.

[24] Frame, *The Doctrine*, 887.

[25] William Perkins, cited in Edmund S. Morgan, ed., *Puritan political ideas, 1558-1794* (Indiana: Bobbs-Merrill, 1965), 56-57.

[26] Rushdoony, *Leviticus*, 307.

[27] C.A. Hodge, *Evangelical theology: Lectures on doctrine* (Carlisle, PA: The Banner of Truth Trust, 1990), 283–284.

[28] Lim & Coffey (eds.), *The Cambridge companion to Puritanism*, (Cambridge: Cambridge University Press, 2008), 339.

[29] Joel McDurmon, "Why Leftists Should Shut Up About Dominionism," *The American Vision*, last modified September 29, 2011, http://americanvision.org/5209/why-leftists-should-shut-up-about-dominionism/.

[30] J. Gresham Machen, "Christianity and culture," 5.

[31] Alfred Edersheim, S*ketches of Jewish social life in the days of Christ*, (Grand Rapids: Eerdmans, 1979), 122–123.

[32] Michael Horton, "Transforming culture with a messiah complex," *9 Marks*, last modified December 2007. http://sites.silaspartners.com/cc/article/0,,PTID314526_CHID598014_CIID2376346,00.html.

[33] This description may sound harsh to some, but based on what I have read of Horton on this subject I think his view of the kingdom is a long way from being reformed and is much closer to Lutheranism; although Luther had a stronger understanding of the role of God's law in society, and viewed the 'two kingdoms, as the temporal and eternal,

not church and state.

[34] Charles Darwin, *Journal of a voyage round the world* (London: T. Nelson and Sons, Paternoster Row, 1890), 496–497.

[35] Horton, "Transforming culture."

[36] Horton, "Transforming culture."

[37] Beeke and Jones, *A Puritan theology*, 773.

[38] J. I. Packer, cited in Beeke and Jones, *A Puritan theology*, 773. Emphasis added.

[39] Beeke and Jones, *A Puritan theology*, 773.

[40] See Beeke and Jones, *A Puritan theology*, 773–775.

[41] Horton, "Transforming culture." Note: It is important to notice that for Horton the field of common grace (whatever he means by that) is not specifically biblical or Christian in the values it expresses culturally, otherwise it would be identical with Christianization.

[42] Isaiah 9:7; Isaiah chapters seven and nine are both worth reading in full and Reformed Christians will be interested to read Calvin's comments on these passages.

[43] Gelasius, "Letter to Emperor Anastasius," in J. H. Robinson, *Readings in European history* (Boston: Ginn, 1905), 72–73.

[44] Frame, *The doctrine*, 862.

[45] Horton, "Transforming culture."

[46] Horton, "Transforming culture."

[47] Horton, "Transforming culture."

[48] Horton, "Transforming culture."

[49] A. C. Grayling, *The good book: A humanist bible* (New York: Walker & Co. 2011), 395.

[50] Horton, "Transforming culture."

[51] R. C. Campbell, *Militant Christianity: Broadman sermons* (Nashville: Broadman, 1940), 46, 54–55.

[52] Beeke and Jones, *A Puritan theology*, 784.

[53] Beeke and Jones, *A Puritan theology*, 785.

[54] Beeke and Jones, *A Puritan theology*, 785.

[55] Beeke and Jones, *A Puritan theology*, 786.

[56] Iain Murray, cited in Beeke and Jones, *A Puritan theology*, 788.

CHAPTER ELEVEN

[1] Isaac Ambrose, cited in R.C. Richardson, *Puritanism in northwest England: A regional study of Chester to 1642* (Manchester: Manchester University Press, 1972), 105.

[2] William Gouge, cited in Charles H. George and Katherine George, *The Protestant mind of the English Reformation, 1570-1640* (Princeton: Princeton University Press, 1961), 459.

[3] Cotton Mather, *A family well ordered,* cited in Edmund S. Morgan, *The Puritan family: Religion and domestic relations in seventeenth-century New England* (1944; Reprint

New York: Harper and Row, 1966), 143.

[4] Richard Weikart, "Marx, Engels, And The Abolition of the Family," *History of European Ideas*, 18 (U.K: Pergamon, 1994), 657–672

[5] Weikart, "The Abolition," 568.

[6] See Richard Weikart, *From Darwin to Hitler: Evolutionary Ethics, Eugenics, and Racism in Germany* (New York: Palgrave Macmillan, 2004), 129ff.

[7] See *Demographic winter: The decline of the human family*, directed by Rick Stout (2008; Salt Lake City: SRB Documentary, 2008), DVD.

[8] Canada, Ministry of Finance, "Ontario Population Projections Update, 2012-2036," *Ontario Ministry of Finance*, last modified July 19,2013, http://www.fin.gov.on.ca/en/economy/demographics/projections/#s4c.

[9] For an informative examination of the degree to which the church has been feminized and abandoned by men in Canada see Douglas Todd, "Faced with feminization churches want to reach men," *Vancouver Sun*, last modified December 15, 2012, http://blogs.vancouversun.com/2012/12/15/faced-with-feminization-churches-wonder-how-to-reach-men/.

[10] For a look at the Puritan view of family see Ryken, Worldly Saints, 73–88.

[11] Sutton, *That You May Prosper*, 140–141.

[12] Michael Wagner, *Standing on guard for thee: The past, present and future of Canada's Christian right* (United States: Freedom Press Canada, 2007), 177.

[13] William D. Gairdner,: *A parent speaks out on the political, economic and social policies that threaten us all* (Toronto: Stoddart Publishing, 1992), ix–x.

[14] Gairdner, *The war against the family*, 5.

[15] The well-known case of pro-life activist and Queen's Diamond Jubilee medallist, Linda Gibbons, is the most prominent illustration on this. See: Deborah Gyapong, "Pro-life activist Linda Gibbons counts on Christ's strength," The Catholic Register, last modified November 1, 2012, http://www.catholicregister.org/news/canada/item/15350-pro-life-activist-linda-gibbons-counts-on-christ%E2%80%99s-strength.

[16] Former Canadian Prime Minister, Pierre Elliot Trudeau, who was anti-Christian to the core, was instrumental in seeing capital punishment abandoned in Canada. On June 15th 1976 he addressed the House of Commons in support of his government's bill for its effective abolition. The bill then passed by a margin of 131 to 124. In this famous speech to the house he seriously misconstrued and caricatured the purpose of capital punishment as 'vengeance' and referred to its use as, 'unreasoning passion.' For him the only reason for using execution was if it achieved a, 'worthwhile social purpose.' Sin, justice, truth and righteousness did not enter his thinking, let alone God's law inherent in the Canadian criminal code. Capital punishment was not wrong to Trudeau because he thought execution was immoral, but because he didn't think it achieved anything sociologically useful to the state. His humanistic hope was in mankind, "It is because I

have an enduring confidence in mankind and confidence in society's ability to protect itself without taking human life, that I am eager to support this bill and vote for the abolition of capital punishment." Of course when the ground of penal philosophy is not God's justice but human pragmatism, as soon as taking life is seen as 'useful' to the state's purpose, executions can and are justified on almost any basis so long as it is serving the state's declared end. For the speech in full see Edward Humphreys (ed.), Great Speeches: Words That Shaped The World (Singapore: Arcturus Publishing, 2009), 139–143.

[17] Karl Marx, cited in Theodore Dalrymple, *Our culture, what's left of it: The Mandarins and the masses* (Chicago: Ivan R. Dee Publishing, 2005), 85.

[18] Dalrymple, *Our culture, what's left of it*, 85.

[19] Richard Weikart, "Marx, Engels and the abolition of the family," 661.

[20] Weikart, "Marx, Engels and the abolition of the family," 661.

[21] American scholar and climate researcher E. Calvin Beisner has pointed out that, "The UN is using fears of global warming as justification for instituting binding, transnational agreements that undermine national sovereignty and give enormous new power to the UN." See: E. Calvin Beisner, 'Ecological Utopia,' Peter Jones (ed.) *The Coming Pagan Utopia: Christian Witness in Tough Times* (Main Entry: Costa Rica, 2013), 76

[22] Julian Huxley, cited in Ian T. Taylor, *In the Minds of Men: Darwin and the New World Order* (Toronto: TFE Publishing, 1984), 424.

[23] Janet Mefferd, 'Geo-Political Utopia,' Jones, *The Coming Pagan Utopia*, 83-84

[24] Cited in Taylor, *In the minds of men*, 425.

[25] Unnamed York University student, letter to author, 2011.

[26] Gairdner, *The War*, 246.

[27] Cited in Wagner, *Leaving God behind*, 91.

[28] Supreme Court Ruling, in the Big M Drug Mart decision [1985] 1 S.C.R. 355, per Dickson J.).

[29] See Wagner, *Leaving God behind*, 95–96. For a full account of the impact of the Charter of Rights and Freedoms on marriage, family and the social order see, Wagner, *Leaving God behind*.

[30] William Eskridge, cited in Alan Sears & Craig Osten, *The homosexual agenda: Exposing the principal threat to religious freedom today* (Nashville: Broadman and Holman, 2003), 96.

[31] Cited in Sears & Osten, *Homosexual agenda*, 96.

[32] Cited in Sears & Osten, *Homosexual agenda*, 96.

[33] Rousas John Rushdoony, *Noble savages: Exposing the worldview of pornographers and their war against Christian civilization* (Vallecito, CA: Ross House, 2005), 98.

[34] "Births and Fertility," *Toronto's Health Status Indicator Series*, City of Toronto, Public Health September 2012, http://www.toronto.ca/health/map/indicators/pdf/

birthsandfertility.pdf, accessed January 2013.

[35] "Births and Fertility."

[36] Carman Bradley, *Pivot of civilization or rivet of life: Conflicting worldviews and same-sex marriage* (Victoria, BC: Trafford, 2004), 122.

[37] Bradley, *Pivot of civilization*, 115–116.

[38] A. Mrozek & R. Walberg, *Private choices, public costs: How failing families cost us all* (Ottawa: Institute of Marriage & Family Canada, 2009), 25.

[39] Mrozek & Walberg, *Private choices*, 5.

[40] Alan Schwarz, "A.D.H.D. Seen in 11% of U.S Children as Diagnoses Rise," *New York Times*, March 31, 2013.

[41] See: David Cameron, Conservative Party Speech, http://www.independent.co.uk/news/uk/politics/tory-party-conference-2015-david-camerons-speech-in-full-a6684656.html accessed November 2015.

[42] "Stressed and Depressed: The Unreported Health Crisis of the Obama Era." *Whistleblower Magazine*, April 2013.

[43] Richard Greenham, *Of the Good Education of Children,* cited in Everett Emerson (ed.), *English Puritanism from John Hooper to John Milton* (Durham, NC: Duke University Press, 1968)153.

[44] James Allan Evans, *The Empress Theodora: Partner of Justinian* (University of Texas Press: Austin, 2002), 23.

[45] Evans, *The Empress Theodora*, 36.

[46] Evans, *The Empress Theodora*, 37

[47] Evans, *The Empress Theodora*, 38

[48] Evans, *The Empress Theodora*, 110-111

[49] Mark Galli, *131 Christians everyone should know* (Nashville: Holman Reference, 2010), 312–314.

[50] "The law and your body." *Kids' Help Phone*. 2013. http://www.kidshelpphone.ca/Teens/InfoBooth/Money-jobs-laws/Laws/The-law-and-your-body.aspx#abortion.

[51] Sarah E. Chinn, *Inventing modern adolescence: The children of immigrants in turn-of-the-century America* (New Brunswick, NJ: Rutgers University Press, 2009). PDF e-book.

[52] Social Justice Policy Group, *Breakdown Britain: Interim report on the state of the nation,* (London: The Centre for Social Justice, 2006).

CHAPTER TWELVE

[1] T.S. Eliot, cited in Ryken, Worldly Saints, 157.

[2] Effective Christian education has taken place throughout the history of Christendom and down to the present in both the church and private school context as well as in the home. I am in favor of all these proven models.

[3] Ebenezer Pemberton, *Sermons and discourses on several occasions,* cited in Perry

Miller and Thomas H. Johnson (eds.), *The Puritans,* rev. ed., vol. 1 (New York: Harper Torchbooks, 1963), 18.

[4] A History of Christian Education, Reed and Prevost, p. 82)

[5] H. C. Porter, *Puritanism in Tudor England* (Columbia, S.C; University of South Carolina Press, 1971), 198.

[6] Ryken, *Worldly saints,* 158.

[7] Cited in Ryken, Worldly Saints, 161.

[8] Ryken, *Worldly saints,* 163.

[9] George Grant, *Technology and empire: Perspectives on North America* (Toronto: House of Anansi Press, 1969), 46, 49.

[10] R. J. Rushdoony, *The philosophy of the Christian curriculum* (Vallecito, CA: Ross House, 1981), 3.

[11] R. J. Rushdoony, *The Messianic character,* 14–15.

[12] R. J. Rushdoony, *The Messianic character,* 43–44.

[13] See Wagner, *Leaving God behind,* 47–83.

[14] 'Committee on Religious Education in the Public Schools of the Province of Ontario' (1969), cited in Michael Wagner, *Leaving God behind,* 60.

[15] Wagner, *Leaving God behind,* 73.

[16] Rushdoony, *Messianic character,* 20, 151ff.

[17] Rushdoony, *Messianic character,* 3.

[18] Rushdoony, *Messianic character,* 3.

[19] Rushdoony, *Messianic character,* 4.

[20] According to *The National Post,* May 24th 2006, with reporter Dan Bjarnason, Scott Murray crunched numbers on illiteracy and administered two major international surveys at Statistics Canada. And what his numbers say is that Canada's situation is particularly shameful when you look at the two worst categories: Nearly fifteen per cent of Canadians can't understand the writing on simple medicine labels such as on an Aspirin bottle, a failing that could seriously limit the ability of a parent, for example, to determine the dangers for a child. An additional twenty-seven per cent can't figure out simple information like the warnings on a hazardous materials sheet, the kinds of warning that set out workplace dangers such as risks to the eyes and skin. In total, forty-two per cent of Canadians are semi-illiterate. The proportion is even worse for those in middle age. And even when new immigrants are excluded, the numbers remain pretty much the same.

[21] Rushdoony, *Intellectual schizophrenia,* 3.

[22] Annual Report of the Ontario Teachers' Association, 1875, cited in Philip Oreopoulos, "Canadian compulsory school laws and their impact on educational attainment and future earnings," (Ottawa: Statistics Canada, 2006), http://www.statcan.gc.ca/pub/11f0019m/11f0019m2005251-eng.pdf, 5.

[23] Grant, *Technology and empire,* 57.

[24] Grant, *Technology and empire*, 57.

[25] Bob Allen, "Millennials losing their religion," *ABP News*, last modified June 25, 2012, http://www.abpnews.com/culture/social-issues/item/7555-millennials-losing-their-religion#.UbevUrnD_IU.

[26] Rushdoony, *Christian curriculum*, 17

[27] Cornelius Van Til and Louis Berkhof, *Foundations of Christian education*, Dennis E. Johnson ed, (Phillipsburg, New Jersey: Presbyterian and Reformed 1990), 4.

[28] Werner Jaeger, cited in John Lennox, *God's undertaker: Has science buried God?*, (Malta: Lion Hudson, 2007), 49

[29] Roy A. Clouser, *The myth of religious neutrality: An essay on the hidden role of religious belief in theories* (Indiana: University of Notre Dame Press, 2005), 19.

[30] Clouser, *The myth*, 19.

[31] Rushdoony, *The philosophy*, 15–16.

[32] Van Til & Berkhof, *Foundations*, 7.

[33] Van Til & Berkhof, *Foundations*, 7–8.

[34] Clouser, *The myth* 131–146.

[35] Morris Kline, cited in Clouser, *The myth*, 141.

[36] Rushdoony, *The philosophy*, 11.

[37] See Clouser's discussion, "A Non-Reductionist Theory of Reality," *The myth*, 237–268.

[38] Christopher J. Small, *Music, society, education* (London: John Caldwell Publishers, 1980), 36.

[39] Small, *Music*, 170.

[40] Small, *Music*, 68.

[41] Rushdoony, *The philosophy*, 15.

[42] J. Gresham Machen, "Christianity and Culture," 8.

[43] Eugene H. Peterson, *Reversed thunder: The revelation of John & the praying imagination* (San Francisco: Harper, 1988), 113

CHAPTER THIRTEEN

[1] The period after the life and work of the eighteenth-century German philosopher Immanuel Kant.

[2] Alister McGrath, *Bridge building: Effective Christian apologetics*, (Ebbw Vale, Wales: IVP, 1992), 9.

[3] Cornelius Van Til, *Christian apologetics*, (Phillipsburg, New Jersey: Presbyterian & Reformed Publishing, 2003), 17.

[4] Machen, "Christianity and Culture," 6. Emphasis added.

[5] John Frame, *Cornelius Van Til: An analysis of his thought* (New Jersey: Presbyterian & Reformed Publishing, 1995), 46.

[6] Presuppositional critique involves analysing the foundational assumptions, or

presuppositions, of a given worldview, and exposing their unintelligibility in accounting for reality.

⁷ P. Andrew Sandlin, "The Genius of the Thought of Rousas John Rushdoony," in P. Andrew Sandlin ed., *A comprehensive faith: An international festschrift for Rousas John Rushdoony* (San Jose: Friends of Chalcedon, 1996), 7.

⁸ This includes mathematics. There is no consensus among philosophers on what numbers actually are. Are they eternal abstract entities; an aspect of logical relations; experientially derived objects of sensation; or just useful tools that relate to nothing beyond themselves, like a shovel or axe? Furthermore all theorems begin with axioms, some of which cannot be proved within the system – they just have to be accepted on faith. This is known as 'incompleteness' proven by Kurt Goedel. As the advent of the 'new math' has revealed, we all come to math with a set of assumptions.

⁹ Rousas John Rushdoony, *By what standard*, (Vallecito, CA: Ross House, 1995), 100.

¹⁰ Rushdoony, *By what standard*, 101.

¹¹ A brute fact is one that is being considered prior to the question of whether it is created and related to all other facts by the will and decree of God. A brute fact is thus to all intents and purposes uncreated, unrelated, meaningless factuality.

¹² Hans Küng, *Does God exist?* (New York: Doubleday and Company, 1978), 68.

¹³ James K. A. Smith, *Introducing radical orthodoxy* (Grand Rapids: Baker Academic and Paternoster Press, 2004), 97.

¹⁴ Küng, *Does God exist*, 15.

¹⁵ Peter Kreeft, *Christianity for modern pagans*: *Pascal's Pensees*, edited, outlined and explained (San Francisco: Ignatius, 1993), 115.

¹⁶ Kreeft, *Christianity for modern pagans*, 17.

¹⁷ Immanuel Kant, *The critique of pure reason: Preface to the second edition*, 1787, (Great Books of the Western World, vol. 42, Encyclopedia Britannica, 1952), 5.

¹⁸ Rushdoony, *The one and the many*, 305–306.

¹⁹ Rushdoony, *The one and the many*, 308.

²⁰ Friedrich Nietzsche, *The will to power in science, nature, society and art* (New York: Frederick Publications), 5.

²¹ Nietzsche, *The will to power*, 550.

²² Nietzsche, "My sister and I," in Oscar Levy ed., *The complete works of Nietzche* (New York: Bridgehead, 1954) 213.

²³ Jean-Paul Sartre, *Being and nothingness: An essay in phenomenological ontology*, trans. Hazel E. Barns (New York: Philosophical Library, 1956), 615.

²⁴ Sartre, *Being and nothingness*, 566.

²⁵ Amy Orr-Ewing, *Is the Bible intolerant? sexist? oppressive? homophobic? outdated? irrelevant?* (Illinois: IVP, 2005), 18–19.

²⁶ Lyotard, cited in Orr-Ewing, *Is the Bible intolerant*, 19.

[27] Alison Leigh Brown, *On Foucault* (Belmont CA: Wadsworth, 2000), 15.

[28] Michel Foucault, cited in Brown, *On Foucault*, 15.

[29] Foucault, cited in Orr-Ewing, *Is the Bible intolerant*, 20.

[30] Foucault, cited in Orr-Ewing, *Is the Bible intolerant*, 20.

[31] Smith, *Introducing radical orthodoxy*, 116.

[32] Orr-Ewing, *Is the Bible intolerant*, 33.

[33] Friedrich Nietzsche, *The will to power*, 84.

[34] Richard Rorty, *Contingency, irony and solidarity* (Cambridge: Cambridge, 1989), 59.

[35] Curtis Chang, *Engaging unbelief: A captivating strategy from Augustine and Aquinas*, (Illinois: IVP, 2000), 19–20.

[36] Derrida, cited in Richard Kearney, *Dialogues with contemporary continental thinkers* (Manchester: University Press, 1984), 124.

[37] Merold Westphal, 'Postmodernism and Religious Reflection,' *International Journal for Philosophy of Religion* 38, 1995, 137.

[38] Don Carson, *Becoming conversant*, 96.

[39] Smith, *Introducing radical orthodoxy*, 89.

[40] Rushdoony, *Systematic theology*, vol. 1, 128.

[41] Barry Taylor, "Converting Christianity: The end and beginning of faith," in Doug Pagitt and Tony Jones, *An emergent manifesto of hope*, (Grand Rapids: Baker Books, 2007), 167. Emphasis added.

[42] Taylor, "Converting Christianity," 165.

[43] Taylor, "Converting Christianity," 169.

[44] Octavius Brooks Frothingham, cited in Rushdoony, *The one and the many*, 366.

[45] Brian D. McLaren, *A generous orthodoxy*, (Grand Rapids: Zondervan, 2004), 92.

[46] Taylor, "Converting Christianity," 168

[47] Carson, *Becoming conversant*, 82

[48] Carson, *Becoming conversant*, 83.

[49] Herbert Ernest Cushman, *A beginner's history of philosophy*, vol. II (Boston: Houghton Mifflin, 1911), 72.

[50] Cushman, *Beginner's history*, 75.

[51] Cornelius Van Til, *The defense of the faith* (Phillipsburg, NJ: Presbyterian & Reformed, 2008), 122–132

[52] Albert Wells, *Pascal's recovery of man's wholeness*, (Richmond, VA: John Knox Press, 1965), 152.

[53] Greg Bahnsen, 'The Reformation of Christian Apologetics', in Gary North ed., *Foundations of Christian scholarship* (Vallecito, CA: Ross House, 2001), 213.

[54] For a more complete discussion of this matter see chapter 14, Men of Athens.

[55] Rushdoony, *By what standard*, 105.

[56] Van Til, cited in Rushdoony, *One and many*, 354.

[57] Smith, 'Introducing Radical Orthodoxy', 181–182. Emphasis added.

[58] Alvin Plantinga, "Augustinian Christian Philosophy," in Gareth B. Matthews ed., *The Augustinian tradition* (Berkley, L.A, London: University of California Press, 1999), 20–21.

[59] Chang, *Engaging unbelief*, 143.

[60] Rousas John Rushdoony and P. Andrew Sandlin, *Infallibility and interpretation*, (Vallecito, CA: Chalcedon Foundation, 2000), 49.

[61] Chang, *Engaging unbelief*, 27.

[62] Chang, *Engaging unbelief*, 153.

[63] Rushdoony, *Systematic theology*, vol. 1, 217.

CHAPTER FOURTEEN

[1] Michael Haykin, *Defence of the truth: Contending for the faith yesterday and today*, (Darlington: Evangelical Press, 2004), 8.

[2] Küng, *Does God exist*, 587.

[3] Küng, *Does God exist*, 594.

[4] Küng, *Does God exist*, 611.

[5] Armstrong, *The battle for God*, xiii.

[6] Armstrong, *The battle for God*, xiii.

[7] That is, a conceptual framework by which a given worldview seeks to account for a given aspect of reality.

[8] Armstrong, *The battle for God*, xiv.

[9] Vinoth Ramachandra, *Faiths in conflict: Christian integrity in a multi-cultural world*, (Illinois: InterVarsity Press, 1999), 127.

[10] John Hick, *God has many names*, (Philadelphia: Westminster, 1982), 58.

[11] Küng, *Does God exist*, 607.

[12] Ajith Fernando, "The Uniqueness of Jesus Christ" in D. A. Carson ed., *Telling the truth: Evangelizing postmoderns*, (Grand Rapids: Zondervan, 2000), 124.

[13] Ronald H. Nash, *Is Jesus the only savior*, (Grand Rapids: Zondervan, 1994), 10.

[14] J. Andrew Kirk, *What is mission*, 129.

[15] Nash, *Is Jesus the only savior*, 24 (footnote 22).

[16] Samir Selmanovic, "The Sweet Problem of Inclusiveness: Facing our God in the Other," in Doug Pagitt and Tony Jones (eds.), *An emergent manifesto of hope*, (Grand Rapids: Baker Books, 2007), 192.

[17] Selmanovic, "The Sweet Problem," 192.

[18] Selmanovic, "The Sweet Problem," 192.

[19] Nash, *Is Jesus the only savior*, 11.

[20] Greg L. Bahnsen, *Always ready: Directions for defending the faith*, (Nacogdoches: Covenant Media Press, 1996), 241.

21 Bahnsen, *Always ready*, 243.

22 Bahnsen, *Always ready*, 244.

23 F. F. Bruce, *The book of the Acts: The New International commentary on the New Testament*, (Grand Rapids: Eerdmans, 1988), 203

24 Bruce, *Acts*, 210.

25 Bahnsen, *Always ready*, 240–241.

26 Bahnsen, *Always ready*, 241.

27 Bruce, *Acts*, 206.

28 Ramachandra, *Faiths in conflict*, 135.

29 R. B. Kuiper, *God-centred evangelism*, (Edinburgh: The Banner of Truth Trust, 1966), 69.

30 Nash, *Is Jesus the only savior*, 138.

31 Ramachandra, *Faiths in conflict*, 167.

32 Alister McGrath, *Bridge-building: Effective Christian apologetics*, (Ebbw Vale: Inter-Varsity, 1992), 49.

33 D. A. Carson, *The gagging of God: Christianity confronts pluralism*, (Leicester: Apollos, 1996), 497.

34 Bahnsen, *Always ready*, 246.

35 Bahnsen, *Always ready*, 248.

36 Küng, *Does God exist*, 523.

37 Carson, *The gagging*, 498.

38 Bruce, *Acts*, 329.

39 Bruce, *Acts,* 334. Emphasis added.

40 McGrath, *Bridge-building*, 49.

41 Bahnsen, *Always ready*, 256.

42 Bruce, *Acts*, 335.

43 Carson, *The gagging,* 499.

44 Bahnsen, *Always ready*, 260.

45 Bruce, *Acts*, 339.

46 Bahnsen, *Always ready*, 261.

47 F. F. Bruce, "Paul and the Athenians," in *The Expository Times* 88 (October, 1976), 11.

48 Bruce, *Acts*, 340.

49 Bruce, *Acts*, 341.

50 Bahnsen, *Always ready*, 272.

51 Bruce, *Acts*, 211.

52 Bruce, *Acts*, 212.

53 Kirk, *What is mission*, 131.

54 Nash, *Is Jesus*, 139.

55 Clark Pinnock, *A wideness in God's mercy*, (Grand Rapids: Zondervan, 1992), 165.

[56] Pinnock, *A wideness in God's mercy*, 96.

[57] Nash, *Is Jesus*, 170.

[58] Ramachandra, *Faiths in conflict*, 167.

CHAPTER FIFTEEN

[1] Bosch, *Transforming mission*, 256.

[2] Richard Marius, cited in Bosch, *Transforming mission*, 256.

[3] Bosch, *Transforming mission*, 256.

[4] Bosch, *Transforming mission*, 257.

[5] Bosch, *Transforming mission*, 259.

[6] Bosch, *Transforming mission*, 260.

[7] Bosch, *Transforming mission*, 261.

[8] Bosch, *Transforming mission*, 259.

[9] This is not to say that all critics of theonomic missiology do so due to the influence of the Enlightenment. Both the Anabaptist and Lutheran tradition within Protestantism offer an alternate approach to mission theology.

[10] Bosch, *Transforming mission*, 267.

[11] Bosch, *Transforming mission*, 267–268.

[12] Bosch, *Transforming mission*, 268.

[13] See Miroslav Volf, *A public faith: How followers of Christ should serve the common good* (Grand Rapids: Brazos Press, 2011).

[14] Volf, *A public faith*, 144–145.

[15] R. J. Rushdoony, *The atheism of the early church* (Vallecito C.A: Ross House, 2000), 38–39.

[16] Volf, *A public faith*, 145.

[17] Volf, *A public faith*, 145.

[18] See Rushdoony, *Atheism of the early church*.

[19] Verkuyl, *Contemporary missiology*, 197–198.

[20] Newbigin, cited in Verkuyl, *Contemporary missiology*, 5.

[21] Abraham Kuyper cited in Owen Fourie, 'The State and the Church: Conflict or Harmony?' *The Journal of Christian Reconstruction: Symposium on the Decline and Fall of the West and the Return of Christendom*, 13 (1994), 294. I was unable to locate the original volume from which Fourie quotes.

[22] Rushdoony, *Systematic theology*, vol. 2, 670.

[23] Rushdoony, *Systematic theology*, vol. 2, 746.

[24] John Calvin, *Calvin's New Testament commentaries: 1 Corinthians* (Grand Rapids: Eerdmans, 1996) 118–119.

[25] Rushdoony, *Systematic theology*, vol. 2, 695.

[26] R.J. Rushdoony, *The institutes of biblical law*, Vol. 2: *Law and society* (Vallecito,

CA: Ross House, 1986), 336.

[27] Rushdoony, *Systematic theology*, vol. 2, 745.

[28] Rushdoony, *Systematic theology*, vol. 2, 745.

[29] Rushdoony, *Sovereignty*, 150.

[30] Roy Porter, *The greatest benefit*, 87.

[31] Rushdoony, *The institutes of biblical law*, vol. 2, 342.

[32] Carl F. H. Henry, cited in Bosch, *Transforming mission*, 404.

[33] Bosch, *Transforming mission*, 404

[34] John Stott, cited in Bosch, *Transforming mission*, 405

[35] Rushdoony, *Christianity and the state*, 2.

[36] Rushdoony, *Christianity and the state*, 2.

[37] Rushdoony, *Christianity and the state*, 2.

[38] Rushdoony, *Christianity and the state*, 2.

[39] Verkuyl, *Contemporary missiology*, 198.

[40] John Frame, 'Foreword,' *Comprehensive faith*, 5.

[41] J. G. Child, 'Christian Reconstruction Movement,' David J. Atkinson, David H. Field ed. *New dictionary of Christian ethics and pastoral theology* (Illinois: IVP, 1995), 227.

[42] Michael J. McVicar, 'The Lord Will Perfect That Which Concerneth Me: The Work of Rousas John Rushdoony,' *Faith For All OF Life*, (Chalcedon Foundation, November/ December 2010), 24

[43] Jefferey A. Ventrella, "Practicing Postmillennialism" in Kenneth L. Gentry Jr ed. *Thine Is the kingdom: Studies in the postmillennial hope* (Vallecito, CA: Chalcedon, 2003), 196.

[44] Ventrella, "Practicing Postmillennialism," 191.

[45] Ventrella, "Practicing Postmillennialism," 209.

[46] C. S. Lewis, *Letters to Malcolm chiefly on prayer* (London: Geoffrey Bles, 1964), 126–127.

[47] "Living together before marriage study: No longer seen as a bad omen,"' *Huffington Post*, last modified March 22, 2012, http://www.huffingtonpost.ca/2012/03/22/living-together-before-marriage-study_n_1372756.html.

[48] Hilary White, "90% of unmarried couples with babies will break up by baby's teens: study," *Lifesite News*, last modified May 23, 2013, http://www.lifesitenews.com/news/90-percent-of-unmarried-couples-with-babies-will-break-up-by-babys-teens-st/.

[49] C. S. Lewis, *The problem of pain*, (London: Fount, 1977), 37–38.

[50] G. Campbell Morgan, *The acts of the apostles* (New York: Fleming H. Revell Company, 1924), 546.

[51] Morgan, *The acts*, 546–547.

APPENDIX 1

[1] Carl Trueman, "Rushdoony, historical incompetence, racism and lunacy," *Reformation 21*, last modified December 20, 2006, http://www.reformation21.org/blog/2006/12/ rushdoony-historical-incompete.php, and "Rushdoony, once again – for the last time," *Reformation 21*, last modified December 31, 2006, http://www.reformation21.org/ blog/2006/12/rushdoony-once-again-for-the-l.php. In these brief articles Trueman exhibits a quintessential English snobbery (that I am all too familiar with as an Englishman), anti-Americanism and an intractable hostility to the Christian Right. The greater concern however is the lack of Christian charity on display in this incredible outburst that dismisses a respected brother in Christ as a mentally ill, anti-Semitic racist. Trueman is a capable and helpful scholar in many respects who can be read to great benefit, but on this issue he appears to have left the measured tools of the historian to one side, in favour of a visceral emotional outburst.

[2] Mark Rushdoony, "A Biographical Sketch of My Father," in Andrew Sandlin (ed*)*, *A comprehensive faith: An international festschrift for Rousas John Rushdoony* (San Jose: Friends of Chalcedon, 1996), 21.

[3] Mark Rushdoony, "A Biographical Sketch," 21.

[4] Mark Rushdoony, "Rousas John Rushdoony: April 25th 1916 - February 8th, 2001," *Chalcedon Report: In Memoriam*, 429 (April 2001), 3. Emphasis added. See also, R. J. Rushdoony, "On Death and Dying," *Chalcedon Report: In Memoriam*, 429 (April 2001), 2.

[5] Mark Rushdoony, "Rousas John Rushdoony," 3.

[6] Mark Rushdoony, *interview by Joe Boot*, March 12 2009.

[7] Cited in Michael McVicar, "First Owyhee and Then the World: The Early Ministry of R.J. Rushdoony," *Chalcedon*, last modified December 2009, http://www.chalcedon. edu/articles/article.php?ArticleID=2894. (I was unable to locate the unpublished text from which McVicar quotes.)

[8] Personal email correspondence of this author with Steve Schlissel, July 18, 2013. A Jew, as well as Rushdoony's close friend, colleague and confidant, Steve Schlissel has said that Rushdoony, at this time in his writing career, believed that a downward revision of numbers slaughtered in the holocaust might be warranted; he apparently thought two million may have been closer to the truth.

[9] Better resources were available that would have given him a more accurate perspective. i.e. Raul Hilberg's, *The Destruction of the European Jews* (Yale University Press, 1961).

[10] Paul Rassinier (1906-1967) was an anti-Nazi French resistance fighter and prisoner of the German concentration camps at Buchenwald and Mittelban-Dora. See Ben S. Austin, "Holocaust denial: A brief history," *Jewish Virtual Library,* accessed August 18 2015, https://www.jewishvirtuallibrary.org/jsource/Holocaust/denialbrief.html. See

also "Paul Rassinier," *Wikipedia,* http://en.wikipedia.org/wiki/Paul_Rassinier.

[11] One of the most revered specialists in Holocaust studies, the Austrian-born Jew, Raul Hilberg, in the third edition of his groundbreaking three-volume work, The Destruction of the European Jews, estimates that 5.1 million Jews died during the Holocaust. This figure includes over 800,000 who died from ghettoization and general privation; 1,400,000 who were killed in Open-air shootings; and up to 2,900,000 who perished in camps. Hilberg estimates the death toll in Poland at up to 3,000,000. Only for the death toll at Belzec does Hilberg provide a precise figure, all the others are rounded. When these rounding factors are taken into account a range of 4.9 million to 5.4 million deaths emerges. Note that the discrepancy in total figures among Holocaust researchers is often overshadowed by that between centres of destruction. One striking example can be seen in the Auschwitz State Museum's significant reduction of the estimated death toll in Auschwitz. A 1980 study by the Historical Department at the Auschwitz State Museum (later approved by the Polish government), led by the Department chair, Franciszek Piper, revised very dramatically their (widely held as grossly inflated) figure of four million (including a large number of non-Jewish Poles) into one million (mostly Jewish). See http://en.wikipedia.org/wiki/The_Destruction_of_the_European_Jews, accessed July 2013.

[12] R.J. Rushdoony, *The institutes of biblical law* (Chicago: The Craig Press, 1973), 588.

[13] R. J. Rushdoony, *Institutes of biblical law* vol. 1, 589.

[14] Paul Rassinier's controversial claims began to take shape in 1950 with The Lie of Ulysses, though his denial of a policy of extermination by the Nazis did not appear until the mid-1960s. For the English-speaking world, he remained in obscurity until 1977 when George Wellers, editor of *Le Monde Juif* magazine, dissected his work, including *The Drama of the European Jews* (1964) in" Reply to the Neo-Nazi Falsification of Historical Facts Concerning the Holocaust," an essay by Wellers included in *The Holocaust and the Neo-Nazi Mythomania,* English edition published by The Beate Klarsfeld Foundation, (1978).

[15] See "David Irving," *Wikipedia,* last modified April 2013, http://en.wikipedia.org/wiki/David_Irving.

[16] R.J. Rushdoony, *The Chalcedon Report* (September 2000). This article was brought to the attention of Carl Trueman by an email correspondent at the time of his 2006 blogs. See Carl Trueman, "Rushdoony revisited," *Reformation 21,* last modified December 21, 2006, http://www.reformation21.org/blog/2006/12/rushdoony-revisited.php. In light of it he seems to back down from his claim that Rushdoony was a Holocaust denier, arguing instead that he was merely an anti-Semitic incompetent. See also: "'Rushdoony and the Holocaust," *The Thinklings,* last modified December 21, 2006, http://thinklings. org/?post_id=3487.

[17] Correspondence with the author, from Steve Schlissel, July 18, 2013.

APPENDIX 2

[1] *Vine's expository dictionary of biblical words*, W.E. Vine, Merrill F. Unger, William White. Jr. (eds.), (Nashville, New York: Thomas Nelson, 1985), 208.

[2] I will not enter here into the theological dispute between cessationists and non-cessationists regarding the sense in which apostles and prophets function or do not function in today's church.

[3] William J. Abraham, *The logic of evangelism*, (Grand Rapids: Eerdmans, 1989), 42.

[4] John H. Armstong, *Five great evangelists: Preachers of real revival*, (Guernsey: Christian Focus, 1997), 239.

[5] Christopher Catherwood, *Five evangelical leaders* (Guernsey: Christian Focus, 1994), 220–221.

[6] Catherwood, *Five evangelical leaders*, 224.

[7] *Billy Graham: God's ambassador: The story of Billy Graham's extraordinary life and ministry*, produced by Bill Carter and Barry Jennings (Spring House Productions, 2006)

[8] *Billy Graham: God's ambassador*

[9] *Just as I am: The autobiography of Billy Graham*, (New York: Harper Collins, 1997), 276–278.

[10] *Billy Graham: God's ambassador*.

[11] Catherwood, *Five evangelical leaders*, 254.

[12] *Billy Graham: God's ambassador*.

[13] Billy Graham, *Just as I am*, 658–659.

[14] *Billy Graham: God's ambassador*.

[15] *Billy Graham: God's ambassador*.

[16] Geoffrey Hanks, *70 great Christians: Changing the world*, (Bath: Christian Focus, 1992), 272.

[17] *Billy Graham: God's ambassador*.

[18] Robert F. Ramey, "Billy Graham: Pathfinder in Evangelism" in John Woodbridge (ed.), *More than conquerors*, (Singapore: Candle Books, 1994), 175.

[19] Tony Lane, *The Lion concise book of Christian thought: Great thinkers of the Christian faith from the first century to the present*, (Reading: Lion Publishing, 1996), 168–169.

[20] Armstrong, *Five great evangelists*, 16.

[21] Harry S. Stout, *The divine dramatist: George Whitefield and the rise of modern evangelicalism*, (Grand Rapids: Eerdmans Publishing, 1991), 204.

[22] Stout, *The divine dramatist*, 212.

[23] Armstrong, *Five great evangelists*, 36.

[24] Charles G. Finney, *The memoirs of Charles G. Finney: The complete restored text*, Garth M. Rosell and Richard A.G. Dupuis (eds.), (Grand Rapids: Zondervan, 1989), 321.

[25] Lane, *Book of Christian thought*, 190.

[26] Lewis A. Drummond, *The evangelist: The worldwide impact of Billy Graham*, (Nashville: Word, 2001), 174.

[27] Keith J. Hardman, *Charles Grandison Finney 1792-1875: Revivalist and reformer*, (Durham: Evangelical Press, 1990), 110.

[28] Hardman, *Charles Grandison Finney*, 114.

[29] Armstrong, *Five great evangelists*, 162.

[30] Hardman, *Charles Grandison Finney*, 114.

[31] Hanks, *70 great Christians*, 260.

[32] Hardman, *Charles Grandison Finney*, 170.

[33] Hanks, *70 great Christians*, 259.

[34] Hardman, *Charles Grandison Finney*, 409.

[35] John Hannah, "Billy Sunday: Acrobatic Evangelist," in J. Woodbridge (ed.), *More than conquerors*, 153.

[36] Janet Lowe, *Billy Graham speaks* (Hoboken: John Wiley & Sons, 1999), 1.

[37] Abraham, *The logic of evangelism*, 9.

[38] Drummond, *The evangelist*, 173.

[39] Catherwood, *Five evangelical leaders*, 274.

[40] Francis Schaeffer, cited in Armstrong, *Five great evangelists*, 245.

[41] Drummond, *The evangelist*, 187.

[42] Catherwood, *Five evangelical leaders*, 267.

[43] Drummond, *The evangelist*, 185.

[44] Drummond, *The evangelist*, 205.

[45] Catherwood, *Five evangelical leaders*, 273.

[46] Armstrong, *Five great evangelists*, 173.

[47] Armstrong, *Five great evangelists*, 197.

[48] Catherwood, *Five evangelical leaders*, 271.

[49] Catherwood, *Five evangelical leaders*, 255.

[50] Drummond, *The evangelist*, 206.

BIBLIOGRAPHY

Abraham, W.J. *The Logic of Evangelism*. Grand Rapids: Eerdmans, 1989.

Agus, Irving A. *Urban civilization in pre-Crusade Europe*. II vols. New York: Yeshiva, 1966.

Allen, Bob. "Millenials losing their religion." *ABP News*. June 25, 2012. http://www.abpnews.com/culture/social-issues/item/7555-millennials-losing-their-religion#.UbevUrnD_IU.

Alter, Robert. *The Five Books of Moses: A Translation with Commentary*. New York: W.W. Norton, 2004.

"An Act to amend the Canadian Human Rights Act and the Criminal Code (gender identity)." n.d.

Antonides, Harry. *Stones For Bread: The Social Gospel and its Contemporary Legacy*. Ontario: Paideia, 1985.

Armstrong, John H. *Five Great Evangelists: Preachers of Real Revival*. Guernsey: Christian Focus, 1997.

Armstrong, Karen. *The Battle for God: Fundamentalism in Judaism, Christianity and Islam*. London: Harper Collins, 2001.

Augustine. *Commentary on Galatians*. Edited by Eric Plumer. Translated by Eric Plumer. Oxford: Oxford University Press, 2003.

—. *Letters: The Works of St Augustine; A translation for the 21st Century*. Edited by John E. Roselle. New York: New City Press, 2001.

—. *The City of God*. Translated by Marcus Dods. New York: The Modern Library, 1993.

—. *The Triumph of Grace: Augustine's writings on salvation*. Edited by N.R. Needham. Ebbw Vale: Grace Publications Trust, 2000.

Bacote, Vincent E. *The Spirit in public theology: Appropriating the legacy of Abraham Kuyper*. Grand Rapids: Baker Academic, 2005.

Bahnsen, Greg L. *Always Ready: Directions for defending the Faith*. Nacogdoches, Texas: Covenant Media Press, 1996.

—. *Theonomy in Christian Ethics*. Nacogdoches, Texas: Covenant Media, 2002.

Bahnsen, Greg L., and Kenneth L. Jr. Gentry. *House Divided: The Break-Up of Dispensational Theology*. Texas: Institute for Christian Economics, 1989.

Bahnsen, Greg. "The Reformation of Christian Apologetics." In *Foundations of Christian Scholarship*, edited by Gary North, 191-240. Vallecito, California: Ross House, 2001.

Bainton, Roland H. *Early Christianity*. Princeton, New Jersey: D. Van Nostrand, 1960.

Baklinski, Peter. "'Social justice' apart from evangelization drives youth away from Christianity, says new study." *Lifesite News*. July 5, 2013. http://www.lifesitenews.com/news/social-justice-apart-fromevangelization-drives-youth-away-from-christianity.

Barber, John. *The Road from Eden: Studies in Christianity and Culture*. Lakeland, FL: Whitefield Publishing,2008.

Barzun, Jacques. *From Dawn to Decadence: 1500 to the Present – 500 years of Western Cultural Life* . St. Ives: Harper Collins, 2000.

Beeke, Joel R. *Puritan Reformed Spirituality*. Grand Rapids: Reformation Heritage, 2004.

Berman, Harold J. *Law and Revolution II: The Impact of the Protestant Reformations on the Western Legal Tradition*. Cambridge, Massachusetts: Harvard University Press, 2003.

—. *Law and Revolution: The Formation of the Western Legal Tradition*. Cambridge, Massachusetts: Harvard University Press, 1983.

Bonhoeffer, Dietrich. *The Cost of Discipleship*. New York: Touchstone, 1995.

Bonta, J., T. Rugge, and M. Dauvergne. "The reconviction rate of federal offenders." Solicitor General Canada, Ottawa, 2003.

Bosch, David J. *Transforming Mission: Paradigm Shifts in Theology of Mission*. New York: Orbis Books, 1998.

Bowen, R. *So I Send You: A Study Guide to Mission*. London: SPCK, 1996.

Bowman, Robert M. "The New Puritanism: A Preliminary Assessment of Reconstructionism,." *Christian Research Journal* 10, no. 3 (1988).

Boyer, Paul S., ed. *The Oxford Companion to United States History*. New York: Oxford University Press, 2001.

Bradley, Carman. *Pivot of Civilization or Rivet of Life: Conflicting Worldviews and Same-Sex Marriage*. Victoria, British Columbia: Trafford, 2004.

Breese, D. *7 Men who Rule the World from the Grave*. Chicago: Moody, 1990.

Breuer, Sarah Dylan. "God's Justice: A Biblical View." In *The Justice Project*, edited by Elisa Padilla, Ashley Bunting Seeber Brian McLaren, 31-36. Grand Rapids: Baker, 2009.

Broton, Hon. Laurel C. *Bill 13, The Accepting Schools Act.* Toronto, Ontario, 2012.

Brown, Alison Leigh. *On Foucault.* Belmont, California: Wadsworth, 2000.

Brown, F., S. Driver, and C. Briggs. *The Brown-Driver-Briggs Hebrew and English Lexicon.* Peabody, Massachusetts: Hendrickson, 1996.

Brown, Michael L. *A Queer Thing Happened to America: And what a Long, Strange Trip it's Been.* Concord, North Carolina: Equal Time Books, 2011.

Bruce, F.F. *The Book of the Acts: The New International Commentary on the New Testament.* Grand Rapids: Eerdmans, 1988.

—. "Paul and the Athenians." *The Expository Times*, October 1976: 10.1177/001452467608800104.

Bruckner, Pascal. "Dazed and Apocalyptic: Why today's secular elites are prophesying a doomsday without redemption." *National Post*, May 22, 2012.

Brueggemann, Walter. "Hope from Old Sources for a New Century." In *Hope for the World: Mission in a Global Context,* edited by W. Brueggemann, 13-26. Louisville: Westminster John Knox Press, 2001.

—. *The Covenanted Self: Explorations in Law and Covenant.* Minneapolis: Fortress, 1999.

Powerful as God: The Children's Aid Society. Internet video. Directed by Esther Buckareff. 2011.

Burnside, Jonathan. *God, Justice and Society: Aspects of Law and Legality in the Bible.* Oxford: Oxford University Press, 2010.

Calvin, John. *Calvin's New Testament Commentaries: A Harmony of the Gospels, Matthew, Mark and Luke.* Edited by David W. Torrance & Thomas F. Torrance. Translated by A.W. Morrison. Grand Rapids: Eerdmans, 1994.

—. *Calvin's Wisdom: An Anthology Arranged Alphabetically.* Edited by Graham Miller. Bath, Avon: Banner of Truth Trust, 1992.

—. *Calvin's New Testament Commentaries: 1 Corinthians.* Edited by David W. Torrance and Thomas F. Torrance. Translated by John W. Fraser. Grand Rapids: Eerdmans, 1996.

—. *Institutes of the Christian Religion.* Translated by Henry Beveridge. Grand Rapids: Eerdmans, 1989.

—. *Institutes of the Christian Religion.* Edited by John T. McNeill. Translated by Ford Lewis Battles. II vols. Philadelphia: The Westminster Press, 1960.

Campbell, R. C. *Militant Christianity: Broadman Sermons.* Nashville: Broadman, 1940.

Campolo, Peggy. "Just Family Values: How Can Christians Advocate Justice for Non-traditional Families." In *The Justice Project*, edited by Elisa Padilla, and Ashley Bunting Seeber Brian McLaren, 129-134. Grand Rapids: Baker, 2009.

Camus, Albert. *The Rebel: An Essay on Man in Revolt.* New York: Vintage, 1956.

Canadian Centre for Justice Statistics. 1996. https://www.ncjrs.gov/App/publications/Abstract.aspx?id=163072.

Carden, Allen. *Puritan Christianity in America: Religion and Life in Seventeenth-Century Massachusetts .* Grand Rapids: Baker, 1990.

Carson, D.A. *Becoming Conversant with the Emergent Church.* Grand Rapids: Zondervan, 2005.

—. *The Gagging of God: Christianity Confronts Pluralism.* Leicester: Apollos, 1996.

Catherwood, Christopher. *Five Evangelical Leaders.* Guernsey: Christian Focus, 1994.

Cavanaugh, Willliam T. "Beyond Secular Parodies." In *Radical Orthodoxy*, edited by C. Pickstock & G. Ward J. Milbank, 182-200. London and New York: Routledge, 2003.

Ast, David, ed. "Challenging Homophobia and Heterosexism: A K-12 Curriculum Resource Guide." *Toronto District School Board.* 2011. http://www.canadianvalues.ca/SCC/TDSB_Equity%20_%20 InclusiveCurriculum_Seepage%2010%20_.pdf.

Chang, Curtis. *Engaging Unbelief: A Captivating Strategy from Augustine and Aquinas.* Downers Grove: Intervarsity, 2000.

Child, J.G. "Christian Reconstruction Movement." In *New Dictionary of Christian Ethics and Pastoral Theology*, edited by David J. Atkinson and David H. Field, 227. Downers Grove, Illinois: Intervarsity, 1995.

Chilton, David. *Paradise Restored.* Fort Worth: Dominion Press, 1985.

—. *Productive Christians In An Age of Guilt Manipulators: A Biblical Response to Ronald Sider.* Tyler, Texas: Institute For Christian Economics, 1981.

Chinn, Sarah E. *Inventing Modern Adolescence: The Children of Immigrants in Turn-of-the-Century America.* New Brunswick, New Jersey: Rutgers University Press, 2009.

City of Toronto. *Births and Fertility.* Public Health, Toronto: City of Toronto, 2012.

Clark, H.B. *Biblical Law: A Text Of The Statutes, Ordinances, And Judgments Of The Bible.* Powder Springs, Georgia: American Vision, 2010.

Clouser, Roy A. *The Myth of Religious Neutrality: An Essay on the Hidden Role of Religious Belief in Theories.* Notre Dame: University of Notre Dame Press, 2005.

Cochrane, Charles Norris. *Christianity and Classical Culture: A Study of Thought and Action from Augustus to Augustine.* New York: Oxford University Press, 1957.

Coffey, John. "Puritan Legacies." In *The Cambridge Companion to Puritanism,* edited by John Coffey and Paul C. H. Lim. Cambridge: Cambridge University Press, 2008.

Billions Behind Bars: Inside America's Prison Industry. Television documentary. Produced by Mitch Weitzner. Performed by Scott Cohn. CNBC, 2011.

Colbert, Don. *What would Jesus eat: The ultimate program for eating well, feeling great and living longer.* Nashville: Thomas Nelson, 2002.

Como, David R. "Radical Puritanism." In *The Cambridge Companion to Puritanism,* edited by John Coffey and Paul C. H. Lim, 241-258. Cambridge: Cambridge University Press, 2008.

Copley, Hamish. "The End to the Death Penalty for Sodomy in Canada." *The Drummer's Revenge.* September 9, 2007. http://thedrummersrevenge.wordpress.com/2007/09/09/the-end-to-the-deathpenalty-for-sodomy-in-canada/.

Crankshaw, Edward. *Gestapo: Instrument of Tyranny.* Ebbw Vale: Wren's Park, 2002.

Cromwell, Oliver. *The Writings and Speeches of Oliver Cromwell: Volume IV, The Protectorate 1655-1658.* Edited by Wilbur Cortez Abbott. Oxford: Clarendon, 1947.

Cushman, Herbert Ernest. *A Beginner's History of Philosophy.* Vol. 2. Boston: Houghton Mifflin, 1911.

Dalrymple, Theodore. *Our Culture, What's Left of It: The Mandarins and the Masses.* Chicago: Ivan R. Dee, 2005.

—. *In Praise of Prejudice: The Necessity of Preconceived Ideas.* New York: Encounter, 2007.

—. *Not With A Bang But A Wimper: The Politics and Culture of Decline.* Chicago: Ivan R. Dee, 2008.

Darwin, Charles. *Journal of a Voyage Round the World.* London: T. Nelson & Sons, Paternoster Row, 1890.

Davies, Philip. "Rough Justice?" In *Bible and Justice: Ancient Texts, Modern Challenges*, edited by Matthew J.M. Coomber, 43-56. Milton Keynes: Equinox, 2011.

Davis, J.C. *Oliver Cromwell.* London: Arnold, 2001.

Denning, Rt. Hon. Lord. *The Influence of Religion on Law.* Edmonton: Canadian Institute for Law, Theology and Public Policy, 1997.

Diewert, Dave. "Living Justly." *Mosaic*, 2009: 5-6.

Dodaro, R. *Christ and the Just Society in the Thought of Augustine.* Cambridge: Cambridge University Press, 2004.

Drummond, Lewis A. *The Evangelist: The Worldwide Impact of Billy Graham.* Nashville: Word, 2001.

Drummond, Lewis. *Spurgeon Prince of Preachers: A New Look at the 19th Century's Greatest Preacher.* Grand Rapids: Kregel, 1992.

Edersheim, Alfred. *Sketches of Jewish Social Life in the days of Christ.* Grand Rapids: Eerdmans, 1979.

Edgar, William. "The Passing of R. J. Rushdoony." *First Things.* August/September 2001. www.puritanboard.com/f54/passing-r-j-rushdoony-35542.

Eidsmoe, John. *Historical and Theological Foundations of Law.* III vols. Powder Springs, Georgia: American Vision and Tolle Lege Press, 2012.

Elniff, Terrill Irwin. *The Guise of Every Graceless Heart: Human Autonomy in Puritan Thought and Experience.* Vallecito: Ross House, 1981.

"Equity Policy." *Hamilton-Wentworth District School Board.* n.d. http://www.peacehamilton.com/pdf/policy.pdf (accessed 2013).

Farah, Joseph. "Suicide in the Age of Obama." *Whistleblower Magazine,* April 2013.

Fernando, Ajith. "The Uniqueness of Jesus Christ." In *Telling the Truth: Evangelizing Postmoderns*, edited by D. A. Carson, 123-137. Grand Rapids: Zondervan, 2000.

Finney, Charles G. *The Memoirs of Charles G. Finney: The Complete*

Restored Text. Edited by Garth M. Rosell & Richard A.G. Dupuis. Grand Rapids: Zondervan, 1989.

Flinn, Richard. "Rutherford and Puritan Political Theory." *The Journal of Christian Reconstruction: Symposium on Puritanism and Law,* 1978: 49-74.

Folger, Janet L. *The Criminalization of Christianity: Read This Book Before It Becomes Illegal!* Colorado Springs: Multnomah, 2005.

Foulner, Martin A. *Theonomy and the Westminster Confession .* Edinburgh: Marpet, 1997.

Fourie, Owen. "The State and the Church: Conflict or Harmony?" *The Journal of Christian Reconstruction: Symposium on the Decline and Fall of the West and the Return of Christendom,* 1994: 277-294.

Fourie, Owen. "The State Reduced to its Biblical Limits." In *A Comprehensive Faith: An International Festschrift For Rousas John Rushdoony,* 193-200. San Jose: Friends of Chalcedon, 1996.

Frame, John. Cornelius Van Til: *An analysis of his thought.* Phillipsburg, New Jersey: Presbyterian & Reformed, 1995.

—. *The Doctrine of the Christian Life: A Theology of Lordship.* Phillipsburg, New Jersey: Presbyterian & Reformed, 2008.

Gairdner, William D. *The Trouble With Canada ... Still.* Toronto: Key Porter, 2010.

—. *The War Against the Family: A Parent Speaks Out on the Political, Economic and Social Policies That Threaten Us All.* Toronto: Stoddart, 1992.

Galli, Mark. *131 Christians Everyone Should Know.* Nashville: Broadman Reference, 2010.

Gardam, Tim. "Christians in China: Is the Country in Spiritual Crisis?" *BBC.* September 11, 2011. http://www.bbc.co.uk/news/magazine-14838749.

Garland, David. *Punishment and modern society: A study in social theory.* Chicago: University of Chicago Press, 1990.

Geisler, Norman L. *Christian Ethics: Contemporary Issues and Options.* Grand Rapids: Baker Academic, 2010.

Gentles, Ian. *Oliver Cromwell: God's Warrior and the English Revolution.* New York: Palgrave MacMillan, 2011.

George, Timothy. *The Theology of the Reformers.* Nashville: B&H, 1988.

Geree, John. *The Character of an Old English Puritan or Non-Conformist.* London: Christopher Meredith, 1646.

Goldberg, Michelle. *Kingdom Coming: The Rise of Christian Nationalism*. New York: W.W. Norton, 2006.

Graham, Billy. *Just As I Am: The Autobiography of Billy Graham*. New York: Harper Collins, 1997.

Grant, George. *Bringing in the Sheaves: Replacing Government Welfare with Biblical Charity*. Windsor, New York: The Reformer Library, 1995.

Grant, George Parkin. *Technology and Empire: Perspectives on North America*. Toronto: House of Anansi, 1969.

Grayling, A. C. *The Good Book: A Humanist Bible*. New York: Walker & Co., 2011.

Gregg, Samuel. "Europe, Immigration, and Merkel's Christian Values." *Acton Institute Power Blog*. November 24, 2010. http://blog.acton. org/archives/20178-europe-immigration-andmerkel%E2%80%99s-christian-values.html.

Gundry, Stanley N., ed. *Five Views On Law And Gospel*. Grand Rapids: Zondervan, 1996.

Gurnall, William. T*he Christian in Complete Armour*. Phillipsburg, New Jersey: Banner of Truth Trust, 1964.

Gyapong, Deborah. "Pro-life activist Linda Gibbons counts on Christ's strength." *The Catholic Register*. November 1, 2012. http://www. catholicregister.org/news/canada/item/15350-pro-life-activistlinda-gibbons-counts-on-christ%E2%80%99s-strength.

H.G.Wells. "Points of View: A Series of Broadcast Addresses." 1930. http://dspace.gipe.ac.in/jspui/bitstream/1/6186/3/GIPE-062996.pdf (accessed June 18, 2013).

Hall, David W. *The Legacy of John Calvin: His influence on the modern world*. Phillipsburg, New Jersey: Presbyterian & Reformed, 2008.

Hanks, Geoffrey. *70 Great Christians: Changing the World*. Bath: Christian Focus, 1992.

Hannah, John. "Billy Sunday: Acrobatic Evangelist." In *More than Conquerors*, edited by John Woodbridge. Candle Books, 1994.

Hannam, James. *The Genesis of Science: How the Christian Middle Ages Launched the Scientific Revolution*. Washington, DC: Regnery Publishing, 2011.

Hardman, Keith J. *Charles Grandison Finney 1792-1875: Revivalist and Reformer*. Durham: Evangelical Press, 1990.

Harris, Sam. "Response to Controversy." *Sam Harris*. April 7, 2013.

http://www.samharris.org/site/full_text/response-to-controversy2.

—. *The End of Faith: Religious Terror and the Future of Reason*. New York: W.W. Norton, 2004.

Harrison, Carol. *Augustine: Christian Truth and Fractured Humanity*. Oxford: Oxford University Press, 2000.

Haykin, Michael A.G. *Defence of the Truth: Contending for the faith yesterday and today*. Darlington: Evangelical Press, 2004.

—. *The Reformers and Puritans as Spiritual Mentors*. Kitchener, Ontario: Joshua Press, 2012.

Hegel, G.W.F. *Reason in history: A general introduction to the philosophy of history*. Translated by Robert S. Hartman. Indianapolis: The Liberal Arts Press, 1953.

Hegeman, David Bruce. *Plowing in Hope: Toward a Biblical Theology of Culture*. Moscow, Idaho: Canon, 2007.

Henry, Matthew. *Matthew Henry's Commentary On The Whole Bible In Six Volumes: Vol. 5 - Matthew To John*. New York: Fleming H. Revell Company, ca. 1935.

Herrick, James A. "C. S. Lewis and the Advent of the Posthuman." In *The Magician's Twin: C. S. Lewis on Science, Scientism, and Society*, edited by John G. West, 235-264. Seattle: Discovery Institute Press, 2012.

Hick, John. *God Has Many Names*. Philadelphia: Westminster, 1982.

Hilberg, Raul. *The Destruction of the European Jews*. Chicago: Quadrangle, 1961.

Hitchens, Peter. *The Rage Against God: How Atheism led me to Faith*. Grand Rapids: Zondervan, 2010.

Hodge, C.A. *Evangelical Theology: Lectures on Doctrine*. Carlisle, Pennsylvania: The Banner of Truth Trust, 1990.

Holland, Tom. *The Forge of Christendom: The End of Days and the Epic Rise of the West*.New York: Doubleday, 2008.

Homophobia is Gay. Internet video. Produced by Thames Valley District School Board. 2010.

Horton, Michael. "Transforming Culture with a Messiah Complex." *9 Marks*. December 2007. http://sites.silaspartners.com/cc/article/0,,PTID314526_CHID598014_CIID2376346,00.html.

House, H. Wayne, ed. *Restoring the Constitution, 1787-1987: essays in celebration of the Bicentennial*. Dallas: Probe, 1987.

Howse, Ernest Marshall. *Saints in politics: The Clapham Sect and the growth of freedom*. Trowbridge: George Allen and Unwin, 1953.

Humphreys, Edward, ed. *Great Speeches : Words That Shaped The World* . Arcturus, 2009.

Huxley, Julian. *I Believe: The personal philosophies of twenty-three eminent men and women of our time*. London: George Allen and Unwin, 1944.

Ignatieff, Michael. "9/11 and the age of sovereign failure." *The Globe and Mail*. September 9, 2011. http://www.theglobeandmail.com/news/world/americas/september-11/michael-ignatieff-911-andthe-age-of-sovereign-failure/article2160153/.

John, J. "A matter of justice." *Philo Trust*. September 12, 2012. http://www.philotrust.com/blog/2012/09/a-matter-of-justice#.UiYaTD_hdbA.

Johnson, Paul. *Intellectuals: From Marx and Tolstoy To Sartre and Chomsky*. New York: Harper Collins, 2007.

Jonas, George. "Supreme Court puts the Final Nail in the Coffin of Religious Freedom." *National Post*. February 28, 2012. http://fullcomment.nationalpost.com/2012/02/28/george-jonas-supreme-courtputs-the-final-nail-in-the-coffin-of-religious-freedom/.

Jones, Joel R. Beeke & Mark. *A Puritan Theology: Doctrine For Life*. Grand Rapids: Reformation Heritage Books, 2012.

Jordan, James B. *The Covenant Enforced: Sermons on Deuteronomy 27 and 28*. Tyler, Texas: Institute for Christian Economics, 1990.

Jordan, James. "Calvinism and the Judicial laws of Moses: An Historical Survey." *The Journal of Christian Reconstruction: Symposium on Puritanism and Law*, 2000: 17-48.

Jue, Jeffrey K. "Puritan Millenarianism in Old and New England." In *The Cambridge Companion to Puritanism*, edited by John Coffey and Paul C. H. Lim. Cambridge: Cambridge University Press, 2008.

Kant, Immanuel. *The Critique of Pure Reason: Preface to the second edition, 1787*. Vol. 42. Encyclopedia Britannica, Great Books of the Western World, 1952.

Kearney, Richard. *Dialogues with Contemporary Continental Thinkers*. Manchester: University Press, 1984.

Keller, Timothy. *Generous Justice: How God's Grace Makes Us Just*. New York: Dutton, 2010.

Keller, Timothy. "Theonomy and the poor: Some reflections." In *Theonomy: A Reformed Critique,* edited by William S. Barker and

W. Robert Godfrey, 263-294. Grand Rapids: Zondervan, 1990.

Kirk, J. Andrew. *The Good News of the Kingdom Coming.* Downers Grove, Illinois: Intervarsity, 1985.

—. *What is Mission? Theological Explorations.* Minneapolis: Fortress, 2000.

Klaiber, W. *Call and Response: Biblical Foundations of a Theology of Evangelism.* Nashville: Abingdon, 1997.

Klinghoffer, David. *Shattered Tablets: Why We Ignore The Ten Commandments At Our Peril.* New York: Doubleday, 2007.

Kreeft, Peter. *Christianity for Modern Pagans: Pascal's Pensees, edited, outlined and explained.* San Francisco: Ignatiius, 1993.

Kuiper, R.B. *God Centred Evangelism.* Edinburgh: Banner of Truth Trust, 1966.

Küng, Hans. *Does God Exist: An Answer for Today.* New York: Doubleday, 1980.

Lagartera, Reece. "Shout Out Against Homophobia, Biphobia, Transphobia and Heterosexism." *Ontario Secondary School Teacher's Federation.* Rainbow Resource Centre. 2010. http://www. osstf.on.ca/adx/aspx/adxGetMedia.aspx?DocID=0c42ad90-0d22-41f4-a6ce-dcba45381e61&MediaID=8241f51ddf44-41ef-8e9a-559ffa3293ed&Filename=shout-out.pdf&l=English.

Lane, Tony. *The Lion Concise Book of Christian Thought: Great thinkers of the Christian faith from the first century to the present.* Reading: Lion, 1996.

Lavoie, Denise. "Freed from his body: U.S judge orders prison officials to pay for inmate's sex change surgery." *National Post,* September 5, 2012.

"Leading Causes of Death, 2000-2004." Statistics Canada, 2008.

Leithart, Peter J. *Defending Constantine: The Twilight of an Empire and the Dawn of Christendom.* Downers Grove, Illinois: IVP Academic, 2010.

Lennox, John. *God's Undertaker: Has Science Buried God?* Lion Hudson, 2007.

Lewis, C.S. *God in the Dock.* Grand Rapids: Eerdmans, 1970.

—. *Letters to Malcolm Chiefly on Prayer.* London: Geoffrey Bles, 1964.

—. *The Problem of Pain.* London: Fount, 1977.

Lewis, Jessica. "Moments of spirituality can induce liberal attitudes,

U of T researchers say." *University of Toronto, Faculty of Arts and Sciences*. February 22, 2013. http://www.artsci.utoronto.ca/main/ newsitems/spirituality-induce-liberal-attitudes?utm_so.

Lim, John Coffey and Paul C. H., ed. *The Cambridge Companion to Puritanism*. Cambridge: Cambridge University Press, 2008.

"Living together before marriage study: No longer seen as a bad omen." *Huffington Post*. March 22, 2012. http://www.huffingtonpost. ca/2012/03/22/living-together-before-marriage-study_n_1372756. html.

Lorentzen, Lois Ann, and Salvador Leavitt-Alcantara. "Religion and Environmental Struggles in Latin America." In *The Oxford Handbook of Religion and Ecology*, edited by Roger S. Gottlieb, 510-534. New York: Oxford University Press, 2006.

Lowe, Janet. *Billy Graham Speaks*. Hoboken: John Wiley & Sons, 1999.

Luther, Martin. *Martin Luther's Table Talk: Luther's Comments on Life, the Church and the Bible*. Christian Focus, 2003.

Macdonald, A. M., ed. *Chambers' Twentieth Century Dictionary*. New Edition. Edinburgh: W. & R. Chambers, 1972.

Machen, J. Gresham. "Christianity and Culture." *The Princeton Theological Review* 11, no. 1, 1-15 (1913).

Mangalwadi, Vishal. *The Book that Made your World: How the Bible Created the Soul of Western Civilization*. Nashville: Thomas Nelson, 2011.

Maqdisi, E Al, and Sam Solomon. *Modern Day Trojan Horse: The Islamic Doctrine of Immigration, Accepting Freedom or Imposing Islam*. Charlottesville: ANM, 2009.

McCarthy, Andrew C. "Islamophobic Hysteria Becomes Conventional Wisdom." *PJ Media*. August 23, 2012. http:// pjmedia.com/andrewmccarthy/2012/08/23/islamophobic-hysteria-becomesconventional-wisdom/.

McDurmon, Joel. "Why Leftists Should Shut Up About Dominionism." *The American Vision*. September 29, 2011. http:// americanvision.org/5209/why-leftists-should-shut-up-about-%e2%80%9cdominionism%e2%80%9d/.

McGoldrick, James E. *Abraham Kuyper: God's Renaissance Man*. Ebbw: Evangelical Press, 2000.

McGrath, Allister. *Bridge-Building: Effective Christian Apologetics*. Ebbw Vale: Intervarsity, 1992.

McLaren, Brian D. *A Generous Orthodoxy*. Grand Rapids: Zondervan, 2004.

McVicar, Michael J. "First Owyhee and Then the World: The Early Ministry of R.J. Rushdoony." *Chalcedon*. December 2009. http://www.chalcedon.edu/articles/article.php?ArticleID=2894.

McVicar, Michael J. "The Lord Will Perfect That Which Concerneth Me: The Work of Rousas John Rushdoony." *Faith for All of Life* (Chalcedon Foundation), 2010: 6-11, 24.

Billy Graham: God's Ambassador: The Story of Billy Graham's Extraordinary Life and Ministry. Directed by Michael Merriman. Produced by Bill Carter & Barry Jennings. 2006.

Molnar, Thomas. *Utopia: The perennial heresy*. New York: University Press of America, 1990.

Montgomery, John Warwick. *Law and Gospel: A Study Integrating Faith and Practice*. Edmonton: Christian Legal Fellowship, 1994.

Morgan, G. Campbell. *The Acts of The Apostles*. New York: Fleming H. Revell, 1924.

Morrill, John. *Oliver Cromwell*. Oxford: Oxford University Press, 2007.

Morrill, John. "The Puritan Revolution." In *The Cambridge Companion to Puritanism*, edited by John Coffey and Paul C. H. Lim, 67-88. Cambridge: Cambridge University Press, 2008.

Motyer, Alec. *Roots: Let the Old Testament speak*. Glasgow: Christian Focus, 2009.

Mrozek, A., and R. Walberg. *Private choices, public costs: How failing families cost us all*. Ottawa: Institute of Marriage & Family Canada, 2009.

Murphy, Edward J. "Conflicting Ultimates: Jurisprudence as Religious Controversy." *American Journal of Jurisprudence*, no. 35 (1990): 129-148.

Murray, Iain. *The Puritan Hope: Revival and the Interpretation of Prophecy*. Bucks: Banner of Truth Trust, 1991.

Nash, Ronald H. *Is Jesus the Only Savior*. Grand Rapids: Zondervan, 1994.

—. *Social Justice and the Christian* Church. Lima, Ohio: Academic Renewal, 2002.

—. *Why the Left is Not Right: The Religious Left: who they are and what they believe*. Grand Rapids: Zondervan, 1996.

Nietzsche, Friedrich. "My sister and I." In *The complete works of*

Nietzche, edited by Oscar Levy. New York: Bridgehead, 1954.

—. *The Will to Power in Science, Nature, Society and Art.* New York: Frederick Publications, n.d.

Noll, Mark A. *A History of Christianity in the United States and Canada.* Grand Rapids: Eerdmans, 1992.

North, Gary, ed. *The Journal of Christian Reconstruction: Symposium on Puritanism and Law* (Chalcedon), 1978.

—. "R.J. Rushdoony: R.I.P." *Chalcedon Report: In Memoriam,* April 2001.

North, Gary. "Hermeneutics and Leviticus 19:19 – Passing Dr. Poythress' Test." In *Theonomy: An Informed Response*, edited by Gary North, 255-294. Tyler, Texas: Institute for Christian Economics, 1991.

—. *Tools of Dominion: The Case Laws of Exodus.* Tyler, Texas: Institute for Christian Economics, 1990.

O'Connor, DJ. *Aquinas and Natural Law.* London: MacMillan, 1967.

Obenchain, Diane B. *The Study of Religion and the Coming Global Generation.* Vol. 3, in *God and Globalisation: Christ And the Dominions of Civilization*, edited by Max L. Stackhouse and Diane B. Obenchain, 59-109. Harrisburg, Pennsylvania: Trinity Press International, 2002.

"Ontario Population Projections Update, 2012-2036." Ontario Ministry of Finance, Government of Ontario, 2013.

Oreopoulos, Philip. "Canadian compulsory school laws and their impact on educational attainment and future earnings." *Statistics Canada.* 2006. http://www.statcan.gc.ca/pub/11f0019m/11f0019m2005251-eng.pdf.

Origen. *Contra Celsum.* Translated by Henry Chadwick. Cambridge: Cambridge University Press, 1953.

Orr-Ewing, Amy. *Is the Bible Intolerant? Sexist? Oppressive? Homophobic? Outdated? Irrelevant?* Downers Grove, Illinois: Intervarsity, 2005.

Orwell, George. *1984.* New York: Signet, 1950.

"OSSTF "Shout Out"." n.d. http://www.osstf.on.ca/adx/aspx/adxGetMedia.aspx?DocID=0c42ad90-0d22-41f4-a6ce-dcba45381e61&MediaID=8241f51d-df44-41ef-8e9a-559ffa3293ed&Filename=shoutout.pdf&l=English.

O'Toole, Megan. "Police need witnesses to nab gang." *National Post,* September 12, 2012.

Pagitt, Doug. "This Is Just the Beginning: Living Our Great-Grandchildren's History." In *An Emergent Manifesto of Hope*, edited by Doug Pagitt and Tony Jones, 303-308. Grand Rapids: Baker, 2007.

Pearse, Meic. *Why The Rest Hates the West: Understanding the Roots of Global Rage*. Downers Grove, Illinois: Intervarsity, 2004.

Pera, Marcello. *Why We Should Call Ourselves Christians: The Religious Roots of Free Societies*. Translated by L.B. Lappin. New York: Encounter, 2011.

Peterson, Eugene H. *Reversed Thunder: The Revelation of John & the Praying Imagination*. San Francisco: Harper, 1988.

Phillips, Howard. "The Renewal of Christendom is R.J. Rushdoony's legacy." *Chalcedon Report,* no. 429 (April 2001): 28.

Pinnock, Clark. *A Wideness in God's Mercy*. Grand Rapids: Zondervan, 1992.

Plantinga, Alvin. "Augustinian Christian Philosophy." In *The Augustinian Tradition,* edited by Gareth B.

Matthews, 1-26. Berkeley: University of California Press, 1999.

Porter, H. C. *Puritanism in Tudor England*. Columbia, South Carolina: University of South Carolina Press, 1971.

Porter, Roy. *The Greatest Benefit to Mankind: A Medical History of Humanity*. New York: W.W. Norton, 1997.

"Public Education Advocates for Christian Equity." n.d. http://www.peacehamilton.com/index.php. *R. v. Big Drug Mart Ltd.* 1 S.C.R. 295 (Supreme Court of Canada, April 24, 1985).

Powell, E.A. and Rushdoony, R.J. *Tithing and Dominion*: Ross House, P.O. Box 67, Vallecito, California 95251.

Ramachandra, Vinoth. *Faiths in Conflict: Christian Integrity in a Multi-Cultural World*. Downers Grove, Illinois: Intervarsity, 1999.

Ramey, Robert F. "Billy Graham: Pathfinder in Evangelism." In *More Than Conquerors*, edited by John Woodbridge. Candle Books, 1994.

Rassinier, Paul. *The Holocaust story and the lies of Ulysses: a study of the German concentration camps and the alleged extermination of European Jewry*. Translated by Adam Robbins. Newport Beach, California: Institute for Historical Review, 1950 [translated and reprinted 1978].

"Realizing the Promise of Diversity: Ontario's Equity and Inclusive Education Strategy Guidelines." *Ontario Ministry of Education.* 2009. http://www.edu.gov.on.ca/eng/policyfunding/inclusiveguide.pdf.

Reisinger, Ernest. *The Law and the Gospel*. Phillipsburg, New Jersey: Presbyterian & Reformed, 1997.

Richard, Lucien Joseph. *The Spirituality of John Calvin*. Atlanta: John Knox Press, 1974.

Robinson, Armin L., ed. T*he Ten Commandments: Ten Short Novels of Hitler's War Against the Moral Code*. New York: Simon & Schuster, 1943.

Robinson, Marilynne. *The Death of Adam: Essays on Modern Thought*. New York: Picador, 2005.

Rorty, Richard. *Contingency, Irony and Solidarity*. Cambridge: Cambridge University Press, 1989.

Rushdoony, Mark. "A biographical sketch of my father." In *A comprehensive faith: An international festschrift for Rousas John Rushdoony*, edited by P. Andrew Sandlin, 21-32. San Jose: Friends of Chalcedon, 1996.

Rushdoony, Mark, interview by Joe Boot. *Live Interview with Joe Boot* Vallecito, California, (March 12, 2009).

—. "Rousas John Rushdoony: April 25th 1916 - February 8th, 2001." *Chalcedon Report*, no. 429 (April 2001): 3.

Rushdoony, R.J. *A Christian Survey of World History*. Vallecito, California: Ross House, 1999.

—. *Chariots of Prophetic Fire*: Studies in Elijah and Elisha. Vallecito, California: Ross House, 2003.

—. *Systematic Theology*. Vol. 1. 2 vols. Vallecito, California: Ross House, 1994.

—. *The Biblical Philosophy of History*. Vallecito, California: Ross House, 1997.

—. *The Mythology of Science*. Vallecito, California: Ross House, 2001.

—. *The Philosophy of the Christian Curriculum*. Vallecito, California: Ross House, 1981.

—. *The Sermon on the Mount*. Vallecito, California: Ross House, 2009.

—. *A Word in Season Vol. 1*. Vallecito, CA: Ross House Books, 2010.

—. *Bringing back the King: The Crown Rights of Christ the King*. Comp. R.J. Rushdoony. 2006. Audio cassette.

—. *By What Standard: An analysis of the philosophy of Cornelius Van Til*. Vallecito, California: Ross House, 1995.

—. "On death and dying." *Chalcedon Report*, April 2001: 2.

—. "Christian reconstruction as a movement." *The Journal of Christian Reconstruction: Symposium on Reconstruction in the Church and State,* 1996: 5-38.

—. "Christianity and Freedom." *The Journal of Christian Reconstruction: Symposium on the Decline and Fall of the West and the Return of Christendom,* 1994: 75-82.

—. *Christianity and the State.* Vallecito, California: Ross House, 1986.

—. *Death and Restitution.* Comp. R.J. Rushdoony. RR10777. n.d. MP3.

—. *Deuteronomy: Commentaries on the Pentateuch.* Vallecito, California: Ross House, 2008.

—. *Exodus: Commentaries on the Pentateuch.* Vallecito, California: Ross House, 2004.

—. "The Centrality of the Atonement." *Faith For All of Life,* March/April 2012: 2-3, 18.

—. *Freud.* Vallecito, California: Ross House, 2006.

—., interview by Bill Moyer. *God and politics: On earth as it is in heaven* PBS. 1988.

—. *In His Service: The Christian Calling to Charity.* Vallecito, CA: Ross House, 2009.

—. *Intellectual Schizophrenia: Culture, Crisis and Education.* Philadelphia: Presbyterian & Reformed, 1961.

—. *Larceny in the Heart: The Economics of Satan and the Inflationary State.* Vallecito, California: Ross House, 2002.

—. *Law and Liberty.* Vallecito, California: Ross House, 1984.

—. *Leviticus: Commentaries on the Pentateuch.* Vallecito, California: Ross House, 2005.

—. *Noble Savages: Exposing the Worldview of Pornographers and Their War against Christian Civilization.* Vallecito, California: Ross House, 2005.

—. *Salvation and Godly Rule.* Vallecito, California: Ross House, 1983.

—. *Sovereignty.* Vallecito, California: Ross House, 2007.

—. *Systematic Theology.* Vol. 2. 2 vols. Vallecito, California: Ross House, 1994.

—. *The Atheism of the Early Church.* Vallecito, California: Ross

House, 2000.

—. *The Foundations of Social Order: Studies in the Creeds and Councils of the Early Church.* Vallecito, California: Ross House, 1998.

—. *The Institutes of Biblical Law.* Phillipsburg, New Jersey: Presbyterian and Reformed, 1973.

—. *The Institutes of Biblical Law: Law and Society.* Vol. II. Vallecito, California: Ross House, 1982.

—. "The Meaning of Theocracy." In *The Roots of Reconstruction,* by R.J. Rushdoony, 63-668. Vallecito, California: Ross House, 1991.

—. *The Messianic Character of American Education.* Vallecito, California: Ross House, 1995.

—. *The One and the Many: Studies in the Philosophy of Order and Ultimacy.* Fairfax: Thoburn Press, 1978.

—. *This Independent Republic: Studies in the Nature and Meaning of American History.* Nutley: The Craig Press, 1964.

Rushdoony, Rousas John, and P. Andrew Sandlin. *Infallibility and Interpretation.* Vallecito, California: Chalcedon Foundation, 2000.

Russell, Bertrand. *A Fresh Look at Empiricism:1927–42* . London: Routledge, 1996.

Ryken, Leland. *Worldly Saints: The Puritans as They Really Were* . Grand Rapids: Zondervan, 1986.

Sabine, G.H. *A History of Political Theory.* Third. New York: Rinehart & Winston, 1961.

Sandlin, P. Andrew. "R.J. Rushdoony: Champion of Faith and Liberty." *Chalcedon Report,* no. 429 (April 2001): 11.

Sandlin, P. Andrew, ed. *The Future of the Conservative Movement: A Chalcedon Symposium.* Vallecito, California: Chalcedon Foundation, 1998.

Sandlin, P. Andrew. "The Genius of the Thought of Rousas John Rushdoony." In *A Comprehensive Faith: An International Festschrift For Rousas John Rushdoony,* edited by P. Andrew Sandlin, 7-20. San Jose: Friends of Chalcedon, 1996.

Sandys-Wunsch, John. "Is the Belief in Human Rights either Biblical or Useful?" In *Bible and Justice: Ancient Texts, Modern Challenges,* by 57-69, edited by Matthew J.M. Coomber. Milton Keynes: Equinox, 2011.

Sartre, Jean-Paul. *Being and Nothingness: An Essay in Phenomenological*

Ontology. Translated by Hazel E. Barns. New York: Philosophical Library, 1956.

Sawyer, Jack W. Jr. "Moses and the Majestrate: Aspects of Calvin's Political Theory in Contemporary Focus." Westminster Theological Seminary, 1986.

Schlissel, Steve. "Personal email correspondence with author." July 18, 2013.

Schreiner, Thomas R. *New Testament Theology: Magnifying God in Christ*. Grand Rapids: Baker Academic, 2008.

Schwarz, Alan. "A.D.H.D. Seen in 11% of U.S Children as Diagnoses Rise." *New York Times*, March 31, 2013.

Sears, Alan, and Craig Osten. *The Homosexual Agenda: Exposing the Principal Threat to Religious Freedom Today*. Nashville: Broadman & Holman, 2003.

Selmanovic, Samir. "The Sweet Problem of Inclusiveness: Facing our God in the Other." In *An Emergent Manifesto of Hope*, edited by Doug Pagitt and Tony Jones, 189-200. Grand Rapids: Baker, 2007.

Singer, Peter. *Animal Liberation*. Second. New York: New York Review, 1990.

Small, Christopher J. *Music, Society, Education* . London: John Caldwel, 1980.

Smith, James K.A. *Introducing Radical Orthodoxy*. Grand Rapids: Baker Academic and Paternoster, 2004.

Social Justice Policy Group;. *Breakdown Britain: Interim report on the state of the nation*. London: The Centre for Social Justice, 2006.

Sproul, R. C. Jr. *Essential Truths of the Christian Faith.* Wheaton: Tyndale House, 1992.

Sproul, R.C. Jr. "What is Theonomy?" *Ligonier Ministries*. May 12, 2010. http://www.ligonier.org/blog/what-reconstructionism-what-theonomy/ (accessed 2012).

Stark, Rodney. *God's Battalions: The Case for the Crusades*. New York: Harper One, 2009.

Stott, J. *New Issues Facing Christians Today*. Third. London: Marshall Pickering, 1999.

Stout, Harry S. *The Divine Dramatist: George Whitefield and the Rise of Modern Evangelicalism.* Grand Rapids: Eerdmans, 1991.

Demographic Winter: The decline of the human family. DVD. Directed by Rick Stout. Produced by SRB Documentary. 2008.

Sutton, Ray R. *That You May Prosper*. Tyler, Texas: Institute for Christian Economics, 1987.

Sutton, Ray. "Whose Conditions for Charity." In *Theonomy: An Informed Response*, edited by Gary North, 231-254. Tyler, Texas: Institute for Christian Economics, 1991.

Swift, Michael. "Homosexual Manifesto." *The Gay Community News*. 1987. http://panindigan.tripod.com/homorev.html (accessed November 2012).

Taylor, Barry. "Converting Christianity: The end and beginning of faith." In *An Emergent Manifesto of Hope*, edited by Doug Pagitt and Tony Jones, 163-170. Grand Rapids: Baker, 2007.

Taylor, Ian T. In *The Minds of Men: Darwin and the New World Order*. Toronto: TFE Publishing, 1984.

Taylor, Rupert. "Will Canada Bring Back the Death Penalty?" *Suite 101*. December 1, 2010. http://suite101.com/article/will-canada-bring-back-the-death-penalty-a315608.

Thames Valley District School Board. "Diversity - Embracing Who We Are." *Thames Valley District School Board*. n.d. http://www.tvdsb.ca/programs.cfm?subpage=188593 (accessed 2013).

"The 10 most dangerous cities in the world." *Urban Titan*. September 2012. http://urbantitan.com/10-most-dangerous-cities-in-the-world-in-2010/.

"The Book of the Laws and Liberties Concerning the Inhabitants of the Massachusetts." In *The Puritan Tradition in America 1620-1730*, edited by Alden T. Vaughan, 161-171. Columbia: University of South Carolina Press, 1972.

"The law and your body." *Kids' Help Phone*. 2013. http://www.kidshelpphone.ca/Teens/InfoBooth/Money-jobs-laws/Laws/The-law-and-your-body.aspx#abortion.

"The Music with the Form and Order of the Service to be Performed at the Coronation of Her Most Excellent Majesty Queen Elizabeth II in the Abbey Church of Westminster on Tuesday the 2nd Day of June, 1953 ." London: Novello & Co., 1953.

Todd, Douglas. "Faced with feminization churches want to reach men." *Vancouver Sun*. December 15, 2012. http://blogs.vancouversun.com/2012/12/15/faced-with-feminization-churches-wonder-howto-reach-men/.

Trueman, Carl. "Rushdoony and the Holocaust." *The Thinklings*.

December 21, 2006. http://thinklings.org/?post_id=3487.

—. "Rushdoony Revisited." *Reformation 21*. December 21, 2006. http://www.reformation21.org/blog/2006/12/rushdoony-revisited. php.

—. "Rushdoony, historical incompetence, racism and lunacy." *Reformation 21*. December 20, 2006. http://www.reformation21. org/blog/2006/12/rushdoony-historical-incompete.php.

—. "Rushdoony, once again – for the last time." *Reformation 21*. December 31, 2006. http://www.reformation21.org/blog/2006/12/ rushdoony-once-again-for-the-l.php.

"Uganda to Pass Anti-Gay Law as 'Christmas Gift'." *BBC*. November 13, 2012. http://www.bbc.co.uk/news/world-africa-20318436.

Unnamed York University student. "Untitled letter to author." 2011.

Van Til, Cornelius. *A Christian Theory of Knowledge*. Phillipsburg, New Jersey: Presbyterian & Reformed, 1969.

—. *Christian Apologetics*. Phillipsburg, New Jersey: Presbyterian & Reformed, 2003.

—. *The Defense of the Faith*. Phillipsburg, New Jersey: Presbyterian & Reformed, 2008.

Van Til, Cornelius, and Louis Berkhof. *Foundations of Christian Education*. Edited by Dennis E. Johnson. Phillipsburg, New Jersey: Presbyterian & Reformed, 1990.

Van Til, Henry R. *The Calvinistic Concept of Culture*. Philadelphia: Presbyterian & Reformed, 1959.

Ventrella, Jefferey J. "Practicing Postmillennialism." In *Thine Is The Kingdom: Studies in the Postmillennial Hope*, edited by Kenneth L. Gentry Jr., 191-222. Vallecito, California: Chalcedon, 2003.

Verkuyl, Johannes. *Contemporary Missiology: An Introduction*. Grand Rapids: Eerdmans, 1978.

Vermigli, Peter Martyr. "Of a magistrate, and the difference between civil and ecclesiastical power (1561)." In *The Zürich connection and Tudor political theology*, edited by W.J.T. Kirby, 75-120. Leiden: Brill, 2007.

Vermigli, Peter Martyr. "Of a magistrate, and the difference between civil and ecclesiastical power (1561)." In *The Zürich connection and Tudor political theology*, edited by W. J. T. Kirby. Leiden & Boston, 2007.

Vine, W.E., Merrill F. Unger, and William Jr. White, . *Vine's Expository Dictionary of Biblical Words*. Nashville: Thomas Nelson, 1985.

Visher, Christy A. *Transitions from Prison to Community: Understanding*

Individual Pathways. Justice Policy Center, Washington, D.C.: The Urban Institute, 2003.

Volf, Miroslav. *A Public Faith: How Followers of Christ Should Serve the Common Good*. Grand Rapids: Brazos, 2011.

Wagner, Michael. *Christian Citizenship Guide: Christianity and Canadian Political Life* . Ottawa: ARPA Canada, 2011.

—. *Leaving God behind: The Charter of Rights and Canada's official rejection of Christianity*. Russell, Ontario: Christian Governance, 2012.

—. *Standing on Guard for Thee: The Past, Present and Future of Canada's Christian Right*. St. Catharines, Ontario: Freedom Press Canada, 2007.

—. *The Anglosphere's Broken Covenant: Rediscovering the Validity and Importance of the Solemn League and Covenant*. Lewiston, Idaho: Gospel Covenant, 2010.

Walsh, Brian J. "From Shock and Awe to Shock and Grace: A Response to Naomi Klein's 'The Shock Doctrine 1'." *Empire Remixed*. University of Toronto, November 26, 2007.

Warfield, B.B. "Jesus Christ the Propitiation for the Whole World." In *Thine is the Kingdom: Studies in the Postmillennial Hope,* edited by Jr. Kenneth L. Gentry, 67-82. Vallecito, California: Chalcedon, 2003.

Watson, Thomas. *The Ten Commandments*. East Peoria, Illinois: Banner of Truth Trust, 2009.

Weber, Timothy P. *On the Road to Armageddon: How Evangelicals Became Israel's Best Friend*. Grand Rapids: Baker, 2004.

Weikart, Richard. *From Darwin to Hitler: Evolutionary Ethics, Eugenics, and Racism in Germany*. New York: Palgrave MacMillan, 2004.

Weikart, Richard. *Marx, Engels and the Abolition of the Family*. Vol. XVIII, in *History of European Ideas*. Pergamon, 1994.

Wellers, George. "Reply to the Neo-Nazi Falsification of Historical Facts Concerning the Holocaust." In *The Holocaust and the Neo-Nazi Mythomania*. New York: The Beate Klarsfeld Foundation, 1978.

Wells, Albert. *Pascal's Recovery of Man's Wholeness*. Richmond: John Knox Press, 1965.

Westfall, William. *Two Worlds: The Protestant Culture of Nineteenth Century Ontario*. Kingston: McGill - Queen's University Press, 1989.

Westphal, Merold. "Postmodernism and Religious Reflection." *International Journal for Philosophy of Religion*, no. 38 (1995):

127-143.

White, Hilary. "90% of unmarried couples with babies will break up by baby's teens: study." *Lifesite News*. May 23, 2013. http://www.lifesitenews.com/news/90-percent-of-unmarried-couples-withbabies-will-break-up-by-babys-teens-st/.

—. "Abandonment of Christian Principles led to Europe's Economic Crisis: Hungarian Prime Minister." *Lifesite News*. November 20, 2012. http://www.lifesitenews.com/news/abandonment-of-christianprinciples-led-to-europes-economic-crisis-hungaria.

Wilberforce, William. "A Letter on the Abolition of the Slave Trade: Addressed to the Freeholders and Other Inhabitants of Yorkshire." London: Luke Hansard & Sons, 1807.

Willson, James M. *The Establishment and Limits of Civil Government: An Exposition of Romans 13:1-7.* Powder Springs: American Vision, 2009.

Wilson, Marvin R. *Our Father Abraham: Jewish Roots of the Christian Faith* . Grand Rapids: Eerdmans, 1989.

Wines, E.C. *Commentaries On The Laws of the Ancient Hebrews.* Powder Springs, GA: American Vision, 2009.

Witsius, Herman. *The Economy of the Covenants Between God and Man: Comprehending A Complete Body of Divinity.* 1822. Reprint, Escondido, CA: The den Dulk Christian Foundation, 1990.

Worthen, Molly. "The Chalcedon Problem: Rousas John Rushdoony and the Origins of Christian Reconstructionism." *Church History* 77, no. 2 (2008): 399-437.

Wright, Christopher. *The Mission of God: Unlocking the Bible's Grand Narrative.* Downers Grove: Intervarsity Press, 2006.

Yoder, John Howard. *The Politics of Jesus.* Grand Rapids: Eerdmans, 1972.

Young, Frances. *The Making of the Creeds.* London: SCM, 1991.

Zuckerman, Arthur J. *A Jewish Princedom in Feudal France 768-900*; New York, N.Y.: Columbia University Press, 1965,1972.

ABOUT THE AUTHOR

Rev. Dr. Joseph Boot (M.A., Ph.D.) is the founding pastor of Westminster Chapel in Toronto and founder of the Ezra Institute for Contemporary Christianity (EICC). He also serves Christian Concern in the United Kingdom as Director of the Wilberforce Academy and Head of Public Theology. Joe is widely recognised as an evangelical cultural theologian and leading Christian apologist. Originally from England, Joe worked with Ravi Zacharias International Ministries for seven years as an apologist based first in Oxford, England and then Toronto, Canada. He subsequently planted Westminster Chapel in downtown Toronto and established the Ezra Institute, a Christian worldview and cultural apologetics think tank, as well as founding one of Canada's first Classical Christian Elementary Schools. Joe has spoken in 25 countries at numerous universities, seminaries, churches, colleges and conferences, from Eton College and Wycliffe Hall Oxford, to Forman University in Lahore, Pakistan. He regularly addresses students, pastors and Christian leaders as well as medical, legal, and business professionals in North America, Britain, and the Middle East and has publicly debated leading atheistic thinkers and philosophers in Canada and the United States.

As a contributing author to Thomas Nelson's major Christian apologetics volume, *Beyond Opinion* (2007), Joe's other apologetic works include *Searching for Truth* (Crossway, 2003; Joshua Press, 2011), *Why I Still Believe* (Sovereign World, 2005; Baker Books, 2006), and *How Then Shall We Answer?* (New Wine Press, 2008).

Joe is Senior Fellow for the cultural apologetics think-tank truthXchange in Southern California; is Senior Fellow of Cultural Philosophy for the California-based Centre for Cultural Leadership and serves as faculty for Alliance Defending Freedom's Blackstone Legal Academy. In 2011, Joe was recognized by Toronto's Centre for Mentorship and Theological Reflection as 'Best Preacher-Apologist' for his contribution to apologetic and expository preaching. Joe is General Editor of the Ezra Institute's journal, Jubilee, and is Chancellor of Westminster Classical Christian Academy, Toronto.

Made in the USA
Coppell, TX
28 December 2020

47196538R00369